Distribution of human physical types in the Old World.

Skin color, hair form, head shape, and other features formerly used to delineate "races" occur in gradients that shade into one another as one moves down or across the map. These distributions show that no clear boundaries can be put around "races." The New World is not shown because its populations of Asian origin are recent arrivals, in genetic terms, and have not yet differentiated very much from one another.

TO BE HUMAN

An Introduction to Anthropology

Alexander Alland, Jr.
Columbia University

JOHN WILEY & SONS, INC.
New York Chichester Brisbane Toronto

Cover Photo: Peter B. Kaplan/Photo Researchers
Endpaper Maps: John Morris
Chapter Opening Illustrations: Mario Stasolla
Photo Research: Kathy Bendo with assistance from Mary Stuart Long
Production Manager: Janet Sessa

Library of Congress Cataloging in Publication Data:

Alland, Alexander, 1931–
To be human.

Includes index.
1. Anthropology. I. Title.

GN25.A44 301.2 79-19497
ISBN 0-471-01747-7

Printed in the United States of America

10 9 8 7 6 5 4 3

PREFACE

This text is the result of teaching and thinking about introductory anthropology for eighteen years at three institutions, one public and two private. In presenting the field as a whole, I have attempted to be fair to the various schools of anthropological theory. Still, this book expresses a very definite and, I hope, coherent point of view. It is basically humanist, with a focus on culture as our species' major adaptation. I see culture neither as a mere abstraction from regularities in behavior nor as a set of norms elicited from informants. I take the long-accepted concept of psychic unity seriously and attempt to ground it in cognitive theory as well as in biological ideas about the evolution of the capacity for culture.

A good deal of this book depends on a biocultural approach to human nature. I am convinced that a theory of culture must be biological in three senses. (1) The capacity for cultural behavior is clearly the product of biological evolution. (2) Culture is itself the product of mind, and mind is not to be taken as an abstract or metaphysical entity. It is the outcome of specific biological processes. Mind is the filter through which perceptions are organized and behavioral outputs constructed. (3) Mental processes and behavior enter into a dynamic interaction with the environment in which all societies are embedded. This interaction results in a constantly changing pattern—the ways in which real people interact on a daily basis with their environment and with each other. Culture faces in two directions. It is a self-regulating system of signs *and* it is a code for behavioral adaptation. Culture is more than the result of environmental adaptation. It is too flexible, too creative, and too systematic for that alone.

This book attempts to introduce students to the necessary anthropological concepts in a coherent and logical way. It builds toward an understanding of how anthropologists analyze their own and others' data so that, by the later chapters, serious anthropological material can be read critically. Unlike most texts, therefore, it provides both the basics and some experience with how professionals within the field actually think and work. Material on American society is introduced throughout the cultural section and is integrated with material on traditional societies in order to provide a truly comparative framework for anthropology as a social science.

The theory of evolution has been given more space here than in most texts. My intention is to ground the student in the basics of the theory before filling in the details of human evolution. Sexism and racism are discussed in the context of biological and cultural questions. The rest of the book follows a relatively standard format; the chapter sequences should fit most course outlines. I have tried to be innovative in content without excessive innovation in structure. I hope that both teachers and students will find the section on ethnography into ethnology useful as an exercise in how anthropological theory and data are manipulated by professional anthropologists.

Boxed material is either more difficult or more detailed than the body of the text. For instance, an optional and more difficult chapter on the evolution of artistic behavior appears as a box in the physical anthropology section. Boxes have also been used to guide the students toward an understanding of anthropological tools. Thus, the kinship terminology section, for example, begins with a box on the manipulation of kinship diagrams and kin terms.

I am indebted to many individuals for the multiple inspirations and encouragement that such a task as this book requires. The manuscript was read in several drafts by a series of anonymous individuals whose advice I have taken to heart. I am sorry that I cannot name them, but I am grateful to them. Among those who can be named I am particularly in debt to Donald L. Brockington and Joel Wallman for many helpful suggestions, on the levels of interpretation, content, and style. I know they will see their hands in the final product. Joel Wallman spent many hours in careful contemplation of the entire manuscript. His unique combination of brilliance and intellectual compulsiveness combined with a broad knowledge of both physical and cultural anthropology has strengthened this book in innumerable ways.

I was particularly fortunate to have the backing and active cooperation of a highly competent staff at John Wiley. Ron Nelson saw this book through several revisions and made a series of insightful and imperative suggestions. Kathy Bendo gathered an enormous collection of illustrations and, with her keen eye, helped me choose the final selection. Joel Wallman and Nat Wander prepared the extensive glossary.

I also owe a great debt to my students, both graduate and undergraduate, who have in many ways taught me anthropology and who, I hope, have learned from me. I am particularly grateful to Larry Hirshfeld, Mike Billig, Nat Wander, Rena Lederman, Scott Atran, John Hennessey, and Jessica Weiderhorn. Let me add that errors of omission and commission are my own.

CONTENTS

A NOTE TO STUDENTS

Anthropology, like any new subject, has its own special set of concepts and vocabulary that must be mastered before you can deal with it as a coherent field. These concepts are introduced to you in a step-by-step and systematic way. Each chapter begins with a set of major and secondary heads that will guide you through its subject matter. New terms are set in **bold face** and discussed immediately in the text. Concise definitions appear in an extensive glossary that can be found at the end of the book. At the end of each chapter you will find a summary of the pertinent material just presented. It might be useful to read the summaries just before and after reading the chapters. Each chapter also ends with a short, annotated bibliography that will guide you toward further reading in the subject. Some chapters contain boxed material that will add somewhat more difficult/or more detailed information to your growing knowledge of anthropology. Other boxes provide useful guides to material presented in the text.

This book is heavily illustrated. Both the diagrams and line art and the photos have been chosen for their clarity and ability to reinforce a point made in the written material.

By the time you get to Chapter 24 you will be able to deal critically with the kinds of materials professional anthropologists actually use in their work. This will give you some real contact with an exciting discipline and prepare you to think in anthropological terms.

CHAPTER 1
WHAT IS ANTHROPOLOGY?

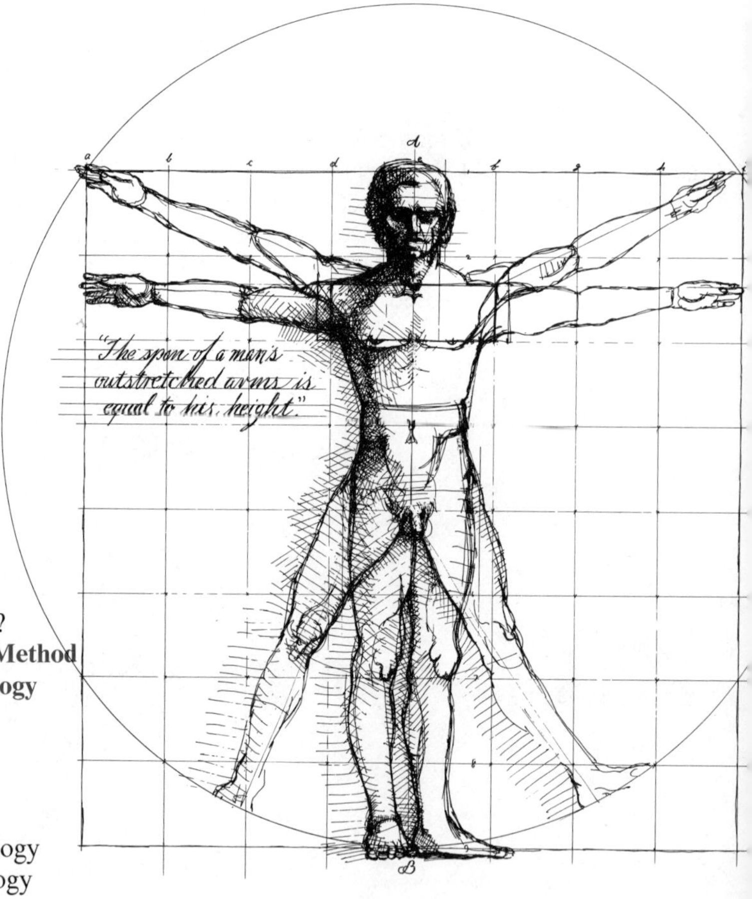

"The span of a man's outstretched arms is equal to his height."

Anthropology, the dictionaries tell us, is the study of humankind, but what does that mean? Certainly many social sciences (like sociology and psychology) as well as history and some branches of biology focus on our species and its behavior. What makes anthropology unique among the human sciences is the way it attempts to define and understand human nature. To do this anthropology faces in two directions. It searches for the origin of human nature in evolutionary biology and the development of social and behavioral differences among the world's peoples in the historical process. Anthropology searches for the rules of human behavior and finds these rules in our biological past as well as our social and cultural present. Anthropology recognizes the fact that humans are members of the animal kingdom, but that a full understanding of human behavior can only come when we move beyond purely biological principles to principles that are unique to our species. What these principles are and how they emerged in evolution provide the focus for this book.

As we shall see our bodies tell us much about ourselves. We are, among all the mammals, the only species that walks fully erect. Our hands are free to touch, carry, and manipulate objects. We have large brains that provide us with excellent sense perception, high intelligence, and good memories. The brain equips us to use our highly efficient communication system known as language. Our biological heritage prepares us to live in social groups and our very survival as individuals depends on this fact. Humans are highly sensitive to social experience. What kind of experience we have tends to shape us and helps determine our life course. In order to better understand the interaction between ourselves as individuals and the social groups to which we belong, we shall enter our discussion of anthropology via two examples. One of these is drawn from a real case; the other is borrowed from fiction. Both illustrate the immense impact of the social experience on human beings.

Walking near his hospital in November 1884, a young British surgeon, Fredrick Treves, strayed into a vacant grocery store that served as a temporary sideshow. There in the dim light of a gas jet Treves saw a pitiful yet frightening human being billed as the "Elephant Man." Suffering from a serious illness that disfigured his face and body, John Merrick was exposed to ridicule for the sum of two shillings. He must have struck the imagination as neither human nor animal—a monstrous freak who inspired curiosity as well as fear and loathing.

Treves's first interest in the "Elephant Man" was medical. Merrick was invited to the hospital, where he was examined by a group of doctors.

I made a careful examination of my visitor. . . . I made little of the man himself. He was shy, confused, not a little frightened and evidently much cowed. Moreover, his speech was almost unintelligible. The great bony mass that projected from his mouth blurred his utterance and made the articulation of certain words impossible. . . .

I supposed that Merrick was imbecile and had been imbecile from birth. The fact that his face was incapable of expression, that his speech was a mere spluttering and his attitude that of one whose mind was void of all emotions and concerns gave grounds for this belief. The conviction was no doubt encouraged by the hope his intellect was the blank I imagined it to be. That he could appreciate his position was unthinkable. Here was a man in the heyday of youth who was so vilely deformed that everyone he met confronted him with a look of horror and disgust. He was taken about the country to be exhibited as a monstrosity and an object of loathing. He was shunned like a leper, housed like a wild beast and got his only view of the world from a peephole in a showman's cart. . . . It was not until I came to know that Merrick was highly intelligent, that he possessed an acute sensibility and—worse than all—a romantic imagination that I realized the overwhelming tragedy of his life.

After Treves's examination, Merrick disappeared for two years. He finally turned up as a derelict in a London police station. A card that

Treves had given him was found among his few possessions. The doctor was summoned and, being a compassionate man, took Merrick under his wing. Merrick was installed in the London hospital, where he found refuge during the last six years of his life.

I very soon learned his speech so that I could talk freely with him. This afforded him much satisfaction, for, curiously enough, he had a passion for conversation, yet all his life had had no one to talk to. I—having then much leisure—saw him almost every day, and made a point of spending some two hours with him every Sunday morning when he would chatter almost without ceasing. It was unreasonable to expect one nurse to attend to him continuously, but there was no lack of temporary volunteers. As they did not all acquire his speech it came about that I had occasionally to act as an interpreter.

Treves, who treated several aristocratic families, was able to interest a group of charitable women in Merrick's case. Soon there was a stream of compassionate visitors to his bedside. Treves described Merrick's transformation in the hospital:

Merrick, I may say, was one of the most contented creatures I have chanced to meet. More than once he said to me: "I am happy every hour of the day." This was good to think upon when I recalled the half-dead heap of miserable humanity I had seen in the corner of the waiting room at Liverpool Street. Most men of Merrick's age would have expressed their joy and sense of contentment by singing or whistling when they were alone. Unfortunately poor Merrick's mouth was so deformed that he could neither whistle nor sing. He was satisfied to express himself by beating time upon the pillow to some tune that was ringing in his head. I have many times found him so occupied when I have entered his room unexpectedly. One thing that always struck me as sad about Merrick was the fact that he could not smile. Whatever his delight might be, his face remained expressionless. He could weep but he could not smile.

The Queen paid Merrick many visits and sent him every year a Christmas card with a message in her own handwriting. On one occasion she sent him a signed photograph of herself. Merrick, quite overcome, regarded it as a sacred object and would hardly allow me to touch it. He cried over it, and after it was framed had it put up in his room as a kind of ikon.

As a specimen of humanity, Merrick was ignoble and repulsive; but the spirit of Merrick, if it could be seen in the form of the living, would assume the figure of an upstanding and heroic man, smooth browed and clean of limb, and with eyes that flashed undaunted courage."

The anthropologist Ashley Montagu has speculated about Merrick's gentle nature. It is his opinion that, when Merrick was very young, his mother was probably loving and affectionate. This care and a shy disposition may have kept Merrick's spirit alive during the period when he lived in a work house and later when he earned his living as a sideshow freak. He may also have been helped by his romantic imagination, which was ultimately satisfied by the friendships instigated by Treves. It was through these contacts that Merrick came to endure his condition and find a certain degree of happiness.

Let us now contrast Merrick's story with that of the fictional monster portrayed in Mary Wollstonecraft Shelley's *Frankenstein.* Since its original publication in 1818 *Frankenstein* has fascinated generations of readers and moviegoers. In the novel, unlike the film, the monster that Dr. Frankenstein patched together learns to talk. Thus he can express his feelings of loneliness and rejection. Like Merrick, Frankenstein's monster was abandoned, but unlike Merrick he was never redeemed by acts of kindness. Frankenstein describes his creation thusly:

How can I describe my emotions at this catastrophe, or how delineate the wretch whom with such infinite pains and care I had endeavored to form? His limbs were in proportion, and I had selected his features as beautiful. Beautiful!—Great God!

His yellow skin scarcely covered the work of muscles and arteries beneath; his hair was of a lustrous black, and flowing; his teeth of a pearly whiteness; but these luxuriances only formed a more horrid contrast with his watery eyes, that seemed almost of the same colour as the dun white sockets in which they were set, his shrivelled complexion, and straight black lips. And the contortions that ever and anon convulsed & deformed his un-human features. . . .

Oh! no mortal could support the horror of that countenance. A mummy again endued with animation could not be so hideous as that wretch. I had gazed on him while unfinished; he was ugly then; but when those muscles and joints were rendered capable of motion, it became a thing such as even Dante could not have conceived.

Because he is abandoned, Frankenstein's creature becomes a ruthless killer. His creator is forced to hunt him down. In the end Frankenstein sacrifices his own life to rid the world of a superhuman evil. Before the horrible climax, however, the monster recounts his brief life and begs for a mate, a modest form of human companionship.

"How can I move thee? Will no entreaties cause thee to turn a favorable eye upon thy creature, who implores thy goodness and compassion. Believe me, Frankenstein: I was benevolent; my soul glowed with love and humanity: but am I not alone, miserably alone? You, my creator, abhor me; what hope can I gather from your fellow creatures, who owe me nothing? They spurn and hate me. The desert mountains and dreary glaciers are my refuge. I have wandered here many days; the caves of ice, which I only do not fear, are a dwelling to me, and the only one which man does not grudge. These bleak skies I hail, for they are kinder to me than your fellow beings. . . .

What I ask of you is reasonable and moderate; I demand a creature of another sex, but as hideous as myself: the gratification is small, but it is all that I can receive, and it shall content me. It is true, we shall be monsters, cut off from all the world; but on that account we shall be more attached to one another. Our lives will not be happy, but they will be harmless, and free from the misery I now feel. Oh! my creator, make me happy; let me feel gratitude towards you for one benefit! Let me see that I excite the sympathy of some existing thing; do not deny me my request!"

At first Frankenstein agrees, but finally he destroys the almost completed female monster. He fears that the couple will return to the human world where further rejection will lead to new acts of terror. The monster then swears vengeance on Frankenstein and promises to destroy his life and happiness.

The novel ends when Frankenstein, who has followed the monster to the arctic, dies after great suffering. The monster, revenged, dies in peace.

Shelley's fiction and the real Merrick teach us about the human condition. Monsters behave monstrously because of attitudes, not because of physical appearance. Nonhuman animals kill or reject a deformed member of their species. Humans may well do so too, but exceptions are possible. Merrick was saved by early love and later by the acceptance of a sympathetic group. He became part of the social world. Frankenstein's monster, rejected and hated because of his physical ugliness, was forced to live in the wilds as an animal. He craved human companionship and begged Frankenstein for a mate as ugly as himself. He wished only to share life with a sympathetic equal. Frankenstein's refusal unleashed the monster's fury and hatred. The monster's only goal became the total destruction of that which he could not share: Frankenstein's social world.

The Frankenstein tale carries a fundamental truth about human nature. It is from the monster's point of view that we come to see what is essentially human: a normal *social* existence. The human body has evolved through time from related animal forms. Our physical structure is a part of our biological heritage. To be fully human, however, we must have positive contact with other humans, first within the context of the family and later within the context of a larger social group. Among all living creatures we, as humans, are most reliant on our fellows. What we finally become depends greatly on those among whom we are raised. It is from them that we learn language and the customs that determine correct behavior.

Human nature does not exist apart from physical development. We have evolved as part of the living world and we are still part of that world. The fact that we are social creatures is itself the result of biological evolution. If we are to understand ourselves, then, we must understand the ways in which our species has been shaped by natural forces. We must also understand how, in each generation, helpless babies become members of society. We must discover what all humans have in common and how differences in behavior develop from this common base. We need to know how different groups of humans have come to master their environment with the help of technological and social forms and how our symbolic activities—language, religion, and art—help us to deal with the natural world and with one another.

The task of anthropology is to answer these questions. It is concerned with our origins and our contemporary behavior. It records and explains the evolution of our species from animal ancestors. It also accounts for biological variation in contemporary human groups. Anthropology seeks to determine what biological and social factors shape our behavior and how, once shaped, such behavior is perpetuated in the social life of particular groups. This is an ambitious task. Its fulfillment requires both a biological and a social-historical point of view. These two points of view come together in the central concept of anthropology: *culture.*

CULTURE

Behavior in the animal kingdom is governed by innate and learned patterns. **Innate patterns** are inborn, automatic responses that occur under appropriate environmental conditions. These innate patterns are most useful for organisms that live in relatively stable environments, spend little time with parental animals, and mature rapidly. A spider never knows its parents and must be able to spin a proper web completely on its own. Web spinning is an innate pattern. **Learning,** gaining knowledge through experience, is most useful among organism that live in variable environments, mature slowly, and have the mental capacity to store and use accumulated information. A learned response is better than an innate one in a variable environment. Under changing conditions an inflexible automatic response might turn out to be useless or even harmful for survival.

Innate and learned behaviors are *not* mutually exclusive. All organisms rely on both behavioral patterns, but higher forms—those with complex nervous systems and well developed brains (warm-blooded animals, for example)—rely on learning much more than lower forms. Later in this book you will see how learning and innate patterns are interrelated. Here I shall note only that learning is particularly important for the survival of the human species. Its importance is increased by the existence among us of language and culture. Language, our communications system, allows us to talk and, through talking (and writing) to learn about the past, the present, and the future. It allows people to learn *without* direct experience. But language is a group phenomenon. It is part of a shared tradition and therefore part of *culture.* **Culture is the major human adaptation.** It provides us with the means of coming to terms with the environment and with one another. It is the part of human behavior that is based on learning, thought, and the use of symbols. **Culture is all of tradition and its expression in behavior.**

The ability to develop and maintain culture lies in the structure of the human brain. Since the brain is the product of evolutionary development, we can think of culture as the product of our specific biology. Culture and language are not innate—they have to be learned—but the ability of normal humans to *learn* language and culture *is* innate. Anthropologists differ over the meaning of this statement, although all agree that it is correct. Some think that culture and language are shaped only by experience. Others think that, because language and culture are rooted in the brain, all languages and cultures must have a common biological base. They also believe that this base affects the way in which specific languages and cultures develop.

Why Is Culture Important?

Humans live in varied and changing environments. Under these conditions innate, inflexible behavior would inhibit adaptation. The wearing of snow shoes in the tropics would be as ludicrous as running naked in the snow would be dangerous. With culture we humans adapt to recurrent situations by benefiting from the accumulated past experience of others and we correct our behavior as new conditions arise.

Culture provides rules for beliefs and social life as well as a means for exploiting the environment. The latter includes rules for making and using tools, for organizing work, and for distributing food and other economic goods. Because culture is a rule system that, among other things, governs behavior, individual members of a society can predict what other members of their group will do in given situations. Thus culture helps to regulate social life.

Although it is flexible because it is learned, culture tends to be conservative. A system of rules that changed at the whim of any individual would lose its effectiveness in the regulation of social life. All aspects of culture can and do change through time, but the change is itself regulated by internal and external restraints. Certain behaviors are not tolerated because they are disruptive to group living; others are not tolerated because they threaten economic survival. Anthropology attempts to discover what it is about culture that is conservative and what it is that brings about change.

Human behavior derives from biological capacities that have evolved through time. Culture and language have their basis in brain mechanisms that determine how we learn and perhaps how we organize what we learn. Learning itself, however, depends on experience and tradition. We are not born destined to speak a particular language, but only with the *capacity* to speak language. We are not destined to behave in a certain way, but only with the *capacity* to learn culture. What language we learn and what culture determines our behavior depend on our social experience. Thus, although culture and language are rooted in biology, they are not biological in the sense that innate patterns are. Culture is the result of biological patterns that allow humans to adapt to the physical and social environment in a unique way. It is based on special learning capacities that are fully mobilized *only* in social life.

Until recently anthropologists concentrated only on the evolution of culture and its expression as learned behavior. **Biological anthropologists** have been concerned with the origin of culture and **cultural anthropologists** have examined its variation in relation to the environment and social life of contemporary groups. At the present time scholars are beginning to probe human nature itself in order to see how it might organize, limit, and direct cultural behavior.

ANTHRO-POLOGY AND THE SCIENTIFIC METHOD

Although culture is the central concept of anthropology, it can be approached from many points of view. Which point of view an anthropologist chooses will determine the way he or she analyzes or explains behavior. All data, all facts, only make sense when they are organized according to some system. An array of red, blue, and yellow triangles, squares, and circles, all varying in size can be grouped according to color, shape, or size. The system of classification chosen determines the membership of the final sets. In science, such systems are necessary steps in the construction of **theories** (general principles) that are used to explain phenomena.

Theories have both explanatory and predictive power. That is, they should make sense out of data and allow one to predict what will happen under a set of stated conditions. Theories affect the choice of data and their organization. A theory might suggest that a particular system of classification is inappropriate for the data chosen. A system of species classification dependent only on the colors of different animals would not be very useful for the theory of evolution.

What theory a scientist chooses to employ will affect the way in which a particular experiment or observation will be interpreted. This is the case because theory guides both interpretation and observation. When it was believed that the sun went around the earth rather than the earth around the sun, observed planetary motions could be made to conform to the geocentric theory by using a complex geometric system. When the theory was reversed, that is, when the sun was put at the center of the planetary system, a different set of predictions and observations was made to support the new theory and explain away the old.

In the physical and natural sciences it is often possible to decide which of two competing theories is the more correct one because they can be tested through experiment. If a single experiment is unable to distinguish between the validity of two different theories, new experiments can be constructed in order to make this judgment. In the social sciences, which include anthropology, it is often difficult to choose among different theories and approaches, particularly because experiments with humans are often difficult to arrange or are impossible to perform for ethical reasons. In addition, data on humans may be particularly ambiguous and difficult to interpret. Often in experiments in plant and animal genetics, parents are bred to their own offspring or a set of offspring to each other. Such experiments and those in which organisms are raised in highly artificial environments make it possible to separate the effects of both heredity and environment on the developing organism. Neither condition can be met in the study of human genetics.

There is one rule, however, that all scientists try to follow. A theory must be stated in such a way that it can be **falsified,** that is, proved false through experiment and observation. The statement "God exists" may be true, but it cannot be falsified. We have no means for determining its scientific validity. In contrast, a theory of the effect of salts on molecular bonding of the water molecule can be tested by **hypothesizing** (making a theoretical supposition) that salts affect the freezing temperature of water. Samples of plain water and water in which various salts have been dissolved are subjected to ever lower temperatures. The temperature at which each sample freezes is noted. If the plain water freezes at higher or lower temperatures than the other samples, the hypothesis is confirmed. This confirmation based on a simple experiment tends to support the more general theory about molecular bonding of the water molecule. If the experiment fails to support the hypothesis, the hypothesis is disconfirmed and the theory is proved false.

Anthropologists are interested in studying, among other things, *beliefs* about ghosts in different cultures, but they do not worry about the possible reality of ghosts. The existence of ghosts cannot be falsified. In attempting to account for the belief in ghosts in various societies, anthropologists construct theories that can be tested. One theory might assume that ghosts are part of religious belief only when aggressive behavior in children is punished by adults. The reasoning is that when individuals are forced to abandon aggressive actions and feelings, they project them on to (that is, attribute them to) imaginary creatures like ghosts. The theory can be falsified through testing. Anthropologists can see whether the frequency of repressed aggression in child training correlates (that is, occurs with) the belief in ghosts. If the correlation does not occur, the theory is falsified and a new one will have to be constructed. Theories can never be proved true, but if they are stated in a falsifiable way they stand as true until they are shown to be false through experiment.

When chemists want to test the boiling point of any liquid, they can do so easily by setting up an appropriate experiment. Very little experimentation is possible in anthropology, however. In addition to the fact that the manipulation of human beings raises serious moral and ethical questions the phenomena we study are often **nonrecurrent**—when a language or a culture ceases to exist it will never occur again. Furthermore, no two human behaviors are exactly the same, and no two occur under exactly the same conditions. Anthropologists can only hope to find sets of *similar* events and *similar* conditions. One of the major advantages of anthropology is the fact that we study different societies around the world living under different sets of historical and environmental conditions. This variation provides a natural laboratory in which different types of behavior can be studied in their proper context. We are not able to create these conditions in the laboratory, but we are often successful in finding them somewhere among the many peoples we study.

THE FOUR FIELDS OF ANTHROPOLOGY

In Europe the biological and cultural sides of anthropology are usually pursued in different university departments. In the United States and Canada anthropology has approached human behavior from the point of view of four integrated fields. These are: **cultural anthropology, physical anthropology, linguistics,** and **archeology.** Each has made its own contributions to the overall field of anthropology. What is more important is the way all have contributed to a unified notion of what anthropology and its theories are all about.

The unity of anthropology comes about largely through the integration of biological concepts drawn from evolutionary theory and the concept of culture as a learned system rooted in our biological nature.

Cultural Anthropology

Cultural anthropology is concerned with the traditional behavior of humans in a social context. Cultural anthropologists study the rule systems and behavior of groups ranging from those of self-contained technologically primitive peoples without their own systems of writing to segments of urban populations. Anthropological studies exist on the Pygmies of the Ituri Forest in tropical Africa, on nomadic cattle-herding peoples of the Middle East, and on middle class Americans in the Midwest of the United States. The focus of cultural anthropology in the past was on exotic peoples with relatively simple technologies. There were three essential reasons for this choice. (1) These societies tend to be small in population and homogeneous in behavior. They are, therefore, easy

A cultural anthropologist in the field. Megan Biesele among the !Kung San, in the Kalahari desert in southern Africa.

to study. (2) Such populations are natural laboratories in which different combinations of environments, technologies, and customs can be studied. Hypotheses relating different sets of variables to one another can therefore be tested. A cultural anthropologist might, for example, wish to know if there is any association between a certain kind of natural resource, let us say fish, and a particular kind of family structure or set of religious beliefs. For another, he or she might wish to test the hypothesis that population size and density are correlated with the complexity of political systems. (3) Cultural anthropology has more than a scientific mission. It is also historical and humanistic. Historians deal only with written records and therefore do not study the many cultures that lack or lacked writing. Anthropologists work to reconstruct the cultural history of such peoples. In this way they extend our historical knowledge back from the beginning of writing, only about 5000 years ago in one small part of the world, to the beginning of human life, now estimated at over five million years before our time.

As they study and record human behavior, anthropologists document disappearing languages and cultures. This information is, of course, scientifically useful, but it is also a treasure of great value for humanity. Each time a language becomes extinct or a way of life disappears, the human species as a whole becomes that much less varied. Cultural variation is one aspect of the human heritage. Anthropologists cannot stand in the way of change, but they can, at least, provide a record that preserves the past and its variety.

Cultural anthropologists study human cultures in their environmental settings. They examine such aspects of social life as child rearing, education, family relations, economy, religion, and art. Cultural anthropologists live for some time, usually for a year or more, with the people studied. When they return from the field, the collected material is written up and published. When anthropologists attempt to generalize about human behavior by comparing the results of many such studies, they convert descriptive data (**ethnographic** data) into **ethnology** (generalizations about human behavior). Ethnology is the goal of cultural anthropology.

Physical Anthropology

Physical anthropologists are human biologists with a special mission—generalizing about human evolution, particularly the evolution of the biological foundations of cultural behavior. Some physical anthropologists study the fossil record in an attempt to document human physical evolution from our early ancestors in order to discover the reasons for variations among groups. While all physical anthropologists ultimately focus on the human species, many specialize in the behavior and **morphology** (physical structure) of our closest relatives, the monkeys and apes. Their goal is to understand the similarities and differences between these forms and ourselves. The study of fossil apes and monkeys combined with studies of living forms helps to fill in missing information. Only bones fossilize, but extinct animals often have close living relatives that stand in for their ancestors. Information on contemporary species and the fossil record together provide a more complete picture of evolution than could be obtained by either type of research alone.

Physical anthropologists study genetic variation among human populations as well as physical adaptation to different kinds of environment. They are interested in such problems as the reasons for differences in skin color, blood

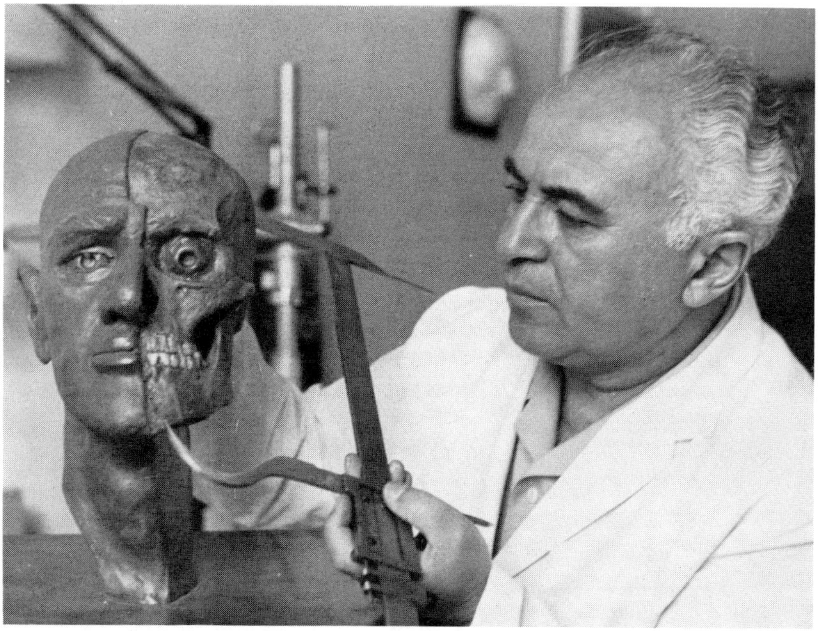

A physical anthropologist at work. Professor Andronik Jagaryan, of Armenia, reconstructs a face from a skull.

groups, or the distribution of body hair. In cooperation with doctors and public health officials they help decide what role genetics plays in human disease or how nutritional factors affect such variables as growth or intelligence. They also study such topics as population size and fertility, growth, the effects of migration on physical adaptation, and crowding.

Linguistics

Linguists are interested in the origin, distribution, and comparative grammar of languages. As language historians they study the relationships among different languages as well as linguistic change through time. They are interested in the reasons behind linguistic change and attempt to discover rules that predict how sound systems and grammars shift. They even attempt to reconstruct dead languages from still-spoken descendant languages.

Today most linguists study a language **synchronically,** that is, at one point in time. Their purpose is to understand language structure, which includes the sound systems as well as grammar and semantics (the relationships between words as well as combinations of words and meaning). Some linguists concentrate on specific languages and attempt to describe and analyze them as completely as possible, others interest themselves in the theory of language in order to derive rules that apply to all languages. While many linguists study languages as abstract entities, divorced from those who use them, there are some who concentrate on language as it is used in speech. These linguists study conversational language in various social contexts as well as dialects spoken by different social segments of larger populations. Linguists are, therefore, interested in languages as self-contained systems and as means of communication. Finally there are linguists who study the relationships between usage and perception, and the relation of these to the development of philosophy and world view.

Archeology

Archeologists are anthropologists who specialize in the reconstruction and analysis of past cultures. Archeologists contribute directly to

A linguist collecting a text in Papua-New Guinea.

A group of archeologists working on an Aztec site in Mexico.

theory in anthropology, and in turn, use anthropological theory in interpreting their data. Archeologists also contribute to culture history. For the most part the cultures they study had no written records. The history must be built up from data left behind in sites that are dug up. Digging in specific sites, archeologists order their data into chronologies of local development that can be worked into regional schemes as material from various sites is compared.

The remains of past cultures are limited to certain classes of objects that are resistant to decay. What remains of a culture is a function of climate, the physical nature of the objects made, and whether or not these objects were destroyed or damaged by such human activities as war and plunder. Archeologists attempt to discover where certain objects and techniques were invented or discovered and trace their **diffusion** (or movement) from a point or points of origin to other cultures. The spatial arrangements of sites and the distribution of sites in and across geographical areas allow archeologists to study settlement patterns. By comparing sites and chronologies, they are able to analyze such activities as trade and warfare. Floral and faunal data allow them to deduce past climates, the diets of local populations, and the origin of plant and animal domestication for specific species. From the characteristics of sites they are able to give physical anthropologists some notion of population size and distribution. Working with material from living societies, archeologists are able to move between contemporary social data and the culture of past societies.

Because they frequently work with data that have considerable time depth, archeologists are able to study long-term change. Since cultural anthropologists rarely have this opportunity, archeologists are uniquely equipped to understand how human populations develop in their historical and environmental contexts. Time depth makes it possible to study environmental deterioration or adaptation to particular conditions. It also makes it possible to relate population growth or decline to technological, environmental, and social factors. In these ways archeologists are able to translate the particulars of history into anthropological generalizations about human behavior.

Outside of anthropology, archeology contributes to a wide range of sciences, including climatology and geology. Floral data, particularly on pollen, can be used to reconstruct past climates and provide a good estimate of prevailing plant cover. Stratigraphic material is useful to geologists. In many cases cultural remains can be used to verify or even establish geological chronologies.

From the recreational and educational points of view, archeology enriches our lives immensely. Archeological museums and reconstructed sites are favorite attractions among a wide spectrum of the public. In many parts of the world (for example, Greece, Mexico, Peru, and Turkey as well as Colonial Williamsburg in the United States) such facilities are major drawing cards for the tourist trade.

Applied Aspects of Anthropology

The four branches of anthropology all have applied aspects. Cultural anthropologists often study change and cooperate with other specialists in the design and development of agricultural and industrial projects, particularly in third world countries. Applied cultural anthropologists have increasingly involved themselves in programs designed to overcome urban problems as well. I have already noted that physical anthropologists often work with doctors and public health officials in order to improve the health profile of a particular social group. Chapter 8 deals with applied physical anthropology in its many aspects including health, nutrition, genetics, and even sports. Applied linguistics is used to develop methods for the study and acquisition of language and contributes to speech therapy programs that deal with such problems as aphasia (disruption of normal speech after stroke), and other speech pathologies, including reading difficulties. Recently, applied linguistics has made a contribution to the legal profession by working on a standard dictionary of legal terminology in the United States. The educational and recreational role played by archeology cannot be exaggerated. Americans in particular are attracted to their past, and archeological analyses as well as site reconstructions have contributed greatly to this interest. Many important reconstructed sites have become part of national parks, monuments, and recreational areas. Archeological exhibits in anthropological and natural history museums are very popular.

The Integration of Anthropology

Anthropology as a discipline has developed in many countries. In Europe, as I noted, the four fields are often taught in different university departments. Physical anthropologists are frequently isolated from cultural anthropologists. Physical anthropology developed out of biology and medicine and cultural anthropology out of geography, philosophy, and psychology. Linguistics has its origin in philology (the study of language and literature) and archeology has its roots in art history as well as biology, particularly paleontology (the study of fossils).

In the United States and Canada anthropologists have successfully maintained a working relationship among the four fields. It is this integrated approach to human behavior that distinguishes modern American and Canadian anthropology from sociology. In the past sociologists studied modern Western societies and anthropologists studied non-Western traditional societies, but this difference has now broken down. Today many sociologists specialize in the social life of third-world countries, and many anthropologists never set foot outside of the urban environment. Today the four-field approach to human behavior is the hallmark of anthropology.

Working together in the same university departments, American anthropologists specializing in the four fields have begun a long journey toward the understanding of the human species. Their scientific analyses and humanistic interests have led to an enrichment of our intellectual and artistic lives.

To know ourselves, however, is, paradoxically, one of the most difficult tasks. We are, perhaps, too close to ourselves for easy access to self-knowledge. Our progress has been slower than the progress of those who probe distant galaxies or submicroscopic atoms. We have, nevertheless, made many exciting and useful discoveries and more are made each year. What we hope to understand in the future provides the challenge for the next generation of anthropologists. This knowledge will come from the close study of both the ordinary and the exotic aspects of our species. We all carry the secret of human existence in ourselves, yet self-discovery is the hardest task of all. Anthropology has set this task as its major aim.

Summary

Anthropology is the study of humankind from a biological and cultural perspective. Anthropology searches for the rules of human behavior and finds these rules in our biological past as well as our social and cultural present. Humans are born with a set of potentialities that are fulfilled only in the context of social life. An examination of two cases, one real and the other drawn from fiction, illustrates the impact of social experience on human beings. John Merrick, the "Elephant Man," lived at the end of the nineteenth century. Afflicted with a disfiguring disease he was exploited by unscrupulous people and exhibited as a freak. Merrick was rescued and befriended by Fredrick Treves, a London doctor who gave Merrick shelter in his hospital. There Merrick, who had, as an adult, never known a real home, found peace. Surrounded with caring people, Merrick displayed a gentle spirit and keen love of art and nature. The anthropologist Ashley Montagu, speculating on Merrick's case suggests that when Merrick was very young, his mother was probably loving and affectionate. He may also have kept his spirit alive through his romantic imagination, which was ultimately satisfied in the many friendships he made while living in the hospital.

Although a fictional character, Frankenstein's monster, as described by Mary Shelley in the original *Frankenstein* novel, also serves to illustrate the role of social life as the foundation of a normal human existence. Frankenstein's monster had a tender heart and high intelligence. His monstrous behavior toward humans began only after he was rejected by his maker, Dr Frankenstein, who found him to be physically ugly and frightening. If the monster had not been deserted by his maker, he might have joined the world of real human beings.

The fact that we are social creatures is itself the result of biological evolution. If we are to understand human behavior, we must understand the ways in which our species has been shaped by natural forces. We must also understand how, in each generation, helpless babies grow up to become members of society. *The task of anthropology is to discover what all normal humans have in common and how differences in behavior develop from this common base.* For this reason anthropologists study how different groups of humans have come to master their environment with the help of technological and social forms and how our symbolic activities—language, religion, and art—help us to deal with the natural world and with one another. Thus anthropology seeks to determine what biological and social factors shape our behavior and how, once shaped, such behavior is perpetuated in the social life of particular groups.

Culture is the major human adaptation. It provides us with the means of coming to terms with the environment and with one another. *It is the part of human behavior that is based on learning, thought, and the use of symbols. Culture is all of tradition and its expression in behavior.* Culture provides rules for beliefs and social life as well as a means for exploiting the environment.

Anthropologists employ the scientific method. Theories, general principles, guide anthropologists in the collection of data, and data tend to support or disprove a theory. Theories have both explanatory and predictive power. That is, they make sense out of data and allow one to predict what will happen under a set of stated conditions. What theory a scientist chooses to employ will affect the way in which a particular experiment or observation will be interpreted. This is the case because theory guides both interpretation and observation. In the physical and natural sciences, it is often possible to decide which of competing theories is more correct because they can be tested through experiment. In the social sciences, which include anthropology, it is often difficult to choose among different theories and approaches. Data on humans may be particularly ambiguous and difficult to interpret.

There is one rule that all scientists try to follow. A theory must be stated in such a way that it can be falsified, that is, proved false through experiment or observation. Theories can never be proved true, but if they are stated in a falsifiable way, they stand as true until such time as they are shown to be false.

Anthropology in the United States and Canada is made up of four fields: cultural anthropology, physical anthropology, linguistics, and archeology. Cultural anthropology is concerned with the traditional behavior of humans in a social context. Anthropologists test hypotheses about behavior and work to reconstruct the cultural history of peoples who do not themselves keep written records. Physical anthropology studies human biology as it relates to human evolution and biological variation in contemporary populations. Linguists are interested in the origin, distribution, and comparative grammars of languages. In addition, they study language acquisition in children and attempt to discover any universal rules that might exist governing all languages. Archeologists are anthropologists who specialize in the reconstruction and analysis of past cultures.

The four fields of anthropology all have applied aspects. Cultural anthropologists are often employed by private and governmental agencies involved in development, particularly in the third world. Recently anthropologists have been employed in increasing numbers to study and develop plans in the urban sector, both overseas and in the United States. Applied physical anthropology ranges over a wide variety of topics from nutrition and disease to sports. Linguists working in the applied field design new methods for studying language and help develop programs to deal with speech pathology. Archeology plays a major role in reconstructing our own past, and many archeological sites have become national and state recreation areas. Archeology also plays a major educational role, particularly in anthropological and natural history museums.

In the United States and Canada anthropologists have successfully maintained a working relationship among the four fields. It is this integrated approach that distinguishes modern anthropology from sociology. In fact the four-field approach can be said to be the hallmark of American and Canadian anthropology.

Bibliography

Cohen, Morris R. and Nagel, Ernest 1934 — *An Introduction to Logic and Scientific Discovery.* New York: Harcourt, Brace, Jovanovich. An excellent introduction to scientific method as it relates to logic.

Fried, Morton H. 1972 — *The Study of Anthropology.* New York: Crowell. An introduction to the field of anthropology with sections on careers, graduate schools, and so on.

Montagu, Ashley 1971 — *The Elephant Man.* New York: Ballantine Books. The original Treves manuscript, plus commentary by Ashley Montagu.

Shelley, Mary W. 1974 — *Frankenstein.* New York: Bobbs-Merrill Co. This edition, edited and annotated by James Rieger, is taken from the original manuscript in the Morgan Library.

PART 1

PHYSICAL ANTHROPOLOGY AND ARCHEOLOGY

CHAPTER 2
EVOLUTION AND GENETICS

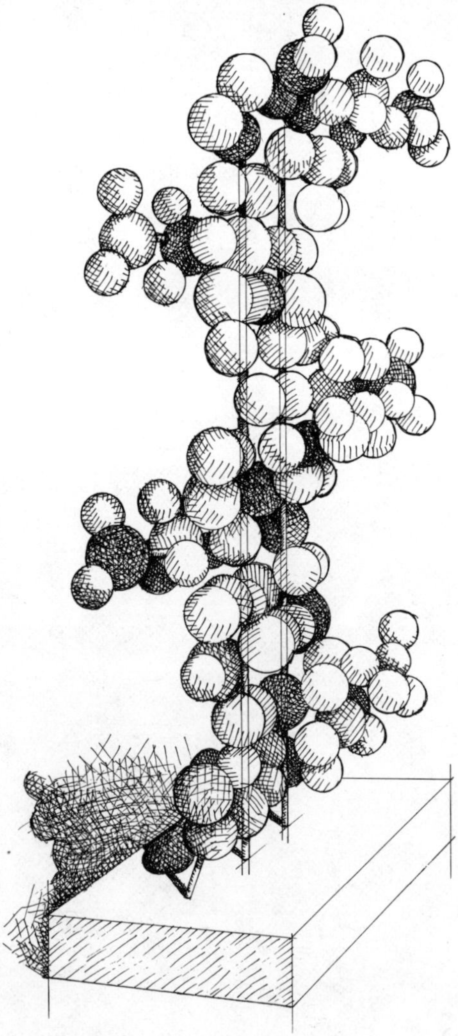

The theory of evolution explains the development and diversification of all life forms including the human species. If anthropologists are to understand our place in nature, they need to know how we are related to other species, why we have diverged from them, and how evolution has shaped us in the ongoing process of adaptation.

The theory of evolution is what scientists call a powerful theory, that is, it can be applied to all cases of development in the biological world, past and present. It is also parsimonious, or economical. With only a few basic principles the theory explains a vast realm of seemingly different phenomena. The principles are these: (1) All life is related. (2) The members of a species (a group of animals or plants that can interbreed and produce fertile offspring) differ from one another in ways that are inherited according to regular laws from generation to generation. (3) Members of a species compete with one another in the context of specific environments. (4) The environment favors, or **selects,** those variants that are most fit and it is these that survive the competition. (5) *Therefore,* differentiation among living forms is the result of a gradual process of adaptation through natural (environmental) selection.

It is important to remember the following points: Variation and competition occur among organisms of a species. Selection always occurs in specific environments, since what is fit in one environment may be unfit in another. The science of genetics has demonstrated that hereditary variation in organisms is accidental. *Organisms do not vary in order to adapt to their environments.* Rather, evolution is the result of random variation in which **adaptation** (adjustment to environmental conditions) occurs only when inherited change accidentally confers an advantage on an organism and its descendants. Evolution is also a slow process in which organisms are shaped gradually by environmental pressures.

The original theory of evolution (as proposed by Charles Darwin) was associated with the principle of the **survival of the fittest** (first proposed by the English philosopher and evolutionist Herbert Spencer, several years before Darwin published his own theory in 1859). Survival of the fittest suggested fierce competition among organisms. It led to the idea of **selective mortality,** according to which the best adapted literally kill off less well-adapted forms. Actually evolution does not work this way. Adaptation really occurs through **selective fertility:** Organisms that are most fit *outreproduce* those that are less fit. Adaptations, after all, have no survival value unless they are passed on. Change is inherited only through genetic transmittal from generation to generation. Those parents with more offspring that survive to reproduce make a greater contribution to succeeding generations than those with fewer such offspring. *Fitness,* therefore, is measured by comparing the fertility of variant forms in a species.

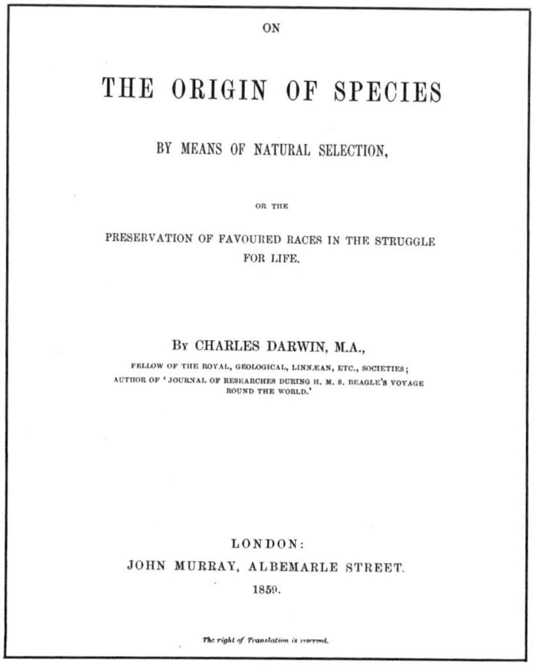
ON

THE ORIGIN OF SPECIES

BY MEANS OF NATURAL SELECTION,

OR THE

PRESERVATION OF FAVOURED RACES IN THE STRUGGLE FOR LIFE.

By CHARLES DARWIN, M.A.,

FELLOW OF THE ROYAL, GEOLOGICAL, LINNÆAN, ETC., SOCIETIES;
AUTHOR OF 'JOURNAL OF RESEARCHES DURING H. M. S. BEAGLE'S VOYAGE ROUND THE WORLD.'

LONDON:
JOHN MURRAY, ALBEMARLE STREET.
1859.

The right of Translation is reserved.

Title page of the first edition of *The Origin of Species,* 1859.

CHARLES DARWIN

Charles Darwin was born in Shrewsbury, England, in 1809, the son of a doctor. He studied medicine at Edinburgh University and then theology at Cambridge. While at Cambridge he became friendly with J. S. Henslow, a botanist. Through Henslow Darwin was invited to serve as naturalist on a research voyage around the world that was to last five years. The trip suited Darwin, who was searching for a career and whose interest in natural history had been awakened by Henslow. Darwin set out from England in 1831 on the *Beagle,* a vessel commanded by captain Robert FitzRoy. During the voyage, which included many side trips on land, Darwin collected specimens and made observations of natural phenomena ranging from geological strata to plant and animal variation. In addition, his journals show a keen interest and sympathy with the native populations of the many countries through which he passed. Darwin's experiences during this voyage were published in his *Journal of Researches.*

While in South American waters the *Beagle* stopped in the Galapagos Islands. Darwin's experience there was crucial for the development of evolutionary theory. Among a wide variety of local flora and fauna, he noted over 26 species of birds unique to the Galapagos. Many were finches. Traveling among the islands, Darwin noted that finch species varied from island to island and from habitat to habitat (see Figure 2.1). He also observed that the different species had adapted to local variations in available food. Apparently the different environments of the Galapagos Islands

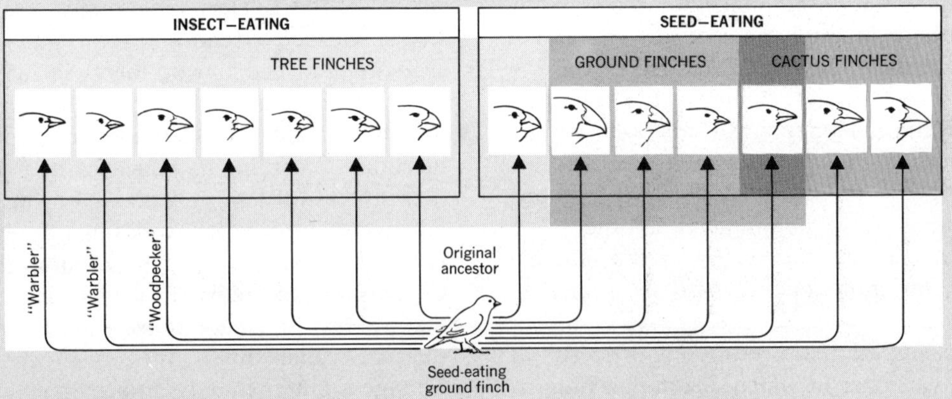

Figure 2.1

Darwin's finches. All of the 14 species of finch shown here radiated from a common ancestor. Each species has adapted to a local environment through behavioral and morphological change.

had shaped the development (or evolution) of these birds, all of which had originated in a mainland species. In adapting to the specific conditions of each island, these birds had become separate species.

Although the idea of evolution came to Darwin during the *Beagle* voyage he did not publish it for several years. His hesitation was based on the desire to muster as much evidence as possible to bolster the theory. Thus for many years he quietly collected support for evolution.

In June 1858 another naturalist, Alfred Russel Wallace, wrote a letter to Darwin and included a paper he had written on the subject of evolution. Wallace's theory was identical to Darwin's. Darwin, who was a scrupulously honest person, sent the paper on to Charles Lyell, a famous geologist and president of the Linnean Society. Lyell, who knew of Darwin's own work, suggested that he, Darwin, write a joint paper on evolution with Wallace. Such a paper was presented to the members of the Society in July of 1858. Darwin's book—*On the Origin of Species by Means of Natural Selection, or the Preservation of Favoured Races in the Struggle for Life*—was published in 1859. In it he presented a large body of data supporting evolutionary theory.

Darwin believed that the human species was part of the evolutionary process and had itself evolved from precedent forms. This part of the theory was excluded from the *Origin of Species* because Darwin did not wish to overly antagonize his potential audience. Finally, however, in 1872 he published *The Descent of Man,* in which the full implications of evolution were discussed and set forth.

Darwin created a revolution in biology. The theory of evolution is now the major driving force in the search for order among living things. At first the details of the process were obscure. But at the beginning of the twentieth century the new science of genetics was shown to provide an explanation of the mechanisms through which evolution operates.

Charles Darwin.

Alfred Russel Wallace, the codiscoverer with Darwin of the theory of natural selection.

ADAPTATION

Adaptation, the process of modification whereby organisms come to fit environmental conditions, is the central concept of evolutionary theory. Organisms that survive in an environment are said to be adapted to that environment. What survives is adapted and what is adapted survives. Such a statement of the concept, however, is merely circular reasoning. To be scientifically useful, adaptation must be measured in such a way that its occurrence can be demonstrated empirically. Such a measure does exist and we have already made its acquaintance. It is called **fitness** and is based on the notion of *selective fertility.* In a given population, if an average organism with one variation (A) outreproduces an average organism with another variation (B) by 10 percent, (A) can be said to be 10 percent more fit than (B). (A produces 110 offspring to every 100 offspring produced by B.) Note that I have said *average* organism. We can never be sure that a *particular* organism, even if it is the most fit organism in a population, will survive and pass its genetic material to the next generation. Chance always plays a role in survival. Even the strongest animal of a species might be killed by a predator, for example.

Adaptation is a limited if powerful concept. We can speak of adaptation only in terms of a single species. We cannot say that bacteria are better adapted than humans because they outreproduce us; we can only say that one variant of a bacterial species is better adapted than another because the one outreproduces the other. We cannot say that one group of a species is better adapted than another if the two groups live in different environmental settings. One setting may be better suited for the species as a whole than another. Adaptation is, therefore, environment-specific.

Since many, if not all, species are widely distributed and therefore occupy varying environments, the process of adaptation is studied in populations. *A* **population** *is a group of organisms of the same species, occupying the same locality, that interbreed among themselves and do not interbreed significantly with other populations.* The members of a population share an environmental **niche** (see Box) and, because they interbreed, they share a common set of genetic material, or **genes.** This set of genes is known as the **gene pool.** The environment affects this gene pool in such a way that the most fit genes are selected, that is, survive. Adaptation, then, takes place as variation in the gene pool is selected out in response to the environment.

Internal and External Adaptation

Organisms are functioning wholes. Their parts and processes are integrated and work together. Even single-celled bacteria are complicated beings in which literally thousands of chemical processes take place. Since organisms are integrated, it can be said that each consititutes a system. Even when evolutionary change occurs, a system must retain its integrity. Any disruption will reduce the fitness of the organism. The maintenance or improvement of a system's integrity can be called **internal adaptation.** Of necessity only certain variations can be adaptive, because they alone will not disrupt the system. Of course, by implication, certain variations may improve the efficiency of the system.

Although organisms must be integrated, functioning systems, evolution as a process takes place only when the environment selects the most fit organisms from a pool of variation. Remember, organisms vary and the environment selects. In general, we should expect more efficient organisms (those that are well-integrated systems) to outreproduce less efficient ones, because the more efficient an organism is the more energy it can put into the reproductive process. When environmental selection occurs we can refer to the process as **external adaptation.**

Clearly, the concepts of internal and external adaptation are but two sides of the same coin. When two organisms compete in an environment, the best integrated (or most efficient) of the two will have the evolutionary advantage.

Variation and Stability

For evolution to occur there must be change. But evolution is more than change, it is adaptation. Adaptations must be retained and passed down from generation to generation. The environment will select new and better-adapted forms that last until they themselves are replaced by even better-adapted forms. What are the mechanisms by which evolution is achieved?

In Darwin's time little was known of evolutionary mechanisms, largely because the science of genetics did not exist. The source of both variation and continuity in evolution is the genetic material. In the reproductive process that underlies evolution, genes (bits of genetic material) are passed down from one generation to the next. In most cases these genes are invariant. They constitute the stable element in heredity. Genes are a chemical system of information by which messages are transmitted from generation to generation. These messages control the development of the organism and determine such traits as hair color or body form. Sometimes, however, the genetic message is changed—always accidentally. But there is no guarantee that the change will confer an advantage. In fact, in most cases the change will have a negative effect on survival. In rare cases, however, the change in message *will* confer an advantage. Any such change, for good or bad, in the genetic message is called a **mutation.** The accidental way they occur is precisely why evolution is a random process.

Organisms are more than the results of heredity, of course. They are also the products of environment. Genes interact with one another and with the environment. Height in humans, for example, has a strong genetic component, yet it is also affected by environmental variables such as nutrition. People who eat little protein tend to be small no matter what their genetic potential, whereas individuals who have an adequate protein diet during their growth period usually attain the maximum height genetically possible for them. For organisms of the same species it is sometimes difficult to sort out differences due to environment and those due to heredity.

An interesting example of the complex interaction between heredity and environment can be seen in Siamese cats, which have peculiar pigmentation. Their bodies are light-colored but the facc, foreparts of the paws, and the tips of their tails have dark areas. In addition, there are two basic color types; seal point and blue point. Seal-point cats have dark-brown extremities while the others display a milder darkening that is almost blue in color. The cat's body provides different environments for the color genes. Both types of Siamese cat are darker at their extremities because these are cooler parts of the body. The gene that controls Siamese cat color is temperature-sensitive and does not produce its full effect on the warmer central parts of the cat. The difference between the seal and blue points is hereditary, however. There is another gene for blue points that dilutes the effect of the Siamese pigment-producing gene, yielding a lighter color in the points. For a similar example, there is a well-known species of snapdragon that produces white flowers when it is grown in the shade and red flowers when it is grown in the sun. There is no genetic difference between the two varieties.

Among humans several diseases are due to genetic factors. Some of these occur in most environments whereas others are quite environment-specific. For example, in some people the tendency to develop diabetes (which is the result of a malfunction of the gland that controls sugar metabolism) is inherited; but if an affected individual is careful to restrict carbohydrates in the diet, the disease may not occur. Diet in this case has an environmental effect on the operation of a gene.

NICHES

A niche can be defined as the place occupied by a specific population *plus* the way that place is exploited by that population. Thus, swallows and bats both eat insects and fly over the same territory, but swallows eat during the day and bats at night. The two species, therefore, occupy and exploit different niches. The niche is a concept involving place, time, and the way in which organisms extract energy from the environment. Animals that graze over the same grassland but eat different plants occupy different niches, as do plant-eaters on the one hand and the carnivores that prey on them on the other.

A niche may be large or small. The grasslands of Africa provide a series of large niches. The surface film on a small pond is also a niche for those animals—water striders, for example—that live on it. Different zones in the water that lie under the surface film provide a set of niches that are exploited by different species.

As we have seen, the same place may provide different niches at different times. Biting flies attack us in the day and mosquitoes at night, although the latter may also be active in deep shadows. Seasonal variation may also bring about a change in the niche. An environmental space may be exploited by one species in the winter and by another in the summer. This is another way in which a single space can provide different niches.

The snail darter, subject of a Congressional hearing, is an endangered species because it occupies a single very small niche. Conservationists have protested the construction of a dam that would eliminate the snail darter's niche and, therefore, kill off the species.

Lions, members of the cat family are carnivores. They occupy a meat-eating niche on the African Plains. Lions feed on various grass-eating species that live in their territory but occupy a niche based on plant eating.

Genotype and Phenotype

Geneticists working in a laboratory can separate genetic and environmental effects. They do so by means of controlled experiments in which either the environment or heredity varies. Animals that are closely inbred (through the mating of sister and brother organisms for several generations) are very similar in genetic material. These animals can be raised in different environments to see how environmental differences affect development. Although we cannot reduce genetic variation among humans through inbreeding (such experiments would be unethical), we can study identical twins, who share the same genetic material. When identical twins are reared apart (when, for example, each twin is adopted by a different family), we have the opportunity to test the effect of environment on the same genetic background. On the other hand, environmental conditions can be held constant. Animals or plants with different genes can be raised under the same conditions to isolate what must then be genetic effects.

The genetic makeup of an organism considered apart from the environment is called the **genotype.** The genotype is the genetic potential of the organism. As the organism matures, its genotype interacts with the environment. The result of this interaction is called the **phenotype.**

The variation that we see in a natural population is actually variation of phenotype. This is so because each organism in the population is the result of its genetic potential and its environmental experience. Since natural selection operates on variation in a population, it follows that adaptation is a process in which the most fit phenotypes are selected. For this reason a genotype may have different selective values in different environments. In populations with low-carbohydrate diets, diabetes should rarely occur even if the genotype for the disease is common. The environmental effect—in this case, diet—will prevent the phenotype, diabetes, from appearing. Since selection only works against the phenotype, diabetes, a high frequency of the genotype will be irrelevant in selection. When carbohydrates are a major component of the diet, the genes for diabetes can be said to **penetrate** (that is, to produce their effect) more frequently. Since the disease has a negative selective value, natural selection will work against the phenotype and thereby reduce frequency of the genotype in the population.

When a population of a particular species enters a new environment, a close fit between the gene pool of the population and the environment has not had time to develop. Provided that some of the variation present in a population has a positive selection value, as time passes the population will come into a better adaptive relation with its environment. Remember that this is not an automatic process. The variation is independent of the environment. Any accidental variation that has positive value will, however, be selected.

The adaptive pattern that emerges as a species accommodates to its environment varies. Some species develop fine-grain adaptations. They become highly **specialized.** As long as the environment remains constant, these species are very efficient, or highly adapted. If environmental conditions change significantly, however, such species may find themselves in serious difficulty. Their phenotypes may shift from highly adaptive to maladaptive (see Box). Thus, while they are efficient in stable environments, they are fragile in the face of environmental change.

A species may *remain* **generalized** vis-à-vis its environment, that is, it can endure a wide range of environmental fluctuations. This adaptive pattern occurs in changing environments. Strong seasonal differences in temperature or rainfall or severe fluctuations in the amount of food available will favor a generalized adaptation. The overall adaptation in a specific environment may be less efficient for a generalized species than for a specialized species. If the environment changes dramatically, however, the generalized species may turn out to have the advantage.

SPECIALIZATION AND GENERALIZATION

Parasites of all sorts are highly specialized organisms. They have adapted to the strict environmental conditions of the hosts on which, or in which, they live. Such parasites as *ascaris,* a roundworm that infests humans, is chemically much simpler than its relatives, the free-living earthworms. If a parasite's host species dies out, the parasite cannot survive since it is adapted specifically to the host's physical and chemical system. The degree of specialization varies. Some parasites can live in only a single host species, while others can infest a wide range of species. When an organism infested with parasites dies, the parasites will either die with it or successfully transfer to another host. Some parasites can live, sometimes in the form of spores, for a long time outside of a host organism, while others must bc transferred directly from host to host.

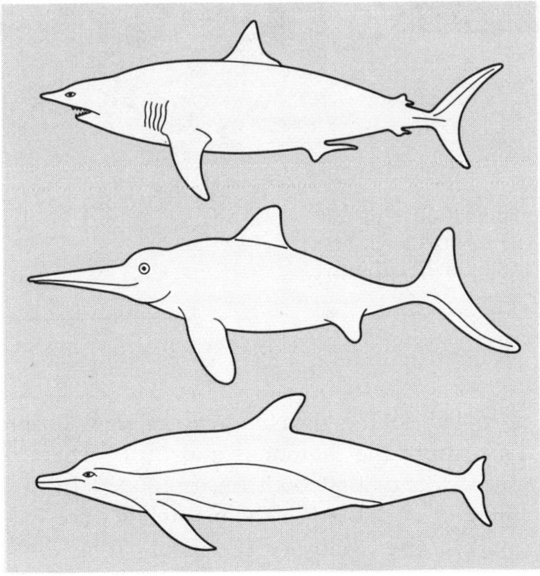

a

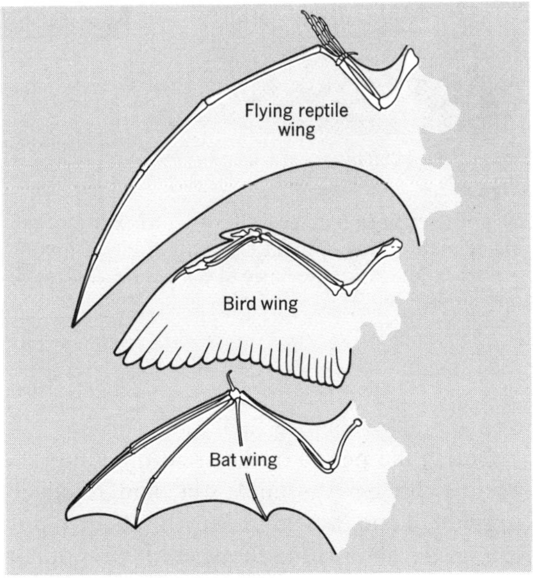

b

Figure 2.2
Reptiles were originally adapted to a terrestrial environment. Through adaptive radiation new forms invaded the sea and flying forms developed. Figure 2.2a shows convergent adaptation to sea life. From top to bottom: shark, sea-dwelling dinosaur, and sea-dwelling mammal. (Adapted from Lull, 1925.) Figure 2.2b shows the development of wings in three lines: reptiles, birds, and mammals. (Adapted from Colbert, 1951.)

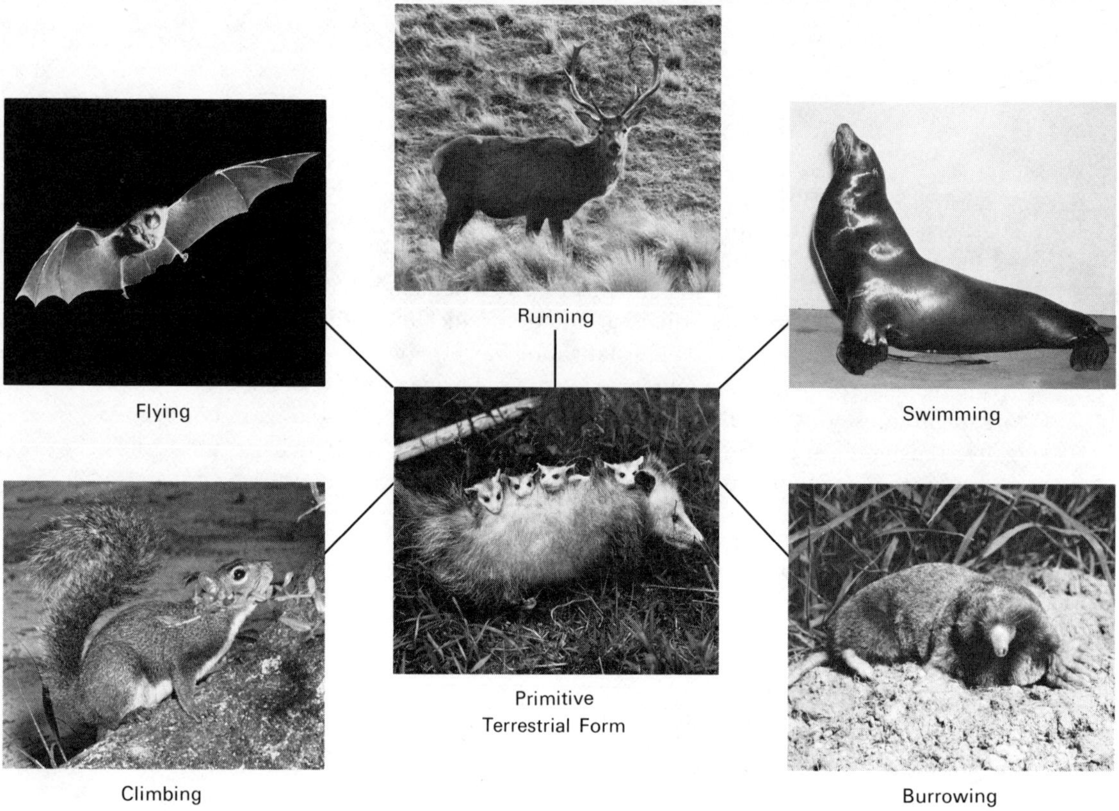

Figure 2.3
Adaptive radiation in the limb structure of mammals. Mammalian limb structures are related to the animal's size and mode of locomotion. The forms shown here are all variations of the basic five-toed, short, flexible limbs found in the primitive opossums.

Adaptive Radiation

During the period of the great dinosaurs the world's climate was mild, wet, and relatively constant. Food was abundant for both plant-eating and flesh-eating forms, and the reptilian population spread into a variety of environmental niches on land and in water. Even flying forms developed. The spread of changing forms into new environments is known as an **adaptive radiation** (see Figures 2.2 and 2.3). The reptiles radiated wherever they met little competition. As long as the climate remained benign and food plentiful, they were successful. Toward the middle of the dinosaur period a series of mutations led to the development of new forms. These were the mammals and birds. There is now evidence that both lines radiated from a common stock. At first the mammals were very small in size. Many of the meat-eating dinosaurs were rather massive animals and preyed upon large forms. Mammals survived, in part, because of their insignificant size. They were literally not worth the effort. As a new type of animal, they came to occupy a wide range of environmental niches that were marginal for reptiles.

SPECIATION

A species is a closed unit. Members of a species can interbreed with one another but not with members of another species. How, then, can the theory of evolution account for the origin of species? The answer is not hard to find.

Selection, over time, produces an ever greater degree of genetic difference between forms. In a single population this difference never becomes great enough to produce speciation, because members of a population breed with one another and spread the variation around the gene pool. The same thing occurs, but to a lesser degree, within the species as a whole. Gene flow (the sharing of genes through interbreeding) among the populations of a species spreads out the variation, and selection acts to bring it back within limits. Thus, interbreeding and selection acting together maintain the integrity of the species.

If, on the other hand, populations of a species become isolated from one another so that no interbreeding takes place among them, and if selection continues to operate, the genetic differences among the populations may become pronounced. If this process continues long enough, speciation will occur. Species cannot interbreed precisely because they are genetically incompatible. As successful populations spread out into new niches, environmental pressures will differ. Selection will then favor the development of locally adapted forms. When these forms become reproductively isolated, speciation will result.

This process is easy to conceive of in space, but it also occurs through time. New forms develop out of old forms gradually, but eventually differentiation becomes so great that we can speak of new species. When we look at the living world, it is hard to see the continuity among species, because each is the outcome of a long process of selection and differentiation. Dogs are like dogs, and cats are like cats. We see no intermediate forms between them. We must also remember, however, that there is a cat family including lions and tigers as well as tabby cats, and a dog family that includes wolves and coyotes as well as domestic dogs. Thus, we can see that there are separate species that belong to the same group of related animals. It is the fossil record, however, that provides us with the necessary evidence for continuity among species. If the record is complete we can trace two different species down to a set of common ancestors.

Simplicity and Complexity in Adaptation

The first forms of life on earth were simple, and complex organisms did not develop until late in the evolutionary process. But we cannot say that evolution is merely a matter of the accumulation or development of complexity in itself. Adaptation does not require increasing complexity. On the other hand, complexity, by its very nature, must always be preceded by simpler forms—even if the reverse is not always true. This must be so for purely logical and mechanical reasons. Complex structures cannot evolve out of nothing.

Selection may favor simplification through changes in certain organs or in chemical processes. If we compare humans and fish, we find examples of both greater simplicity and greater complexity in both groups. Fish, for instance, have many more bones in their skulls than humans. As the skull evolved, it became simpler and better adapted to anatomical (internal adaptation) and environmental (external adaptation) conditions. Three small bones in the jaw of the fish migrated into the ear to become the anvil, hammer, and stirrup of the mammalian inner ear. This mechanism is an adaptation for hearing on land. On the other hand, the central nervous system of humans is much more complex than that of fish. Both forms share parts of what are referred to as the old brain, or *archeopallium,* but mammals have developed a new area called the *neopallium.* The neopallium is most advanced in humans. It consists, primarily, of the gray matter of the brain (also known as the cerebrum). Without it our perceptual mechanisms would be much less well developed, we could not think very much, and we would not be able to talk at all.

Pigs are well-developed mammals that precede humans in the fossil record. Although pig brains are more advanced than fish brains, pig brains do not compare with ours. On the other hand, the pig's digestive system is equipped to synthesize all of the *amino acids* (constituents of protein) necessary for animal life. Pigs are able to convert incomplete plant protein into complete animal protein. The conversion process, however, is expensive; it requires energy. Carnivorous (meat-eating) animals and omnivorous (meat- and plant-eating) animals like humans get some of their amino acids from meat and some plants and do not have to synthesize them. The loss of this synthesizing ability is a simplification that promoted efficiency. This development brought morphological and behavioral changes as well. Since these changes led to a highly efficient form of energy capture, they were worth the effort. But as usual, only when environmental conditions were favorable. One necessary condition was the presence of herbivores on which the carnivores could feed.

Fossils and Evolution

The fossil record combined with the science of genetics provides the evidence for the theory of evolution. Fossils are useful not only because they reveal a substantial part of a family tree, but also because they provide a good idea of time sequence and the spatial distribution of forms. Fossils tell us, for example, that some of the ancestral forms of elephants lived in what is now the Arctic and that the camel and other large mammals now extinct were once native to the New World.

In related fossil forms genetic differentiation provided the basis for change, according to the same rules that apply today. But remember that genetic changes are random events that are generally of small *quantitative* and *qualitative* significance. It is for this reason that evolution requires a tremendous amount of time. The earth has been in existence for over four billion years. Life appeared before the middle of that period. During the three or so billion years of evolution many species have become extinct. These were forms that lacked the necessary variations to adapt to changing environments. Some species disappeared because climatic changes produced a hostile environment. Others disappeared in some regions of the world because they were unable to compete with new, more efficient forms. That is what happened to the first mammalian forms, the marsupials, or pouched mammals. These animals give birth to very immature and fragile offspring that must enter the mother's pouch for further maturation. The placental mammals, because they have hardier offspring, are more efficient than marsupials and have replaced them in most parts of the world.

The exceptional cases in which marsupials have survived provide further evidence for the theory of evolution. Most marsupials are limited to the Australian subcontinent. They arrived there over a land bridge from Asia that disappeared before the development of placental mammals. Left alone as the only mammalian forms in Australia, marsupials flourished, and many species can be found there today.

Genetics and Evolution

Some opponents of evolutionary theory do not accept the fossil record as evidence. They claim, for example, that genetic change cannot be deduced from fossils. The science of genetics, in fact, provides the missing evidence for selection among living forms. Laboratory experiments with artificial selection show how hereditary patterns can be changed. If a geneticist takes into the laboratory a segment of a wild or naturally occurring population, the genetics of that population can be manipulated at will. For example, the wild population of fruit flies has a high frequency of a trait know as red eye. From time to time white-eyed flies appear in small numbers. Under laboratory conditions the white-eyed forms can be bred to the exclusion of the red-eyed forms. After a few generations of inbreeding, populations of white-eyed fruit flies can be developed. Of course, now and then red-eyed forms will appear through mutation. But the scientist can control their number by eliminating any new red-eyed insects that appear. Under laboratory conditions the white-eyed population will thrive. If these flies are allowed to go wild, however, in a few generations the red eyes will soon predominate again. Under natural conditions selection favors red-eyed fruit flies.

The process of evolutionary change has also been seen under natural conditions. In preindustrial England a light-colored form of the moth *Biston betularia* was common in the Midlands. This species had a tendency to alight on the lichen-covered surfaces of tree trunks. Since the wing color matched the lichen background, light moths were camouflaged against their natural predator, a species of bird. A dark-wing form of this moth also occurred, but selection kept its frequency low. Dark moths alighting on the lichen-covered trees were natural targets for birds. They occurred in the population because of mutation. As soon as they appeared, they were eaten by the birds. When the Midlands were industrialized, the air became highly polluted. Smoke from the coal furnaces soon covered the lichen and the trunks turned black. Under these changed environmental conditions the light moths became good targets for the birds. The dark forms were now camouflaged. In a short time the frequencies of the two colors of moth reversed. The light forms became rare

Biston betularia. In preindustrial England the dark form was selected against because it stood out on lichened tree trunks. With the coming of industrialization the trees became soot covered and the dark form acquired an advantage over the previously superior light form.

and the dark forms became common. Variation that had previously been disfavored by the environment was now favored. The moth species could continue to survive under changed conditions, but only with a change in the frequency of the newly adaptive trait. Because of the promptings of environmentalists the air in the Midlands has been cleaned up in recent years, and the light-colored moths are apparently making a comeback.

Studies of living populations support the hypothesis that Darwin used to account for speciation. There is one more problem to be solved, however. If evolution depends on random events, how is it that the fossil record shows any evidence of progressive adaptations at all? The theory should account for differentiation, but evolution also implies an orderly development of improving adaptations. The answer lies in the logic of the process. Once a certain kind of adaptation is selected, any variation that improves its quality will also be selected.

The primate hand began as a rather crude instrument, capable of grasping, that was equipped with a rudimentary thumb placed opposite the fingers. The **opposability** of the thumb is a major feature of primate-hand architecture. In its fully developed form the thumb-hand combination allows us to grasp objects firmly. The development of the fingers and the thumb, including the increase in finger-tip nerve endings, can be traced by examining the fossil record and living primates that represent various evolutionary grades (see Figure 2.4).

The same progressive trend can be seen in the development of the mammalian brain from the earliest mammal forms to the human species. As long as the gene pool of a population contains variation and as long as some of that variation includes improvement of an already existing adaptation, evolution will appear to go in a particular direction. Adaptation within a particular species is not a never-ending process, however. There are chemical and structural limits to any particular adaptation. When these limits are reached, species become stable.

Sources of Evolutionary Change

Evolution is more likely to develop from some generalized type than from a specialized form. A species that is well adapted and specialized within a narrow environment is unlikely to give rise to a new line. Generalized forms, on the other hand, may produce a new adaptive trend because their structures are not firmly fixed in relation to environmental requirements.

The first amphibians to invade the land could live in many niches as long as they remained close to the water. As time progressed, differentiation occurred and various amphibian forms arose. When reptiles developed from amphibians they were freed of the need to spend part of their life cycle in the water. New land surfaces opened up to the reptilian line. The first reptiles spread rapidly and gave rise to continuing variations. The reptiles were so successful that some of them returned to the water to become fish-like icthyosaurs, while others became the first vertebrates to take to the air. When the majority of reptiles died out, the land was cleared for the rise of mammals, which in their turn became the major vertebrate types.

Negative Selection

Most environmental changes have a negative effect on species, particularly when fine-grain adaptations have developed over time. For example, the invasion of an environmental niche by a new species can be disastrous for established species. This is one reason why the United States Department of Agriculture is so careful about the importation of plants and meat products. An uncontrolled type of plant, if

Figure 2.4
Adaptive radiation in the hands and feet of primates (pre-monkey forms, monkeys, apes, and humans).

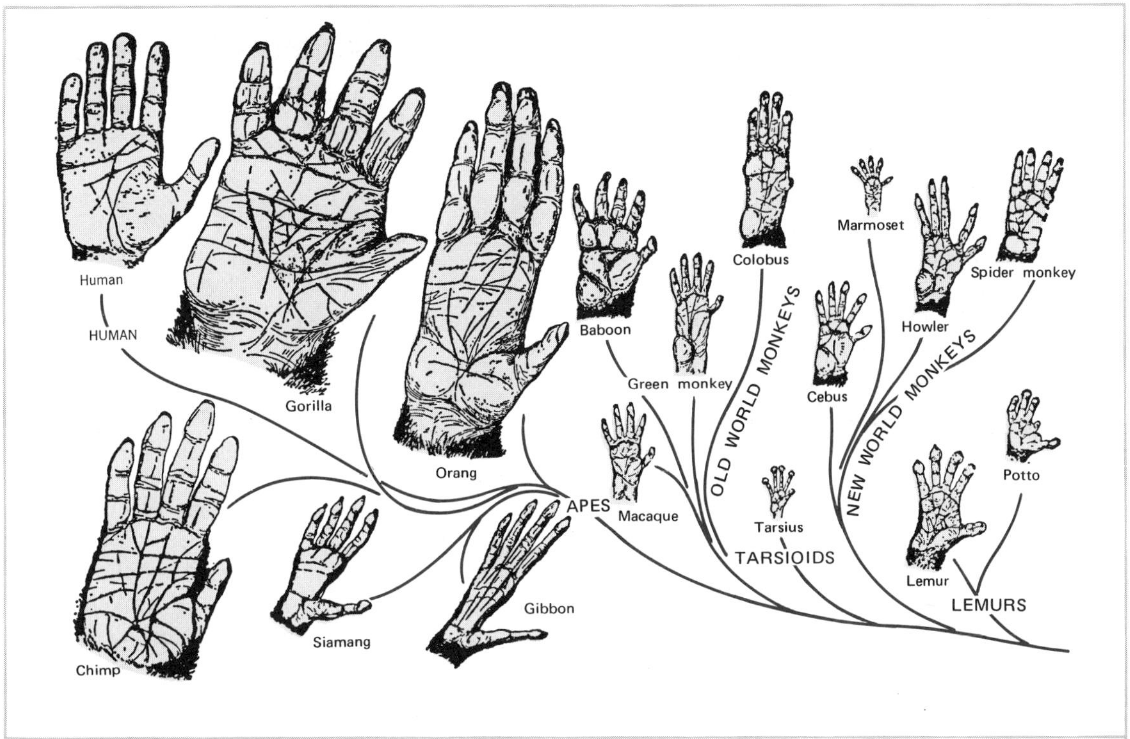
Human
HUMAN
Gorilla
Orang
Chimp
Siamang
Gibbon
APES
Baboon
Green monkey
Macaque
Colobus
OLD WORLD MONKEYS
Tarsius
TARSIOIDS
Marmoset
Cebus
Howler
Spider monkey
NEW WORLD MONKEYS
Potto
Lemur
LEMURS

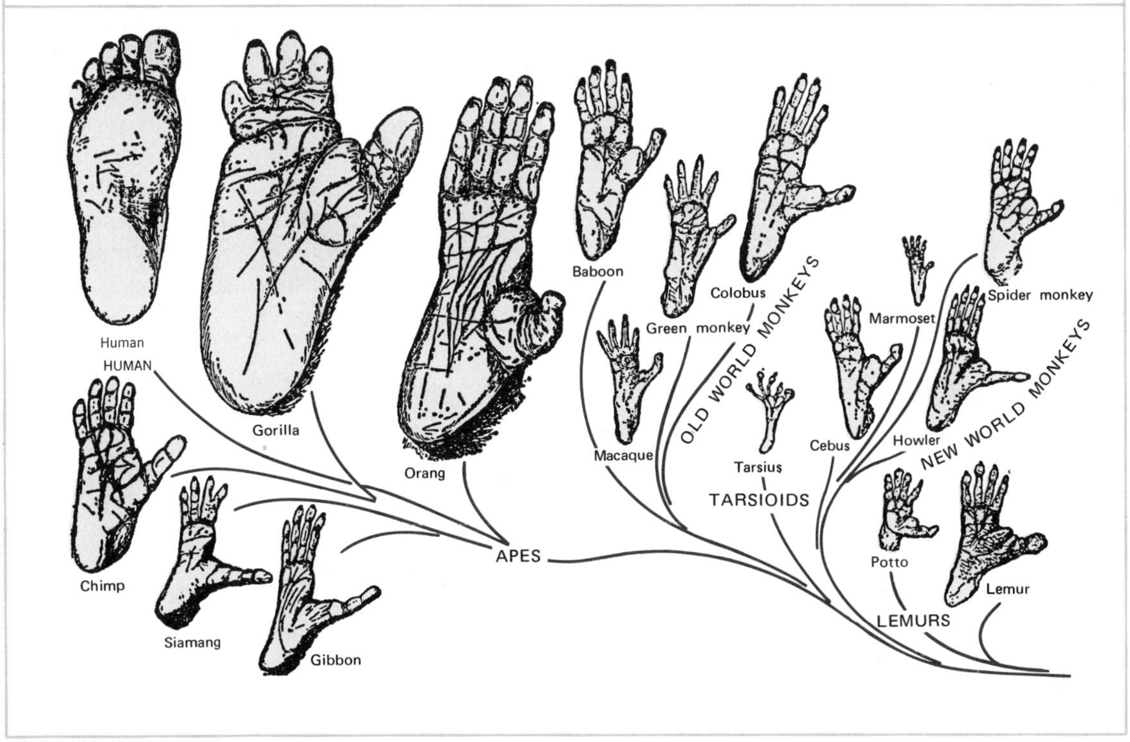
Human
HUMAN
Gorilla
Orang
Chimp
Siamang
Gibbon
APES
Baboon
Green monkey
Colobus
Macaque
OLD WORLD MONKEYS
Tarsius
TARSIOIDS
Marmoset
Cebus
Howler
Spider monkey
NEW WORLD MONKEYS
Potto
Lemur
LEMURS

it were to go wild, might replace species useful for humans. In addition, plants often harbor dangerous parasites. Recent history has seen the accidental importation of harmful species into this country. The beginning of the twentieth century saw the arrival of the Japanese beetle, and more recently the fire ant, native to Africa, has become a plague in much of the South. While introduced species may have a negative effect on established forms, they may themselves flourish because their own natural enemies do not live in their adopted environment.

GENETICS

We have now examined the theory of evolution from an overall biological perspective. What remains is to take a closer look at various branches of genetics in order to fully understand the interplay between populations, their genes, and those forces in the environment that together shape the evolutionary process.

Every living organism is a self-regulating system, structured to maintain normal life processes under varying conditions. To maintain its system every organism must complete a large number of chemical reactions in which material from the environment is taken in, broken down, and rebuilt according to the organism's requirements.

Every living organism has a finite existence. The continuation of a species through time depends on reproduction. While single-cell organisms, such as bacteria, need only reproduce exact copies of themselves, multicellular forms face the additional problem of constructing various organs containing specialized cells. The architect-and-engineer of biological structure is the hereditary material that directs the operation and reproduction of each individual organism. It is heredity that insures continuity between generations.

DNA

The control mechanism of the cell, and hence of the organism, is found in the nucleus. It is known as **deoxyribonucleic acid (DNA).** DNA has both stable and variable parts. The stable part consists of alternating molecules of sugar and phosphate linked together in two chains. These chains are joined together by a series of chemical bases (**thymine, adenine, cytosine, guanine**) attached to one side of each chain. These bases join the two chains in such a way as to produce a ladder-like effect (see Figure 2.5). The ladder itself is twisted, forming a structure known as a **double helix.** Although the sugar-phosphate components are identical in structure, the sequence of bases varies along the length of the molecule. The base sequence on one chain controls the base sequence on the other. This is true because the four bases can join together only in two pairs. *Thymine* and *adenine* form one pair, *cytosine* and *guanine* the other. If one chain contains the sequence thymine-thymine-cytosine-guanine then the other chain *must* contain the opposite sequence adenine-adenine-guanine-cytosine.

DNA is the major constituent of the **chromosomes,** the information packets of the cell. These microscopic structures, in the nucleus of the cell, each contain sequences of shorter units, the **genes,** which are the fundamental hereditary units of the organism. Genes themselves are made up of long sequences of base triplets (that is, a sequence of three bases) that act as units of a code. The bases, adenine, thymine, cytosine, and guanine are the four letters of the code. Each triplet "spells" one of 20 amino acids used by the cell in the synthesis of proteins essential to the chemical processes that maintain the structure of the organism.

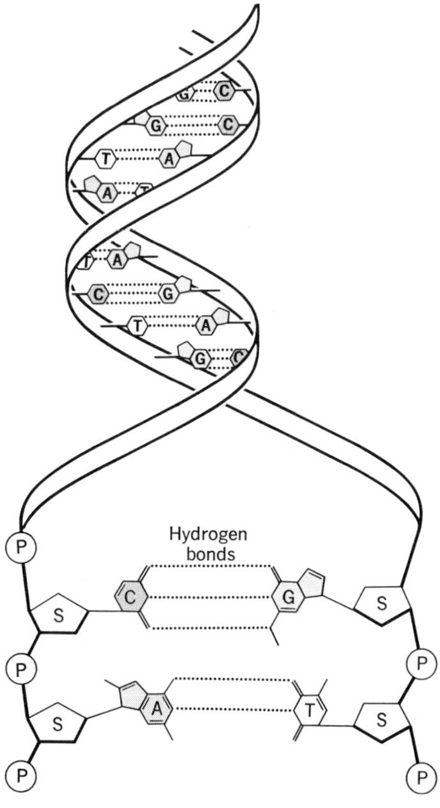

Figure 2.5
A schematic diagram of the DNA molecule. (A = adenine, C = cytosine, G = guanine, T = thymine, P = phosphate, S = sugar.)

DNA is an information system. It contains the rules for the operation of the cell. This operation, however, requires another substance to transmit the coded message from the chromosomes in the nucleus to a special place in the cell where necessary chemicals are synthesized. These chemicals are all proteins and are used in normal cell functions. The transmitting substance—**ribonucleic acid,** or **RNA**—occurs in two forms, each of which has a special role in the chemical-building process. Like DNA, RNA contains four bases linked to a sugar-phosphate chain, but the base **uracil** is substituted for thymine. RNA occurs as a single chain; bases are not paired across a bridge as in DNA.

One form of RNA, known as **messenger RNA,** carries a code message from the DNA of the nucleus to special areas of the cell known as **ribosomes.** Chemical synthesis takes place in these structures. Messenger RNA occurs in long chains that contain the messages for the coding of single proteins. As such it acts as a template for another kind of RNA called **transfer RNA.** Transfer RNA carries small pieces of proteins, amino acids, that will be fitted together in the formation of specific protein molecules. Short strands of transfer RNA pick up these amino acids and line up on the messenger RNA to form the coded protein unit. When the process of synthesis is complete, the newly formed molecule is released by the RNA and is ready to begin its activity in the cell (see Figure 2.6).

In protein synthesis DNA acts as the architect, messenger RNA as the blueprint, and transfer RNA as the construction engineer. DNA also controls the reproduction of the cell.

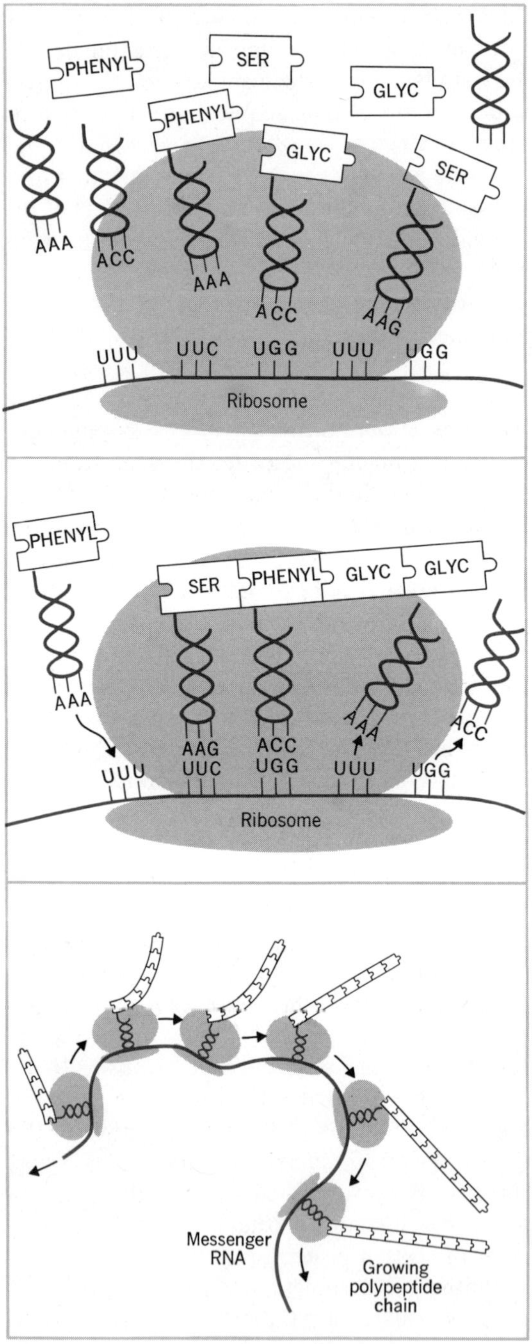

a

b

c

Figure 2.6

Transfer RNA and messenger RNA operate in protein synthesis. (a) The messenger RNA contains a sequence of bases complementary to the DNA strand that it "copied." (b) The messenger RNA moves out of the nucleus of the cell and attaches itself to a ribosome. (c) Units of transfer RNA, joined to their particular amino acids, gather along the messenger RNA on the ribosome. As the amino acids form a chain, the transfer RNA molecules are released.

Since cells reproduce by division, DNA must somehow correctly duplicate itself to appear in each daughter cell. This need explains why DNA is a double-stranded molecule rather than a single-stranded molecule like RNA. In reproducing itself the DNA molecule first separates into two single strands. The strands themselves do not break apart and no information is lost. Remember, thymine can only link with adenine and cytosine can only link with guanine. In order to reproduce accurately, each strand of DNA must rebuild the opposite strand (see Figure 2.7). DNA therefore is not just an information-bearing system; it is an information-bearing system *capable of accurate replication.*

Gene Mutations

Evolution depends on change, however, so the DNA molecule must be subject to change as well as accurate reproduction. New proteins can only be constructed from new messages. From time to time accidental variations do occur in the process of DNA reproduction. These accidents are known as **gene mutations.** Instructions for making a protein can be significantly altered if only one code word (one triplet) is changed. Such a slip can mean that one amino acid is substituted for another in the protein chain. A well-known example of such a mutation in humans is provided by the fatal disease known as **sickle-cell anemia.** Normal hemoglobin (the red substance in the blood that transports oxygen and carbon dioxide) contains 574 amino acids arranged in two sets of paired chains. The *sixth* amino acid on one set of these chains is *glutamic acid.* The sickle-cell mutation leads to the substitution of another amino acid, *valine,* for the glutamic acid. This produces *abnormal hemoglobin S* and the disease, sickle-cell anemia (see Figure 2.8).

Chromosomal Changes

Gene (or point) mutations are not the only kind of variation that occurs in hereditary material. Gross changes in chromosome structure are also possible. These occur in sexually reproducing organisms during the formation of **gametes** (eggs in the female and sperms in the male). Each normal human has 46 chromosomes. (Chromosome number varies from species to species.) Twenty-three of them come from the mother via her egg and 23 from the father via his sperm. Each set of 23 controls the same traits. For example, a gene on one of the father's chromosomes controls eye color as does a **homologous** (or matched) gene on one of the mother's chromosomes. The normal human being has 23 pairs of matched (homologous)

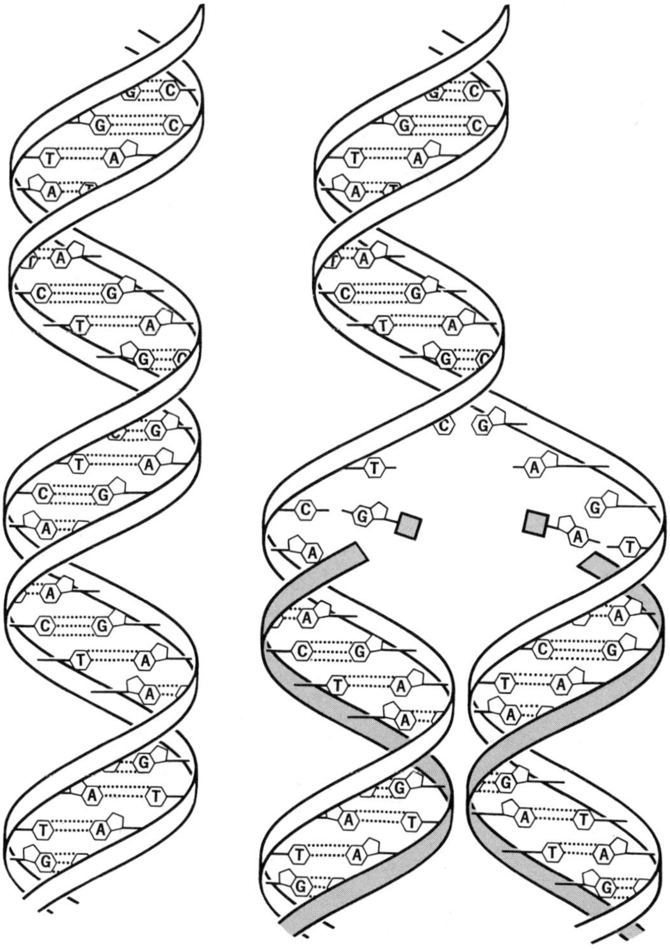

Figure 2.7
The double helix model of DNA (left) and its replication (right).

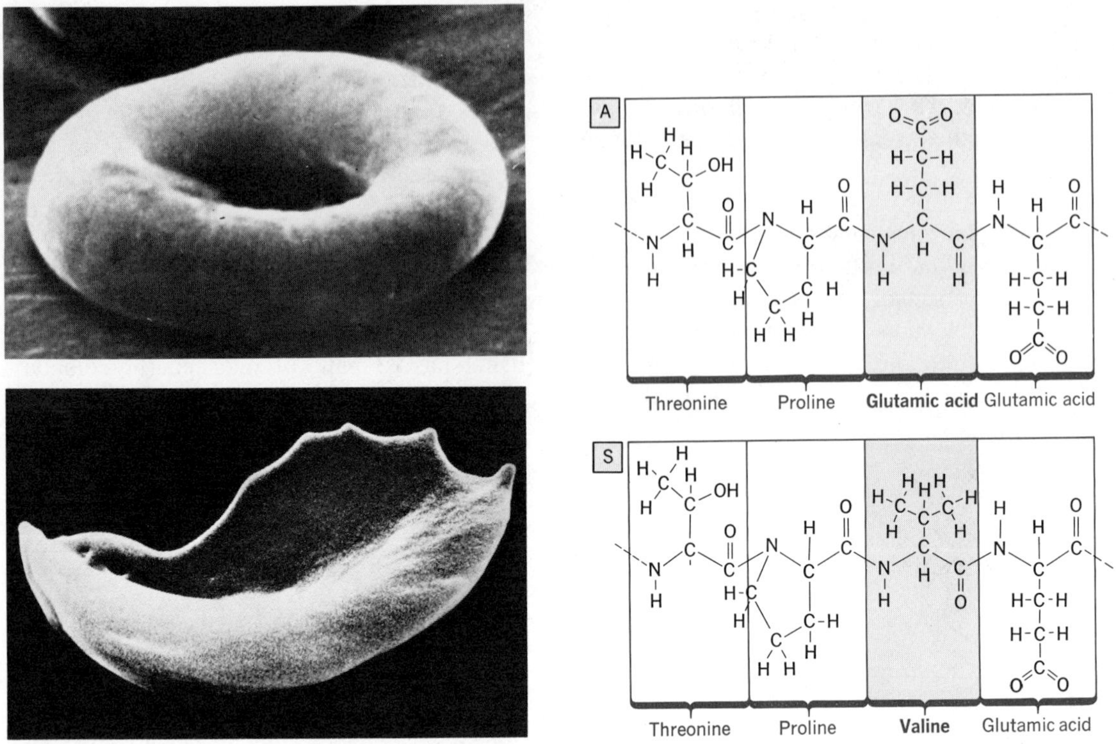

Figure 2.8

Corresponding sections of the normal hemoglobin molecule (A) and the sickle cell hemoglobin molecule (S) showing the substitution of valine for glutamic acid. The photos show a normal red cell and one with the sickle-cell trait.

chromosomes. It is important to note that while these chromosomes are matched (each pair controls the same traits), they are not identical. One homologue may contain a gene that produces brown eye color and the other homologue may contain a gene that produces blue eye color. What color eyes an infant will end up with depends on the way in which these two homologous genes, or **alleles** (variant forms of a gene that controls a specific trait), interact with each other. We shall see below how this interaction takes place.

Single-celled organisms and all the cells of complex organisms except those cells that produce gametes reproduce *asexually*. To become two, the "mother" cell merely divides in half producing two "daughter" cells. The DNA in such organisms need only reproduce itself by dividing once and rebuilding two new DNA molecules. This process is called **mitosis** (see Figure 2.9).

In the process of egg or sperm formation (**gametogenesis**) (see Figure 2.10), the parental set of 46 chromosomes must be reduced to 23. If sperm and egg cells were formed by mitosis, every offspring would get 46 chromosomes from each parent and, therefore, would have 92 chromosomes. The next generation would have 184 and so on. The number of chromosomes is, however, kept constant from generation to generation by a process known as reduction division, or **meiosis.** Meiosis takes place only in the

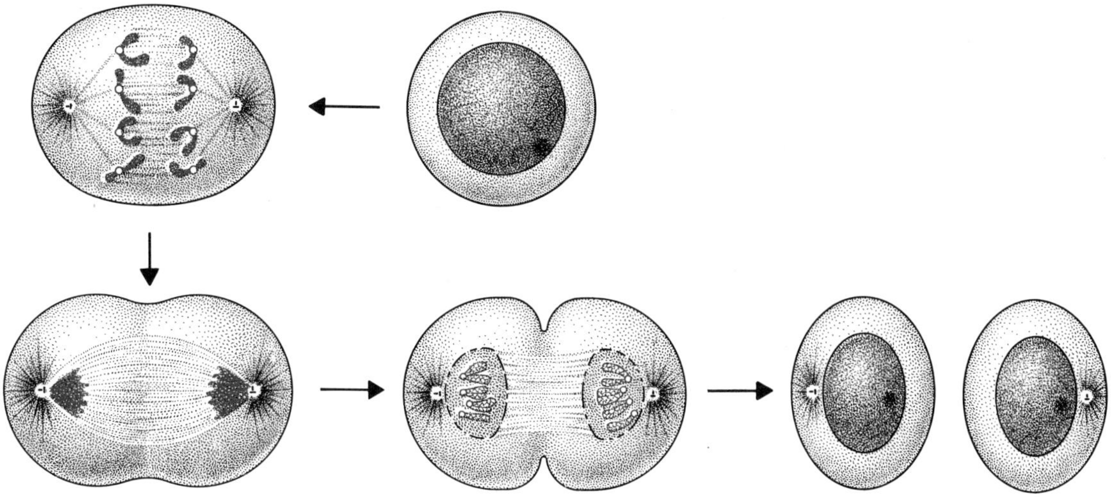

Fig. 2.9
The various phases of mitosis.

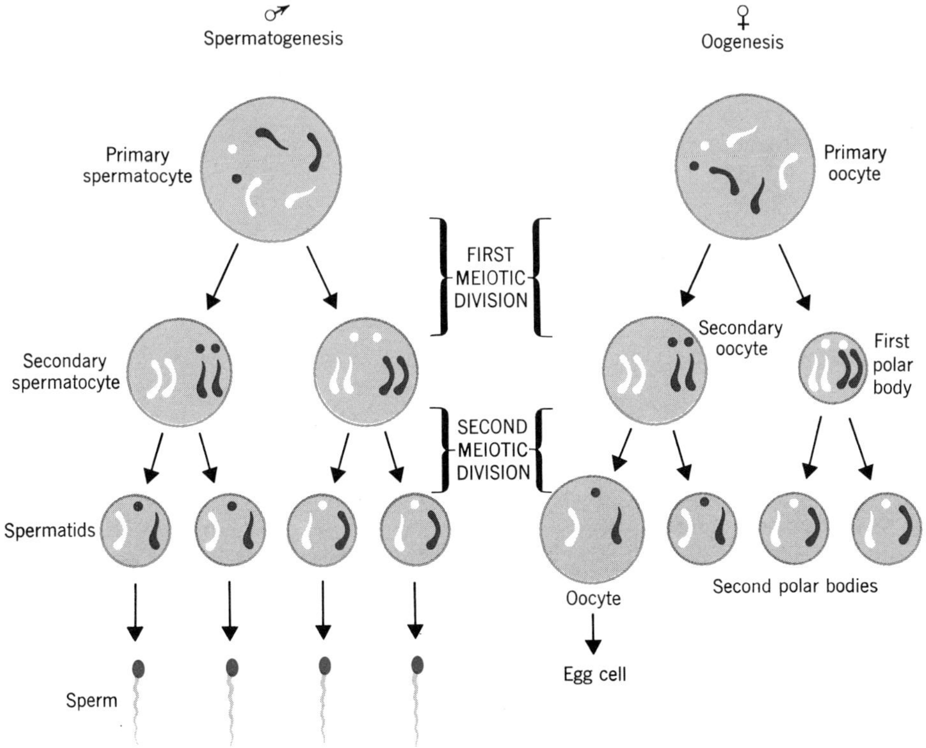

Figure 2.10
Gametogenesis or meiosis showing the formation of sperms and egg. Note: one primary spermatocyte produces four sperms, while one primary oocyte produces only one egg plus three polar bodies.

formation of gametes. Remember, asexual reproduction is known as *mitosis;* reduction division that takes place in the formation of gametes is known as *meiosis.*

It is during the reduction of chromosome number from 46 to 23 that various accidents can occur (see Figure 2.11). A piece of one chromosome may break off and join another. This is known as **translocation.** Pieces of chromosomes may break apart and rejoin in reversed form. This is known as **inversion.** When a chromosome breaks, a piece may be lost and what is called **deletion** may result. Finally, one homologue may end up with a segment of its sister homologue, in which case a particular gene segment is repeated twice. This is known as **duplication.** Duplication may account for the increase in hereditary information that has taken place during the course of evolution, because duplication adds genetic material to a chromosome. If this information later changes through mutation, it may control new traits.

Any change in genetic information can lead to a significant change in the hereditary message. The action of genes depends partially on their placement in the DNA chain. Thus, any one of these chromosomal changes can lead to changes in an organism's heredity.

Another kind of change, in this case a reshuffling of alleles, can occur during meiosis. This is known as **crossing over** (see Figure 2.12). In meiosis each homologous chromosome lines up with its mate. Each homologue then produces an exact copy of itself. This results in four chromosomes known as **tetrads.** As the process of reduction division proceeds, these tetrads will separate and each will end up in a different cell. Reduction division produces four sperms in males and one egg plus three small cells that will die off in females. During the formation of tetrads pieces of chromosomes may cross over each other, break apart, and rejoin. Thus, a part of homologue *A* may exchange pieces with homologue A^1. This exchange leads to a reshuffling of genetic material although it does not produce new traits. If, for example, a brown-eye gene and a blond-hair gene are on

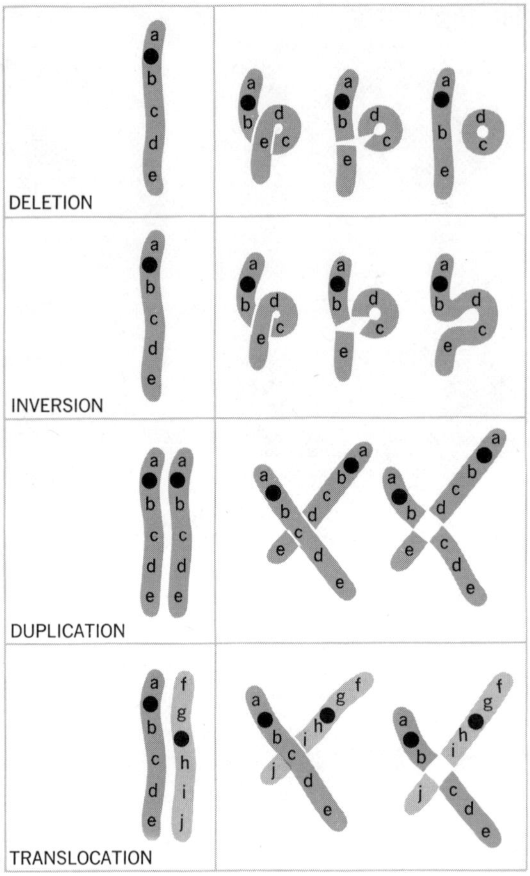

Figure 2.11
Various types of chromosome rearrangement.

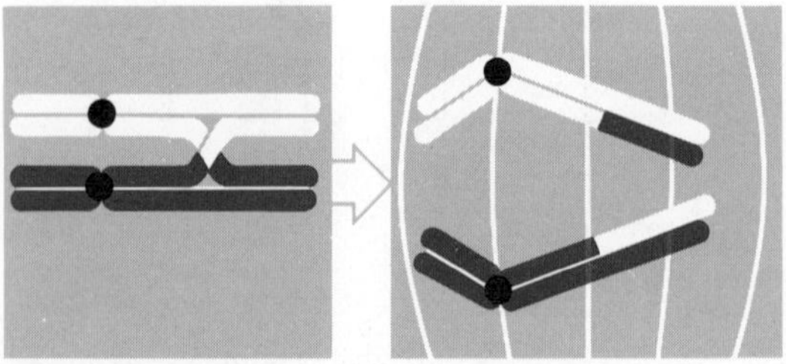

Figure 2.12
Crossing over during meiosis.

different parts of homologue *A*, and a blue-eye gene and a brown-hair gene are on A^1, a crossover of the two homologues might lead to a joining of brown eyes with brown hair on *A* and blue eyes with blond hair on A^1.

One other kind of mistake sometimes occurs during meiosis. An egg or sperm may end up with extra chromosomes or it may be missing chromosomes. If a sperm ends up with 46 instead of 23 chromosomes and if the egg with which it unites is normal, the offspring will have 69 chromosomes, too many for normal functioning. The process of chromosome duplication is known as **polyploidy.** Polyploidy in plants is often useful, for it can lead to a larger and more vigorous type. Many domesticated plant species such as cotton, corn, and wheat are polyploid varieties of ancestral wild types. In animals, however, polyploidy is harmful and can lead to gross malformation, sterility, or death.

Mendelian Genetics

Long before the chemistry of the gene was discovered, scientists had begun to understand how heredity and environment interacted to produce specific types of organisms. Anthropologists continue to use these principles as they study human variation and the heredity of the many plants and animals useful to human life.

In the 1850s the Abbé Gregor Mendel discovered that genes are integral units. They may act in combination, sometimes producing intermediate effects, but they never mix. Mendel's experiments, which lay undiscovered until the beginning of the twentieth century, concerned hereditary transfer in sexually reproducing organisms. Mendel used the common pea plant. The pea is convenient because it reproduces abundantly and has easily marked, distinctive traits. In his search for the secret of genetic transmission, Mendel studied seven traits, among them: *plant height* (tall vs. short); *seed color* (green vs. yellow); and *seed texture* (smooth vs. wrinkled). Mendel was careful to use plants of pure strain, those that breed true from generation to generation. Plants with various variations of the three traits were crossed (tall, green, wrinkled with short, yellow, smooth, for example). Each **parental generation** produced a first filial generation, known in genetics as the **F_1 generation.** Members of the F_1 generation were crossed with each other to produce an F_2 generation.

Mendel found that in the F_1 generation some variations failed to appear. A yellow crossed with a green, for example, produced only yellow plants. But when F_1 plants were crossed with each other, the green reappeared in 25 percent of the offspring. Thus, Mendel discovered that the yellow gene could mask the effect of the green gene. Mendel's analysis of these experiments led him to conclude that some genes of the same trait (color, for example) are **dominant** over others. In this case, yellow is dominant over green. The green gene reappeared in the F_2 generation because in 25 percent of the cases no yellow gene was present in the offspring. Because it is masked by yellow, green is **recessive** to yellow. Mendel also found that a cross between green and yellow, tall and short, or smooth and wrinkled never produced intermediate forms. Traits could be masked but they never blended.

Segregation. When a variation of a trait reappears in a breeding experiment, it is said to have **segregated out.** The process, known as the **law of segregation** (see Figure 2.13), is as follows: Each parent plant contributes one allele for a trait. Each offspring, therefore, contains two alleles for the trait. These alleles are donated at random, so each has as good a chance as the other to turn up in the offspring. If two pure-strain plants with opposite variations are crossed (a yellow with a green, for example), the cross can be represented as *YY* (yellow parent) $\times$ *gg* (green parent). All the F_1 offspring will be *Yg*, since all possible combinations of parental genes will give the four identical products (*Yg, Yg, Yg, Yg*). All the offspring will be yellow because the yellow allele is dominant over the green allele. Now, if two of the F_1 plants are crossed with each other ($Yg \times Yg$) the following results will occur: *YY, Yg, Yg, gg*. Twenty-five percent of the offspring will be *gg*, or green.

When the two alleles of a gene are the same in an organism (*YY* or *gg*), the organism is said to be **homozygous** for that gene. When the two alleles are different (*Yg*), the organism is said to be **heterozygous** for that gene.

Not all alleles occur in simple dominant-recessive relationships described above. Some alleles are **codominant.** When codominant alleles occur together in the heterozygote, they produce an intermediate effect. Working with sweet pea flowers, for example, if we cross red homozygous plants with white homozygous plants ($RR \times WW$) the F_1 generation will have 100 percent pink plants. This looks as if the alleles themselves had blended! We already know that DNA does not work this way, however. Mendel's law of segregation works just as well in this case as it did in his other experiments. If we cross the F_1 plants with each other ($RW \times RW$), the F_2 generation will produce 25 percent red plants, 50 percent pink plants, and 25 percent white plants (25 percent *RR,* 50 percent *RW,* and 25 percent *WW*). The alleles did not blend, but they did work together to produce an intermediate effect. We can see the same process operating in humans. The ABO blood system contains three alleles known as A, B, and o (see Figure 2.14). A and B are codominant and both are dominant over o. Since each individual can carry only two of the three alleles, the following genotypes are possible: AA, Ao, AB, BB, Bo, oo. These yield four phenotypes, A, B, AB (the codominant form), and o (the recessive form).

Independent assortment. During the formation of gametes, chromosomes sort out at random independently of one another. During his experiments with pea plants Mendel discovered that the various traits could recombine independently. He observed all possible combinations of tall or short plants with green or yellow, smooth or wrinkled seeds. This random combination of separate traits (on dif-

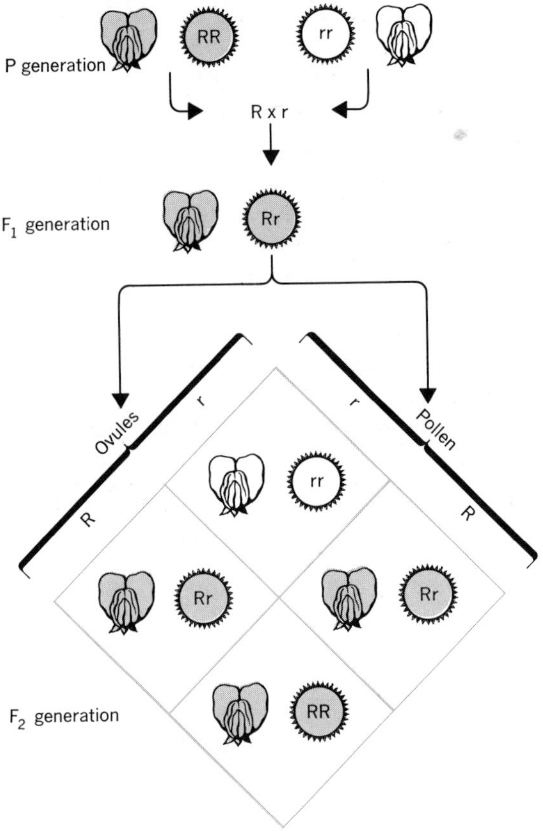

Figure 2.13
Mendel's law of segregation. A cross of red and white flowers produces all red flowers in the F_1 generation. In the F_2 generation the white form reappears unchanged.

Genotype	Phenotype
AA, Ao	A
BB, Bo	B
AB	AB
oo	o

Figure 2.14
Phenotypes and genotypes of the human ABO blood group system showing a codominant relationship between alleles A and B with allele o recessive to both.

ferent chromosomes) is known as the law of **independent assortment** (see Figure 2.15). However, genes that occur on the same chromosome stay with that chromosome during gametogenesis unless crossing over occurs. Thus genes on the same chromosome do not assort independently. Mendel was lucky. He discovered the law of independent assortment because the seven traits he experimented with all occurred on separate chromosomes. Curiously, the pea plants with which Mendel worked have only seven pairs of chromosomes.

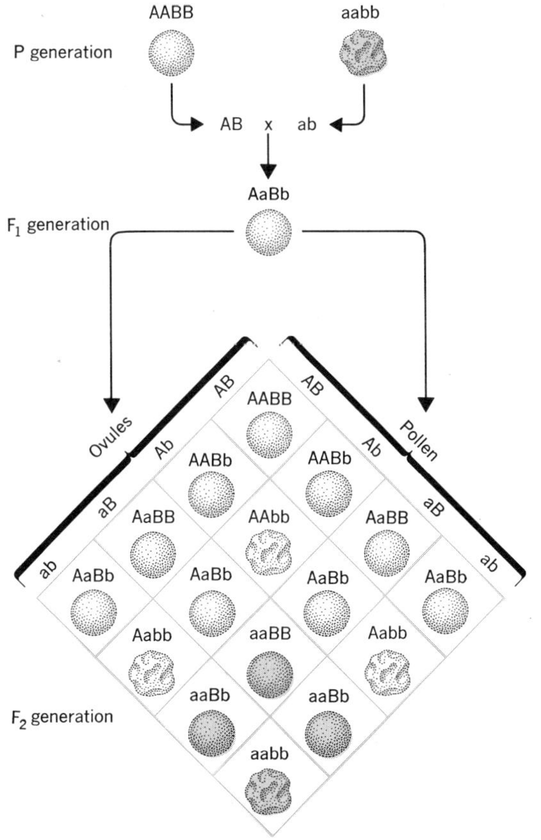

Figure 2.15
Mendel's law of independent assortment. Strains of peas with yellow and smooth seeds and with green and wrinkled seeds are crossed. A and a represent yellow and green, and B and b smooth and wrinkled surfaces, respectively.

Sex Linkage

The sex of an organism is determined by a special set of chromosomes, designated *X* and *Y*. In humans if an individual inherits one *X* from the mother and one *X* from the father, she will be female. If an individual inherits one *X* from the mother and one *Y* from the father, he will be male. The *YY* combination is impossible since females only carry *X* chromosomes and males must be *XY*. This difference explains why men determine the sex of offspring.

The *X* chromosome is longer than the *Y* chromosome. It carries more information. In fact, it is likely that the only information carried on the *Y* chromosome is sex determination. If a trait is carried on the portion of the *X* chromosome that is missing on the *Y* chromosome, it is said to be **sex-linked.**

Sex-linked traits may be recessive or dominant (see Figures 2.16, 2.17 and 2.18). Red-green color-blindness and hemophilia in humans are sex-linked recessive traits. Since women have two *X* chromosomes, they must be homozygous for a sex-linked trait if it is to appear in the phenotype. Males, on the other hand, can be affected if their single *X* chromosome carries the trait. More males than females will be affected because a single dose will be more likely to occur than a double dose. Therefore, most people affected with red-green color blindness and hemophilia are men.

When a trait is sex-linked dominant, more

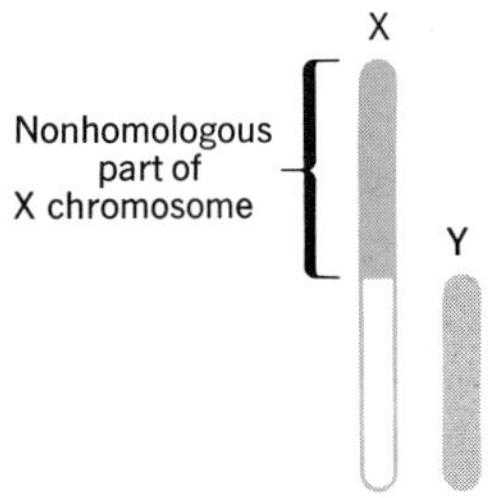

Figure 2.16
The *X* and *Y* chromosomes showing section of the *X* chromosome missing on the *Y* chromosome.

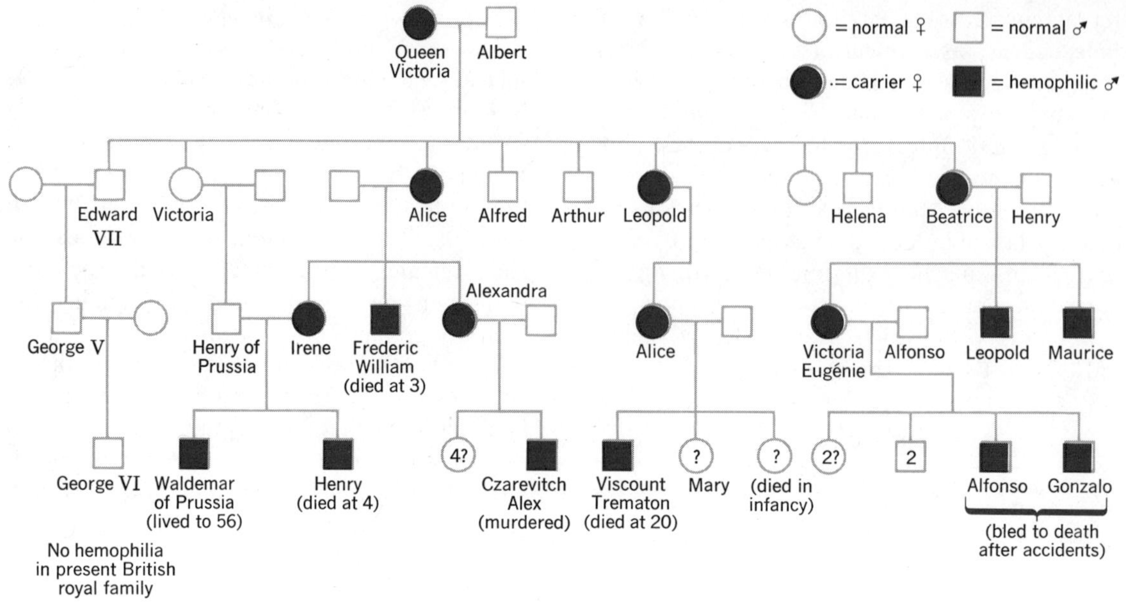

Figure 2.17

Genealogy of Queen Victoria of England showing the transmission of a sex-linked recessive trait, hemophilia.

women than men will be affected, because women have twice the chance to get an affected *X*. Remember, women have two *X* chromosomes, men only have one (see Figure 2.18).

Polygenes

Not all traits are controlled by a single gene at a single place (or **locus**) on the chromosome.

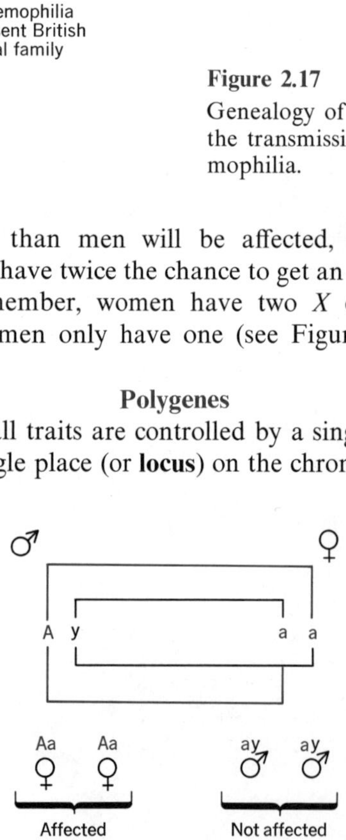

Figure 2.18

Diagram of the transmission of a sex-linked dominant trait. Note the affected women and the absence in this case of affected men.

Many traits are in fact **polygenetic** and are controlled by several genes at different loci. Skin color in humans is an example of this (see end paper). Height is another. Imagine that height is dependent on three gene loci and that there are dominant and recessive alleles at each locus. The several possible gene combinations will produce different heights. If the tall genes are dominant over the short genes, then the tallest individuals have at least one dominant gene at each of the three loci. On the other hand, the shortest individuals will be homozygous recessive at all three loci. Between these extremes there will be a distribution, or range, of heights. The situation will be even more complicated if the alleles at each locus are codominant. In this case the tallest individuals have to have the tall allele at each locus in a double dose. They will have to be homozygous for tall for all six alleles.

Polygenetic traits produce a gradation from one extreme to the other in a population.

POPULATION GENETICS AND EVOLUTION

We are now ready to put genetics and evolutionary theory together. To do so we must see how genetics and the environment operate together on populations.

Evolution implies that beneficial changes in genetic structure are preserved in living forms and passed down to the next generation during the reproductive process. Within any species there must be a certain rigidity that preserves evolutionary gains as well as a certain flexibility that provides the material for further adaptation. The process of evolution takes place within a population, for the population shares both a gene pool and an environment. The evolution of populations is studied through **population genetics** and **ecology** (the relationships among groups of organisms and their environment). The basic model of population genetics consists of organisms containing a hypothetical single gene with two alleles [*A*] and [*a*].* The population is assumed to be unaffected by either mutation or selection. Under these conditions the frequencies of the two alleles (their percentages in the population) will remain stable from generation to generation. No mutation (and therefore no variation) occurs and selection does not favor either allele. If [*A*] occurs in 90 percent of all organisms and [*a*] in 10 percent, the 90:10 ratio will continue from generation to generation. This expectation is expressed by the Hardy-Weinberg law, which predicts that in stable environments gene frequencies will remain the same from generation to generation (see Box).

The Hardy-Weinberg law provides the basis against which all observations and experiments are made. When deviations from stability in the frequencies of any allele are found, they have to be accounted for. Mathematical formulas exist that make it possible for the population geneticist to determine what evolutionary forces are acting to change gene frequencies. Although I will not go into the mathematics of population genetics here, I will discuss the processes that produce change.

Major Evolutionary Factors

Mutation. Mutation provides the raw material for evolution, but new mutations are extremely rare. In general, mutations occur back and forth in already existing alleles. For alleles [*A*] and [*a*] mutations occur in both directions. That is, [*A*] mutates to [*a*] and [*a*] back-mutates to [*A*]. Mutations occur at known, measurable rates. The mutation from one allele to the other ([*A*] to [*a*], for example) may be more frequent than the reverse process. Nevertheless, if the mutation rates are constant, and they usually are, the frequencies of the two alleles will eventually stabilize, or come into equilibrium. The higher change-over from [*A*] to [*a*] than from [*a*] to [*A*] will produce a large pool of [*a*] that will balance the difference in the mutation rates.

Selection. As I have already noted, selection is also a measurable process. The environment has a selective effect on the two alleles, favoring one and disfavoring the other. The measure is fitness, or reproductive success. If the environment exerts a constant selection pressure on a population, one of the two alleles will tend to disappear after several generations of selection. If, however, as is usual, mutation also occurs (constantly adding new negative alleles to the population), selection and mutation will also come into equilibrium. Then the rates of the two alleles will

*For convenience, I'm showing alleles in brackets. Dominant alleles are in capital letters, recessive alleles are in lower case letters.

remain constant from generation to generation. New selection pressures, however, will lead to new frequencies.

Gene flow. When individuals migrate alone or with others from their original population into another and have children with members of the second group or their own migrating group, they have contributed their genes to the gene pool of the new population and can influence its genetic constitution and hence its evolution. This process can introduce previously absent alleles or alter the frequency of those already present. **Gene flow** tends to counteract the tendency of isolated populations to diverge genetically due to random forces, just as a small but steady exchange of air between two rooms of different temperature will reduce their temperature difference. When gene flow takes the form of a regular one-way stream of migration along a string of lineally distributed adjacent populations, a clinal distribution of particular alleles, discussed below, can result.

Genetic drift. Genetic drift refers to several related processes in which gene frequencies are altered as the result of chance forces. Since, unlike selection and mutation, which have consistent trends and allow for prediction, such changes cannot be predicted, they are said to produce random "drift" in gene frequencies. What these random processes share in common, aside from their chance nature, is their potential for substantially altering allele frequencies between generations in small populations, eliminating some alleles entirely and raising the frequency of others to 100 percent.

The most common of such processes is perhaps the least easy to understand. It results from the fact that, within single families, the ratio of genotypes among offspring is often different

The Hardy-Weinberg equilibrium

Parental Generation

Alleles	Frequency	Numerical Frequency	Genotypes	Frequency in Population
A	p	.90	AA	p^2
a	q	.10	Aa	2pq
			aa	q^2
A + a	p + q	1.00	AA + Aa + aa	1

Offspring from Random Matings

Parents M F	Frequency of Mating Type	Frequency of Offspring AA	Aa	aa
AA × AA	p^4	p^4		
AA × Aa Aa × AA	$4p^3q$	$2p^3q$	$2p^3q$	
AA × aa aa × AA	$2p^2q^2$		$2p^2q^2$	
Aa × Aa	$4p^2q^2$	p^2q^2	$2p^2q^2$	p^2q^2
Aa × aa aa × Aa	$4pq^3$		$2pq^3$	$2pq^3$
aa × aa	q^4			q^4
Total	1	p^2	2pq	q^2

THE HARDY-WEINBERG LAW

If we consider alleles [*A*] and [*a*], every individual in a population will have two alleles in one of three possible combinations: homozygous dominant *AA*; heterozygous *Aa*; and homozygous recessive *aa*. Since each parent can donate only one allele to an offspring, parental gametes will be either [*A*] or [*a*]. The problem of gene frequency in successive generations is similar to the toss of a coin. In coin tossing we have two possibilities, a head or a tail. In our genetic problem we have two alleles [*A*] and [*a*]. In tossing coins the combined probability of both kinds of toss (heads or tails) is equal to unity or one. The same is true of alleles [*A*] and [*a*]: $A + a = 1$. If the frequency of [*A*] is .90 then the frequency of [*a*] must be .10, if [*a*] is the only other allele at that locus. Of course. $.90 + .10 = 1.00$. The probability of tossing a head or a tail is always 50 percent, since heads and tails occur with equal frequency. A coin has as many heads as it has tails (one of each). If our alleles [*A*] and [*a*] occurred in equal frequencies (.50 each), probabilities of these genes in the combinations *AA, Aa,* and *aa* would work out like a coin tossing problem. Since we have chosen to use .90 as the frequency of [*A*] and .10 as the frequency of [*a*], the situation is different. The probabilities of the combinations *AA, Aa,* and *aa* occurring will depend on the frequencies of [*A*] and [*a*] alleles in the population. If we let p equal the frequency of the [*A*] allele and q equal the frequency of the [*a*] allele, then the three possible combinations of the two alleles will follow the formula $p^2 + 2pq + q^2 = 1$. This is the case because the chance of getting two heads in a row is equal to the probability of getting a head on any one toss times the chance of getting a head on any one toss. ($.50^2 = .25$). Getting two *A*'s together (*AA*) is the same as getting two heads in a row. The chances of getting *Aa* is equal to $2pq$ because it involves the possibility of getting an [*A*] combined with an [*a*] or an [*a*] combined with an [*A*]. In coin tossing this is the same as getting a head first ([*A*] first) and then a tail ([*a*] second) and getting a tail first ([*a*] first) and then a head ([*A*] second). Thus [*A*] times [*a*] and [*a*] times [*A*] is equal to 2*Aa* or, in terms of probabilities, $2pq$. Finally, the probability of getting the *aa* homozygous combination is equivalent to getting the *AA* homozygous combination, but since its frequency in the population is different from the frequency of [*A*], its probability is q^2.

A simple problem may make it easier to understand how this formula works. Let us consider a population in which the allele [*A*] occurs with a frequency of .7, and the allele [*a*] with a frequency of .3. Then, by the formula $p^2 + 2pq + q^2 = 1$, we get:

$$.7^2 + 2(.7 \times .3) + .3^2 = 1$$
$$.49 + .42 + .09 = 1$$

The frequency of the [*A*] and [*a*] alleles will be the same in every generation because the distribution and recombination of alleles will follow the Hardy-Weinberg formula. Stated as a law the Hardy-Weinberg formula produces a stable model of allele distribution and frequency in each generation.

from the statistically *expected* ratio. For example, if an *AA* woman and an *Aa* man have children, the expected ratio of offspring genotypes is 1 *AA* : 1 *Aa*. Frequently, however, such a mating might produce only *AA* children simply because none of the father's [*a*]-bearing sperm cells (constituting 50 percent of them, the others bearing the [*A*] allele) happened to unite with the mother's egg cells (all of which, of course, contain [*A*] alleles). Now, in a large population, such chance deviations in genotype ratios within individual families will tend to cancel one another out, since a roughly equal number of families will experience deviations in the opposite direction. In very small populations, on the other hand, it is not unlikely that, simply by chance, most of the deviations in a given generation might be in the same direction and thereby appreciably change the frequency of one allele relative to the other(s) at a locus. If, in the next generation, the chance deviations happened again to go in the same direction, the frequency of the already scarcer allele would be further reduced, possibly even eliminated.

The second type of genetic drift is known as the **founder effect,** which occurs when a small number of individuals emigrate from a population in order to found a new one. Such a group, simply because of its small size, would very possibly not have exactly the same gene frequencies as the original population, for the same reason that a randomly chosen sample of 10 marbles from a jar containing 500 red ones and 500 white ones might not contain exactly 5 red and 5 white ones. Intuition should tell you that such chance variations in sample proportions are increasingly smaller with increasingly larger samples. The founder effect, then, which involves a small population budding off from a larger one to start a new community, is a case of genetic "sampling error" and results in gene-frequency differences between the original and founder groups and between their respective offspring generations.

The third major type of genetic drift is called the **bottleneck effect.** This is the result of a substantial reduction in population due to natural disaster such as flood or earthquake. If the group surviving this temporary "bottleneck" is small in number, then the situation is precisely the same as under the founder effect, as the new population might differ substantially from the original in gene frequencies simply because of its small size.

Social Selection

Social regulations that affect the potential reproductive capacities of individuals may interfere with their actual biological fitness. They may increase or decrease fertility. Thus a **polygynous** man (a man with several wives) may have more children than a monogamous man, even if the latter has selectively "better" genes. On the other hand the custom of **celibacy** (sexual abstinence) will lower the fertility of those who practice it to zero, provided of course, they obey the proscription on sexual intercourse.

The principles of population genetics assume random mating, yet in human groups marriage rules and incest prohibitions create mating patterns that are far from random. Where social classes exist or where individuals have different ranks, mating patterns may be strongly affected by social rules. Often, social groups are **endogamous**—that is, mating occurs within the group. Rules of **exogamy** also exist that force individuals to marry outside of their group.

It is probable that, because of the small size of human groups during most of our history and the effects of social selection, nonrandom mating and genetic drift have produced a great deal of the variation in contemporary human populations. Much of human diversity may be due to accidental and social factors rather than to the operation of natural selection.

Adaptive Polymorphism

One might expect selection always to favor a single allele over all others at the same locus. Under this condition one allele would be more common than the others. Frequently, however, two alleles occur at high frequencies relative to each other. This event can happen when the heterozygote is favored over either homozygote—that is, when [*Aa*] has an advantage over both [*AA*] and [*aa*]. For [*Aa*] to be common both alleles ([*A*] and [*a*]) would have to be common. Thus, a heterozygote advantage leads to a high frequency of heterozygote individuals and, as a consequence, both alleles are maintained in substantial frequencies.

An example of this phenomenon, known as **adaptive polymorphism,** has been found in human populations living in Africa. The chemical structure of normal hemoglobin is controlled by the dominant allele [*HbA*]. Remember that the mutant allele [*HbS*] also occurs. In homozygotes this mutation produces sickle-cell anemia. Sickle-cell anemia is usually fatal in young adulthood. It lowers fertility and therefore has a negative selective value. Heterozygotes [*HbAHbS*] normally have a lowered fitness as well because their red blood cells contain *some* abnormal hemoglobin. In certain parts of Africa (see Figure 2.19), the [*S*] allele occurs in high frequency. This is surprising because for homozygotes the allele is just as fatal in Africa as it is in other parts of the world. There is an explanation, however. Medical research has shown that the heterozygote for sickle-cell anemia is resistant to the deadly *falciparum* form of malaria. The [*S*] allele is common only in those regions where *falciparum* malaria is also common. There, individuals who are homozygous dominant [*HbAHbA*] have no sickle-cell anemia, but many sicken and die of malaria. Individuals who are homozygous recessive [*HbS HbS*] get sickle-cell anemia and die. Individuals who are heterozygous [*HbA HbS*] have a mild form of sickle-cell disease but are resistant to malaria. Their fertility is, therefore, greater than that of the homozygotes of both groups, thus accounting for the high frequency of both alleles.

Clines

Theoretically, populations are closed units, breeding uniquely within the group. In reality, however, there is always some interbreeding among adjacent populations, leading to an exchange of genes from population to population. This exchange is known as **gene flow.** Gene flow keeps the genetic distance between populations low enough to prevent speciation. Imagine a series of populations A,B,C,D,E,F,G,H distributed geographically from north to south. It is easy to see in this model how interbreeding can take place among adjacent populations.

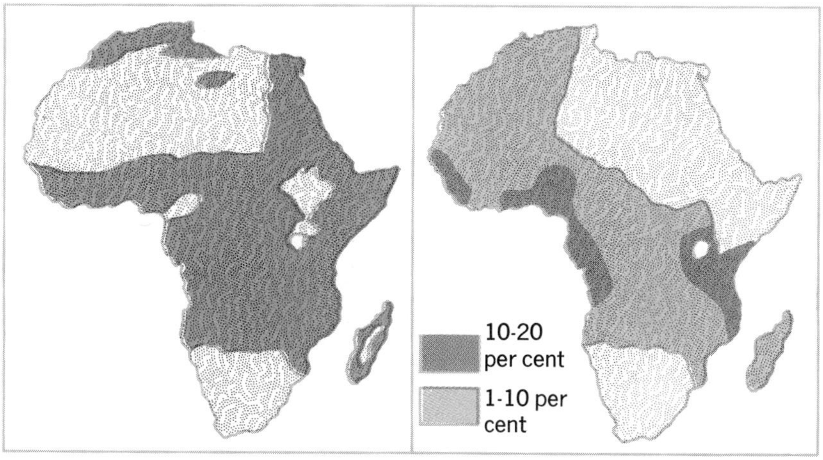

Figure 2.19

Maps of Africa showing (left) the distribution of falciparum malaria and (right) the distribution and frequency of the sickle-cell allele.

The model also shows that interbreeding among distant populations is unlikely. It cannot occur unless migration takes place. If population B breeds with population A and population C, there will be gene flow from B to both A and C, as well as from A and C to B. Given enough time, genes from A will flow all the way to H and genes from H will flow all the way to A. There will, however, be more A genes in B than in C, in C than in D, and so on. If gene flow occurs and if a certain high-frequency allele in A becomes progressively less frequent from A to H, we are in the presence of a **cline.** *A cline is a gradient in the distribution of a gene or a trait through space from population to population of the same species* (see Figure 2.20). In humans, skin color is clinally distributed in a north-south gradient. Light skin occurs in the north and skin color becomes progressively darker as we move southward to the equator.

Clines may also result from the operation of natural selection. A regular change in skin color, for example, suggests adaptation to gradual climatic differences that occur as one moves from north to south.

Clines mark the distribution of specific traits. In widely distributed species clines do not all flow in the same directions, because clines reflect the selective effect of different environments and different genetic histories of specific traits and populations. Thus, although a skin-color cline runs from north to south, a cline for blood type A runs from east to west, from Asia to Europe; the frequency of A, high in eastern China, diminishes as we move westward.

When gene flow is interrupted because a linking population in a cline becomes isolated from the rest of the chain, speciation may occur (see Figure 2.20). The different selection pressures acting on the separated populations are no longer counteracted by gene flow.

Summary

Anthropology is concerned with the place of the human species in the natural world. While humans are unique in many ways, we are also part of the animal kingdom and share many features with other members of that kingdom. In order to understand ourselves, we need to know what it is we have in common with other species and what makes us different. From a biological perspective it is the theory of evolution that provides us with this information.

Evolution is a process by which species have come to differ, one from another. Most differentiation comes about through adaptation, the accomodation of organisms to their environments. Adaptation is the central concept of evolutionary theory. Members of a species vary. Different variations are not equally successful in specific environments. The environment selects the most fit variations through a process known as selective fertility. In the context of a specific environment the most fit organisms outreproduce the less fit organisms of the same species.

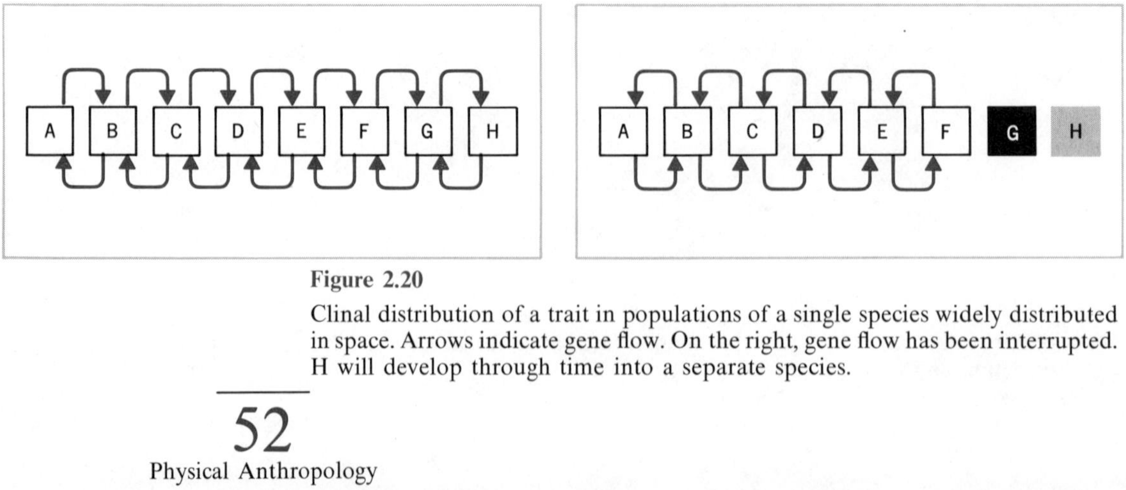

Figure 2.20

Clinal distribution of a trait in populations of a single species widely distributed in space. Arrows indicate gene flow. On the right, gene flow has been interrupted. H will develop through time into a separate species.

Organisms do not vary in order to adapt. Variation is a natural part of life, but it is based on imperfections in the genetic code that controls the inheritance of traits. When an accidental variation confers a selective advantage on an organism, that organism may outreproduce forms that do not carry that variation.

Organisms are the result of their specific genetic structure as it develops in the context of a specific environment. Genes (the genetic material) do not operate alone, and their effects on an organism may differ widely depending on environmental influence. The genetic makeup of an organism is known as the genotype. The expression of this genetic makeup in a real living organism is known as the phenotype. The phenotype is the result of genes plus the environment. Since natural selection can only work on organisms (on what is there), it can only work on phenotypes. Natural selection, then, selects the most fit phenotypes in the context of specific environments.

Speciation (the differentiation of organisms into biological groups that can only breed among themselves) is a gradual process. It occurs when different populations of a single species are physically isolated from each other. As selection exerts different pressures on these populations, they begin to differ genetically. When genetic differentiation reaches a certain point, populations become genetically incompatible, that is, they can no longer produce fertile organisms if and when they interbreed. In most cases fully evolved species do not even attempt to interbreed under natural conditions.

The evidence for evolution comes from both the fossil record, which shows a gradual but increasing amount of differentiation among the remains of once-living forms, and the science of genetics, which studies variation in living organisms. Evolution depends on a certain degree of continuity (adaptations are passed down from generation to generation) and a certain degree of variation (new adaptations must occur if evolution is to occur). The chemical molecule DNA provides the key to both stability and variation. DNA controls the chemical processes that each cell in an organism must perform in order to live. It also controls the reproductive process in which genetic material is passed on from one generation to another. In most cases DNA reproduces itself accurately so that genetic information continues to be the same from generation to generation. Sometimes this information contains accidental mistakes. These mistakes are called mutations and provide the basis for change.

DNA is the major constituent of the gene, the unit of hereditary material. The fitness of a gene (its effect on fertility) depends on its penetrance (its expression in the phenotype) and its selective value in a specific environment. Adaptation as a concept is meaningful only when populations (subgroups of species living and interbreeding in a specific environment) are examined in the context of their environments. In fact, adaptation is measured by the concept of comparative fitness and can be demonstrated only when one genetic variation can be shown to outbreed another competing genetic variation.

Evolution occurs with changes in the genetic makeup of populations. It is due to a small number of processes, some of which interact with one another. Genetic variation derives ultimately from mutation, change in the genetic material itself. Selection is the process whereby the environment favors some of this variation over others. Gene flow among populations tends to reduce differences in gene frequencies. Genetic drift, accidental changes in gene frequency, may occur for a variety of reasons, particularly in small populations, and tends to promote genetic divergence between populations.

Where selection has been operating for some time, one allele (or variant form) of a gene might be favored over another. In this case, one will occur in high frequency and the other in low frequency. Sometimes the frequency of two or more alleles is surprisingly high. Such a situation is called polymorphism. A special case of this phenomenon is known as adaptive polymorphism. Adaptive polymorphism occurs when the heterozygote has a selective advantage over both the dominant and recessive homozygotes. In certain parts of Africa the heterozygote carrier for sickle-cell anemia has an advantage over the normal dominant homozygote, who is sensitive to falciparum malaria, and the homozygote recessive, who is subject to the disease sickle-cell anemia. The heterozygote displays a mild form of anemia and is resistant to malaria. This fact keeps the [*S*] allele in high frequency in such populations.

Evolution is a relentless process in which material from the environment is converted into organisms. Reduced to its essentials, evolution is the history of the development and spread of DNA through space and time. This spread takes place as accidental changes in DNA structure produce variations that have a selective advantage in particular environments. Most changes in DNA are harmful, however, and all adaptations are tentative. They may be replaced by better adaptations, or they may lose their selective value if the environment in which they occur changes.

The nineteenth-century writer Samuel Butler once said that a chicken is the egg's way of producing another egg. Put in a modern form and generalized to all species, we might say that the organism is DNA's way of producing more DNA.

Bibliography

Darwin, Charles 1958 (orig. 1859) *The Origin of Species.* New York: New American Library. This is the original statement of the theory of evolution.

Darwin, Charles 1871 *The Descent of Man and Selection in Relation to Sex.* New York: Random House. Darwin includes humans in his theory of evolution.

Eiseley, Loren 1961 *Darwin's Century.* Garden City, New York: Doubleday Anchor. The history and development of evolutionary theory with its complete cast of characters.

Livingstone, Frank B. 1958 Anthropological Implications of Sickle Cell Gene Distribution in West Africa. *American Anthropologist* 60: 533–562. The relationship between gene frequency, adaptive polymorphism, and culture.

Mendel, Gregor 1948 (orig. 1866) *Experiments in Plant Hybridization.* Cambridge: Harvard University Press. A report of the first recorded genetic experiments by the founder of genetics.

Merrell, David J. 1962 *Evolution and Genetics: The Modern Theory of Genetics.* New York: Holt, Rinehart and Winston. An excellent synthesis of modern genetics and evolutionary theory.

Scientific American, 1978 *Scientific American* (Sept. 1978). A special issue on evolution including articles on the mechanisms of evolution, chemical evolution, the evolution of behavior, human evolution, and adaptation.

Watson, James D. 1970 *Molecular Biology of the Gene.* New York: Benjamin. Genetic chemistry from the codiscoverer of DNA structure.

CHAPTER 3
BEHAVIORAL EVOLUTION

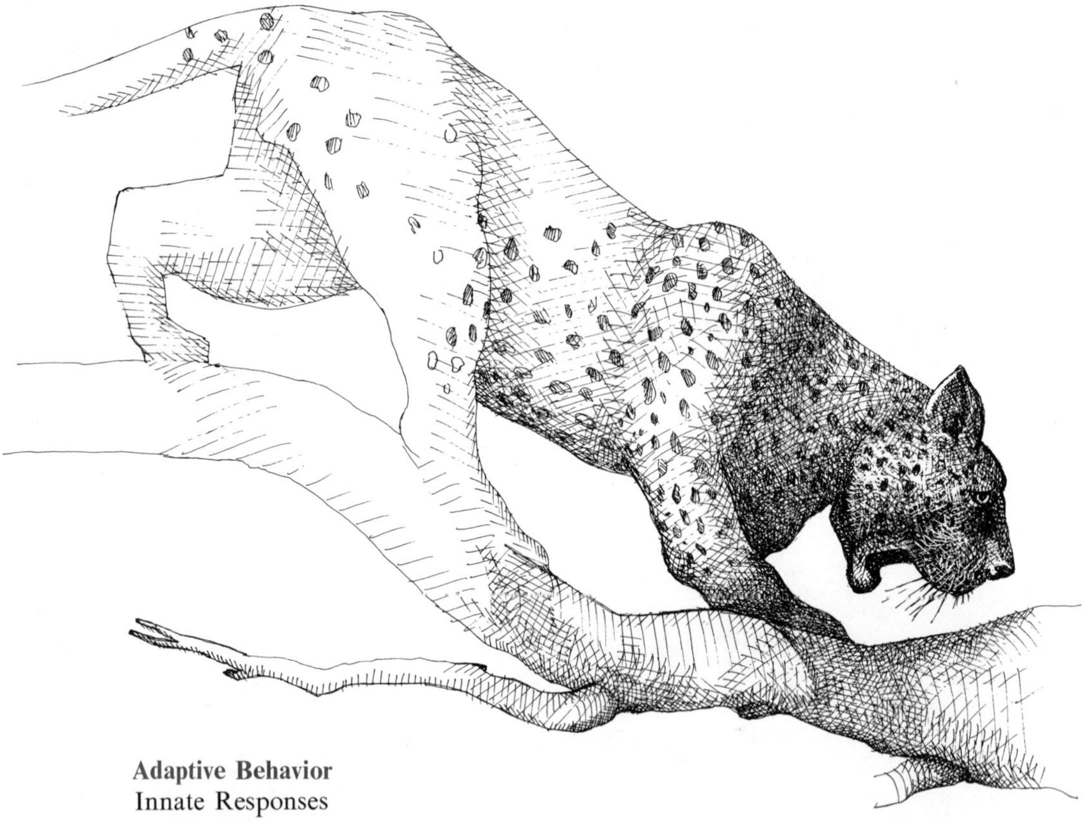

ADAPTIVE BEHAVIOR

No matter how specialized, all organisms must be able to adjust to normal environmental variation—changes in temperature, for example. (What is tolerable for an organism, that is, how much variation it can adjust to, depends on the degree of specialization achieved during the evolutionary process.) The adjustments that can occur during such environmental variation involve **self-regulation,** the maintenance of stability under varying conditions. Self-regulation is achieved through the interplay of internal chemical reactions and external behavior. When, for example, a warm-blooded animal responds to cold by raising its chemical activity and producing more body heat, a chemical change in internal regulators has occurred. When the same animal seeks shelter from the wind, or a sunny spot in which to warm itself, it is responding to environmental variation with an adaptive change in behavior.

Two major types of adaptive behavior have evolved in the animal kingdom. These are **innate responses** and **learning.** With the exception of a few very primitive organisms, both types of behavior play a role in adaptation. The degree to which innate responses and learning contribute to the adaptation of an organism varies by species.

Innate Responses

In simple, one-celled organisms even innate behavior is limited. These organisms can respond only to a small number of stimuli and, in general, such responses are quite simple. Certain protozoa, for example, react to light, to the acid content of the media in which they live, and to gas concentration. They respond to a noxious stimulus with an increase in random motion. If an organism thereby moves away from the stimulus, it slows down. Although inefficient, this behavior eventually leads the organism away from the irritating stimulus. This type of response is known as **kinesis** (Figure 3.1). It is one of the simplest forms of behavior.

More complex organisms have developed behaviors that allow them to move directly toward positive or directly away from negative stimuli. These responses are known as **taxes** (Figure 3.2). Fruit flies, for example, are *geotaxic negative;* they respond negatively to gravity and fly upward. Many flying insects are *phototactic*

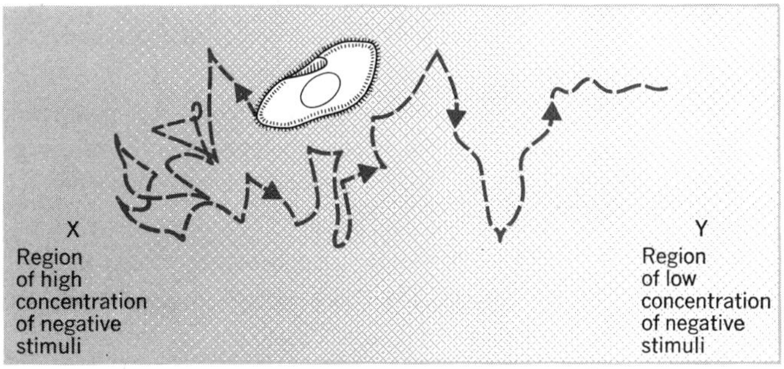

Figure 3.1

Kinesis in a paramecium. As the organism approaches a region of high concentration of negative stimulus, it speeds up. The further away it moves from the negative stimulus the slower its movement. This type of random movement will eventually remove the organism from the negative stimulus.

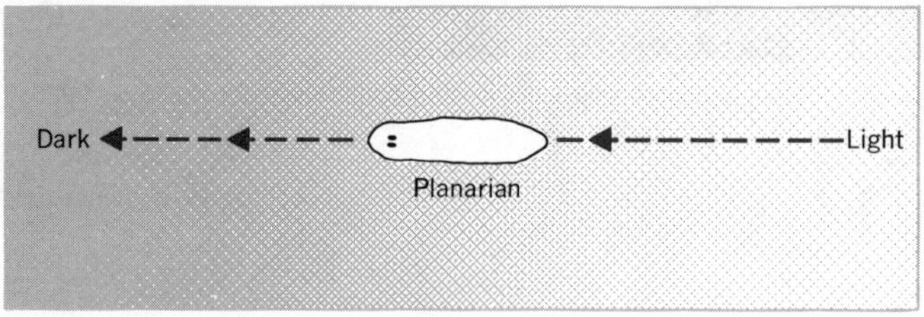

Figure 3.2
Phototactic negative response in a planarian. The organism is stimulated to move in the direction of darkness.

positive; they fly towards the light. The house mouse will tend to run around the walls of an open space; it only ventures into the open if food is present and even then hesitantly. The last example demonstrates that even innate behaviors can be complex and dependent on different **releasing mechanisms** in the environment. The mouse will follow the walls of a room automatically unless another behavior is released. The presence of food suppresses the first behavior and releases another.

Innate behavior may include very complex and organized responses. Web spinning in spiders and nest building in birds are examples. Complex behaviors of this type lead to an adaptive alteration of the environment. The spider web is an artificial product of behavior that enhances its manufacturer's ability to feed itself. A bird's nest offers "unnatural" protection for its young.

An innate behavior is triggered by some stimulus in the environment in combination with an appropriate chemical state within the organism. The behavior can only occur when both conditions exist. Organisms that respond in this way are born with a built-in behavioral system that is resistant to change. The evolutionary advantage of such behaviors is due to their automatic quality. They occur spontaneously the first time environmental conditions are appropriate. New innate responses do not arise automatically during the lifetime of an organism. Because such responses are genetically programmed, new ones must await the occurrence of genetic change. It is for this reason that innate responses lack flexibility in the face of environmental challenges.

Learning

Behavioral flexibility depends on another capacity of organisms, learning. Almost all animals are capable of learning from their environment and of modifying their behavior accordingly. Learning provides an organism with a high degree of behavioral flexibility. The learning process is a source of variation in behavior and is as important to evolution as the development of any morphological trait or any genetically determined behavioral trait.

How much an animal can learn, as well as what it can learn, is partially controlled by its heredity. In higher organisms, in which learning is a very important part of the adaptive process, learning can lead to a cataloging and reorganization of the environment. A dog, for example, may learn on his own that people in uniform react differently to him when he is running loose from the way other people react to him. Or he may come to discriminate between different neighborhood children on the basis of their friendly or cruel behavior. He may learn which dogs or cats to avoid and which people are likely to give him a bone, which a kick.

Animals that learn, particularly mammals, also learn by playing. Play is an excellent way to learn because it usually occurs in a safe context.

When young baboons play-fight, they are watched over by adults. If one of the young emits a cry of pain or alarm, an adult will step in and break up the game. Human children often learn a great deal about adult behavior by playing such games as house. Among hunting and gathering peoples young boys often hunt insects with toy bows and arrows. They learn adult skills without facing adult dangers.

Animals can learn directly from their environment or they can learn from other animals. The latter occurs more frequently among social species, but among some solitary species of birds, adolescent males learn the mating call from distant mature males. In the primates, particularly among social monkeys and apes, social learning can be so patterned and so extensive that the behavior of individuals in one troop can differ significantly from the behavior of individuals in another troop of the same species.

Although it is convenient to separate innate and learned behavior, it is often difficult to do so in real situations. Learning and innate processes often occur together. Ducks, for example, will learn to follow any noisy moving object presented to them within a certain period after hatching. This process is known as **imprinting.** Under normal circumstances the first noisy moving object a baby duck comes in contact with is its mother, and the response is perfectly adaptive. Observations of baby ducks in the wild would never reveal the variable aspect of imprinting. Nor could such observations reveal that imprinting occurs only *within* a very specific time period. If young ducks are isolated for a few days and are then presented with an appropriate stimulus (even their own mother), they will not imprint. The learning in this case is under the strict control of a genetic process. Genes do not determine *exactly* what is learned but they certainly do determine the type of behavior learned and when it can be learned.

Web spinning in spiders is a complex innate behavior.

There is evidence that something similar to imprinting occurs in humans. Up to about the age of ten, it is very easy for children to learn to speak a second language without a foreign accent. In fact, very young children can become truly bilingual—that is, they may become completely proficient in two (and even more) languages. After a certain age this ability is reduced; it is even lost in adults. This does not mean that adults cannot learn a second language. Of course, they can; but they cannot, in most cases, learn to speak it as well as a native. There is also evidence that children brought up in total isolation (by psychotic parents, for example) find it very difficult to learn *any* language if they are not exposed to normal speech before they reach adolescence.

Recent experiments with newborn human infants suggest that early skin-to-skin contact between mother and offspring can have a profound effect on later development. The effect in this case is reciprocal—that is to say, behavioral changes can be seen in both mothers and their babies. When infants and mothers have such contact for a few hours in the first days after birth, mothers are more attentive later to the needs of their children and the children show accelerated development. The positive response of infants in this case rewards the mother and encourages her to continue such behavior. The

Mammals are animals with high learning capacities. Here, trained pigs perform at a county fair and a killer whale performs at the Vancouver, British Columbia Aquarium.

Kittens learn adult behavior through play-fighting.

These young geese have imprinted on the Nobel-prize-winning ethologist Konrad Lorenz.

accelerated development in infants may be based on a combination of genetically programmed imprinting and associated learning. More experiments and observation of this process must be done to clarify the details of this process.

The amount an animal can learn, the complexity of the learned response, and the complexity and subtlety of the stimuli that can be discriminated under learning—all these differ according to species *and* according to early experience. Certain animals are capable of solving more difficult problems than others. The types of solution attempted by various species also differ. The comparative psychologist M. E. Bitterman has studied problem solving in a range of animals from fish to rats; he finds that fish are unable to change responses when learning conditions are changed. Thus, if a fish is given food when it presses button A but not button B, it will continue to press button A even when the experimenter reverses the conditions, withholding food when A is pressed and giving it when B is pressed. Rats, on the other hand, soon learn to switch responses from one stimulus to another. Bitterman has also found that turtles fall in between fish and rats in their ability to reverse responses.

THE INTEGRATION OF BEHAVIOR AND EVOLUTION

Morphological Evolution and Behavior

Behavior does not evolve as an independent system. The evolutionary goodness-of-fit between an organism and its environment includes internal adaptation. An important aspect of internal adaptation is the harmony that develops between morphology and behavior. Dogs, for example, are strong-jawed, swift runners capable of tracking game animals for long distances. Behaviorally, they are social animals that hunt in packs. A group of dogs can bring down large grazing animals. Cats lack the endurance and long-range speed of dogs, but they are more graceful and can therefore move silently as they stalk their single prey. Cats usually kill alone. A single cat is a likely match for most animals up to twice its size. Dogs, on the other hand, cannot bring down a large animal alone; they snap at their prey and dart away. They protect themselves by feints and dodges. If dogs hunted alone, their prey might well escape, but as manifested in group behavior their technique is highly effective.

Sensation and Behavior

Behavioral adaptations tend to follow the same rules as morphological ones. Some animals are highly specialized while others adapt behaviorally in a general way. Animals that learn well tend to be generalists—that is, they can easily adapt to varying environments—at least in comparison with animals that rely heavily on instinct. The development of behavior, whether innate or learned, is a genetic process, since learning capacities, if not what is learned, are under genetic control.

All behavior requires specializations that are related to the functioning of the nervous system. For it is the nervous system that controls the reception of stimuli from the environment, converting them into sensations and producing the behavioral responses that follow. Sensory reactions are called **afferent** responses, the behavior that flows from them are called **efferent** responses. Sensations relay information about the environment to centers in the nervous system that initiate appropriate efferent responses.

Sensory discrimination varies from species to species just as much as morphology and behavior. Sensation is one other aspect of internal adaptation that contributes to the coherence of the organism as a functional system. Biting insects such as mosquitoes are sensitive to the carbon dioxide expired by their prey. Leeches are highly sensitive to minute quantities of blood dissolved in water. Ticks are activated by slight changes in temperature that occur when their hosts approach. Some animals can see only moving objects. Bees can respond to ultraviolet light, which is invisible to humans. Dogs and cats can smell very low concentrations of various chemicals in the air. Birds of prey have keen vision. The primates, the group to which we

Wild dogs hunt in groups or packs. Here they bring down a hartebeeste.

belong, have a relatively poor sense of smell but good hearing and vision. The primates are the only mammals that have wide-range color vision. Our hands are good grasping organs not only because of their architecture, but also because the fingertips are equipped with a rich supply of nerve endings. Our fingertips are highly developed sensory organs.

Members of the cat family are often solitary hunters. They stalk their prey and then spring at it with a swift-killing movement.

Innate Behavior, Learning, and Selection

I have already noted that both learning and innate responses are the product of evolution. I have also pointed out the relative advantages of each and their interdependence. One other important fact about learning that has confused discussions of evolution needs to be discussed. While it is clear that the capacity for learned responses is based on genetic mechanisms, what is learned in specific instances is not genetic in origin. *Nonetheless, the environment exerts a selective effect on learned behavior.*

The environment is not a conscious presence. When an organism behaves, the environment does not "know" whether the behavior is innate or learned. In either case, however, the behavior has either a positive or a negative adaptive value in the context of the environment. Positive behavior has two effects.

(1) It helps the organism in some way. In higher animals the selective value of the behavior may be directly perceived by the animal

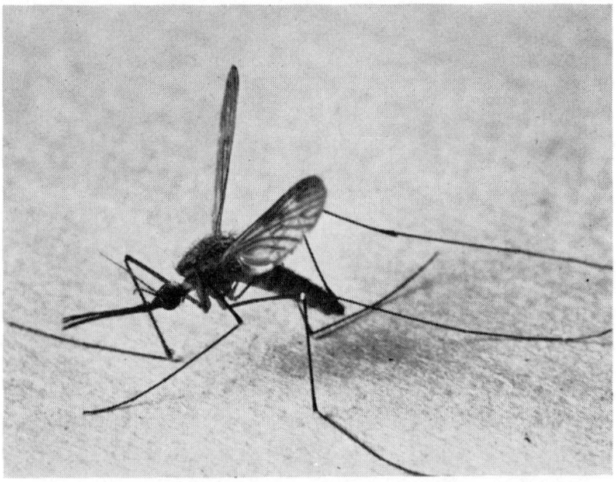

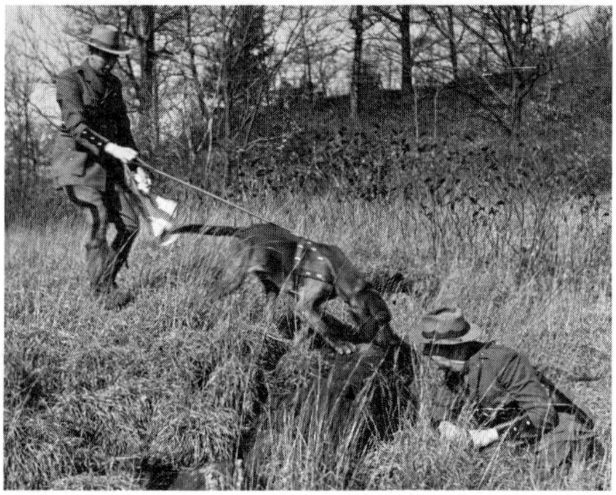

Sensory modes are developed differentially in different organisms. Mosquitoes are highly sensitive to carbon dioxide levels in the air and find their victims in this way. Hawks have keen eyes and hunt visually. Bloodhounds have a keen sense of smell that can be used to follow a scent trail. Bats use high-pitched signals much like radar to find their way through the air.

itself. It is "aware" that the environment has "rewarded" an appropriate response. Experimental psychologists use this awareness when they train rats in a laboratory. They "shape" behavior by rewarding those responses they wish to develop and by ignoring those responses that do not fit the sought-after pattern. Nature works the same way, if only in a metaphorical sense. Good (that is, adaptive) responses are "rewarded," poor (that is, maladaptive) responses are "punished" or "ignored." (2) If the behavior is adaptive, it contributes to the fitness of the organism and therefore to the contribution it will make to the next generation. The learning itself will not be passed down to the next generation, but animals that learn better than others will have a selective advantage. Thus, learning capacities evolve; they are environmentally selected.

The important point is that behavioral traits that look alike need not have the same source. An aggressive response in one species may be innate or partially innate. In another species it may be completely learned. Both species have to have the *capacity* for aggressive responses, but in the second aggression will only occur *when* it is learned. The stimuli that provoke aggression will be learned as well. Since environment shapes behavior for both innate and learned responses, we should expect to find similar responses in similar environmental conditions. We cannot tell merely by observing animals in the wild whether or not a response is innate. This is one reason why it is dangerous to assume that parallels between human behavior and animal behavior have the same bases. Our nervous system is the most complex in the animal world. We have the greatest learning capacity and excellent memory storage. In addition, we are the only species that has language and culture. These adaptations make learning a highly efficient means of coping with the environment. In most cases, innate, and therefore rigid, responses would serve the human species poorly because of the varied and changing environments in which we live.

Despite these remarks, I do not reject all notions of inborn patterns. Rather I wish to point out that facile analogies between human behavior and lower animals may reflect our folklore more than they reflect scientific facts.

Studying Behavioral Evolution

In the early days evolutionary studies were limited to the field of **paleontology,** the study of fossils. The fossil record was probed and ordered into temporal sequences. Later, genetics began to make its contribution. More recently, biologists have begun to study animal behavior under natural conditions. Sometimes they document exactly what happens as animals live their lives out undisturbed by humans. Some-

The behavior of a pigeon is shaped by rewarding correct movements.

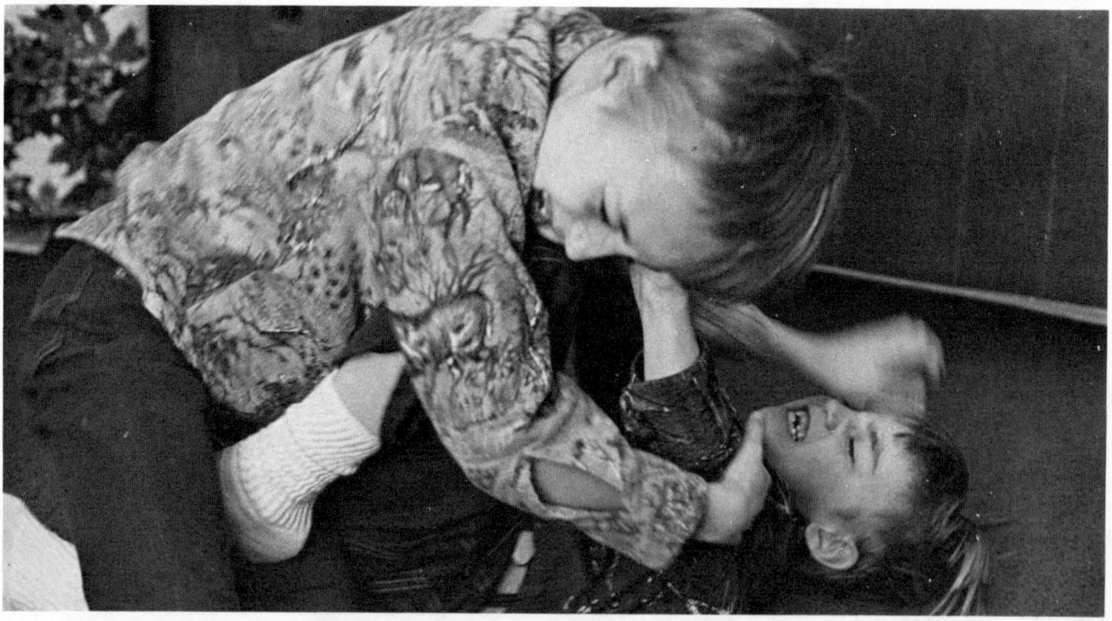

Aggression is common in the animal world. While the capacity for aggression may be biologically determined, its occurrence and form are often the result of learning. Here we see two male elephants fighting and two children fighting. The elephants are attempting to establish territory. The children may be fighting for a variety of reasons, none of which can be predicted from biological facts.

times they manipulate environmental conditions in order to enhance our understanding of behavior. This field, known as **ethology,** has taught us much about the relations between animal morphology and behavior. Among the leading ethologists are the Nobel prize winners Niko Tinbergen, Konrad Lorenz, and Max von Frisch. Tinbergen, famous for his studies of wild bird behavior, has analyzed such patterns as sexual displays, responses to predators, and territoriality. Lorenz has also worked with birds, studying sexual patterns, territoriality, and aggression. Max von Frisch has conducted a series of experiments and observations with honey bees. These demonstrate that bees use an effective communication system to signal the location of nectar to members of the hive.

THE PROBLEM OF ALTRUISM

Evolution depends on selective fertility. Therefore, an organism that sacrifices itself for the "good" of another puts itself at an evolutionary disadvantage, since premature death is an obvious limitation to fertility. When a mother bird diverts a cat away from her nest full of fledglings and is killed, she is acting altruistically. Her behavior saves the young birds but she loses her life in the process. Such behavior is even more surprising when it occurs, as it does, among young siblings who have not yet reproduced. Yet sacrifice, or **altruistic** behavior, is found in many species. This fact confronts the study of behavioral evolution with a paradox that has plagued it for years.

One solution to this paradox is offered by the theory of group selection. According to this view, populations with altruistic members are better adapted (as whole populations) than populations without such members. Altruistic animals enhance survival by sacrificing themselves for the good of the entire group. In group-selection theory competition and adaptation both occur on the level of entire populations. This theory creates several problems. It takes the process of adaptation away from organisms (the real gene packages in any population) and places it on a higher level, that of the group. Yet we know that selection acts on individual organisms. For altruism to spread through a species by this means, it would have to evolve through competition between genetically isolated groups. These groups would have to differentiate from one another (at least in the frequency of the altruistic trait) and, therefore, little gene flow could be present. This, however, is a condition for speciation. For group selection to work, there would have to be enough gene flow to maintain the integrity of the species but not so much as to stop the competition between

THE PROBLEM OF TERRITORIALITY AND AGGRESSION

Territoriality (the defense of living and/or breeding space by an individual organism or a group of organisms against another organism or group of organisms) is a widespread phenomenon in the animal kingdom. **Aggression** (the unprovoked attack of an organism on another organism of the same species) has been widely reported among such animal groups as insects, fish, birds, and mammals. It is often confused with defense, behavior in which an animal responds to attack. In some instances the term **agonistic** behavior is used to describe *both* aggressive and defensive reactions. Since territories are often established through aggressive behavior and defended agonistically, aggression has often been linked to territoriality. Both are assumed to have survival value, since the successful organism is able to establish a territory and gain access to breeding. The capacity for aggression and territorial behavior is widespread in the animal kingdom. It can be argued, however, that learning plays an important role in the manifestation of these responses in any given situation. It can also be argued that while the capacities are biologically based, the appearance of such behavior is dependent, at least in some species, on learning. When the conditions for such learning are absent, the behaviors themselves may not occur. The notion that territoriality and aggression are innate, automatic responses in the human species has been explored by several popular authors, among them Konrad Lorenz and Robert Ardrey.

Lorenz is probably the best-known **ethologist.** I do not wish to fault his work with lower animals, but I must caution you about his statements concerning humans. Lorenz's book *On Aggression* was a best-seller. It has influenced the thinking about humans of many individuals, including some biologists. There are many books in this vein. Robert Ardrey has had great success with a series of books: *The Territorial Imperative, African Genesis, The Social Contract,* and most recently *The Hunting Hypothesis.* These books fall into a trap noted in the discussion of learned versus innate responses. When these authors find a behavioral similarity between lower animals and humans, they jump to the immediate conclusion that this behavior in all species is innate. Analyses of this type appeal to readers because they are simple and perhaps because they treat social problems with a certain fatalism. If one can argue that territoriality and aggression are inborn patterns, then programs designed to solve social and international problems may be a waste of time and effort. The same argument has been applied to the biology of IQ. Those who believe that certain races are inferior in intelligence use **biological determinism** to speak against integration and educational programs designed to equalize opportunity.

It would be foolish to deny that territoriality and aggression are widespread in human populations, but they are not universal traits. In addition, their expression (how, when, and why they occur) varies tremendously from culture to culture. These differences in cultural behavior involving aggression or territoriality cannot be explained biologically.

Authors like Ardrey and Lorenz have tended to equate individual psychological traits such as aggression with such social phenomena as war. Wars may involve aggression, but they need not. Wars are often planned by generals and politicians far removed from actual battle scenes, for reasons that are social rather than psychological. Soldiers on the front lines sometimes kill aggressively, but killing in warfare may also be caused by fear of the enemy or fear of punishment by officers. A good soldier is one who does what he is told, who follows orders. The "overly" aggressive combatant is a danger to himself and his fellows.

altruistic and nonaltruistic populations. Even if these conditions could be met (as has been pointed out by the mathematical geneticist James Crow), the evolution of altruism on the basis of group selection would take an enormous amount of time, more time than it has taken many higher organisms to develop into separate species. Apparently the problem of altruism requires a simpler answer.

In the 1960s a biologist, W. D. Hamilton, suggested that altruism could be accounted for through selection on the level of the individual organism. Biologists were encouraged to consider what has come to be known as the **inclusive fitness** of an organism and its genetic relatives. If, in sacrificing itself, an organism protects its own close kin (siblings, offspring, and so on), it would also protect a significant part of its own genetic heritage, because all organisms share genes with their relatives. If part of this common genetic heritage is an innate disposition to protect kin, then **kin selection** (the protection of kin through altruistic acts) could account for the evolution of such behavior (see Figure 3.3). The notion of kin selection has been systematized in a formula: Selection $= k < \frac{1}{\bar{r}}$. This means that kin selection will work when the altruist's loss is smaller than the recipient's gain and where the recipient is a relative of a certain degree. In the formula $\bar{r}$ is the mean coefficient of relationship (a father has a higher coefficient than an uncle; an uncle is genetically closer than a cousin); k is the ratio of altruist's cost to recipient's gain.

An additional hypothesis to help account for altruism has been developed by R. Trivers. According to his concept of **reciprocal altruism,** a social organism that saves a member of its group at one time may itself be saved by that group member at another time. The mathematical problems involved in measuring reciprocal altruism, however, have lead some biologists to question its validity.

Although most biologists and many anthropologists accept the concept of kin selection as an important and probably valid hypothesis to account for the evolution of altruistic behavior in nonhuman species, many scholars in both fields question its applicability to humans. The anthropologist Marshall Sahlins, for example, has examined a wide range of data from preliterate societies and finds that the degree of genetic relationship within any individual's social group is often lower than the degree of genetic relationship between the individual's group and competing groups. Sahlins believes that altruistic behavior in humans can only be explained as a cultural phenomenon. Sahlins has in turn been criticized by Richard Alexander, a biologist, for ignoring k in the kin-selection formula (k = altruist's cost in relation to recipient's gain). This is an important point, because social and genetic relations in human societies are very complex, and many factors are likely to contribute to any genetic outcome. The problem with k in the analysis of human behavior, however, is that it is probably not a measurable quantity. Too much elusive data over too much of a time span would have to be collected through observation to get even a partial estimation of k.

Many anthropologists argue that altruism among humans is the result of our species' spe-

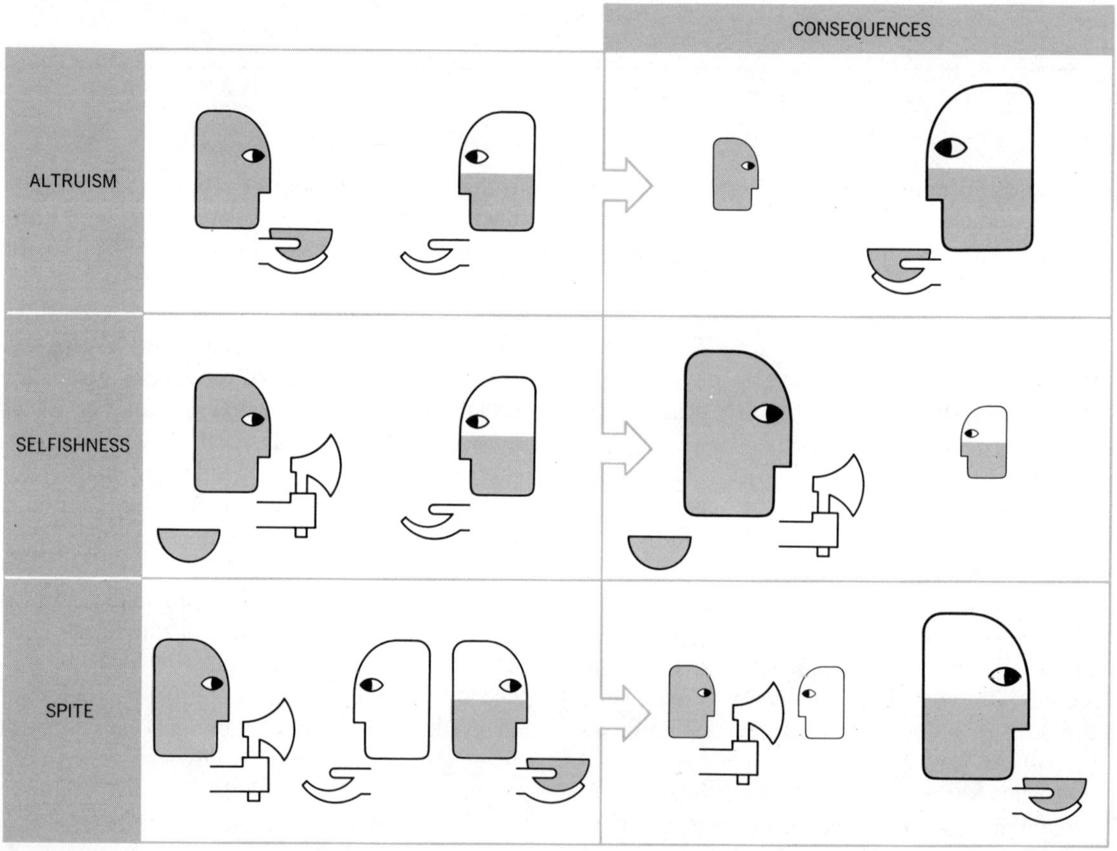

Figure 3.3
The conditions that give rise to altruism, selfishness, and spite by means of kin selection. The relationships shown are between an individual and his brother. The fraction of genes in the brother shared by common descent is indicated by the darkened half of the face. Positive behavior is indicated by a cup and negative behavior by an axe. In the case of altruism the altruist lowers his own genetic fitness but raises his brother's. In the case of selfishness the selfish individual reduces his brother's fitness but enlarges his own. In the case of spite an individual lowers the fitness of a genetically unrelated competitor. While he has a neutral or negative effect on his own fitness, he raises the fitness of his brother. (Adapted from Wilson, 1975.)

cific adaptation—*culture*—and so reflects cultural rather than biological rules. The application of a strictly genetic model to altruism among humans is the result of confusion between the roles of genetics and learning, in this case cultural learning, in the human adaptive process. That kin selection may have given rise to altruistic behavior in the course of evolution does not mean that it continues to operate in human societies, even though altruistic behavior is very much an aspect of human behavior. It is highly possible that the genetic mechanism has been replaced by a cultural mechanism.

The problem of altruism as well as a set of other questions concerning the behavioral evolution of many social species has led recently to the emergence of a field known as **sociobiology.**

SOCIOBIOLOGY

The year 1975 saw the publication of a massive book, *Sociobiology,* by the Harvard biologist Edward O. Wilson. *Sociobiology* attempts to demonstrate a relationship between genetically programmed behavior in lower animals and *some* aspects of cultural behavior in humans. The arguments in *Sociobiology* grow out of the problem of altruism and its solution in kin selection. Kin selection is used to explain a wide variety of human behavior that might otherwise seem strange or at least difficult to explain with the usual evolutionary principles. Wilson's book attracted immediate attention and was both praised and attacked. Some anthropologists and biologists saw *Sociobiology* as a great synthesis of our knowledge about behavioral evolution and ethology. Others saw it as an affirmation of simple biodeterminism like that of Lorenz and Ardrey, a step backward toward the denial of cultural variables in human behavior.

Most of the debate has focused on the last chapter, *Man: From Sociobiology to Sociology.* In this chapter, Wilson suggests that a good deal of human behavior can be explained on the basis of behavioral-biological principles derived from the study of lower animals. Not only does Wilson attempt to trace the origin of human traits in lower animals, he also argues that contemporary behavior can, in part, be explained on the basis of behavioral genes. On the other hand, he recognizes the fact of culture and says, "It is part of the conventional wisdom that virtually all cultural variation is phenotypic rather than genetic in origin."

Reviewing the role of genetics in the transmission of culture, Wilson is forced to admit that the evidence is negative. "Yet despite the plausibility of the general argument, there is little evidence of any hereditary solidification of status . . . cultural evolution is too fluid."

In spite of this conclusion, however, Wilson clings to the notion that genes have a direct and immediate effect on culture: "Although the genes have given away most of their sovereignty they maintain a certain amount of influence in at least the behavioral qualities that underlie variation between cultures."

Wilson claims that genes control such behavioral traits as introversion-extroversion, personal tempo, psychomotor and sports activities, neuroticism, dominance, depression, and the tendency for certain types of mental illness. He says that if even a small part of the variance in these traits between populations is due to genetics, heredity could predispose societies toward cultural differerences.

Wilson points out that one of the major features of human social groups is the variety of individual differences. "The hypothesis to consider, then, is that genes promoting flexibility in social behavior are strongly selected on the individual level." I do not think that it is possible to argue against the last statement. The development of culture and human social behavior must have been aided by genetic selection for behaviorally polymorphic (variable) populations. But this is a far cry from the claim that specific genetic differences among the members of different populations lead to cultural change! The history of human development, since the emergence of *Homo sapiens,* has been one of cultural change based on environmental and social facts that can be documented. This development is, in fact, one major subject of cultural anthropology.

In *Sociobiology* Wilson tends to employ the same analogies between human and animal behavior that are found in the work of ethologists. The following terms are used in reference to animal behavior: absenteeism in parental care, adoption, polygamy, moralisitc aggression, caste, slavery, warfare, altruism, division of labor, dialects, begging, monogamy, infanticide, xenophobia, leadership. Although these have become standard terms in the description of animal behavior, their widespread use obscures the differences that exist between animal behavior and the human cultural behavior to which they apply directly. The pervasive **anthropomorphism** (interpreting the nonhuman in human terms) in Wilson's book is not unique, but in the context of sociobiology it serves to undermine scientific understanding.

There are other, perhaps more serious problems in *Sociobiology*. Among these are the following:

1. Although Wilson admits that human social evolution is largely cultural, he does not clearly separate the biological origins of specifically human traits from the operation of these traits in the fully evolved species. It is one thing to understand the biological roots of culture and quite another to equate culture to genes.
2. As I have stressed before, "Mother Nature" does not know whether a particular trait is genetic, learned, or a combination of these. Parallel behaviors found in different species may depend on different mechanisms. Selection will favor adaptive traits whatever their origin.
3. Wilson notes that the evolutionary function of the organism is the production of more DNA. This is correct. It means, among other things, that the evolutionary process involves the transformation of environment into organisms. Wilson forgets, however, that with the emergence of *Homo sapiens,* environmental energy is *diverted into much more than organisms.* Humans use energy to produce nonconsumable "wealth," which is distributed unevenly in society. This arrangement *may* sometimes contribute to the selective advantage of some individuals, but to think that this is always the case is to indulge in a vast oversimplification. While we are certainly biological creatures, subject to evolutionary forces, we must also consider historical (nonbiological) facts in the development and differentiation of human culture.
4. Although Wilson is to be complimented for discussing such exclusively human traits as language and art, he tends to build his case on a series of continuities between lower and higher animal forms. Even though he

notes that many of the important human traits are either shared with only *some* primates or are unique to our species, he loses sight of the basic discontinuities between species. Bees, after all, do not have language even if they do communicate in sophisticated ways, and we do not have stingers in our tails. There *is* continuity in the biological world, but in order to understand the evolution of a particular species we must concentrate on that species' adaptations.

It must be emphasized, in defense of Wilson and others who attempt to study human behavioral biology, that some cultural anthropologists have tended to exaggerate the liberation of *Homo sapiens* from biological control. For these individuals the emergence of culture means that humans have become totally separated from the biological evolutionary process. Yet everything we do has its biological underpinnings. We must meet the problems posed by our environment in order to survive as living creatures. In most cases, cultural means are used to attain biological ends, but although the behavioral vocabulary of humans is large, it is not infinite. That we can, under appropriate circumstances, act aggressively is related to ancient patterns that are embedded in the brain. These patterns are, however, in no way instinctive. In humans their expression is modified by higher brain functions and cultural learning.

In answer to his critics, Wilson has written: "There is no doubt that the patterns of human social behavior, including altruistic behavior, are under genetic control, in the sense that they represent a restricted subset of possible patterns that are very different from the patterns of termites, chimpanzees and other animal species." (*New York Times Magazine,* Oct. 12, 1975)

This is a perfectly acceptable statement, but it is different in tone from much of *Sociobiology.* The book speaks of genes for altruism and talks about direct biological control of major differences in cultural behavior. The *New York Times* article is well within the mainstream of thinking among those who recognize the role of both biology and culture in the evolution of human behavior. As Stephen Jay Gould put it in his review of *Sociobiology* (*Natural History* magazine, May 1976):

If this is all that Wilson means by genetic control, then we can scarcely disagree. Surely we do not do all the things that other animals do, and just as surely, the range of our potential behavior is circumscribed by our biology. We would lead very different social lives if we photosynthesized (no agriculture, gathering, or hunting—the major determinants of our social evolution) or had life cycles like those of certain gall midges."

What Gould and others, including myself, object to is the stronger argument that social behaviors such as spite, aggression, xenophobia, conformity, homosexuality, and sexual differences are all under strict genetic control.

This criticism is not meant to read biological studies out of the analysis of human behavior. In order to fully understand the complex mix of cultural and biological interactions that have led to human behavior, we need to maintain a focus on human biology. We need to document both the continuities and discontinuities between ourselves and other species. But a human behavioral biology that rests only on comparative studies will fall short of the mark. We also need a true human ethology that will concentrate on those patterns that are species-wide. These include certain aspects of emotional expression as well as such specifically human traits as language and art.

Summary

Survival is not just a matter of physical evolution. Organisms respond in a variety of ways to environmental fluctuations. These responses consist of internal, physical-chemical changes—such as increased or decreased rates of circulation and the secretion of hormones such as adrenalin that mobilize the body for defensive action—and external, behavioral adjustments—such as seeking the sun when the body is cold and avoiding it when the body is too hot. The capacity to respond to environmental variation is inherited and depends on a variety of biological systems.

Animals face many problems besides environmental variation. They must eat and reproduce. Some must establish and defend territories. Many must nourish and care for immature offspring. These problems are solved through behavioral adaptations. Some organisms, spiders and birds, for example, are able to alter their environment through the operation of genetically programmed behavior. Thus, web spinning and nest building are programmed into the species. Such social responses as mating displays that precede sexual union are also frequently genetic in origin. Another important means of behavioral adaptation involves learning. As an organism becomes familiar with its environment it learns where to find food sources, how to defend itself, when to avoid certain dangers. Learning is a powerful adaptive tool in complex environments because it allows for a great deal of flexibility in behavior.

Most organisms display both genetically controlled and learned adaptive behaviors. Many behaviors are of a mixed type; this can occur when an animal is programmed to learn a behavioral pattern during a specific period in its development. Imprinting in ducks (the following of mother duck or some artifically presented substitute) involves a behavioral pattern that must be learned within a short period after hatching. It is possible that the ability to learn language in humans is partially dependent on a genetically based timing mechanism.

Although learning itself is not genetic, the capacity to learn and the type of learning that an animal can master are under partial genetic control. The amount of environmental stimulation that occurs during early growth also affects learning capacities.

Behavioral adaptation is dependent on such factors as morphology (the physical characteristics of an organism), its perceptual mechanisms, its activity levels, and the kind of genetic and learned responses it is capable of. What an organism does not perceive it cannot respond to. Some animals can only see moving objects. Bees respond to ultraviolet light, which is invisible to humans. Dogs can smell minute concentrations of various stimuli that are unnoticed by humans. The morphology and behavior of animals have evolved together so that there is a relative goodness-of-fit between behavior and hardware. Cats are built to hunt alone and dogs are built to hunt in packs.

The fact that a particular type of behavior is genetic in one species does not guarantee that it is genetic in another species. Learned responses can be just as adaptive as genetic ones, and natural selection has no way of distinguishing between the two. Remember that variation comes from organisms and that the environment selects. The environment is therefore blind to the origin of such variation. The environment will favor adaptive variations whether they be genetic, learned, or a combination of the two.

One of the major paradoxes of evolutionary theory concerns that aspect of behavior known as altruism. If selection depends on survival, how can behavior that involves sacrifice become fixed in species? Evolutionists have attempted to deal with this problem for many years. It was first suggested that altruistic behavior evolved on the level of groups. If a group of organisms contained altruistic members, it was reasoned, it would have an advantage over groups without such members. This theory soon ran into theoretical difficulties related to the fact that evolution is a process involving individual organisms. Recently it has been suggested that altruism can become part of a species' genetic heritage if sacrifices are made for genetic relatives that carry some of the genetic material of the altruist. For selection to favor altruism, there must be a certain relationship between the degree of genetic sharing and the loss suffered by the altruist to the benefit of the recipient of an altruistic act. Such a process is known as kin selection.

Thinking about the problem of altruism has led many biologists and anthropologists to consider the biological foundation of a wide range of behaviors. A school known as sociobiology has recently emerged that suggests that a wide range of animal and human behaviors can be at least partially explained on the basis of genetics, particularly as a function of genetically controlled altruism. Sociobiologists recognize that learning and culture play a role in the evolution of behavior, but feel that the biological model has not been adequately explored. Critics of sociobiology feel that culture and learning are the overriding forces in human behavior and have attempted to show, with some success, that sociobiological models applied to human societies do not work.

Bibliography

Alland, Alexander, Jr. 1972 — *The Human Imperative.* New York: Columbia University Press. An answer to the popular biology of Lorenz and Ardrey.

Ardrey, Robert 1961 — *African Genesis.* New York: Atheneum. The aggression hypothesis for human evolution presented dramatically.

Ardrey, Robert 1970 — *The Social Contract.* New York: Atheneum. Society and culture from the perspective of popular biology.

Bitterman, M. E. 1960 — Toward a comparative psychology of learning. *American Psychologist.* 15:704–712. The evolution of learning capacities in different grades of organism.

Fuller, J. L., and W. R. Thompson 1960 — *Behavior Genetics.* New York: John Wiley and Sons. The classic text on behavioral genetics.

Lorenz, K. 1966 — *On Aggression.* New York: Harcourt, Brace, Jovanovich. The original biological explanation of human behavior on the basis of instinctive aggression by one of the founders of ethology.

Sahlins, M. 1976 — *The Use and Abuse of Biology.* Ann Arbor: University of Michigan Press. A strong critique of sociobiology, which has itself been highly criticized by some biologists.

Scott, J. P. and J. L. Fuller, 1965 — *Genetics and the Social Behavior of the Dog.* Chicago: University of Chicago Press. Classic study of the interaction between genes and environment in the behavior of five species of dog.

Wilson, E. O. 1975 — *Sociobiology: The New Synthesis.* Cambridge, Mass: Belknap Press of Harvard University Press. The original book on sociobiology by one of its main proponents.

Wilson, E. O. 1978 — *On Human Nature.* Cambridge, Mass: Harvard University Press. Wilson's discussion of the application of sociobiology to human evolution and contemporary behavior.

CHAPTER 4

EVOLUTION THROUGH PRIMATES

In this chapter I will examine a series of evolutionary changes running from single-celled organisms to the emergence of modern humans, *Homo sapiens.* Evolution, as we have seen, is a complex process of environmental accommodation through internal and external adaptation. Here I will discuss only those major features that bear upon human evolution. Before reading this chapter you should examine the tables on pp. 78, 79. One presents the classification scheme used by biologists, with the human species as the example. The other shows the sequence of geological time periods as related to animal evolution.

Evolutionary sequences are determined primarily from the fossil record, which in vertebrates (animals with bony skeletons) is almost exclusively limited to such hard material as bones and teeth. Bones, however, tell us a great deal about the form and structure of animals. Muscles and other soft tissues leave their imprints on bone, and experts can reconstruct a good approximation of an entire animal from its skeleton alone. Comparisons of reconstructed fossils and related living species allow deductions to be made about behavior as well. Teeth are particularly useful in the analysis of fossils. In many cases they are the only parts of an animal to survive. Tooth structure and size as well as the number of particular kinds of teeth (grinding versus cutting, for example) provide behavioral and dietary clues. Carnivores (meat eaters) for example, have a different kind of tooth structure from that of herbivores (plant eaters).

The investigation of the fossil record and the analysis of related living forms are used by scientists to provide a sequential record of both physical and behavioral development. Such data teach us about the degree of relatedness among organisms and the development of particular kinds of adaptation through space and time. When analyzing the fossil record, scientists attempt to relate data on plants and animals to the specific facts of the environment. These last are determined in cooperation with geologists and climatologists, who aid in the reconstruction of past environmental conditions.

THE CELL

The first organisms were undoubtedly unicellular (single-celled). Although unicellular organisms by their very nature cannot have organs, which develop from different types of cells, they are by no means simple. Protozoa, the least complex form of animal life, show a sharp differentiation between the nucleus and the rest of the cell. In addition, the nonnuclear area, the *cytoplasm,* contains specialized parts that perform specific metabolic functions. We have already met one of these—the ribosomes, where protein is synthesized.

All organisms higher than unicellular forms are constructed of differentiated cells with special functions. The first complex organisms to evolve were loose aggregates of cells whose functions were determined by their locations. These organisms—as are their living relatives such as sponges—were little more than a colony of semi-independent cells. Further evolution led to a more coherent organization of cellular structures: true organs such as heart, lungs, and stomach. This development was a major step in evolution since it required complex transformations in the genetic code.

Cellular Differentiation

Since every organism begins as a single cell containing the DNA passed down from its parents when the fertilized egg begins to divide, each subsequent new cell can only receive identical information. Each cell in the body can be seen as the daughter, granddaughter, great granddaughter, and so on, of the original mother cell. How, then, do cells with the same genetic information develop into such specialized organs as livers, eyes, and brains? Although the process is far from fully understood, it seems clear that differentiation depends on genetic processes.

Cellular differentiation requires the development and elaboration of a timing mechanism that directs the process in an orderly way. The emergence of specific organs in fetal development, for example, must follow an architectural plan according to which certain types of cells emerge first. These cells become the building blocks for further elaboration as the fetus becomes more and more like the organism it will be at birth. During fetal growth genes responsible for differentiation remain inactive until it is time for them to trigger specific localized changes. Such genes are coded to change particular target cells, and they operate only during specific stages of development. Timing mechanisms of this sort operate after birth as well, particularly among those organisms that go through various types of change during the maturation process. This is true of those insects, for example, that pass from a larval to an adult stage. The spectacular changes that take place as a caterpillar finally emerges into an adult butterfly or moth are controlled by genetic mechanisms of this type.

While much remains to be discovered about

Classification of the human species. The classificatory terms (Kingdom, Subkingdom, etc.) are listed in order of increasing specificity.

Level of Classification	Name	Descriptive Remarks
Kingdom	Animalia	Animals
Subkingdom	Metazoa	Multicellular
Phylum	Chordata	Nerve cord
Subphylum	Vertebrata	Spinal column, bony skeleton
Superclass	Tetrapoda	Four-limbed
Class	Mammalia	Warm blood, four-chambered heart, live birth, mammary glands, hair
Order	Primates	Prosimii, Old and New World monkeys, apes, humans
Suborder	Anthropoidea	All of above except Prosimii
Superfamily	Hominoidea	Apes, fossil humans, living humans
Family	Hominidae	Fossil humans, living humans
Genus	*Homo*	Fossils in genus *Homo* and modern humans
Species	*sapiens*	Modern humans but including Neanderthal fossils
Subspecies	*sapiens*	Living humans

Geological time and animal evolution.

Millions of years ago	Era	Period	Epoch	Animal forms
	CENOZOIC	Quaternary	Recent Pleistocene	Age of *Homo sapiens*
1.5–7		Tertiary	Pliocene	Large carnivores
7–26			Miocene	Apes, grazing animals
26–38			Oligocene	Large grazing mammals; apes appear
38–53			Eocene	Early horses
53–65			Paleocene	First primates and carnivores
65–135	MESOZOIC	Cretaceous		Age of reptiles; extinction of dinosaurs; marsupials; insectivores
135–190		Jurassic		Dinosaur radiation; small mammals
190–225		Triassic		First dinosaurs; primitive mammals
225–280	PALEOZOIC	Permian		Reptiles evolve
280–345		Carboniferous Pennsylvanian Mississippian		Age of amphibians; reptiles appear
345–400		Devonian		Age of fish; amphibians appear
400–430		Silurian		Fish evolve
430–500		Ordovician		First fish; invertebrates predominate
500–570		Cambrian		Age of marine invertebrates
	PRECAMBRIAN			Earliest fossils

the way in which developmental genes are turned on and off, we do know that the process is determined, at least in part, by the internal environment, particularly the spatial relationships among the cells of the developing organism. Thus, genes in cells on the outside of a mass begin to direct one process while genes located in cells inside a mass will direct another

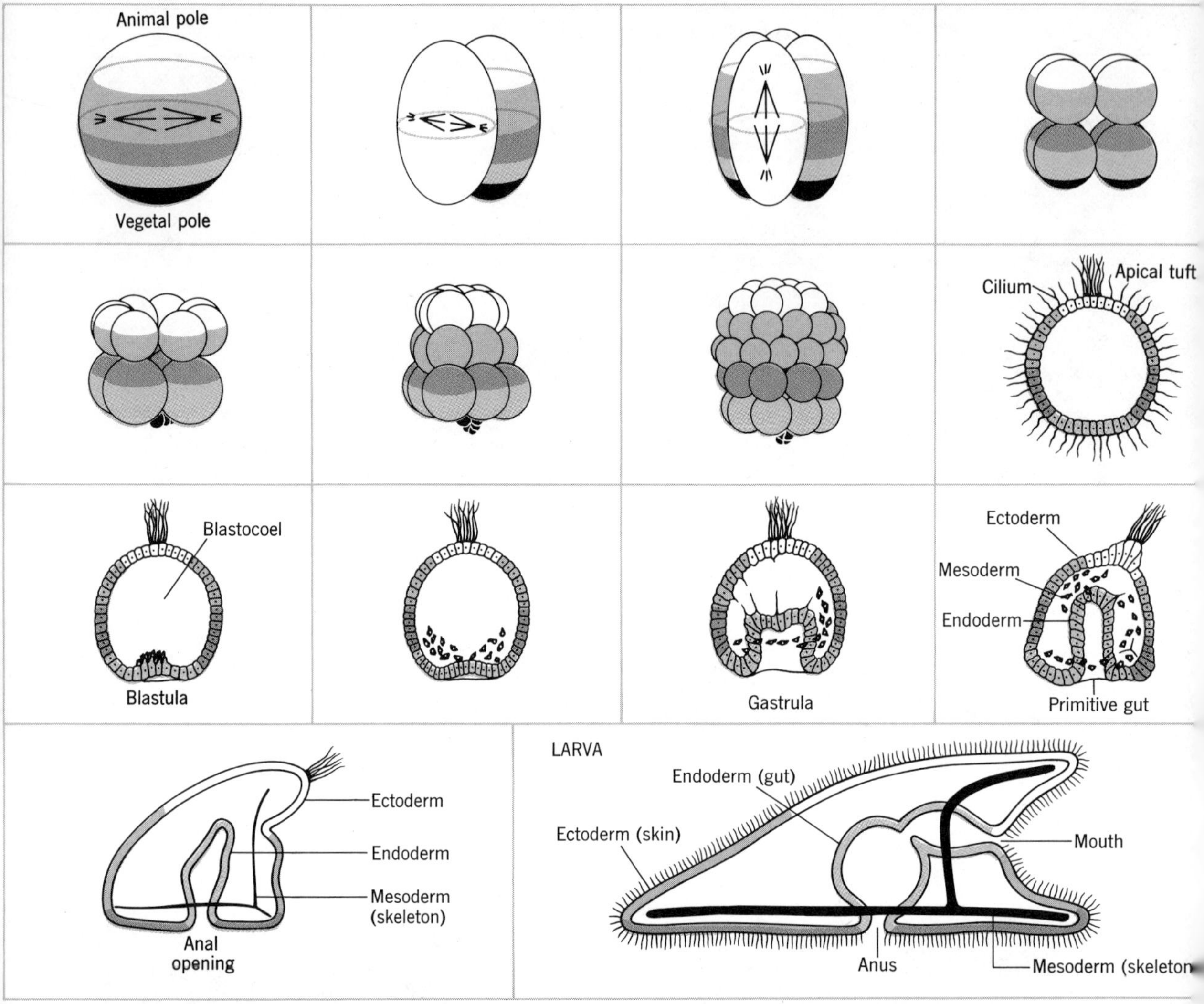

Figure 4.1
Cellular differentiation in a complex organism: the sea urchin. The egg divides repeatedly to produce a hollow ball of cells known as the blastula. One side of the blastula folds in forming two layers. Cells then migrate between the two layers to form a third layer. The three-layered stage is known as the gastrula.

(see Figure 4.1). As an organism becomes more complex, more and more differentiation occurs. New local environments are created that affect the expression of genetic information. All of this, of course, is part of internal adaptation. Note that even in internal adaptation it is the *interaction* between gene and environment that determines the outcome of the genetic process. The environment in this case is a cell and its surrounding cells, as they move through time.

THE MAJOR STAGES OF EVOLUTION

Life began in the sea. The saline (salt) content of our blood reflects that origin. The cell, which is highly dependent on moisture, must have had little difficulty maintaining a liquid balance in a watery environment. When the land surfaces were invaded, life forms had to develop protective mechanisms against dessication. Several means evolved. Small animals such as insects have an **exoskeleton,** a hard layer on the outside of the body. It protects against water loss and provides support as well as protection for the body. An exoskeleton is unsuitable for large animals, however. All the large land forms developed out of sea-dwelling **vertebrates** (see Figure 4.2); vertebrates are animals that have **endoskeletons** (supports on the inside). For architectural reasons the bony endoskeleton is far better suited to large animals on land than the exoskeleton. It is so good an architectural plan, in fact, that it allowed such enormous animals as the brontosaurus and other dinosaurs to develop. These animals, descendants of wet-skinned amphibians, developed dry skins that acted as envelopes for the internal wet cellular environment.

Another early development in the line that led to mammals and ourselves was **bilateral symmetry** along the vertical axis. Some early forms are totally asymmetrical while others are **radially symmetrical** (see Figure 4.3). Star fish are a good example of the latter form.

Nervous System and Skeletal Evolution

A growing complexity of the central nervous system occurs all along the line leading from lower to higher forms of animal life. While costly to maintain and organize, a complex nervous system offers organisms a gamut of behavioral adaptations that have high survival value. In the development of humans, as well as of all vertebrates, a long nerve chord forms, running down the back (dorsal) side of the organism with a swelling of nervous tissue at the head end. This swelling becomes the brain. There are a few **chordates** (animals with dorsal nerve chords) that have no skeletal systems and no back bones. Most, however, do have a spinal column that protects the delicate nervous system. The spinal column became the framework for the support and attachment of other bones as the skeletal system evolved.

Sharks and some other primitive fish lack true bones and their skeletons are made of cartilage. The bony skeleton began with the evolution of fish. It was one major adaptation necessary for the emergence of large land forms.

The Emergence of Limbs

Today the most common fish are ray-finned. These have flexible fin structures supported by thin cartilaginous spines. Among the early fish some had what are called *lobe fins* (see Figure 4.4). These fins are supported by bones much like the bones in our hands and feet. The lobe-fin fish also had a breathing mechanism that allowed them to breathe in both water and air. In ray fins these primitive lungs developed into swimming bladders. In the lobe fins they served as the basis for the true air-breathing lung. The lung and the bony fin are both what paleontologists refer to as **preadaptations** for land dwelling. If you compare the form of a lobe-fin fish with a reconstruction of the first amphibians you will note very little anatomical change. The lobe-fin fish provided the pattern for the first land vertebrates: amphibians (see Figure 4.4).

Land Vertebrates

The amphibian adaptation to land was tentative and imperfect. Amphibians must breathe through the skin as well as through the nose. In order to respire correctly they must keep the skin wet. In addition, amphibians cannot breed on land. All must lay their eggs in water. These hatch into larval forms that must continue to

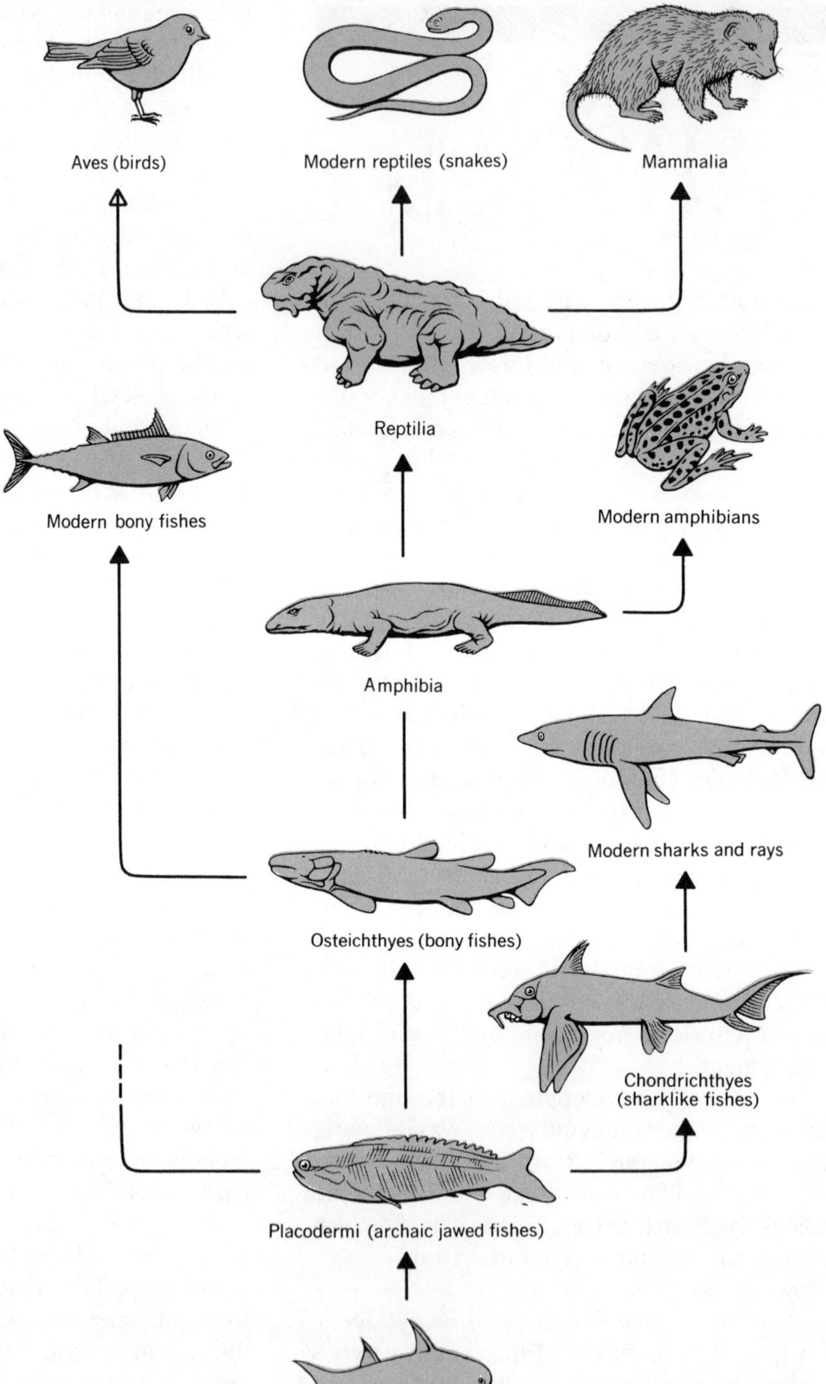

Figure 4.2
Evolution of the vertebrates from the jawless fishes.

develop in a liquid environment. Only adult amphibians can leave the water and only then for short periods. Of course, no living forms are totally independent of water. All must replenish their body fluids or die from dehydration.

However, the next stage in land adaptation, which culminated with the dinosaurs, was a decrease in the dependence on water. The reptiles represent this stage (see Figure 4.5). Reptiles lay eggs with hard shells. The reptile embryo still develops in a watery environment but this environment is contained within the egg. When the eggs hatch, the young can live on the land immediately and do not pass through a larval stage. Adults have dry skins and breathe, as we do, directly into the lungs. There are, of course, reptiles (as there are mammals) that live in the water, but they returned to the sea and required further evolutionary modifications.

Homeothermy

Reptiles have cold blood and are, therefore, highly dependent on external climatic conditions. Reptiles, like other cold-blooded organisms, are sluggish on cold mornings and can begin normal activity only after they have warmed themselves in the sun. Sometime during the middle of the great dinosaur age, a series of genetic changes led to the development of constant body temperature, or **homeothermy,** in the two lines that were to become birds and mammals. Homeothermy consumes a great deal of energy. Its evolutionary justification is that homeothermic animals can act independently of external temperature and support more complex nervous systems. Mammals and birds replaced the reptiles as the major land vertebrates only after severe climatic changes.

Warm blood requires a very active metabolic

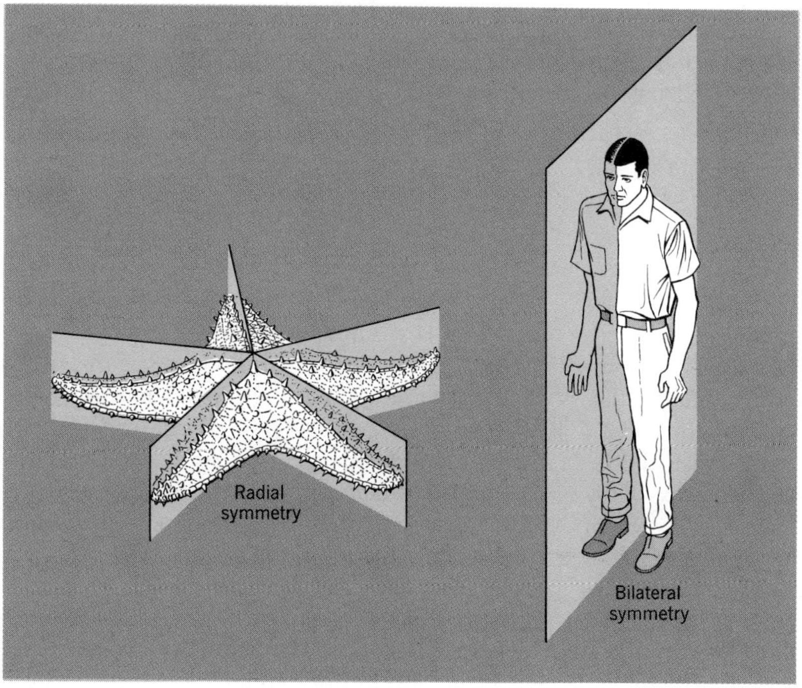

Figure 4.3
Radial symmetry (star fish) versus bilateral symmetry (human).

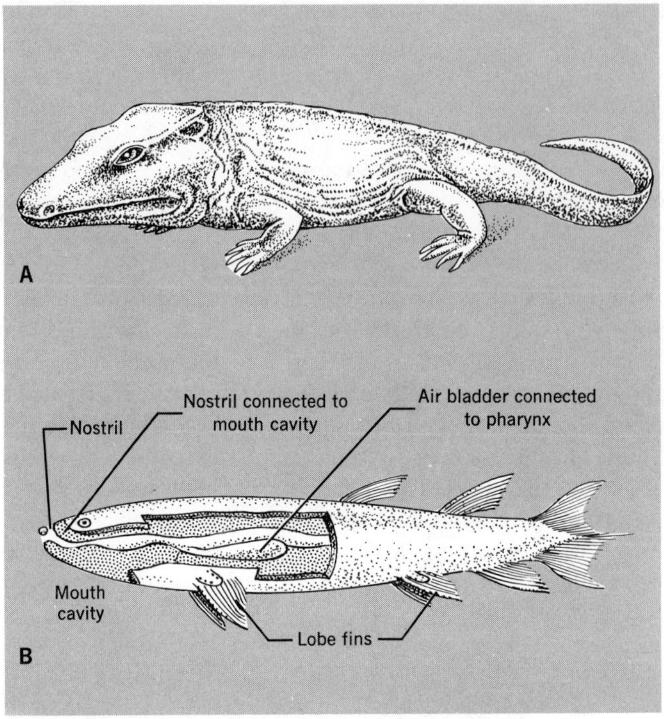

Figure 4.4
Evolution of the amphibia from the lobe-fin fish. Top shows a labyrinthodont amphibian about two feet long. Bottom shows a crossopterygian fish dissected to show three preadaptations for land dwelling. Note the overall similarity in body structure between the two organisms.

system. More fuel is required to keep the organism alive. This need in turn increases the need for physical activity and food getting. Metabolism depends on good oxygen transport and the rapid elimination of waste gases from the blood. Improved circulatory mechanisms must, therefore, develop along with homeothermy. The reptilian heart has only three chambers. Oxygen and carbon dioxide are only partially isolated during circulation. In birds and mammals a four-chambered heart allows for the complete isolation of oxygen-rich arterial blood and venous blood that carries waste gases to the lungs. Homeothermy, increased activity, and a more efficient metabolic system create the necessary internal environment for an enrichment of the central nervous system. The increased need for a high degree of behavioral efficiency (in order to feed the expensive system) demands a more complex central nervous system. There is, therefore, a relationship between homeothermy and development of the central nervous system. The mammalian brain is a major advance over the reptilian brain. Most of this development occurred in the **neocortex,** the most recently developed part of the brain. It is there that learning and information-storage take place and it is there that thinking developed.

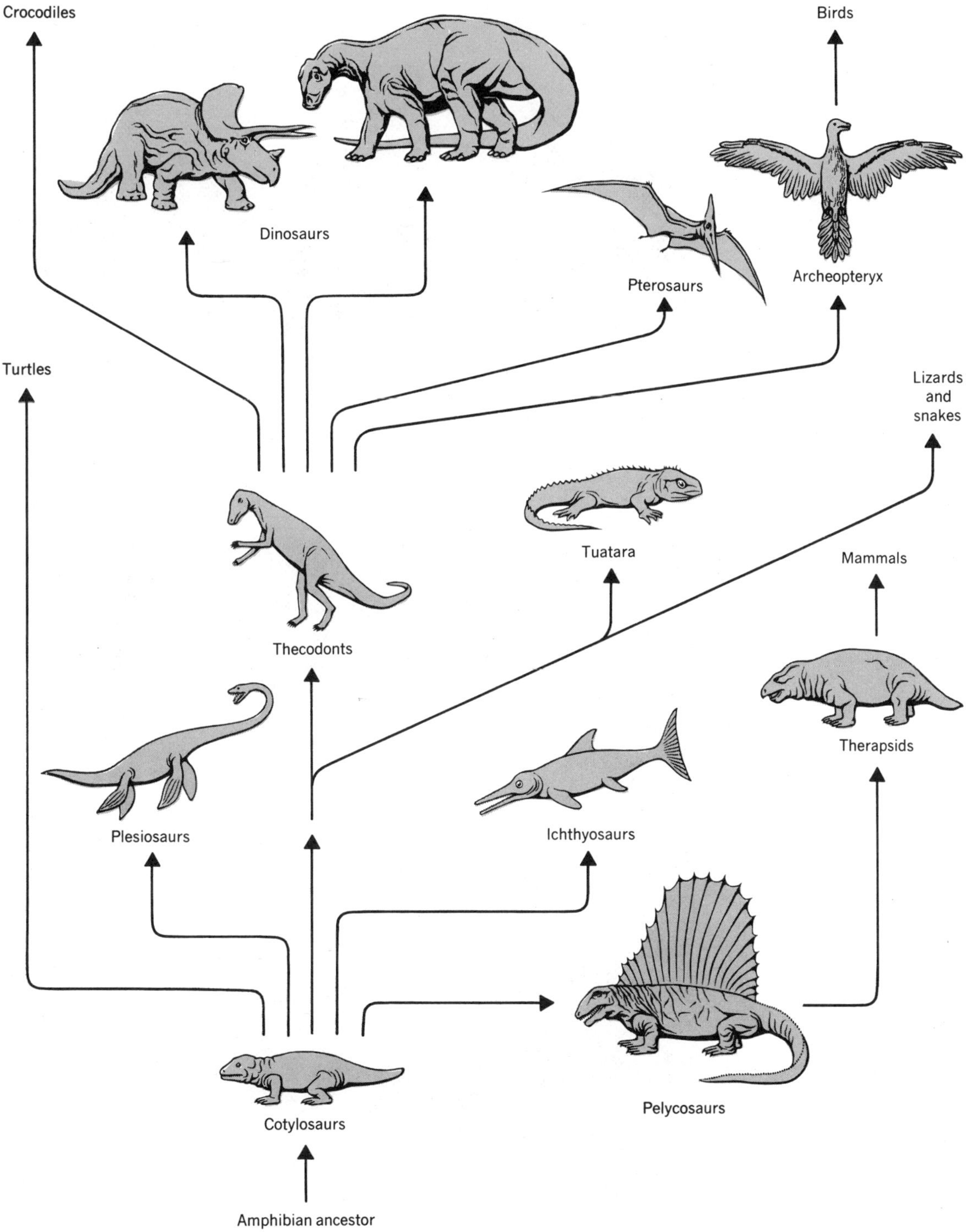

Figure 4.5
Evolution of the reptiles from an amphibian ancestor.

Iguanas must regulate their body temperature by seeking the warmth of the sun. The polar bear is a homeothermic animal and can maintain its body temperature under severe conditions of cold.

Mammals

Mammals, of course, are characterized by live birth, after a complex process of fetal development, and by mammary glands with which the female nourishes her young. The class Mammalia contains a wide variety of animals (see Figure 4.6), including such divergent forms as rodents, the large herbivores (cows, deer, horses, sheep, etc.), such carnivores as the cat family, as well as the bats, and the primates (prosimians, to be described below, monkeys, apes, and human beings). Each order within the class Mammalia has developed its own special adaptations. The fact that all mammals share the traits of live birth and mammary glands creates an important set of social requirements that lead in humans to the emergence of language and culture. Young mammals are born quite immature and are dependent for some time on their mothers. Nursing creates a close bond between infant and mother. This protective relationship gives the young animal time to learn about its environment before it must strike out on its own. Dependence on adults, particularly the mother, is common among all mammals. The length of the immature period, however, increases with brain evolution and reaches its full development with the primates and particularly humans. In addition to providing protection, the dependency period among primates apparently has an effect on the development of social bonding among members of a group. Monkey infants deprived of their mothers under laboratory conditions develop severe personality problems that affect their ability to interact normally with their fellow animals.

The Primates

The primate order is a continuation of the mammalian line. Primates include such premonkey forms as tarsiers, lemurs, and lorises; the monkeys, the apes, and human beings. Primates are characterized by a tremendous increase in central nervous system development, an acute visual system, and by **prehensile** (grasping) hands.

The fossil evidence suggests that the primate line developed from a group of small and currently insignificant mammals known as **insectivores.** These are sharp-eyed ground and tree-dwelling animals that feed on insects. Recently it has been proposed that the development of keen vision facilitated the stalking of small prey in a complex visual environment of leaves, sticks, and other disruptive elements. In order to feed successfully, these animals had to grab their prey with quick, sure movements. Because they fed on flying insects, insectivores needed to pinpoint their victims in the visual field. **Stereoscopic vision** provides an excellent means for meeting this adaptive requirement. The ability to see colors would also have been helpful to such organisms, for color vision allows the eye to distinguish prey from background. All higher primates have stereoscopic color vision.

Sometime early in primate evolution the precursors of today's living monkeys and apes took to the trees. In the trees stereoscopic color vision would continue to be highly adaptive. Tree-living animals must be able to judge distances as they move, sometimes leaping or jumping, from branch to branch. Because these primates spent most of their time in the trees, the sense of smell decreased in importance. Ground scents were no longer followed in the search for food. Improved vision is dependent not only on eye structure but also on a reorganized neocortex. Visual centers of the primate brain show increased development, while centers connected with olfaction (smell) show a decrease.

The larger primates developed good grasping appendages, which enabled them to survive in the trees. The fossil record and living forms show an early development of a grasping hand equipped with an opposable thumb. This development also accompanied changes in the brain. The fingers equipped with rich nerve endings became sensitive organs that could pass information on to the brain. In addition, the primates developed good eye-hand coordination. Touch and vision could be used in combination to monitor and manipulate the environment. Increased monitoring of the environment through touch and vision, feedback between

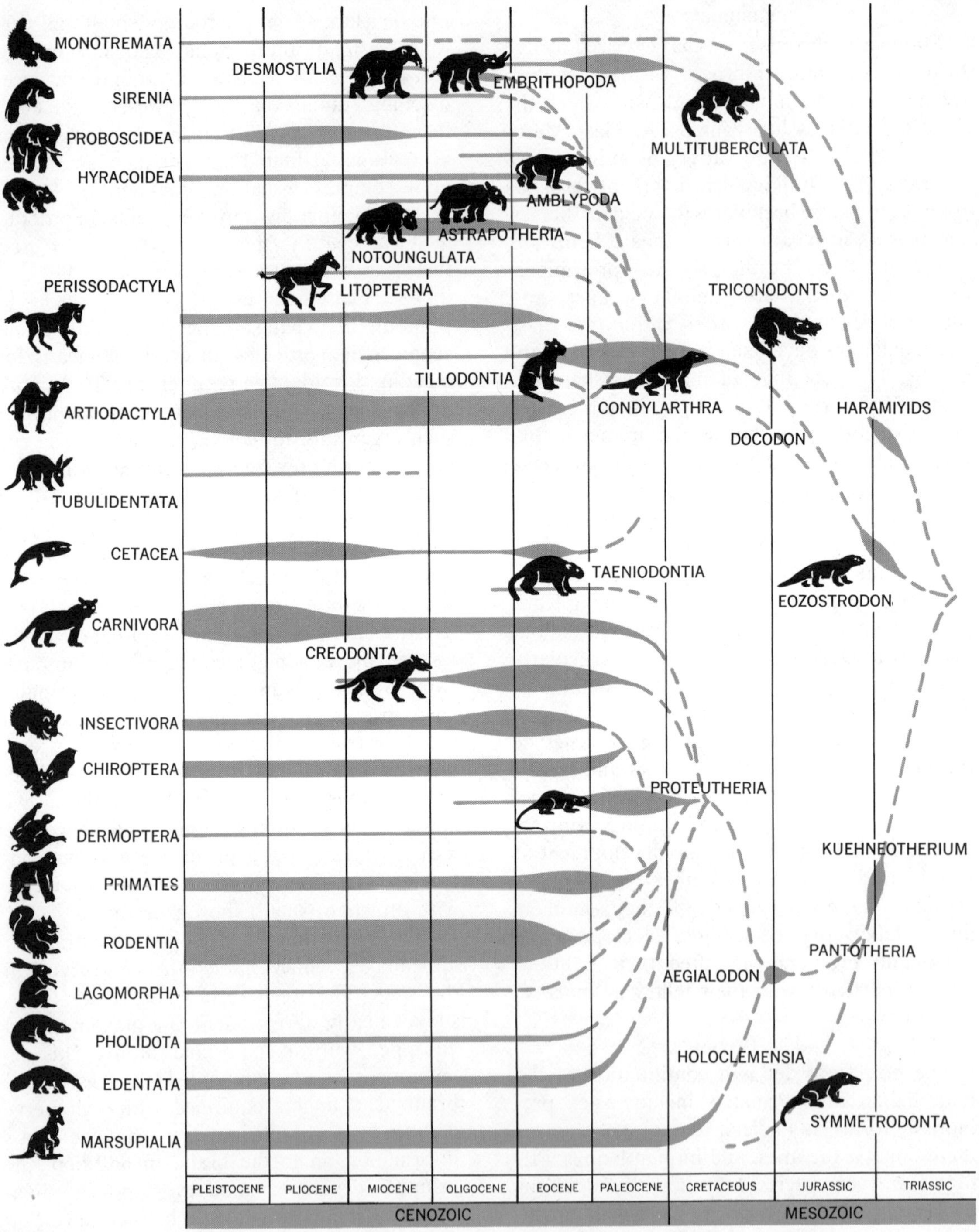

Figure 4.6

Mammalian evolution from a reptilian ancestor. (Adapted from "The Evolution of Multicellular Plants and Animals," by James W. Valentine. Copyright © September 1978 by Scientific American, Inc. All rights reserved.)

these two sensory modes, and the need to make fine-grain perceptual discriminations—these developments led to an increase in the size of the brain as well as to its reorganization. Changes in cerebral size and organization display a constant trend in primate development from the earliest to the most recent forms. A consequence was an increase in **intelligence,** that is, the ability to learn and to understand new or trying situations. The apes, which emerge just before us in the fossil record, are highly intelligent creatures and can be taught an amazing array of skills. As we shall see later, apes can even be taught to use human sign language, although it is argued whether or not they use it the same way we do. In any case, the learning capacities of apes have led some experts to conclude that they have mental capacities very close to our own.

The primate skeleton has also became modified in ways that were compatible with **arboreal** (tree-dwelling) life. The generalized flexible limbs of the mammalian class were retained. The trunk lengthened. Changes in posture occurred. Although most primates are **quadrupedal** (they walk on all fours), they tend to sit upright. This posture frees the hands for manipulative activities. Differences in limb length and further modifications of the hand and foot structure took place with the development of different forms of locomotion. Some primates move through the trees primarily by jumping and hopping, particularly small, primitive forms. Apes can move swiftly through the trees by swinging from arm to arm when the occasion demands. A specialized form of swinging locomotion called **brachiation** developed in gibbons. Brachiation became an efficient means of locomotion only with certain modifications of the limb system. Gibbons have long arms and short legs. They have well-developed hands with which they catch and grasp the branches; their shoulders and shoulder muscles are specially developed for the long rhythmic swings that are characteristic of this movement.

Not all primates remained in the trees. As is so often the case in evolution, adaptive radiation eventually led to a return of some forms to an earlier mode of existence—for primates, ground-dwelling. Today the ground-dwellers include baboons, rhesus monkeys, langur monkeys, and humans. Ground-dwelling monkeys do spend some of their time in trees or in cliffs, depending on the environment, and they have not lost their ability to move rapidly and gracefully. Their hands show some modification for quadrupedal support but also remain good grasping organs.

PRIMATE EVOLUTION

The tree shrews (Tupaiidae) are considered by some to be the earliest known primates. These animals lie on the boundary between insectivores and true primates. Tree shrews are followed by a series of related animals, all accepted as primates and all more primitive than the monkeys. These are the **Prosimii.** Living relatives of these prosimians, or premonkeys, are the tarsiers, the lorises, and the lemurs. The lemurs occupy a position among the primates that marsupials occupy among placental mammals. Lemurs are found only on the island of Madagascar and appear to be a remnant group surviving because no higher primate forms ever arrived to compete with them.

Above the Prosimii are two major groups of true monkeys. These are the **Catarrhini,** or Old World monkeys, and the **Platyrrhini,** or New World monkeys (see Figure 4.7 for their distribution). The New World monkeys are divided into two groups: the **Cebidae** and the **Callithricidae.** The Cebidae are similar in form to Old World monkeys and the two groups constitute an example of parallel evolution. Although they differ in some features, they are anatomically quite similar in spite of their independent evolution from New and Old World prosimian forms.

Most New World monkeys live in deep jungles and have become well adapted for tree living. Those New World monkeys classed as cebids have prehensile tails that provide an additional grasping organ. This characteristic is not found in any Old World monkey.

Old and New World monkeys also differ in tooth number. Paleontologists note teeth according to a **dental formula.** This formula is derived from counting the different kinds of teeth in one half of the upper and one half of the lower jaw. All primates have a series of teeth specialized for different functions. The **incisors**

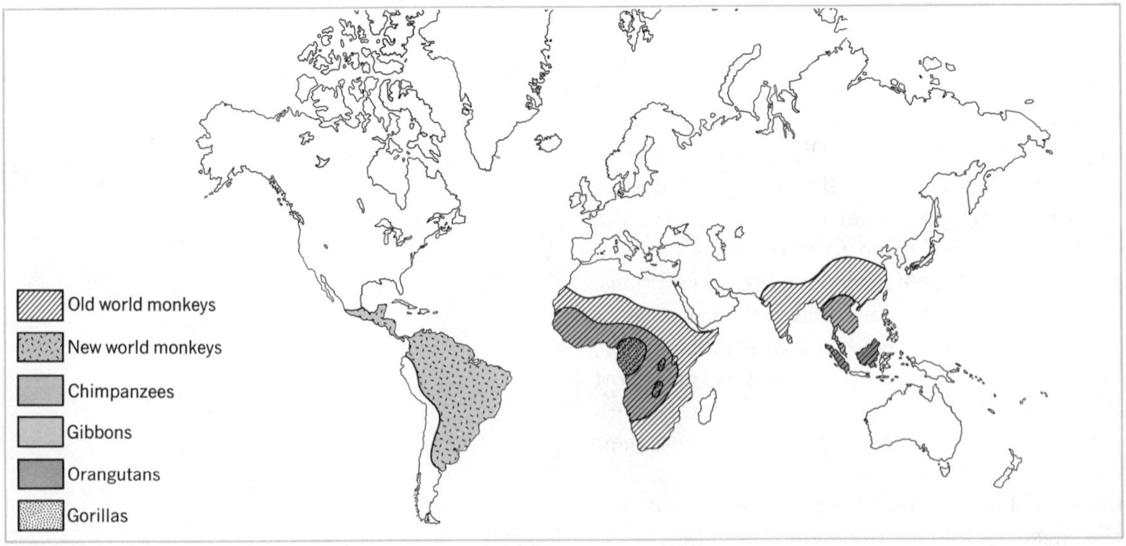

Figure 4.7
Distribution of New and Old World monkeys and apes.

A

B

C

D

E

F

Some typical primates.

A

Reed lemur, Madagascar, a prosimian.

B

Galago (bush baby) West Africa, a prosimian.

C

Baboons, Africa, Old World monkey.

D

Vervet monkey, Africa, Old World monkey.

E

Squirrel monkey, South America, New World monkey.

F

located at the front of the mouth are cutting or shearing teeth. Directly behind these are the **canines** (one on the upper side and one on the lower side.) These are dagger-like and can serve as weapons or aggressive displays. Behind these are small grinding teeth known as **premolars,** and behind these the larger grinding **molars.** Old World monkeys, apes, and humans have a dental formula that includes two incisors, one canine, *two* premolars, and three molars on each side of both upper and lower jaws. The New World monkeys have two incisors, one canine, *three* premolars, and three molars. Dental formulas are written as follows: $\frac{2:1:2:3}{2:1:2:3}$ Old World monkeys and $\frac{2:1:3:3}{2:1:3:3}$ New World monkeys. The line divides the teeth of the upper from the lower jaw and the types of teeth are read out from front to back. Remember that the formula describes only one half the jaw. To find the total number of teeth for a species you must add both the upper and lower rows and multiply by two. Thus, humans have 2:1:2:3 = 8 plus 2:1:2:3 = 8; (8 + 8) = 16 (2) = 32. New World monkeys have a full complement of 36 teeth.

The dental formulas for the prosimians are highly variable and are useful in determining species differences.

The Apes

The are only four living genera (plural of *genus*) of ape, represented by the **gorilla,** the **chimpanzee,** the **orangutan,** and the **gibbon.** The latter two live in South Asia while the chimp and gorilla live in Africa (see Figure 4.7). Three of these genera are considered to be close relatives of humans and, because of their size, are referred to as the great apes. The other, the gibbon, is a more distant relative. None of the apes have tails.

All of the apes are forest creatures and normally shy of humans. They are fruit-eating and leaf-eating animals, but chimps, at least will kill small game. Among the primates the great apes are the most intelligent, except for the human species. As you might expect, they have larger brains in proportion to body weight than monkeys.

Most people who are at all familiar with the apes know them from zoos and circuses. Young chimps are good performers. They learn well, are affectionate, and love to show off. When they grow up, however, they tend to become rather moody and unpredictable. Retired performers frequently end up in zoos, where they may be seen lying listlessly about in their cages. Chimps rarely show their intelligence under these conditions. In the wild, however, they

Classification of the primates.

Order	Primates								
Suborder	Prosimii			Anthropoidea					
Infraorder	Lemuriformes	Lorisiformes	Tarsiiformes	Catarrhini				Platyrrhini	
Superfamily	Lemuroidea			Hominoidea			Cercopithecoidea	Ceboidea	
Family				Hominidae	Pongidae	Hylobatidae	Cercopithecidae	Cebidae	Callithricidae
Example	lemur	loris galago	tarsier	Homo humans	gorilla chimpanzee orangutan	gibbon	Old World monkeys	New World cebids	marmosets

Apes are the primates closest to humans.
A
Chimpanzee, Africa.
B
Gorilla, Africa.
C
Gibbon, Southeast Asia.
D
Orangutan, Southeast Asia.

A

B

C

D

retain their lively curiosity and social grace. Confinement in zoos is probably a dulling (and if chimps were human we could say a "dehumanizing") experience for so intelligent an animal.

Gorillas and orangs also deteriorate in zoos. Both species become fat and tend to sleep away much of their time. The orang has an exaggerated tendency to obesity and in zoos is reduced to a sack of fur and skin filled to overflowing with fat.

Humans have been interested in the great apes ever since their discovery. Early zoological texts sometimes confuse them with humans or describe them as part human. *Orangutan* in Malay actually means *old man of the forest.* When apes were first brought to zoos they became immediate crowd-pleasers. They look enough like us to arouse curiosity, and their performances are taken as a parody of human behavior. As circus performers chimps are clothed and taught to mimic human actions. We are pleased by our ability to control and train wild beasts, to domesticate them. And we laugh and wonder at the close approximation these creatures are to ourselves.

Comparison of Apes and Humans

Although the great apes are indeed like ourselves in many ways, major differences also exist between the two groups of primates. Fully erect bipedal walking is the major **locomotive** form only for humans. Walking erect frees the hand for carrying and allows it to be used for a variety of tasks during locomotion. Apes are well adapted to forest life, while humans probably evolved in a grassland environment. (The human adaptation to forests, particularly among hunters and gatherers, is a late development dependent on culture.) Although it is true that some apes occasionally use very primitive tools, tool use is pervasive only in the lives of humans. While traditions (shared patterns of learned behavior) exist in both monkey and ape societies, its full flowering occurs only with the emergence of culture, a specifically human characteristic. The development of social roles (nurturance, defense, and some sharing behavior) occurs among many primate species, yet it is much more highly developed and complex among human groups. Further, the division of labor along sexual lines in economic activity is a human characteristic that binds males and females together in an important human way.

The human brain is characterized by major developments in the frontal lobes (see Figure 4.8), which are important in behavior requiring foresight and planning. Changes also occur in the parietal lobes located behind the frontal lobe at the sides and top of the brain. These are related to speech development and the ability to integrate information. Humans have a highly developed capacity to use and combine information gathered from the many senses at our disposal. This high-level integration is a specialized feature of human brain evolution.

Primate Fossils

The fossil record of primates begins in the **Paleocene** epoch about 69 million years ago. Found in North America and western Europe, these early forms were squirrel-sized animals similar to living *Tupaiidae.* Although they display some primate features, particularly the flexible limb structures characteristic of monkeys, apes, and humans, paleontologists argue over their classification. This argument rests on the ambiguity you would expect to find in any transitional form.

The first fully unambiguous primates, (the prosimians), came into their own during the **Eocene** epoch, which began about 58 million

Figure 4.8
Side views of primate brains. (a) Lemur; (b) Old World monkey; (c) chimpanzee; (d) human. The occipital area at the back of the brain that controls vision is relatively large. The area of motor control is larger in the higher primates and particularly in humans than it is in lower primates. The same is true of the temporal and parietal lobes. (Adapted from Buettner-Janusch, 1973.)

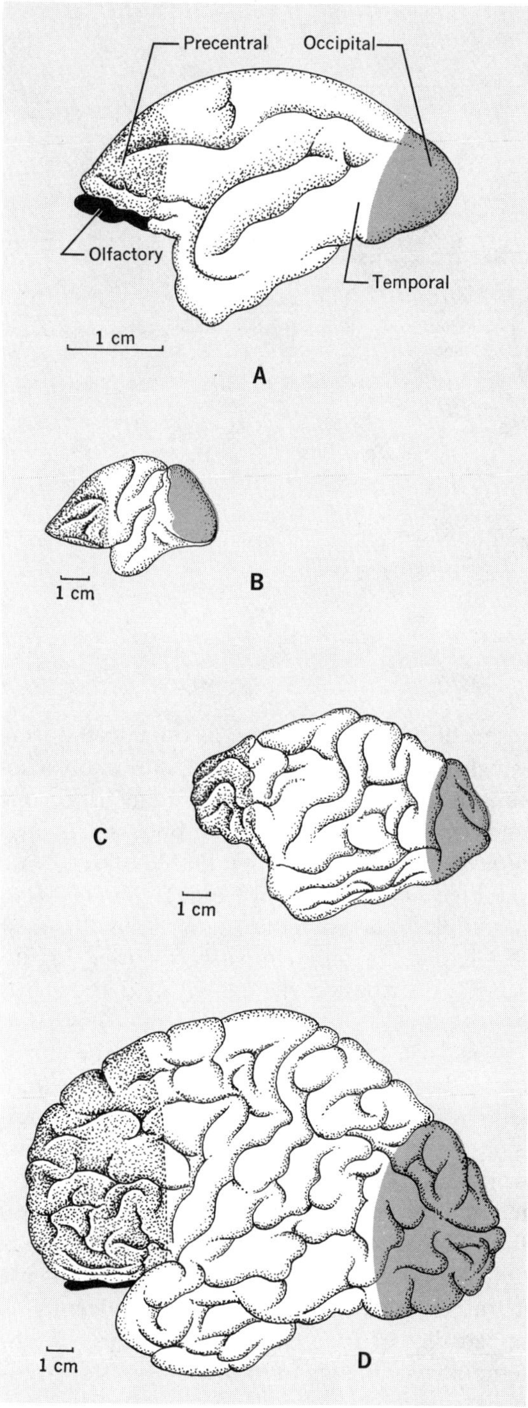

years ago and lasted perhaps 20 million years. As might be expected, the spread and development of the primate order was accompanied by adaptive radiation. As new niches were invaded, variations in basic primate skeletal architecture and size appeared. Although they were probably more widely distributed, Eocene forms have been found in North America, Europe, and Asia. Regardless of particular niche-specific adaptations, Eocene fossil primates display evidence of a shift away from smell to vision as a primary sense. This shift is indicated by a shortening of the snout and changes in the orbit, the bony socket that protects the eye. Their teeth were small and unspecialized. Finger bones of a North American form, *Notharctus,* indicate that the primate grasping hand had already appeared (see Figure 4.9).

Evidence of the development and radiation of anthropoid as opposed to prosimian forms appears in the **Oligocene** epoch, between about 38 and 25 million years ago. The Oligocene was a period of general cooling. The tropical forests of the mid-latitudes disappeared. The fossil evidence indicates that the primates retreated southward with the forests and established themselves in South America and Africa. The ancestors of New World monkeys appear in South America at this time. In North Africa, particularly in the fossil beds of the Fayum (in Egypt), evidence of Old World monkeys is found in great profusion. Parallel selection pressures of an arboreal environment in both regions of the world led to the development of genetically distinct but highly similar anthropoid forms. There were differences, however. Due to climatic factors South American forests remained dense while African forests tended to be somewhat broken. This difference was to be crucial in the evolution of apes. It undoubtedly also contributed to the emergence among New World monkeys of such highly arboreal adaptations as prehensile tails and the elongated limb structure characteristic of spider monkeys. The most recent evidence shows the emergence of anthropoids about 40 million years ago in Southeast Asia. The fossils found in Burma in

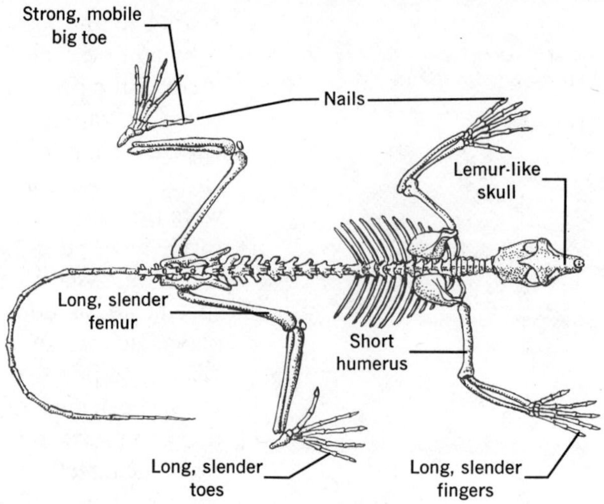

Figure 4.9

Reconstruction of the skeleton of Northarctus, a North American lemuriform primate from the Eocene. (After Gregory, 1920.)

1978 resemble both monkeys and apes and may represent a common ancestor of both groups. The certain place of these finds in primate evolution awaits further analysis.

Among the important Fayum finds were *Propliopithecus,* a small ape-like form; *Parapithecus,* a small animal that may be the ancestor of Old World monkeys; and *Aegyptopithecus.* One particularly good specimen of *Aegyptopithecus* (an almost complete skull with only the lower jaw missing) was found by Elwyn Simons, a Yale University paleontologist. Simons believes that Aegyptopithecus is directly ancestral to modern apes and humans.

The next important set of developments in primate evolution came during the **Miocene** epoch, which lasted from about 25 to 5 million years ago. Africa and the Eurasian continent were connected by a land bridge at that time, and the anthropoids moved outward from Africa toward the east. Shifts in the African climate gave rise to mixed forests and grassland. The Miocene saw the further development of Old World monkeys, but it is most important, in terms of human evolution, as the epoch during which modern apes appeared. Important Miocene forms are *Pliopithecus* (found in Europe and a probable ancestor of gibbons), *Gigantopithecus* (an enormous ape that continued into the Pleistocene epoch in China), *Ramapithecus* (a middle-to-late-Miocene form to be discussed in Chapter 6), and *Dryopithecus.* (See Figure 4.10 for distribution of *Ramapithecus* and *Dryopithecus.*)

The earliest *Dryopithecus* finds may be ancestral to both ape and human lines. A later find, *Dryopithecus africanus,* diverged from the common stock. Richard Leakey, a paleontologist working in East Africa, suggests that it was on its way to forming a lineage of apes. The dental forms of *Dryopithecus* are particularly important. Molar and incisor size and shape indicate a rather generalized dentition, reflecting a mixed diet of fruit, stems, and leaves. If contemporary evidence from observations of chimpanzees can be used to deduce the *Dryopithecus* diet, they probably also ate meat occasionally.

Little is known about the *Dryopithecus* skeleton other than the skull (see Figure 4.11). Information that is available comes from *Dryopithecus africanus,* which, it has already been noted, is considered to be a divergent stock. This form was apparently monkey-like in limb structure, but more fossil material will have to be forthcoming before we can be sure of its locomotor patterns.

The fossil evidence on primate evolution shows the emergence of this group in Africa and its rapid spread throughout the tropical and semitropical world. As new niches were invaded, forms diverged to meet new adaptive challenges. The major primate adaptations—including the development of high intelligence, acuity of vision, and the hand—were retained. Brain evolution is a constant feature of primate adaptation, with development and differentiation toward higher intelligence from lower to higher forms. Further deductions about primate evolution and relationships to the emergence of the human species can be made from an examination of the structure and behavior of living primates.

Summary

In this chapter we have examined evolution from the perspective of nonhuman primates, with some indications of our own adaptive history. Major features of primate evolution include the following characteristics:

1. *Multicellularity.* Specialized groups of cells differentiate during fetal development into skeletal structure, internal organs, organs of perception, the circulatory system, the nervous system, connective tissue, and so on.
2. *Chordate-vertebrates.* Bony skeletons have evolved with a spinal column protecting a nerve chord running from the well-developed brain down the length of the back.
3. *The mammalian adaptation.* Defining characteristics are homeothermy (shared with birds), live birth, hair, a four-chambered heart which increases the efficiency of oxygen transport and waste-gas removal, and mammary glands for the nourishment of

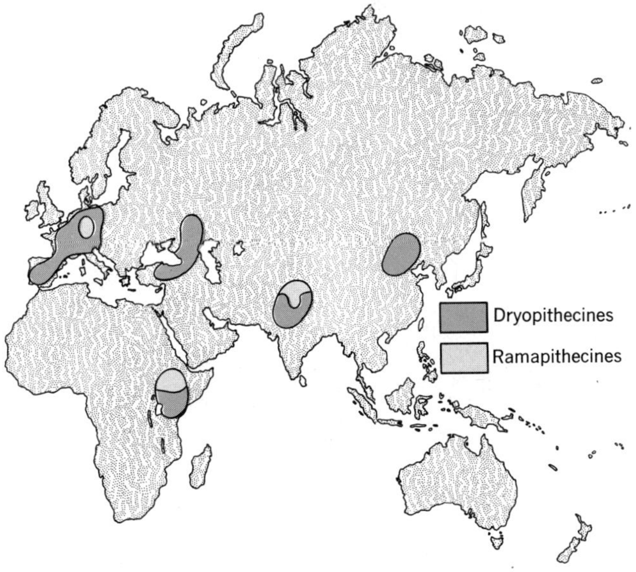

Figure 4.10
Distribution of Ramapithecus and Dryopithecus in the Old World.

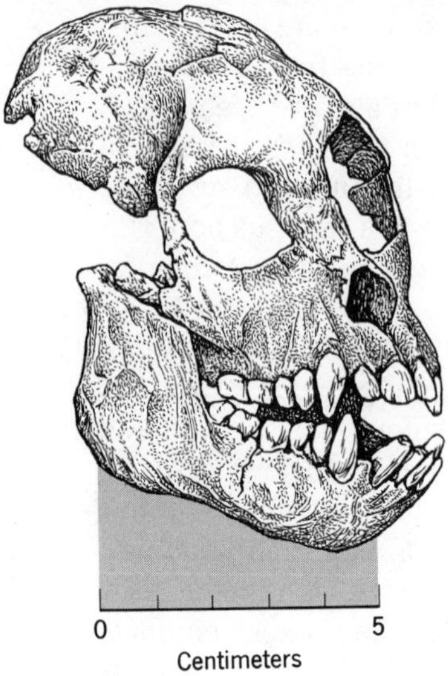

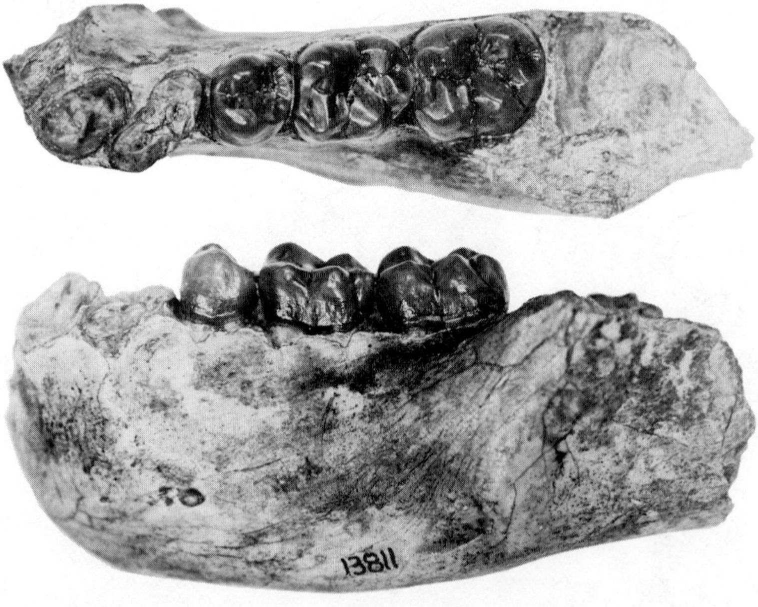

Figure 4.11
The late Oligocene and Miocene fossil ape *Dryopithecus. Dryopithecus* is a good candidate for the ancestor of contemporary apes. It is also possible that hominids were an offshoot of one early *Dryopithecus* form. The photographs show two views of *Dryopithecus sivalensis.* This fragment of a lower jaw is about 7 cm long.

the young. Among mammals there is a considerable development of the brain, particularly the neocortex, and learning is very important in behavior.

4. *The primate adaptation.* Olfaction (the sense of smell) has been reduced and vision centers in the brain have increased. Stereoscopic color vision appears. The hand has developed as a grasping tool. This has involved the flattening of claws into nails, the development of the opposable thumb that works against the fingers and the increase of nerve endings in the fingers, which provide a high degree of sensitivity. The hand is capable of both power and precision grips. The latter is facilitated by the development of excellent eye-hand coordination, which allows us to monitor manipulative activities. Primate young are dependent on their mothers for long periods, allowing for the development of strong social ties and learning.

The fossil record of primates begins in the Paleocene epoch about 69 million years ago. Early primates are found in many parts of the world, including Western Europe and North America. The first to appear are primitive prosimians apparently related to small insect-eating mammals represented today by the South Asian tree shrews.

The Eocene epoch, beginning about 58 million years ago, yields fully unambiguous primates from most of the world. They are all prosimians, but there is strong evidence from the fossil record that they have begun the adaptation to arboreal life that saw a reduction in the snout and the sense of smell, the price paid for improved vision.

The higher primates, the anthropoids, including the monkeys and apes, first make their appearance in the Oligocene about 34 million years ago. The evidence during this epoch is limited to tropical areas of the world.

The ape group developed in the Miocene epoch about 25 million years ago. Important finds come from Africa, India, and, most recently, China. Hominid evolution may have also begun in the Miocene, but this is a subject of debate.

Bibliography

Clark, W. E. Le Gros 1966 — *History of the Primates.* Chicago: University of Chicago Press. An excellent introduction to primate morphology and evolution.

Leakey, R, and R. Lewin 1977 — *Origins.* New York: E. P. Dutton. An interesting account of fossil discoveries, ecological adaptation, and the rise of culture. The early chapters deal with fossil primates.

Romer, A. S. 1945 — *Vertebrate Paleontology.* Chicago: University of Chicago Press. The classic work on general vertebrate paleontology.

Simons, E. L. 1972 — *Primate Evolution.* New York: Macmillan. A major figure in primate paleontology discusses primate evolution in simple terms.

Stirton, R. A. 1959 — *Time, Life, and Man: The Fossil Record.* New York: John Wiley & Sons. An excellent general introduction to evolution through the fossil record.

CHAPTER 5
PRIMATE BEHAVIOR

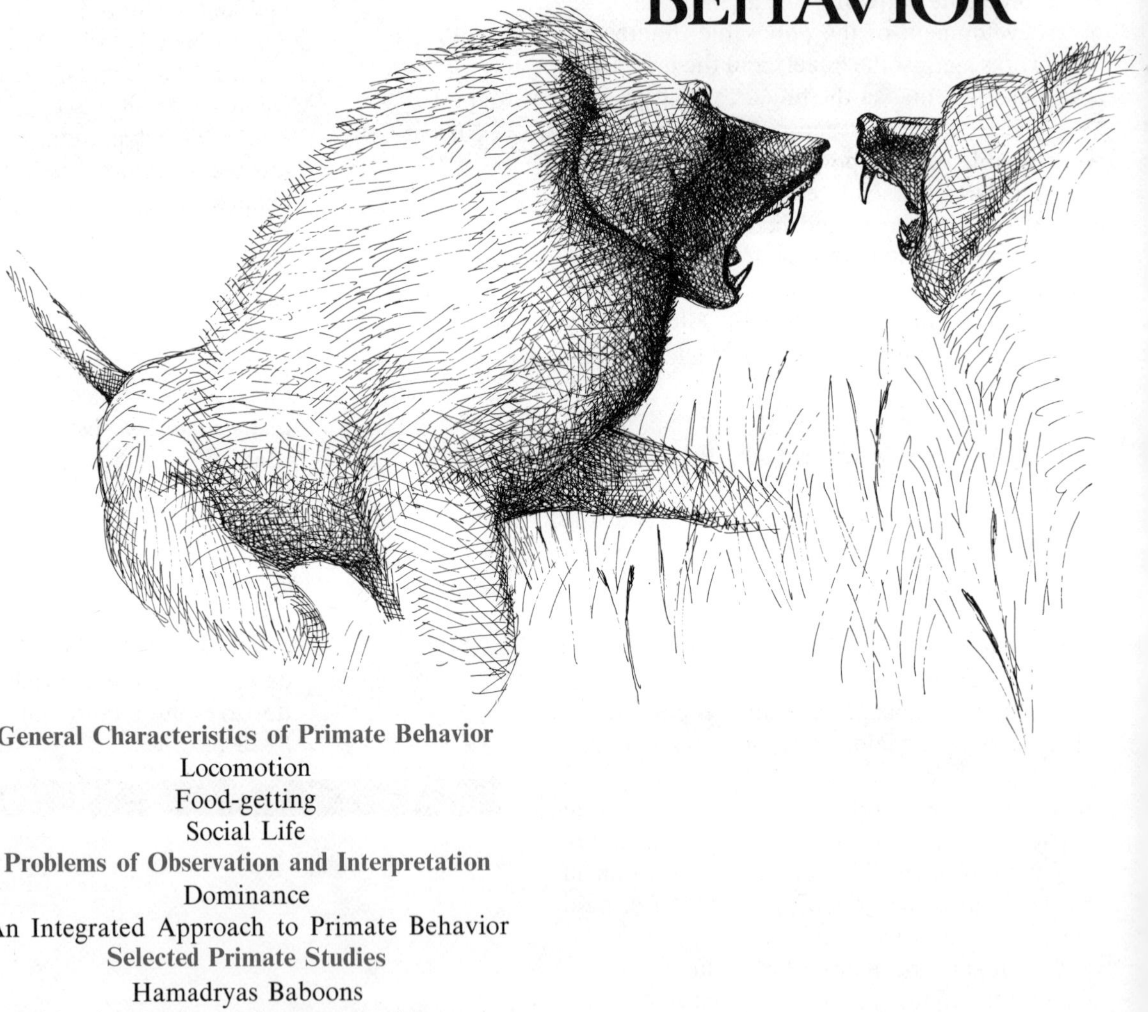

Physical anthropologists attempt to unravel the evolution of our species. In order to do this, they must, like detectives, use any scraps of available relevant material. They reconstruct behavioral change from anatomical features such as teeth and limb bones, which provide clues about dietary habits and locomotion. They make other behavioral inferences from climatological and botanical evidence as well as from the observation of living primates. Because many major fossil types of primates are represented by living descendants, anthropologists can make deductions from living species back to fossils. In this way they can attempt to reconstruct both soft body parts and behavior.

Behavioral studies must be approached with caution, however. Contemporary primates live in environments that differ in unknown ways from those originally occupied by their fossil ancestors. In addition, many of the behavioral differences we see in living members of the same species, particularly between groups, are due to learned adaptations.

Primate behavior is studied primarily for the following reasons: (1) Primate studies contribute to comparative psychology. They provide data on variation within and between species. Thorough study of a range of different primate species allows us to make generalizations about the behavioral capacities of the primate order as a whole. (2) The study of different primate species, graded according to evolutionary change, can be used to unravel the sequence of evolution of primate behavior. (3) The behavioral study of several groups of the *same* species illuminates the degree to which behavior is modified by environment *and* learning. The observation of groups under natural conditions, in combination with laboratory experiments, provides data on behavioral flexibility, learning, and, in some cases, the development of tradition in primate groups. (4) Some physical anthropologists study nonhuman primates to understand the evolution of human behavior. These scholars have usually focused on two different types of primate. The first are ground-dwelling monkeys. These animals live in large social units under conditions that might parallel those faced by early humans. Other scholars prefer to concentrate on the great apes, particularly the gorilla and the chimpanzee. Among all the primates the genetic distance between these species and ourselves is the smallest. They are indeed our closest relatives. Gorillas and chimps are also the most intelligent of the primates. In addition, chimps are the only primates for which tool using has so far been established.

This last reason for studying primates must be approached with particular caution. Monkeys and apes cannot stand in for early humans. We and they have specialized under different sets of environmental conditions. As *contemporary* forms the monkeys, the apes, and humans have *diverged* from a set of common ancestors. From an evolutionary perspective the divergences are probably more important than the similarities.

GENERAL CHARACTER-ISTICS OF PRIMATE BEHAVIOR

Locomotion

Locomotion among primates is highly varied. Different patterns can be correlated with body size and environmental adaptation. The two major adaptive patterns reflect arboreal and ground-dwelling modes. Within each there are variations. Small forms with light bodies, particularly prosimians, jump and leap through the trees. Vertical clinging is also characteristic of these animals. Larger animals—monkeys and apes—must have well-developed grasping hands and feet. All forms are able to climb and grasp with ease and all display a tendency for **orthograde** (trunk-erect) posture at rest. Many Old and New World monkeys run and climb on the branches of their arboreal environment, moving from branch to branch by leaping. The spider monkey, *Ateles,* however, has developed a specialized form of locomotion known as **semi-brachiation** (arm swinging). This animal is striking for its exceptionally long arms and thin hands. The spider monkey's fingers are elongated and its thumbs are small. The chest is broad and the shoulder blade has been modified to accommodate the weight of the body as it is suspended from the arms. These are locomotor adaptations. Spider monkeys also have prehensile tails, which they use for support and to grasp objects.

True **brachiation** (swinging in wide arcs with the arms) is found only among the gibbons. These animals spend over ninety percent of their time in the trees, moving in graceful loops that carry their bodies from limb to limb. Gibbons have exceptionally long arms and short trunks. The hand is long with long fingers. The shoulder bones and muscles are well adapted for hanging and swinging (see Figure 5.1).

Chimps do sometimes swing by the arms, but gorillas, except the very young, lighter animals, for obvious reasons move rather cautiously through the trees, climbing with all four limbs. The orangutan also climbs in this way and uses its arms over its head for suspension (Jolly, 1972). Unlike gibbons, chimpanzees and gorillas spend a good deal of time on the ground. Although both can move bipedally, the most common form of locomotion is **knuckle-walking.** These animals have long arms and short legs. The body is held at an angle with the head higher than the hind end. The weight of the body is carried by a curled-under second finger. The bones and ligaments of the wrist in these animals are adapted to this special form of locomotion.

Food-getting

Almost all primates are **omnivorous.** Recent observations of baboons and chimpanzees reveal that on occasion both species eat meat, which they obtain through scavenging or hunting. Leaf-eating is common among monkeys that live in the high tropical-forest canopy, particularly in South America. Baboons eat grass stems, which they pull up with their hands and scrape off with their incisor teeth. Geladas eat grass blades, insects, and seeds. These monkeys have small incisors and large molars that provide a grinding surface for food requiring good mastication. The insect-eating tarsiers have sharp incisors, with which they can seize their prey, and sharp molars, which function to tear insects apart. Fruit-eating primates, such as gibbons, have broad incisors for shearing and biting and broad molars for crushing.

Social Life

Most primates are social animals, but the degree of social life and group size depend on their ecological adaptation. Allison Jolly (1972) divides primate species into ecological grades with different habitats. These correlate roughly

A

B

C

D

E

Locomotion among primates.

A

Branch running (tree-shrew, an insectivore).

B

Vertical clinging and leaping (ring-tailed lemur).

C

Brachiation (gibbon).

D

Knuckle walking (gorilla).

E

Ground-walking quadrupedalism (macaque).

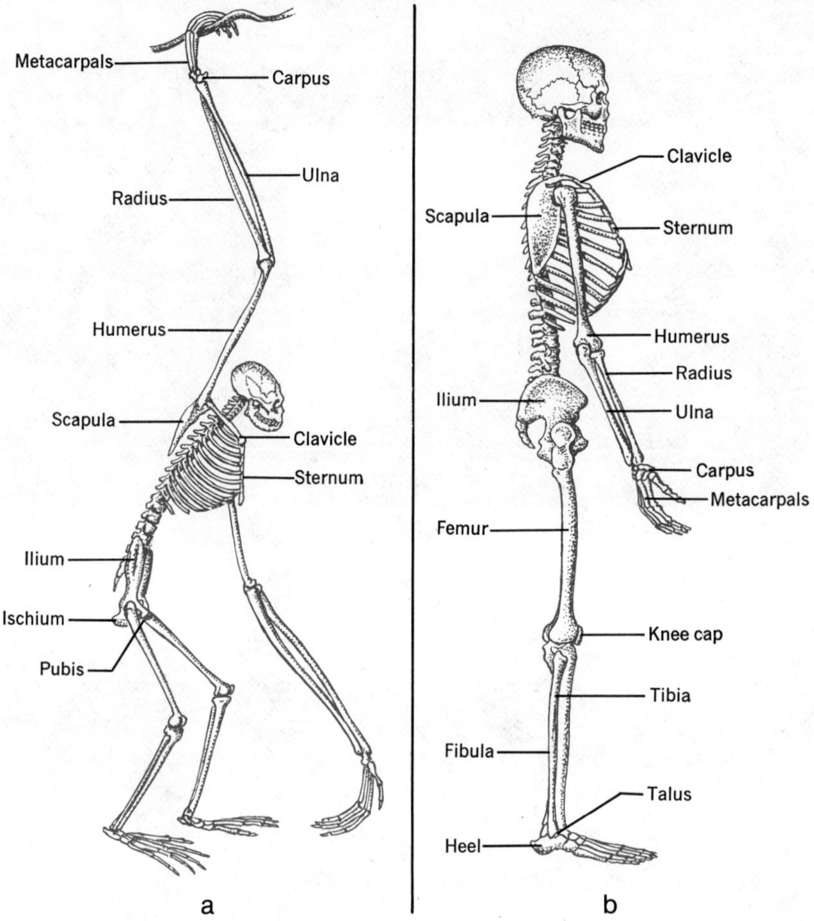

Figure 5.1
Comparison of (a) gibbon and (b) human skeletons showing specializations for brachiation (gibbon) and bipedalism (human). Note in particular the length of legs and arms in both species as well as differences in hands, feet, and pelvises.

with group size and structure, home-range size, and the degree of spatial separation that exists between groups. Jolly distinguishes the following grades and types of social group:

1. *Nocturnal* primates (particularly prosimians) are mostly solitary. Some live in overlapping individual ranges with the range of a male overlapping those of one or more females.
2. *Arboreal leafeaters* tend to live in small groups. One-male harems also occur. These animals have small home ranges and highly ritualized behavior for spacing. The behavior is often vocal. The howler monkey, which uses sound to define living space, has a specialized bone in the throat that serves as a sound box.
3. *Arboreal omnivores* live in one-male harems or small groups, with the exception of squirrel monkeys and talapoins, which may live in groups of up to 100 animals. The

extent of their home ranges is not well known, but they move around more than leaf-eating monkeys.

4. *Semiterrestrial leaf-eaters* include only two species—the langur and the gorilla. These animals live in small groups and have small home ranges.
5. *Semiterrestrial omnivores* are divided into forest and savanna dwellers. These, with the exception of the chimpanzee, are primarily Old World monkeys. They form larger groups than tree dwellers and have much larger ranges. Intergroup avoidance is common and aggressive encounters between troops are rare.
6. *Arid country forms* live in single-male units (see section on hamadryas below) but may sleep in larger social units.

Most primate social groups are graded by sex and status. Dominant animals are often males. Group structure is maintained through real and symbolic aggressive encounters. The symbolic encounters may take the form of various types of sexual and aggressive display behavior and call behavior. Group cohesion is maintained through such behaviors as social grooming and mutual defense from predators. In addition, as Jolly suggests, most social primates apparently enjoy group living.

Grooming in a family of langur monkeys (India).

PROBLEMS OF OBSERVATION AND INTER-PRETATION

Primate studies are only as good as the observations made by scientists. In the early days, when primates were observed in zoos, many false impressions were created by the artificial living conditions. Zoo animals do not behave the same way as animals that live in the wild. These differences range from aggressive displays and territoriality to care of the young. Female gorillas, for example, have to learn to be good mothers. In the wild they learn from the experience of other females. In zoos they do not know how to treat their offspring. In one zoo a female that had recently given birth was seen dragging her baby around the cage by one leg. Successful breeding in zoos requires the keepers to act the role of normal mothers!

Observation (what is seen and noted) depends on theory and on the categories of behavior that a scientist has chosen to study. Such concepts as aggression, play, and timidity have to be made **operational,** that is defined in behavioral units that can be observed and counted. The scientist must distinguish differences in behavior that occur in different circumstances. Early studies of primates in the field were based on crude observational criteria. Recent studies have been more sophisticated and have often led to new interpretations.

We humans tend to look at animals as reflections of ourselves. This tendency is particularly true in observing primates because they share many of our anatomical features and, in zoos at least, are good at mimicking human behavior. Even their natural behavior often seems quite human. We frequently think of animals as metaphorical humans. People all over the world have developed folk tales in which animals speak and do many of the things humans do. There is a danger in this attitude for science. When human motives are projected onto animals, we may not be able to understand the animals as they are. If we use animals as metaphors for ourselves, we run the risk of reinforcing old prejudices and blocking scientific discovery.

A good deal of the early work in primate ethology was marred by a singular lack of objectivity. Much harmless material was further distorted by popularizers, who emphasized aggression, male dominance, and territoriality. Little was said about cooperation, learning, and the role of females in group dynamics. Primatologists projected what they were sure were universals about human behavior onto monkeys and apes. They found what they expected to find and used their findings as proof of the very ideas they began with.

Dominance

Let me take dominance, the relative position of an individual in a social hierarchy, as an example. In a summary of studies on this subject, Gina Bari Kolata notes that the concept of dominance was first used many years ago to describe the pecking order among chickens (Kolata, 1976). Early observations showed that flocks of domestic birds are organized socially on a hierarchical basis. This hierarchy is established in the flock by aggressive encounters. After a series of such encounters some birds become dominant over others. Once established, the pecking order tends to remain stable. As long as individual birds keep their place in the flock, fighting is reduced.

When primate studies began, researchers transferred the concept of dominance to monkeys and apes. "Pecking orders" were "found" among most species studied in the wild. Soon the notion of dominance was linked to the idea of reproductive success. The hypothesis was that the more dominant male monkeys would have greater or exclusive access to females and therefore would have a genetic advantage over less dominant males. If this were true, it would demonstrate a means for the rapid selection of certain genes. The implication, of course, is that dominance and aggression have both been positively selected in primates. Recent studies, however, have shown that the concept of dominance is often poorly defined and that measuring it is no easy matter. Kolata cites Irwin Bernstein of the Primate Research center at Emory University, who showed that various measures of dominance do not agree with one another. In his work Bernstein ranked captive monkeys in relation to previously used measures of dominance: sexual mounting, grooming, aggression, and responses to aggressive behavior. He found that these measures of dominance do not produce consistent results. Another researcher, Thelma Rowell of the University of California at Berkeley, suggested that "dominance" may be a creation of the observer. It must be emphasized, however, that this is a matter of some dispute among scientists.

As to breeding success and dominance, the evidence shows that different species reflect different patterns. In some species dominance *can* be linked to breeding success, but in others it *cannot.* Clearly, not all primates fit the original dominance hypothesis. It cannot be argued, therefore, that humans as primates must reflect a universal primate pattern. There is no such pattern.

Ground-dwelling rhesus monkeys were tested for paternity to see if there was a correlation between dominance and reproductive success. The results showed that some low-ranking and even adolescent males fathered as many offspring as the highest-ranking males. This study also found that *female* monkeys had a good deal of choice in mate selection. Earlier male-centered studies had assumed that females were passive in the face of male dominance.

Bernstein's study indicates that male rank as well as reproductive success may be related to female choice. Which monkey a female *decides* to mate with helps to establish the male's position in the troop and affects overall fitness. If so, the notion of dominance is turned on its head!

Donald Sade of Northwestern University provided Kolata further evidence for the role of females in the establishment of social structure in monkey troops. He found that rhesus monkeys live in matriarchal societies. Females remain in the troop into which they were born, while an overwhelming percentage of male monkeys leave before they reach maturity. Females tend to acquire dominance ranks equal to those of their mothers. Those few males that remain in their natal troop also tend to inherit dominance rank from their mothers, but if they move on to another social unit they may improve their rank. Several primate ethologists studying rhesus monkeys have suggested that acceptance in the new troop as well as potentially attained rank will depend on female acceptance. Bernstein suggests that the length of time a male stays with a particular troop and the rank he achieves are directly correlated with the reception he receives from females. He will father many young if he stays with a troop for a long time. This fact will lead automatically to a correlation between rank and reproductive success, but rank for a male will not be the *cause* of his reproductive success.

Only *some* primate groups have dominance hierarchies, and those without them survive; hierarchies are apparently not a crucial aspect of behavior for all primate species. Where hierarchies are found they undoubtedly play an adaptive role, but just exactly what this role is must be determined in individual cases. Social behavior is integrated, and one aspect of it—such as dominance hierarchies—cannot be understood in a vacuum.

An Integrated Approach to Primate Behavior

Jane B. Lancaster has taken an integrated approach to primate behavior in an attempt to understand the adaptive significance of different patterns. She isolates five basic aspects of social organization that occur in different forms and combinations among different species. These

Aggression and dominance in baboons. (Top) Dominant males establish their position in the troop through nonfatal aggressive encounters with subordinate males. (Bottom) The dominant male has first access to food.

basic aspects are the following: (1) dominance; (2) the mother-infant bond, which creates a mother-infant subunit; (3) the sexual bond between males and females; (4) the separation of roles between adult and young primates; and (5) the separation of roles by sex.

Lancaster notes that dominance has an adaptive value because it allows members of the social group to predict the outcome of an interaction between two animals competing for a scarce resource (food, space, or a sexually receptive mate). Although dominance is based on aggressive encounters, it promotes tranquility by organizing social interaction. Lancaster agrees that dominance is not prominent among all primate groups and points out that it is most pronounced in ground-dwelling species. She also recognizes that environmental differences influence the degree of dominance behavior even within the same species. She points out, for instance, that a species of baboon studied by Irven DeVore in the Kenya grasslands and by Rowell in the forests of Uganda differs markedly in aggression and dominance behavior. Highly structured dominance relations occur only among the savannah-dwelling baboons.

Lancaster believes that the most basic theme to be found among primate social relations is the mother-infant bond. This is the first social tie to be formed in the life of the individual and it often serves, as we have seen above, as a model for other social relations. It also provides the basis of the matrifocal unit that is the core of many primate social groups. In her own field studies of vervet monkeys Lancaster found that coalitions of females could be formed against dominant males if the males offended the females by attempting to take control of a food source or frightening an infant. These coalitions are formed outside of the dominance positions of individual monkeys. Even low-ranking females would chase males that had frightened one of their offspring.

The sexual bond between males and females is highly variable among primates. In most species mating is promiscuous, while in some more or less permanent bonds develop. When the latter pattern occurs Lancaster believes that it must have some special adaptive significance. We shall see below how male-female bonds among hamadryas baboons can be explained in this way. Lancaster notes that among gibbons the sexual bond between mating pairs is particularly strong. Gibbons live in small groups that consist of a single male-female pair and their immature offspring. These families live in small territories, which they protect from other such groups. These territories contain enough food to maintain the family through the annual cycle. Lancaster compares this pattern to the family structure of small birds and mammals, particularly in the tropical habitat, suggesting that it serves to create a protective environment for the nurturance of the young.

For Lancaster the most important adaptation of the higher primates, including monkeys, apes, and humans, is the division of roles between adults and immature animals. Primates are slow to mature and offspring remain dependent on adults for long periods. It is during the maturation process that social identity is formed and reinforced through behavioral encounters within the group. In addition, young animals learn a great deal about their environment and their place in the social group through play behavior. Young animals can play freely with each other because they are protected by adult animals.

The separation of roles by sex among different primate species is another highly variable trait. In many species this division is minimal, beyond the fact that the females care for infants. In tree-dwelling monkeys the male is often aloof from young animals and can even be said to be *loosely* attached to the social core of the group. Among ground-dwelling monkeys, however, the male is often larger and stronger than the female and is equipped with large, slashing canines that are used in the defense of the troop. Role differentiation is not extended to economic activities as it is among humans. In most cases adult males and females in a group eat the same foods. The only interesting exception is the hunting by baboon and chimpanzee males.

Lancaster summarizes her discussion of these five axes of social organization by noting that each species—and perhaps even each different population of the same species occupying different habitats—has its own unique combination of these elements, all of which contribute to the formation of the social system. Attention to only one of these axes at the expense of the others leads to an incomplete and perhaps false picture of social life and the adaptation of each group to its particular environmental setting.

SELECTED PRIMATE STUDIES

We can see that the most useful primate studies are those that investigate the adaptation of individual species. When a species is studied under natural conditions, we learn not only about real behavior but also about how it operates in the environment. This information is essential for evolutionary analysis.

Hamadryas Baboons

Hans Kummer has studied hamadryas baboons in Ethiopia. In an interesting book, *Primate Societies,* he compared his own field work with work of other students of baboon ethology. By analyzing differences among different species that live in different environments, he was able to reconstruct the evolution of certain specific social patterns.

Kummer notes that locating sleeping areas, finding food, and avoiding predators are the major problems faced by primate groups. The social behavior of the several species reflects the different solutions to these problems that have evolved. Kummer uses the hamadryas baboon as an example of a probable **phylogenetic** change in which a general baboon social pattern was modified by the selection pressures of a specific environment.

The social organization of baboon troops is similar throughout Africa. Typically the population of any geographic area is divided into mutually avoiding groups. Fighting occurs only when two such groups attempt to stay in the same sleeping area. During the day baboons range on the ground, feeding on plant material, particularly grass stems. At night they take to a safe sleeping area. On the great plains of East Africa they usually select trees, in which the animals can perch, away from marauding pred-

(Top) A hamadryas band, consisting of several males, each with his females. (Bottom) A hamadryas one-male unit. The male is "aggressing" against his female in order to keep her within his unit.

ators. In the more arid, treeless areas of Ethiopia, baboons sleep in niches in steep cliff faces.

It is usual among baboons that, aside from the mother-infant pair, there are no permanent subgroups within specific troops. During ovulation a female will associate with a male for both mating and grooming. In general, the dominant male of a troop will have first access to the receptive female, but she may have succeeding relations with other males.

The hamadryas is the *only* deviant from this pattern among the five species of African baboon. The hamadryas female is locked in a permanent bond with a male consort. Males, for their part, frequently have several females. The hamadryas male keeps his females by attacking those that stray from the group. After a few such attacks the female submits to her particular mate. Several one-male groups plus single males form a hamadryas band. Usually two such bands form a troop, the large sleeping group described below.

Kummer suggests that this departure from typical baboon social structure results from an ecological adaptation to the arid conditions of the hamadryas environment. Their environment is less rich in food than the East African grasslands. Since the ancestors of the hamadryas were already social creatures, a behavioral modification in the direction of solitary life was unlikely. Instead, the one-level baboon society was modified to a three-level society, which consists of the one-male-plus-females unit, the band, and the large troop.

The independent one-male group appears as the optimal foraging unit, just large enough to include one male protector, but small enough to find enough food for every member without covering inordinate distances. . . . On the other hand, the one-male units must gather at the cliffs in numbers far exceeding nondesert baboons. The social solution is the troop. The band represents an intermediate level between the small foraging and large sleeping units. Its ecological functions are not immediately evident; the band is quite possibly a vestigial unit for the hamadryas baboon, that is, a remainder of the ancestral baboon group.

Kummer examines each level in greater detail. He notes that the troop is not a genuine social unit, since interaction is limited to the members of each band. Troops exist on the basis of mutual tolerance. They could, therefore, have evolved with little difficulty. The core adaptation, and the most deviant social form among baboons other than the hamadryas, is the one-male group. Kummer reasons that it took longer to evolve than the troop. The herding technique used by males to maintain their control over females is similar to the technique used by all baboon females to control their infants. Kummer suggests that males "get away with this behavior because dominance is strongly ingrained in all baboons and because they are larger and stronger than females. *Bonding* [permanent social relationships] is also incipient among baboons. Dominant males defend access to sexual partners and mothers generally do not let other females handle their offspring."

The major shift in hamadryas baboon social behavior requires a high motivation among males to bond permanently with more than one female rather than with a single female only during her oestrus period.

Hamadryas females have also changed their behavior. While other baboon females take flight from an aggressive male, the hamadryas female will approach her male consort when he adopts threat behavior. This reaction, however, can be easily learned. When females of other baboon species are put into a hamadryas troop they soon adopt this new response. Kummer suggests that male possessiveness, on the other hand, has a genetic base. It remains a persistent form of social behavior in captive colonies even when the monkeys are subjected to different environmental conditions.

The hamadryas adaptation is a social solution to the problem of food-getting in a limited environment. The new social process, however, creates its own problem in baboon group dynamics. The one-male group increases the risk of conflict between jealous males. This potential risk has itself led to a further adaptation.

A male does not claim *a female if she already belongs to another male. . . . Hamadryas baboons in evolving a system of one-male units in adaptation to their environment, also evolved a mechanism to cope with the concomitant problem of highly possessive males; possessiveness was complemented by a "respect" for possession.*

Kummer links and contrasts the hamadryas adaptation to human evolution by noting that both species have evolved stable family units that are themselves embedded in larger social groups or bands. But there is a key difference between the two species. Unlike females among other primates, the human female is sexually receptive, that is, may be desirous of sexual intercourse with males whether she is ovulating or not. Hamadryas male baboons are attracted to their females even when they are not in estrus and receptive. Thus, in the hamadryas baboon a nonsexual attraction links males and females in permanent bonds. Whereas the human female may have changed to become permanently "attractive," the hamadryas male that changed to become more permanently "attracted."

The pattern of sexual receptivity in the human female certainly played an important role in the early phases of human evolution. Once bonding occurred, however, it must have been reinforced by such nonsexual factors as sharing and the division of labor. Economic factors must have been important in the formation of both the human family and larger social groups.

I find Kummer's approach to primate behavior congenial because he takes a balanced view of the role of genetics and learning in the development of primate adaptations. His work on the hamadryas baboon is useful because the origins of particular adaptations are not prejudged according to some deterministic theory. He illustrates clearly how environmental selection leads to behavioral changes, some of which are genetic and some of which are learned.

Tradition in Monkeys: The Japanese Macaques

The role of learning is indeed important in primate behavior. Evidence now exists demonstrating that individual monkeys and apes learn from each other as well as from the environment. In some cases learning leads to significant changes in social behavior, which are passed down from generation to generation. Learning of this type is very much like culture, although it is not as highly developed in monkeys and apes as among humans. A particularly interesting case involving the development of a culture-like tradition in monkeys has been noted by Japanese scientists working with macaques, a species of monkey.

In 1952 scientists at the Japan Monkey Center on Koshima Island began to leave pieces of sweet potato around for a troop of macaques living in a seminatural setting. The area soon became both a feeding and a breeding ground. One year later a two-year-old female was observed washing the sand off a potato in a nearby fresh-water stream. This custom spread rapidly through a large part of the troop. Soon the washing shifted to the sea. Apparently the animals learned to combine the advantage of washing the sand off their food and salting it. Most of the young monkeys learned this behavior, but only about 18 percent of the older animals adopted it. Among those monkeys that did adopt potato washing were several females who taught it to their young. Thus a habit that had initially spread horizontally among the monkeys of a particular generation began to pass vertically as a tradition. A learned adaptation was preserved through transmission to the next generation.

The move to the sea introduced young monkeys to a new environment. They soon learned to swim. One monkey even swam to another island. Others began to pick edible seaweed from the inshore bottom.

Japanese macaques washing food.

The Gombe Chimps

Chimpanzees are a particularly interesting species to study. They are, like gorillas, highly intelligent animals. These two species are probably the closest to humans in mental ability. Unlike gorillas, chimpanzees live in rather large and diversified social groups in which a great deal of vocal and physical communication takes place. They live in areas (of Africa) that are more accessible to researchers than the home territories of gorillas and are easy to observe. Since chimpanzees, gorillas, and humans represent advanced stages in primate evolution and because all three species are highly intelligent, comparative studies of these primates can shed light on the evolution of culture. Because we and the apes developed in different environments, environmental differences may be used to partially account for the divergences between humans and these simian species. As you will see, both chimpanzees and gorillas have a similar vocabulary of calls, yet the frequency with which these are used in social behavior differs markedly between the two species. Both group structure and environment appear to play a role in these differences.

Primatology has been greatly enriched in the past several years by long-term, patient observation of chimpanzees under slightly modified natural conditions. All zoologists and anthropologists owe a particular debt of gratitude to Jane van Lawick-Goodall for her continuing observation and analysis.

The Gombe Stream Chimpanzee Research Center is located on the shores of Lake Tanganyika in Tanzania. The animals in the center are protected from hunting and other forms of human molestation. Although the chimpanzee troops studied at Gombe Stream have all been native to the area, they have been attracted to the observation station by plentiful supplies of bananas left for them in feeding boxes. The feeding and the presence of human observers have been the only unnatural elements introduced into the research.

Chimps are naturally curious animals and they soon accustom themselves to the presence of observers. Eventually they even become active participants in the lives of their human guests. This relationship has allowed Goodall to record an amazing series of previously unknown data about chimpanzee life, including the discovery that these animals use simple tools and, on occasion, eat meat.

Chimps love to eat termites, and they get at the insects by stripping the leaves off small twigs and pushing them into termite holes. Some of the insects adhere to the twigs when they are withdrawn from the holes and the chimps lick them off. The tools are crude but suited to their task. Chimps also hunt small game; the young of many of the larger mammals such as wild pigs that inhabit the area are captured, killed, and shared by members of the troop.

Like many other (but remember, not all) primates, chimps display dominance. Rank in the troops is established by aggressive displays and reinforced by social grooming, in which subservient animals groom more dominant members. Goodall had the opportunity to observe a change in hierarchy that was facilitated by a clever use of empty kerosene cans left around the camp area. Goodall notes that in 1963 a chimp she had named Mike was almost at the bottom of the rank order of his troop. One day, as five males, including three high-ranking animals, were sitting grooming each other, Mike walked over to the camp tent and picked up two empty kerosene cans. He then sat down and stared at the other males. Soon he began to rock from side to side and emit a series of calls.

As he called, Mike got to his feet and suddenly he was off, charging toward the group of males, hitting the two cans ahead of him. The cans, together with Mike's crescendo of hooting, made the most appalling racket: no wonder the erstwhile peaceful males rushed out of the way. Mike and his cans vanished down a track, and after a few moments there was silence.

This performance was repeated several times until Mike was approached by one of the males. Soon most of the other males were grooming him. Only the most dominant male, Goliath, stayed away. Goodall suggests that Mike used his superior intelligence and a strong desire for dominance to work himself into a position of

Chimpanzees playing. Note the facial expression, which is a play signal.

leadership. She asks herself whether Mike would have attained high status without the cans and answers that he probably would have. Getting to know the chimps had convinced her that they had different personalities and different degrees of intelligence.

It is also clear from her description that high intelligence allowed a rather complex social organization to develop within the troop. Although the members of a chimp community move about "in constantly changing associations . . . [and] the society seems to be organized in such a casual manner, each individual knows his place in the social structure—knows his status in relation to any other chimpanzee he may chance upon during the day."

This social structure demands a large vocabulary of gestures that the animals use to signal their knowledge of position within the group. Without such a system, aggressive encounters would be much more common and disruptive. If social complexity has an adaptive function in chimpanzee societies—and it appears that it does—then it would be facilitated by the development of high intelligence. High intelligence, in turn, allows for the development of increased complexity. There is, therefore, a circular adaptive relationship between individual intelligence and sociability. This same process must have played an important role in human development, but in humans it led to even higher intelligence and greater social differentiation. Chimps are on the verge of culture, but they do not have either culture (in the sense of complex symbolism) or true language.

Chimps not only display dominance and aggression, they are also affectionate creatures. "When a chimpanzee is suddenly frightened he frequently reaches to touch or embrace a chimpanzee nearby, rather as a girl watching a horror film may seize her companion's hand. Both chimpanzees and humans seem reassured in stressful situations by physical contact with another individual." Chimpanzees need each other and the social group of which each member is only a part.

The Shy Mountain Gorilla

Ever since its discovery the gorilla has fascinated people. For most it is a savage creature of great power. It is no accident that King Kong was a supergorilla, endowed with both strength and primitive compassion. The gorilla in the popular mind is both a superbeast and, at least partly, a superman.

It was not until 1959 that we began to get a true picture of gorilla behavior under natural conditions. It was then that George Schaller undertook his remarkable study of the mountain gorilla in the Eastern Congo.

Gorilla troops vary in size from two to 30 animals. There are more females than males in the group, and ages range from infants (0–3 years), to juveniles (3–6 years), to adults. Adult males can be divided into two groups; the blackbacked males (6–10 years) and silverbacked males (over 10 years). The latter are the dominant animals. Average group size is about 16. Unlike many monkeys, gorillas display *no* territoriality. Groups often intermingle and aggressive encounters are very rare. Schaller notes that during his study as many as six groups frequented the same section of the forest.

Unlike chimpanzees, gorillas have never been observed to eat meat. Their diet consists exclusively of leaves, bark, pith, and fruit. They feed as they move through the forest, covering from 300 to 15,000 feet per day. The movement occurs at a leisurely pace.

Each gorilla group is led by a silverbacked male. Dominance, which is not strongly marked, appears to be a function of body size. Older males dominate younger males and females. Females dominate juveniles. When more than one silverback male occurs in a group, they arrange themselves in a linear hierarchy, but females are not so ranked. Unlike chimpanzees, gorillas rarely display dominance and their grooming does not appear to have any social significance. The sexual drive appears to be very low. Schaller observed very few incidents of sexual intercourse. In the two cases actually observed the males were *not* dominant animals.

The aggressive reputation that humans attribute to gorillas is probably based on casual observations of chest beating and occasional charges, as well as attacks by wounded or startled animals. For one ignorant of the degree of bluff in such displays, the effect must be quite frightening. Yet the gorilla tends to be more bluff than bite. Aggressive signals range in intensity from mild to strong displays. Schaller lists them in order of increasing intensity: "(1) an unwavering stare or a sudden turn of the head; (2) an incipient charge indicated by a forward lunge of the body; (3) a bluff charge over 10 to 80 feet, either silent or roaring; and (4) actual physical contact in the form of biting or wrestling."

As is true among all species with aggressive signals, there is also a set of submissive responses. These include turning away from an aggressing animal and cowering the head downward, with the arms and legs tucked under the abdomen. Schaller notes that gorillas can be easily stared down and that attacks can often be thwarted by looking aggressive males straight in the eye. On the other hand, people who run from a charging animal are likely to be bitten in the back. In general, gorillas can be thought of as the gentle primate giants of the forest.

Comparing Species: Chimpanzee and Gorilla Communication

Ethologist Peter Marler has compared gorilla and chimpanzee communication and related the differences to social organization in both species. Both chimps and gorillas have a vocabulary of calls that are similar in number and acoustic (sound) features. There are only three gorilla sounds that have no equivalent in chimps. The major differences in communication occur in the use of calls by specific members of the troops. Vocalization among chimps is distributed through all age classes and both

Mountain gorillas led by a silverbacked male.

sexes. Among gorillas three specific calls are restricted to adult males, which also produce the majority of all but one of the calls.

Chimps live in large, dispersed groups, "containing adult males, with members recombining from day to day in different subgroupings of adult males, females and young. They also spend much time alone." Gorillas live in more coherent groups, most frequently with one adult male member. Vocalizations within the group reach over much shorter ranges than among chimps. "The compactness of the group is such that they confront such exigencies as predator detection, dissemination of alarm and defence as a group rather than on an individual basis. This difference in within-group organization provides some basis for speculating about the social significance of differences in their vocal behavior."

Among gorillas separations are brief and reunion rituals are rare. Such rituals are common among chimps. Since the gorilla troop spends most of its time together, males are able to make many communicative decisions for the group as a whole. Among the more dispersed chimps, all sex and age classes (except infants) must cope as individuals with a range of environmental and social situations that gorillas experience as a group. Marler suggests that "The strong individuality and loudness of pant-hooting (one frequent chimpanzee call) may aid in maintaining organization of the dispersed chimpanzee group and in between-group relations."

In recent years the number and sophistication of primate studies has increased. As we learn more about our close relatives, we come to see how naive our original impressions were. Each species has its own set of adaptations that fit closely with its environmental experience. If there is an overall primate pattern, it is reflected in the high degree of intelligence found throughout the order as well as in the sociability of all the higher primates. Sociability implies cooperation and, perhaps, a certain amount of aggression. Some friction occurs in most, if not all, social groups. It also implies communication and social differentiation. The behavior of one of the primate species, however, cannot be used as the model for other species. In addition, parallel forms of behavior cannot be attributed automatically to either instinct or learning. Environmental selection can operate on both, in different times, and under different conditions.

As smart as they are, none of our primate relatives have developed true language and culture. Without these powerful new adaptations they are bound to a certain degree of innate patterns. Humans may display the vestiges of a few of these innate responses, particularly as newborns, but culture has freed us from most of them. Culture provides the basis for a difference in kind rather than a difference in degree between ourselves and other primates.

Summary

Primate behavior is studied to test hypotheses about the evolution of human behavior and to reconstruct possible steps in the series of behavioral adaptations that resulted in the human pattern. The study of primates also contributes to the field of comparative psychology, providing information on a range of specific capacities within and between species. Careful field and laboratory studies of different species, particularly when these are placed in their proper evolutionary grade, provide some notion of the direction of behavioral evolution in the primate order. Laboratory and field studies of the same species under different conditions helps to unravel the role of environment and learning in the behavioral process.

Primate studies have concentrated on such factors as locomotor patterns, feeding behavior, sexual and social relations, as well as communication. Of particular interest are the ways in which these patterns are integrated with one another and with the environment of each species. In some cases it can be shown that the same physical equipment and behavioral capacities are expressed differently because of environmental and social conditions. This is apparently the case for differences in vocalization between chimpanzees and gorillas.

The chimpanzees in this group are hooting in response to strangers.

Behavioral studies are difficult because the units of analysis may be hard to define. Before a concept such as aggression can be used, for example, it must be operationalized. That is, it must be defined in such a way that it can be observed unambiguously and counted. Sometimes prior assumptions about behavior obscure the real dynamics of social life. Different definitions of aggression and dominance, for example, have led to contradictory results. The concentration on one type of behavior at the expense of others can also lead to a biased picture. Early studies of primates in the wild were restricted for the most part to aggression, territoriality, and dominance. Little was said about cooperation and the role of females in group structure.

In this chapter we have looked at four selected primate species, the hamadryas baboon, the Japanese macaque, the chimpanzee, and the gorilla. The hamadryas have been studied in the wild and the peculiarities of their social behavior have been compared to that of other baboon species. Of particular interest among the hamadryas is the male-female group, which contrasts to group formation in other baboons. Hans Kummer suggests that the general baboon behavioral pattern was modified as an adaptation to an arid environment in which food is scarce. He believes that the tendency for males to form a permanent relationship with one or more females is genetic in origin. On the other hand, he suggests that the bonding of females to males is based on learning. This is confirmed when female baboons of other species are introduced into hamadryas groups and adopt the typical hamadryas pattern.

The Japanese macaque colony provides interesting information on the role of learning in the formation of social hierarchies and suggests that traditional behavior can emerge in primate societies. Young Japanese macaques learned to wash the sand from sweet potatos provided by experimenters. Such washing was not a trivial behavior, since it made the potatos edible. At first potato washing spread among monkeys of the same generation; later it was passed down from mothers to their offspring. With that, it had become part of tradition. Potato washing provided access to a new food resource.

The Gombe chimpanzees studied by Jane van Lawick-Goodall live under seminatural conditions. They are attracted to the study area by banana boxes where they have access to a plentiful food source. The Gombe chimpanzees have provided many insights into primate behavior. Goodall was the first person to document tool use among chimps, and more recently she has noted both hunting and meat-eating as well as aggressive encounters between hostile groups.

George Schaller studied mountain gorillas under totally natural conditions. During the length of his pioneering study Schaller followed gorilla bands through the forest. He discovered that gorillas are rather shy creatures that live in groups ranging from two to 30 animals. Dominance among gorillas appeared to be a function of body size and groups were led by large silverback males.

Peter Marler, noting the difference between gorilla and chimpanzee social groups and the dispersal patterns exhibited by the two species, uses these factors to explain differences in vocalization. Among gorillas adult males produce the majority of calls, while among chimps communication is quite democratic, and chattering occurs throughout the social unit. Marler notes that among chimps separations are common and reunions vocal. Gorillas, on the other hand, rarely separate, and males make most of the communication decisions for the group. While communication within these two species may be due to social and environmental factors, neither of them has developed true language. Language is a strictly human capacity.

Bibliography

Jay, P. C. Editor 1968 — *Primates: Studies in Adaptation and Variability.* New York: Holt, Rinehart and Winston. A good collection of articles on primates.

Jolly, A. 1972 — *The Evolution of Primate Behavior.* New York: Macmillan. An excellent but somewhat mistitled introduction to the behavior of contemporary primates.

Kawai, M. 1965 — Newly acquired precultural behavior of the natural troop of Japanese monkeys on Koshima islet. *Primates.* 6:1–30. Report on food washing as a cultural trait.

Goodall, J. van Lawick 1972 — *In the Shadow of Man.* New York: Dell. Popular account of chimpanzee society.

Kolata, G. B. 1976 — Primate Behavior: Sex and the Dominant Male. *Science,* Vol. 191, 9 Jan. 1976, pp. 55–56. Review and critique of aggression and dominance studies in a variety of primate species.

Kummer, H. 1971 — *Primate Societies: Group Techniques of Ecological Adaptation.* Chicago: Aldine. Excellent review and comparison of environmental and genetic effects on primate social behavior.

Lancaster, J. B. 1975 — *Primate Behavior and the Emergence of Human Culture.* New York: Holt, Rinehart and Winston. An excellent short account of primate behavior and its relation to human behavior and culture.

Marler, P. 1976 — Social Organization, Communication, and Graded Signals: the Chimpanzee and Gorilla. In *Growing Points in Ethology,* edited by P. G. Bateson and R. A. Hinde. Cambridge: Cambridge University Press. An excellent comparative study of communication systems in two primate species.

Schaller, G. B. 1963 — *The Mountain Gorilla.* Chicago: University of Chicago Press. Report on field work with a gentle primate species.

CHAPTER 6
THE EVOLUTION OF HOMO SAPIENS

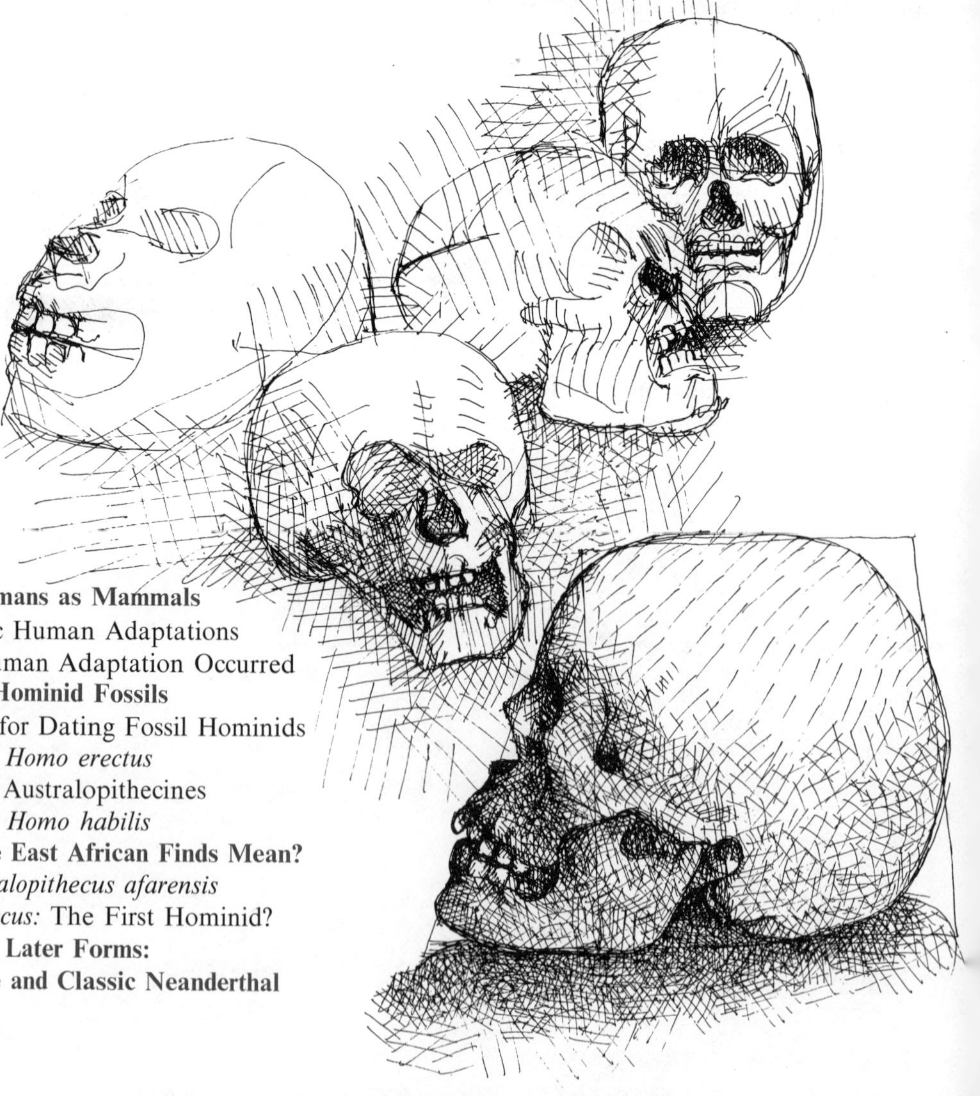

HUMANS AS MAMMALS

Modern *Homo sapiens* evolved through the retention of certain basic mammalian and primate patterns, the elaboration of others, and the development of new morphological and behavioral adaptations. Although human evolution does involve some spectacular physical changes, these are surpassed by our major behavioral adaptation—the development of language and culture. Both language and culture, however, depend on genetic patterns and are rooted in biology.

All mammals are equipped with warm blood, an efficient circulatory system, including the four-chambered heart, and an elaborate neocortex (the major portion of the gray matter of the brain). Mammals are well programmed for active life and are suited to a wide range of climates. All are good learners and adapt to local environments through a combination of inborn and learned behaviors. Learning as an adaptation is enhanced among all mammals by exploration and play. Through exploration the young learn to map the environment. Through play, a safe means for practicing adult behavior, they learn to interact with other animals and to deal with the natural setting.

All mammals, except the primitive monotremes and marsupials, have live birth; they are **viviparous.** The female nurses her young at the breast. Nurturing insures food and protection for the young and aids in the development of sociability.

Humans have retained the flexible upper limb that is a feature of all generalized mammals. In addition, we have retained the primate grasping hand with its opposable thumb. Humans, like monkeys and apes, have traded claws for flattened nails and have a rich network of nerves in the fingers. These aid in touch and manipulation. Like all primates humans have good eye-hand coordination. Human vision is well developed. As do other primates, we have stereoscopic vision—that is, the field of view for each eye overlaps the other and the brain merges the two slightly different images, thus providing a three-dimensional view of the world. Unlike most mammals, but like the other primates, we see the world in color. Humans have also inherited the upright sitting posture so common in primates.

Specific Human Adaptations

Major changes that have occurred in human evolution include the enlargement of the brain case (see Figure 6.1). The frontal region of the skull rose, the temporal region (just above the ears) ballooned and the occipital region (the back of the skull) filled out and became rounded. These changes, of course, accompanied increased brain size and a reorganization of brain centers.

Other changes in the skull include a shortening of the face, with a reduction in tooth size, particularly the incisors and canine teeth. Changes in muscle attachment and size have been associated with other modifications in skull architecture, including a reduction of the bony ridge over the eyes (the *supraorbital torus*), a thinning out of the lower jaw along with the development of a protruding chin, and an increase in the size of the *mastoid process* (a bony protuberance just behind the ear). The *foramen magnum,* the hole at the base of the skull through which the spinal cord joins the brain, has moved forward to the center of gravity for the skull, in keeping with the evolution of upright posture.

The spinal column and the pelvis have altered in ways that enable upright posture and bipedalism (see Figure 6.2). The spinal column has developed a series of curves that strengthen the back. The major change is the development of a lumbar curve at the base of the spine just above the pelvis. This curve is not genetic, however; rather, it forms in normal individuals as a result of upright posture and walking. The pelvis has developed into a bowl that helps to support the abdominal organs (see Figure 6.3). The shaft of the pelvis (the *ilium*) has become shortened and has twisted forward. A modification of the *ischium* (the lower rear part of the pelvis) accomodates shifts in muscles necessary for bipedal locomotion. The lower limbs (see Figure 6.4) have become longer in relation to the upper limbs and have lost some of their flexibility. The leg has developed into a strut for walking and modification of the foot also facilitates walking. The big toe has swung into line with the other toes and is no longer opposable. The foot is long and arched both across its width and along its length.

All of these changes are related to two aspects of behavior: 1) upright posture and bipedalism, and 2) the development of language and culture. These two sets of behaviors are thought to be closely linked. Bipedalism frees the hand to work and to carry. The development of dexterity and an increase in the number and difficulty of the things that the hand can do are thought to be linked to brain development and intelligence.

We must remember, however, that like most primates, the human being is also a social creature. The change in sexual receptivity (noted in chapter 5) was probably related to the development of pair bonding, (the establishment of male-female couples) and the development of the human family. Many anthropologists deduce that social behavior was as important as the hand (if not more important) in the emergence of higher intelligence and speech. The development of a division of labor by sex and a certain degree of social differentiation based on age and ability undoubtedly played a role in the evolution of the brain, which in turn fed back into the further development of social elaboration.

Nonhuman primates cooperate in defense and sometimes in feeding. Their social groups are marked in many cases by dominance hierarchies. Human groups are more complex and human cooperation more multifaceted. Humans cooperate in hunting and gathering, in child care, in aggressive behavior, in defense. Adults teach the young and the old often teach adults. Some individuals are wise in the way of nature and others wise in the symbolic sphere. Humans share things and ideas to a degree unknown among all the other animals. Humans are less aggressive within the group than many other primates and are also able to enter into mutually useful and satisfying relations with other social groups. Heightened cooperation is facilitated by our knack for symbolic communication and also by the realization that inter- and intragroup cooperation has important benefits.

Cooperation was facilitated by changes in the endocrine system that reduced intragroup aggression as well as by the development of symbolic communication. Modification in the endocrine system also affected **secondary sexual characteristics,** reducing some differences between males and females and increasing others.

How The Human Adaptation Occurred

Anthropologists argue over what part or parts of anatomy and behavior altered first when the ancestral line that led to humans began to diverge from other primates. The first modern, coherent attempt to account for the pattern of divergence was published by Sherwood Washburn in the late 1950s. Washburn suggested that the first step in **hominization** (the development of humans) occurred with true bipedal locomotion, accompanied by the skeletal changes noted above. Bipedalism freed the hand. Any increase in hand use would be at least partially dependent on higher intelligence so that brain development would be associated with the increased sophistication of fine-grain manual dexterity. According to this theory increased intelligence led to the invention of manufactured tools, and tools made the species less dependent on large canine teeth for aggression and defense. Improved tools provided an evolutionary advantage for any group possessing them. Since technological advance would depend on better brains, better tools implied selection for better brains. This entire process operated as a complex feedback system that, once begun, would proceed rapidly toward the final outcome: modern *Homo sapiens.*

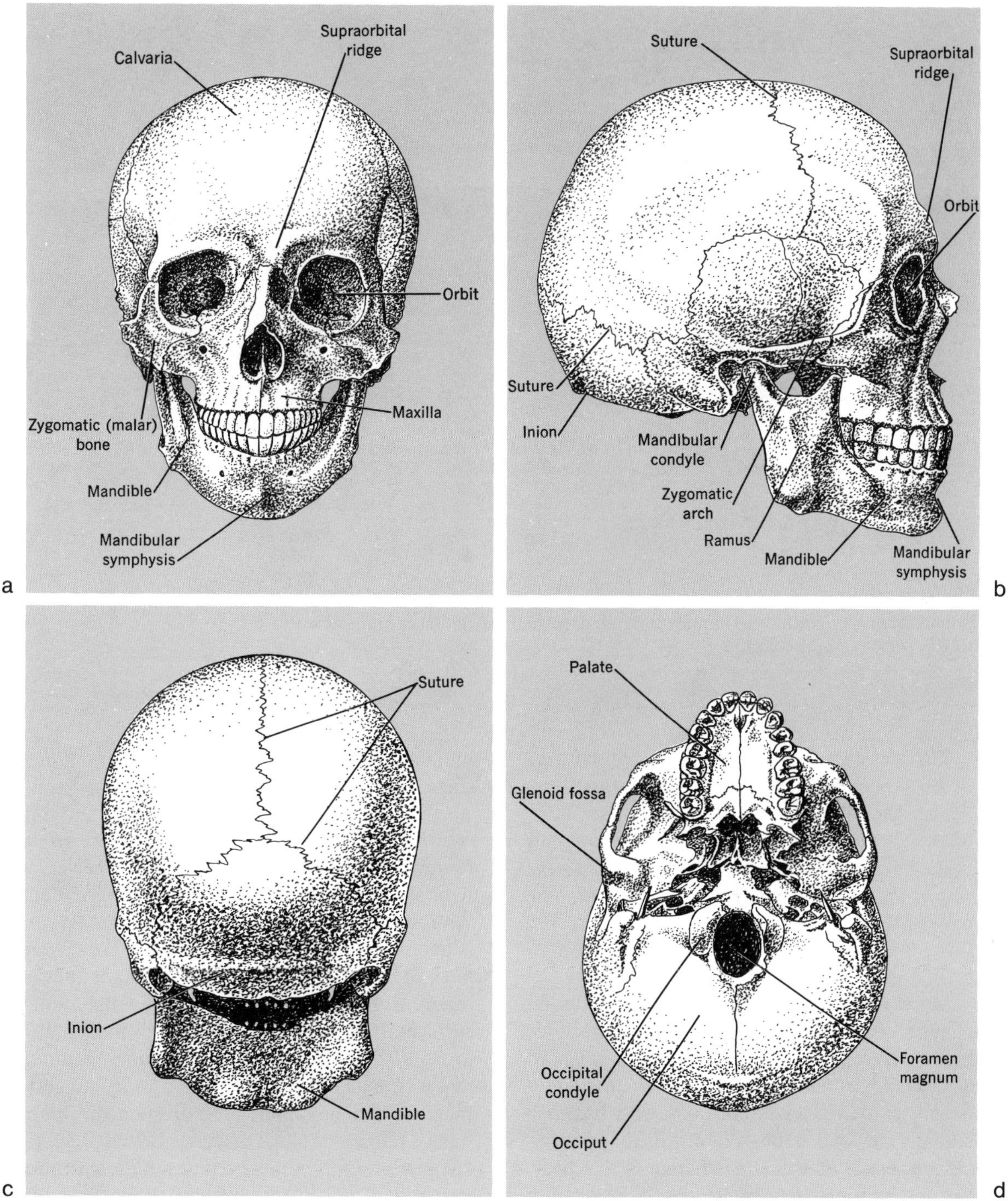

Figure 6.1

Four views of the human skull: (a) Front view, (b) side view, (c) back view, (d) bottom view. (Adapted from J. Buettner-Janusch, *Physical Anthropology*. New York: John Wiley, 1973.)

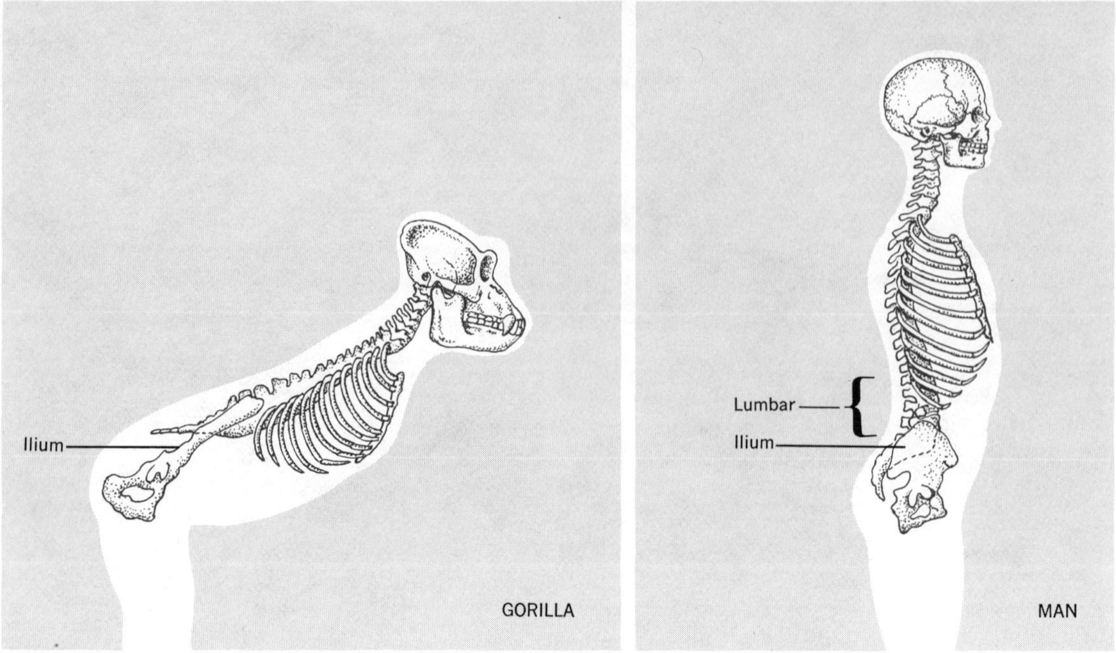

Figure 6.2
Spinal column of gorilla and human compared. Note the differences in the curves of the two vertebral columns.

This was an appealing theory and at the time of its publication it agreed with the fossil evidence. The first fully erect hominids had skeletons well developed for bipedalism, but their brain development, *at least as measured by the size of the brain,* appeared to lag behind. The major problem with the theory was the fact that these fossils already had more or less modern teeth.

More recent discoveries show that dental change occurred before either bipedalism or brain development. Clifford Jolly, a physical anthropologist who has examined the fossil evidence for dental evolution and who has also studied the food habits of certain living monkeys, suggests that the first change in the direction of hominization came with a change in tooth structure. Jolly relates this change to diet. He notes that modern baboons (*papio*) living in East Africa have large incisors and rather small molars. This pattern fits well with baboon diet since these animals eat the soft parts of grass stems. The grass is plucked by hand and the stem is scraped between the incisor teeth to remove the edible portion. Another species of baboon (*theropithecus*), living in a different environment, is dependent on seeds for its nourishment. Seed-eaters need to push their food back onto the molar teeth with their tongues in order to grind it efficiently on the flat molar surfaces. Interestingly, *theropithecus* has smaller incisors than its East African cousins and, as might be expected, larger molars. Jolly suggests that the first **hominids,** creatures on the main line of human evolution, were also seed-eaters. He goes on to hypothesize that a later shift to a partial dependence on meat may have served to select further skeletal changes. He correlates these later changes with bipedalism and tool using. Both traits would be adaptive for even part-time hunters, given the basic primate physical structure.

Kathleen R. Gibson and Sue Taylor Parker, both physical anthropologists, have offered a more complex set of hypotheses to account for the development of high intelligence and social behavior in early hominids. They suggest that three behavioral factors and one environmental factor were linked in the evolutionary process. Important to their hypotheses is the notion that hominid development occurred in a mosaic (that is, variable) environment with seasonal access to a wide range of edible foods. Many of these foods, they believe, had to be extracted by cutting, breaking, or crushing with some kind of tool. Gibson and Parker refer to this technology as extractive food-getting. They note that extractive food-getting is not exclusive to primates and have studied the behavior in a wide range of animals, including vultures, which use stones to break ostrich eggs, and otters, which use stones to break open shell fish. While such crude tools need not be culturally modified, their use does require a certain amount of insight. The animal must "realize" that food can be obtained only through the extractive act. Lower animals such as vultures and otters use tools on only a limited range of

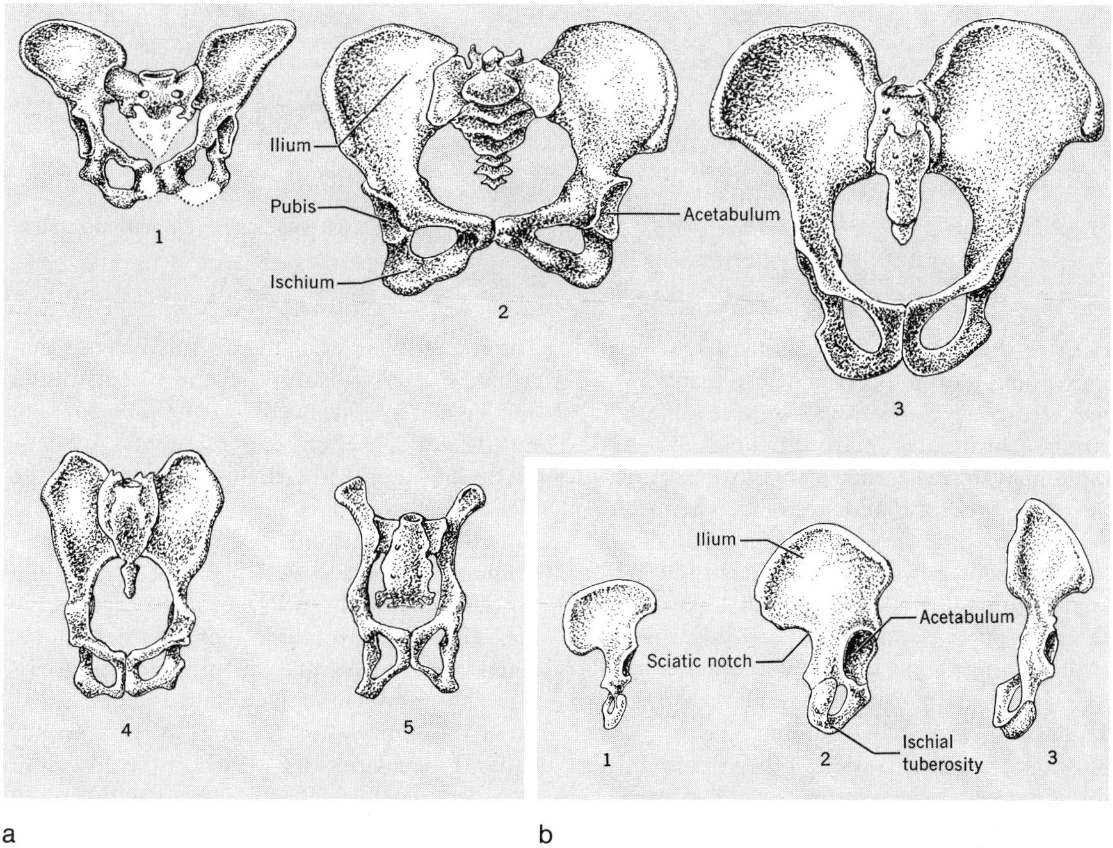

Figure 6.3

Pelvises. (a) Ventral view of (1) *Australopithecus,* (2) *Homo,* (3) gorilla, (4) gibbon, (5) lemur. Note the similarities between *Australopithecus* and *Homo* and the ways both differ from other primates. (b) Side view of the pelvises of (1) *Australopithecus* (2) *Homo,* and (3) gorilla.

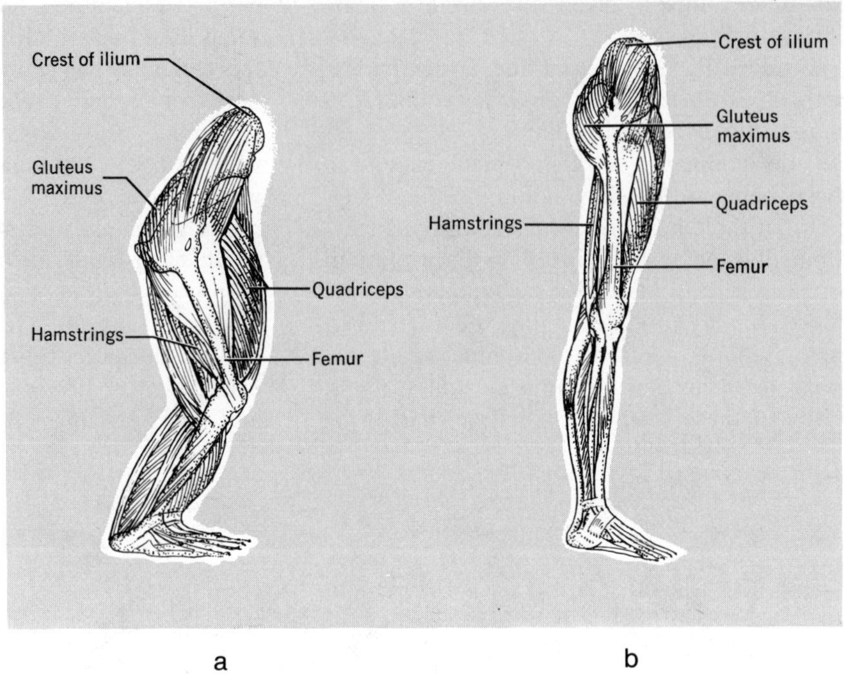

Figure 6.4
Lower limbs of (a) gorilla, (b) *Homo.* The leg of *Homo* has developed into a strut for bipedal walking.

resources. In a mosaic environment the technique would have to be extended to many food types, some of which would require different extractive techniques. Early hominids, for example, may have learned early to crack nuts and seeds, peel fruit, and cut meat. The extension of extractive food-getting to a range of seasonal resources would insure a constant food supply during the year. The behavior would require an increase in cognitive ability.

Gibson and Parker include two other behaviors in their adaptive complex. These are missile-throwing and shelter-building. Again these behaviors are seen in species other than hominids. Chimpanzees and gorillas, for example, build sleeping nests in trees, and chimpanzees have been observed to throw objects at predators. Improvements in accuracy in missile-throwing and the use of missiles in hunting as well as defense would depend on improved coordination as well as increases in intelligence. The use of complex materials for the construction of shelters would also require cooperation and higher intelligence. Recent evidence from East Africa of shelters, apparently built by Australopithecines, early hominids, supports the idea that this behavior could have developed from patterns already established in nonhuman primates. In fact, one of the most interesting aspects of the Gibson-Parker hypotheses is the idea that early hominid behavioral patterns could have developed out of preexisting primate patterns. Under environmental selection these became elaborated into more complex cultural behaviors, all of which favored and were favored by high intelligence and insight.

The Gibson-Parker theory can easily be integrated into the growing agreement among physical anthropologists that social cooperation in the context of permanent groups was a major feature in the hominid adaptation from its beginning. Extractive food-getting in a variable environment would tend to stimulate both the sharing of resources and a true division of labor, in which some members of the group provided one type of resource and other members provided another type. We shall now see how Ralph Holloway, also a physical anthropologist, treats brain development and the development of human social life.

Holloway accepts Jolly's version of early hominid evolution, but has gone on to suggest that brain development, particularly a reorganization of cerebral centers, occurred early for the human brain (see Figure 6.5). Holloway has personally studied almost all of the available hominid fossil material in the world. Although the brain is covered by several layers of material that insulate it from the skull, Holloway has attempted to get some notion of brain structure from the muted imprints left by the brain on the inside of the skull. He has made, or has had made, casts of the inside of the brain case of monkeys, apes, and hominid fossils. Holloway believes that he has evidence for early changes in the brain, including the development of language centers.

Holloway's ideas have been disputed by those who feel that human brain evolution is primarily a matter of increasing size. These scholars, particularly Harry Jerison, note that early hominids had rather small brains and that intermediate forms display intermediate cranial capacities. On the basis of these findings, Jerison suggests that hominization was a long process of gradual cerebral development in which increasing brain size was the major variable.

Holloway counters by arguing that even the earliest tool-using hominids had reorganized brains. In particular, he has found evidence in an early fossil for a speech area that is completely lacking in chimpanzee brains. Holloway notes that the earliest hominids were rather small creatures (they weighed about 50 pounds) and that their small brains can be explained by overall body size. He believes that a brain very much like ours developed early, that it was derived from the primate brain through reorganization, and that increases in brain size throughout the fossil record can be explained by increases in body weight *and* further cerebral development. To support this viewpoint, Holloway cites evidence that **microcephalics** (abnormal humans with brains only slightly larger than the apes') have many of the brain functions of normal individuals. Microcephalics are impaired, but some of them, at least, are able to use language.

Holloway suggests the following sequence in the development of hominization:

Stage 1: The early phase. This saw an emphasis on social behavior adaptations associated with bipedalism, endocrine function, and the reorganization of the brain.

Stage 2: Middle stage. A refinement of stage 1.

Stage 3: Elaboration of culture with a positive feedback between brain organization and culture.

Holloway suggests that stage 1 included the development of the sexual division of labor as well as other forms of cooperation. Cooperation

A gelada baboon (*theropithecus*), the species used by Jolly in constructing his theory of seed-eating and hominid evolution.

was facilitated by modifications in the endocrine system, which could have led to a reduction in aggression, permitting groups to live together more densely. These changes may also have affected growth rates, slowing down the maturation process. Delayed maturation in turn led to a longer dependency period of offspring.

Holloway relates his **endocasts** (molds taken from the inside of the skull) to the development of social dynamics. He concludes that the development of language is more closely related to social relations within the group than to hunting, although hunting may well have played a role in the development of language. He also sees a change in brain organization involving a decrease in the visual cortex with an increase in the **association cortex;** the latter enhanced the ability to make complex discriminations among environmental cues. This development of the association cortex also was responsible for an increase in memory and foresight, both of which contribute to our ability to cope effectively with the environment and with one another. Holloway also suggests that in stage 3 the positive feedback between brain development and cultural complexity was mediated by an increase in the maturation period. Increasing the length of the maturation process produces a longer dependency period during which the child learns from and is protected by adults.

If you have followed the arguments already presented in this book, it should be no surprise that I favor Holloway's interpretation. In my view, it explains, in a well-reasoned and logical fashion, a great deal of evidence from the fossil record (to be examined next), the living primates, and what we know about brain function in normal and certain debilitated humans. I wish to point out, however, that these ideas, although based on the best available evidence, are tentative. Current discoveries tend to support Holloway, yet the fossil record is still rather poor, especially for the earliest representatives of the human line. Even the best theories can be thrown into disarray by new discoveries.

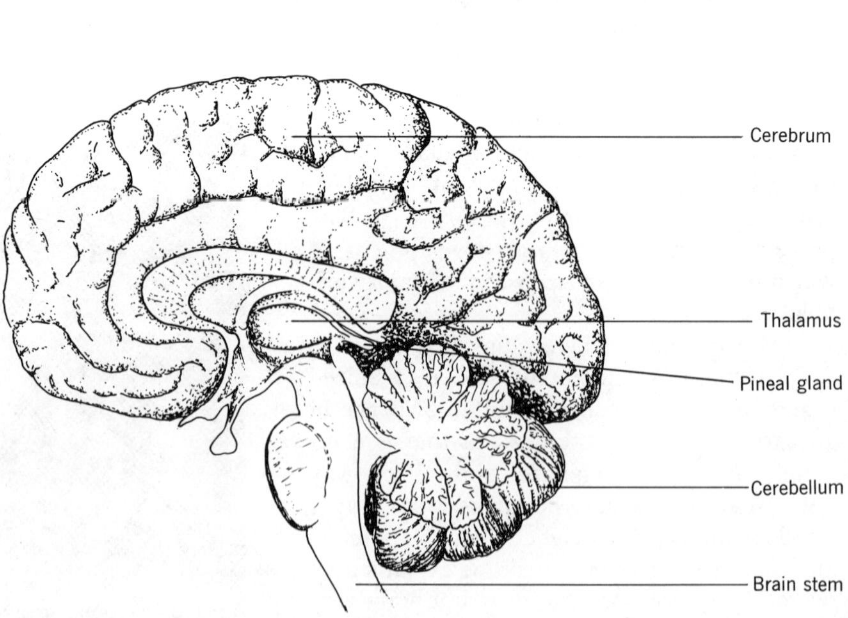

Figure 6.5
The fully evolved human brain, showing major parts.

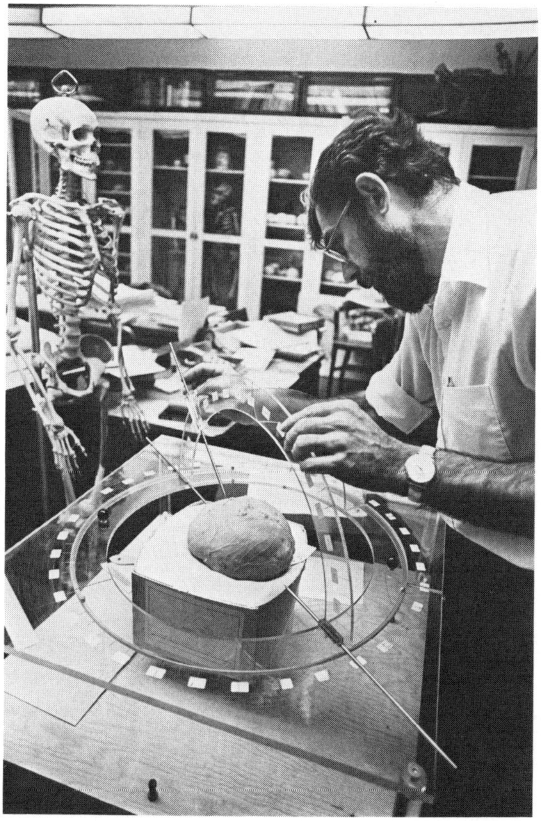

Professor Ralph Holloway in his laboratory working with a brain endocast.

HOMINID FOSSILS

Frameworks for Dating Fossil Hominids

While the great apes, the long series of fossil species leading to modern humans, and modern humans themselves are grouped as **hominoids,** only members of the human line are referred to as **hominids.** In classification a distinction is made between the **Hominoidea** (apes and humans) and the **Hominidae** (human line alone). In this chapter we are concerned with the Hominidae, or hominids.

Our knowledge of human evolution is based on what we know of the fossil record and the comparative anatomy of living forms. To be useful, fossils must be accurately dated. Geological and cultural materials are used in the dating process as well as a series of techniques, some based on chemistry and physics, and some based on stratigraphy (the natural layering that occurs as geological deposits accumulate through time). The complexities of dating techniques will be discussed in the archeological section of this book. Here I will examine the geological framework into which fossils are placed. The late Pliocene and the Pleistocene are the major periods of human evolution, although one important and early form, *Ramapithecus,* appeared in the Miocene and continued into the early Pliocene. Newly discovered fossils from East Africa and Ethiopia push the dates for fossil hominids back to around 5 million years ago. The Pleistocene itself runs from about 1.9 million to about 10,000 years ago. We are now living in what geologists and anthropologists call the Recent epoch.

The Pleistocene is generally divided into a series of glacial and interglacial periods. Although glaciation occurred only in the northern and central parts of the Northern Hemisphere the development of large ice sheets led to a general lowering of sea level. Conversely, interglacials saw a rise in the seas and the drowning of coast lines. Thus, glacial and interglacial periods can be used (with some difficulty and great caution) to date material found in the tropical and semitropical parts of the world. The glacial periods provide useful sequences for the placement of fossil and cultural evidence of human evolution. We know in which order they occurred, but unless other methods are used their absolute dates are difficult to establish.

From oldest to youngest, the Old World glacial and interglacial periods can be placed in the following sequence. The first Pleistocene glaciation was the Donau, which began about 1.8 million years ago. This was followed by the Donau-Günz interglacial. The next glacial period was the Günz, about one million years ago. The next interglacial was followed by the Mindel glaciation, dated to about 800,000 years ago. After yet another interglacial, lasting in this case for several hundred thousand years, the ice sheets once again moved downward over Europe. This fourth glacial period is known as the Riss. After the usual warming trend and glacial retreat, the last advance of the ice occurred. This is known as the Würm glacial. It began about 100,000 years ago and lasted until the Recent epoch.

European fossils can be easily placed within these glacial periods, which are associated with relatively clear geological strata. The most important recent fossil finds, however, come from Africa, and other important fossils come from Asia and Southeast Asia. These are dated by the newer chemical and physical techniques and then placed in an overall sequence that is matched to the glacial periods in Europe.

Since I am going to discuss the fossil record in historical perspective, that is, in the order in which the fossils were discovered, it will be helpful for you to consult the sequence of fossil evolution found on page 133. It places the major discoveries in their proper chronological and taxonomic framework. I have chosen the historical approach to show how the process of discovery itself affects the interpretation and classification of evidence concerning human evolution.

Let us now turn to the fossil record. The first discoveries of prehuman hominid fossils were made in the middle of the nineteenth century before the publication of Darwin's *Origin of Species.* These were the **Neanderthal** finds in Germany. At first these fossils were thought to be diseased representatives of modern humans. The gradual acceptance of evolution and the publication of *The Descent of Man* by Darwin in 1871 led to a reexamination of these finds. Let us see what Thomas Henry Huxley, a contemporary of Darwin and an evolutionist, had to say about them. First, he noted differences between Neanderthals and modern humans.

In truth, the Neanderthal cranium has most extraordinary characters. It has an extreme length of 8 inches, while its breadth is only 5.75 inches, or, in other words, its length is to its breadth as 100:72. It is exceedingly depressed, measuring only about 3.4 inches from the glabello-occipital line to the vertex. . . The large supraciliary [*supraorbital*] *ridges give the forehead a far more retreating appearance than its internal contour would bear out . . .*

Huxley goes on, however, to support a modern view of these fossils.

In conclusion may I say, that the fossil remains of Man hitherto discovered do not seem to me to take us appreciably nearer to that lower pithecoid form, by the modification of which he has, probably, become what he is. And considering what is now known of the most ancient races of men; seeing that they fashioned flint axes and flint knives and bone-skewers, of much the same pattern as those fabricated by the lowest savages at the present day, and that we have every reason to believe the habits and modes of living of such people to have remained the same form from the time of the Mammoth . . . til now, I do not know that this result is other than might be expected.*

*Pithecoid means apelike.

The evolution of *Homo sapiens*.

Years (before Present)	Geologic Periods	Periods of Glaciation	Emergence of Hominid Forms
10,000	Recent		*Homo sapiens sapiens*
100,000	Upper Pleistocene	Würm	
	Middle Pleistocene	Riss-Würm Interglacial	*Homo sapiens neanderthalensis*
		Riss	
500,000	Lower Pleistocene	Mindel-Riss Interglacial	
1,000,000		Mindel	*Homo erectus*
	Beginning Pleistocene	Günz-Mindel Interglacial	
		Günz	
		Donau-Günz Interglacial	
		Donau	
2,000,000	Pliocene		*Homo habilis* and *Australopithecus* (coexisting since the middle Pliocene)
3,000,000			
			Australopithecus afarensis
4,000,000

Where, then, must we look for primaeval Man? Was the oldest Homo sapiens *pliocene or miocene, or yet more ancient? In still older strata do the fossilized bones of an ape more anthropoid, or a Man more pithecoid, than any yet known await the researches of some unborn paleontologist?*

Time will show. But, in the meanwhile, if any form of the doctrine of progressive development is correct, we must extend by long epochs the most liberal estimate that has yet been made of the antiquity of Man.

As these remarks reveal, Huxley noted the

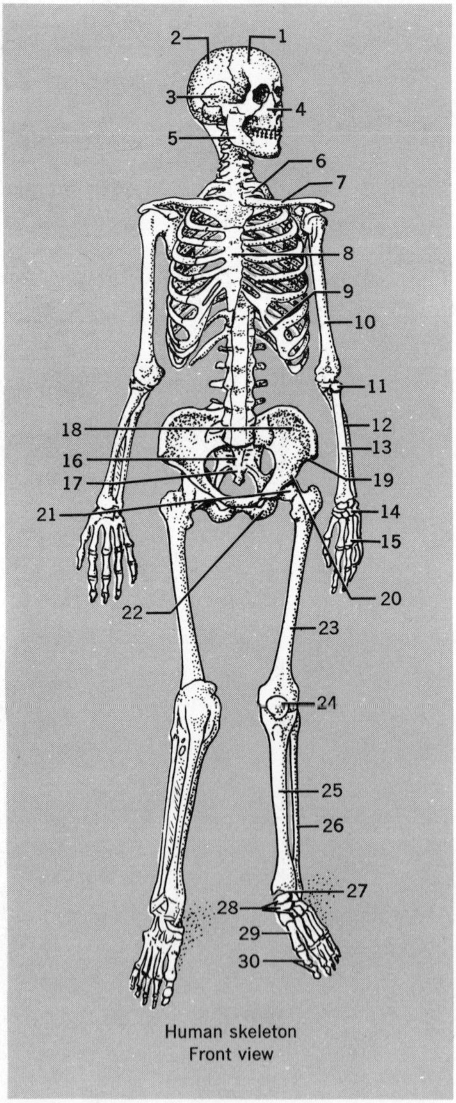

a

1. Frontal
2. Parietal
3. Temporal
4. Maxilla
5. Mandible
6. First rib
7. Clavicle
8. Body of sternum
9. Twelfth rib
10. Humerus
11. Head of radius
12. Ulna
13. Radius
14. Carpal bones
15. Metacarpal bones
16. Sacrum
17. Coccyx
18. Ilium
19. Anterior superior iliac spine
20. Anterior inferior iliac spine
21. Head of femur
22. Pubis
23. Femur
24. Knee cap
25. Tibia
26. Fibula
27. Ankle bone
28. Tarsal bones
29. Metatarsal bones
30. Phalanges

Figure 6.6
The human skeleton. (a) Front view, (b) back view. Major bones are shown.

differences between Neanderthal fossils and modern *Homo sapiens* yet he recognized how close to ourselves the Neanderthals were. Other interpretations of these fossils tended to exaggerate their aberrant form. In fact, one of the reconstructions of the Neanderthal, made by a French paleontologist, suggested that this hominid was unable to walk fully erect. We now know that this was a gross error.

As Huxley suspected, the Neanderthals alone did not allow evolutionists to reconstruct even the barest outlines of human evolution. Shortly

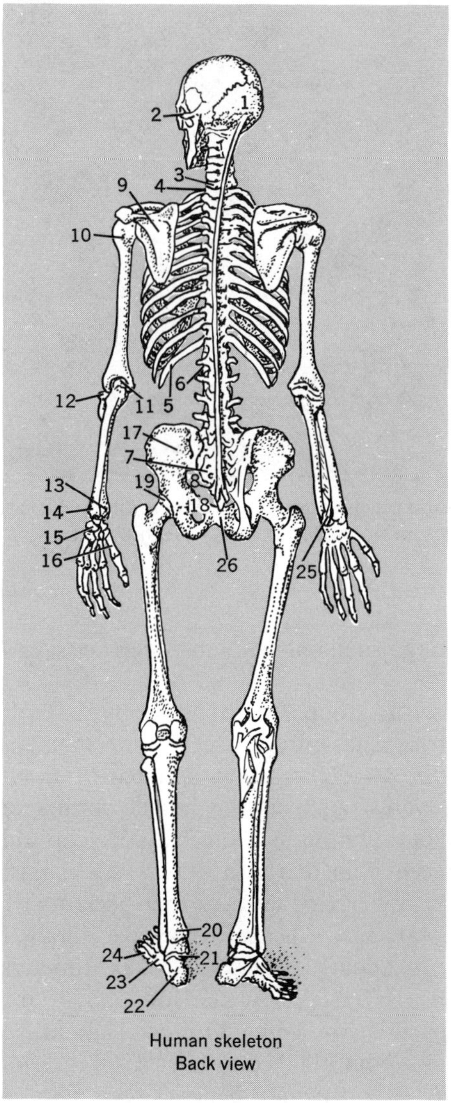

Human skeleton
Back view

b

1. Occipital
2. Arch of zygoma
3. Seventh cervical vertebra
4. First thoracic vertebra
5. Twelfth rib
6. First lumbar vertebra
7. Sacrum
8. Coccyx
9. Shoulder blade
10. Head of humerus
11. Point of elbow
12. Head of radius
13. Base of radius
14. Head of ulna
15. Bones of the wrist
16. Bones of the hand
17. Hip bone
18. Spine of ischium
19. Head of femur
20. Medial ankle bone
21. Ankle
22. Heel
23. Metatarsal bones
24. Phalanges of the toes
25. Wrist joint
26. Pubic symphysis

after the original Neanderthals were found in Europe, an ancient primitive jaw was found near Heidelberg in Germany. Although this discovery was to make sense later when it could be compared with other finds, as an isolated fossil it could only lead to idle speculation about human origins. What it did do even then, however, was to provide further evidence for Darwin's theory within the human line itself.

Homo Erectus

The next fossil species was discovered at the end of the nineteenth century by the Dutch physician Eugene Dubois. Inspired by a desire to find the missing link* and convinced that it was in Java, Dubois went straight to the source and found his fossil! In the 1920s a similar species was found in China, and later in the 1940s G. H. R. von Koenigswald went back to Java to find more complete specimens of the Dubois species. At first the Java fossil was named *Pithecanthropus erectus* and the related China specimens *Sinanthropus pekinensis.* This kind of naming exaggerates the differences between the two types. The China and Java finds were too much alike to belong to two separate species, not to mention genera. In addition, both finds, although more primitive than Neanderthals, were close enough to modern *Homo sapiens* to be included in the genus *Homo.* But some human paleontologists have a tendency to exaggerate the special nature of their own finds and to treat them as if they were unique. At any rate, a later reform of human taxonomy, made possible by a larger sample, put the Java and the Chinese finds into the genus *Homo* and gave both of them the species title *erectus.* They are now distinguished only by subspecies classifications.

Tools found on the surface at Olongasaillie (Africa) closely resemble Acheulian tools found in Europe.

The *erectus* group, which now includes finds from Africa and Europe (see Figure 6.7), including the Heidelberg jaw, is dated to about 500,000 years ago, although one primitive member of this group is about 750,000 years old and a recent find (early in the 1970s) in East Africa pushes *erectus* even further back, to 1.5 million years ago. *Erectus* fossils have a cranial capacity of about 750–1050 cubic centimeters (cc), which is just below the low end of the range for modern *Homo sapiens.* That range runs from about 1000 cc to over 1700 cc, *with absolutely no correlation between these normal capacities and intelligence. Erectus* stood fully erect, hence its name, and has been found in

*In the early days of speculation on human evolution it was believed that a single missing link existed that would unite the ape and human lines at their point of divergence. Evolution, however, is a process of gradual divergence as adaptation to specific environments shapes the developing species. There is no missing link, but rather a long series of related fossils that display different adaptations to environmental variables as well as development through time toward the fully evolved human species.

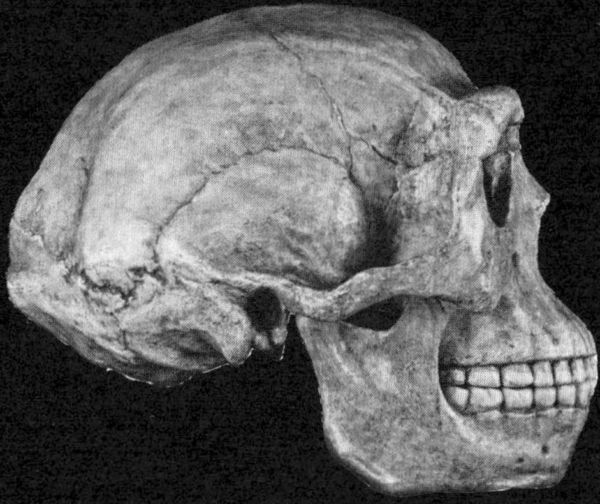

A

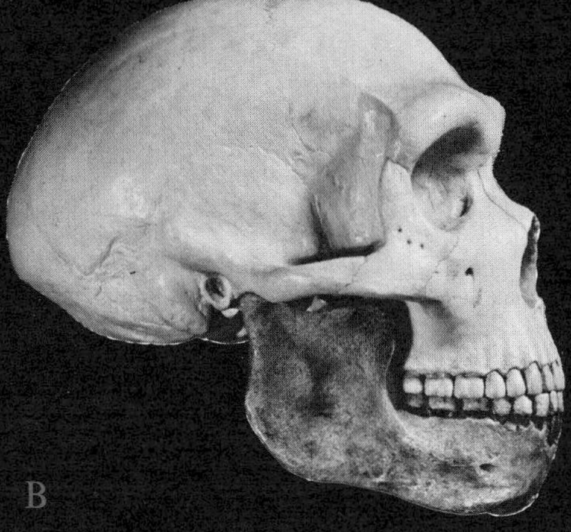

B

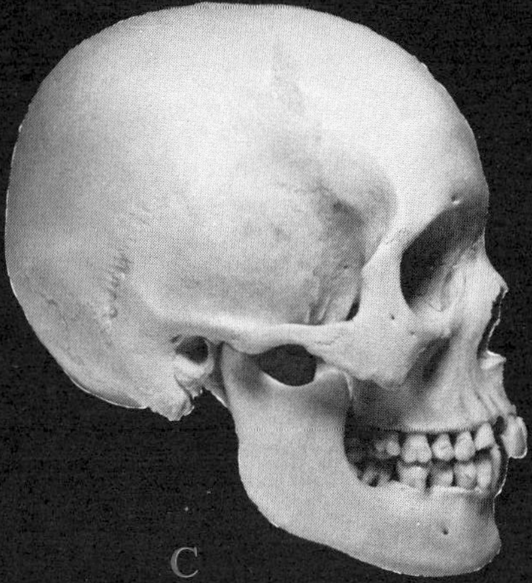

C

Homo erectus.

A

The China find (formerly called *Sinanthropus pekinensis*).

B

The *Heidelberg* jaw with reconstructed skull.

C

Modern *Homo sapiens* for comparison.

D

Chellean hand ax, and

E

Acheulian cleaver, both tools associated with *Homo erectus.*

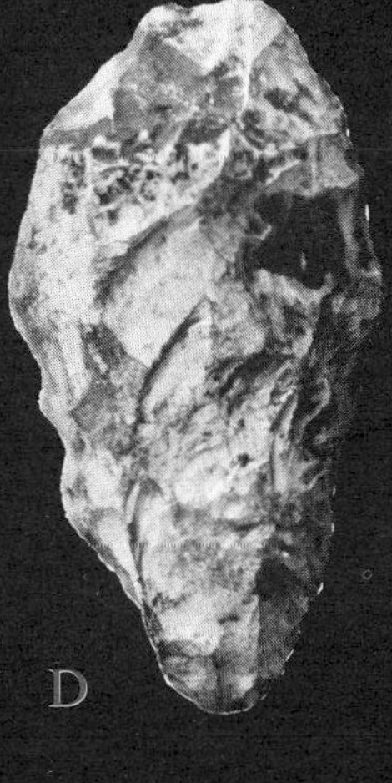

D

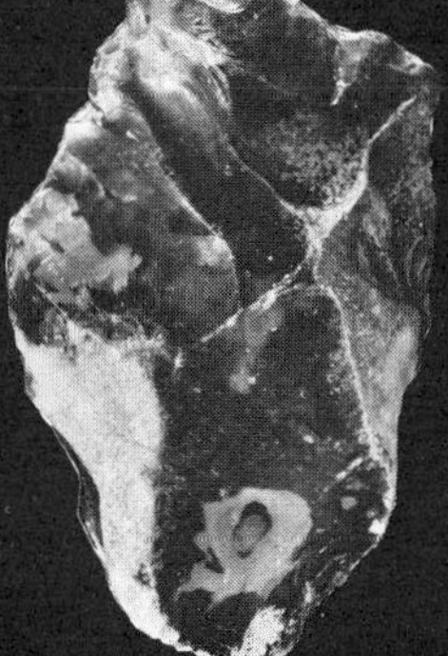

E

association with some stone tools known as hand axes, although their exact use is unknown. These tools were shaped from a core of stone; the best were made from flint, by chipping.

The erectus skulls are primitive in that they are thick-boned and massive. They have rather large supraorbital or brow ridges (bony protuberances over the eyes) and lack chins. Their teeth are larger than those of modern *Homo sapiens* but are similar in form. Their postcranial bones (other parts of the skeleton) were very close to modern *Homo sapiens.*

The Australopithecines

Another series of finds came to light in Africa beginning in the year 1924 (see Figure 6.8). These hominids are now known as the **australopithecines,** although they also went through a complicated stage of taxonomic overkill. The first fossil in this series was found by Raymond Dart. It included the face and part of the skull as well as a natural endocast of an apparently young anthropoid creature. Dart named it **Australopithecus africanus** (*southern ape of Africa*). Standing alone, this fossil was difficult to categorize. Although the skull was quite modern in appearance—at least in such features as facial length, reduced brow ridges, and a large brain in relation to face size—the fact that it was from a juvenile led to controversy. The skulls of young primates often look more advanced than those of adults because they have less strongly developed features. A baby chimpanzee skull, for example, looks much more human than does an adult chimpanzee skull. In addition, the en-

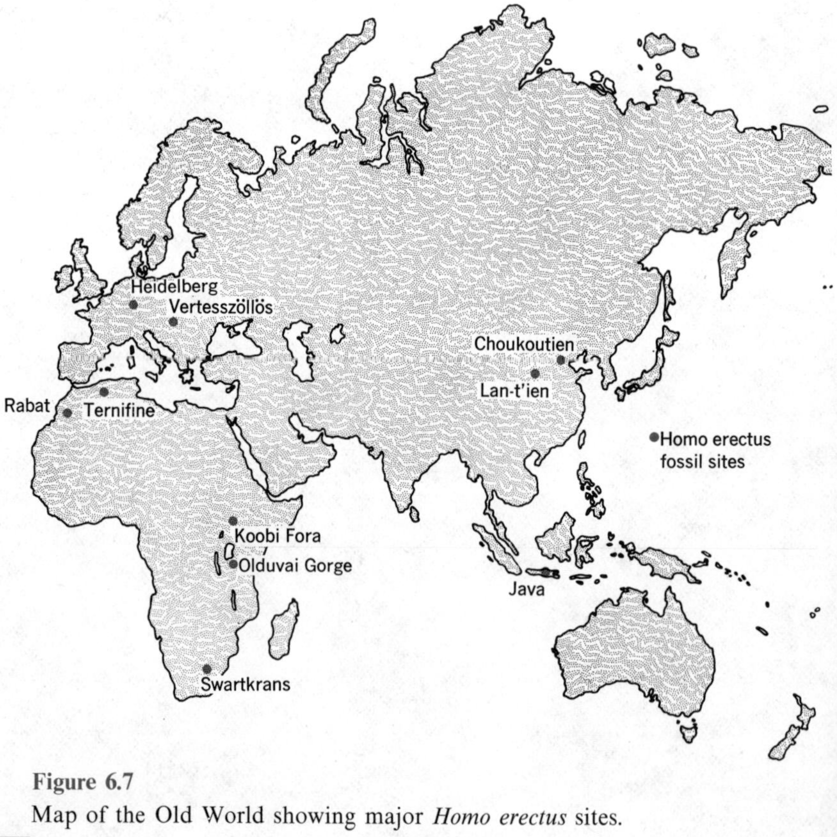

Figure 6.7
Map of the Old World showing major *Homo erectus* sites.

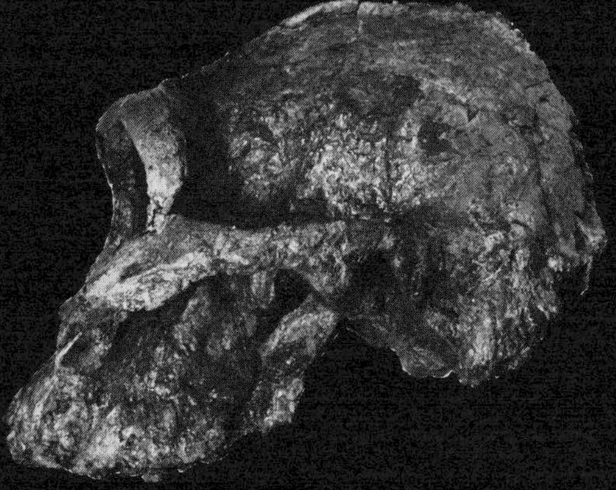

A B

C D

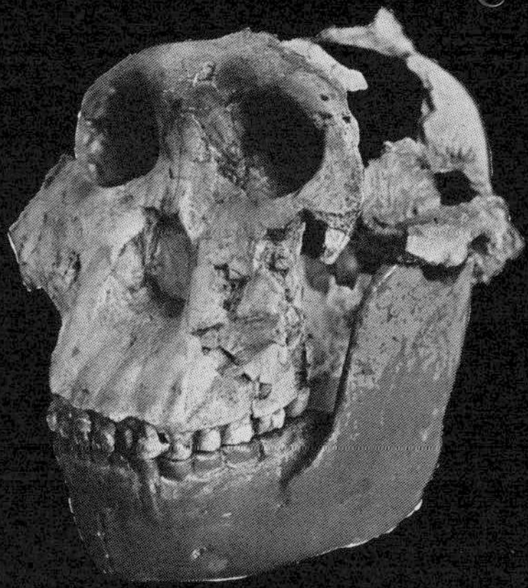

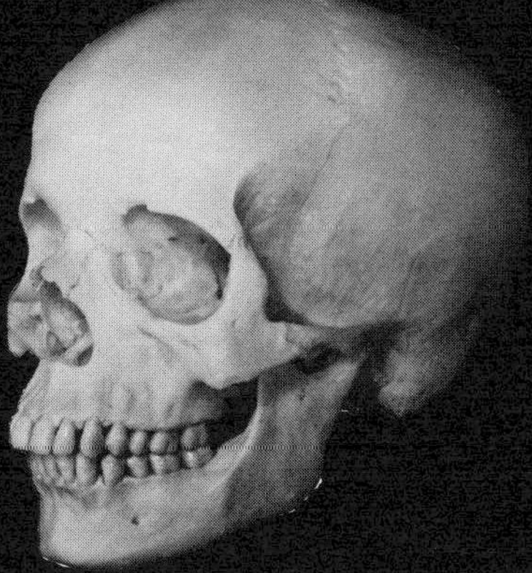

E

The Australopithecus group.

A

The gracile form of Australopithecus (*Australopithecus africanus*).

B

Robust form of Australopithecus (*Australopithecus robustus*).

C

Zinjanthropus boisei.

D

Modern *Homo sapiens.*

E

An Oldowan chopper from East Africa.

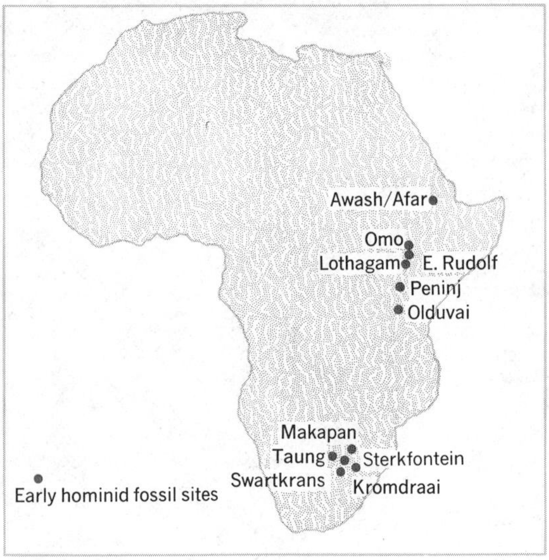

Figure 6.8

Map of early hominid fossil sites in Africa.

tire series of *Australopithecus* finds from South Africa were difficult to date. They were discovered in chalk strata that gave no clear indication of geological period. Dating techniques that now exist were not available at the time.

Between 1936 and the 1950s a bewildering series of australopithecine fossils was uncovered in South Africa by Robert Broom and his students. Some of these appeared to be quite modern in form, while others were more primitive. Postcranial material of the more advanced types suggested that these animals stood erect and were fully or almost fully bipedal. Their pelvises and leg bones were almost identical to those of *Homo sapiens.* The *foramen magnum* was as far forward as in modern humans. By the time several specimens had been collected, it was apparent that they fell into two groups, now classified by most paleontologists as *Australopithecus africanus* and **Australopithecus robustus.** The gracile, or slight, form (*africanus*) has large incisors relative to the premolars and molars, very small brow ridges, a surprisingly high vault above the brow ridges and a cranial capacity of about 450 cc. The robust form is characterized by a more rugged skull. The premolars and molars are very large relative to the incisors and the cranial capacity is larger (about 530 cc). The *foramen magnum* is further back than in *africanus.* The larger brain size was probably related to greater size and weight, relative to the gracile form, rather than to an advance in intelligence.

The tooth structures of *africanus* and *robustus* have suggested to some physical anthropologists that they were adapted to different environmental niches. The large grinding teeth of *robustus* suggest a vegetable diet, while the more human-like pattern of *africanus* makes an omnivorous diet at least possible.

In 1959 Louis and Mary Leakey burst upon the scene with the first of what was to become a

Olduvai Gorge with Mary Leakey.

long series of fossil finds from Olduvai Gorge in Tanzania. A good part of a skull was found on what had been the floor of a living area; the skull was in association with broken animal bones and primitive stone tools classified by anthropologists as pebble choppers (**Oldowan** culture). These are simple tools made by crudely striking chips off of a large pebble with another pebble. Such chipping produces a primitive but effective cutting surface. This fossil, named *Zinjanthropus boisei* by the Leakeys, appears to be an East African relative of *Australopithecus robustus.* It is very rugged, with a massive face, almost no forehead at all and a crest of bone (**sagittal crest**) running lengthwise down the middle of the skull vault. These crests are found in gorilla males and serve as support for massive jaw muscles. Later a massive lower jaw that matched the *Zinjanthropus* skull was found in another site.

New dating techniques plus associated animal remains made it possible to demonstrate that the Olduvai fossils were Pliocene and therefore *could* be antecedent to *erectus.* They could be on the main line of human evolution.

Homo habilis

Olduvai Gorge has proved to be a mine of fossil types. Since the discovery of *Zinjanthropus* the Leakeys have found other specimens of both the gracile and robust types. In addition, they found another hominid type that, in their eyes at least, was more advanced than *A. africanus* and at least as old. This fossil was put into the genus *Homo* and named *Homo*

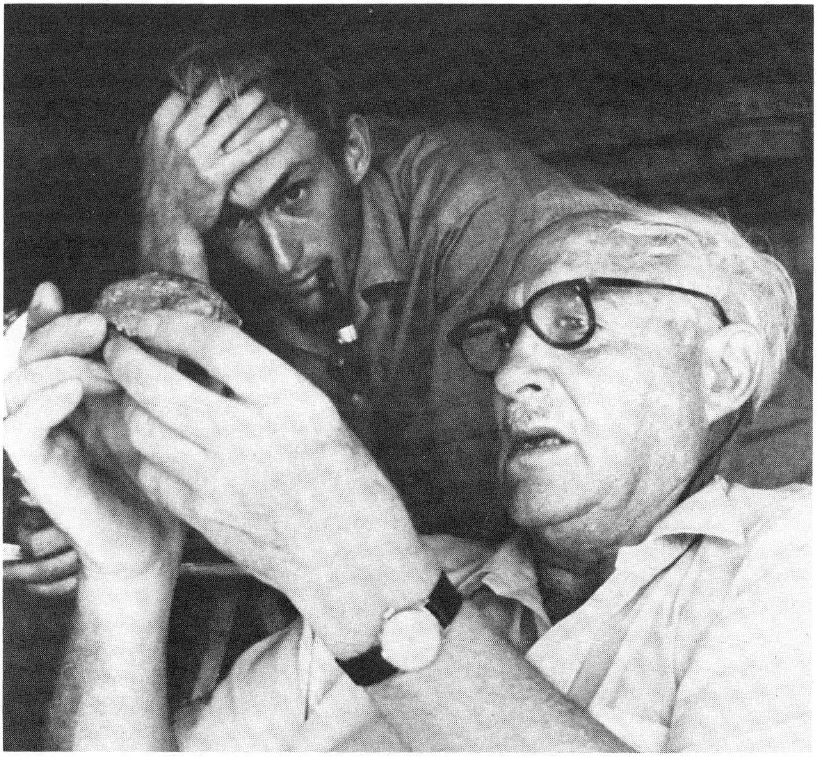

Louis and Richard Leakey discuss a fossil.

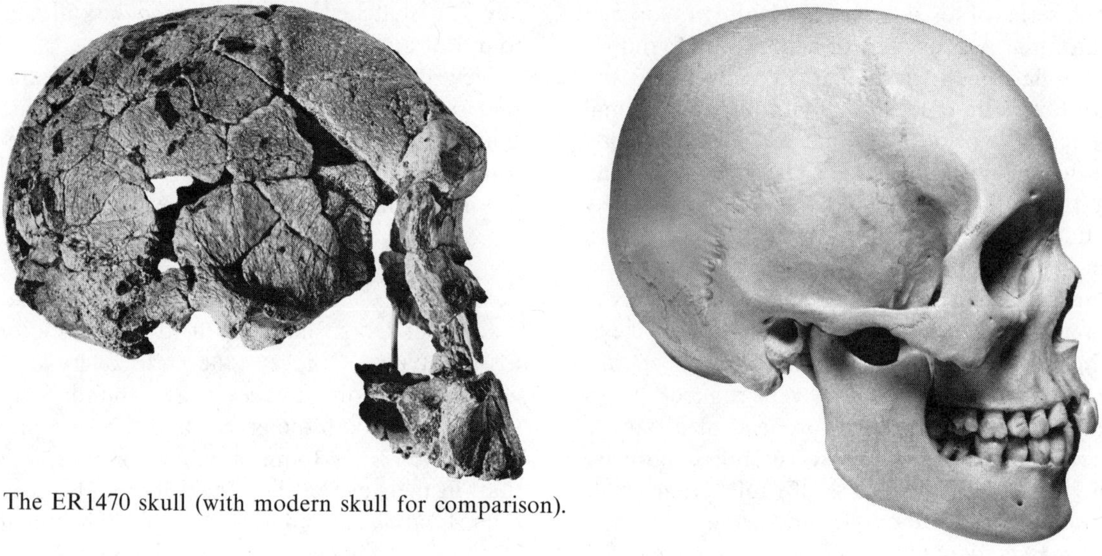

The ER1470 skull (with modern skull for comparison).

habilis. One of two *habilis* finds was probably an adolescent with a cranial capacity of 652 cc—very large, indeed, for an early form. Taken alone with no other confirming evidence, *habilis* was classified by most physical anthropologists as a gracile type of australopithecine.

Meanwhile, at Omo in Ethiopia and later at East Lake Rudolf (now Lake Turkana) in Uganda, the dates for *Australopithecus* were pushed further and further back. Robust forms dating from about 2–3 million years ago were found at Omo, and another site has yielded a date of 5.5 million years before the present. A skull found at Lake Turkana by Richard Leakey, the son of Louis and Mary, dating to about 2.9 million years has advanced features putting it with either *habilis* or an even more progressive type (this date is now disputed). The skull, known as E. R. 1470, has an estimated cranial capacity of 775 cc. At Hadar in Ethiopia tools have been found in association with *A. africanus* fossils dated to about 2.6 million years ago.

WHAT DO THE EAST AFRICAN FINDS MEAN?

Paleoanthropologists now have enough specimens of hominid fossils to draw some conclusions about the first stages of human evolution. It appears that *Homo* appeared as a descendant of a previous, more primitive type. The hominid line is complicated by the coexistence of two other fossil groups, the robust and gracile forms of *Australopithecus.* Some believe that both early *Homo* and *A. africanus* used tools. The evidence suggests that *Homo* eventually outbred the other forms and replaced them to become the unique precursor of modern humans. This is confirmed by another recent find of Richard Leakey's. In late 1975 he found an *erectus* in East Africa that is contemporaneous with at least some of the *Australopithecus* material!

Australopithecus afarensis

The very latest finds from Hadar in Ethiopia and Laetolil just to the south of Olduvai Gorge have forced yet another reevaluation of early hominid evolution. The Laetolil fossils found in the middle and late 1970s date to somewhere between 3.6 and 3.8 million years ago. The Hadar finds are the result of field work in the Afar triangle in Ethiopia begun in 1972 and continuing until 1977. These fossils date from between 2.6 and 3.3 million years ago. The latter have produced a particularly rich collection of cranial and postcranial material. The remains of between 35 and 65 individuals were recovered. Nearly all portions of the skeleton are represented and one specimen known as "Lucy" from Afar locality (coded as A.L. 288) consists of about 40 percent of a complete skeleton.

As described by D. C. Johanson and T. D. White, both physical anthropologists, these fossils can be grouped together under the name *Australopithecus afarensis.* They are small-brained but erect-walking members of the *Australopithecus* group. Their dates and morphology suggest that they are ancestral to both the gracile and robust forms of *Australopithecus.* If this interpretation is correct, *A. afarensis* lies below a major split in hominid development. One line gave rise to *Homo habilis;* this in turn evolved into the *erectus* group, which itself finally evolved into the modern *sapiens* forms. The other line gave rise to *Australopithecus africanus;* this evolved into *Australopithecus robustus,* which eventually became extinct. This hypothetical pattern suggests that at least two hominid lines coexisted in Africa for a rather long period, but that the gracile and robust species of Australopithecus both lie on a side branch of the path toward modern humans.

A. afarensis represents another major piece in the puzzle of early hominid evolution. If Johanson's and White's interpretation is correct, *afarensis* tends to clear up the rather messy picture created by the many gracile and robust specimens, the place of the South African finds (which now appear to be on the line between gracile and robust forms), and the controversies about the true status of *Homo habilis.* The latter is now a good bet to be a true member of the line that led through *erectus* to modern *Homo sapiens.* The fact that *afarensis* was erect-walking and small-brained confirms the notion that erect posture was a major early feature of hominid evolution. Bipedalism once again appears to underlie the shift towards higher intelligence. Apparently, once the hands were free to carry and manipulate objects, brain reorganization and expansion followed rather rapidly.

Johanson's and White's interpretation has already been challenged by Richard Leakey, who suggests that the Hadar and Laetolil finds are not uniquely different from the other *Australopithecus* fossils. At present, however, many

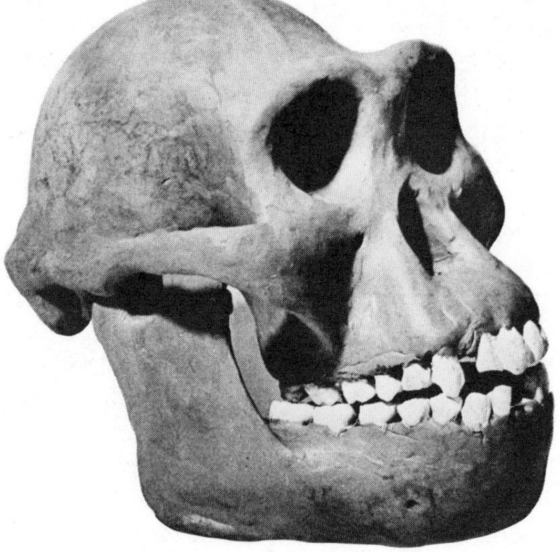

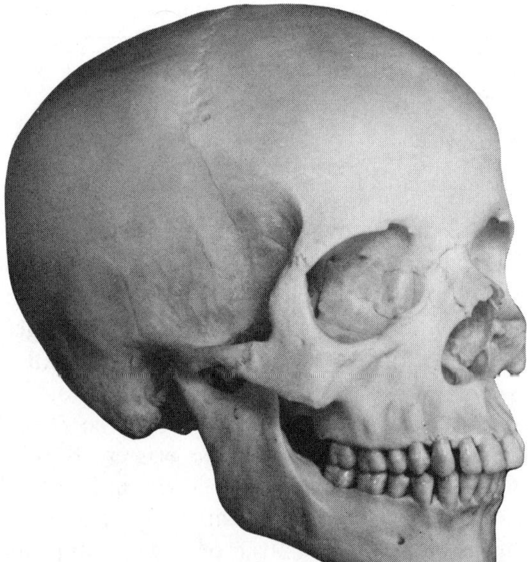

Australopithecus afarensis compared with modern *Homo sapiens.* The skeleton of "Lucy" (*A. afarensis*), indicates upright posture and bipedalism in an early hominid form.

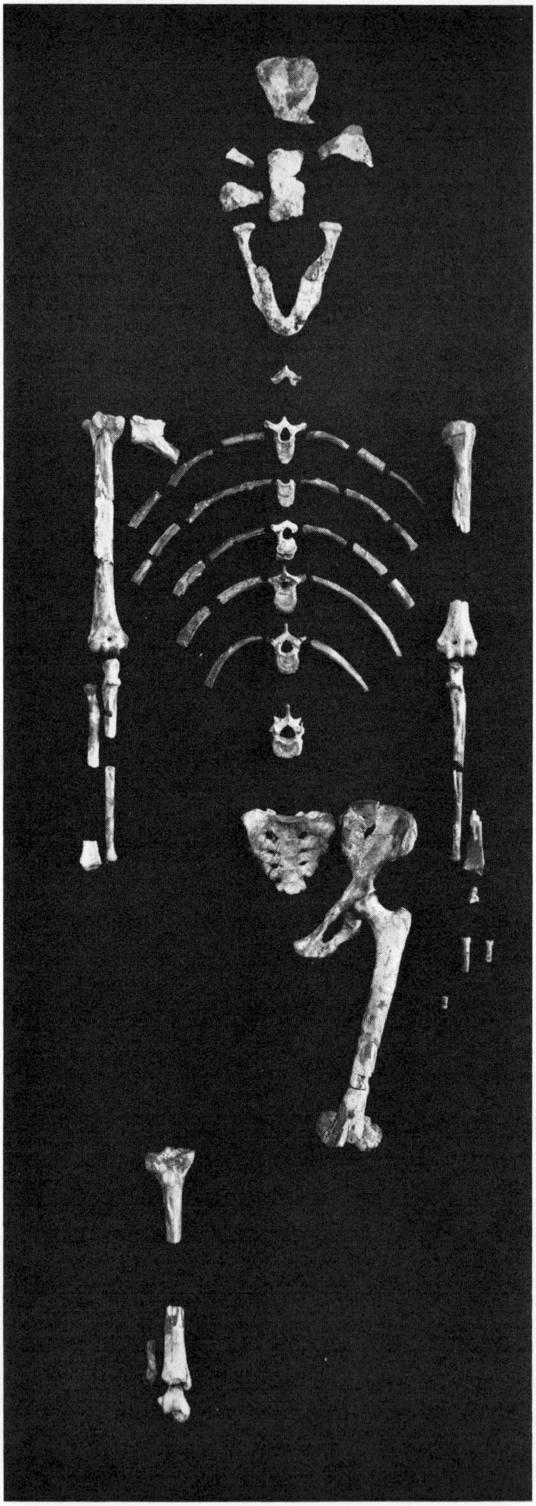

physical anthropologists favor the interpretation of *afarensis* as ancestral to the two hominid lines described.

Ramapithecus: The First Hominid?

While the early and middle periods of hominid evolution are beginning to make sense, we have very little data on the beginning of the divergence that led to the great apes on the one hand and *Homo sapiens* on the other. The one clue we do have consists of teeth and jaw fragments from the Siwalik Hills of India and from Miocene deposits in Kenya (see Figure 6.9). The Indian specimens are known as *Ramapithecus* and the African finds were named *Kenyapithecus africanus* by Louis Leakey. According to Elwyn Simons and David Pilbeam of Yale University, the Indian and African finds belong in the same genus, and most physical anthropologists now refer to them both as *Ramapithecus.* Although these remains are fragmentary, they are quite hominid in appearance. The dental arch is parabolic and therefore human-like. The molars and premolars also follow the human pattern. Although the Indian find lacks canines, the jaw fragments suggest that the canines were small. Recently *Ramapithecus* fragments have turned up in Europe and the Chinese report the discovery of a complete skull.

Ramapithecus is the find used by Jolly to suggest that hominization of the dental arch and teeth must have occurred before the development of tools. *Ramapithecus,* which dates to between 15 and 10 million years ago, has not been found in association with any artifacts. Unfortunately, so far we have no fossils in the period from *Ramapithecus* to the early *Homo* and *Australopithecus* finds. In addition, we lack the postcranial bones of *Ramapithecus.*

Judging from presently available fossil evidence, the hominid line diverged from the other primates sometime in the Miocene. The first change may have been in tooth structure, but until we have cranial and postcranial evidence we cannot be sure what they were like. The link

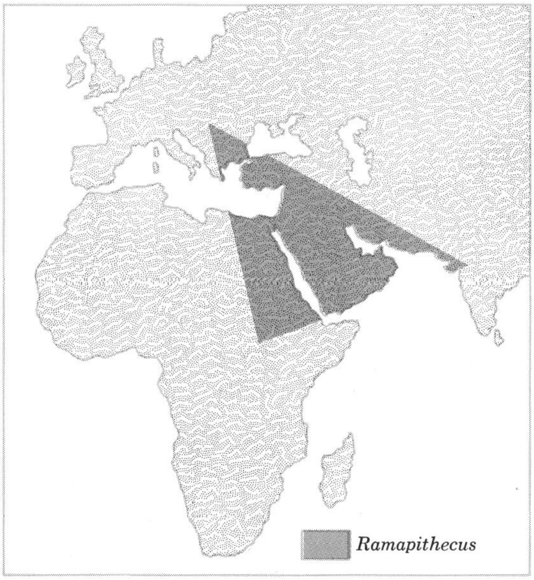

Figure 6.9
Map of *Ramapithecus* sites in Africa and the Middle East.

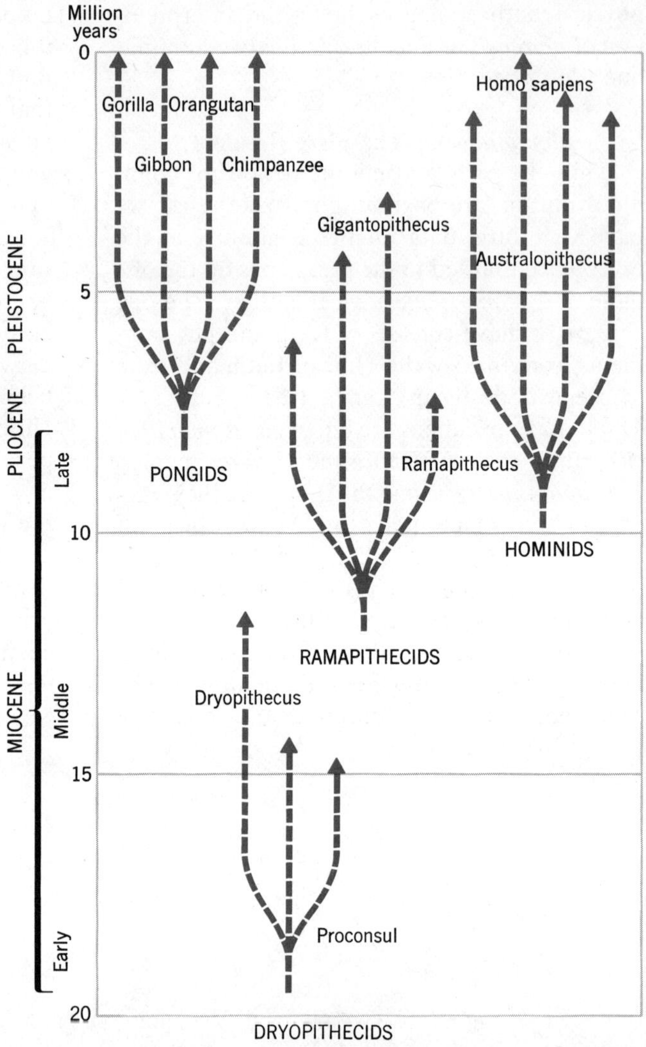

Figure 6.10

Current theories of hominid evolution. Note the multiple lines and lack of connections between fossil types. This indicates variation and slow development among evolving forms. (Adapted from "Rearranging Our Family Tree" by David Pilbeam, in *Human Nature,* June 1978. Copyright © 1978 by Human Nature, Inc. Used by permission of the publisher.)

Figure 6.11

Hominid evolution showing changes in skull form, jaws, pelvises, locomotion, and brain size. (Adapted from *Scientific American.*)

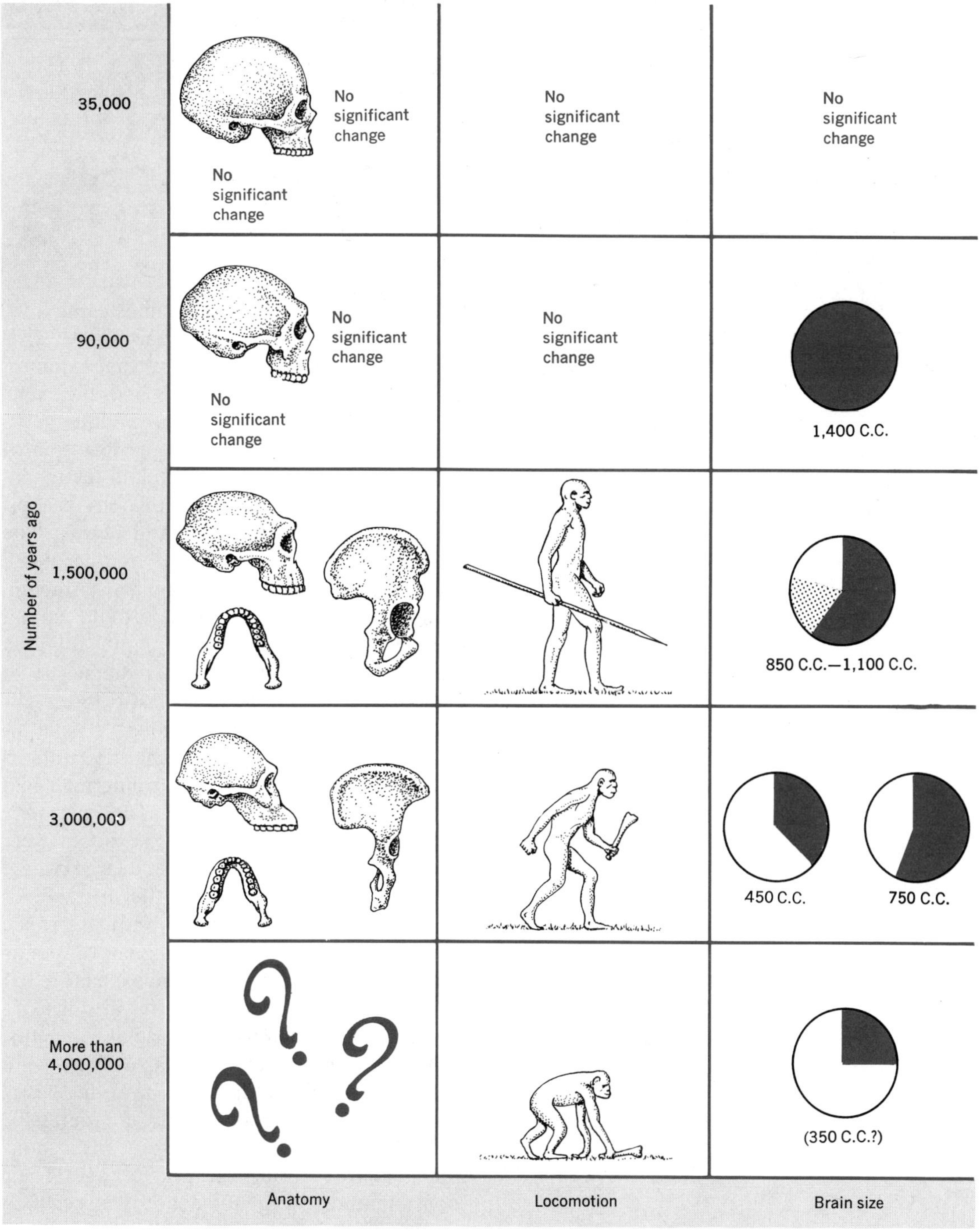
Number of years ago
35,000
No significant change
No significant change
No significant change
No significant change
90,000
No significant change
No significant change
No significant change
1,400 C.C.
1,500,000
850 C.C.—1,100 C.C.
3,000,000
450 C.C.
750 C.C.
More than 4,000,000
(350 C.C.?)
Anatomy
Locomotion
Brain size

(or links) between *Ramapithecus* and *Homo* is missing; it could even be a hominid much like the gracile *Australopithecus*. The genus *Homo* may have appeared as long ago as about 3 million years, to be rapidly followed by the evolution of *erectus* forms. These dispersed widely in migrations that took them from Africa into Europe and Asia. The related hominids (*Australopithecus africanus* and *Australopithecus robustus*) continued to survive for some time, along with the first *Homo* types—perhaps *habilis* and certainly *erectus*.

LATER FORMS: PROGRESSIVE AND CLASSIC NEANDERTHAL

Most of the early Neanderthal finds came from central Europe (Germany, France, and Italy). Most were badly documented so that a certain amount of ambiguity surrounds both their dating and reconstruction. By the middle 1950s enough evidence existed for a physical anthropologist, F. Clark Howell, to explain the evolutionary significance of two apparent groups, named by some *progressive* and *classic*. The progressive types had a high, rounded skull vault, a rather small brow ridge, and a smooth, rounded occipital region, the back of the cranial vault. Some of them also had chins, although this trait is no longer taken as diagnostic of modern *Homo sapiens*. The classic forms appeared somewhat cruder (although I have already noted that some of these characterizations were prejudiced). The classic Neanderthals had large skulls with thick bones. The *zygomatic arch* (cheek bone) and the brow ridges were massive. Although these forms had large cranial capacities (even higher than the average for modern humans), the forehead was low and the skull quite long. The occipital region was not as rounded as in both the progressive Neanderthal and modern *Homo sapiens*. It was also heavily marked by the remains of muscle attachments.

Howell suggested that the classic forms were the result of genetic drift. His hypothesis was that a rather small population of progressive Neanderthals had been trapped in a nonglaciated area during the last ice age. Their robust features were not adaptive specializations, merely exaggerations of the more normal Neanderthal pattern.

We now have a large sample of Neanderthals

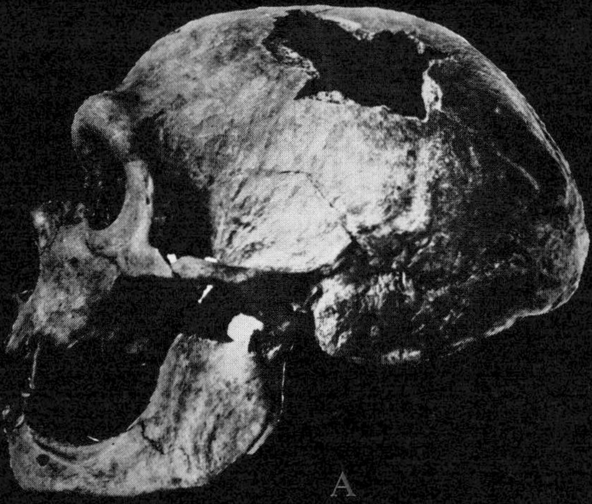

A

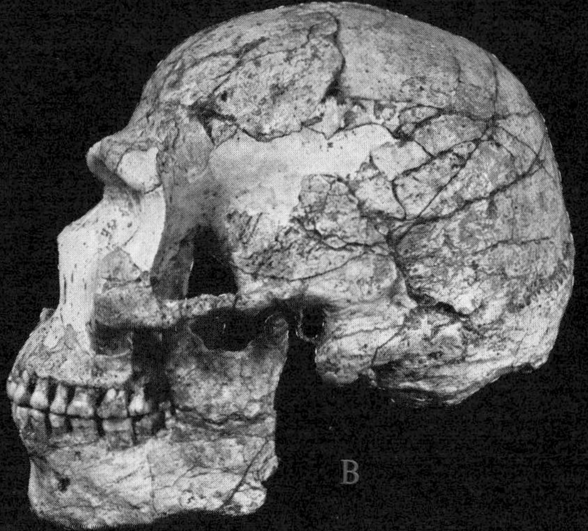

B

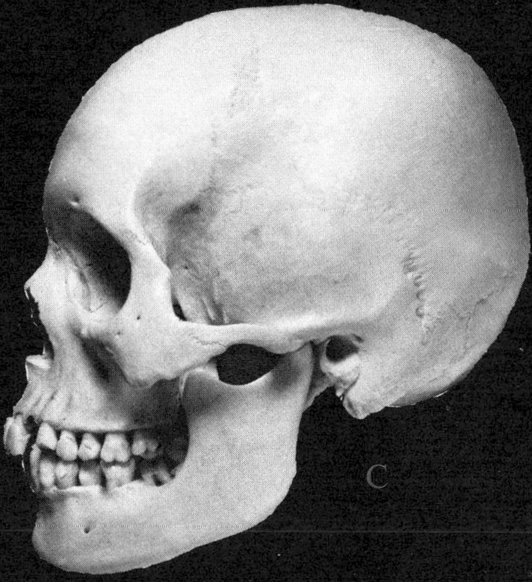

C

D

Neanderthal.

A

Classic Neanderthal skull.

B

A "progressive" Neanderthal from the Near East, Skhul 5.

C

Modern *Homo sapiens* for comparison.

D

Mousterian tools associated with Neanderthal fossils.

from all over Europe and the Middle East (see Figure 6.12). Finds from Mount Carmel in Israel (Skhul and Tabun) are progressive types that date from about 30,000 and 40,000 years ago. Tabun appears to be midway between Neanderthals and modern humans. Some physical anthropologists have speculated that Tabun represents a hybrid population. In the late 1950s Ralph Solecki found nine Neanderthals in Shanidar Cave in Iraq. These dated to about 45,000 years ago and shared many features with the classic Neanderthals.

We are suffering from an embarrassment of riches. The data show clearly that Neanderthals were a widely dispersed, highly variable group. This condition is, of course, not unlikely. Populations of hunters and gatherers are small. When they are also widely dispersed with little gene flow, they are subject to drift as well as local selection pressures. It is possible that the classic forms represent an isolated group that diverged slightly from the rest of the type through drift. We must not, however, exaggerate the differences between the classic and progressive Neanderthals or even between both of these and modern *Homo sapiens.* Most physical anthropologists now agree that the differences among all three are slight enough to classify all Neanderthals as *Homo sapiens.* Some use a subspecies classification to separate the Neanderthals from modern forms. These individuals now refer to Neanderthal as *Homo sapiens ne-*

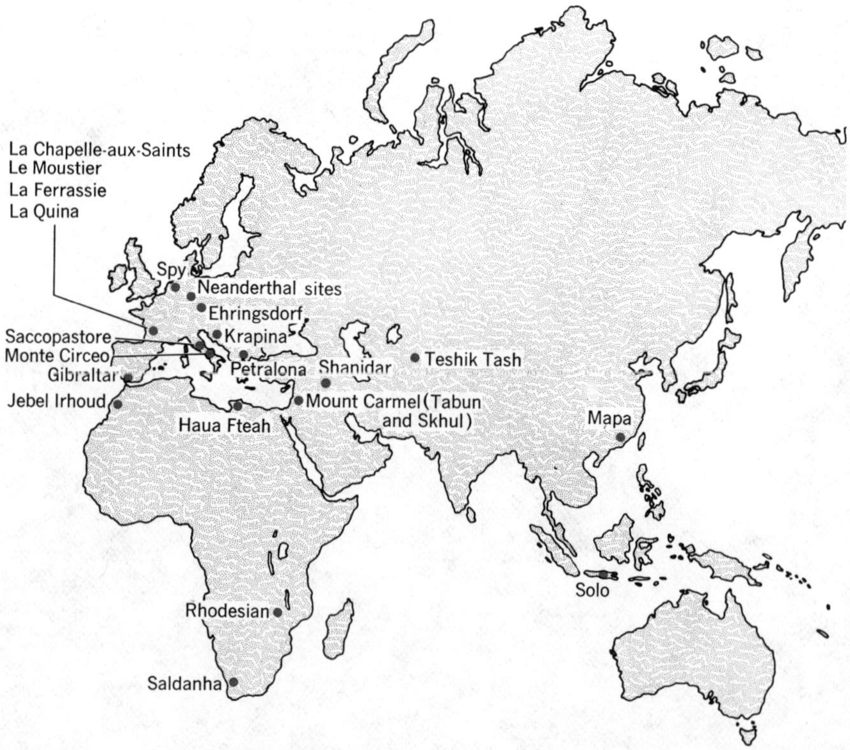

Figure 6.12
Major Neanderthal sites.

anderthalensis and ourselves as ***Homo sapiens sapiens.***

The Neanderthal finds are associated culturally with a tool kit known as Mousterian, named for the site in France where these tools were originally found. At first archeologists thought that the break between this culture and later tools associated with morphologically modern humans was absolute. More recent work shows a gradual gradation from one tool tradition to another. This evidence mitigates against the notion, popularized by the novel *The Inheritors,* that a "brutish" Neanderthal was replaced in Europe by more advanced modern *Homo sapiens* coming from the East.

There is *some* evidence that even the progressive Neanderthals were preceded in Europe by a more modern version of *Homo sapiens.* Two fossils dating from about 250,000 years ago show features that may indicate their ancestral relationship to both later Neanderthal types. These are *Steinheim* and *Swanscombe,* from Germany and England, respectively (page 153). Steinheim is a badly crushed but rather complete specimen of, probably, a female skull. It has a high, rounded and therefore modern forehead and the typical modern rounding at the back in the occipital region. It also has massive brow ridges. Cranial estimates are difficult for this fossil because of its crushed form, but there is some agreement that 1150 cc is not far off the mark. Swanscombe consists of two parietals and an occipital bone. These date from the second interglacial. Lacking its face, we have no notion about its mouth, cheeks, or brow ridges. What we do have indicates the same kind of high-rounded vault found in the Steinheim specimen. Both Steinheim and Swanscombe *could* be ancestral to the Neanderthals.

Two fossil fragments were found in Fontéchevade, France in 1947. These are associated with so-called Tayacian tools (used by modern *Homo sapiens*). The fragments consist of a small portion of frontal bone (but lacking the brow region) and a piece of the top of the skull. Fontéchevade is difficult to date and reconstruct. Holloway suggests that the three forms—*Steinheim, Swanscombe,* and *Fontéchevade*—may all represent a population of *Homo sapiens* slightly preceding or contemporaneous with Neanderthal populations.

Two other related—and somewhat aberrant—Neanderthal types have been found in East and South Africa. These are the *Rhodesian* skull (and thigh bone) and *Saldanha* man. The first dates from about 30,000 to 40,000 years ago and the latter may be a bit older. Both are extremely rugged skulls with the most massive brow ridges found to date. The cranial capacity has been estimated at about 1300 cc and is therefore well in the range of modern *Homo sapiens.* It is probable that these fossils represent other isolate populations of the highly variable Neanderthals.

When the ice of the last glacial period retreated northward, the entire Old World was inhabited by *Homo sapien sapiens.* Cultural differentiation began to intensify at the end of the Mousterian, and by the time modern *Homo sapiens* had emerged a wide variety of tools and tool types could be found distributed regionally. By about 15,000 years ago, cave dwellers in France and Spain (**Cro-Magnon** people) had begun to paint lively murals on cave walls (page 152). As human populations spread, they diversified genetically. Each became the product of different evolutionary forces: natural selection, mutation, gene flow, and drift. These produced what are now known as "racial" types.

Summary

Human evolution is marked by the retention of certain basic mammalian and primate characteristics as well as the development of new morphological and behavioral adaptations. Current theory suggests that the first shift toward hominization involved changes in dental morphology as an adaptation to seed-eating. This shift may have occurred with *Ramapithecus* or some related and as yet undiscovered fossil. A further shift in diet to include meat eating may have led to further changes in skeletal, muscle, brain, and behavioral characteristics. Hunting in a small primate must have required cooperative behavior as well as sharing. The hunt itself was aided by the ability to use tools and to carry objects in the hands. This ability is related to true bipedalism, a characteristic of fossils after the *Ramapithecus* group. Cooperation in social behavior and an increase in communicative capacities must have been associated with changes in brain organization and endocrine levels. Pair bonding between males and females was stimulated by the shift in females from a rutting season to permanent receptivity. Shifts in social behavior included a division of labor by sex, and perhaps by age, the cooperation of the male in nurturance of the young, particularly through a contribution to food-getting and -sharing, and the development of true language.

Hominid development occurred during the late Pliocene and Pleistocene epochs (the former beginning about ten million years ago). The Pleistocene is difficult to date because the epoch itself is defined by the presence of the genus *Homo,* and the argument over just what fossils are *Homo* is still a burning issue in physical anthropology.

Although this chapter has treated the fossil record historically, I will review it here in terms of its true evolutionary sequence. The group of fossils including the highly variable *Australopithecus* group, the possible *habilis* species of the genus *Homo,* the *erectus* group, early *sapiens,* Neanderthals, and late *sapiens* falls into a sequential order.

Most physical anthropologists agree that the early Pleistocene fossils classified as australopithecines can be divided into two groups. The group known as *Australopithecus africanus* had many features that bring it close to *Homo sapiens.* It had a rather flat face, with a rounded brain case and a cranial capacity (when corrected for overall body size) well above that of fossil apes and monkeys. Pelvic bones of the *africanus* group suggest fully erect posture. Other postcranial material, particularly leg and foot bones, tends to confirm bipedalism, although the foot may not have reached its final hominid form in this species. *Australopithecus robustus* had a massive skull, with small incisors and large molars, suggesting a vegetarian diet. Its face protruded more than that of *africanus* and its skull was rather flat, with less development of the cranial vault.

Louis Leakey, digging in East Africa, is re-

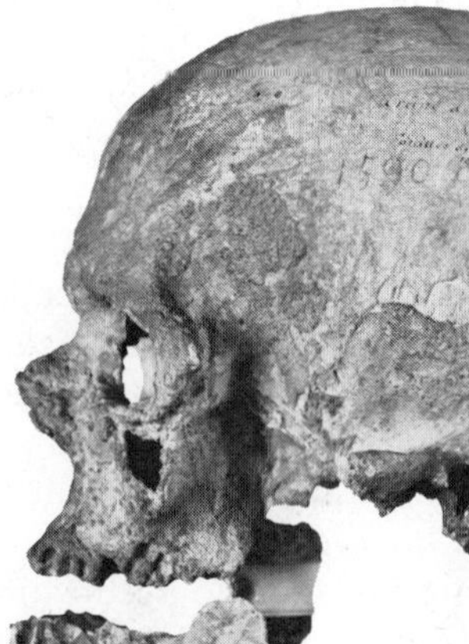

Cro-Magnon, a fully evolved *Homo sapiens sapiens.* Cave painting from Altamira in Spain, done by Cro-Magnon people.

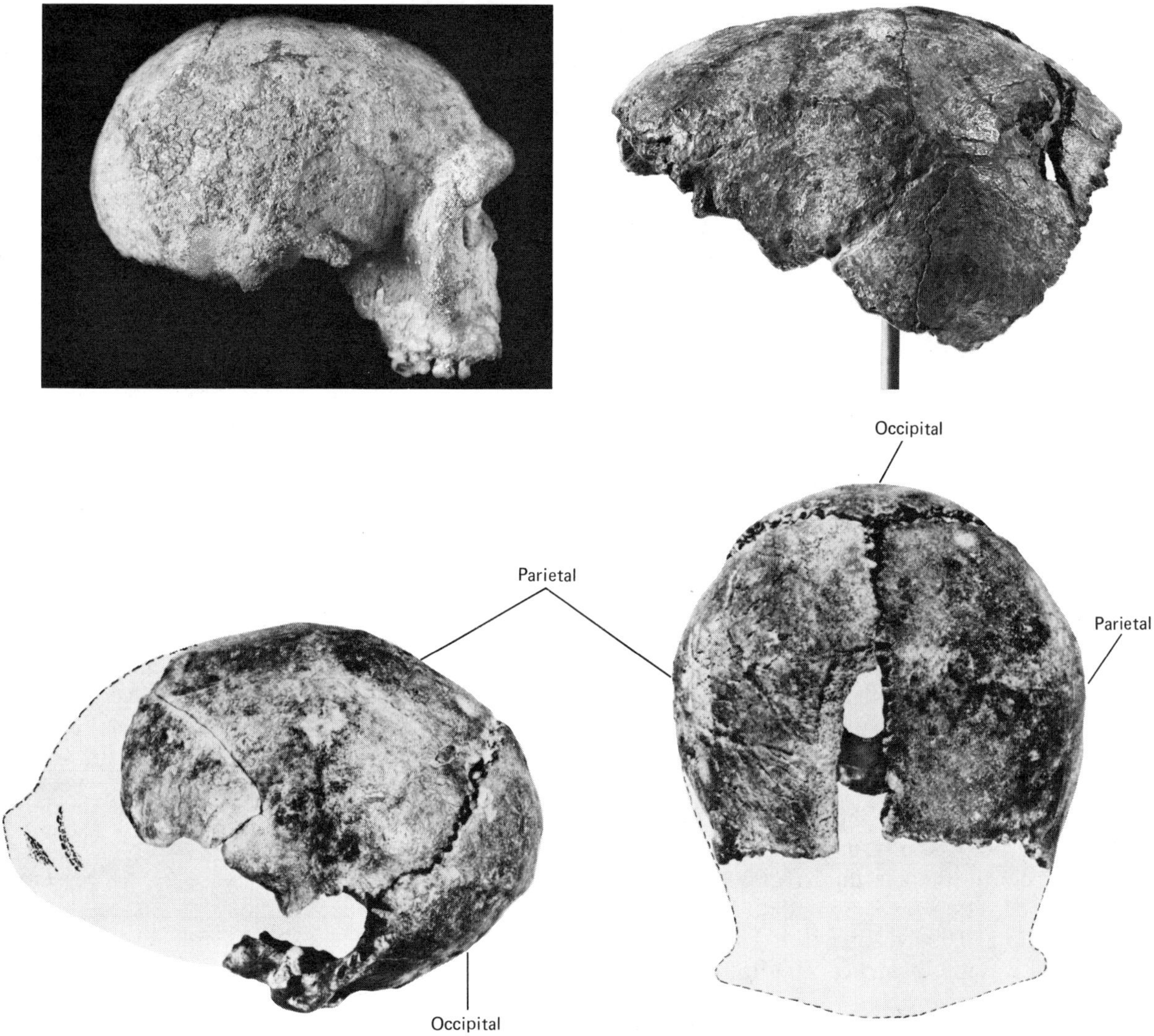

Possible pre-Neanderthal representatives of *Homo sapiens* in Europe. (Top left) Steinheim (uncrushed side), (top right) Fontéchavade. (bottom) Swanscombe (side and top views).

sponsible for the discovery of a large number of robust and gracile australopithecines. One of these fossils appeared to Leakey to be more advanced than even the *africanus* group. This fossil, which he called *Homo habilis,* has an estimated cranial capacity of 650 cc, which is large for an early form. While Leakey put *habilis* in the genus *Homo,* many other physical anthropologists continue to classify it under the genus *Australopithecus.*

A skull found at East Lake Turkana in Kenya by Richard Leakey (the son of Louis and Mary Leakey) has caused a controversy similar to that caused by *Homo habilis.* Known as E. R. 1470, this skull has an estimated cranial capacity of 775 cc. Some physical anthropologists believe that E. R. 1470 is a member of the genus *Homo* and that it displaces both types of *Australopithecus* in the main line of hominid evolution. Other physical anthropologists would classify it with the *africanus* group, suggesting that it represents one end of what is probably a rather large spectrum of variation in cranial capacity. To add to the confusion over these early hominids, tools have been discovered at Hadar in Ethiopia in association with *Australopithecus africanus,* dated to about 2.6 million years ago.

The most recent find at Hadar in Ethiopia, *Australopithecus afarensis,* dating from between 3.6 and 3.8 million years ago, has forced a reevaluation of early hominid evolution. *A. afarensis* was a small-brained, erect-walking hominid that is believed by many to be ancestral to *A. africanus* and *A. robustus* on the one hand and *Homo habilis* on the other. If this is the case, the direct hominid line includes *A. afarensis* and *A. robustus* and *A. africanus* are side branches.

Fully erect forms with large but varying cranial capacities were discovered at the turn of the century and a bit later in Java and China. At first these were given different genus and species classifications, but they are now known as *Homo erectus.* Recently, finds in North and East Africa confirm the fact that *erectus* was widely distributed. The *erectus* group dates from about 700,000 to 350,000 years ago.

There is some evidence that fully modern *Homo sapiens* appeared as early as 250,000 years ago. Two fossils, Steinheim and Swanscombe, found in Germany and England respectively, may be ancestral to later Neanderthal forms that are associated with cultural materials dating from about 50,000 years ago.

The earliest discovered Neanderthal fossils appeared to be rather distant relatives of modern *Homo sapiens.* Although their cranial capacity was measured as larger than that of modern humans, their skulls were low and rather flat across the cranial vault. One reconstruction based on a diseased thigh bone suggested that they did not walk fully erect. At the present time, we have a very large sample of Neanderthal fossils. Some anthropologists would divide them into two groups, progressive and classic, suggesting that the progressive types precede the classics and give rise to modern *Homo sapiens.* The classic types are assumed by these scholars to be the result of genetic isolation during a late glacial period. Other experts assume that the Neanderthals were a highly variable population and that the differences we find among the existing skulls are the result of a sample rich enough to reveal the range of variation. It is now generally agreed that all of the Neanderthals were close enough to modern humans to classify them as a subgroup of *Homo sapiens—Homo sapiens neanderthalensis.* In contrast, we are now classified as *Homo sapiens sapiens.*

While the early stages of hominid evolution are not clear, and it can be fairly said that confusion reigns over the relationships among early forms, no one any longer questions the basic outline of human development from a primate ancestor. The hominid divergence began sometime in the Miocene and was relatively complete by the late Pleistocene.

Bibliography

Holloway, R. 1974 — Fossil Man in the Old World. In *The Old World: Early Man to the Development of Agriculture.* Edited by R. Stigler. New York: Saint Martin's Press. A concise outline of fossil evolution by a leading figure in physical anthropology.

Holloway, R. 1975 — The Role of Human Social Behavior in the Evolution of the Brain. *Forty-Third James Arthur Lecture on the Evolution of the Human Brain, 1973.* New York: The American Museum of Natural History. A synthesis of human mental and behavioral evolution based upon endocasts of fossil hominid skulls and data on primate brains.

Huxley, T. H. 1896 — *Man's Place in Nature.* New York: D. Appleton and Co. Darwin's leading advocate in the nineteenth century discusses evolution and human fossil forms.

Johanson, D. C. and T.D. White 1979 — A Systematic Assessment of Early African Hominids. *Science* 203: 321–330. First major publication describing the new fossils from Hadar and Laetolil in East Africa.

Jolly, C. 1970 — The Seed Eaters: A New Model of Human Differentiation Based on a Baboon Analogy. *Man* 5:1–26. Presentation of the seed-eating hypothesis.

Leakey, R. and R. Lewin 1977 — *Origins.* New York: E. P. Dutton. Well-written review of hominid evolution.

Pilbeam, D. 1972 — *The Ascent of Man.* New York: Macmillan. An introduction to human evolution from a leading paleontologist.

Washburn, S. H. 1967 — Tools and Human Evolution, In *Human Variation and Origins.* Edited by W. S. Laughlin and R. H. Osborne. San Francisco: W. R. Freeman. Discusses the relationship between tools, reduction of tooth size, and brain evolution.

CHAPTER 7

HUMAN DIVERSITY; RACE AND SEX

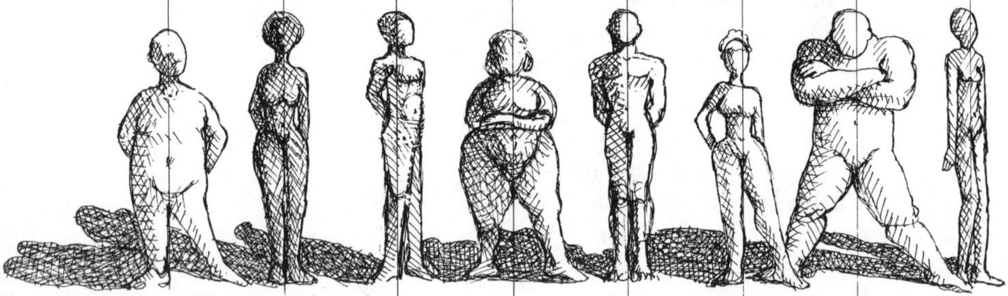

THE CLASSIFICATION OF HUMAN DIVERSITY

Homo sapiens spread rapidly throughout the Old World and then sometime between 40,000 and 20,000 years ago (the dates are disputed) populations began to cross a land bridge between Asia and Alaska. Migrating hunting and gathering bands rapidly moved across the new continent and eventually down as far as the very tip of South America. As these populations spread they diversified.

At least as early as Herodotus, in the fifth century B.C., Europeans were aware that in other parts of the world humans existed who had physical characteristics different from theirs. Early descriptions of such people were often fanciful and exaggerated certain features. Sometimes, distant populations were characterized as half-human. Nonhuman primates were also frequently described with human characteristics. The lines between humans and beasts were blurred. In the nineteenth century these physical descriptions were often used to prove that non-Europeans were inferior creatures, and they provided an excuse for slavery and a particularly brutal kind of racism.

The eighteenth and nineteenth centuries saw the rise of biological sciences, including the birth of physical anthropology. Darwin's theory of evolution gave an impetus to the study and classification of human groups. Because of this initial interest in classifying human diversity, the concepts of race and subrace gained currency. The human species was compartmentalized. A system was created into which various human types could be ordered. The largest units with the greatest difference between them were called races, and each race was subdivided. The actual number of races and subraces differed from observer to observer. The field was soon cluttered by "lumpers" and "splitters." The lumpers favored three to five races. The threefold classification included blacks, whites, and yellows; those who preferred five groups added Australian Aborigines and American Indians. Splitters cannot, themselves, be classified. Some added only a few "races," while others were not satisfied until the human pie had been divided almost a hundredfold. Typically, whites, or Caucasoids, were divided into Nordics, Alpines, and Mediterraneans, but even these groups were sometimes split into subtypes.

At first, racial classifications were based on such visible characteristics as skin color, hair color and form, eye color and shape, body height, and head shape. Although all of these components have a genetic aspect, many of them are also subject to environmental variables. When various blood groups and other more stable genetic traits were discovered, they were used to confirm or disprove racial relationships.

The advent of human genetic studies led to a reform of racial classification. It was soon noted that human groups do not differ absolutely in genetic traits. One rarely finds groups that are the exclusive carriers of particular genes. Rather it is the *frequency* of alleles that varies from group to group. In addition, a new look at visible variations revealed that the races do not really fit into neat boxes. White skin color blends gradually into black skin color among a chain of populations from the far north of Europe into Africa (see Figure 7.1 and the endpaper). Similarly, the frequencies of blood-group genes change gradually from Asia westward toward Europe into Africa (see Figure 7.2). These observations led to a shift in the approach to racial classification from absolute typologies (closed units) to what has come to be known as *populational thinking.* Populationists see races as overlapping groups that differ one from another in the frequencies of a gene or genes. In fact, many of those associated with

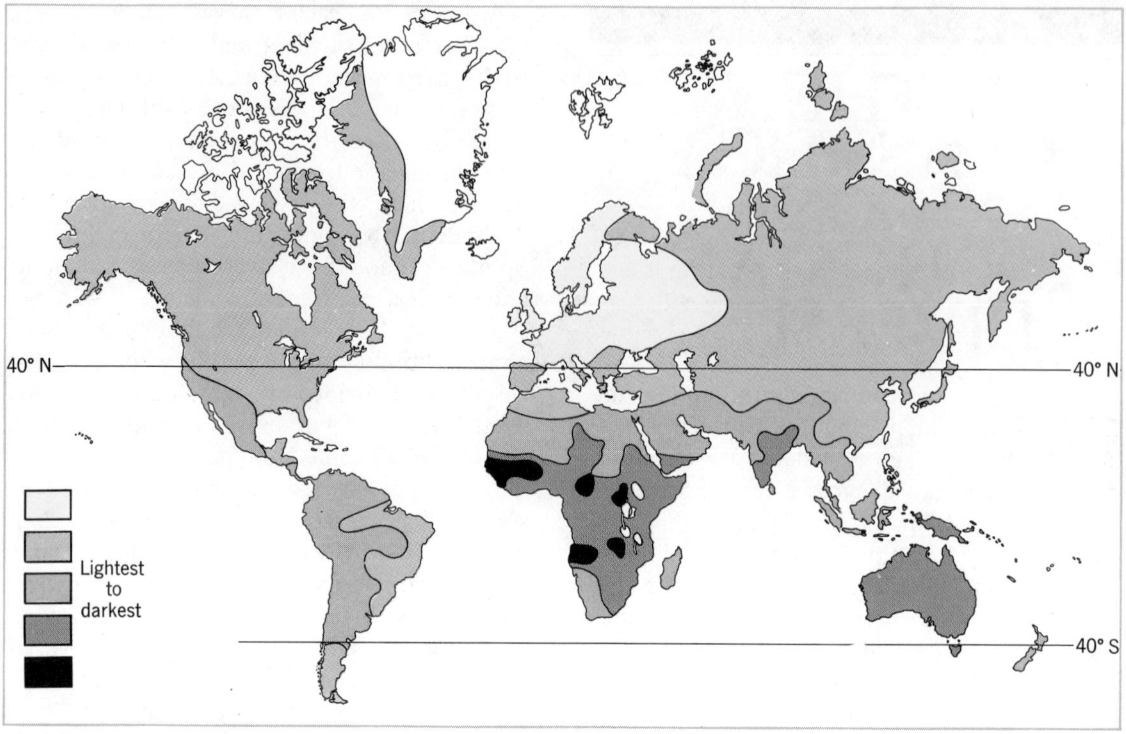

Figure 7.1
Skin color clines. Note the general north-south increase in dark skin, which is more pronounced in the Old World than in the New World.

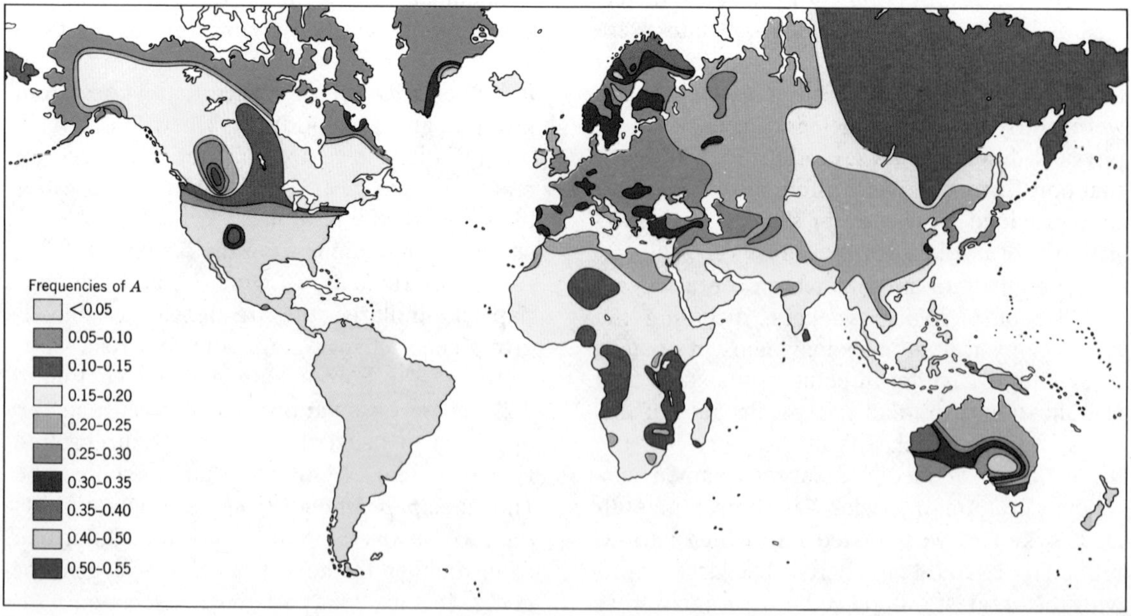

a

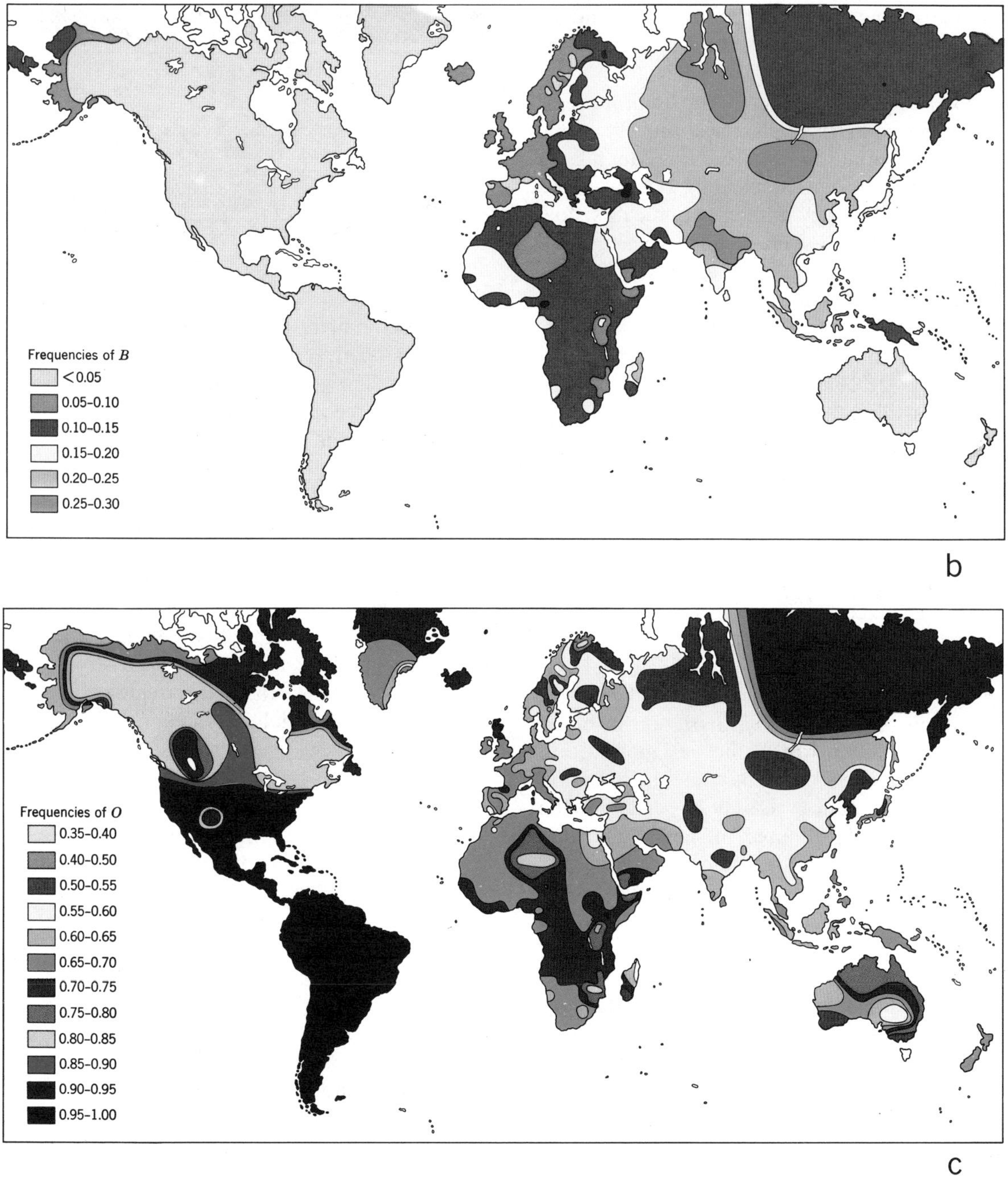

Figure 7.2

Distribution frequencies of three major blood types in the ABO system. (a) The distribution of type A, (b) the distribution of type B, (c) the distribution of type O. (From J. Buettner-Janusch, *Physical Anthropology*. New York: John Wiley, 1973.)

this school have taken the logical step of defining races as *populations* that differ in gene frequencies.

Populational thinking is an improvement over older systems of classification, but it has two shortcomings. (1) It continues to take a static view of race. Classification systems alone can never tell us why differentiation exists, how it developed, and where it might be heading. Human diversity is clearly a part of human evolution. To understand variation we must understand the processes that bring it about. To study human evolution we need a dynamic approach. (2) The word "race" implies that a group exists between the level of the population and that of the species. For such a group to have biological reality, it must differ more from any other such group than individuals within each group differ among themselves. Put in genetic terms, we can say that the genetic distance between races has to be greater than the genetic distance between the individual members of the populations concerned. A population geneticist, Richard C. Lewontin, has analyzed the genetic distribution of nine blood systems. He found that, of the total variation in blood types around the world, the variation within populations was 85 percent while the variation between populations was only 15 percent! If the word "race" were limited in meaning to real biological differences, it would not matter that the populationists equate race with population. To do so is redundant and unnecessary, but not unscientific. Unfortunately, the term "race" has a social meaning as well. This meaning is often at odds with biological facts. If we maintain the word "population" to mark groups that differ in gene frequencies, we will clarify the difference between biological thinking about human diversity and social concepts that often rest on folklore and racism.

THE REASONS FOR HUMAN VARIATION

Since human diversity is the result of evolution, it must be analyzed by employing evolutionary principles. These are, mutation, selection, drift, and interbreeding (gene flow). The study of genetic variation in the context of specific environments can tell us about selection. There is evidence, for example, that dark skin is an adaptation to strong sunlight, and that, white skin is an adaptation to weak solar radiation. Skin color is implicated in the production of vitamin D in the skin through stimulation by ultraviolet radiation and susceptibility to skin cancer. Black skin protects individuals from strong ultraviolet radiation, which is carcinogenic, but cuts down on vitamin D production, while white skin is cancer-sensitive as well as a better producer of vitamin D. A reduction in vitamin D production in regions of high sunlight intensity might be an adaptation as well, since an overdose of this vitamin can itself cause disease.

In the Old World, including Europe, Asia, and Africa, there is a skin-color cline that runs from north to south. Light skin occurs in the north and skin color becomes progressively darker as one moves toward the equatorial regions. The darkest Africans and the unrelated Melanesians, of New Guinea and nearby islands, are found in the regions of most intense ultraviolet radiation. Not only are the sun's rays more direct over the equator, but the ozone layer that protects the skin against ultraviolet is thinner in these regions. The correlations between skin color are better in the north-south gradient that runs from Europe to Africa than in Asia. Very light-skinned people are found in northern Europe and very dark people in equatorial Africa, but in Asia there are no populations as light as the fair-skinned Scandinavians. Still, the correlation does hold: Northern Asiatics are much lighter than southern Asiatics, and the degree of darkness in skin color follows a path that runs from north to south.

In addition to the hypothesis that light skin favors the production of vitamin D and that such production is an adaptation in areas with low ultraviolet intensity, it appears that light skin is also an adaptation to cold. There is evidence that deeply pigmented skin is more sensitive to freezing than white skin. Since the species evolved in the tropics, whites, who originated in the north of Europe, can be thought of as depigmented humans.

Africans and Melanesians are much darker than South American Indians, some of whom live in the same latitude as black people. If natural selection favors dark skin in the tropics, why are these native Americans so light? The probable answer is that they have not yet spent enough time in the tropics for the full effects of natural selection to take place. Even so, South American Indians do tend to be darker than genetically related populations found in North America.

Another possible set of adaptations related to different environments concerns body proportions and the shape of certain body parts. Africans living in hot, dry areas tend to be very tall and thin. This anatomical structure is an effective way of getting rid of excess heat. On the other hand, Eskimos tend to be rather short and relatively fat. While diet undoubtedly plays a role in body shape (Eskimos tend to eat a great deal of fat), such a body structure does tend to preserve heat. Eskimos, who are an extreme example of a northern-Asian body type, have less surface area in relation to body volume than the thin, tall Africans. Eskimos and others of the northern-Asian type have small noses, high cheekbones, flat faces, and rather stubby fingers and toes. These features indicate a possible adaptation to cold. All of them tend to reduce freezing in those parts of the body that are most susceptible to heat loss. In addition, Eskimos and other Asians have less body hair and much less hair on the face than many other human populations. Since moisture from the breath tends to catch in facial hair and freeze under conditions of extreme cold, relative beardlessness would appear to be an adaptation to cold as well.

There is some indication that different blood groups, particularly in the ABO series, can be linked to different diseases. This association might indicate that differential blood group frequencies in human populations may be related to selection. This hypothesis is clouded, however, by the fact that most of the associated diseases—cancer and ulcers, for example—tend to occur after the reproductive age and would therefore play no selective role.

Drift as a Cause of Variation

Until the advent of agriculture, which at its earliest dates to only about 10,000 years ago, human populations were quite small. In most environments a hunting and gathering economy implies migration and frequent fissioning of groups. These are perfect circumstances for genetic drift. Different studies of populations in such distant areas as Australia and Italy provide evidence for the hypothesis that genetic drift has played a major role in human differentiation. Once drift occurs, the gene frequencies of separate populations may continue to differentiate because natural selection works on existing gene frequencies. If these frequencies are different, the conditions for selection will also be different. In these cases, and there must have been many of them during the course of human evolution, drift would be a major factor in producing genetic change. The absence of blood group B in Native Americans is an example of drift. Once populations diverge through drift, they may continue to differentiate through the action of selection.

Interbreeding

Human populations are not closed units. All human populations can interbreed and, given the opportunity, they frequently do. This gene

(Left) These people, Galla from Ethiopia, are well adapted to heat. They are good radiators because their skin surface area is high in relation to their body volume, thus allowing excess heat to escape easily. (Right) The Eskimos are anatomically adapted for heat retention. They are short and relatively heavy. They have less body surface in relation to body volume than the Galla. In addition, they have short fingers and toes, broad flat faces, small noses, high cheek bones, and the man has scant beard growth. All of these characteristics inhibit freezing of exposed body parts.

flow leads to genetic intermixture: the production of populations with new gene frequencies. Intermixture has occurred on a worldwide scale. Peaceful contact and warfare have both contributed to gene flow. Populations in the New World provide several instances of genetic mixture. Many black Americans carry genes from European and African populations. (So do many "white" Americans.) Latin American populations show various degrees of African, European, and Native American genetic admixture. Such interbreeding, combined with cases of genetic isolation where relatively little interbreeding has occurred, produce highly variable populations within the confines of a single country. Such hybrid populations can provide material for the operation of natural selection.

Mutation

Mutations play an insignificant role in differentiation. Mutation rates tend to be specieswide—that is to say we should expect to find the same mutation rates in all human populations. Mutation *alone* does not produce population differences.

Can Populations Be Grouped into Races?

Jean Hiernaux, a French physical anthropologist, has attempted to group African populations into races. After assembling data on genetic variation and morphological traits from several hundred African populations, Hiernaux subjected them to computer analysis. If some populations were genetically closer to one another than to some other population groups, clusters would emerge from the data. Hiernaux found a small number of populations that could be clustered, but in general clustering did not occur. Lewontin's and Hiernaux's data tend to demonstrate that the category "race" as a meaningful biological unit does not exist.

The study of human diversity has been helped by the development of high-speed computers. The kind of analysis in which hundreds of variables are compared would have been impossible only a few years ago. This technological advance has not been matched in the thinking of those biologists and physical anthropologists who cling to the notion of race. Most of these use a perfectly acceptable definition of the race concept—race = population—but they frequently go on to talk as if race were a biological entity separable from populations. In many instances after this definition is given, they discuss such problems as genetics and IQ, assuming that blacks and whites in the United States constitute two populations. Populations, however, are inbreeding groups. Both blacks and whites in the United States have their origin in a large number of populations from different parts of Africa and Europe. Breeding patterns in the United States do not show that either group now constitutes a *single* large inbreeding population. The misuse of these terms in popular literature can only serve to confuse laymen. Because politicians are laymen when it comes to these issues, misuse can lead to laws or appropriations based on old-fashioned ideas of race.

RACE AND IQ

The clearest case of abuse has occurred in relation to IQ and race. Ever since the concept of IQ (or the Intelligence Quotient) was developed at the beginning of the twentieth century, some individuals have attempted to apply it to racial differences, usually with the assumption that certain races are superior to others.

It is not surprising that this point of view continues to exist, although the concept of race has, itself, been called into doubt. It is the *social* rather than the *biological* concept of race that operates in these arguments. Ironically, not only race is at issue here. The notion of IQ as a measure of innate intelligence has also been questioned. Some psychologists have even begun to doubt that the concept of intelligence itself is a meaningful category. Let me begin, however, by discussing intelligence.

The Problem

If we follow the line taken by American behaviorist psychology, the problem of definition can be sidestepped. We simply define intelligence in terms of the means used to measure it: Intelligence is what IQ tests measure. These tests are designed so that individual performances can be ranked. The rankings can be standardized against an average score in order to determine whether an individual falls above, at, or below the mean. When rankings are ordered and compared in terms of "racial" identity, it appears that certain "races" do better than others as a group. What are compared are the average scores of different groups. Testing in the United States reveals that blacks, Indians, and certain ethnic groups (themselves often classified as races) score lower than whites. Japanese and Chinese score higher than whites.

Class differences also appear in test results. Lower-class individuals tend to score below middle- and upper-class individuals. These results have been used to support the theory that society rewards intelligence. Bright individuals are said to rise into upper income categories. Such a society is called a **meritocracy.** Advocates of meritocracy suggest that any attempt to interfere with "natural selection" will favor mediocrity and therefore harm society at large. As you will see shortly, meritocracy theorists are close to those who consider race rather than class to be a critical genetic variable in performance.

Let us return to the tests themselves. Several studies have shown that IQ tests are subject to a wide range of invalidating factors. Among these are cultural variables that give one group of test-takers an advantage over another. This is a complex phenomenon. Questions may be culturally biased, or they may be asked in culturally biased ways. Then, too, middle-class Americans tend to be familiar with the process of taking tests; experience alone allows them to score well. Studies have shown that the race and the class of individuals administering tests also affect the performance of different categories of test-takers.

Intelligence tests are designed, in theory, to measure such abilities as spatial relations, reasoning, verbal fluency, and mathematical ability. These are the variables educators feel are crucial in predicting how students will do in school. Because our school system is geared to middle-class success, however, these tests may merely confirm the notion that middle-class children will do well in an educational system tuned to their particular needs.

The Jensen Argument

The most notable recent attempt to relate performance on IQ tests to race was a paper by Arthur Jensen, "How much can we boost I.Q. and scholastic achievement?" published in the *Harvard Education Review* in 1969. Coming at a time of shifting economic and political priorities, the Jensen article had a tremendous impact on educators and the lay public.

Noting a consistent difference in the mean IQ's of whites and blacks, Jensen suggested that only about half the difference could be attributed to environmental effects. Thus, of 15 points of difference, Jensen said about 7 to 8 points were due to inherited factors. He arrived at this figure by examining a large number of race and IQ studies. In most cases the expected deficit among blacks was demonstrated. He then examined studies of twins reared apart to get some notion of the hereditary component in IQ. Since identical twins have exactly the same genes, differences between them are attributed to environmental effects. A look at the twin data convinced Jensen that heredity must play a significant role in IQ. He arrived at this conclusion because the average (mean) differences in IQ among twins reared apart are consistently lower than the mean differences among nontwin siblings reared apart. To interpret these studies Jensen used a statistical measure known as heritability. **Heritability** is a measure of the genetic component in a variable trait, that is, it tells what percentage of the variation is due to heredity.

What Jensen overlooked in the twin studies is the fact that, even among twins reared apart, the environments for both children may be more similar than the environments of sociological racial groups in the United States. In addition, by focusing on mean differences in twins reared apart he ignored cases in which the IQ difference was very high. Yet deviations from the mean are important because they may occur precisely where environmental differences produce their full effects.

A great deal of confusion among lay people is created by the use of the technical term heritability. Heritability does *not* measure the degree to which heredity determines a trait. Instead, it is a measure of comparative variation. It tells us what relative contributions genes and the environment together make to the variation of a trait under known environmental conditions. If conditions vary between two populations, heritability measures in one group are not applicable to the other. Although Jensen informs his readers that the concept of heritability is not applicable to between-group studies, he uses it anyway. Another point: given different environmental conditions, the penetrance of a gene or genes will vary. Even if the genetic contribution to IQ were the same in all human populations, the effect of the environment on the expression of the genes still might differ. We estimate, for example, that the genetic component in height among humans is about 80 percent. Japanese before World War II were much shorter than Americans. After the war a change in the Japanese diet led to a rapid increase in average height. The genetic component did not change, but environmental conditions produced an effect that brought average height of Americans and Japanese closer together.

There are many errors in the Jensen article. Some are based on misreporting the results of other studies. Others are based on misrepresentations. Still others are based on faulty biological reasoning. The use of heritability is one. Another is Jensen's acceptance of race as a valid biological subdivision of the human species.

The geneticist I. I. Gottesman discussed the geographic range of populations in Africa from which slaves were imported to Charleston, South Carolina during the period 1733-1807. (These data appear, curiously enough, in a book edited by Jensen and two psychologists, Martin Deutsch and Irwin Katz. The book, incidentally, is dedicated to the memory of Martin Luther King.) Borrowing his data from the historical work of William Pollitzer, Gottesman points out that slaves came from the following different populations: Senegambia 20 percent; Windward Coast 23 percent; Gold Coast 13 percent; Whydah-Benin-Calabar 4 percent; Congo 17 percent; and Angola 23 percent. This distribution covers more than 1000 miles of coast line and extends up to 600 miles inland. The genetic populations and ethnic groups from which the slaves were taken were by no means homogeneous.

In the United States it is a curious oversimplification to talk as if there were single white and black populations. American whites have their origins all over Europe and represent several populations. Blacks are equally varied. According to Gottesman, "The variation observed in the studies reviewed . . . are probably valid and reflect the genetic heterogeneity of Negro Americans living different geographical and social distances away from their white neighbors. Such heterogeneity prevents us from speaking validly of an average 'Negro American' with an x percentage of white genes." Gottesman goes on to say, "At the present time Negro and white differences in general intelligence in the United States appear to be primarily associated with differences in environmental advantages."

I have already noted that Jensen cites an overall deficit of about 15 IQ points among blacks, with 7.5 points attributed to genetics. Yet on page 100 of his report we find this:

In addition to these factors, something else operates to boost scores five to ten points from first to second test, provided the first test is really the first. When I worked in a psychological clinic, I had to give individual intelligence tests to a variety of children, a good many of whom came from an impoverished background. Usually I felt these children were really brighter than their IQ would indicate. They often appeared inhibited in their first visit to my office, and when this was the case I usually had them come in on two to four different days for half-hour sessions with me in a "play therapy" room, in which we did nothing more than get better acquainted by playing ball, using finger paints, drawing on the blackboard, making things out of clay, and so forth. As soon as the child seemed to be completely at home in this setting, I would retest him on a parallel form of the Stanford-Binet, a boost in IQ of 8 to 10 points or so was the rule; it rarely failed, but neither was the gain very often much above this. So I am inclined to doubt that IQ gains up to this amount in young disadvantaged children have much of anything to do with changes in ability. They are largely a result simply of getting more optimal conditions . . . I would put very little confidence in a single test score, especially if the child is from a poor background and of a different race from the examiner.

It is important to note that the conditions under which Jensen retested his children were not met in the studies he cites. If the deficit he notes is consistent in disadvantaged children, then all the IQ differences noted between blacks and whites in the United States may be subsumed under a combination of testing errors and environmental effects.

More recently, an educational psychologist, Rick F. Heber, began an experimental study of low-IQ parents and children in the city of Milwaukee, Wisconsin. He drew a sample of mothers in the community with IQ scores below 75. The children of these mothers were divided into experimental and control groups. The control group was left alone, while the experimental group received various types of remedial education. At the end of one phase of the experiment, the IQ levels of the experimental group showed a significant increase to an average of 125! It should be noted that these children went from subnormal to above average in IQ scores. Heber is a cautious researcher and admits that his study is not yet complete. The preliminary results do, however, tend overwhelmingly to support the position that IQ differences between groups can be attributed to environmental variables.

Jensen models much of his work on that of the late Cyril Burt, who carried out a series of IQ studies in England.* Even before Burt's time, English psychologists engaged in statistical studies of intelligence. Because English society was, until recently, relatively homogeneous from the genetic point of view, the concerns of English psychologists focused on differences between the upper and lower classes. Their studies were stimulated by the founder of modern statistics, Sir Francis Galton. Galton was a believer in meritocracy. He assumed that high-intelligence individuals clustered in the upper class and that membership in the lower classes could be equated with low intelligence. Galton also suggested a difference in fertility between the two classes. He believed that lower-class individuals were outbreeding the upper classes. Putting these two hypothetical data together, Galton reasoned that the overall intelligence of the English population would drop through time. Notions of this sort led to the foundation of **eugenics** societies in England and the United States. These organizations were devoted to the improvement of human genetics through "proper" breeding. They also campaigned against what they considered dysgenic (or detrimental) effects, such as the supposed outbreeding of the intelligent by the less intelligent.

Generations of studies in Britain have failed to show the predicted drop in overall IQ. There is no absolute relation between class membership and intelligence.

The English were concerned with I.Q. and class, because until recently their population was divided along class, not racial lines. When the IQ argument was transported to the United States, it underwent a mutation. Race was substituted for class. Jensen's study reflects this change, but curiously it also demonstrates the continuity between the two views of IQ. In the end of his report we find Jensen suggesting that high-IQ blacks are concentrated in the middle class while low-IQ blacks are found among the lower class. He also notes that lower-class blacks have high fertility and middle-class blacks low fertility. Like Galton he reasons that if this breeding pattern continues, the IQ deficit of low-class blacks in relation to middle-class blacks will widen. He also suggests that the overall IQ of blacks as compared to whites will drop through time. There is no more evidence for this effect among blacks in the United States than among British whites.

*Recent evidence has been uncovered to suggest strongly that Burt faked some or all of his data! An analysis of his statistical procedures indicates that his results were much too close to his expectations. It looks as if he created the statistics to match his hypothesis. This possibility is supported by the fact that researchers can find no records concerning the identity or careers of several of Burt's collaborators. It now appears as if Burt invented them himself and wrote articles as well as defenses of his theories in their names.

SOCIOLOGY OF RACE

Popular ideas concerning racial identity are based on a wide range of nonbiological criteria. In some, but not all, cases, these do reflect selected phenotypic differences and would seem, on the surface at least, to have some justification in biology. Phenotypes, however, are often a poor guide to underlying differences and similarities. In addition, the perception of differences among individuals is highly subjective and may be affected by purely social, cultural, economic, and even political factors.

Racial classifications in the United States are derived from social definitions and confused with biological categories. An individual is Indian, for example, if he or she is a registered legal inhabitant of an Indian reservation or is on the roles of The American Indian Service. This is the rule even if the person has no phenotypic characteristics normally associated with Native Americans. Individuals may label themselves as members of some "racial" group or they may be so labeled by others. When a self-defined Native American looks white, the individual will be forced to remind others of his or her "racial" category.

Establishing Identity

If a phenotypically white individual acts according to the rules of another group, he or she may become identified with that group. If such a group is considered a race by society at large, then the individual is defined as a member of that race. When I was an undergraduate at the University of Wisconsin, I met a blue-eyed, blond man with a Polish last name who was a **shaman** (native medical practitioner) among the Winnebago, a Native American group.

In some parts of the United States it is socially valuable to be an "Indian," especially if one is not *too* Indian. Distant ancestry from some Native American people adds to one's overall prestige. It provides evidence for one's "Americanness."

Being black in the United States rarely confers any advantage. The definition of blacks,

Jews are often referred to as a race yet these New York blacks practice the Jewish religion.

Thomas M. Cook, born 1883, although of mixed parentage, was officially classified as a Cherokee. Lillian Gross was one-eighth Cherokee, phenotypically "white," but classified as Indian by the Bureau of American Ethnology.

however, depends on social and historical events. Since there is no legal obligation for the United States government to care for blacks on established reservations and because black ancestry has rarely provided a political advantage, phenotypically white individuals have little, if anything, to gain from claiming black ancestry.

Biologically, black populations in America are hybrid. Their gene pools derive from Africa and Europe, and to a small extent from Native North America. The category "black" includes individuals who claim to have or can be shown to have black ancestry. Unlike Caucasians, who can remain white and be part Indian at the same time, a person who is said to have any black ancestry is categorized as black. One of the folk myths associated with this notion of blackness is the idea that individuals who are phenotypically white can have black babies if there are any African genes in their ancestry. No one ever talks about blacks having white babies if there is any white ancestry in the family tree. The difference reflects a crude racism in which the "return" to blackness is seen as a throwback, or a return to a "primitive" trait. In fact, this notion is linked to the socially accepted idea that, in mixed marriages between individuals of different races or classes, the children belong to the group classified within the culture as socially inferior. This is known as **hypodescent.**

The Latin American Case

In Latin America racial categories based on color are more complicated than in the United States. Instead of two types, white and black, there are several. These range along a continuum from white at one end to black at the other. Individuals are classified as mulattoes (half white, half black), as octoroons (one-eighth black), and so on. Of course, no one bothers to determine what the real quantities of "black" and "white" genes are because the system is only pseudobiological. In fact, in classifying individuals such nonbiological characteristics as dress, speech patterns, and education figure in the "racial" determination.

The anthropologist Marvin Harris showed to a sample of Brazilians a series of pictures in which various facial features such as lip form, hair form, color, and eye shape were varied in different combinations. Each subject was asked to classify the individuals in the pictures by race. Harris found that agreement among his subjects was very low. "Race" turned out to be an ambiguous category.

Race as Folk Category

The ambiguity in racial classification occurs because the concept of race is a folk category clothed in the respectability of biological language. The criteria used for placing individuals into races are not really determined by biological principles. In fact, so-called racial categories vary historically and culturally. In different times the term "race" has been applied to individuals with the following characteristics: (1) having a certain aggregate of phenotypic traits (blacks that look "black"), (2) belonging to a particular religion or culture or both (Jews), (3) belonging to a certain nationality (Irish), or (4) belonging to some linguistic group (Aryans).

Historically, certain terms have been applied to individuals that have nothing to do with their genetic background. Hitler, for example, chose to emphasize the Aryan myth of German ancestry. Yet the word "Aryan" refers to a linguistic group originating in India. Ironically, the only ethnic group living in Europe and speaking an Aryan language is the Gypsies. Yet Gypsies were classified by the Nazis along with Jews as inferior people and were subject to genocide.

Behavioral characteristics have come to be associated with races. These may be seen as positive or negative, depending on the context and the word chosen. Jews, for example, are sometimes referred to as intelligent and sometimes as crafty, people of Scottish ancestry can be frugal or stingy, Irish can be light-hearted or irresponsible, and so on.

Not all such behavioral characterizations are wrong, although many are; but when they are correct they reflect cultural and not biological patterns. There *are* cultures in which individuals are expected to be shy, withdrawn, and diffident, and contrasting cultures in which individuals are expected to be flamboyant and aggressive.

American blacks show a range of phenotypes reflecting different degrees of population mixture.

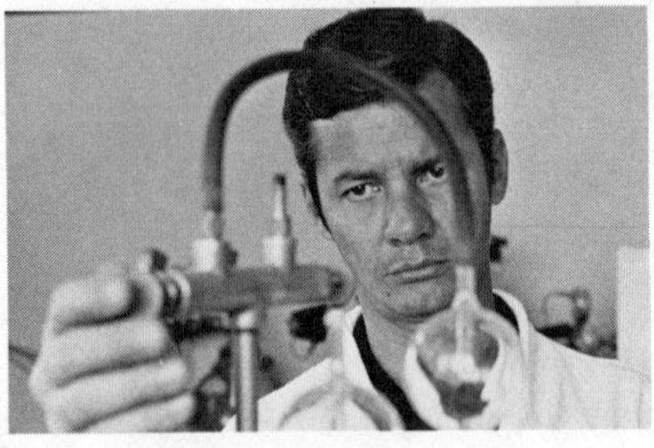

In Brazil each of these individuals would be given a different "racial" classification. The classification to which they might be assigned will depend on judgments about their social-class position, income, quality of dress, and estimated education. In addition, Brazilians acting as classifiers will not agree among themselves on the "racial" type to be assigned to each individual.

This Nazi propaganda is anti-Jewish and anti-Catholic. It employs physical and social stereotypes to characterize members of both groups.

Cultural Misunderstandings

People from one culture may misunderstand the behavior of people from another culture. French and Americans, for example, have a totally different attitude toward bodily elimination. We tend to be rather prudish about exposing the body in public. Elimination is a private act strictly segregated by sex. In France, however, one is likely to see men, and sometimes women, urinating along the roadways in full view of passing traffic. Occasional coed bathrooms do exist in French cafés, although the women's part is restricted. Women entering a private cabinet may walk by men who, urinating, have their backs turned to passing traffic. The frequent invasion of toilet facilities by cleaning women all over Europe is a source of embarrassment to American men.

These differences often lead to the assumption on the part of American tourists that Europeans are somehow less moral than we are. But there is a real confusion here. The French and other Europeans separate elimination and sex. We tend to merge these categories. The physical equipment used in both activities is partially the same, so the potential for misunderstanding is always present.

Race and Aesthetics

Racists attempt to convince us that physical characteristics are markers for innate behavioral differences. One's own group is often seen as physically beautiful, but it is also described as virtuous, intelligent, brave, honest, healthy, and so on. The opposite characteristics are attributed to other groups. Racists forget that aesthetic standards are relative and that different concepts of beauty can lead to equally pressing claims to superiority. The pervasiveness of using aesthetic standards to categorize races is so strong that members of a subordinate group may come to feel inferior. It took a long time for black to be beautiful in the United States. The conviction that black *is* beautiful is a very important part of black liberation. The growing awareness of blackness as a positive virtue has led to self-pride among many blacks. Afro hair styles are now more common and such beauty aids as bleaching cream are less popular than they were not too many years ago.

Racial Myths

Each country has its own set of racial myths. In the United States blacks make up the largest minority group. It is no wonder that so many of our racist notions apply to them. One of the major sources of mythmaking is the old description of Africa as the "dark" continent inhabited by savages. Africa was compared unfavorably with Europe, which was said to be the focus of technological development and civilization. Although modern technological society is, of course, a product of recent Western European culture, civilization did not develop in Europe. Every one of the major innovations that contributed to the rise of early urban civilization took place in the Middle East among people of mixed genetic heritage, the product of gene flow from Europe, Asia, and Africa. Besides, it is likely that civilization arose where it did because of social and environmental factors. Evidence for the separate development of civilizations in the Middle East, China, and the New World (all in the context of similar environments) supports this point of view.

During the European medieval period, Africa south of the Sahara was cut off from direct contact with Europe. The West African coastline is almost devoid of good harbors and the open Atlantic cannot be compared with the Mediterranean as a trading lake. In addition, with few exceptions, African rivers are navigable only for short distances from the sea. Still, the great desert was crossed by trading caravans, but it was the traders who controlled what got in and out of black Africa. For centuries the trade consisted primarily of slaves, salt, and gold. In spite of the attenuated contact, great trading empires did develop in West Africa, around strategic locations along trade routes. From the sixth century AD to about 1500, these empires developed and declined as the struggle raged for control of major caravan routes. The cultures of these empires were equivalent in many ways to those of Europe of the same period.

The Portuguese finally managed to navigate down the west coast of Africa in the fifteenth century. When they established trade relations with coastal peoples, the states of the interior were short-circuited. With their trade cut off they soon declined. Imagine what would have happened to Venice, which became great as a mercantile power, if for some reason it had been suddenly deprived of its trade.

Race and "Primitivism"

The notion that some peoples are biologically primitive has been disproved over and over again. Individuals who come from technologically primitive cultures rapidly learn to adapt to new ideas. Lives have changed overnight with the transition in the "third world" from preindustrial society to industrial society. This is clearly not a question of genetic adaptation, but simply one of learning.

"Positive" Racism

Even racists are willing to grant some good qualities to the groups they despise, but positive beliefs may reflect wishful thinking or poor understanding. The tolerance and sense of humor attributed by many white Americans to black genes dissipated rapidly with the rise of the civil rights movement. The development of black pride did away with the image of blacks as passive and subservient.

Many Americans are convinced that blacks have a genetic gift for music and dance. Blacks are said to excel particularly at rhythmic music. While it is true that jazz and other forms of American popular music have their roots in black culture, musical ability *per se* is not the same thing as tradition. Although music is an important part of West African culture, only a small minority of West Africans are outstanding musicians. Musical ability is distributed in African populations the same way it is distributed in other parts of the world. But because the culture values music, a large number of talented people get the opportunity to express their abilities.

SEXISM

It is almost always the case that when we find strong economic and/or political distinctions between groups, we also find a biological theory to account for the supposed inferiority of the subordinate group. It should be no surprise, therefore, that sexual differences are also cast in this light. The continuity between racism and sexism is apparent in the thinking of many individuals. Michael Gelfand, a South African doctor and researcher, has compared women and blacks. He says that both groups have a low frequency of both idiots and geniuses. Like blacks, he suggests, women tend to fall into a middle range. They are mediocre!

Women and Power

As with race, a set of behavioral characteristics has been attributed to the biological nature of women. Because these have been taken as genetic truths, they are used to justify economic discrimination against females. The position imposed on women by society is then used as an illustration of their "innate" characteristics. As is commonly the case, the result of a social process is used as its cause.

In the preindustrial world and in many non-Western cultures, women have wielded a considerable amount of power. While they infrequently occupy high political office, they may exert political power indirectly. In some cases, but not all, economic participation, *particularly when ownership of resources is also included,* goes together with social and political power.

This has not been true in the industrialized West. The notion of female inferiority has weighed heavily on our social and legal system. Even though women made up a good part of the labor force in the textile factories in eighteenth- and nineteenth-century Europe and made major contributions to the development of frontier society in the early days of the United States, Western society has tended to put women in the historical role of child-bearer and housekeeper. Like other members of the labor force women have rarely controlled the productive forces of society. In our contemporary consumer-oriented culture housewives function as buyers. They crystallize the demand side of production. A good deal of the millions spent on advertising is aimed specifically at the housewife. At the same time women are kept away from the centers of political and economic power. When they do work, and many women work, they generally remain in inferior positions and rarely get equal pay for equal performance.

Sexist Stereotypes

Notions about women are varied and complex. They run from the supposed positive idea that females are good at such things as motherhood and, by extension, that they make good teachers and nurses, to the negative characterization of women as less intelligent and more emotional than men.

Women are often seen as more animal-like than men. Their biological status is confirmed by the act of childbirth. It is women who menstruate and it is women who nurture babies at the breast. From this reality men sometimes fabricate the myth of female inferiority. Women, like animals, it is said, are less intelligent and more emotional than men.

IQ tests for sexual differences show ambiguous results. Women as a group tend to score well on some intellectual tasks and score poorly on others. Women excel in languages, for example, but do poorly in mathematics. Women are sometimes characterized as more sensitive than men and, therefore, as more artistic. Yet, there are fewer successful artists among women than among men. This lack of success is then used to suggest that women are less ambitious than men.

Men are said, by some, to form strong bonds among themselves. In our culture these are translated directly into successful political, social, and economic groups. Male bonding, it is suggested, is a trait that comes from man's

A B

E F

Women in various cultures. Women have different degrees of economic and social power depending not upon how hard they work, but rather on the degree to which they control resources. The notion that women form social bonds among themselves less readily than men is belied by these illustrations of women at work in different cultures.

A

Burmese women students at an agricultural school study sugar cultivation.

B

Highland Peruvian women winnowing barley in the village of Chimu.

C

Indian women of the Xingu river in the Mato Grosso, Brazil, pounding manioc.

C

D

G H

D
Women drawing water in India.
E
A Nepalese woman twining thread.
F
Nenet women (Siberia) making fur clothing.
G
A Western Nigerian woman crushing manioc.
H
Vietnamese women crew members sailing a sampan along the Mekong River.

hunting past and continues to be adaptive in the modern world. Women, on the other hand, respond to the *pair* bond and are linked to their children.

Broad statements about bonding actually fly in the face of a great deal of data from the world's peoples. Women do form female groups ranging from secret societies (see Chapter 17) through coffee klatsches (a function of American culture and not biology) to the League of Women Voters. More recently, the rise of the women's liberation movement has shown how well women can organize to pursue socioeconomic goals. Women usually do not go on weekend hunting parties because our culture does not sanction this activity as a standard form of female recreation. Women do perform well, however, in team sports and, in fact, are capable of entering into every phase of life that is opened to them. That they can do so successfully is ample testimony to the skill and persistence women can muster in the pursuit of their goals.

Attitudes Toward Women's Liberation

It is true that many women reject the goals of women's liberation. Some men and women use this fact as evidence that women neither want nor have the capacity to perform as equals in society. The likely explanation for this lack of enthusiasm among some individuals is that women, like men, are the product of culture. They are feminized by a whole range of institutions that begins with the family, continues with our educational system, and finishes with standardized middle-class notions of feminine success: marriage, a good and successful husband, proper children. Yet a crisis often occurs in the life of an American woman when her children grow up. She finds herself trapped in an empty house with little to do and no training with which to enter the economic life of the community.

Biological Differences

I do not mean to suggest that there are no biological differences between men and women. Several are obvious and others have been demonstrated through scientific research. None of the evidence, however, can be used as an excuse for sexual discrimination, because none of it demonstrates that women are inferior to men.

Men on the average are larger and physically stronger than women. The latter fact has to be clarified immediately, however, by noting that this strength only applies to short-term physical activity. Over the long haul women have better physical endurance than men. Women live longer than men, they have lower frequencies of heart attack, and less hypertension. This female superiority may be related to such biological factors as natural stress resistance in women and such cultural factors as the particularly high stress that men face in the business world.

Women on the average have a better sense of smell than men. There is some evidence that they hear better, at least at the upper range of the scale. Women are more resistant to cold than men. Sexually based differences in the nervous system may also exist. The central nervous system of all mammals works in combination with the endocrine hormonal system. Nerves work fast, but their action extinguishes rapidly. The endocrine system is slower acting but is more sustained. Together, these two ways of mobilizing behavior form a single integrated unit known as the **neuroendocrine system.** The endocrine system itself is one of the chemical bases of sexual differentiation. Although the hormones found in men and women do not differ completely (both sexes carry both male and female sex hormones), the ratios of these hormones do differ in normal men and women. Since endocrines affect many aspects of normal physiology, differences in hormonal balance have some effect on behavior.

Because hormones, like genes, act only in combination with the environment, we can expect evolutionary pressures to favor different behavioral phenotypes in both sexes under different environmental circumstances. Culture is a major part of our environment. It must, therefore, have a strong influence on behavioral differences. Research on sexual differences runs into the same difficulties as any research that attempts to separate out genetic and environmental effects. The only thing we can say at present about behavioral differences based on sex is the following: *The average female at birth is potentially different from the average male at birth. Although we do not know what these average potential differences might be, we do know that they will be subject to modification by culture. Potential sexual differences in behavior, although real, may be overridden by cultural factors.*

From a purely biological perspective men are more expendable than women. We do not have to be reminded that it is females and not males who bear children, but what is not so obvious is that a few males can sexually service many females. In so many instances among other species selection has produced gaudy males and rather bland females—particularly bird species. Birds have color vision and rely on visual cues for mating. The gaudy male is the sexual target of the female, but because he is highly visible, he is also the target of predators. The female is camouflaged or at least unobtrusive. Her survival chances are higher, therefore, than those of the male. This makes sense, of course, since it is she who must ultimately produce the next generation.

Paradoxically, sexism may derive in part from the value biological evolution and culture places on females. When this value is translated culturally, men may convert women into objects. The first step in this process may have occurred with the emergence of hunting as a male task. This aspect of the divison of labor protects women from unneccessary danger. The **incest taboo** (prohibitions on marriage with certain relatives) universal in all societies, stimulates the exchange of women in marriage. The process of exchange increases the probability that women will become *valuable objects,* the pawns of matrimonial exchange. If women are seen as valuable objects they are treasured and protected, but may also be dehumanized. When women become objects, sexism is born. As in the case of race, sex becomes the basis of social discrimination. Obvious external biological characteristics are taken as evidence for unproven behavioral differences. The only way we shall ever come to know which behavioral differences, if any, are characteristic of specific groups is when our society develops full social equality. For only then will the environment allow individuals to express their full genetic potential.

Summary

Humans are among the most widely distributed of living species. It is not surprising that such geographical dispersion has led to a wide range of phenotypic differences among the world's populations. In attempts to make sense out of this variation, anthropologists derived different kinds of classifications based in part on geography and in part on visible physical characteristics. A series of "racial" classifications developed ranging from three categories (white, black, yellow) to over 50. These classifications assumed that races were real biological units existing between the level of the population on the one hand and the species on the other. Some thinking about race also assumed that such units reflected absolute biological differences among the various types. Racial classification was originally based on such external phenotypic characteristics as skin color, hair form, eye color, stature, and head shape. In the 1950s the emphasis shifted to easily studied genetic markers such as blood groups. It soon became apparent that no blood group was the exclusive property of a specific race. Different populations had different frequencies of the common set of human blood groups. This discovery led to the populationist notion of race; according to this view races were classified as populations differing one from another on the basis of gene frequencies. Typological thinking about race gave way to populational thinking about race. Yet if races were in fact groups between the level of the individual population and the species, it would have to be shown that the genetic distance between one race and another was greater than the genetic distance between populations clustered into the same race. There is a great deal of genetic evidence now available to show that this is not the case.

Populations, however, do differ one from another on the basis of genetic variation. This variation is probably due to all the evolutionary factors discussed previously in this book. Mutation has produced genetic variation and this variation has been subjected to the specific selection pressures of different environments. Because human populations have been small for much of their history, drift has undoubtedly played an important role in diversity as well. In addition, since migration and interbreeding are also characteristic of our species, genetic variation cannot be understood without attention to gene flow as well. Each population's genetic pattern is the result of a complex combination of these factors acting in different degrees and at different times.

Many physical anthropologists now consider the term race to be synonymous with the term population. The use of the term in and out of anthropology, however, creates a confusion between what it means in strictly biological language and what it means in a social context. In biology the word is redundant and therefore unnecessary, because there is no real difference between a race and a population. In social usage the word is ambiguous. It has a flexible set of meanings, only a few of which reflect even partial biological facts. Thus, in American society a phenotypically white person can be categorized as a member of the white or Indian "race." This kind of classification is only tenuously related to biology, through remote ancestry and the identification an individual claims through personal history. Many Native Americans who are phenotypically white identify themselves as Indians for cultural, historical, and political reasons.

The notion of race has often been identified with attitudes of superiority and inferiority. Dominant social groups often categorize the dominated as "racially inferior." Social differences are often thought to reflect biological differences even when subordinate individuals can be shown scientifically to be biologically indistinguishable from members of the dominant group. Not all groups *are* biologically identical, but real biological differences cannot be assumed to reflect either superiority or inferiority. Differences in performance on IQ tests between so-called racial groups appear to be due more to social than to biological differences, and in most cases the biological status of the racial group is dubious in the first place.

What has been said of thinking about race is also true of thinking about sex. Real differences between men and women are obvious, but these obvious differences are often used consciously or unconsciously to create a folklore about sex differences that has no basis in fact. The folklore is more often than not used to justify a set of discriminatory practices. The fact that differences exist does not mean that the differences can be ranked on a scale of inferiority and superiority. Nor do they mean that every idea associating women with one set of characteristics and men with another is in any sense correct.

Bibliography and Suggested Reading

Alland, A., Jr. 1973 — *Human Diversity.* New York: Doubleday/Anchor. A review of human diversity and "race" from the biological and sociological points of view.

Bodmer, W. F., and L. L. Cavalli-Sforza 1970 — Intelligence and Race. *Scientific American.* 223: 19–29 Review of arguments on race and IQ.

Burt, C. 1961 — Intelligence and Social Mobility. *British Journal of Statistical Psychology.* 14:3–24 The notion that social class and IQ are related to genetics.

Gottesman, I. I. 1968 — In *Social Class, Race, and Psychological Development.* Edited by Deutsch, Katz, and Jensen. New York: Holt, Rinehart and Winston. An argument against correlations between race and IQ, with an examination of black and white populations in the United States.

Harris, M. 1964 — *Patterns of Race in the Americas.* New York: Walker and Co. Race prejudice and racial discrimination in historical context.

Harris, M. 1970 — Referential Ambiguity in the Calculus of Brazilian Racial Identity. *Southwestern Journal of Anthropology.* 26:1–14. An analysis of Brazilians' perceptions of phenotype in their own diverse population.

Heber, R. F. and R. B. Dever 1969 — Research on Education and Habilitation of the Mentally Retarded. In *Social-Cultural Aspects of Mental Retardation.* Edited by H. C. Haywood. New York: Appelton-Century-Crofts. Study of environment and mental retardation.

Hiernaux, J. 1968 — *La Diversité humaine en Afrique subsaharienne.* Editions de L'institut de Sociologie. Brussels: Université Libre de Bruxelles. Mathematical analysis of data on African populations showing that most cannot be clustered into units between population and species.

Jensen, A. 1969 — How Much Can We Boost IQ and Scholastic Achievement? *Harvard Educational Review.* 39:1–123. Suggests that IQ is related to race and based largely on genetic inheritance. Sparked controversy on this issue.

Livingstone, F. 1958 — Anthropological Implications of Sickle Cell Gene Distribution in West Africa. *American Anthropologist.* 60:533–62. Classic paper on interaction among culture, environment, and a genetic polymorphism.

SPECULATIONS ON THE EVOLUTION OF ARTISTIC BEHAVIOR

Darwin's theory of natural selection established that all living forms are linked together in a great chain of being. *The Descent of Man,* published in 1871, put the human species firmly in the animal kingdom and showed that our closest living relatives were monkeys and apes. Resistance to Darwin came from theologians who felt that evolution removed humans from the realm of special creation. In spite of this resistance, during the early part of the twentieth century, evolution became fully established within biology and anthropology. In anthropology, however, the concept of culture was used to set humans apart from other species.

I do not wish to dispute the view that culture is *our* major adaptation or that it is rooted in our biological past. In fact, this is a primary message of this book. Neither shall I argue, however, that such biological factors as instinct can be used to explain the behavior of humans, either as individuals or as members of social groups. Instead, I think it is important to realize that culture is bound by certain biological constraints that determine its outer limits. I believe that cultural traditions are built on a foundation of universal, inborn, biological patterns that shape and limit our perceptions and our thinking. It is these universal patterns that provide all humans with basic mental processes, what anthropologists have long referred to as the **psychic unity** of the species. In order to fully understand human behavior it is necessary to understand this biological substratum. To do so we must search for unity in the face of diversity which has outer limits. If psychic unity is based in our biology, then diversity must be bounded by a more profound commonality.

To analyze psychic unity we must concentrate on those behaviors that are strictly human. In my analysis, therefore, I will abandon simple analogies between the behavior of lower animals and ourselves. Aggression and territoriality will be laid aside. Instead, I will focus on the foundations of culture and its expression in communication and artistic creativity. Let us begin with a relatively simple form of communication, the expression of emotions nonverbally.

Irenaus Eibl-Eibesfeldt, a German ethologist and student of Konrad Lorenz, has suggested that emotional expression in humans is inborn and species-wide. He has filmed the emotional expressions of individuals in a wide range of societies. He has also investigated such expression in adults born blind and deaf. In both lines of inquiry Eibl-Eibesfeldt has found evidence that universal patterns exist. In addition, he has data showing that more complex pancultural messages can be transmitted nonlinguistically. These messages involve facial expressions that communicate such information as "leave me alone" or "I am interested in you." Other researchers interested in nonverbal communication have noted that humans respond to a wide range of very subtle cues, *some* of which may be pancultural. There is, for example, evidence that eye-pupil size is perceived subconsciously as a sexual signal: a narrow pupil is a negative sign; a wide pupil is positive, inviting sexual advance. Signals of this type would be adaptive because they would allow important communication to take place across the barriers of culture and, possibly in some cases, between a mother and her preverbal infant. This type of research has just begun and it is too soon to make firm statements about the extent and significance of such possible inborn patterns.

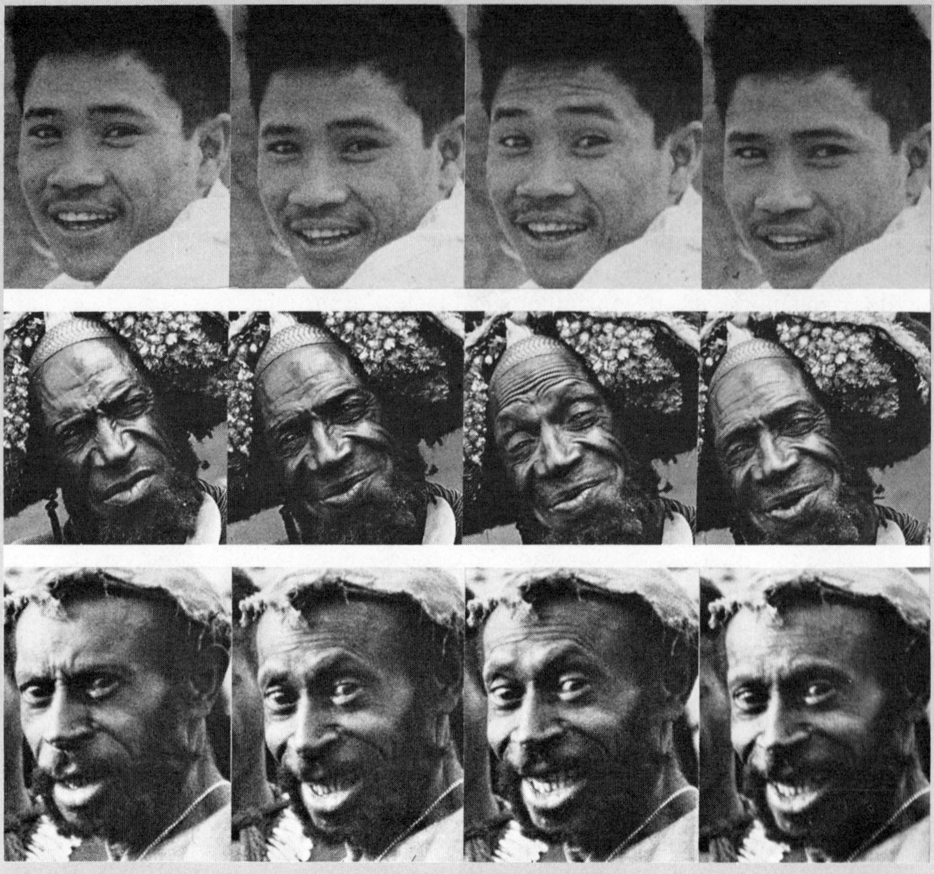

Cross cultural similarities in emotional signals. Eyebrow-flash during greeting in Bali (top row) and in Papua-New Guinea.

ARTISTIC BEHAVIOR

Artistic behavior (dancing, music, dramatic performance, the creation of oral or written literature, the production of painting, drawing, and sculpture, as well as the appreciation of all of these) is universal in human social groups. Not all of the arts exist everywhere nor do all humans produce or appreciate art, but some form of art can be found in every society. Although some weak claims can be made for the existence of artistic behavior in lower animals (some birds decorate their nests, some birds "sing", and some birds as well as primates produce rhythmic movements during certain social interactions), I do not believe that the evidence is convincing. Art as we understand it is a very special form of communication that requires symbolic transformations that appear to be beyond the capacities of nonhuman animals. The existence of art throughout human culture requires some kind of explanation. Its wide distribution suggests, at least on the surface, that artistic behavior must be adaptive in some way. Under close examination, however, we run into serious problems with the simple hypothesis that art is biologically adaptive.

Art as a cultural phenomenon *may* be adaptive in many circumstances, yet adaptation must be measured in terms of fitness. We have no evidence to show that artists of any type have a higher fertility than nonartists. In our own society artists may have a lower average fertility than the members of the population at large. That art may be psychologically rewarding for an individual does not imply that it confers a selective advantage. The problem of the evolution of artistic behavior, therefore, must be approached from the viewpoint that artistic behavior in itself may not have been selected in the evolutionary process. Instead, it may be the result of the accumulation and merging of other adaptive traits.

In discussing art we must make a clear separation between those factors in our evolutionary past that make art possible and art itself as it is practiced in human society. The development of the capacity for artistic behavior is a biological question, while the development of art in the context of society is a socio-historical question.

Before examining the specific adaptive responses that led to art, I shall discuss some other more general features of the human organism that contribute to the patterning we see in the various arts. None of these involves direct selection in favor of artistic behavior. They are, like the organs of speech, qualities and traits that were selected for specific functions, such as physical manipulation, bipedalism, and high intelligence.

The hand is a highly specialized organ. As we have seen, bipedalism and erect posture have freed the human hand to carry and manipulate objects with a finesse reflected only partially in some of our primate cousins. The hand itself is a prehensile organ with an opposable thumb. Its complex articulation allows us to grasp objects with ease. Because of its architecture and the rich nerve endings in the fingers, the hand is capable of both a power grip, with which things are firmly held, and a precision grip, which can be used to manipulate small objects with great care. It is this precision grip that allows for the production of fine detail in drawing, painting, and sculpture, as well as the playing of musical instruments.

Another development important to our overall adaptation is well-tuned eye-hand coordination. The human nervous system is patterned so that the eye can monitor what the hand does in great detail. Through complex feedback controlled by special brain centers, the hand operates on the basis of instructions formed from visual patterns.

Humans have retained limb flexibility in the upper extremities, including full rotation of the arms. We can also turn our hands over. Flexibility in the lower limbs has been sacrificed somewhat with the development of bipedal locomotion, and, of course, as our feet have developed we have lost the use of the primitive primate hands on the lower limbs. Still, with proper exercise, a good deal of flexibility is also available in our legs, as manifested in dancers and acrobats.

Our ability to see color and judge distance may be part of our early primate heritage. Humans, like birds, are quite color conscious; other non-primate mammals are either color-blind or are only sensitive to a small range of what to us is the visible spectrum. The first primates or their immediate ancestors were small insect-eating animals that had to accurately perceive both the distance and the color of their prey as they stalked it in an environment rich in vegetation. Three-dimensional color vision probably continued to be advantageous for tree-dwelling primates, the next stage in the development of our evolutionary line. We have seen that stereoscopic vision has an obvious value for animals that move rapidly through an arboreal environment—jumping, leaping, and swinging from limb to limb. Poor judgment of distance there can lead to instant disaster. Visual acuity allows complex and subtle art styles to develop in visual arts and dance. It evolved with the growth and increasing complexity of the visual centers in the brain.

On the negative side, the olfactory centers of the brain, so highly refined in such ground-dwelling animals as members of the dog and cat families, are much attenuated in humans. For this reason, ethologists have, until recently, almost totally ignored chemical signaling among animals, concentrating instead on visual signals. Scents are, however, very important even to some primates, particularly those living in the dense forests of South and Central America. In those environments visual signals are not as effective a means of social communication as chemical traces. Evidence for communication through odors has recently come from laboratory experiments in which captive animals are exposed to sample secretions from other animals of the same species. Humans, however, are apparently insensitive to the subtle differences between their own species' male and female smells.

This is not to say that scents have no part to play in human behavior. Our own culture has both positive and negative associations for particular odors. Food preparation involves both taste and odor, and the perfume industry could not exist if smell had no stimulating effect. Still, our sense of smell is much less powerful than that of many other species, and our ability to recall particular smells when they are absent is quite limited. It would be surprising, then, if smell became a central concern of artists, for it occupies only a small place in our symbolic life.

Hearing is also well developed in humans. Although we are not as sensitive to pitch and loudness as some species (dogs, for example), we can hear subtle differences in these aspects of sound as well as difference in timbre (the quality of sound). These perceptual abilities are all exploited in music along with a sense of rhythm.

Let me now turn to my central topic: the evolutionary development of artistic behavior.

Artistic behavior depends on the following adaptive traits: (1) *exploratory behavior and play* (found in all mammalian species as well as among other species in other phyletic lines); (2) *a sense of rhythm and balance,* which may be referred to generally as *form;* (3) *fine-grain perceptual discrimination of visual and auditory patterns coupled to large memory capacity and long-term memory storage;* and (4) *transformation-representation,* which includes such linguistic processes as metaphor, that is, the creation of new meanings through association. Transformation-representation, at least as fully developed, is a process exclusive to the human species.

Exploration and Play. The first trait (or traits, although I choose to merge them) is of undoubted selective advantage for a species equipped with high learning capacity. Exploration coupled to a high capacity for learning allows an organism to map its environment, while play provides a controlled experience for environmental manipulation. Play is, of course, a widespread characteristic of mammals in general and primates in particular. We must, however, distinguish between games and play. Play is the larger and more inclusive category. Play is an activity that is self-rewarding. One plays for the sake of playing rather than for rewards external to playing. While play need not be structured, games are structured events that involve playing. Games may have formal structures (as in chess or cards) or informal structures (as in playing cops and robbers or playing house).

The human hand is capable of both precision and power grips. The precision grip allows humans to make highly decorated delicate objects.

Irven DeVore in his film on the behavior of baboons captures their play. The young play-fight silently under the careful eyes of adults that stand ready to intervene should any of the players emit a cry of pain. Anyone who has had a pet puppy or kitten is familiar with the play patterns that make up so much of these animals' behavior. Puppies and kittens are fearless as they attack bits of string, shoes, or other objects that can be pushed around or manipulated. Anything that moves is animated and then conquered by them. Cats, at least, later apply this behavior to real hunting. Dogs, as house pets, are restrained in this activity, but those animals used for hunting get a chance to practice their acquired skills. These are sharpened through training, a process that they thoroughly enjoy because, for them, it is just another aspect of play.

Sigmund Freud saw creative behavior as a continuation of and a substitution for the play of childhood. In his essay *The Relation of the Poet to Day-Dreaming,* Freud said the following:

. . . every child at play behaves like an imaginative writer, in that he creates a world of his own or, more truly, he rearranges the things of his world and orders it in a new way that pleases him better. . . .

Now a writer does the same as a child at play; he creates a world of fantasy which he takes very seriously; that is, he invests it with a great deal of affect [emotion], *while separating it sharply from reality.*

. . . when a man of literary talent presents his plays, or relates what we take to be his personal day-dreams, we experience great pleasure arising probably from many sources. How the writer accomplishes this is his innermost secret. . . . The writer softens the egotistical character of the day-dream by changes and disguises, and he bribes us by the offer of a purely formal, that is, aesthetic, pleasure in the presentation of his fantasies.

Play is one biological property that makes art possible in the human species, but culture determines a particular tradition and its stability through time. Play as an aspect of art appears in all cultures, but the degree of freedom allowed in the game of art (its formal rules) varies. Egyptian art, for example, changed very little during the many centuries of dynastic rule. Oriental art has shown much less formal change than Western art in the same periods. How much freedom an art tradition allows is linked to such cultural factors as the purpose for which works of art are produced (the style of Russian icons, for example, tends to remain very stable), the role of the individual artist in society, and the set of formal rules that surrounds artistic production.

Rhythm and Balance: Form. The second factor is response to form. There is abundant evidence that animals are sensitive to certain spatial configurations. Many of these shapes trigger such specific behaviors as species recognition or flight reactions; young ducks, for example, will show a fear reaction when a schematic hawk-like image is passed over them. Other patterns appear to stimulate pleasurable reactions, as do pictures of immature animals presented to humans of all ages and schematic human faces presented to babies. Apart from these obviously adaptive social responses there is evidence that among primates, at least, art-like form-creating behavior may occur under laboratory conditions. Such behavior, although artificially stimulated, may reflect brain-based preferences for certain types of spatial arrangement, for what I should like to call "good form."

Desmond Morris and others working with various primates have stimulated animals to mark paper with pencil or paint. The activity appears to some degree to be ordered. Apes produce fan-like patterns, and after some time and experience with a medium, their "compositions" become more and more complex, involving elaborations of the basic design. Color balance may also improve with practice. More significant, however, is the reaction of primates to a surface marked with squares placed on different parts of an empty painting surface. When a square is centered, an animal will tend to paint within it, maintaining the centrality of the design. When the square is placed on the upper left-hand side of the surface, the animal will tend to limit its design to the lower right-hand corner. Placing the square in different corners elicits responses that suggest concern for design balance—indeed, design balance based on inversion and opposition.

In his book *The Naked Ape* Morris suggests that music, dance, and plastic art might be manifestations of an exploratory drive. He derives an interesting series of rules that he believes govern such behavior: (1) Investigate the unfamiliar until it becomes familiar. (2) Impose rhythmic repetition on the familiar. (3) Vary this repetition in as many ways as possible. (4) Select the most satisfying of these variations and develop them at the expense of others. (5) Combine and recombine these variations with one another. (6) Do these all for their own sake.

If this proposal is correct, there may well be a link between exploratory behavior and play on the one hand and response to form on the other. The imposition of order and a preference for certain shapes are two separate ways of coding environmental information. Such coding allows for accurate memory storage and easy retrieval as well as a means for the rapid discovery of disturbances in remembered patterns.

There is some evidence—although it is much more scattered than the evidence concerning play and exploratory behavior—that some mammals other than primates may be acutely aware of spatial relations and the arrangement of the elements of their environment. Domesticated wolves and coyotes reared as pets in the home become agitated when even small objects are dislocated from their habitual positions. The agitation generated by changed conditions of the field tends to restimulate environmental exploration and sets the animal on guard against potential danger; thus, the adaptive nature of the behavior is obvious.

Pattern Recognition and Discrimination. Humans are, of course, equipped with a highly developed capacity for pattern recognition and discrimination, the third trait relating to art. Such a capacity allows for the coding of useful information. One vital category of information is the subtle differences in facial patterns that allow unambiguous social discriminations within and among groups. The complex nature of human social interactions is facilitated by this ability. Its operation however, also depends on long-term memory storage of complex data, another feature of the human mind. Such pattern discrimination and stored memories can be transmuted into artistic behavior and the development of an artistic tradition.

Although humans are capable of discriminating and storing a wide range of visual information, the accuracy of recall tends to vary with the stimulus. We are able to retain minute details of facial features much better than architecture and landscapes, although our powers of retention even for them are also extraordinary. When it comes to accurate reproduction, we tend to be much more tolerant of deviations or mistakes in natural scenes or buildings than in faces. Slight deviations in a portrait drawing change the face. Although a person might still recognize a distorted portrait, the deviations will be noted. During the summer of 1975 I did a great deal of drawing in a small village in southern France. My landscapes were quite successful, and villagers unhesitatingly recognized and appreciated local scenes. I found it much harder to represent people, particularly faces, and in many cases my portraits were judged as poor but recognizable, or unrecognizable. I do not think that these differences in reaction can be explained by differences in ability to represent. Rather, I think that they were due to a differential tolerance to errors in depicting landscapes and faces. Since facial recognition is so much a part of our social life, depending on the coding

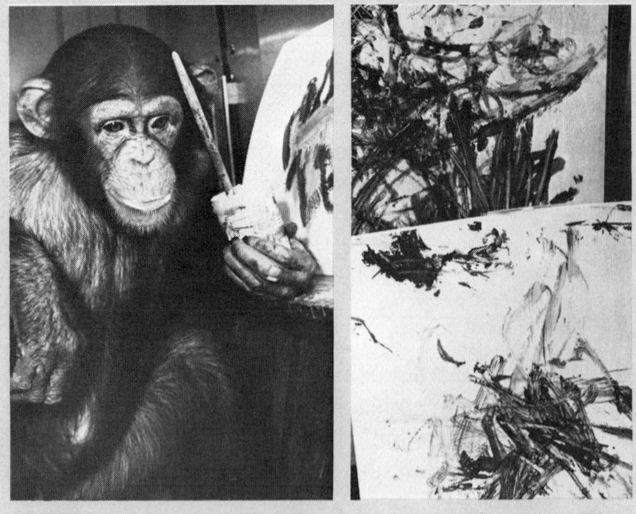

Chimpanzees can be stimulated by humans to paint. They apparently enjoy playing with form, and while their pictures are crude they are not mere scribbles.

and recall of minute differences, it might well be that both coding and storage mechanisms in the brain act differentially for facial and other patterns.

Transformation-Representation. The final factor in our evolutionary development that gave rise to art is what I call transformation-representation. All art consists of a process of representing, even if what is represented is only form or emotion. When an artist chooses to produce an art work, he or she must make a series of decisions concerning the means of representation. Expression is limited and controlled, at least partially, by the particular art form employed. It is impossible for an artist to represent without transforming in some way as well. Transformation, however, is not just a limiting factor. *It is in the process of transformation that objects and ideas become art.* The entire process of transformation-representation rests on the development of human language as opposed to other forms of communication. This is just as true for painting and music as it is for prose and poetry. Art is a type of communication involving form. Art is based on our symbolic-linguistic capacities but it is not language.

Human language, as opposed to communication in lower animals, depends on the ability to apply arbitrary symbols to objects and concepts, and to manipulate these symbols by means of a grammar so as to produce thoughts that are independent of time and place. That is to say, humans can think backward to past events or forward to possible future events. Through speech we can communicate about the real world and about imaginary worlds. We do this also through our art. But art more than language deals with the emotional realm of human experience. Artistic expression is a byproduct of the development of our major adaptive form of communication, language.

Defining Art. Art may now be defined as play with form, the end of which is the production of some aesthetically successful transformation-representation. This statement, of course, immediately raises a new question: what do I mean by aesthetically successful? I mean that the work stimulates an emotional response in the creator and, it is hoped, in some communicant as well. That is to say, art as communication produces a successful transaction between the producer of the "signal" and an audience. What is communicated in these transactions is the subjective aspect of experience. Art *can,* of course, communicate verbal messages, but it is distinctive as an aspect of human behavior because it *always* communicates experience that has no direct linguistic expression in the spoken language.

The pleasurable element in artistic expression and appreciation derives from its basis in play and the response to form. There is some evidence that aesthetic judgment by experts (people who are artists or connoisseurs) in different cultures is similar. The psychologist Irvin Child has developed a standardized test of artistic appreciation that has been given in such culturally diverse places as the United States, Japan, Fiji, and Greece with similar results. A different test showed that art experts in New

A

B

C

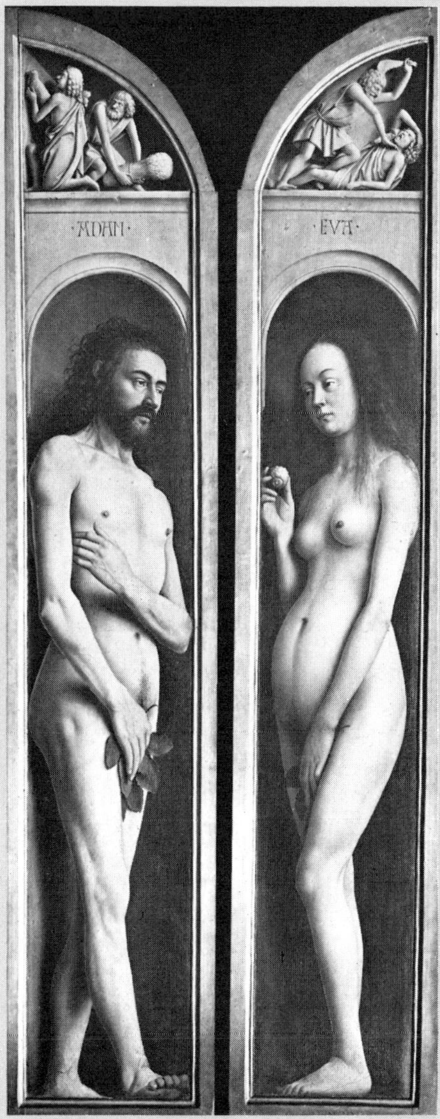

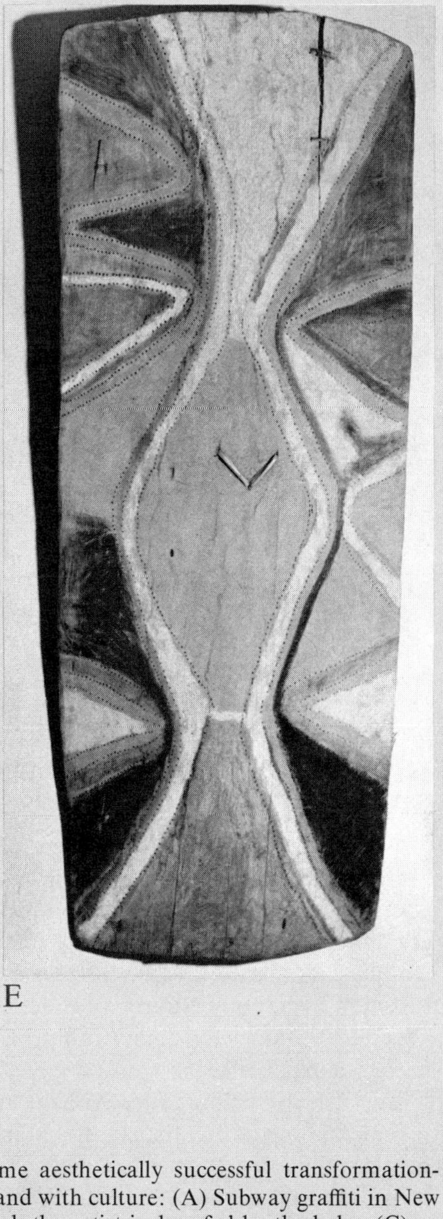

E

D

Art is play with form, the end of which is some aesthetically successful transformation-representation. The game of art shifts with time and with culture: (A) Subway graffiti in New York, (B) a work by the sculptor Marisol in which the artist is dwarfed by the baby, (C) an abstract painting by Franz Kline, (D) Adam and Eve by the Flemish painter Jan van Eyck; (E) Maring (New Guinea) war shield.

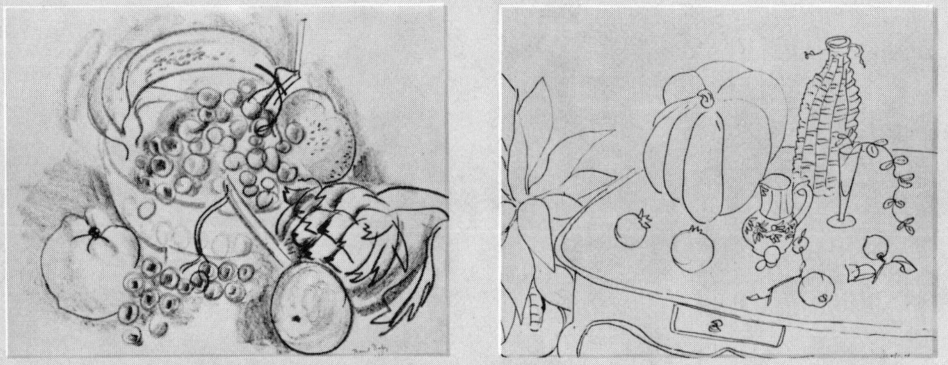

Cross-cultural aesthetic-judgment test devised by Irvin Child of Yale University. Subjects are asked to choose what in their opinion is the best of paired illustrations.

Haven, Connecticut and Zaire made similar evaluations of a series of African masks. These tests suggest that humans who are interested in art share certain common responses that may be based on biological patterns. People who are not interested in art do not make the same judgments. The difference may arise because the phenotype *art expert* involves both biological and cultural elements. People who are not trained to appreciate art are not likely to pay much attention to it. Such training of course, need not be formal; it might simply come with experience as individuals are exposed to various forms of artistic expression.

Music as a Special Case. In a series of lectures at Harvard, published as *The Unanswered Question,* Leonard Bernstein attempted to link linguistic theories of universal grammar to music. Bernstein likened musical structure to grammar and both the grammar and "meaning" of music to emotional pleasure. He notes, however, that while language primarily involves *messages,* music is aesthetic or nothing. In analyzing Mozart's Symphony Number 40, Bernstein attempts to show how a basic grammar generates the notes and orchestration of the music, producing its overall aesthetic effect. He notes that, while the music is governed by basic rules, it becomes beautiful when these rules are violated in ways that are specific to the genius of Mozart. Bernstein goes on to suggest that the emotional impact of great music comes from the interplay between the rules (the basic structure) and the ways these are manipulated and even broken by a composer of genius. What this means is that we are presented with a series of pleasant surprises set against a background of expectations. Unfortunately, Bernstein is unable to explain why Mozart is able to produce his own unique set of aesthetically pleasing violations while other composers using the same basic rule system might fail. We have yet to discover what makes great art great even when we agree on which art is great and which is not. Yet Bernstein does raise an important question about the relationship between the transformational aspect of art and that which is transformed. When the two aspects of art (that which is represented and its representation) are no longer linked, only chaos results. The successful artist finds ways of maintaining the connection, but in an aesthetically pleasing way. Using music as a case in point is instructive because it shows that what is represented may be a set of rules or conventions rather than a concrete object such as a house or a tree. It may be that the artistic process is difficult to grasp fully, precisely because it is a basic part of our brain structure. Although we carry our brains inside our heads, we know very little about the way in which they function, particularly in the symbolic realm.

Bibliography

Alland, A., Jr. 1977 — *The Artistic Animal.* New York: Doubleday/Anchor. A discussion of the biological background of art.

Bernstein, L. 1976 — *The Unanswered Question: Six Lectures at Harvard.* Cambridge, Mass.: Harvard University Press. An attempt to relate music to contemporary linguistic theory.

Caillois, R. 1968 — Riddles and Images. *Yale French Studies.* 40:148–58. A look at riddles as aspects of the creative process.

Child, I. and L. Siroto 1965 — Bakwele and American Esthetic Evaluations Compared. *Ethnology* 4:349–69. Cross-cultural study of aesthetic judgment showing agreement among American and Bakwele experts.

Gardner, H. 1975 — *The Shattered Mind.* New York: Knopf. A book about aphasia, with a section on creativity.

Freud, S. 1959 — The Relation of the Poet to Day-Dreaming. *Collected Papers.* Edited by E. Jones. New York: Basic Books. Freud looks at poetry as reflection of unconscious thought.

Iwao, S., and I. Child 1966 — Comparison of Esthetic Judgment by American Experts and by Japanese Potters. *Journal of Social Psychology.* 68:27–33. Cross-cultural study of aesthetic judgment showing significant agreement among art experts in several cultures:

Moore, O. K. and A. R. Anderson 1960 — Autotelic Folk Models. Paper presented at the meeting of the American Sociological Association, New York, 1960. An examination of games as learning situations. Includes art as a game.

Morris, D. 1962 — *The Biology of Art.* New York: Knopf. A look at the origins of art in the painting of chimpanzees. One of the earliest studies of this type.

Morris, D. 1967 — *The Naked Ape.* New York: McGraw-Hill. A comparison of human and animal behavior with some ideas about common origins. There is a section on creativity.

CHAPTER 8

APPLIED PHYSICAL AND MEDICAL ANTHRO-POLOGY

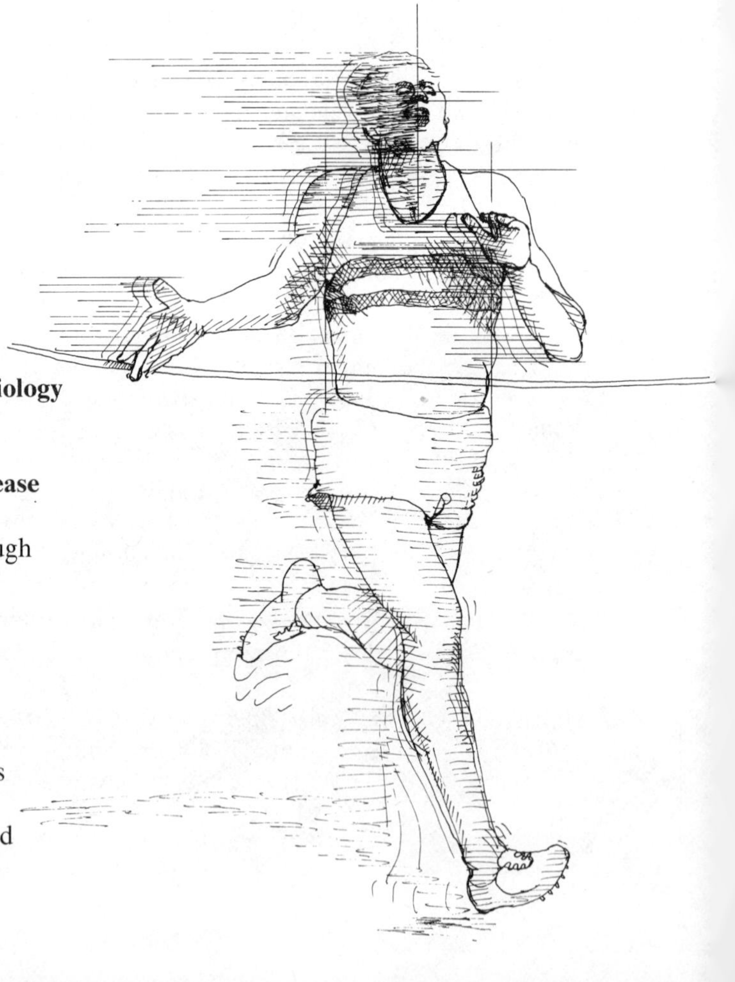

All sciences have both research and applied aspects. Basic discoveries in physics, chemistry, and biology often lead to technological advances in industry and medicine. Physical anthropology, too, has a direct bearing on modern life. A physical anthropologist may be concerned with such matters as health and nutrition, genetic disease, and even the planning of practical items ranging from comfortable furniture to safe machines. Although some anthropologists work specifically in applied fields, basic research may also contribute to the solution of practical problems. Scientists can never tell in advance when a basic discovery will have some value in the everyday world.

Medical anthropology deals with the relationships between health and disease on the one hand and biological and cultural variables on the other. While most medical anthropologists are trained in cultural anthropology (with additional training in public health), some are physical anthropologists. Many medical anthropologists are engaged in basic research, but they also do a great deal of applied work. Because medical anthropology deals, at least in part, with human biology and because medical anthropologists often work with physical anthropologists, this field will be discussed here in the context of applied work.

BIOLOGY AND CULTURE, CULTURE AND BIOLOGY

So far in this book we have traced the path of human evolution that led to the emergence of culture as our major adaptation. Culture has evolved through a long process of selection and interaction with the environment. Since humans made the first tools, they have altered the natural world. When the environment is changed, new selective conditions are created. Thus, culture itself can affect genetic and other biological patterns. The shift from hunting and gathering to cultivation for example, led to major changes in dietary patterns. It also led to permanent settlements and is related to population growth. These two factors create significant environmental changes that are directly related to disease. Permanent settlement and high population density increase the risk from infectious disease. Settled populations remain close to their refuse, including the waste products of their own bodies, and higher population density increases the possibility that disease will spread from individual to individual.

Any cultural practice that affects the environment can change the conditions under which disease organisms and their carriers breed and contact humans. Cutting the forests in West Africa produced an environment compatible with the breeding patterns of the mosquito that carries falciparum malaria. As the disease increased in frequency in local populations a shift occurred in genetic selection as well. Individuals heterozygous for sickle-cell were resistant to malaria and were therefore favored in the selective process. Thus, a cultural practice changed the relationship between human populations, a disease organism via a carrier insect, and ultimately, the genetic patterns of those populations. Medical anthropologists are now studying the context in which this disease occurs in Americans of African descent in order to understand the conditions under which individuals suffer attacks. It is hoped that these studies will lead to new kinds of treatment.

Irrigation agriculture in the tropics creates the conditions for the chronic occurrence of schistosomiasis, a parasite disease carried by a species of snail. The schistosoma parasite passes part of its life cycle in the snail and part in humans. Irrigation works provide perfect environments for snail breeding, while work patterns that foster body contact with water allow the parasite to invade the human host through the skin. Schistosomiasis is a major chronic disease in Africa, Asia, and parts of South America.

The rise of industrialism with its rapid technological change has severely altered the world's environment in a very short time. Recently we have become aware of the dangers of chemical pollutants in our air and water and their relationship to the increase in cancer rates. Industrialism is also associated with crowding and new work patterns that have been related to increases in such stress conditions as hypertension and heart disease. Work patterns can also produce such stress diseases as ulcers and even nervous breakdowns.

Modern technology has also led, through the development of new medical techniques, to the diminution of certain diseases. Tuberculosis, which was a common threat in the urban environment in the nineteenth century, is almost extinct and smallpox is about to disappear. Leprosy, which used to infest Europe, is limited to a few tropical areas, and the great plague epidemics of the Middle Ages are remembered only through literary and historical sources.

Let us now take a closer look at various aspects of applied physical anthropology and medical anthropology as they touch on specific problems. Some will involve disease and others will concern practical aspects of modern life.

POPULATION GENETICS

Physical anthropologists working in population genetics contribute to our general knowledge of adaptation under different environmental conditions. They also investigate the effects of marriage and other cultural practices on the genetic structure of populations, as well as the role of genetics in disease. Scholars who are interested in the interaction between genetics and changing environments study genotypic and phenotypic trends.

The various blood types in the ABO system are distributed unevenly in human populations (see Figure 7.2). Blood group A, for example, occurs in higher frequency in Asian than in European populations. Genetic drift is probably responsible for the disappearance of blood type B in Native American populations. The various blood types of the ABO system have been correlated with different diseases ranging from ulcers to certain types of cancer. Although drift probably plays a considerable role in blood-group distributions, environmental selection may also be related to population differences in blood-type frequencies.

Another important blood group difference is the Rh factor. Individuals are born with or without an Rh blood antigen: Rh+ or Rh−. (Because this trait is produced by multiple alleles on three different loci, intermediate forms also occur.) When an Rh+ man and an Rh− women produce offspring, the woman may become pregnant with an Rh+ fetus. When this occurs, her body responds to its Rh antigen by producing antibodies antagonistic to her offspring. Recently a series of medical techniques has been developed to prevent this incompatibility from developing. Rh genes are distributed unevenly among human populations. Rh− tends to be higher in frequency among Asians than among Europeans. An interesting exception to this is the high frequency of Rh− genes found among the Basques of Spain and France. This suggests that the Basques represent an isolate population within Europe.

Whether or not particular genes associated with disease penetrate, that is affect the phenotype, is closely related to environmental factors. If, for example, a dietary factor that increases the risk of genetic penetrance is absent in a culture, the disease is unlikely to occur. On the other hand in these cases normal selection pressures against the gene are also absent so that it may attain higher frequency than in populations with diets allowing the gene to penetrate, cause the disease, and be partially eliminated.

Data Problems

Because population genetics depends on genealogies that are assumed to reflect true mating patterns, a physical anthropologist working in an exotic culture may need to study the social structure closely. It is often necessary to determine whether genealogies actually reflect genetic family lines. In some societies genealogies are used as part of the ideological system to bolster claims about ownership of land or titles. Under these conditions family lines may be "faked" in order to conform to some economic or political goal. In certain societies in which adoption is very common, it may be very difficult to find out who a child's biological parents are. The geneticist must never assume that the legal father (*pater*) of a child is its biological father (*genitor*). Patterns and frequencies of extramarital sex, which vary from culture to culture and within cultures by social class and caste, must be taken into account. Many anthropologists assumed that Indian castes would show characteristics of breeding populations because in theory, at least, they are endogamous (marriage can only take place within the group). In some regions of India, however, such genetic barriers appear to be less than airtight. Marriage may, in fact, not occur across caste lines, but extramarital relations may.

TRACKING DOWN THE CAUSE OF DISEASE

Causes of Disease

Diseases have variable causes. Among these are infectious agents (viruses, bacteria, various worm parasites, for instance), stress (due to overexertion—psychological, physical, or both—and/or exposure to abnormal environmental conditions as of altitude, temperature, and humidity), normal breakdown of the organism due to old age, environmental sources (as with some cancers, black lung disease due to exposure to coal dust), and psychological sources (as with neuroses, psychoses, and psychosomatic disorders producing physical symptoms). Furthermore, none of these categories are airtight. In many cases multiple factors enter into the etiology (cause) of specific pathological conditions and their particular frequencies in different populations.

Physical and medical anthropologists have contributions to make to the study of all these types of disease. Certain populations are resistant to specific disorders while others have high morbidity (the rate of affected individuals). Both resistance and susceptibility are related to a number of physical and environmental factors. The nutritional base in a particular culture or segment of a culture (diets differ by class, age, religion, and sex) will have a significant effect on disease rates, as will work loads, the type of work performed, and exposure to particular environmental dangers. Finally, a disease may be genetic or resistance to it may be due to genetic factors.

Frequently the etiology of a disease is difficult to determine in modern urban culture. Where populations are large and where significant differences exist in such variables as work, social class, and nutrition, the situation may be too complex to make a determination of what factors contribute to a particular condition. Small-scale societies with fewer variables provide the laboratory for etiological studies. Physical and medical anthropologists can work in combination with medical and public health personnel in the context of such societies; together they all make a significant contribution to unraveling the cause of and providing preventive means against a wide range of disorders. At the present time a great deal of research is being carried out on the relationship between nutrition and heart disease. Much of this research involves the study of small, isolated populations with different stress loads and diets. Heart disease and the condition known as hypertension appear to be caused by stress as well as diet. Again, anthropologists are currently involved in studies that may link these disorders to food intake, work loads, ratio of leisure to work, crowding, degree and types of social interaction, and overall quality of life in different populations.

Solving a Medical Mystery through Anthropology and Medicine

If we suspect that a disease is due to some genetic defect, we must determine whether the allele is dominant, recessive, or codominant, whether sex-linked or autosomal. In addition, we will want to know whether the source is an allele on a single locus or if it is polygenetic. When these factors are determined, we will be able to measure the frequency of the disease-causing allele or alleles in the population.

What appear to be genetic disorders, however, may in fact be due to other causes. Sometimes the solution to an exotic local problem has major consequences for medical theory. Such was the case with *Kuru,* a strange disease of the central nervous system that affected only one very small population in the highlands of New Guinea. As we shall see, this disease turned out not to be genetic, but for a long time the genetic hypothesis appeared to be the most logical.

Kuru occurred among the Foré people in New Guinea. It was discovered in the 1950s when the territory was opened to Europeans. Kuru was always fatal. It was a degenerative disease of the brain that began with mild symptoms and progressed until affected individuals were no longer able to care for themselves. Death usually resulted from other causes (pneumonia, for example) but was directly linked to the disease.

At first glance Kuru appeared to follow a complicated genetic pattern. It occurred only among Foré. It did not appear to be infectious because neighboring peoples with whom the Foré had contact never got it. Foré who moved away from the highlands often came down with the disease several months after leaving their homes. Kuru had a regular, if peculiar, age and sex distribution. It affected children of both sexes but only women among adults. No cases were found among adult men. If Kuru were genetic, it would have to have some adaptive value. Its high frequency suggested some sort of adaptive gain in hypothetical carriers.

The initial hypothesis offered to account for Kuru suggested that it was due to a dominant gene, the penetrance of which was affected by sex hormones. Dominance was hypothesized because Kuru occurred in every generation, and common dominant traits tend to appear in this pattern. It was thought to be linked to hormones because of its sexual distribution in the population: adult men were protected, it seemed, by the suppressive effect of male sex hormones.

In the early 1960s Jack and Anne Fischer, both cultural anthropologists who worked in medical anthropology, published a theoretical article on the probable cause of Kuru. They broke with the genetic hypothesis, citing evidence from Foré culture that could account for the observed pattern. First, the Fischers noted that Foré men lived in relative isolation from both women and children. Mature men slept and ate in men's houses while women and children of both sexes lived in the same hut. Second, they noted that the Foré were cannibals. Third, the Fischers pointed out that the Foré were one of the few ethnic groups in the world

Kuru victims. Kuru is a slow virus disease once thought to be genetic in origin. Its infectious origin was first suggested by anthropologists and proved by the Nobel-Prize-winner Dr. Carleton Gajdusek.

practicing **endocannibalism** (Foré ate Foré, but only under special conditions). The eating of a deceased relative was considered an act of piety. The people who died of Kuru were eaten by their grieving relatives; the part eaten was usually the brain. The Fischers speculated that women and children had contact with undercooked infected brain matter during its preparation. The men would eat of the Kuru victims after the women had brought fully cooked brains to the men's house. Thus, they suggested, Kuru was an infectious disease maintained by a rather rare custom.

The Fischers' hypothesis interested a young medical researcher, Dr. Carleton Gajdusek. The only difficulty with the idea that Kuru was infectious was the fact that Foré women and children who had moved away from their home territory in healthy condition did sometimes come down with the disorder. Before beginning his research, Gajdusek searched the literature for diseases that had a very long incubation period. He found one, a disease of sheep called scrapie. Gajdusek was intrigued because scrapie is viral and affects the central nervous system in ways very similar to Kuru. Microscopic examination of brain material from Kuru victims showed lesions that were strikingly like the lesions of scrapie.

The next thing Gajdusek did was to obtain some material from the brains of Kuru victims and inject it into chimpanzees. Then he waited, and waited! After what seemed like an inordinately long period for an infectious organism to take effect (about 18 months), the chimpanzees came down with Kuru. Its viral origin was demonstrated.

The discovery of Kuru opened up a whole new field of medical research into a group of disease organisms now known as *slow viruses.* It seems possible that several conditions thought to be genetic in origin are actually due to these organisms; among the unproven candidates are muscular dystrophy and multiple sclerosis. A nervous disorder known as Crutchfeld-Jacobs disease has been proved to have a slow virus origin. The Fischers' hunch plus the dogged research of Gajdusek have already paid off for more cultures than just the Foré. Gajdusek was awarded the Nobel Prize in medicine for his work on slow viruses.

This story has a happy ending in another sense too. Kuru is now an extinct disease. Cannibalism has ceased in the Foré area and with it Kuru has disappeared into the annals of medical history.

APPLIED PROBLEMS

Nutrition

The United Nations publishes world-wide average nutritional requirements for proteins, calories, minerals, and necessary vitamins, yet we do not really have good comparative nutritional data for different populations. We do know that some of the world's peoples live without serious difficulty well below some of the published "minimum" requirements. It is very likely that physiological adaptation affects the adjustment of nutritional needs. Some people, paradoxically, may have high nutritional requirements because they are used to a diet rich in certain nutrients. Additional factors—climate, work loads, age, sex, and genetics—play a role in nutrition. Physical anthropologists working with nutritionists are only beginning to scratch the surface of this complicated and interesting field. Better data on nutrition can have far-reaching benefits for all of the world's people.

J. Cravioto, E. R. Delicardie, and H. G. Birch (1966), in a study of the effects of nutrition on brain function, offer strong evidence that early episodes of malnutrition, particularly protein deficit, can have long-range, sometimes permanent, effects on intellectual performance. The research was carried out in Guatemala among peasant populations where malnutrition is common. After eliminating hereditary factors, they found an extremely high correlation between poor nutritional status and small stature. Small and tall children were then compared in a series of psychological tests which suggested that both reversible and irreversible brain damage may result from malnutrition. Recent experiments with nutritional supplements show that a good deal of this intellectual deficit can be overcome, provided it is caught early enough.

Energy and Work

Good measures of economic efficiency require good data about the amounts of actual energy (measured in calories) that is expended in different tasks by people of different physical characteristics in different environments. Yet cultural anthropologists, human ecologists, and geographers interested in energy production and use know very little about these matters. The information would also be of use to those interested in nutrition because work load is directly tied to metabolism. A wide range of laboratory machines has been designed to measure energy expenditure under different conditions of work. Recently physical anthropologists have taken portable versions of these machines into the field. They have yielded information on the effects of different body types

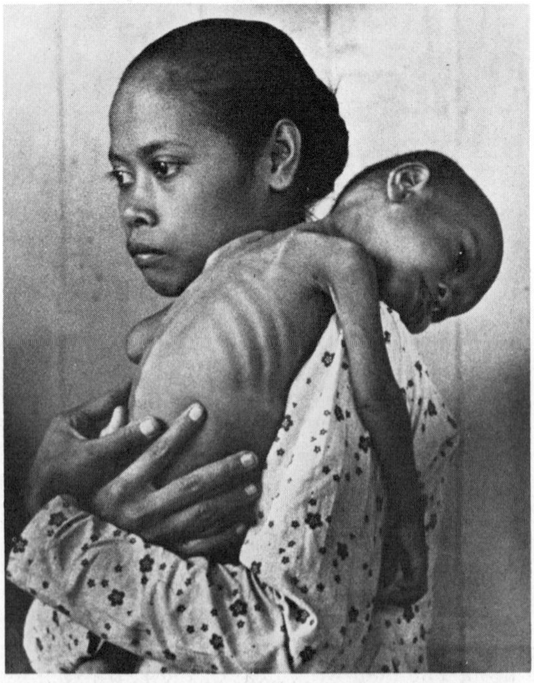

Malnutrition is a major problem of world health. Medical anthropologists can make a contribution to the alleviation of such problems by analyzing eating patterns, studying economic relationships, and helping to devise programs of change.

on work efficiency and the range of possible adaptations that occur under extreme climatic conditions. Work efficiency and metabolism vary genetically *and* through physiological adaptation. We are beginning to learn how these two factors combine in populations that live under extreme conditions. Much information, for example, has been gathered by the physical anthropologist Paul Baker among the high-altitude populations of the Andes.

An important aspect of work activity involves the ability of the body to take in and use oxygen. When individuals who are physically fit are compared to sedentary, or inactive, individuals, large differences are found in oxygen uptake. This difference is apparently due to the capacity of the organs of circulation, the oxygen-transporting capacity of the blood, and other physiological factors in tissues. The physically fit have an enhanced ability to use oxygen. This is the reason why jogging is now encouraged in our own population, which has a tendency for overeating and underactivity. Jogging under the advice of doctors has recently become one means of treating certain kinds of heart condition.

Measuring metabolic activity in the field. A Peruvian farmer walks through his farm wearing a machine that measures metabolism. Metabolic rates are dependent on such factors as body type, nutrition, climate, altitude, and degree of exertion. Data of this sort are collected by physical anthropologists in the field to test a wide range of hypotheses concerning human adaptation.

Environmental Adaptation

When traits occur in clinal distributions, they frequently reflect adaptations to environmental gradients. Knowledge of genetic adaptation to climatic factors provides practical information that can be used to protect nonadapted individuals from specific environmental hazards.

Most of the world's people now live in rapidly changing environments. In order to understand the effects of change on populations we need to continuously monitor such variables as population density, pollution, nutritional change, and alterations in patterns and intensity of work. Each of these can be expected to affect life expectancy, fertility, physical and mental health, disease rates, and even such vague concepts as physical well-being.

In spite of tremendous progress in medical technology, disease has not been eradicated. Nor will it ever be. As medical science conquers certain diseases, other less common ones appear to increase in frequency. Some of this change is merely due to increased longevity. As people live longer, the risk that they will die of heart attack or cancer increases. After all, humans are mortal and must eventually die of something. On the other hand **epidemiology** (the study of disease patterns and frequency) has shown that changes in life style lead to new health problems. Modern life with its tensions has led to a rise, particularly among active middle-aged people, in hypertension and various forms of heart disease. Ulcers are also correlated with a person's mental state. For a long time it has been known that ulcers are common among executives who live and work under great pressure.

A shift from poverty to affluence may decrease the incidence of protein malnutrition but increase the rate of arteriosclerosis (hardening of the arteries). There was apparent evidence that large amounts of animal fat in the diet were directly linked to this disease. We now know that fat alone does not tell the whole story. Populations that have increased fat intake but live outside of the mainstream of modern economic life continue to have a low incidence of arteriosclerosis. Tension and diet acting together contribute to the new disease pattern.

Arteriosclerosis is very uncommon among Eskimos, who live on what is probably the most fat-rich diet in the world. Hypertension and arteriosclerosis have been shown to be infrequent among Italian peasants with a high-carbohydrate and high-fat intake. Certain villages studied over several years show an increase in these conditions without a significant change in diet. Apparently, stress is the factor here. Villagers who used to live out of the mainstream of modern industrial life recently entered the consumer world. Higher work loads, financial insecurity, and increased desires for consumer goods have an apparent effect on health.

Physical anthropologists working with medical researchers have a large role to play in the never-ending study of the interaction between species and environment. These studies range from the analysis of data on small isolated populations like the Foré to material on modern industrial society.

Physical anthropologists interested in stress and nutrition are now or have recently been in the field studying populations that have shifted from rural to urban areas in India, Peru, and the Sudan in East Africa. Stress and work load studies have been carried out in India, as well as many nutritional investigations.

Growth

One of the curious facts uncovered by several generations of measurement is the increase in the average height of Americans over the last 100 years. Growth patterns of this sort have been documented in other parts of the world as well. Developmental studies over a long time allow physical anthropologists to predict population trends and make recommendations to the manufacturers of a wide range of industrial products. The subfield of **somatology** (the study of size and shape in humans) has long been a part of physical anthropology. In addition to studying such simple variables as growth, somatologists analyze head shape and size, limb length, and other body proportions. Without these measurements and the trends they reveal, designers would have only a crude notion of the average, as well as the range of variation, in the body proportions of the people for whom they plan. Proper use of physical anthropology in industry can lead to more rational production through a range of sizes for products as different as clothes and furniture.

Another trend picked up by physical anthropologists working in different parts of the world has been a general lowering of the age of **menarche** (first menstruation) (see Figure 8.1). No one is yet sure how permanent and widespread this change is, nor what is causing it, but it does certainly have implications for fertility. The sooner a woman can have babies, the more babies she can have in her lifetime. (This is true, of course, just so long as the age of menopause is not also lowered.) A reverse process, *late menarche,* is associated with malnutrition, as is *amenorrhea* (the stopping of menstruation before menopause). Poorly fed populations often have decreased fertility, although the association between diet and fertility only occurs under extreme conditions of deprivation. Physical anthropologists need to gather data of this sort and make comparisons with previous trends on an ongoing basis. Possible associations with climate, work patterns, and diet need to be taken into account.

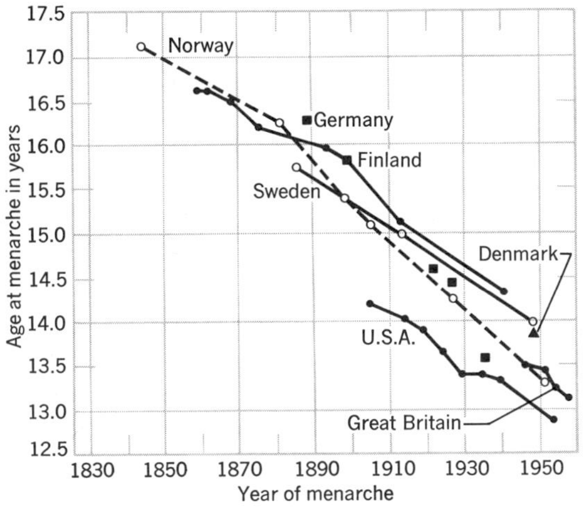

Figure 8.1

Decrease in the age of menarche in selected western countries from 1830 to 1950. (Source: J. M. Tanner, *Growth at Adolescence.* Oxford: Blackwell Scientific Publications, 1962.)

Blood Chemistry and Genetics

Since the discovery of blood groups and other blood serum proteins, scientists have been interested in the genetic variation of these traits among populations. Physical anthropologists have been particularly active in this field. In addition to new blood groups, new types of hemoglobin are discovered almost monthly. Although most of these are rare, some appear in elevated frequencies among some populations. Many of these discoveries have no consequences for such medical practices as blood transfusions; still, new sources of incompatibility are frequently found, particularly among patients who require whole blood. The continual gathering of information on blood components increases our basic knowledge about human evolution and provides potentially useful information about immunochemistry (the body's chemical defense system against foreign proteins) that may have applications in the study of virus diseases and cancer.

Blood-group analysis also occasionally finds its way into the courtroom. While a person's blood group can never be used to prove parenthood, it can be used to disprove it. If, for example, an offspring is type O (genotype OO) and a man is AB, AA, or BB, there is no chance that the man could be the father. On the other hand, a heterozygote with the phenotype A or B (genotypes AO and BO) could produce an O child with an A, B, or O mother. Obviously, an A or B male could produce an A or B child, and an AB child would be the result if one parent donates A and the other B. Paternity cases therefore often use blood-group analysis as one basis of argument about alleged fatherhood.

In addition, blood-group membership can be used in court in attempts to establish the innocence or guilt of individuals suspected of leaving traces of their own blood at the scene of a crime.

Physical anthropology has made other contributions to the law. For example, techniques used for identifying the sex, age, and population classification of a skeleton have been applied to the investigation of crimes.

Sports

Studies of exertion and stress, nutrition and energy all contribute to our knowledge of physical abilities and the means for improving them. Many sports have become dependent on scientific research, as the limits of physical endurance are stretched and extended. Physical anthropologists could have a direct role to play in the development of successful training programs for competitive sports. For instance, training programs for athletes could be improved through research and application. Factors to be considered would include proper types of exercise and appropriate schedules, proper diet, and the use of special machines for strengthening the body. Anthropologists could also participate effectively in both preparation for competition and finding the most efficient means of expending energy during an actual sports event.

The Ethics of Basic and Applied Physical Anthropology

Whatever its practical applications, physical

anthropology, like other basic sciences, flourishes in an atmosphere of open inquiry. When too much emphasis is placed on immediate practical results, research may flounder. Since we never can know when and how major discoveries will be made or what applications abstract knowledge may bring us, open science is really the best method for the achievement of eventual practical success.

On the other hand, like all scientists, physical anthropologists must act responsibly. While information should be freely shared, half-proven or suspect hypotheses should not be publicized until adequate data are available. Any scientific discovery has potential uses in the world of ideas and practice. Tentative notions that are subject to misuse (in, for example, such areas as "race" and IQ) should not be prematurely published, and the misuse of correct data should be monitored by scientists themselves so that the public can be warned. The claim that science is value-free does not extend to the use made by both scientists and the public of the results of scientific work. It is not correct to say that what is done with a discovery is of no concern to the discoverer. This was the original mistake committed by Frankenstein in Mary Shelley's novel. Responsibility and ethics demand that the children of science remain the recognized offspring of their parents.

Summary

Physical anthropology has a wide range of practical applications. In this chapter I have tied these applications to a branch of cultural anthropology known as medical anthropology because both fields share a concern with health and disease.

One common area of applied physical and medical anthropology concerns health and disease in different populations living in different cultural and ecological, or environmental, conditions. Both fields study disease rates and attempt to relate them to such conditions as work load, nutrition, stress, genetics, and the local environment. Both fields also study diseases of unknown origin in an attempt to pinpoint their causes. This research can have wide-ranging significance beyond an individual discovery. Thus, the analysis that led to an understanding of Kuru, a disease limited to a single population in the New Guinea highlands, opened up a new field of slow virus research. This research suggests that diseases once thought to be genetic may be due to slow viruses.

Physical anthropology has uncovered the complex relationships between the genetic disease known as sickle-cell anemia and the cultural conditions that led to its increase in certain West African populations. Medical anthropologists are now studying the context of this disease in Americans of African origin in order to understand the conditions under which individuals suffer attacks. These studies may lead to new kinds of treatment.

Cooperating, physical and cultural anthropologists combine biological and cultural data as they research such fields as population genetics. Their professional awareness that genealogical relationships involving social factors as marriage, exogamy, and endogamy may not completely reflect biological reality helps them avoid traps that might otherwise confuse culturally naive biologists working alone.

Applied physical and medical anthropologists are concerned with the role of nutrition in the well-being of the world's populations. Nutritional requirements are not well standardized for different biological and cultural groups. This is a problem of some importance, since it is known that nutrition affects both mental and physical performance in a variety of ways, including fertility. The well-being of particular populations, even beyond questions of health and disease, is affected by the degree of physical and psychological stress present. Stress factors may be both environmental (altitude, temperature, humidity, for example) or cultural (degree of crowding, type of work, ratio of leisure to work, food intake, and a series of social factors that affect the quality of social interaction).

Problems associated with health and disease will never be eliminated, although changing cultural patterns affect the kind and frequency of disease present in a population at any given time. Research that links changing disease patterns to historical factors is an important aspect of medical and applied physical anthropology.

Applied physical anthropology has a role to play in nonmedical fields as well. Judgments about the genetic identity, age, and sex of skeletal material is often made by physical anthropologists who can serve as expert witnesses in legal cases. In addition, the analysis of such genetic markers as blood-group membership is used in legal cases attempting to establish the innocence or guilt of individuals who are suspected of leaving traces of their own blood at the scene of a crime. Blood typing can also be used in establishing paternity, although newer methods have been recently developed. Contributions to industry are possible through long-range studies of trends in size and body type for specific populations. These allow manufacturers to make predictions about size distributions in clothes and furniture. Even the field of sports has something to gain from applied work in physical anthropology, although little has been done in this area so far. Training programs for athletes including such factors as proper exercise types and schedules, diet, and the use of special machines for strengthening the body can all be improved through research and application. Physical anthropologists can use their expertise to develop programs in a wide range of competitive sports.

Bibliography and Suggested Readings

Alland, A., Jr. 1970 — *Adaptation in Cultural Evolution: An Approach to Medical Anthropology.* New York: Columbia University Press. An ecological and evolutionary look at health, hygiene, and disease in human cultures.

Baker, P. T. editor 1979 — *The Biology of High Altitude Peoples.* Cambridge: Cambridge University Press. Articles on adaptation to high altitudes.

Baker, P. T. and J. S. Weiner 1966 — *The Biology of Human Adaptability.* Oxford: Clarendon Press. A series of articles discussing research needs and results in such fields as stress biology, growth, population genetics, and work. There is a wide coverage of geographic areas.

Buettner-Janusch, J. 1959 — Natural Selection in Man: The ABO (H) Blood Group System. *American Anthropologist.* 61:437–56. Blood groups and disease.

Cravioto, J., E. R. Delicardie, and H. G. Birch 1966 — Nutrition, Growth, and Neuro-Integrative Development: an Experimental Ecological Study. *Pediatrics.* 38: no. 2 part II: 319–72. An examination of the effects of malnutrition on intelligence.

Foster, G. M. and B. G. Anderson 1978 — *Medical Anthropology.* New York: John Wiley and Sons. An introduction to the field of medical anthropology for anthropologists and health professionals.

Williams, G. R., A. Fischer, J. L. Fischer, and L. T. Kurland 1964 — An Evaluation of the Kuru Hypothesis. *Journal génétique humaine.* 13:11–21. A cultural hypothesis concerning the origin and spread of the disease Kuru among the Foré of New Guinea.

CHAPTER 9

DIGGING TO KNOW AND UNDERSTAND THE PAST

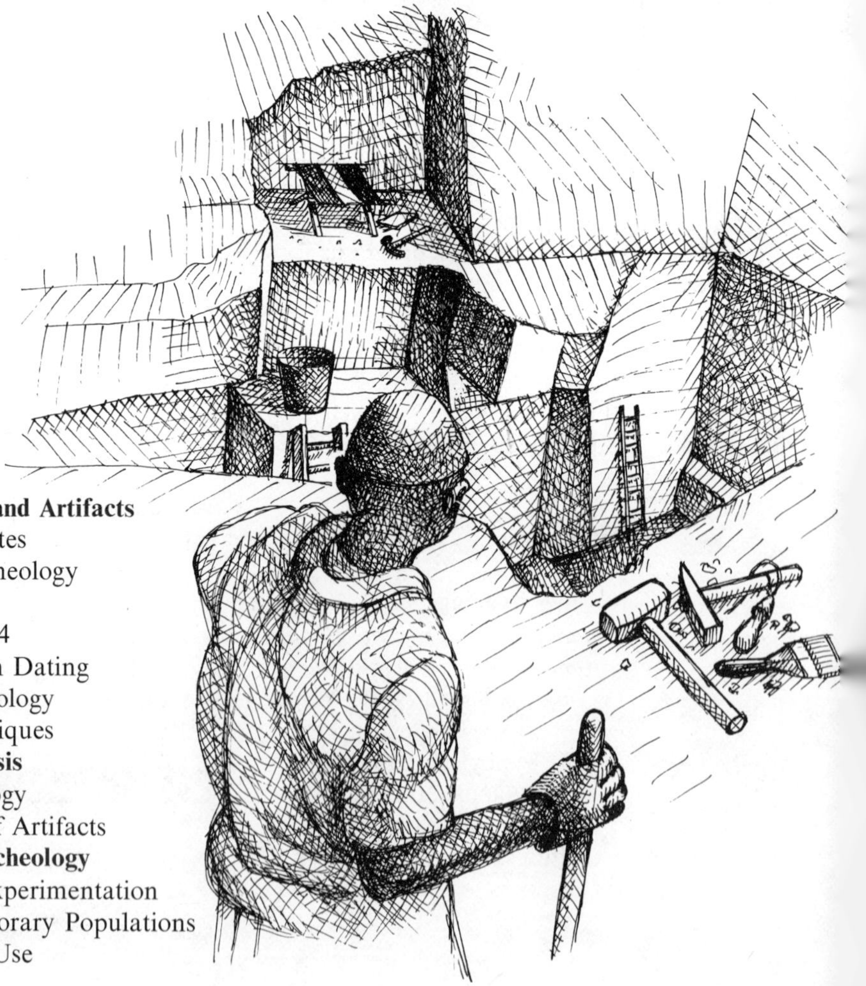

Archeologists are anthropologists (and art historians) who work with the remains of past cultures. Although archeology has a set of special techniques, the theoretical approach is within the mainstream of anthropology. Archeologists contribute to, and borrow from, current ideas and theories within the wider discipline. Their work increases not only our understanding of the past but also our knowledge of the structure and dynamics of culture.

Ever since our first ancestors emerged as culture-bearing animals, the earth has been marked with permanent traces of their and our life patterns. The materials and inferences drawn from these traces as well as their distribution in space and time constitute the subject matter of archeology.

ARCHEOLOGICAL SITES AND ARTIFACTS

Archeologists dig and analyze **sites** (the places where cultural and other remains of human activity are found). A site may contain the remnants of habitations, religious structures, burials, storage facilities, garbage pits, and places for the manufacture of cultural materials. Things made and/or used by the occupants of sites are called **artifacts.** The found objects and remains may be of bone, stone, wood, metal, clay, fiber and other plant materials, and leather. What is preserved in a site and what is lost depend on climatic conditions that have affected the site and its materials over time, the intrinsic durability of the materials (stone and fired clay are highly durable, whereas fiber, leather, wood, and even metal may decay rapidly in all but the driest places), and the treatment they received by their makers or users.

Finding Sites

Jacques Barrau, a French botanist and ecologist, once decided to dig a site in southern France near Mount Ventoux in Provence. His major goal was to test ideas about environmental adaptation among prehistoric people. Although not himself an archeologist, his familiarity with both ecology and cultural anthropology plus training in archeological techniques qualified him for this work. All he needed was a site. Barrau knew the area well. He had studied its past and current climate, the lay of the land, the direction and location of water courses, and the local flora and fauna. As he walked near the contemporary village of Brantes, he asked himself where a band of hunters and gatherers might camp. The criteria he chose included water courses, natural protec-

An archeological crew working at Chan Chan in Peru. Note the mapping and systematic way the site is being dug.

tion, wind direction, and distance from possible hunting grounds. After a short survey he decided to dig in a spot just below the village (see Figure 9.1). The first test pit he dug yielded artifacts dating from about 4000 BC, or, as archeologists usually put it, 6000 BP (before the present).

Barrau's discovery and others like it demonstrate that archeological sites are not randomly distributed over the landscape. People do not decide to live just anywhere. Today with mass transit, automobiles, water and power lines, and relative peace, new cities and towns can be constructed in practically any location, but in former times defense, access to water and natural resources, as well as access to trade routes were all important criteria for deciding where to build a village or even set up a temporary camp. Archeological sites are usually found through systematic research that takes these factors into account.

During the hunting and gathering stage of technology the sites of human settlement were dictated by the presence of water and game animals. Some sites can be found in rock overhangs (rock shelters) and caves, but open sites exist as well. Hunting and gathering peoples were—and still are—closely dependent on the climate, which affects both vegetation and animal life. During and between the ice ages, human populations moved along with changing vegetation patterns. When, for example, central Europe was cold, the landscape was dominated by **tundra** vegetation—lichens, mosses, and some grasses. Reindeer and other animals that

Members of Jacques Barrau's crew digging in Provence.

occur in large herds abounded. Because herd animals are easy to hunt and yield large kills, many human settlements were relatively permanent. When the ice retreated northward, the tundra gave way to **boreal** (northern) forests. The reindeer lost their food resources and moved out, to be replaced by deer, wild cows, and other solitary *ungulates* (hoofed mammals) as well as other mammals. Large fauna still occurred but in smaller numbers and, more importantly, as solitary animals rather than in herds. Hunting became harder and human settlements thinned out, becoming less stable. With further climatic changes human populations shifted to the coasts, where shellfish and other easily gathered forms of marine life were abundant. For these and other reasons archeologists must understand climatic variation when searching for sites relating to a particular age and technology.

Deduction is not the only means by which archeologists find sites and decide where to dig. They often survey an area on the ground, from the air, and sometimes from both perspectives. Such surveys provide useful data on site distribution and therefore **settlement patterns.** Surveying has become standard in archeological work, but in many cases only sample sites from a survey will actually be dug.

Sometimes artifacts accidentally turn up and are reported to a local university or museum. Cave explorers often find the remains of human habitation when they investigate a previously unexplored cavern. In 1948 in southern France, two Boy Scouts followed their dog down a hole in the ground. It opened into a cave that had

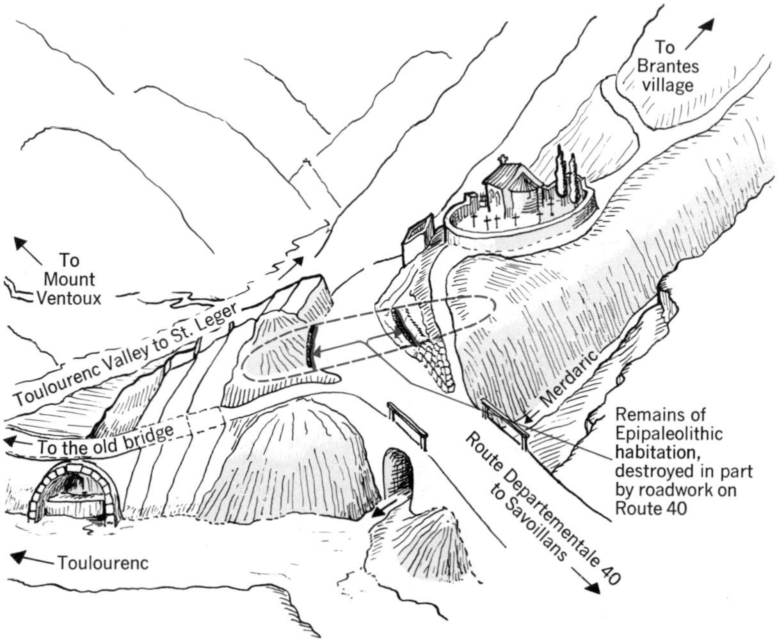

Figure 9.1
Map of Jacques Barrau's site in Provence showing surrounding geographic features. (From original drawing by Jacques Barrau.)

A prehistoric rock shelter at La Colombière in France. Sites of this type provided shelter for Paleolithic hunters.

gone unnoticed for several thousand years! This particular cave, Lascaux, was later found to be decorated with the best preserved, and perhaps the most beautiful, cave paintings in all of Europe.

Farmers plowing their fields may come upon archeological material. In cities the digging of foundations or the construction of subways may lead to important discoveries. Finds are particularly likely in such ancient cities as Rome, Athens, and Mexico City, but archeological remains have also turned up in New York. When the World Trade Center was under construction the remains of a sunken European sailing vessel turned up in the excavation. Manhattan Island was inhabited long before European colonization and remains of these habitations are still found occasionally.

Although the majority of sites are found by the systematic work of archeologists, the public should know that accidental discoveries can be very important. These, however, should always be reported to professionals. A site is much more than the artifacts found within it. Archeologists are careful to document the spatial and temporal distribution of findings at a site as well as their relative and absolute frequency. These data are just as important as the artifacts themselves, for they are key facts in archeological analysis.

Space and Archeology

Every site, of course, occupies a finite space. In addition, different sites may be related to one

An assistant maps a hunting and gathering site. Although this is a camp site of living people, an anthropologist uses the same map and survey techniques employed by archeologists. This material can be used by archeologists to compare prehistoric and modern sites of this type.

An urban archeological site. Excavating an Aztec pyramid in the heart of Mexico City.

another through cultural similarity. The geographical distribution of such sites provides vital information. Archeological surveys are often undertaken to determine the distribution of sites in a particular region. In many cases only some of these will actually be dug. Since sites bear cultural remains, their distribution documents the geographic distribution of cultures. When a site is dug, the dimension of time is added to the dimension of space. It is, therefore, crucial for the archeologist to keep a detailed three-dimensional map of a site as it is dug. This map will locate the **features** (major characteristics of the site such as houses, graves, and other structures), artifacts, and such remains as animal and plant materials.

All site maps are oriented from a particular reference point. This may be a surveyor's pin or a particular permanent feature of the site. The map itself is marked with a set of squares, a grid, that corresponds to grids laid out on the site. The archeologist may decide to dig every square or take a sample of squares from the grid pattern. The decision depends on the type of site to be dug as well as finances and time available.

Since digging introduces the dimension of depth, archeologists must decide how to document their downward movement through successive layers. The definition of layers may be arbitrary (often three to six inches each), but it may also be matched to the natural **stratigraphy** (the study of natural geological deposits). These features may include clear-cut differences in soil type or artifact style. The key thing about the layers is consistency. Once a measure has been

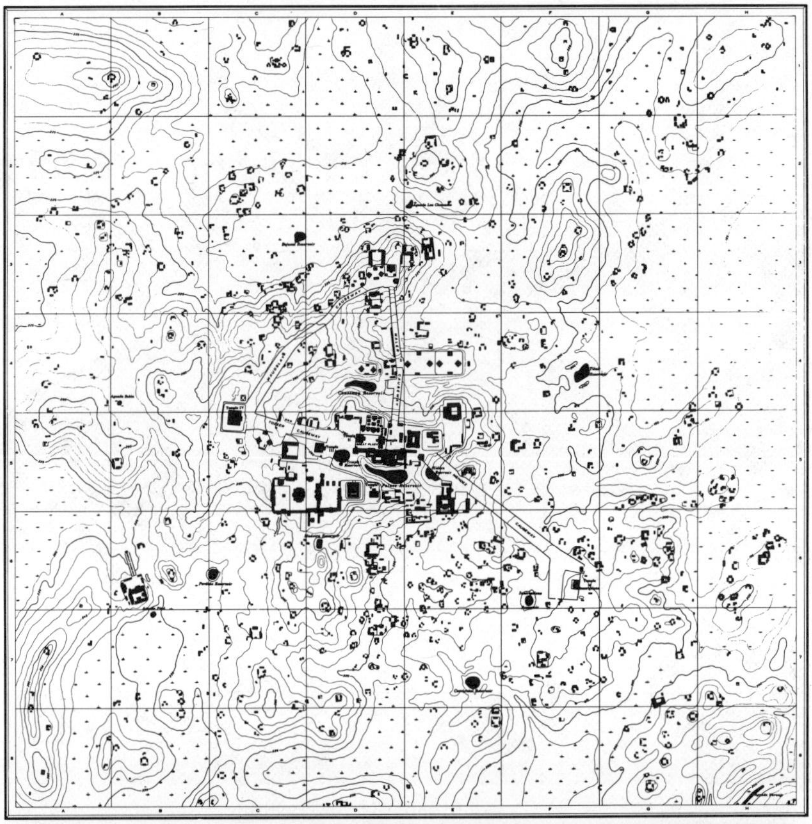

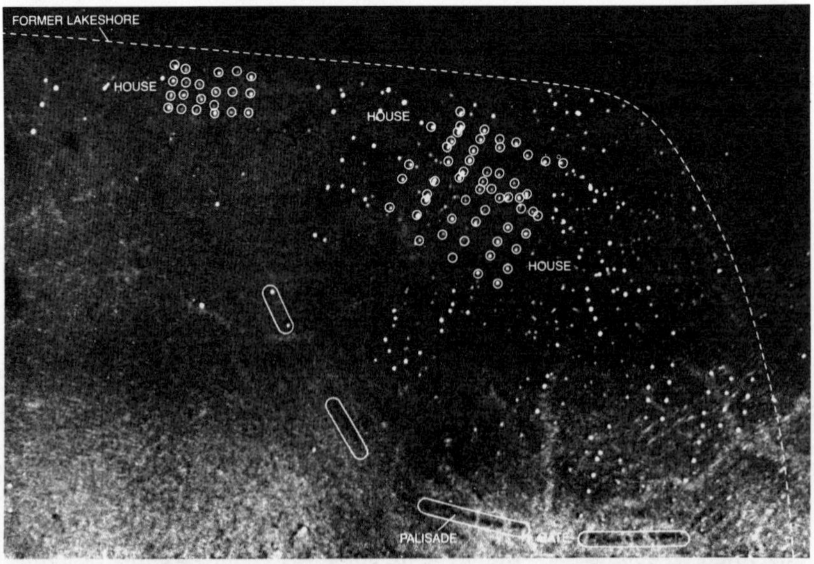

Site maps of complex and simple sites. Top: map of Tikal, a Maya site in Yucatan. Bottom: a relatively simple village site in Lake Palandru in France. The village has been drowned in a lake but can be seen and mapped from the air. (Top, University Museum, University of Pennsylvania. Bottom, from "Lake-Bottom Archaeology" by Aimé Bocquet. Copyright © February 1979 by Scientific American Inc. All rights reserved.)

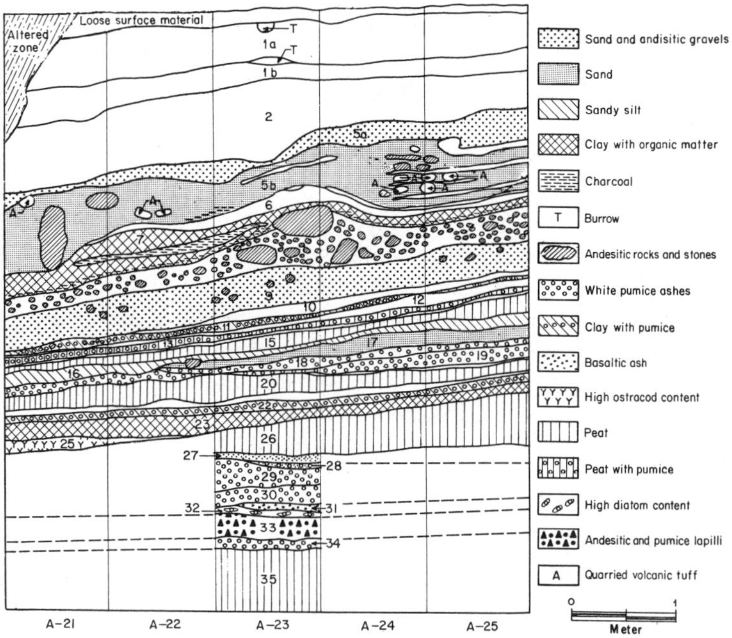

(Left) A stratigraphic marker at Chan Chan, Peru. (Right) Stratigraphic map of the site of Zohapilco in Mexico. The numbers refer to natural strata and excavation units. (Right, from "Early Sedentary Economy in the Basin of Mexico," Christine Niederberger, *Science,* Vol. 203, p. 134, Fig. 3, 12 January. Copyright 1979 by the American Association for the Advancement of Science.)

chosen, it is used throughout the dig. Every layer is labeled and artifacts found within them are cataloged separately. By using a surface grid and numbered layers, the archeologist can prepare a three-dimensional catalog of the site and the artifacts found within it. For example, if an artifact is found in square B-3 on the map in layer six, it will be bagged and labeled with that information. The location of important features, artifacts, and other site material will also be drawn onto the map to show their location *in situ* (in place).

DATING

Time is as much a concern as space to the archeologist. Sites are carefully mapped and their location in a region is recorded as well. Then once a site is dug, the artifacts and other material must be dated in order to analyze the prehistory of an area. A spatial-temporal picture of a culture or a series of cultures can be built up in this way, showing the rise, spread, and decline of particular traditions. Several methods for dating exist. These are divided into two types: **relative dating** (relative chronologies) and **absolute dating** (absolute chronologies). In many cases these two types of dating blend. An absolute date for one layer of a site may be used to anchor the chronology for the other layers in that site or other sites.

In general, relative dating is based on the sequential formation of sediments. When a site is undisturbed, the oldest material lies at the lowest levels, the newest at the top. Although archeologists cannot tell from these layers how old each one is, they can construct a relative sequence. Relative dating can be based on either real sedimentary layers and differences between associated artifacts or on arbitrary levels established by the archeologist. In many cases materials from sedimentary layers can be integrated with similar materials from sites with arbitrary layers.

Carbon-14

Several techniques for the establishment of absolute chronologies exist. Perhaps the most common is radiocarbon or **C^{14} dating.** Natural carbon occurs in three isotopic forms (C^{12}, C^{13}, C^{14}). One of these, C^{14}, is unstable and therefore radioactive. It decays through time, emitting radiation, and becomes C^{12}. Carbon-14 decays at a known rate, which is measured in half-lives (the amount of time it takes for half the amount of C^{14} present in a sample to decay to C^{12}; the figure for carbon-14 is 5568 years). Knowing this rate of decay is useful because all life forms contain carbon. During its life an organism absorbs both C^{14} and C^{12}. When it dies, the absorption of carbon ceases, and the C^{14} begins to decay into C^{12}. Since the rate is constant, it is possible to measure the ratio of the two isotopes of carbon in a sample of material to determine when the source of the material died and ceased to absorb carbon. Any organic material will do, and archeologists often use small amounts of wood or bone found in sites. Recently, a technique has been developed for dating iron by means of C^{14}. All iron contains small amounts of organic carbon with which it combines during smelting. This carbon can be retrieved and subjected to an analysis similar to that used on bone and wood.

Radiocarbon dating is quite accurate but not completely so. When a radiocarbon date is out of line with expectations, you must not assume that a great new discovery has been made. Absorption rates of C^{14} are not totally constant. Recently techniques have been developed to account for some of the inconsistencies.

Potassium-Argon Dating

Potassium-argon dating is useful for materials older than those that can be dated by C^{14}, which is good for only about 30,000 years BP. Potassium-argon dating pushes chronological techniques back into the millions of years. It has been successfully employed on the Australopithecine fossils and other old hominid materials from East Africa. With this technique archeologists analyze the surrounding rock rather than a fossil or an artifact itself unless, of course, the artifact is made of stone. They must, therefore, be certain that the rock to be dated is correctly associated with a specimen. Like C^{14} dating, the potassium-argon method is possible because of radioactive decay, in this case an isotope of potassium that decays to argon.

Dendrochronology

Dendrochronology, or tree-ring dating, is the most accurate technique available, but it is useful only in a very few areas of the world. During

A radiocarbon-dating laboratory.

growth a tree produces a series of concentric rings as the trunk diameter increases with age. One can tell the age of a tree at cutting by counting the rings, but care must be taken to determine whether or not a particular species forms one or two rings a year. Some species of tree are highly sensitive to temperature and moisture during the growing season, and each year's new rings reflects the seasonal conditions. In warm, wet years there is extensive growth and the rings are wide. In cold, dry years there is little growth and the rings are narrow. Through the fluctuations from year to year a tree develops a "fingerprint" of growth. An archeologist can take advantage of this pattern to date wood taken from a site. An absolute chronology can be established with overlapping ring records (see Figure 9.2). Starting with living trees of known age, the archeologist can work backwards with older wood samples that overlap each other. The overlap is used to relate the date and growth of one sample with another. Of course, it is necessary to use wood from trees that grew under the same climatic conditions in the same geographic area.

Tree-ring dating has been particularly useful in the southwestern United States, where trees of tremendous antiquity can be found. The bristlecone pine that grows in the mountains of California can live up to 5000 years. In fact, tree rings from this species have been used to correct dating for C^{14}.

Tree-ring dating in an archeological site requires substantially thick specimens. These are most likely to come from wood used in house construction. In southwestern Pueblos, wood served as roof beams, so tree-ring analysis has been possible. Unlike radiocarbon dating, tree-ring dating is accurate to the season of the year in which the tree was cut down. Unfortunately for archeologists, roof beams were valuable material and they were apparently often salvaged from old buildings and used in new constructions. The result is some ambiguity in the use of this dating technique.

Varve analysis is an absolute dating technique similar to tree-ring dating. Varves are pairs of differing sedimentary layers that form in repeated alternations reflecting a seasonal cycle. The layers differ in chemical composition, grain

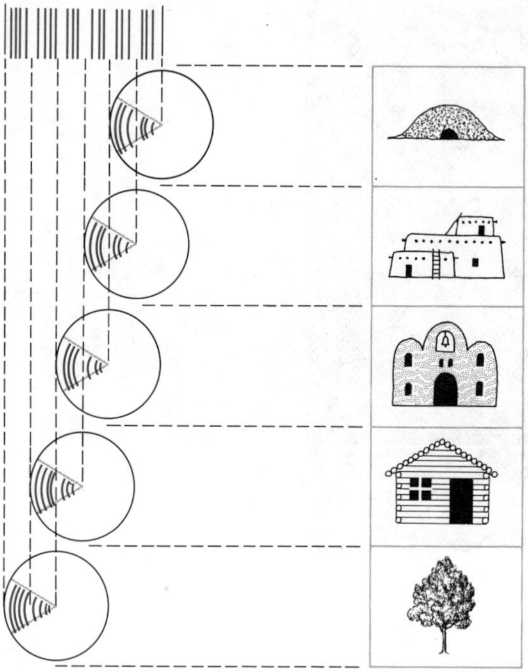

Figure 9.2
Tree-ring dating (dendrochronology). The rings from a contemporary tree are matched against the rings of successively older trees found in archeological sites. (Adapted from J. Deetz, *Invitation to Archeology*. New York: Natural History Press, 1967.)

size, or color according to seasonal variations. For example, a lake in a glacial region may have a heavy layer of pale-colored heavy silt during the warm season and a thin layer of fine clay during the winter. Varve dating is useful in the analysis of cultural materials found in association with lake dwellings and has been extensively used in Europe.

Newer Techniques

Archeologists are constantly on the lookout for new methods of absolute dating. Working in cooperation with chemists and physicists, archeologists have recently added a series of new techniques to their dating arsenal.

Obsidian hydration.

Obsidian, volcanic glass, when available, is a favorite material for the manufacture of artifacts by members of those cultures that depend on stone for many of their tools. It is hard, can be worked rather easily, and when struck with the proper technique produces a razor-sharp edge. Obsidian mined in a particular geographic area absorbs moisture at a constant rate. The rate of absorption (hydration) varies with climate, soil chemistry, and solar radiation. Hydration produces the laying down of a layer, or patina, on the surface of the obsidian. By measuring the thickness of this layer, an archeologist can determine the date at which an artifact was made. **Obsidian hydration dating** must, of course, be corrected for each geographical zone.

Archeomagnetism.

Over the course of centuries the earth's magnetic field changes. The locations of the magnetic poles vary and even reverse over time. These shifts have been studied and dated by geologists. The wandering of the poles can be traced in such human-made artifacts and structures as pottery, fired-brick house walls, kilns, and hearths. What these have in common is their clay content and the fact that, when clay is heated, ferric (iron) particles within it align themselves with the contemporary magnetic field. When the clay cools the iron retains the magnetic-field orientation. If the position and orientation during firing can be determined, the clay can be dated using **archeomagnetism** by comparing it with magnetic orientation data provided by geological research.

SITE ANALYSIS

The material, consisting of artifacts and other remains, found in a site is known as an **assemblage.** In order to understand an assemblage an archeologist must analyze it from many perspectives. For example: What is the range (diversity) of the remains found in a particular site and how does this range compare with the ranges in other sites? In what frequency do different materials occur? What are the stylistic features of artifacts? Where do artifacts and other materials occur in the site? What changes in distribution occur through time—for instance, when (in what layer) does pottery first appear? What animal and plant species are found in the site? Are they the remains of wild or domestic species?

Climatic data may also come from the identification of animal matter. Certain marine species, for example, from both fresh and salt water, live within precise temperature limits.

For floral and faunal analysis archeologists usually turn to experts in those fields; they also seek the aid of chemists and geologists. Chemistry can provide clues to the techniques used in the manufacture of metal and clay artifacts as well as the characteristics of stone used in making tools and other objects. Geologists provide data on climate and other features of the site at the time of its occupation.

Palynology

Climatic analysis of a site may be provided by the examination of microscopic pollen grains, which are highly resistant to decay. Each plant from a pollen-bearing species leaves characteristic grains. The collection and examination of pollen from a site (a technique known as **palynology**) provides a means for determining what plants grew there as well as the relative frequency of different species. The most common species will in general have left the most pollen and the least common will have left only small amounts of pollen. Of course, the amount of pollen produced by different plants also varies, but since this is a known factor it can be corrected for during the process of analysis. Since plant species are highly dependent on such climatic factors as temperature and rainfall, their remains can provide a good indication of the climate during the time a site was occupied. The archeologist can also obtain a picture of climatic change by taking a pollen sample in the form of a core drilled into the site from the surface. This core can be compared with the stratigraphy of the site, and different cultural layers can be correlated with changes in climate. Since pollen is a light material, it may be blown into an area from far away. Thus, sites may be contaminated to a significant degree by plant

An archeologist sorting pollen samples for palynological analysis.

material that actually grew in a climate different from that of the site. This possibility must be taken into account during palynological analysis. The safest method is to use different techniques to establish climatic data. Tree rings, as we have seen, are also good indicators.

Classification of Artifacts

In order to make sense of their finds, archeologists must systematically classify artifacts. To do this, they establish typologies, that is, they group artifacts with the same attributes into types. Tools of various styles or pots of various manufacture and form, for example, can be grouped into types. Typing can be based on such factors as assumed use, overall style, and decoration. We can type pots and pans in contemporary kitchens, for example, by their use (frying pans versus casseroles versus stew pots), by the materials out of which they were manufactured (glass, stainless steel, ceramics), or by their decoration.

The establishment of typologies is sometimes difficult. The archeologist must always consider many different features of the objects to be classified. Sometimes, for example, what are at first invisible features must be used along with such obvious features as decoration. The temper (material such as sand grains, bits of broken pottery, shells, and other forms of grit used to reduce shrinkage and strengthen pottery) may differ from site to site or from time period to time period, even when the decorative style remains the same. The archeologist must decide whether this difference is important enough to separate pottery fragments with different tempers into different types. As you can see, this is a matter of scientific judgment.

The orderly assessment of types within sites and their occurrence in different sites allow the archeologist to reconstruct the distribution and development of a culture or cultures in an area. The spatial and temporal limits of certain artifact types signal the geographic and temporal limits of a culture.

EXPERIMENTAL ARCHEOLOGY

Edward B. Tylor (1832–1917), a great English anthropologist, was curator of ethnology at Oxford University. The major task of a curator is to collect, preserve, and classify materials. Tylor was not satisfied with these tasks alone. He wanted to know how items of material culture in his collection were used by their makers. In order to find out, he made copies of artifacts in the museum's collection and put them to use. From this experimentation Tylor was able to make inferences about the actual employment of artifacts in the daily life of the peoples who had manufactured them.

A similar technique has been developed in modern archeology. The archeologist interested in the uses to which a particular tool was put will produce exact copies and use them on different materials: wood, stone, bone, or hide, for example. The archeologist will chip, chop, scrape, or dig with the tool until it displays wear. The artifact will then be examined microscopically and the wear marks carefully studied. These will be compared with the wear marks on the original tool in order to make inferences about its use. Tools may also be copied and used to test their efficiency for different tasks. Louis B. Leakey, for example, copied Oldowan tools found in his East African sites to see how efficiently they could be used to cut through hides and to butcher meat.

Historical Sites and Experimentation

James Deetz is currently engaged in what is known as historical archeology. He digs at Plymouth Plantation in New England, where he studies and reconstructs the daily life of some of America's first settlers. From historical data, including written records, accurate dates and sequences can be established for much of the material. As a result Deetz can test hypotheses concerning archeological theory and method in general. For example, his analysis of motifs on gravestones in the New England area (see Figure 9.3) has allowed him to test a method used in relative dating known as **seriation.** Seriation is based on the notion that new styles become popular only gradually, remain popular for a certain period, and are then gradually replaced by even newer forms. The relative frequency of various motifs used on artifacts from different sites can be arranged on a curve showing the least popular (fewest occurring) and most popular (most occurring) styles. When curves from different sites are compared, those that are similar are assumed to be closest in time. Since the relative absence of a particular style indicates *either* its beginning *or* the end of its popularity, popularity curves alone cannot be used to decide which end of the curve represents the oldest or youngest material. This can be decided, however, with some success by making hypotheses about the logical development of styles themselves. In many, if not all cases, a set of styles can be arranged in order of complexity on the assumption that the simplest forms precede more elaborate forms.

At Plymouth and in its surrounding areas Deetz tested both seriation and hypotheses about style succession by comparing the frequencies of motifs on gravestones with known dates. He arranged style sequences in a logical order that he believed reflected relative age as well and then checked these against real dates. There was a high correlation between his assumed sequences and the historical records.

The work at Plymouth has also led to an accurate restoration. The Plymouth Plantation is an active museum containing restored build-

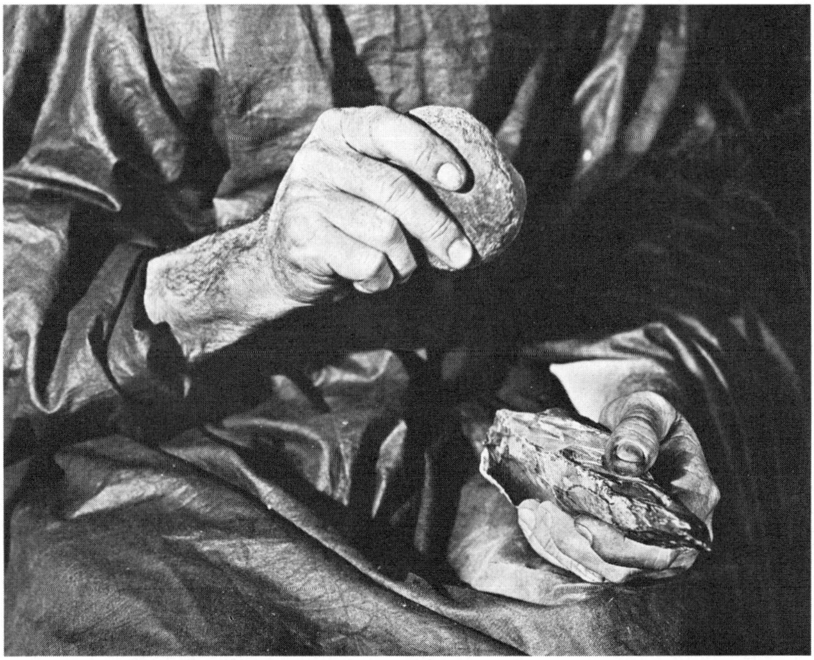

An archeologist making a stone tool. Such tools may be used on a variety of materials and the wear patterns compared to actual artifacts. In this way archeologists can determine how prehistoric tools were used.

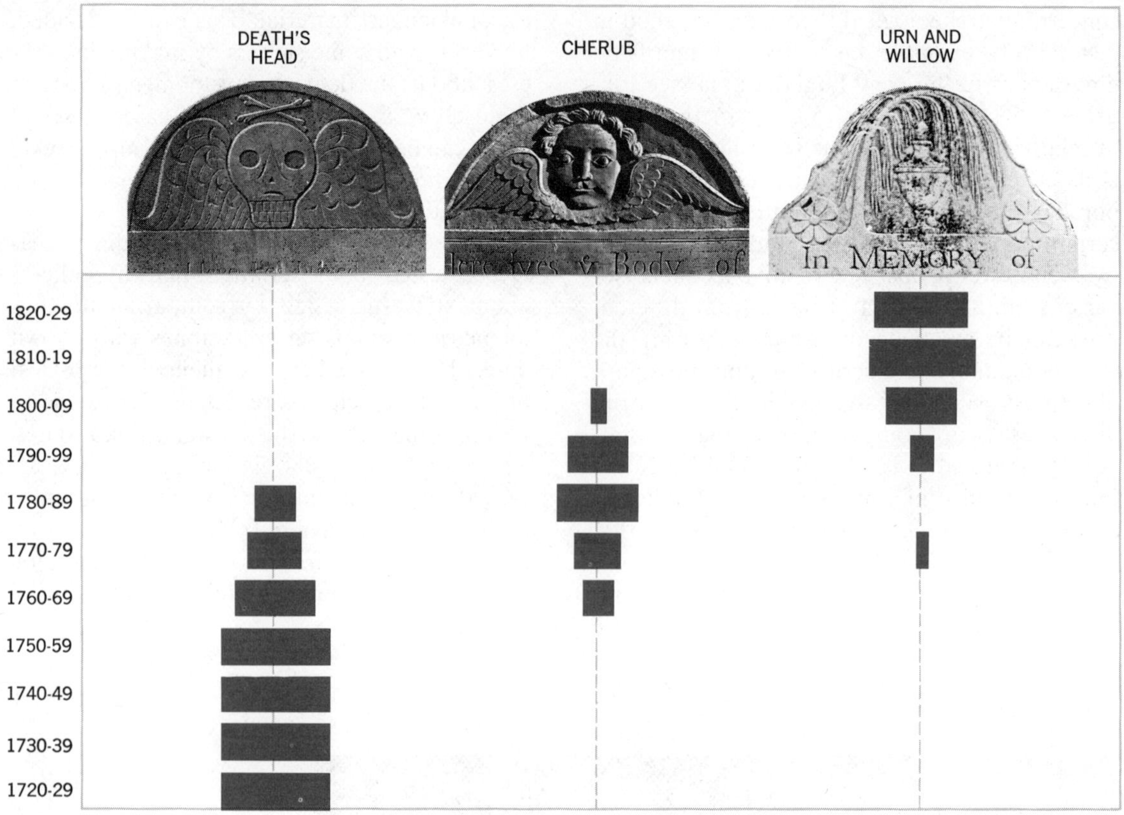

Figure 9.3
An example of seriation using artifacts with known dates. Tombstones from a New England cemetery provide excellent curves through time. (Adapted from J. Deetz, *Invitation to Archeology.* New York: Natural History Press, 1967.)

ings and their artifacts. Museum personnel dress in period costumes and are trained to demonstrate various aspects of daily life as they were lived at the time the Plantation was a functioning institution. These exhibits and activities bring to life an important aspect of Colonial America. The Plymouth Plantation has become an important educational and recreational center, visited every year by many thousands of interested people.

Archeology and Contemporary Populations
The archeologist's understanding of the life of past cultures is enriched by the analyses of contemporary peoples studied by cultural anthropologists. Many clues, ranging from how a tool was used to religious beliefs and practices, are provided by data collected from societies whose technological level and environmental setting are parallel to those of past cultures. For experimental purposes it is possible to study an active village in the present and then analyze it as if it were an archeological site. A researcher can note how dwellings and other structures are placed, where certain activities take place, where certain kinds of refuse accumulate, and so on.

Computer Use

By using computers archeologists can catalog certain environmental and cultural conditions that they believe are crucial to settlement in a particular area. Using these data the computer predicts where on a map certain kinds of sites should occur. These predictions can then be tested against actual archeological research. Another way to use computers is to feed them incomplete data on an area and ask where more materials crucial to particular hypotheses might be located. Since computers are essentially fast counters, they can be used to analyze the frequencies of multiple remains in the light of hypotheses on manufacture, settlement pattern, or use. They can also provide accurate estimates of stylistic distributions in time and space.

Archeologists use their data and their varied methodologies to reconstruct whole cultures, to place them in temporal (time-based) sequences, and to test hypotheses about cultural development. As new techniques emerge and as more data accumulate, archeologists from all over the world contribute to our understanding of prehistory and culture.

Summary

The branch of anthropology that deals with the remains of past cultures is archeology. Archeologists contribute to anthropological theory by creating and testing hypotheses about the structure and dynamics of culture. They also document the historical process in specific regions of the world through careful excavation

Plymouth Plantation, a restored site in New England. Such restorations provide educational and recreational facilities for a wide public.

and analysis of settlement patterns (the distribution of populations through space and time), sites (the places where cultural remains are found), artifacts (cultural remains), and other evidence of human habitation such as waste products and both animal and plant material.

Archeological research is not a haphazard process. Sites are found, dug, and analyzed with the latest scientific techniques, some of which are developed by archeologists and some of which are borrowed from chemistry, physics, and geology. Sites are mapped and a careful record is kept of the place and depth of every feature and artifact found. Sites vary in type. They may contain the remnants of habitations, religious structures, burials, storage facilities, garbage pits, places for the manufacture of cultural materials, places where game was killed and butchered, or a combination of any of these.

The objects found in sites vary by the materials, styles, and techniques used in their manufacture. Some material—such as bone, stone, and fired clay—is more likely to be preserved than artifacts made of plant fibers, animal skins, and wood. The techniques and styles of artifacts are useful in classifying them into types. Such types may be used as markers for specific cultures, the distribution of which can be traced in time and space. The material (artifacts and other remains) found in a site is known as an assemblage. The archeologist analyzes an assemblage for the range of diversity it contains as well as for its possible relationship to other assemblages. The assemblage reflects an aspect of cultural coherence that single artifacts cannot, because the assemblage provides some notion of the culture under investigation as a whole.

An extremely important aspect of archeology is dating. Temporal relationships within and among sites is crucial for the analysis of culture sequences and the dynamics of cultural development. Several kinds of dating techniques have been developed. Some of these result in relative chronologies (in which sequences can only be ordered from older to younger), while others can be used to produce absolute dates. When an absolute date is determined for a set of artifacts it can sometimes be used to anchor a relative dating sequence into an absolute sequence.

Relative dates are based on stratigraphic analysis. In undisturbed geological and cultural strata newer materials overlie older materials. This is why archeologists keep a careful record of the depths at which specific materials are found. Absolute dating involves several techniques. The most common are: potassium-argon for very old sites; C^{14} analysis for sites up to 30,000 years old; tree-ring analysis for sites of moderate age in which good samples of wood can be found and linked into tree-ring data from living specimens. Archeologists are always looking for new dating techniques in order to expand the range of artifacts that can be dated and the time depth of the dating process. Newer techniques use changes in the earth's magnetic field, the rate of chemical change in such materials as obsidian, and the carbon deposited in iron during the smelting process.

Archeologists, in their attempt to reconstruct as accurate and complete a picture of past cultures as possible, work in cooperation with experts from many fields. These experts help them analyze plant and animal material found in sites and to reconstruct climatic conditions prevailing at particular times during a site's occupation. The analysis of plants and climate are aided by a technique known as palynology. This involves the collection and identification of pollen collected by taking depth cores from a site. Different levels of the core can be correlated with cultural levels in the site. Each level will contain pollen from plants that grow under specific soil and climatic conditions. Palynological analysis must take into consideration the possibility of site contamination; therefore, different techniques of analysis are best combined to produce a consistent picture.

Experimental archeology is an important means of deriving evidence about the living style of past cultures and the use to which specific artifacts were put. Particular tools can be made by the archeologist out of the same materials found in sites. The process of making tools provides insights into the original techniques of manufacture. Such tools can also be used on a variety of materials and the wear marks on them can be compared to the wear marks on actual artifacts. This kind of analysis can provide the archeologist with information on how and on what materials tools were used.

The digging of historical sites with known dates provides archeologists with a means of testing new dating hypotheses. The technique known as seriation, for example, has been tested by James Deetz at the Plymouth Plantation, an historical site in New England. Seriation is based on the principle that new styles become popular only gradually, eventually reach a certain level of acceptance, and then become obsolete. The relative frequency of styles from several sites can be arranged on a curve illustrating the degree of their popularity in each location.

Our understanding of past cultures is increased by the study of living peoples. Information ranging from how a tool was used to religious beliefs and practices is collected from societies whose technological level and environments are parallel to those of past cultures investigated by archeologists.

The use of modern computers has allowed archeologists to count and organize vast arrays of data that would have been difficult to deal with in the past. Computer analysis can provide frequency analysis of many artifacts and other remains that can be used to make judgments about changing patterns of use, and accurate estimates of stylistic distributions in time and space.

The employment of archeologists in National Parks and public historical settings contributes to our national heritage. Reconstructed sites such as the Plymouth Plantation provide educational and recreational facilities for a wide public.

Bibliography

Binford, L. R. and S. R. Binford 1968 (editors) — *New Perspectives in Archeology.* Chicago: Aldine. A collection of articles discussing a range of the newer techniques, some of which are controversial, in archeological analysis.

Butzer, K. 1971 — *Environment and Archaeology.* (2nd edition) Chicago: Aldine. Good material on dating, particularly for the Pleistocene.

Fagan, B. M. 1978 — *Archeology: A Brief Introduction.* Boston: Little, Brown. An up-to-date and concise introduction to archeology, with good chapters on methods.

Michaels, J. W. 1973 — *Dating Methods in Archeology.* New York: Seminar Press. Full range of dating methods discussed.

CHAPTER 10
FROM HUNTING AND GATHERING TO DOMESTICATION

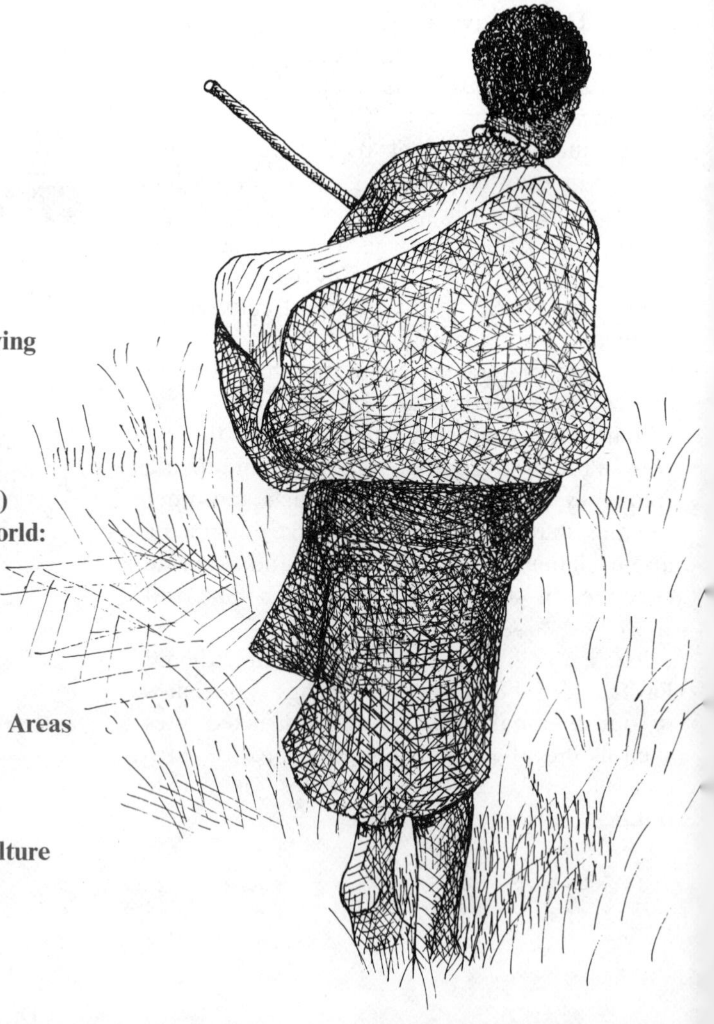

There is little doubt that the genus *Homo* evolved in Africa. Fossils and tools have been found in a series of sites from Ethiopia all the way down to South Africa. Although there is some controversy about which fossil types made the first tools, there is no longer any argument over the cultural status of these tools. They were manufactured and used by some form or forms of hominids.

Before I begin the discussion of tools and the rise of culture, one fact must be emphasized concerning the artifacts that remain for analysis. The earliest examples of culture that we have are stone tools. This does not mean that other materials were not used in the manufacture of tools and other artifacts, but merely that stone survives when other more perishable materials like bone, wood, and fiber tend to decay with the passage of time. It is probable that many early cultures employed tools and artifacts made of perishable materials, but these do not remain in the archeological record.

THE ORIGINS OF CULTURE: HUNTING AND GATHERING, THE DIVISION OF LABOR, SHARING, CARRYING

Using archeological data as well as data on primate behavior, the archeologist Glynn Isaac has attempted to reconstruct those environmental conditions and behavioral traits that gave rise to the hominid line:

The work of the archeologist in drawing inferences from such data is made possible by the fact that at a certain stage in evolution the ancestors of modern man became makers and users of equipment. Among other things, they shaped, used and discarded numerous stone tools. These virtually indestructible artifacts form a kind of fossil record of aspects of behavior, a record that is complementary to the anatomical record provided by the fossil bones of the tool makers themselves.

By comparing men and apes Isaac attempts to isolate those behaviors that set the human species apart from its primate relatives. The differences that he considers of greatest importance are the following:

1. *Homo sapiens* is bipedal. Human hands and arms are free to carry objects and food from place to place. Not so among the apes.
2. Humans communicate by means of language, which, as we have seen, allows us to exchange information about past and future

events. Language can also be used as a device to settle arguments and order social relations within the group. Isaac points out that, although apes communicate, they do not have language.

3. Food-getting among humans is cooperative. Group members work together, at least in part, in obtaining food, and more important, food-sharing is an aspect of human subsistence patterns. In some instances apes may share meat, but the sharing is passive rather than active. Several apes may feed on the same carcass, but they eat vegetable food individually on the spot.
4. Human social groups have a home base. Individuals can move independently away from this base in hunting and gathering activities and then return to it. The base is the focus of group social life. Apes have no such home base. Troop members maintain social coherence by moving together.
5. Humans devote more time than other primates to getting meat, a high-quality source of protein. Apes hunt and glean meat sporadically, but hunting is not a major feature of their subsistence behavior.
6. Unlike our ape cousins we prepare food in various ways. It is cut, ground, crushed, and sometimes cooked. Food is acquired and prepared by humans with the aid of various kinds of equipment. This equipment, even among the most technologically backward peoples, is much more complex than the simple tools manufactured on the spot and used sporadically by some apes. Isaac notes that the Tasmanians—a hunting and gathering group, exterminated in the nineteenth century, that was noted for a very simple technology—manufactured clubs, digging sticks, and spears of wood, made a variety of stone tools, and carried objects in such containers as baskets, trays, and bags. They also had fire.

Features of social organization also contribute to the human adaptation. Of major importance is the bond between a male and a female or females. This bond implies a great deal more than sexual union. Economic cooperation, a division of labor by sex, and joint childrearing are all aspects of long-term male-female bonding among humans. Beyond these immediate family groups, the development of kinship patterns implies the emergence of complex forms of social organization. Language and the ability to postpone food consumption, which facilitates sharing, contribute to the complex and lasting nature of human social groups.

Turning to the puzzle of ape-hominid divergence, Isaac suggests that a major feature of this divergence was the adaptive development of food-sharing. He then goes on to demonstrate how archeological evidence and inferences from this evidence can be used to build a case for the evolutionary emergence of the hominid line.

Since 1970 Isaac has been co-leader with Richard Leakey of a team of archeologists and paleontologists working at Koobi Fora on the northeast shore of Lake Turkana (formerly Lake Rudolf) in northern Kenya. They have used their data, combined with earlier material from Olduvai Gorge, to reconstruct technological and behavioral aspects of emerging cultures.

Three types of site have been dug and analyzed. Type A sites contain scattered sharp-edged broken stones produced by deliberate strong blows. Type B sites contain the same artifacts in association with the bones of a single large animal. Type C sites contain these artifacts in association with the remains of several different animal species. These sites, which date between 2.5 and 1.5 million BP, demonstrate that there was at least one kind of hominid in the area that "habitually carried objects such as stones from one place to another and made sharp-edged tools by deliberately fracturing the stones it carried with it." In one site Isaac and his collaborators found hippopotamus bones and stone tools:

Among the hippopotamus bones and in the adjacent stream bank we recovered 119 chipped stones; most of them were small sharp flakes that, when they are held between the thumb and the fingers, make effective cutting implements. We also recovered chunks of stone with scars showing that flakes had been struck from them by percussion. In Paleolithic tool classification these larger stones fall into the category of core tool or chopper. In addition our digging exposed a rounded river pebble that was battered at both ends; evidently it had been used as a hammer to strike flakes from the stone cores.

The provocative thing about these artifacts, besides their obvious cultural significance, is that they were found in sediments that naturally contain no stones larger than a pea. This suggests strongly that stone was carried there from somewhere else. Furthermore, the association between the bones and the batch of artifacts, including the hammer stone, implies that the tools were manufactured on the spot in order to butcher the animal, which may or may not have been killed by the tool makers themselves. Isaac believes that the low level of technology represented by the tools present in the site points to scavenging rather than hunting.

At a type C site known as KBS the researchers found a large number of artifacts and the bones of many species in an area 16 meters in diameter. Geological evidence showed that the site was located on the sandy bed of a stream that formed part of a small delta. This may have been a pleasant, shady spot for the gathering of early hunters. The accumulation of bones representing many species suggests that killed or scavenged animals were transported to KBS for butchering and possibly distribution. Sites at Olduvai tend to confirm the conclusions drawn from the KBS assemblage.

A type A site at Olduvai appears to have been a quarry. It contains chert, an excellent material for the manufacture of stone tools. Stone was mined and worked in these sites and probably carried out for use elsewhere.

Combining this evidence with observations of ape behavior and ethnographic evidence on contemporary hunting and gathering populations, Isaac has constructed a model of early hominid social and economic life. He points out that the transport of food is associated with the sexual division of labor. The result of such a division is an increase in the variety of food consumed by a group. Generally, it is the females of the group who gather vegetable food and the men who contribute the major portion of meat. In most contemporary groups of this type, the men and women engage in their special economic activities in sexually segregated units. Food gathered by each type of unit (hunter or gatherer) is then brought back to the home base and distributed. Isaac believes that the division of labor led to the development of food carrying. The division of labor itself appears to be connected to the bearing and carrying of offspring. Encumbered with children, women would be more efficient in gathering activities that require neither speed nor long treks away from the home base. The addition of meat to the diet may have been the kick that moved the group toward the division of labor, transportation of food, and foodsharing. None of this, however, could have developed without the invention of manufactured tools.

In terms of evolutionary dynamics the model suggests that a group whose members were able to exchange food and information would have a selective advantage over groups without that capacity. Food-sharing, then, and the behaviors associated with it, would have furthered the development of exchange relations that are the social glue of human groups. These relations call for the ability to judge a range of possible outcomes affecting future behavior. Thus, after food-sharing had become part of the human cultural vocabulary, the ability to plan must have provided a selection pressure for the evolution of intellect.

Isaac believes that his model also explains the development of human marriage arrangements. He speculates that since each member of the male-female couple tapped different resources, which were then shared by the social group, "a mating system that involved at least one male in 'family' food procurement on behalf of each child-rearing female in the group would have a clear selective advantage over, for example, the chimpanzees' pattern of opportunistic relations between the sexes."

THE PALEOLITHIC (OLD STONE AGE)

The earliest human cultures are associated with stone tools, not because other materials were unavailable (except smelted metal), but because stone artifacts are the most likely to survive the ravages of time.

Early cultures in the Old World are classified under three long periods of stone (*lithic*) technology: **Paleolithic** (Old Stone Age); **Mesolithic** (Middle Stone Age); and **Neolithic** (New Stone Age), which is also associated with the rise of plant and animal domestication.

The Lower Paleolithic

Now that we have examined a hypothesis that attempts to explain the dynamics of hominid evolution on the basis of archeological evidence and inferences from nonhuman primate and human populations, let us turn to a description of early tools and their development through time and space.

As we have seen, the first tools were very crude. In most cases they resemble naturally chipped rock and can be distinguished from it only with a trained eye. The earliest tools come from the Kenya shore of Lake Turkana and from Omo in Ethiopia. The Kenya finds have been dated to about 2.6 million BP and the Omo finds to about 3 million BP. This **Oldowan** tool tradition takes its name from Olduvai Gorge where the first specimens were found by Louis Leakey. Oldowan tools, also called **pebble choppers,** were made by a simple process known as **percussion flaking.** A rock, often a water-rounded pebble, was held in one hand and struck with another rock (hammer stone). These tools were also shaped by hitting them against a large anvil stone. In either case the tool maker modified the shape of the original rock in order to create an all-purpose tool with a working surface for chopping, scraping, and cutting.

Oldowan pebble tool.

Richard Leakey and his team digging at Koobi Fora, one of the earliest tool-bearing sites in the world.

To judge from the artifacts and animal bones found at Oldowan sites, the first tool-using hominids were collectors, scavengers, and hunters. Their tools were used to obtain and prepare food. Although Oldowan tools are very crude, Louis Leakey (who was an expert at making his own Oldowan artifacts) showed that they could be used efficiently to skin and butcher animals and prepare the meat obtained from them.

Recent finds at Hadar in Ethiopia dated tentatively to about 2.5 million BP call into question the status of the Oldowan tradition. The tools found at Hadar are more complex than Oldowan tools (some of them are worked on both sides and appear to be quite sophisticated). If the dates for Hadar are verified, we shall have to accept the existence of an advanced tool tradition existing at least contemporaneously with the users of Oldowan artifacts.

Further Developments. The evolution of stone tools (their progressive refinement and growing diversity) depended on the choice of stone, the development of knapping techniques (shaping by breaking off pieces with quick blows), the degree of retouching (secondary flaking to refine the shape), and the preparation of the stone from which tools were to be manufactured. The first tools consisted of stones that were only slightly retouched on one surface. When a tool was formed by removing flakes it is called a "core" tool. The "waste" flakes struck off these cores frequently had sharp cutting edges and could also be used as knives and scrapers. As manufacturing techniques improved through time, both core and flake tools were refined. Tool makers began to choose the kind of stone they would use. There is evidence that high-quality stones were sometimes transported far from their place of origin. Flint, chert, and obsidian came to be the preferred materials. These rocks yield extremely sharp edges and each, because of predictable fracture patterns, can be shaped to preconceived specifications. All that is needed is the proper technique. An increase in the control used to shape stone tools led to the manufacture of specialized instruments. Eventually tool kits included such objects as projectile points, knives, blades, scrapers, drills, chisels, and hole punchers.

By 500,000 BP the genus *Homo* was well established in the Old World. Fossils of *Homo erectus* have been found in China, Southeast Asia, Africa, and Europe. In Asia, where evidence for the use of fire and cooking is found for the first time, Oldowan-like choppers continued until late in the Paleolithic. In Africa and Europe, on the other hand, Oldowan tools gradually gave way to more carefully shaped forms. Characteristic of this new development (the **Chellean-Acheulian** tradition, named for

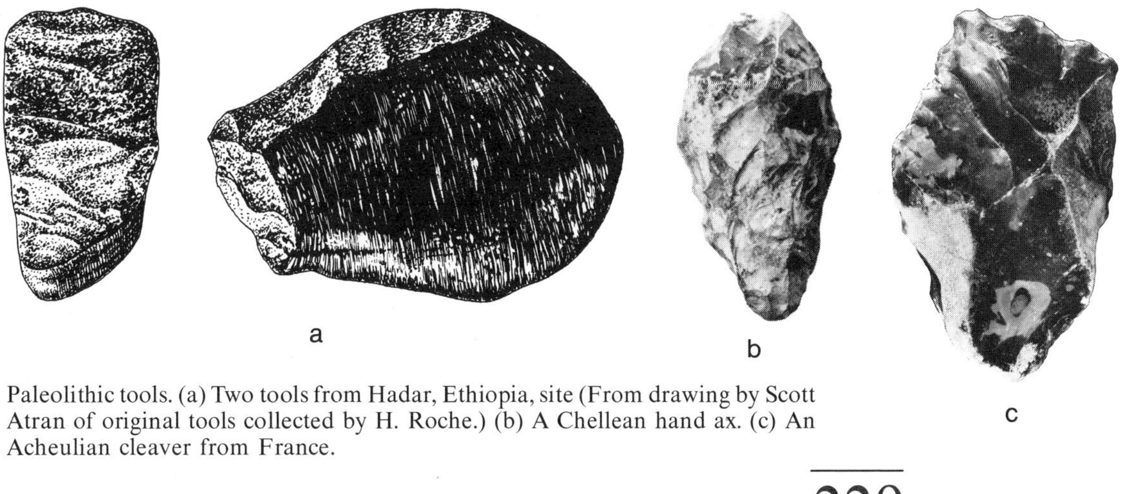

Paleolithic tools. (a) Two tools from Hadar, Ethiopia, site (From drawing by Scott Atran of original tools collected by H. Roche.) (b) A Chellean hand ax. (c) An Acheulian cleaver from France.

sites in France) is the bi-faced **hand ax.** This was manufactured from good-quality stone by striking pieces off a core with a hammer stone. The entire surface of the core was worked to produce a tear-shaped object (four to 16 inches in length) with sharp sides and a pointed end. Although the earlier Chellean forms were less well shaped than later Acheulian axes, both represent the development of a single tool type, and both were made with considerable control. Retouching was regular rather than uneven.

A technique known as *soft flaking* was introduced sometime during this period. Instead of a hammerstone, a piece of wood, bone, or antler was used to shape the edges of the tool. This produced smaller and more even flakes. With this technique cores and flakes could be shaped with great precision. The tool kit could be expanded to include new types of utensils.

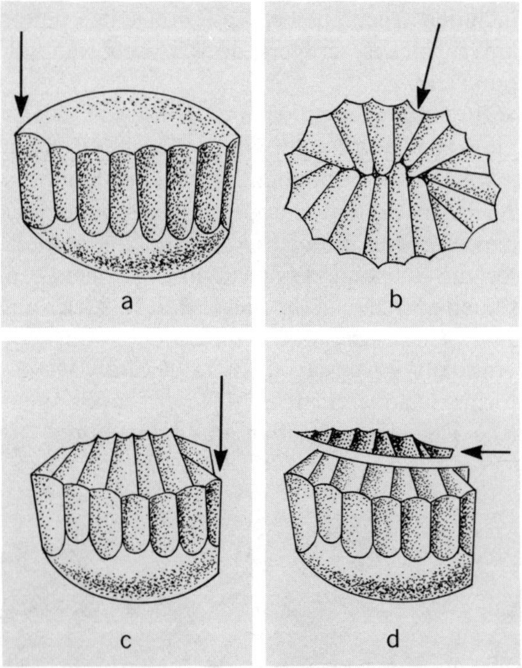

Figure 10.1
The Levalloisian technique. (a) Side view showing how the edge of the core is trimmed. (b) Top view showing how the top surface is trimmed. (c) Side view showing the striking platform (the place from which the tool will be struck). (d) Side view showing how the tool is struck off the core.

The Middle Paleolithic

By about 100,000 BP the distribution of cultures in the Old World became quite complex. Populations increased and spread out geographically and tool-making technologies became more sophisticated. With a growing control over technology and a growing knowledge of the environment (which can be inferred from studying this technology), populations increased their adaptive efficiency. New niches were invaded and experience within these niches in turn stimulated the development of new adaptive strategies. The Middle Paleolithic in comparison with the Lower Paleolithic was an age of specialization.

The Middle Paleolithic is marked by the development of an innovation in tool manufacture. The **Levallois** technique introduced the preforming of the stone core (See Figure 10.1). It apparently developed in southwest Africa and spread from there into Europe. The Levallois technique allowed tool makers to use cores more efficiently and to control the production of flakes that were then manufactured into tools. It was during the Middle Paleolithic that flake tools came to occupy a predominant place in the tool kit. The ability to control stone working coupled to experience in new environments led to a great expansion in the number of tool types produced. François Bordes, for example, one of France's leading experts on the Paleolithic, has identified 60 different tool types within the European tradition known as Mousterian. The Levallois technique was frequently used in the preparation of Mousterian tools.

The Mousterian. The major industry of the Middle Paleolithic in Europe and North Africa is the **Mousterian,** named for a site in France (see Figure 10.2). This technology is associated with *Homo sapiens neanderthalensis.* The Mousterian can be di-

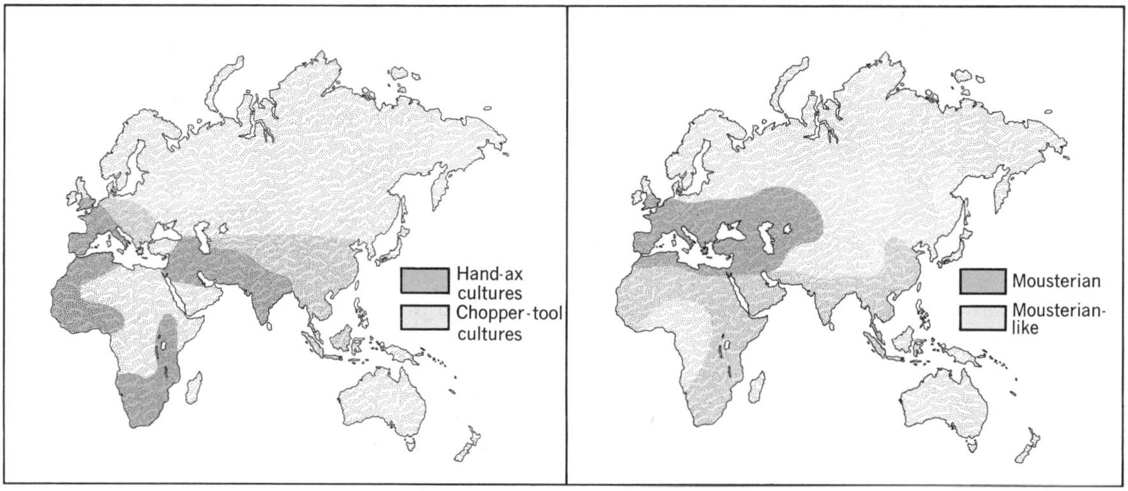

Figure 10.2
The distribution of hand-ax, chopper-tool, Mousterian, and Mousterian-like cultures.

vided into four or five separate traditions, as determined by the frequencies of artifact types (hand axes, scrapers, projectile points, and serrated, saw-like tools known as denticulates). Some sites, for example, have no hand axes and a very high percentage of scrapers, while others have some hand axes and a lower percentage of scrapers. Some are associated with the Levallois technique while others are not. These differences have led to considerable argument among archeologists. Some say that the variation in tool kits is due to their place in a temporal sequence—that is to say, they occupy different times in the evolution of an overall Mousterian culture. Others believe that the variation reflects differences among specific cultural groups, that each variation merely represents stylistic differences. Finally, it has been argued that differences in tool frequencies reflect differences in adaptive strategies, the ways in which local populations exploited their specific environments. Whatever hypothesis is correct—and the latter is compatible with the first two—the argument reinforces the necessity of studying frequencies as well as styles in artifact assemblages. Again we can see that archeology is more than the mere collection of exotic artifacts.

Mousterian scrapers from France. These tools are associated with *Homo sapiens neanderthalensis.*

Evidence from various Neanderthal-Mousterian sites shows that both empathy (caring for each other) and religious beliefs had developed among these populations. Ralph Solecki, a Columbia University archeologist, while digging at Shanidar Cave in Iraq found the skeletal remains of a man, about forty years old at his death, who showed clear indications of congenital deformation as well as old injuries. Solecki surmises that this man could not have survived on his own and must have been dependent on the group for food and protection. At the same site Solecki uncovered clear evidence of a religious burial. One grave contained the remains of eight species of flower. Nearly all of them have been shown to have medicinal properties.

The Upper Paleolithic

The Upper Paleolithic, dating from about 37,000 BP, is associated with *Homo sapiens sapiens* (the fully modern form of human) and *blade* tools. Blades are flake tools at least twice as long as they are wide. Once again, the development of an industry or technique, this time blade industries, can be associated with an improvement in core preparation. In addition, a new retouching method, **pressure flaking,** developed in this period. Instead of *striking* at the flake during retouching, pressure was exerted along the edge of the tool with a piece of bone or antler (see Figure 10.3). This allowed the worker to remove small regular chips from the flake as the tool was brought to its final shape. In the Upper Paleolithic humans were able to produce blades of great uniformity and, to our eyes, at least, great beauty. The most spectacular of all the blade cultures in Europe is known as the **Solutrean.** Solutrean laurel-leaf blades were almost perfectly formed. They ranged in size but were uniformly thin in relation to their length. One blade, found in France, is 13 inches long and only about a quarter of an inch thick.

Bone and antler tools become common in the Upper Paleolithic. Wood was also used. Evidence and logic indicate that these materials were used earlier. What is important about their place in the Upper Paleolithic is their range and variety. As stone tools improved in quality and became specialized, they could in turn be used to shape other materials. One particular innovation was the development of the **burin,** or chisel, a stone tool that could be used for efficient working of hard bone or antler (see Figure 10.4). Burins appeared in the Mousterian but

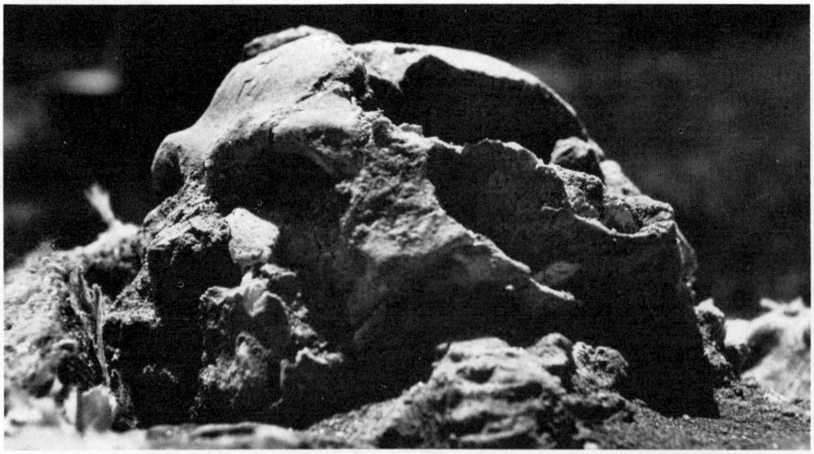

Shanidar Man. A Neanderthal found by Ralph Solecki. This find is particularly interesting because it provides evidence of intentional burial.

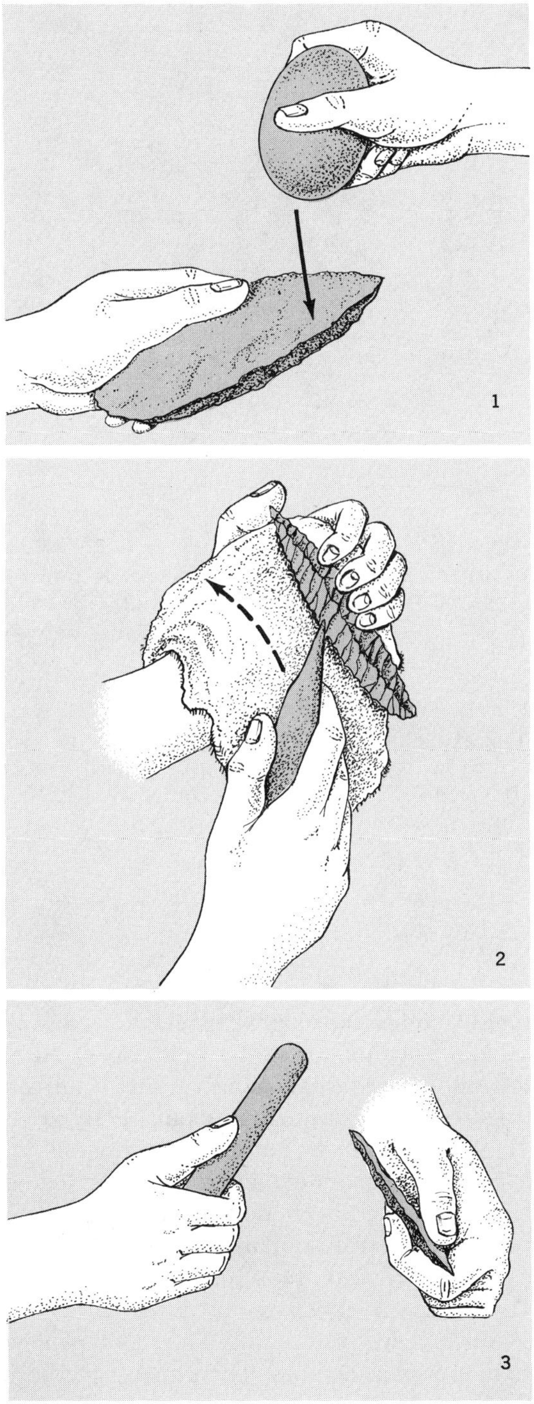

Figure 10.3
Percussion versus pressure flaking. (1) Tool is shaped by hitting it with a hammerstone. (2) Tool is held against a soft surface and retouched by pressing against it with a piece of bone, wood, or antler. (3) A form of percussion flaking known as *soft flaking*. The tool is held in a special manner and hit with a soft hammer of wood or bone. (Adapted from F. Bordes, *The Old Stone Age* New York: McGraw-Hill, 1968.)

increased in frequency during the Upper Paleolithic.

Cultural evolution implies the development of advanced forms of adaptation *and* increasing differentiation. The Upper Paleolithic is very complex and many traditions can be documented from the archeological record. In southwestern France two cultures, the **Aurignacian** and the **Perigordian** (see Figure 10.5) ex-

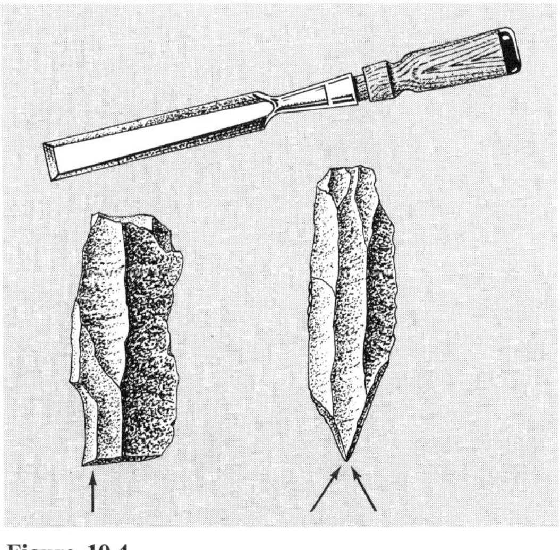

Figure 10.4
A burin or chisel-like tool. Burins appear in the Mousterian and become common in the Upper Paleolithic. (Adapted from R. J. Braidwood, *Prehistoric Men,* 8th ed. Chicago: Scott-Foresman, 1975.)

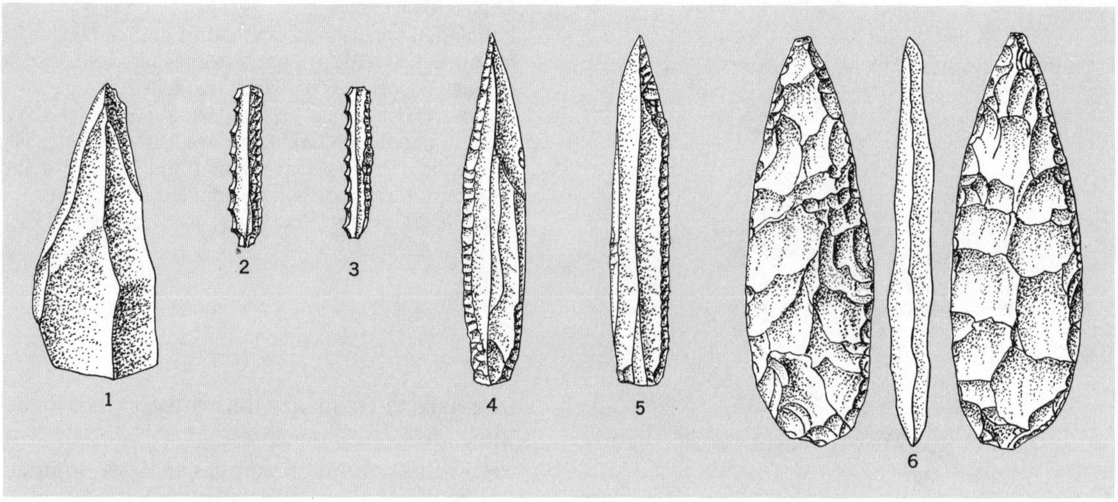

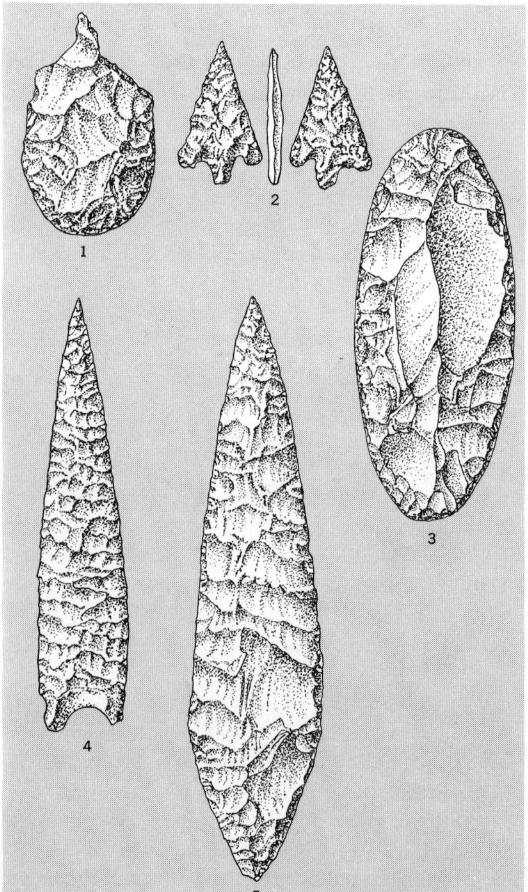

Figure 10.5

Typical tools of the Perigordian culture in Europe: (1) burin; (2, 3) denticulated blades; (4, 5) gravette points; (6) bifacial point. (Adapted from F. Bordes, *The Old Stone Age*. New York: McGraw-Hill, 1968.)

Figure 10.6

Typical Solutrean tools from Europe: (1) awl; (2) arrow point; (3) scraper; (4, 5) spear points. (Adapted from F. Bordes, *The Old Stone Age*. New York: McGraw-Hill, 1968.)

isted almost side by side. Both contain Mousterian-like tools, showing a connection with their Middle-Paleolithic past. These are followed in the same geographic area by the Solutrean (Figure 10.6), dating from about 21,000 BP to 17,000 BP. In eastern Europe a tradition known as **Gravettian** and identified with the hunting of mammoths has been documented. The final stage in the European Paleolithic was the **Magdalenian** (Figure 10.7), dating from about 17,000 BP to 10,000 BP.

Abstract designs have been found on pebbles from Aurignacian sites. These may have been the beginning of art, but representational painting and sculpture first appeared in the Magda-

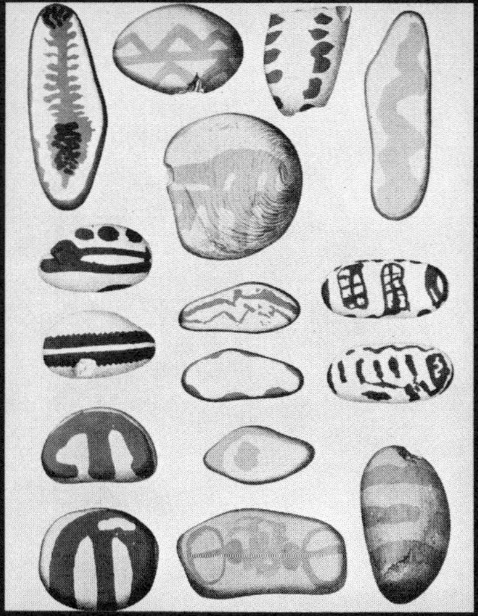

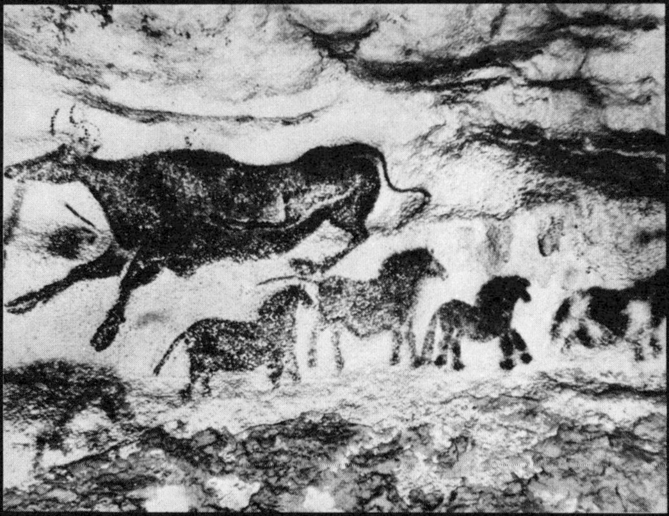

A B
D C

A

Decorated Pebbles from Mas d'Azil in France. These first indications of art from Paleolithic humans come from the Aurignacian culture.

B

Cave paintings from Lascaux in France. Wild cow and small wild horses.

C

Stags, possibly swimming.

D

An Upper Paleolithic "Venus," possibly a fertility figure.

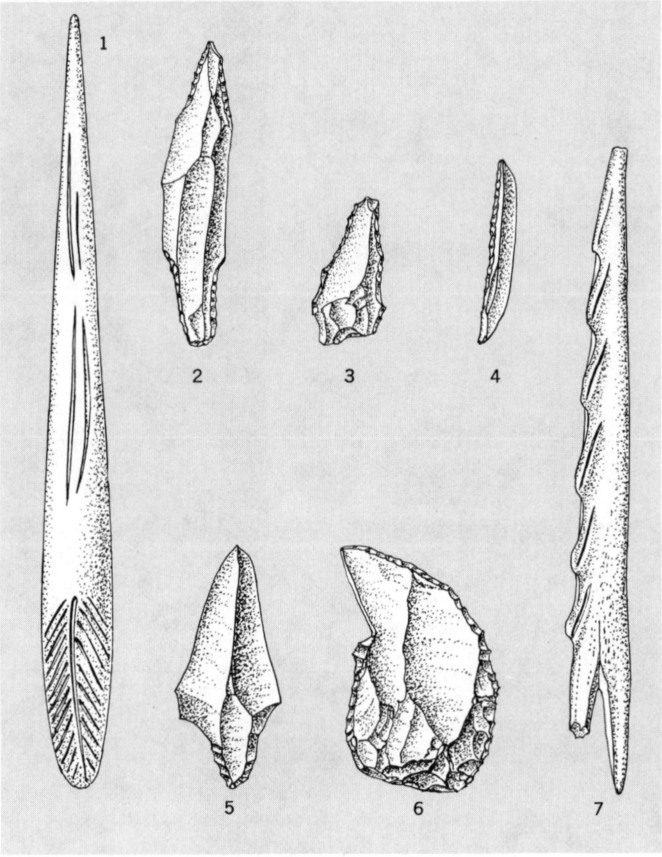

Figure 10.7

Typical Magdalenian tools from Europe: (1) bone point; (2) tanged point; (3) scraper; (4) backed blade; (5) tanged point; (6) burin; (7) bone harpoon. (Adapted from F. Bordes, *The Old Stone Age*. New York: McGraw-Hill, 1968.)

lenian culture. The Magdalenian people decorated bone tools, carved and sculpted animal and human forms, and painted on cave walls. Spectacular murals can be seen to this day in caves in southern France and Spain. One motif of this art was wounded animals. This has led some anthropologists to speculate that the art had a magical function. Wounded animals may have been painted just before a hunt to insure success. "Pregnant" animal paintings suggest fertility magic. Sculptures of fat, big-breasted females dating as far back as 25,000 BP add strength to the notion that fertility cults may have played a role in Upper-Paleolithic religion. Although human figures are rare in cave painting, many of those that do exist show what may be shamans (curers and priests) dressed in ceremonial costume, perhaps in the act of performing some ritual. Whatever its absolute meaning, Upper-Paleolithic art suggests that humans in full control of symbolic activity were using that activity in an attempt to influence the course of events. Adaptation already involved a symbolic as well as a technological approach to the problems of life.

THE MESOLITHIC (MIDDLE STONE AGE)

The Paleolithic in Europe was an age of advancing and retreating ice. Climatic variation over time led to migrations as well as changes in technology. By 10,000 BP the last glacial period was coming to its end. Sea levels rose and coastlines changed markedly. Large herd animals moved northward and easily killed game became scarce in the developing forests of southern and central Europe. Populations during this period tended to cluster along coastlines and on the shores of lakes and rivers where fish and shellfish were common and easily obtained. Gathering probably played an increasingly important role, although it had always been part of the human adaptation along with hunting. The necessity to fish, to gather vegetable resources, and to hunt scarcer and smaller meat "packages" probably stimulated the development of new technologies. Ground and polished stone tools, particularly axes and adzes, made their appearance, although chipped stone continued to be used. Evidence of boats appears in Mesolithic sites as do small projectile points, which hint that the bow and arrow are innovations of this period. The first domesticated animal, the dog, also dates from this time. The most characteristic Mesolithic tool is the **microlith** (small stone). These fine chips were small, hard blades. They could be hafted to arrow shafts with resin or set in rows on sickle-like wooden shafts. The latter could be used to harvest wild grains.

Mesolithic peoples were probably rather sedentary. Big-game hunters must follow animals. Fishers and gatherers do best when they stay put in small village settlements, where they come to understand the lay of the land and the distribution of seasonal resources. In many cases the Mesolithic adaptation included seasonal movement back and forth between hunting camps in the winter and fishing camps in the summer. Patterns of this sort still exist in some isolated groups of Native American hunters and gatherers, particularly Eskimos. Although Mesolithic culture in general was characterized by the presence of microliths, several subcultures have been identified. Among these are the **Maglemosian** (in the bog country of England and Scandinavia), **Azilian** (in the forests of France and Germany), and the **Tardenoisian** (located generally farther south in Europe in scrub forest). The particular distribution of these three cultures in different environments suggests adaptation and specialization to local conditions.

HUNTING AND GATHERING IN THE NEW WORLD: PALEOINDIAN CULTURES

During the glacial periods a land bridge existed between Asia and Alaska. The date that this bridge was first crossed by humans is a point of argument. Estimates range between 70,000 and 18,000 BP. In any case it occurred *after* Eurasians had adapted to living in the cold North. The culture of these early Americans, or *Paleoindians,* was dependent on wood, bone, and stone tools. Hunting and gathering was the dominant subsistence pattern. Paleoindian sites often include the bones of extinct animals. Many of these were large mammals similar to those hunted by populations in the Old World. Game hunted by humans at this time included reindeer, elk, musk oxen, mammoths, mastodons, bison, and antelope.

The earliest known reliably dated tools from the New World come from sites in Mexico and Peru. These are choppers and scrapers. A cave in Peru has been found to contain a cultural sequence that runs from about 22,000 to 450 BP. The lowest level has yielded bones of an extinct ground sloth. Projectile points (sound evidence for hunting) come from North America, ranging from as far south as New Mexico all the way up to Nova Scotia. These artifacts, dating from about 11,000 to 9500 BP, are known as **Clovis** points (see Figure 10.8). Clovis points have been found in association with the bones of mammoths and horses, both of which were extinct in the New World at the time the Spanish arrived.

The western part of the United States was also inhabited by a people who apparently specialized in the hunting of bison. This culture is marked by the distinctive **Folsom** point which is *fluted,* that is, it bears a longitudinal flake scar on both sides (see Figure 10.8). These flutes were undoubtedly an aid in the hafting process, allowing the point to be firmly attached to the shaft.

Clovis sites are generally found near bogs and other stagnant water sources. Interestingly, many of these sites contain artifacts made from materials that could only have come from many miles away. Such distributions suggest either wide territorial movement or trade. Archeologists believe that Clovis hunters ambushed mammoths along their feeding routes and followed the wounded animals to the watering sites toward which they would naturally retreat.

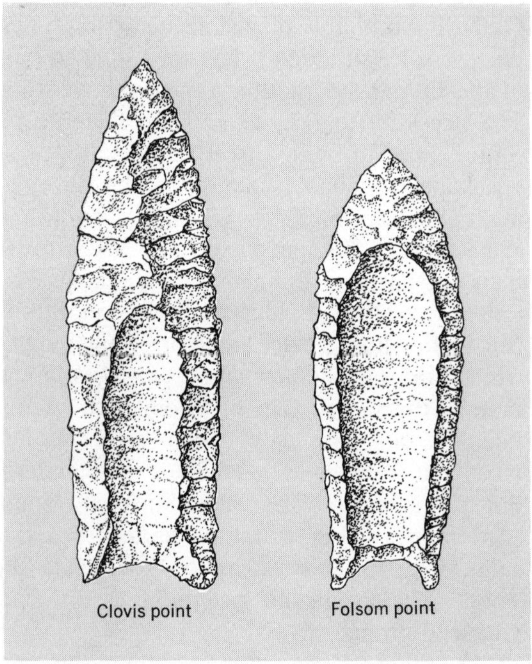

Figure 10.8

New World Paleoindian tools: Clovis (left), Folsom (right). (Adapted from G. H. Bushnell, *First Americans: The Pre-Columbian Civilizations.* New York: McGraw-Hill, 1968.)

This theory explains the location of Clovis points at watering sites. Folsom sites, in contrast, are often located at the foot of cliffs. It is assumed that these hunters stampeded herds of bison, driving them towards a cliff edge where, in a panic, they would fall off to be butchered by the hunters' companions below. Bison were also apparently killed by driving them into dead-end canyons where they could be easily slaughtered.

So far I have only discussed Paleoindian *kill sites* associated with a hunting technology. Other sites associated with the same cultures contain a variety of ground stone tools. These were probably used for woodworking and the processing of various plant materials. This addition to our knowledge of Paleoindians indicates the usual mix of hunting and gathering as a form of human adaptation.

THE NEOLITHIC (NEW STONE AGE)

The Mesolithic evolved slowly into the Neolithic with the development of plant and animal domestication. Stone tools became highly diversified and in the Old World were ground and polished to shape for the first time. The Neolithic was a period of village settlement for agricultural peoples, and one of nomadism for animal herders. Mixed herding and agricultural

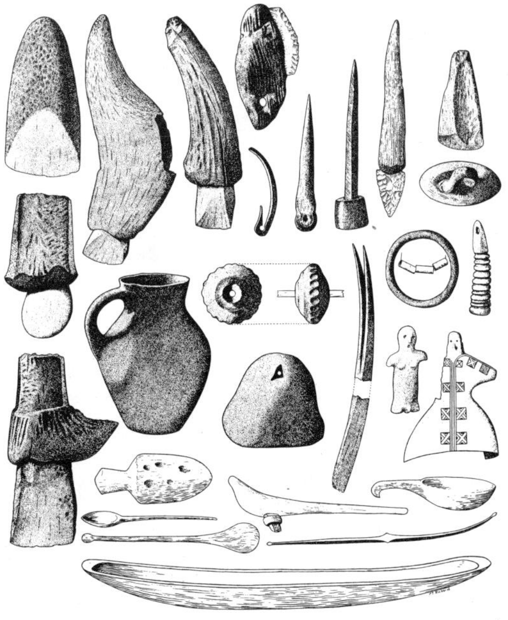

A selection of Neolithic tools from Europe. Note the hafting of stone axes in bone, antler, and wood, various wooden objects, and the doll-like figures made of clay.

Cultural development (in Europe) from the Lower Paleolithic to the Neolithic.

Years (before present)	Geological Epochs and Glacial Stages	Climate	Hominid Form	Cultural Phases (in Europe)	Tool Types (in Europe)
	RECENT				
5000		Cold temperate		NEOLITHIC	
10,000		Cold, but warming		MESOLITHIC 10,000	Bow and arrow
15,000		Very cold		Magdalenian	Eyed needles, cave art, reindeer-antler artifacts
20,000	Late Würm		*Homo sapiens sapiens*	17,000	Extraordinary pressure-flaking; willow-leaf and laurel-leaf lance points.
				Solutrean	
25,000				21,000	
		Cool temperate			Smaller knife blades
30,000				UPPER PALEOLITHIC	Ivory wedges for splitting wood and bone Most skillful flintworking
35,000	Main Würm	Very cold			First true boneworking (pins, awls, light spearheads)
				Aurignacian Perigordian	Earliest blade cultures
40,000				37,000	Slender, straight, keen-edged flakes
45,000					
50,000	Early Würm				
60,000					Wooden hafts added to stone tools Multifunctional tools, thick, heavy flakes
		Cold		MIDDLE PALEOLITHIC	Improved techniques of manufacture
70,000			*Homo sapiens neanderthalensis*		
80,000					
	Interglacial				
90,000					
				Mousterian 100,000	Small, bifacial hand axes
	UPPER PLEISTOCENE		*Homo erectus*	LOWER PALEOLITHIC	Large hand axes
125,000	MIDDLE PLEISTOCENE				

Adapted from J. E. Spencer and W. L. Thomas, *Introducing Cultural Geography,* 2nd ed. (Wiley, 1978).

settlements were also common in the Middle East and parts of Asia, particularly India and China. Pottery made its appearance during the Neolithic. In fact, pottery used to be diagnostic of this period, along with domestication and a certain tool technology. We now know that these three cultural elements do not necessarily appear at the same time or in the same sites. Indeed, contemporary populations in Papua-New Guinea and other parts of the world had both plant and animal domestication as well as polished stone tools before contact with Europeans, but they lacked pottery.

The Neolithic tool kit varied widely by geographic setting, prevailing economy, and local ecology. The Neolithic was a time of cultural diversification that itself gave rise in turn to civilization and urbanism.

DOMESTICATION

In the course of cultural evolution two developments stand out above the rest. These are: (1) plant and animal domestication, which occurred in the Neolithic, and (2) the development of social stratification (social inequality in its many forms) leading eventually to the state as a political entity. Neither appears suddenly. Rather they are the result of gradual processes. The roots of domestication can be found in the resource management of nondomesticated forms. The roots of social stratification can be found in ecological and technological factors as well as in social processes. Social stratification and the rise of the state will be taken up in the next chapter. For the remainder of this chapter I will examine domestication.

Animal Domestication

Dogs. The dog is probably the most ancient domesticated animal. Dogs are social creatures and readily accommodate to a group. When raised by humans, dogs develop attachments that would normally be directed toward members of their own species. The domestication of the dog (in the Mesolithic) may have been an accidental process of mutual accommodation. Wild dogs probably attached themselves to human habitation sites, scavenging garbage. For humans, dogs are useful because they provide warning signals of approaching danger. Proximity could have produced mutual tolerance and led to the eventual taming of the wild species. Even today dogs are prized in lowland South America by warring groups who fear the silent raids of their enemies. The attachment of dogs to their human masters and to a home territory, as well as their alertness, continues to make them a valuable asset. These qualities are often exploited in contemporary society with the training of watch and guard dogs.

Other animals. The domestication of animals other than dogs occurred after the close of the Mesolithic under conditions of expanding population and climatic change. Before we examine these conditions, let us look at the way in which some contemporary populations that hunt interact with their prey. Such ethnographic data provide clues to the origin of domestication.

Many of the world's peoples who lack true domesticates occasionally keep and raise baby animals either as food or as pets. Where technology precludes food preservation and storage, the keeping of live animals maintains a food source that can be used when needed.

In New Guinea, among peoples with a developed agriculture, wild and semi-domestic pigs tend to feed on abandoned gardens where forage is abundant and relatively easy to root out of the soil. In other parts of the world gardens tend to attract wild animals such as deer and other ruminants. Even where cultivation is not

Domestic pig in Papua-New Guinea.

practiced, humans and animals may tend to frequent the same wild plant resources. Such an area may become a feeding station for the animals and a hunting ground for humans. A shift in human behavior could lead toward incipient domestication. If, for example, hunters limited their kill to mature males, preservation of the flock could be enhanced. Such a conservation

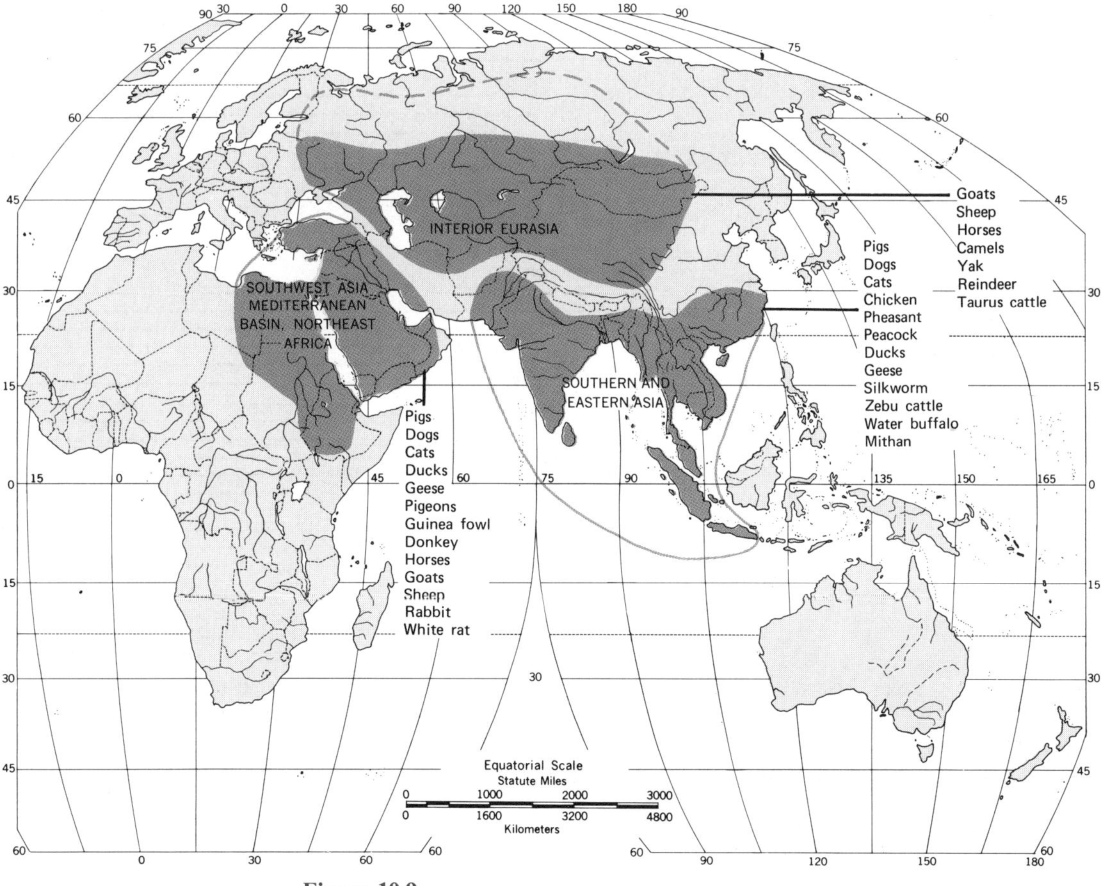

Figure 10.9
Major regions of first animal domestication in the Old and New Worlds. (Adapted from J. E. Spencer and W. L. Thomas, *Introducing Cultural Geography,* 2nd. ed. New York: John Wiley, 1978.)

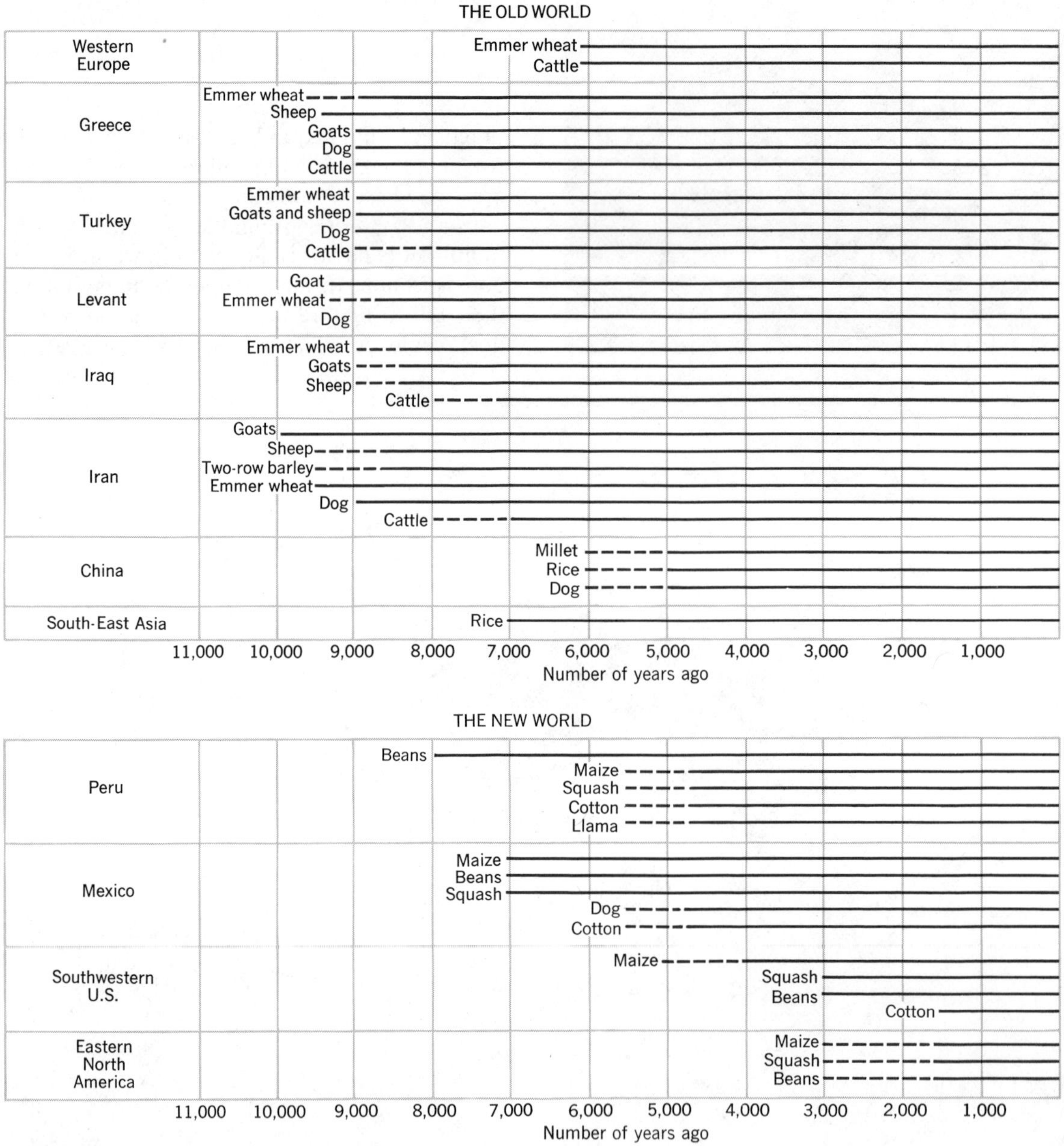

Figure 10.10
Earliest occurrence of plant and animal domesticates in the Old and New Worlds.

strategy is practiced today in many of our states to assure a steady supply of wild game.

Mammalian game species in the United States are, in most cases, limited to nonherding species such as deer, moose, and bear. These are unlikely candidates for domestication. Animals that live in permanent herds are potentially easier to manage and economical to care for than solitary species. Thus, in terms of resource management it makes sense to continue to hunt solitary species but, under certain conditions, to domesticate herding animals. Domestication produces a more stable and dependable food supply than hunting, particularly when human groups are expanding and therefore straining wild resources.

Once animals are even partially tamed, the process of domestication has begun. Dependence can result simply from the removal of a species from its natural habitat. Taking plants or animals out of their home range can produce automatic dependence. Under new environmental conditions transplanted species may have to be cared for in order to survive. Once such a dependency relationship has been established, *artificial selection* may produce significant biological changes in the species. Humans may begin to select certain qualities that increase the economic value of the species. This process need not be the fruit of conscious planning. It can result from resource management strategies that were initially based merely on convenience. The movement of wild species from their natural habitats to proximity with human settlements was probably one of the first steps in the process of domestication. As artificial selection increased the economic value of the captured species, they became more and more dependent on human care; they became domesticated.

Plant Domestication

Ethnographic and archeological data on the human treatment of wild plants add to our knowledge of the origin of cultivation. There is, for example, evidence that certain wild plants were helped along by humans before true domestication occurred. In the Southwest of the United States, Native American groups irrigated stands of wild grasses. In other parts of the world certain wild species are favored over others by weeding out unwanted plants.

Attention to wild plants is in no way surprising. They constitute a major source of food among most of the world's nonagricultural peoples. At first their importance was partially ignored by anthropologists, most of whom have been male and have tended to focus on the hunting aspect of hunting *and* gathering. Hunting is usually a male activity. It is more spectacular than gathering, but gathering is, in most cases, the major source of necessary calories. In fact, hunting and gathering as a mode of subsistence may, as we have seen, provide the basic reason for the division of labor by sex. Women as gatherers provide necessary calories, usually with relatively little energy expenditure. Men provide high-grade (complete) protein, but with great energy expenditure. Societies forced to rely on hunting alone might suffer from a calorie deficit. Those that relied strictly on gathering might suffer from protein malnutrition. Dietary balance is provided by a combination of these two modes of subsistence and by cooperation between the sexes.

It was once felt that hunting and gathering are always arduous and that societies practicing this mode of subsistence are burdened by food shortages and hard work. Studies in the 1960s demonstrated that most societies of this type actually live under rather easy circumstances. In many cases contemporary hunting and gathering peoples are aware of agriculture yet resist it as a form of economic activity. The Hadza of Tanzania, for example, were resettled on agricultural land by the government in an attempt to provide them with stable resources and to bring them into the "modern" world. The Hadza resisted this effort, preferring to continue their seminomadic hunting and gathering mode of life. They realized that work loads associated with agricultural activity were much higher than those required by hunting and gathering.

Throughout the preagricultural period of cultural evolution the world's population was small enough to prevent both overcrowding and game depletion. Although hunting and gathering do not usually allow for long-range resource management or a means for storing food, game and wild crops were generally available in adequate quantities. Under conditions of overall low

Modern hunters and gatherers. A Hadza camp in Tanzania.

population density, when individual groups grew too large for local resources they merely divided and each came to occupy its own new territory. As long as the balance was maintained between resources and population, a minimal effort could provide for daily needs.

In general, hunting and gathering societies are unstratified, that is, there is no marked social distinction between members of any one group. Although a division of labor exists in these groups based on age and sex, they are relatively egalitarian in all other respects. Under these conditions what is produced is generally consumed directly and in relatively equal amounts by members of the group. Thus, environmental energy is converted into organisms just as it is among nonhuman species. Even with the development of stratification (castes, classes, or other forms of social distinction), it is still the rule that environmental energy must be transformed into organisms. In such societies, however, *not all energy is thus transformed.* Egalitarian societies (hunting and gathering groups) but *not* stratified societies fit the model of simple biological evolution, with its direct equation between the number of organisms in a niche and the means these organisms have of successfully converting environmental energy to their own organic needs. Anthropologists must account for a basic change in cultural strategy in which simple and direct adaptations gave way to complex relationships among humans and between humans and their environments. In many parts of the world domestication is implicated in this change.

Domestication is more than just an accommodation between humans and resources—plants, animals, or both. It also involves considerable social change. Settlement and the working of land, for example, imply some notion of property, whether it be communal or individual. The development of property relations affects inheritance and social relations between members of the local group. In order to understand the process of domestication, besides knowing how wild species became transformed, we also need to know what kinds of incentive for change occurred.

Population increase under restrictive environmental conditions that produce shortages provides a major clue to this process. Environmental change may also be a major factor in the shift toward domestication. Long-term climatic change may stimulate people to move and to innovate. Over the long time run of the Paleolithic in Europe, for example, climatic shifts led to changes in the animal population and parallel changes in technology and settlement patterns.

Archeologists and geologists estimate that by 10,000 BC most environments of the world had been occupied, excepting the arctic regions, the Amazon basin, and the Caribbean and Pacific Islands. The end of the glacial periods saw a rise in sea level and a submerging of many sea coasts. River systems were drowned at this time and many river basins were converted into estuaries. The latter were rich in marine resources (fish and shellfish). Although fishing and the gathering of other marine resources is a kind of hunting and gathering, the payoff is usually much higher and more stable than that provided by the hunting of land mammals. Larger and more permanent settlements can be supported by fishing than by land hunting. This technological change led to the development of permanent settlements. Even inland there was a great increase in the variety of food resources. As animals became less common, the gathering of plant food probably became more important. The archeologist Kent Flannery, who has written a great deal on the development of domestication in the Old and New Worlds, points out that this was a period of experimentation in which new ways were sought to expand the local food supply. New techniques were developed for making some types of plant edible. Populations also began to settle in areas where certain abundant wild plants such as wheat and barley grew naturally.

The hilly-flank theory. Robert J. Braidwood, an archeologist, suggested in the late 1940s that domestication began in the Near East on a zone of hills that is located to the north of the so-called *Fertile Crescent* (the land bounded by the great river systems of the Near East—the Tigris, Euphrates, and the Nile—see Figure 10.11). Braidwood reasoned that the hill areas were the locus of the wild grasses, wheat and barley, which were tamed by peoples living in early villages. Once domesticated these plants could have been brought down into the river valleys where they could flourish as floods renewed soil fertility each year.

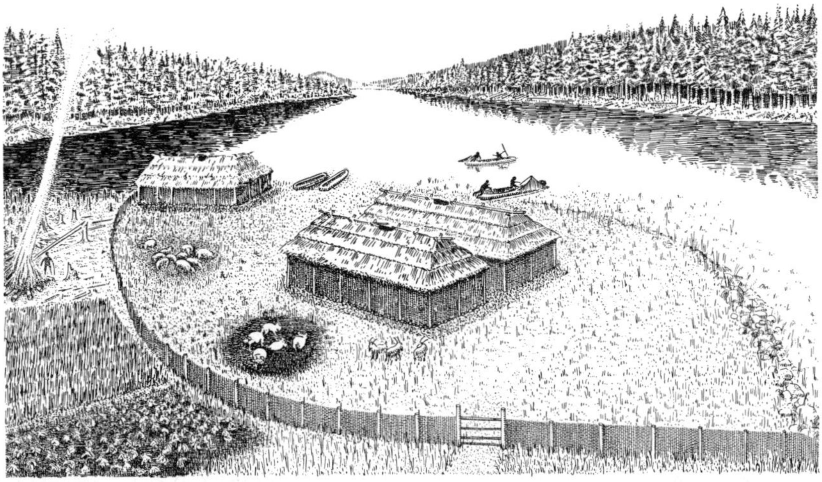

Reconstruction of an early European agricultural village, French Neolithic (From "Lake-Bottom Archaeology" by Aimé Bocquet. Copyright © February 1979 by Scientific American, Inc. All rights reserved.)

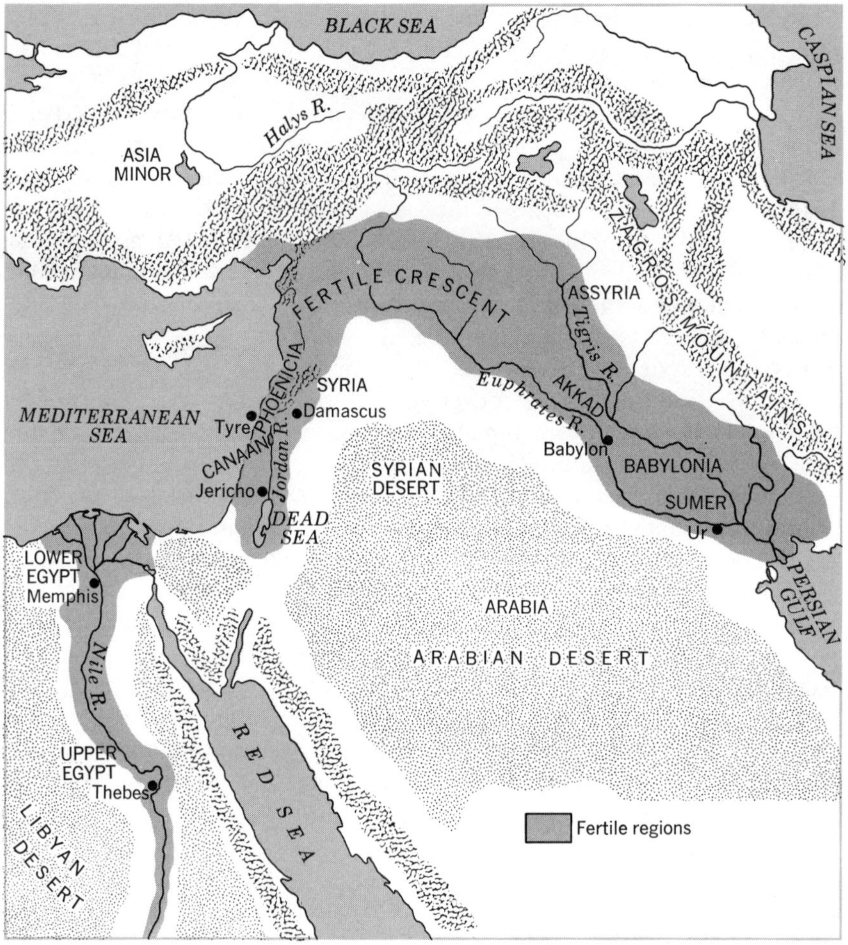

Figure 10.11
The Fertile Crescent, the area in Southwest Asia in which grains were first domesticated.

Flannery's view. Kent Flannery objects to this view, pointing out that populations living in areas abundant in wild grain are not likely to move toward the domestication of that resource. They are, he suggests, perfectly content to exploit it as a wild product. Flannery believes that agriculture began in the drier areas around the margins of these wild grain habitats where the productivity of the land could only be raised by deliberately planting grains. One of the constants in this speculation is that population increase within the context of stable villages exerted pressure for innovation and improvement in food-getting technologies.

According to Flannery, by 7000 BC the first carbonized remains of domestic forms of grain occur in archeological sites. These traces are accompanied by technological evidence for a heavy reliance on grain. Such items as storage facilities, ovens for roasting grain, flint sickles used in harvesting, and tools for separating the grain from the chaff are found. None of these are new innovations. Instead, they mark a grad-

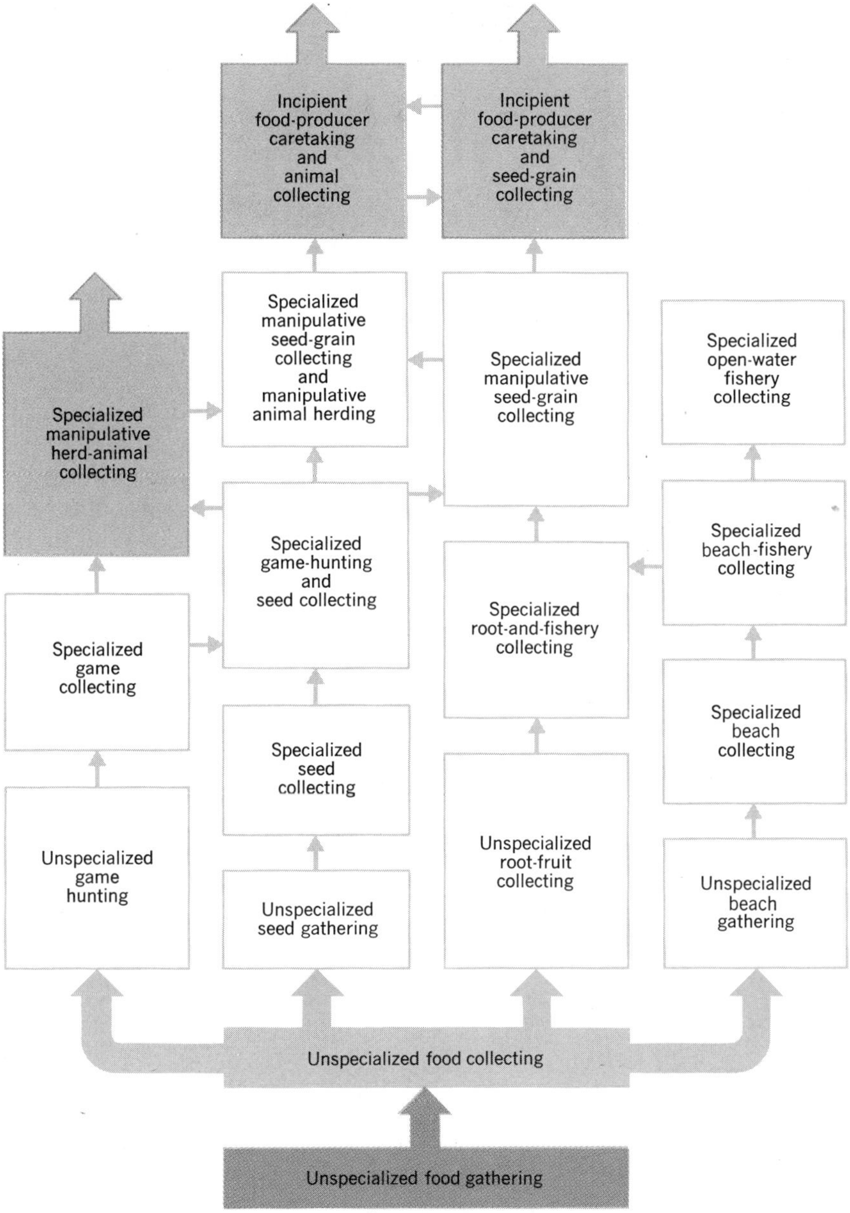

Figure 10.12

The evolution of subsistence strategies from food gathering to incipient food production. (Adapted from J. E. Spencer and W. L. Thomas, *Introducing Cultural Geography,* 2nd ed. New York: John Wiley, 1978.)

ual shift from increased exploitation of wild to domestic plant resources. The whole process rests on gradual intensification of resource use. The cultural complex noted by Flannery is associated with the Mesolithic *Natufian* culture of the Near East. Microliths from this culture show polished wear marks indicating that they were used to harvest wild grain. Flannery believes that experimental domestication occurred in productively marginal areas where increasing population stimulated the development of new subsistence strategies. At first, wild plants were cared for. Later, some were moved into new environmental zones and, as we have already seen, became dependent on humans for their success. The growing management of agricultural and animal resources allowed for continuous permanent settlement and relatively high population density. These, in turn, became the preconditions for the development of civilization.

THE RISE OF DOMESTICATION IN SELECTED AREAS

The Near East

There is evidence of domestic animals in the Near East from as far back as 11,000 BP. The most important animals were pigs, goats, sheep, and cattle. By 8000 BP animal husbandry had already become quite diversified. With the exception of the pig, each animal was domesticated in a different geographical area. According to Dexter Perkins and Pat Daly, experts on animal domestication in the Near East, cattle were domesticated on the Anatolian plateau, sheep in the uplands of Turkey and Iraq, and goats in the mountains of Iran. These authors suggest that as long as meat was the major resource taken from animals, a single domesticate was adequate. Each of these species, however, has its own valuable secondary products. Sheep provide wool, goats provide milk, and cattle provide milk and hides. When these products became known throughout the area, the keeping of multiple species became desirable.

Agriculture also began in the Near East sometime between 10,000 and 7500 BP. Herders collected wild grain as they moved with their flocks across their territory, and, as we have seen, the Natufians harvested wild grains. Agriculture in this area was based on the domestication of three grains: einkorn wheat (*Triticum monococcum*), emmer wheat (*Triticum dicoccum*), and barley (*Hordeum vulgare*). These domestic species are easy to identify and distinguish from their wild cousins. One of the major occurrences in the domestication of these species was a change in the *spike* (the seed-bearing part of the plant). In wild forms the spike is brittle, an adaptation that facilitates the scattering of seeds. This characteristic is not favored by humans, however, who prefer a spike that will remain attached to the stem during harvesting. Artificial selection for a tough spike early in domestication produced a major change that was disadvantageous for wild plants; the seeds of the tough-spiked grains *must* be sowed by hand. Another result of human intervention was an increase in the size of the seed pod or fruiting body, achieved in many cases by exploiting polyploid varieties of the plants. The earliest type of cultivation in the Near East was dry farming (without irrigation). Both temporary settlements and permanent villages appear in the archeological record.

Perkins and Daly document the changes that took place at Tepe Ali Kosh in southwestern Iran. During the earliest phases of occupation (9000–8750 BP) houses were made of unfired clay bricks and floors were of stamped mud or clay. The major food resource at this time was wild seeds. Emmer wheat and barley were grown, but they constituted only one-third of the total volume of plant food. The people of Tepe Ali Kosh herded domestic goats, but meat was mainly provided by hunting. By 8750–8000 BP the architecture had become more elaborate. Emmer wheat and barley provided more than ninety percent of the plant food consumed. Goats continued to be the only domestic animal, and hunting continued to provide a major portion of the meat supply. Trade became extensive at this time. Later, multiple domestication developed, and Perkins and Daly believe that it might have been stimulated by trade between Tepe Ali Kosh and the Iranian plateau as well as the Persian gulf.

By 7500 BP intensive agriculture was the major subsistence pattern in the Near East. Trade was common and all four domestic animals were widespread, although the pig was never as important as cattle, sheep, and goats. By 7000 BP population pressure apparently forced people into lowland areas and irrigation agriculture developed. This new technology, which in turn increased productivity, led to further increases in population.

Asia

According to Kwang-chih Chang, an archeologist who specializes in China, domestication emerged in the Yellow River Valley from a Mesolithic hunter-fisher culture. The first crops were varieties of millet. Animals included the pig and the dog and small quantities of cattle and sheep. Chang believes that rice was first cultivated in South China or Southeast Asia. It appears for sure about 5000 BP in southern China and also in the Indus Valley in India.

Early farmers lived in villages, but there is evidence that they shifted their locale frequently. If so, then cultivation depended on slash-and-burn techniques. In **slash-and-burn** horticulture forest land is cleared by cutting and burning, planted, harvested, and then abandoned for several years of fallow during which it has time to renew itself.

The New World

Although New World cultigens are different from their counterparts in the Old World, and although few animals were tamed, the pattern of domestication is similar to that found in other regions of the world. Domestication in Mexico took place between 9000 and 3500 BP, with villages appearing late, around 4000 BP. Maize, beans, and squash were the major crops. Cultivation developed among small seminomadic groups in several areas. Archeologists speculate that in Mexico as in the Near East cultivation began as an attempt to widen the area in which plants could be successfully maintained. On the other hand, population pressure may not have been the major source of stimulation. Highland Mexico is an area of extreme environmental variation, with widely scattered resources and large seasonal differences in rainfall. In addition, droughts are common, so there are wide swings in the availability of resources in good and bad years. Populations in this area tended to exploit a wide range of limited and seasonal resources. The major resources included:

1. *Maguey* (a cactus with an edible body and upper-root system).
2. *Cactus fruit* (from four species of organ cactus appearing late in the dry season).
3. *Tree legumes* (mesquite, found on the valley floors, bearing edible fruit during the June-to-August rainy season).
4. *Wild grasses* (maize and foxtail grass).
5. *White-tailed deer* (a major food resource in ancient times).
6. *Cottontail rabbits* (available all year long).

The major adaptation to this environment before the advent of cultivation depended on taking advantage of seasonal resources. Since many of the exploitable resources became available at the same time of the year, choices had to made about which to exploit. One means of dealing with many resources is the division of labor among the sexes. We have already seen how useful this policy can be in providing a balance between protein and necessary calories. More complex situations require a series of time-management choices, referred to by Kent Flannery as *scheduling.* Scheduling was determined by the population's judgments about good and bad years in relation to specific plants and animals. This was not a hit-or-miss process. Rather, scouts were sent out to survey the environment and report back on conditions. This procedure was necessary because ripening and abundance varied from season to season. From the point of view of resource management, the scheduling process, plus the variation in quantity of all resources, made it unlikely that specialization in a single resource would develop. The overall adaptation was generalized.

Generalization preserves flexibility and, under the proper conditions, allows for experimentation and changes in basic adaptive patterns. According to Flannery, the adaptive situation in Mesoamerica changed with a series of genetic mutations in plants that were already a part of the subsistence system. These were the wild grass maize (*zea maize*) and beans. Flannery believes that attempts to increase the areas in which these plants could grow were not successful until the mutations had occurred. The following modifications in the existing wild plants were adaptive for humans:

1. Beans became more permeable in water, thus they became more edible. Beans are particularly important since, as a legume, they supply lysine, an essential amino acid lacking in maize. Beans also developed a limp pod that did not shatter when ripe. The seeds thus remained in the pods rather than being scattered. This development is analogous to the change that occurred on the spikes of Old World grain crops.
2. While most of the wild grasses remained unchanged, maize underwent a series of important transformations. The cob became larger. When transported around the highlands, it came into contact and crossed with a related species (*Zea tripsacum*), producing a hybrid form. Thereafter, it changed radically: Cob size, number of cobs on a plant, number of kernel rows, and number of kernels all increased.

When this happened, subsistence strategies shifted in the arid highlands. Grass harvesting grew in importance at the expense of other food-procurement systems. When grasses were *planted,* the system became even more complex; now there was a planting season in the spring and a harvest season in the fall. Planting thus came into competition with the gathering of spring-ripening wild plants, while harvesting produced a similar conflict in the fall. In addition, harvesting interfered with the rainy-season hunting of deer and peccary (a wild pig).

The result was a change from a generalized procurement system to a specialized one. It brought about rescheduling as well. Certain previously practiced seasonal activities were either abandoned or rescheduled. A new emphasis was placed on those activities that did not interfere with cultivation. Cultivation itself led to more permanent and larger settlements, each of which contributed to the development of civilization in the New World.

No one knows when cultivation and domesti-

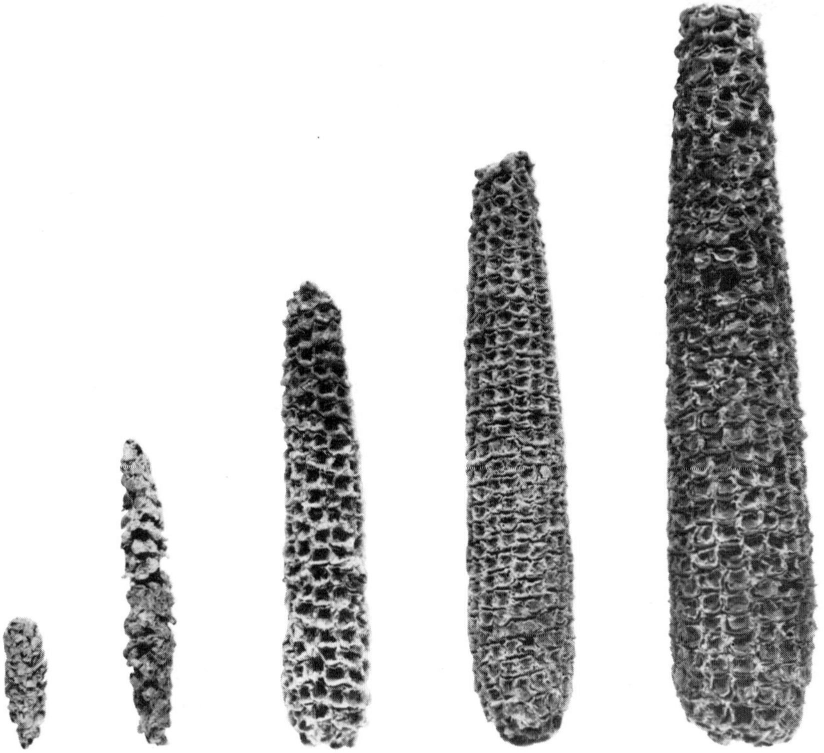
The evolution of maize in the New World. The oldest domesticated forms (on the left) share many characteristics with their wild cousin. Through hybridization the plant becomes larger and stronger. More and more rows of kernels occur in cobs and more cobs appear on single plants.

cation of animals began in Peru. We do know that food production began in the highlands around 7500 BP, where beans appeared before they did in Mexico. The Peruvians also domesticated the guinea pig, which was raised as a food animal, and both llamas and the related alpaca, the only large mammals tamed in the New World.

THE WORLDWIDE DEVELOPMENT OF AGRICULTURE

When archeologists first discovered evidence of cultivation in the Old and New Worlds, it was confined to a rather small central area. In addition, all the domestic **cultigens** (domesticated plants) were grains. The original model for the origins of cultivation was thus based on the notion of a specific center where ecological conditions were appropriate for the new adaptive patterns to emerge. Grain crops were reasonably thought to be the first cultigens because they provide a relatively high protein content (including most of the essential amino acids) and they store well.

Among the world's major crops, however, there is another whole group that does not fit this pattern. These are root crops, such as potatoes, sweet potatoes, yams, taro, and manioc (known to us in one form as tapioca). All of these crops are quite deficient (in varying degrees) in essential amino acids and, in most cases, are difficult to store. Manioc is a partial exception to this since it stores rather well in the ground. On the other hand, root crops have very high yields and are relatively easy to grow. On the island of Ponape in Micronesia, yams (used for ceremonial purposes) may attain weights of over 200 pounds.

In general root crops are associated with tropical climates (potatoes and sweet potatoes are an exception) and slash-and-burn cultivation (see Figure 10.13 for distribution). In this type of cultivation, as you have seen, an area of forest is cut and the trees burned off. The burning cuts down on weeds and provides some ash fertilizer. Crops are planted on the cleared fields for one or two seasons. The fields are then allowed to lie fallow, that is, they are abandoned until the forest restores itself. The process may then be repeated. Fallow periods vary widely in different parts of the world, depending on soil fertility and population density. When a fallow cycle is interrupted too soon, however, the trees may not regenerate and permanent grass land may be the result.

Normally, populations practicing this type of cultivation must have a great deal of land available to them since the largest portion of it will be lying fallow at any one time. Slash-and-burn cultivation properly managed, however, requires little labor compared to plow agriculture and has relatively high yields. When there is enough land and population density is low, it is an efficient system. Slash-and-burn cultivation has been widely studied by cultural anthropologists since it is the major form of economic activity in most of the world's tropical areas. In addition to root crops, some grains—particularly dry, or hill, rice (a form of rice that does not need to grow in water)—are grown by this method. Archeological evidence shows that the slash-and-burn technique was widely distributed in prehistoric times as well. The most spectacular cultures based on this subsistence pattern were those of the lowland Maya of Guatemala and the Khmer who built Angkor Wat in Cambodia.

A very few scholars, mostly geographers under the influence of a major figure in geography, Carl Sauer, believe that root rather than grain crops were the first cultigens. Discoveries in Southeast Asia support this position in part, for it is probable that root crop domestication developed in this area independently of grain domestication.

Root crops. (a) Women in the Amazon Basin of Brazil prepare manioc. (b) An Indonesian man carries sweet potatoes to market.

a

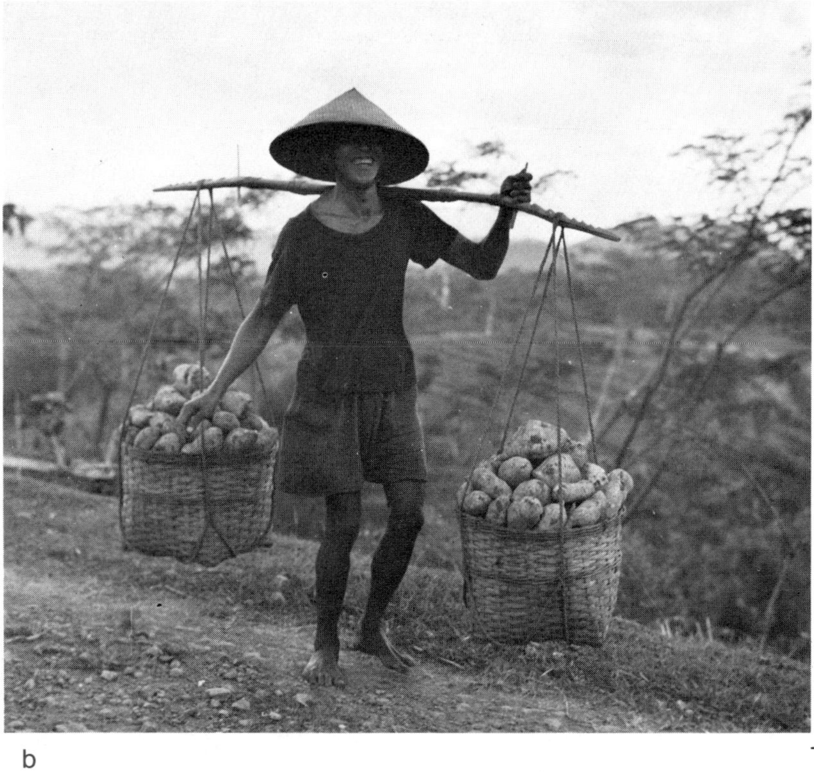

b

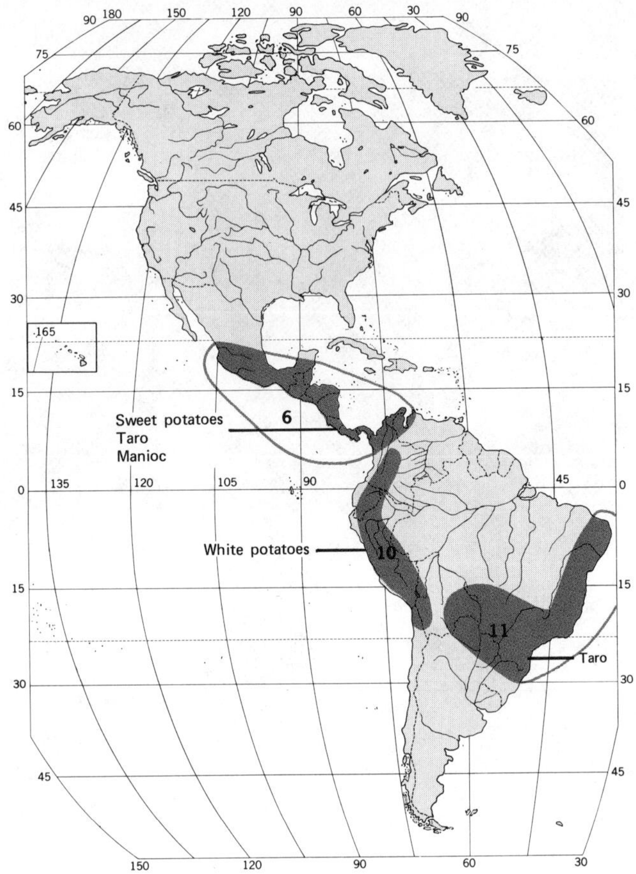

Technological Developments

Agriculture and **sedentarism** (permanent settlement) led to a series of technological developments. In the Old World agriculture is generally associated with pottery from the beginning. In the New World pottery did not develop until well after domestication occurred, but it did emerge and flourish as a major technological, ritual, and artistic item in New World culture. The settlement of populations in permanent villages probably stimulated trade between them. Resources from different areas as well as ideas could be exchanged for the mutual benefit of all concerned. As agriculture developed, its own technology increased in sophistication. Dry farming gave way to irrigation in suitable areas. Farming tools improved and the plow was developed. Permanent dwellings made of sun-dried brick emerged in the Near East, and woven clothing appeared for the first time in many parts of the world in which domestication was practiced. Sheep were exploited for their wool and cotton was raised for spinning.

Social Structure

Large permanent settlements—and the population of even the earliest agricultural villages was large compared to nomadic hunting

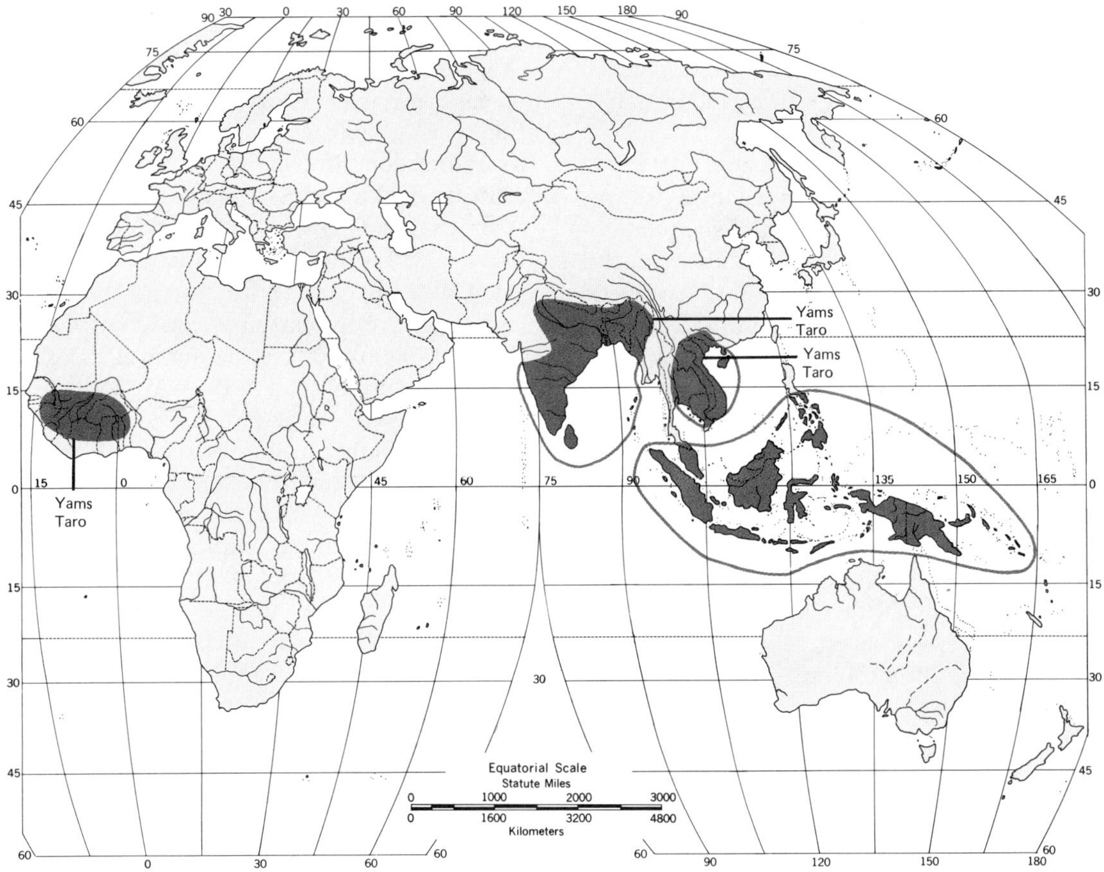

Figure 10.13
The world-wide domestication of root crops.

bands—imply changes in social organization. Land became valuable with cultivation and population increase. Title to land had to be organized on a permanent basis, as did the work process. In many cases organization for defense had to be established. Nomadic hunters and gatherers performed their basic economic tasks as a group divided only by sex and age. Within the new agricultural settlements families and larger kin groups emerged as the foci of economic activity. While hunting and gathering populations do differ from one another, cultural diversification began in earnest with the emergence of domestication. Local environmental conditions, in combination with the specific animal and plant species exploited, gave rise to different technological innovations both in tools and in the ways in which work was organized. Permanent settlement, increases in population, warfare, and trade all stimulated new forms of the division of labor and the eventual emergence of social stratification.

Summary

The early stages of culture are reconstructed through the analysis of the fossil record, primate behavior, and archeological remains. In an examination of the early African materials the archeologist Glynn Isaac has attempted to reconstruct both the environmental conditions and behavioral traits that were most important in the development of our species and its major adaptation—culture.

Isaac notes that the major features that separate humans from apes are: bipedalism (freeing the hands and arms for carrying), communication through language (which allows for the sharing of information about the environment and the mediation of social relations), cooperative food-getting behavior and the sharing of food (reinforcing social bonds and improving economic efficiency), a home base that can be left by individuals (which serves as the basis of social coherence), meat eating as an important part of the diet (providing a high-quality protein), and the preparation of food with tools of various kinds.

Isaac also notes several features of social organization that contribute to the adaptation of *Homo sapiens.* The most important of these are: (1) pair bonding between males and females, which implies an economic as well as a sexual union, a division of labor by sex, and joint child rearing, and (2) the development of kinship beyond the immediate family group, which implies complex forms of social organization.

Isaac considers food-sharing important for the development of the division of labor. The division of labor stimulated the carrying of different types of food, which were then made available to the group. Food was contributed to the group by both hunters (usually men) and gatherers (usually women). Isaac's theory suggests that a group whose members were able to exchange food and information about the environment would have a selective advantage over groups without that capacity.

Culture history reflects a long period in which hunting and gathering, and in some cases fishing, were the exclusive forms of economic activity. The longest period of human existence was the Paleolithic (Old Stone Age), which has been divided by archeologists into three subperiods (the Lower, Middle, and Upper Paleolithic). The Lower Paleolithic is characterized by crude stone tools dating to about 2.6 million years ago. These Oldowan artifacts are pebble choppers made by a simple process known as percussion flaking. (A recent find at Hadar in Ethiopia of more complex tools may force a reclassification of Oldowan tools as the first artifact type known. The Hadar tools are more complex than Oldowan tools, and if they can be firmly dated to the suspected 2.5 or so million years, they will considerably change the archeological picture for early humans in Africa.)

By 500,000 years ago members of the genus *Homo* were established in the Old World. Tools associated with *erectus* fossils have been found in China, Southeast Asia, Africa, and Europe. In Asia tools remain rather crude forms of choppers, but in Africa and Europe Oldowan tools give way to more complex forms. The most characteristic tool from this period in Europe and Africa is the bi-faced hand ax (the Chellean-Acheulian tradition).

By about 100,000 years ago the distribution of cultures in the Old World is quite complex. This period, which begins the Middle Paleolithic, is marked by the development of the Levallois technique. This technique, characterized by the preparation of a core before striking flakes from it, enhances the quality of manufactured stone tools. The Levallois technique was frequently used in the preparation of Mousterian tools associated with the remains of *Homo sapiens neanderthalensis.* The Mousterian tradition includes a complex array of specialized tools including hand axes, scrapers, projectile points, and serrated, saw-like tools known as denticulates.

The Upper Paleolithic begins about 37,000 years ago. It is associated with the modern form of *Homo—Homo sapiens sapiens*—and is characterized by blade tools. These are flake tools at least twice as long as they are wide. Blade manufacture was facilitated by the development of a new technique of manufacture. Instead of striking at the flake during its retouching (percussion flaking), the maker exerted pressure along the edge of the tool with a piece of bone or antler. This allowed the toolmaker to have greater control over the shaping process. This technique became so refined that blades of great size and beauty could be manufactured. The most spectacular of these come from the Solutrean culture of Europe. In addition to stone, tools of bone, wood, and antler are common from the Upper Paleolithic. This period also saw a large increase in the types of tools made. Among the many innovations was the burin or chisel. These tools appeared in the Mousterian but increased in frequency during the Upper Paleolithic.

The Upper Paleolithic is too complex to summarize. It saw the development and diversification of many cultures, each of which can be characterized by a specific tool kit. Among the Upper Paleolithic cultures were the Aurignacian and Perigordian of southwestern France. These were followed by the Solutrean. In eastern Europe archeologists have documented a tradition known as the Gravettian, which has been associated with mammoth hunting. Cave art and sculpture are associated with the Magdalenian culture from western Europe that began sometime around 17,000 years ago.

The Paleolithic was followed by the Mesolithic (Middle Stone Age), characterized by climatic variation, the domestication of the dog, the invention of the bow and arrow, and the movement of many populations to coastal and lake areas, with an increase in fishing as an economic activity. Mesolithic peoples probably lived in settled villages, since fishers and gatherers do well when they stay put. The development of sedentarism (permanent villages) increases the ability of people to know their local environment, which in turn may lead to an increase in exploitative activity. The Mesolithic, therefore, may have been a time of innovation.

The dates for the settlement of the New World are under intense discussion among archeologists. Estimates range from as far in the past as 70,000 years to as recently as about 18,000 years ago. It is agreed, however, that humans entered the Western Hemisphere across a land bridge from Asia (at the Bering Strait) and that the first Americans were hunters and gatherers. Two well-known Paleoindian cultures from the southwest of the United States are identified by projectile points of particular types. One of these, Clovis culture, is associated with bog and other stagnant water sites. The other, Folsom culture, is associated with sites at the foot of cliffs. It has been hypothesized that Clovis hunters ambushed mammoths along their feeding routes, whereas Folsom hunters drove bison off of cliffs to their deaths below. Both Clovis and Folsom assemblages contain ground stone tools probably used in the processing of various plant materials. As is generally the case with people who hunt, gathering probably played an important part in the subsistence of both Clovis and Folsom peoples.

Plant and animal domestication occurred in the Neolithic (New Stone Age). The first domesticates may have been animals that lived near and exploited the refuse of human habitations. There are several theories concerning the development of plant domestication, but the most likely one is that the management of wild species gradually led to the development of cultivated species.

In the late 1940s Robert Braidwood developed the hilly-flank theory of domestication. He suggested that plant domestication in the Middle East began in a zone of hills located to the north of the Fertile Crescent. He believed that wild grasses growing in these hills were domesticated there and eventually brought down to the valleys where cultivation became intensive.

Kent Flannery objected to this theory on the grounds that populations living in areas with abundant wild grains would be unlikely to domesticate them. The underlying assumption here is that people have to be stimulated to give up one sure technique for an untried new method. Flannery suggests that experimental domestication occurred in productively marginal areas, where increasing population stimulated the development of new subsistence techniques. At first, wild plants were cared for. Later, some were moved into new environmental zones, where they became dependent on humans. Further experimentation led to the selection of plants with characteristics favorable to human use. These characteristics made the plants even more dependent on human care, and they could no longer grow successfully in the wild where they would be overcome by weeds.

There is evidence for domesticated animals in the Near East as far back as 11,000 years ago. By 8000 years ago animal husbandry had become diversified and many species can be found in the archeological record. Plant domestication also began in the area about 10,000 years ago with the development of several grain crops.

Domestication in Asia occurred in two zones. One—China—saw the development of pig husbandry, millet, and, later, rice cultivation. The other zone, in the tropical regions of Southeast Asia, saw the development of root crops such as yams and taro. Rice appears in China about 5000 years ago and in the Indus Valley of India about the same time.

The domestication of plants in the Valley of Mexico took place between 9500 and 3500 years ago. Maize, beans, and squash were the major crops. Although archeologists speculate that in Mexico cultivation began, as it did in the Near East, as an attempt to widen the area in which plants could be successfully grown, population pressure may not have been a major stimulus for this change. Instead, plant domestication may have been the outcome of two types of change: genetic changes in certain key plants (particularly beans and the ancestors of maize) and changes in the way a highly varied environment was exploited by humans. Flannery suggests that environmental exploitation shifted from a generalized form, in which many species were used, to a more specialized one with an intensive focus on the new types of plants.

The domestication of plants and animals led to a series of technological and social developments, including larger, more permanent settlements and widespread trade. Since land became valuable with cultivation, permanent title eventually developed in some areas, probably those where land was itself a scarce resource. Larger permanent settlements and trade led to the development of more complex economic specialities, contributing to a highly diversified division of labor and eventually social stratification.

Bibliography

Bordaz, J. 1968 — *The Old Stone Age.* New York: McGraw Hill. A review of stone-tool traditions.

Braidwood, R. and G. Willey 1962 — *Courses Toward Urban Life.* Chicago: Aldine. Material on permanent settlements and the origin of domestication.

Bushnell, G. H. S. 1968 — *The First Americans.* New York: McGraw-Hill. Review of American Indian culture from the earliest settlements to civilization.

Chang, K. C. 1963 — *The Archeology of Ancient China.* New Haven: Yale University Press. China from the Paleolithic to the rise of civilization.

Flannery, K.V. 1968 — Archaeological Systems Theory and Early Mesoamerica. In Betty Meggers (ed.) *Anthropological Archaeology in the Americas.* Washington, D.C.: Anthropological Society of Washington, pp. 67–87. The concept of resource scheduling as it relates to the origin of domestication in the New World.

Isaac, G. 1978 — The Food Sharing Behavior of Protohuman Hominids. *Scientific American.* 238:90–109. An archeologist speculates about hominid evolution on the basis of evidence from archeology, paleontology, primate behavior, and ethnographies of contemporary hunting and gathering populations.

MacNeish, R.S., editor 1973 — *Early Man in America.* San Francisco: Freeman. A set of articles covering theory and data on settlement and subsistence in early New World populations.

Perkins, D., Jr. and P. Daly 1974 — The Beginning of Food Production in the Near East. In *The Old World: Early Man to the Development of Agriculture.* New York: St. Martin's Press. An outline of early food production in the Near East with material on key sites.

Stigler, R., editor 1975 — *Varieties of Culture in the Old World.* New York: St. Martin's Press. A collection of articles on Africa, Europe, the Near East, the Far East, and Australia and the Pacific.

Ucko, P. J. and G. W. Dimbleby, editors 1969 — *The Domestication and Exploitation of Plants and Animals.* Chicago: Aldine. A broad series of articles on domestication and its implications for cultural evolution.

Ucko, P. J. and A. Rosenfeld 1967 — *Paleolithic Cave Art.* New York: McGraw-Hill. A critical examination of explanations of cave art.

CHAPTER 11
THE RISE OF THE STATE

Stratification and State Formation
Rank and Stratification
States and Urban Centers
Civilization
The Origin of Stratification
Population as Motor
Technology as Motor
Social Structure as Motor
Criticisms of These Theories
Theories of the Rise of the State
Conquest
Trade
Ecological Confinement
Circumscription, Warfare, and Population Increase
Hydraulic Agriculture
States of the Old and New Worlds
The Mesopotamian State
Olmec and Maya in the New World
The Valley of Mexico
Peru

Social stratification, and particularly the rise of the state, are related to significant technological developments that increased the human capacity to capture and use environmental energy. Stratification, however, is associated not only with increased energy extraction but also with an unequal distribution and consumption of that energy. In stratified societies, who gets what is determined by social rules. The change from relative equality, which we see in most hunting and gathering societies, to inequality is a major transformation of culture. This transformation must have occurred before the evolution of the state, for social stratification is associated with many agricultural and pastoral societies.

The unequal distribution of environmental energy changes and complicates the evolutionary process. In strictly biological evolution—and perhaps cultural evolution as well before the development of stratification—adaptation involves the ability of organisms to convert environmental elements into themselves. In biological evolution energy flows into organisms, maintains them, and fuels the reproductive process. In stratified human societies a good deal of extracted energy is diverted to certain social groups, particularly elites (such as rulers, upper classes, high castes), and is used to bolster their position in a system of inequality.

The reasons behind the transition from egalitarian to stratified societies are not completely known, although technological change and demographic (population) factors are certainly important. The major problem is wrapped up in a chicken-or-egg-first argument. No one is sure what factors sparked this major change in the development of culture. Before I examine the theories that have been proposed to account for the rise of stratification and the state itself, I must define a set of necessary terms. These are: *rank, stratification, state, urbanism,* and *civilization.*

STRATIFICATION AND STATE FORMATION

Rank and Stratification

Inequality in social relations can be divided into two major types: **rank** and **stratification.** *Rank* refers to differences in prestige but not to political power. Many societies have "big men" who through their actions have gained prestige among their fellows. In ranked societies, however, this prestige is rarely translated into power, that is, control over others. In *stratified* societies, individuals with higher social status exercise real power over individuals of lower status. This power is displayed in the political, social, and economic arenas. As a result, low-status individuals have less access to the material fruits of society. They may be forced into actions that benefit the higher social group. Inequality may also be more or less passively accepted as a fact of life.

Social class and **caste** are different types of social stratification. In a class society, one group controls the means of production. It directs the productive process and controls access to its output. Castes are hierarchically organized, occupation-specific groups. The members of individual castes perform certain economic tasks and exchange their own production or services for those of other castes. They are also **endogamous,** that is, marriage must take place within each caste. In India, where the caste system is most fully developed, it is supported by a complicated set of religious beliefs that reinforce the division of society into a set of rather rigid categories.

States and Urban Centers

The **state** is distinguished from other types of society by social stratification in which coercive authority is manifested in a government through its power to tax, to raise an army, and to enforce laws of its own making.

In *nonstate* societies, legal and political decisions are usually determined within and between kin groups. An act against an individual is commonly seen as a *wrong* (in our own legal terminology as a **tort**) against the individual's kin group. Punishment takes the form of personal or kin-group retribution. In the case of murder, for example, the murderer, and usually his or her kin group, owes a debt to the social group of the murdered person. It is they—not the whole society or a government—who seek redress by means of kin-based negotiations. In nonstate societies kinship determines social relations. A person's status or place is defined in terms of membership in a network of kin relations.

In states, social relations are often based on economic status and occupation. Kinship may continue to play a role, but it is usually secondary. In a state, loyalty is owed to the state itself. As an entity the state is usually defined in terms of its territory. Its citizens are those free individuals who are born within its borders and granted state citizenship by the rule of law. In the state, law as well as political control is managed by rulers and their agents. Although some acts are still defined as torts, it is the state that renders legal decisions. In addition, the notion of **crime** appears. Crime is defined as an act against the state, to be punished by the state. Thus, murder in the United States is not a personal matter. It is a crime and a state court judges the act and sets the punishment.

Urbanism refers to the way of life of population centers that are complex, permanent settlements with large numbers of residents. Characteristically, urban centers are inhabited by full-time craft and business specialists and religious functionaries who rely on others for food produced in rural areas. Urban centers are the focus of religious and symbolic life as well as

A reconstruction of a New World urban center, Tenochtitlan, on the site of present-day Mexico City.

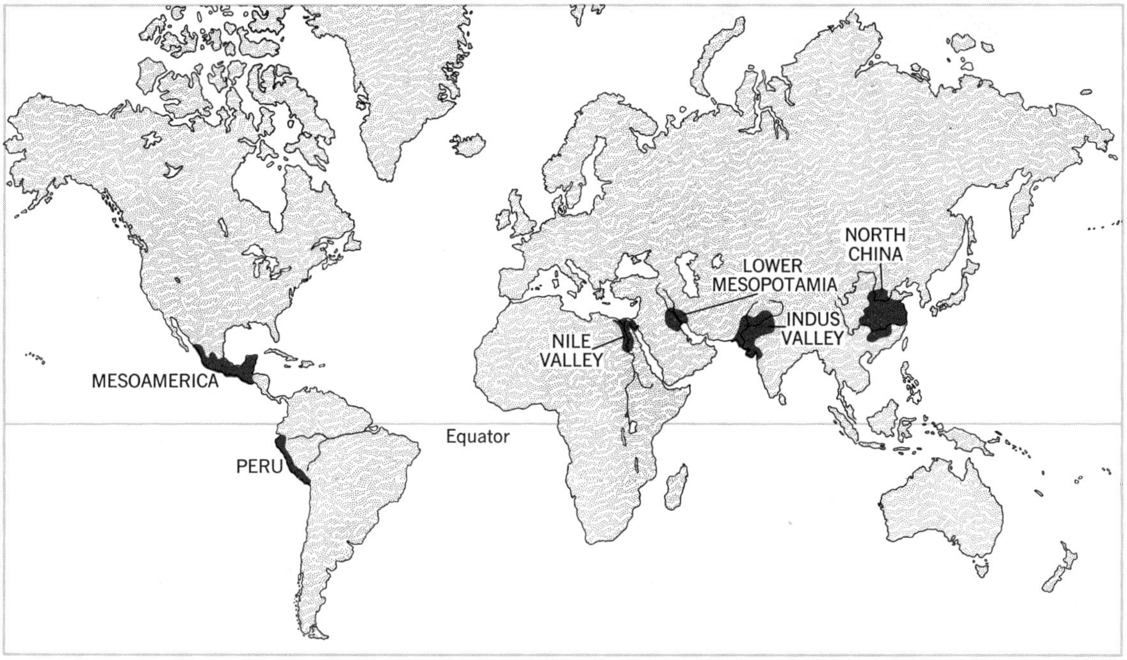

Figure 11.1
The distribution of early civilizations.

the heart of economic activity. They are also often the seat of political and legal power.

State organization and urbanization both contribute to the development and flowering of the arts. Architecture, music, visual art, dance, literature, and medicine all tend to flourish in the context of stratified urban society.

The early states of the Middle East (with the exception of Egypt) were *city-states,* or urban civilizations, as was the Aztec state in the Valley of Mexico. At the end of the Middle Ages in Europe, city-states existed in Venice, Rome, and Florence as well as in the north of Europe.

At the present time, with such minor exceptions as Monaco and Singapore, states consist of national territories of varying size that encompass a range of cities, towns, and villages as well as rural areas. While they continue to be economic centers for trade and manufacturing, modern cities may or may not be political and cultural centers also.

Civilization

The term **civilization** implies both urbanism and state formation. Civilizations are characterized by high population density *usually* concentrated in urban centers, a complex division of labor with full-time nonagricultural specialists, social stratification, full-time government officials, extensive trade, a full-time army, a national religion frequently tied to the ideology of state power, and a high development of the arts as well as science. Writing is often used by anthropologists and historians as a criterion for civilization, but not all societies that should be characterized as civilizations had writing. The most notable example of a civilization without a writing system was that of the Inca in Peru.

THE ORIGIN OF STRATIFICATION

Now that I have defined the key terms, I can turn to the origin of stratification and the rise of the state. Most scholars agree that there are three key variables in social evolution. These are population, technology, and social structure. All three exhibit significant changes with the emergence of stratification and again with the emergence of the state. All three are assumed to play some role in culture change. A fourth variable, the environment, provides the context for cultural developments and undoubtedly exerts a selective force on them. Argument centers around the question of which of the first three variables are independent (or causative) and which are dependent (or resultant).

Let us now examine each of the three variables as a possible motor for cultural evolution.

Population as Motor

The theory favoring population assumes that population growth is a natural process and occurs under all conditions. It further assumes that as a society begins to strain the **carrying capacity** of its environment (the number of people that a given environment and technology can support without leading to environmental degradation), it will be stimulated automatically to respond to need. Three responses are possible under these conditions. (1) A society may begin to practice some form of population control in order to check its growth and restore its balance with its environment. (2) A society may expand its territory or divide with the migration of a part of it away into new territory. In either case the effect would be a reduction in the number of individuals per unit of area and a return to balance with environmental variables. (3) Members of a society may be stimulated to innovate new technological means for meeting the demands of increased population. Innovation can involve either the development of new tools and techniques, or new ways of working, or both. In the case of the work force, production can be improved through changes in social structure, particularly the way in which work is organized and controlled. Since territory is never infinite, it is assumed that sooner or later option two would no longer work and populations would resort to technological change to solve their problems. Option one, of course, does not require increased production since it leads, in theory, to a stable population.

Technology as Motor

This theory assumes that population tends to come into automatic equilibrium with its environment and a given technological means of exploiting it. Growth will only occur, according to this theory, when technological change allows it to happen. Thus technological change is seen as a force for the development of increased population. This growth is then assumed to stimulate a new kind of social organization which is necessitated by greater numbers.

Social Structure as Motor

According to this theory no society is a perfectly functioning unit in which each element of behavior fits perfectly into a system like that of a living organism. Contradictions are, therefore, bound to occur as parts of the system come into conflict. These contradictions are resolved through changes in social organization that have implications for both technology and population. In addition, it is assumed that each time one set of contradictions is resolved new ones are created that will continue to generate cultural change. This theory is discussed at length in Chapter 24, particularly in relation to the Kachin of Burma.

Criticisms of These Theories

Recently some anthropologists have begun to question the idea that population *normally* increases to match or exceed the carrying capacity of an environment. Benjamin White, in a thesis written at Columbia University, argues that social groups have always been capable of controlling their numbers. Techniques range from various sexual taboos to infanticide and geronticide (the killing of old people). For instance, postpartum sex taboos (strictures forbidding sexual intercourse for varying periods after the birth of a baby) are common in Africa and act to limit population growth. Infanticide is common among South American Indians, and abortion is also common among many of the world's ethnic groups. In the past the Eskimos practiced geronticide.

Another means of population control is to raise the age at marriage for women. The older a woman is before she can marry and bear children, the less children she will be able to bear. In addition, delayed marriage increases the span of years between generations. The retardation of generations is a powerful brake on population growth. Just as population can be controlled, it can be stimulated to grow under certain circumstances. Neither growth nor stability is an automatic process.

White's thesis examines the dynamics of population in Java under Dutch colonization. He shows that the rapid growth of the Javanese population can be linked directly to the development of a colonial system in which labor needs were increased. The Dutch plantation system was based on low capital investment and a consequent demand for labor. In order to meet this demand as well as to feed themselves, the Javanese had to increase their labor force. The only way they could do this was to increase their population. Population growth was a response to a social system that required high productivity with little technological input.

A similar case can be documented for Ireland. During the height of the colonization of Ireland by the English, the latter made severe labor demands on the Irish population. Irish peasants were required to work their English lord's farms where cattle and grain were raised. Since the English made few capital investments in Irish agriculture, labor input was very important. The system was labor-intensive (based on manual work) rather than capital-intensive (based on investment). Because children could begin to work early and were a cheap source of labor, large families were favored. For the Irish peasant the output, or gain, from child labor was higher than the cost of having children. The age at marriage dropped significantly during this period of colonization and no birth control was practiced. The Irish population rose rapidly. With overcrowding, overcropping, and exploitation the Irish peasant became dependent for nourishment on potatoes and a little milk. These were produced at home on small-scale holdings. Then famine struck. The potato blight, which had previously hit the European continent, came to Ireland in the 1840s. The intensively planted fields were rapidly infected and the blight became worse than it had been elsewhere. The famine produced many deaths and stimulated emigration. Soon afterwards a demographic adjustment began to occur. Although, for religious reasons, the Irish were loath to practice any form of birth control, the marriage age took a sharp turn upward. As the span between generations lengthened, population growth declined.

The Javanese and Irish experiences apply to the modern world in which stratification has long since occurred and where colonial exploitation is a fact of life. While these cases show that population growth and stability are not automatic processes and that they can be related to technological and political forces, they cannot be used to argue for or against any one particular process in the *original* development of stratification or state formation.

Technological change may well lead to an increase in carrying capacity by improving the means of extracting energy from the environment. It may therefore allow for an increase in population, but such an increase is not automatic. New technology can also be used to reduce the amount of energy that goes into productive activities without increasing overall production. When this occurs, carrying capacity is not raised, at least in actual practice. We tend to see technological innovations as a means for increased production because the capitalist system is based on growth.

The adoption of new technologies is not an automatic process in culture. People are often reluctant to change from a time-proven system to one that might result in unanticipated problems. When new technologies are adopted, however, they may contribute not only to population growth but also to shifts in social organization. The development of the factory system in Europe at the beginning of the Industrial Revolution led to the destruction of home-based industry and the formation of a working class that became dependent on factory owners for employment.

The notion that contradictions in social organization provide the *universal* motor for change is equally unconvincing because our data can only be drawn from contemporary cases in which stratification has already occurred. A hard look at the archeological evidence as well as the data from a wide sample of contemporary societies suggests that stratification is the result of a complex interaction among all three variables and that none of them can be taken alone as the motor for change. Both stratification and the rise of the state are most likely due to historically and culturally different combinations of these factors in each specific case. Nonetheless, these variables along with environment are all central elements in the development of complex society.

THEORIES OF THE RISE OF THE STATE

States are marked by complex forms of stratification as well as a shift away from kinship-based social organization to territorial organization. The three variables of population growth, technological change, and social structure interacting with the environment have been used in all discussions of state formation. Additional factors have been suggested for this important development. The following theories of state formation are either of historical importance or are currently among the most popular.

Conquest

According to the conquest theory, states form when one people or ethnic group overwhelms another in war, moves into the territory of the conquered people, and subjugates them. The immediate result is two classes, one of which governs the other. This theory has been applied to Africa, to explain a set of "conquest" states said to have arisen, particularly in the eastern part of the continent. Any archeological evidence of invasion (a sudden change in technology and art style coupled with signs of marked social distinction) tends to fit this theory, but it is too simplistic. For one thing, it suggests that the invading group had a complex military organization and desire for territorial expansion usually found in already evolved state societies.

Trade

The development of trading centers along strategic routes often leads to the emergence of state organizations. Before European shipping reached the West Coast of Africa, great trading empires had developed on the fringes of the Sahara desert. These states were located along caravan routes (see Figure 11.2). They were able to control the movement of goods both from the forest areas northward and from the Mediterranean and the desert southward. When Europeans finally established contact with the West African coast at the end of the fifteenth century, these trading states were short-circuited and died out. They were followed, however, by the development of great coastal empires that were also dependent on trade.

This theory certainly is backed up by historical evidence. But the kind of large-scale trade that stimulated state development was itself dependent to a degree on the previous existence of trading states. Commerce undoubtedly played a role in the development of *pristine* states (the first states uninfluenced by the processes of diffusion from other states), but it cannot provide an exclusive solution to the problem of state formation.

Ecological Confinement

The theory of ecological confinement is identified with the work of V. Gordon Childe, a great English archeologist who worked in the second quarter of this century. Childe was particularly interested in European Neolithic culture and Middle Eastern civilization. He was an evolutionist who attempted to apply to culture the approach that Darwin had applied to the evolution of life. Childe demarcated a series of great behavioral transformations (Childe called them revolutions) that took place during cultural evolution. The first of these was the *origin of culture* itself. Culture as *the* human adaptation was seen as the major force that separates humans as a species from all other animals. The second revolution was the *discovery and development of plant and animal domestication.* The third revolution was the *development of civilization* (urban centers, the state, full-time specialists, writing). The fourth major change was the *industrial revolution.* Each of these revolutions marked an evolutionary advance. Each produced an increase in the capacity to extract energy from the environment. The increasingly efficient means of harnessing energy allowed greater numbers of humans to live successfully in environments that were coming increasingly under the control of cultural forces. Childe proposed population size as a mark of adaptation, a notion very close to Darwin's idea of selective

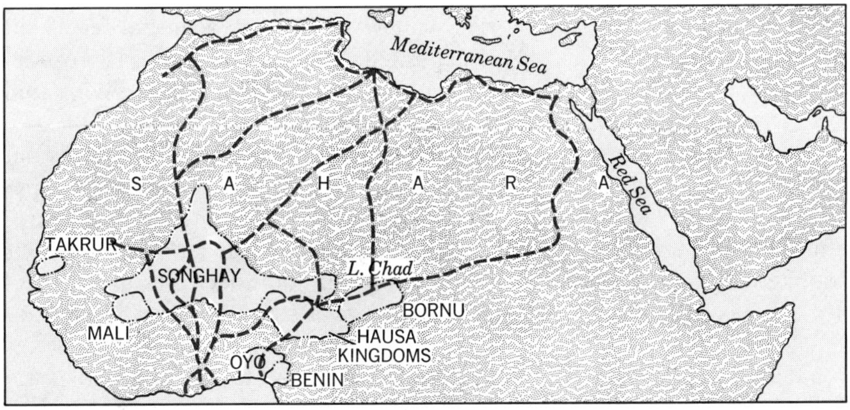

Figure 11.2

Early trading empires in the Sahara region of Africa. The dashed lines show major trade routes. These states were eclipsed when European traders discovered a sea route to the West Coast of Africa.

fertility. In the biological theory animals that outreproduce other animals of the same species in the same environment are the better adapted members of that species. Instead of comparing selective fertility rates in contemporary populations, an impossible task for archeology, Childe saw increasing technological efficiency as equivalent to increasing genetic efficiency. Instead of comparing fertility within populations at one point in time, Childe compared population data from the same culture through time and correlated increases with energy transformation.

Childe was aware that evolutionary theory requires a close look at the interaction between species and environment. The source of change comes from within the species (or better, the population), but it is the environment that exerts a selective influence on variation. Variations that increase efficiency are favorably selected. Those that decrease efficiency are negatively selected (rejected). Childe paid a great deal of attention to the environment in which the first Old World civilizations arose. He attempted to extract from his data those features of environment-culture relations that could produce this important transformation.

There is a key difference between evolution among nonhuman species and cultural evolution. Genes can be exchanged between populations only through interbreeding, but culture traits can be shared through borrowing. This difference has to be taken into account in constructing a theory of cultural evolution. Childe was aware that culture traits can be transmitted by **diffusion** (borrowing) and that cultural adaptation is, therefore, different from genetic adaptation.

Childe assumed that after the first civilizations had arisen in the most likely environmental settings, the new cultural ideas generated could diffuse to less adequate environments. Secondary civilizations would be the result of borrowing. They, in turn, would undergo change under the influence of the local environments as well as those historical processes that are stimulated by trade and warfare. His major conclusions about the rise of primary (or pristine) civilizations were the following:

1 In order for population to increase, there had to be an adequate subsistence base. This base developed in the precivilization period with the development of plant and animal domestication.
2 There had to be some reason why increasing populations also led to increasing density, because the first civilizations in the Middle East were assumed to have developed in the context of urban centers. In general, Childe reasoned, when space is available, migration or local expansion takes care of increased numbers. In urban centers there is a significant increase in local density. The city is essentially a crowded place in comparison to farming land and villages. Childe noted that early civilizations in the Middle East all developed in river valleys (the Nile, the Tigris and Euphrates) that were surrounded by deserts. People could spread along the rivers but were hemmed in on both sides by arid and uncultivable land. This fact, however, raised another problem. With a relatively primitive technology, in which fertilizer and crop rotation were unknown, how could populations reach large numbers on a limited amount of arable land? The answer is that these particular river valleys flood every year and fertile silt is deposited. This natural fertilization process leads to a yearly renewal and continual high agricultural yields.
3 Cities are not populated by rich farmers but rather by full-time craft and economic specialists who are not themselves food producers. They have to rely on others for their food supply. In addition, cities are characterized by social stratification whereby political power and therefore access to resources and manufactured goods are unevenly distributed. Social classes develop. Childe reasoned that these fertile but spatially limited valleys lacked certain necessary resources. The lack stimulated trade

between centers, each of which had access to different resources. Trade in such items as salt and raw materials for industry could be augmented by manufactured goods, which stimulated the development of craft specialties. As trade increased in volume and frequency, traders became full-time specialists. Their enterprises grew and they were forced to employ assistants. As trade increased, some means of keeping a tally of income and outgo became necessary. Childe suggested that it was this kind of mercantile activity that gave rise to a crude notation system that eventually became true writing.

Landsat mosaic of photographs of the Nile Valley and surrounding areas. The Nile shores are fertile, but the river valley is hemmed in by deserts.

4. Social stratification was stimulated by three factors: a) a growing difference in wealth among individuals with different professions, b) the development of slavery with the use of war captives as workers, and c) the need in an area that depended on annual flooding to keep good seasonal records and to assure, through religious activity, the coming of the life-sustaining flood waters. Under these conditions a religious hierarchy could develop that would eventually exert considerable political power over the entire population. From insuring rain and predicting flood levels, the priests could move on to assuring victory in war and good health. These three forces working together could produce a three-class society: a religious aristocracy at the top, a population of free citizens in the middle, and war-captive slaves at the bottom.

State organization has certain adaptive advantages over simpler social forms. Political and military actions are coordinated and controlled by strong leaders. A permanent or semipermanent army is available to wage wars of defense and aggression. People owe their loyalty not to kin but to an abstract entity personalized by leaders and defined by a territory: the state. A state can mobilize considerable power and use it to expand political control. It was not long, therefore, before the first city-states began to expand and become empires. In wartime, empires are formidable military entities. In times of peace, they dominate a wide trade network that spreads ideas and goods beyond the immediate geographic area. Cultures that do not respond by organizing similar states are easily absorbed by the dominant power; thus, state organization as an adaptation spreads.

This is the picture of the Mediterranean

Evidence of a class structure in ancient Egypt. Maidservants attending ladies at a banquet.

world that Childe drew. Considering the time in which he worked and the data then available to him, his theories were of major importance. Nonetheless, he committed errors of both commission and omission. The technological transformation from simple agricultural societies to states is only revolutionary by hindsight. Once the process has been accomplished the differences between the two stages appear clear, distinctive, and very large. It is more likely, however, that the economic, environmental, and social processes that governed the transformation to state organization were slower and more complex than those envisioned by Childe. In addition, Childe tended to neglect rather large differences between the civilizations that grew up along the Tigris and Euphrates rivers and the state that rose along the Nile. Egypt was never really urban, although the other states certainly were. Childe also tended to rely too heavily on diffusion *within* the circumscribed area of the Fertile Crescent to explain the rise of civilization there. It is more likely that a series of independent developments in different parts of the Mediterranean world all contributed to the rise of state societies. Diffusion was integral to the process, but early on well before the first states emerged. Remember, Childe tended to see both the development of domestication and the rise of civilization as revolutions. He implied rapid and spectacular change. Later archeological evidence has shown that these changes were the result of slow accumulations, tentative borrowings, and experimentations.

Circumscription, Warfare, and Population Increase

The anthropologist Robert Carneiro has refined and modified Child's ecological-confinement theory. He suggests that states did indeed arise in areas where populations were hemmed in by environmental or demographic conditions.

In such areas population pressure cannot be reduced through migration. In addition, when people become adapted to a particular environmental zone they are reluctant to leave it, for migration will demand a new set of adaptations. As population increases in circumscribed areas, pressure builds up on available resources. Exploitation of resources is intensified and means are developed for controlling their distribution. These means often include the formation of political elites who regulate overall production and distribution. Population increase and resource scarcity also lead to competition between groups, which eventually results in warfare. Wars are won by superior military organization, and states provide these organizations. Any innovation (social or technological) in the direction of state formation would provide an instant military advantage and may therefore be a powerful means of cultural adaptation. Such cultural selection is enhanced by the power of the state to control production and distribution.

Hydraulic Agriculture

The theory of hydraulic agriculture, associated with the name of Karl Wittfogel, a historian, attempts to account for the development of one particular kind of state known as **oriental despotism.** This social form is characterized by a bureaucratic and despotic government that exerts tight control over its subject population. Oriental despotism is marked by a tremendous centralization of power in the hands of the ruling class. Wittfogel believes that this type of social organization resulted from the need for irrigation technology in areas where the distribution of water had to be controlled by pumping. Under these conditions efficient distribution would require tight bureaucratic control. This control could then be extended to other aspects of social and political life. Since irrigation agriculture, particularly rice agriculture, is tremendously productive, this system, once established, could support a vast population. The larger the population, the greater the need for strict management of resources. Thus, a technological advance was assumed to produce both a particular kind of sociopolitical system and a population explosion.

It is important to note that Wittfogel did not assume that all systems of irrigation led to oriental despotism, only those in which water had to be raised above its source with the aid of pumping devices. For example, the vast, impressive irrigation terraces of the Ifugao of the Philippines are excluded from the hypothesis. These artificial features of the landscape stretch for miles and miles up and down the mountainous country. The Ifugao terraces, however, were built during the course of several hundred years. Irrigation in this area depends on the *downward* flow of water from mountain streams. Adequate water exists to irrigate each field and the water is distributed naturally by the force of gravity. The Ifugao have no state organization, and the hydraulic hypothesis does not predict that they should.

On the other hand, there is no good evidence that all despotic states resulted from the technological development described by Wittfogel. Although irrigation is implicated one way or another in most, the evidence for pumping is often not present. We cannot criticize Wittfogel for the nondespotic nature of nonhydraulic irrigation societies, but we can demand evidence for a hydraulic technology when despotism is found. In addition, it is not at all clear that the social system described by Wittfogel came *after* the institution of hydraulic technology. Nor can we be sure that population increased *only* as the result of the particular technological and political factors Wittfogel singled out.

The question is, can a class division of some sort occur *prior* to technological change? Can a preadaptive form of social organization exist that can easily give rise to a class structure under the proper set of conditions? There is at least one archeologist who thinks this is possible.

In his book, *The Evolution of Urban Society,* Robert Adams examines the rise of civilization in the Middle East and Mesoamerica. A number of evolutionary similarities leads Adams to conclude that parallel processes occurred in

Although the Ifugao construct impressive terraces used in extensive irrigation, they do not have a despotic government—nor should they, according to the hydraulic hypothesis, since water in their system is distributed by gravity. China, on the other hand, provides the type case of Oriental despotism. Chinese agriculture depends on pumping and the strict control of water resources.

these geographically distant areas. Adams acknowledges the influence of environment and technology in the development of civilization, but he feels that archeologists have tended to ignore social factors. He criticizes Wittfogel's hydraulic hypothesis, pointing out that widespread irrigation systems followed on, rather than preceded, the social systems found in despotic states. He then suggests that certain social forms already present in prestate societies could serve as the basis for the emergence of a social hierarchy.

We have already seen that one of the mysteries in anthropology is the origin and development of social stratification. Hunting and gathering societies as well as many horticultural societies are egalitarian, with little or no social differentiation. The only potential for inequality in these cultures lies in the division of labor. Men and women perform different tasks, as do younger and older group members. Although women are exploited in many societies, it is unlikely that the division of labor by sex could lead to class structure, which in all cases involves both sexes and members of each class. What about the older-younger distinction? In an egalitarian society the young may, for a time, serve the old, but since they move through the system as they age, youths can expect eventually to occupy the positions held by their elders. This division is too fluid to produce permanent differences in social status. There are, however, some societies that recognize the superior position of older men not only in terms of age but also in terms of heritage. That is, a line of senior men (the oldest son of the oldest son of the oldest son) may be given certain rights over junior lines. This can occur in societies in which the distinction between elder and younger siblings is strongly marked and where relative age grants certain privileges to oldest brothers and/or sisters. Members of a senior line (the eldest sons of an eldest son of an eldest son, etc.) may have higher rank than the members of other lines. Such a form of ranking is known as **conical clan** organization. The sometimes slight status differentiation exhibited by this system may be the source of real stratification under changed technological conditions with an uneven distribution of resources and unequal access to land. Adams argues that conical clan organization contains the seeds of class stratification. He sees it as a preadaptation for the development of true classes. The latter emerged, he claims, with increases in productivity and population size in the environments provided by both the Fertile Crescent *and* the heartlands of Mesoamerican civilizations. Adams cites evidence for the existence of conical clan organization in both areas prior to the rise of classes and what archeologists call civilization. The vast differences in access to resources that are characteristic of classes were due to the initial differential access to these resources based on rank differences among clans. As productivity increased with the development of irrigation agriculture, and as trade came to play an important role in the development of wealth, already existing differences became wider and more solidified.

None of the theories presented here is completely satisfactory. Proponents of Wittfogel's hypothesis argue that even small shifts in the direction of hydraulic irrigation will lead to the social changes predicted by the theory. These minor technological changes, they claim, might not be easily seen in the archeological record. In Adams's favor, production as a social process is more than just the extraction of energy from the environment. It also involves social relations among people. What begs explanation is why, in some societies, certain groups lose control over production and come to be controlled by others. The seeds of this process would appear to be sown in the social process itself. Hydraulic irrigation does demand strict organization and increased numbers. It does result in increased productivity. But why, we must ask, does productivity have to be significantly increased? Rising population does not provide the answer, because it appears to be the result and not the cause of irrigation agriculture. When class differentiation occurs, one class may coerce another into producing more and consuming less. Increased production will then benefit the dominant class and so widen the economic and social distance between them and the subservient class. As long as the dominant class controls the means of production, they will succeed in dominating society. History tells us that the dominance will continue until the means of production have changed and new social groups organize around economic activity.

STATES OF THE OLD AND NEW WORLDS

As we have seen, states formed in several parts of the world independently. Centers can be found in the Near East, the Indus Valley in India, the Yellow River Valley in China, on the Gulf Coast of Mexico, and on the coast of Peru. In the New World as in the Old, a series of states succeeded one another through time. Let us now examine a few key cases of state development in the Old and New Worlds.

The Mesopotamian State

The development of agriculture and animal husbandry in the Middle East gave rise to sizable permanent settlements. Intensive agriculture on the fertile plain between the Tigris and Euphrates rivers was able to support large concentrated populations. Sometime between 6000 and 5000 BP cities began to grow out of village clusters. By the end of this period civilization based on the city-state had emerged with its full range of characteristics: writing, temples, full-time craft specialists, markets, class stratification, militarism, complex art, and trade.

The data on Mesopotamian civilizations come from archeological excavations, which have provided extensive information on settlement patterns, ground plans of temples, houses, burials, and the development of technology and material culture. These excavations have also yielded many written records, including myths, tales, and epics as well as more mundane materials such as business transactions and legal documents. Although pictographic writing had appeared by 5400 BP, most of the oldest translatable texts date from around 4500 BP. By that time a city was conceived to be the property of the gods and was maintained on their behalf. With the full flowering of the Mesopotamian city-state, the gods came to symbolize collective identity. The citizens and the priests of each city were responsible for the care of their deities. The deities in turn assured prosperity and protected their subjects from loss in war and such natural disasters as flood and drought. This relationship between gods and humans was so central to the ideology of state power that when a city was taken in war, the conquerors would immediately destroy its temple.

The temples had considerable power, both religious and economic. It is not known, however, how important priests were in the political life of the early state. In the beginning there was apparently a distinction between secular and religious authority. A kind of primitive democracy was maintained through the persistence of kin groups, within which important decisions were frequently made. This is a feature of prestate organization. These kin groups were responsible for public works and supplied men for the army. As an institution they stood between the individual and the state.

As the city-state grew in size and importance, the priests came to dominate a wide range of activities. It was their function to regulate irrigation. In addition, they sponsored an array of enterprises in the temples. These included stone and metal workers, carpenters, weavers and tailors, as well as artists. These craft specialists embellished the temple and its priests and created the lavish props used in state ceremonies.

Class stratification developed slowly in Mesopotamia. For a long time land was probably held by kin groups rather than by individuals. Nonetheless, it may have been these groups that provided the basis for the eventual emergence of stratification. We have already examined Adams's notion that the existence of a conical clan, one in which a senior line dominated, was a preadaptation for a class structure. If this clan status was connected to control over land and other forms of property, a senior line could have begun to prosper at the expense of junior lines. As this process continued, certain kin groups could then dominate production and emerge as a class.

This evolution may have been accelerated and directed by an increase in warfare. The need for tight military organization led to the emergence of full-time generals and a standing army. Traditionally the military role had been dominated by the kin groups. It was out of this military leadership that the kingship developed. Apparently, Mesopotamian states were characterized by a political struggle between priests and secular authority, both of which originally came from senior lines. On one side the priests controlled ritual life, on which successful agriculture and a good deal of temple-centered commerce depended; on the other side, the secular royalty controlled the army and political authorities.

Anthropologists argue over the dynamics of Mesopotamian state organization. Most agree that the initial kick was provided by high productivity in a setting of sedentary village life. The dispute centers around the evolution of stratification and centralized political control. Some agree with Adams that a class structure emerged from a preexisting social form, while others employ the hydraulic hypothesis to account for political domination by religious authority.

Whatever solution may finally be agreed upon, there is no doubt that the rise of the Mesopotamian states produced a momentous shift in social organization and a tremendous increase in production. The rise of the state led to completely new forms of social roles, ranging from full-time craft and religious specialists to a career military. Ownership shifted from property held in common by kin groups to private land. Private ownership, in turn, provided the basis of a class structure.

Olmec and Maya in the New World

Before the appearance of written documents in Mesoamerica, state organization is signaled by the existence of large public buildings. These structures require a large and well-organized

The ancient site of Babylon (Mesopotamia) in present-day Iraq.

labor force for their construction and maintenance. In the New World as well as the Old the earliest archeological evidence of social evolution toward the state consists of monumental buildings and large stone sculptures.

Civilization began later in the New World than in Mesopotamia. The earliest ceremonial centers appear around 3000 BP. The **Olmec** created the first Mesoamerican civilization and their influence can be seen in all subsequent state organizations in that region. The Olmec inhabited the Gulf Coast of Mexico between 3500 and 2500 BP. Little is known of them as a people, although they left behind a highly distinctive art, manifested in sculptures ranging from small jade objects to huge monumental stone heads. The characteristic image is a human infant with jaguar-like features.

Major Olmec sites are found in southern Veracruz and Tabasco, states of present-day Mexico. This area is characterized by high rainfall. During the Olmec period it was covered by tropical forest and swampy lowland river basins. The largest Olmec site, La Venta in Tabasco, was built on an island in a sea-level swamp and consists of a clay pyramid 240 by 420 feet at the base and 110 feet high. Lesser structures appear to the north of the pyramid. Large stone heads and tall, flat monuments (**stelae**) also in stone were found at the site. Since there is no naturally occurring stone on the island, it must have been imported. The most likely quarry is 80 miles to the north! Since these sculptures weigh up to 50 tons, the stone out of which they were carved must have been floated to the island on the river systems of the area. Such activity must have required the labor of many people working together under well-organized directors.

A massive stone head characteristic of Olmec civilization.

The Olmec were apparently warlike, and their warriors invaded the Mexican plateau. Their influence extended even farther. Olmec artifacts can be found over a wide area extending southward 500 miles into El Salvador. A culture similar to that of the Olmec flourished in the Valley of Oaxaca in southern Mexico. This is known as Monte Alban, dating in its initial phase from about 2500 BP.

According to Richard Adams, Olmec society was based on two social units, an elite responsible for the development of the arts, religion, and politics and a "folk component." While the former lived in and near the complex ceremonial centers, the latter lived in dispersed hamlets and villages. The folk component supported the elite through slash-and-burn horticulture.

The development of ceremonial-political centers in the context of slash-and-burn cultivation implies trade and possibly warfare. Such centers are expensive to maintain, but they can provide the political means for the organization of military forces as well as market centers for the exchange of goods coming from different regions. The importance of Olmec religion and its influence over a wide region was also enhanced by the existence of these large and impressive sites in which elaborate ceremonies could be staged.

Maya civilization, also influenced at least in part by the Olmecs, began to develop around

A Mayan clay figurine from Jaina Island (left). The Maya site of Tikal in Guatemala (right).

200 AD in the lowlands of the Yucatan peninsula. Complex stepped platforms characterize Maya architecture. These were topped by heavily decorated, multichambered buildings. The sites also contain ball courts for sporting events that were integrated into ceremonial life. Maya sites contain many trade goods, and graves varying from simple to elaborate, signaling social stratification. The scale of the architecture once again indicates some form of tight political organization.

Until recently the Maya case presented a puzzle for anthropology. The evidence suggested that the Maya were dependent on slash-and-burn maize cultivation for their subsistence needs. We have already seen that this type of horticulture involves relatively low population density, yet Maya centers were large and had permanent inhabitants. It is possible that the fertility of Maya land was such that it could support a rural peasantry as well as city dwellers, with surplus production used to feed the latter. Recent discovery and analysis strongly support the argument that Maya horticulture was supplemented by **arboriculture,** the cultivation of tree crops, specifically, the ramon tree. This tree produces a high yield of nuts that are rich in calories and protein. At the Maya site of Tikal there is a strong correlation between the distribution of house mounds and the ramon tree. It was also discovered that a particular type of underground chamber in these sites (a *chultun*) is ideal for the storage of ramon nuts. Experimental storage of ramon nuts and maize in chultuns demonstrated that maize would rot there within two weeks while the nuts remained in edible condition for up to 18 months.

The Valley of Mexico

Irrigation was not absent in Mesoamerica, and it played a role in the development of civilizations in the highland valleys of central Mexico. The earliest and most spectacular of these was **Teotihuacan,** the remains of which still dominate the landscape about 40 miles from Mexico City. The great pyramids at Teotihuacan thrust up above the plain. Teotihuacan was a true city, complete with satellite towns. At its zenith it was populated by somewhere between 120,000 and 200,000 people.

The valley of Teotihuacan comprises about 100 square miles of bottom land situated to the northeast of the main valley of Mexico. The area was fertile, and springs apparently provided water for irrigation. The site proper, occupying about eight square miles, was urban in every sense of the term. It was, in fact, larger than Rome in the time of the Caesars. The largest structures at Teotihuacan are the Pyramids of the Sun and the Moon. The former is 700 feet long on each of its four sides and over 200 feet high. Most of the other buildings at Teotihuacan are residential. The largest are palaces that served the lords of the city. Smaller dwellings found in several neighborhoods served as housing for the common people. Two large main streets, one of which was known to the Aztecs (a later civilization) as the Avenue of the Dead, intersected at a large square which served as a market place and municipal center. The latter contained administrative buildings and temples.

Teotihuacan began its rise in about 2200 BP. It dominated the area until around 1300 BP, when it may have been destroyed in war. The invaders are unknown, but by 600 AD Teotihuacan's domination of Mesoamerican culture was ended. It continued to influence future states, however, and the Aztec king Moctezuma as well as other leaders made pilgrimages to its ruins. Some authorities have suggested that Teotihuacan's downfall might have been influenced by climatic changes that brought increasing aridity to the area.

The next period of Mexican history was dominated by warfare and shifting alliances.

The site of Teotihuacan in the Valley of Mexico.

According to Coe, this was a time of population movement and the development of small conquest states that split up as fast as they arose. Out of this confusion came the Toltec confederacy. The Toltecs, who were to become a dominant force in the Valley of Mexico and elsewhere, including Yucatan, were originally different tribes which joined forces, no doubt in a military alliance. The center of Toltec power was Tula, a city much smaller than Teotihuacan. Like most centers in the Valley of Mexico, Tula was dominated by pyramids, but none reached the scale of those at Teotihuacan. The largest of these, known as Pyramid B, is decorated on four sides with bas-reliefs of jaguars, coyotes, and eagles representing the warrior orders. In general, Toltec public art is violent. To the north of Pyramid B is the so-called "serpent wall", decorated with painted friezes. Toltec soldiers are depicted in stone everywhere at Tula. On the other hand, representations of the gods are rare. Tula, like Teotihuacan, fell in war, and the city was sacked and burned.

After the fall of Tula anarchy reigned in the Valley of Mexico. The time was ripe for the rise of a new state. In the jockeying for power the **Aztecs** suddenly appeared. The land these newcomers moved in upon was already occupied by civilized peoples, and for several years they lived a precarious existence as serfs of the dominant people in the area. Eventually a group of them settled in the swamps of a large lake (Lake Texcoco) where Mexico City is now situated. In 1367 they began to serve as mercenaries for the expanding Tepanec kingdom. This state was ruled by Tezozomoc, who put the Aztecs under his protection. In 1426 Tezozomoc was succeeded by his son, who attempted to destroy growing Aztec power. Instead, the Aztecs defeated the Tepanecs and took control over the Valley of Mexico. Under the leadership of Tlacaelel, the Aztecs consciously created an ideology of superiority. The sacred books of conquered rival people were destroyed and the Aztecs set out to write their own history. This latter phenomenon is, interestingly, paralleled in the Roman Empire. The great poet Vergil was commissioned by the rulers of Rome to compose an epic based on Homeric legends. This work, the *Aeneid,* served as the charter for Rome.

Great Aztec stone calendar found in the main plaza of Mexico City in 1790. It weighs about 25 tons and is 12 feet in diameter.

Aztec ideology centered on warfare and human sacrifice. War captives were thought to be necessary to feed the sun and keep it in the sky. This ideology supported the Aztec empire, which was a militaristic expansionist state, with power divided between priests and the king.

As their power increased, the Aztecs built the great city of Tenochtitlan, founded about 1250 AD. At its height the city contained about 60,000 houses. Moctezuma, the last king of the Aztecs, lived in a palace with 300 rooms. The local economy was supported by a great agricultural innovation, **chinampa** cultivation. Chinampas were artificially constructed islands in Lake Texcoco. Farmers in boats took mud from the bottom of the lake and used it to fertilize growing plants. Green manure (plant material) and human feces were used as supplemental fertilizer. This form of intensive agriculture produced high yields. Lake Texcoco itself provided another important plant resource. The high level of organic material in the lake supported an algae known as *spirula,* a rich source of high-grade protein. Along with beans it insured a good supply of essential amino acids and a balanced diet.

As noted above the Aztecs practiced human sacrifice on a rather large scale. They believed that the sun god demanded blood for nourishment. Victims, who were war captives, had their living hearts torn out of their bodies. These were offered to the god and the bodies were eaten by members of the elite. The anthropologists Michael Harner and Marvin Harris have suggested that this cannibalism functioned to supply a significant segment of the population with scarce protein. This argument is probably faulty since the Aztec diet was not particularly poor in protein. Cannibalism, which was supported by religious belief, certainly served political ends. It was a means of terrorizing and therefore controlling conquered peoples, but it was also a major element in a complex symbolic and ritual system.

Peru

Peru can be divided into two main geographic regions in which states arose. These are the arid coastal valleys cut by mountain rivers and highland valleys separated by plateaus and high mountains. Irrigation is absolutely necessary for intensive agriculture in the lowlands. In the mountains there was less need, although terracing and irrigation did increase yields.

The evolution of Peruvian civilizations in both regions is divided into three main periods called Formative, Classic, and Postclassic. The Formative is marked by the clustering of small agricultural villages around a ceremonial center. Material culture reveals a variety of activities ranging from stone carving and sophisticated pottery making to gold work and fine weaving. Shared religious ideas and symbols spread rapidly over extensive geographic areas. In the central Andes a style known as Chavin became popular. Chavin motifs include jaguar and serpent deities worked into highly distinctive designs. During the Late Formative a great deal of technological experimentation occurred as well as regional development of particular cultural styles. Regional developments suggest the consolidation of ideas over a geographic area that extends beyond local villages. It indicates an evolution towards a centralized type of culture and political organization.

The Classic period saw the rise of local states. Intensive agriculture based on irrigation became common and provided a base for expanding populations. Craft specialization and luxury goods point toward full-time occupations and a class structure. Priests exercised political power and warfare was common.

Warfare was common in the Postclassic period as well. Wide trade networks also existed, goods were produced on a mass basis, and large urban centers arose. The highlands came under the domination of the highly successful **Inca** state, while the coast was dominated by the **Chimu.** The Chimu capital at Chan Chan had a population of around 50,000.

Like the Aztec state the Inca empire was the final outcome of a long process of shifting power among a series of political entities. The Inca state came to dominate the highlands only after 1476, and it was destroyed by the Spanish in 1534. The Inca had their beginnings in the small tribal nation of Urbamba. From simple origins it grew to become the largest state in all of the New World. Imperial expansion began under Pachacuti Inca Yupanqui, who ruled from 1438 to 1471. He gained control of the southern highlands, and then, with the aid of his son and heir, he brought much of the coast and highlands as well as a part of present-day Ecuador under his control. The Chimu empire on the coast was subjugated under his rule. Successor kings added areas that are today the southern Peruvian coast, southern Bolivia, and the northern parts of Argentina and Chile.

The Inca success can be attributed to genius in political and military organization. They were the master bureaucrats of the New World.

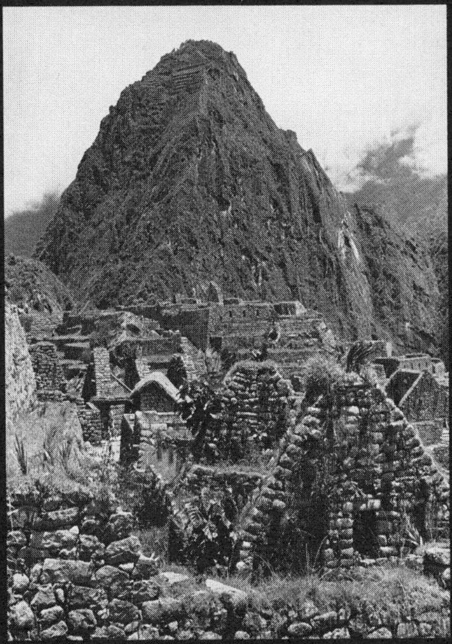

A B

C D

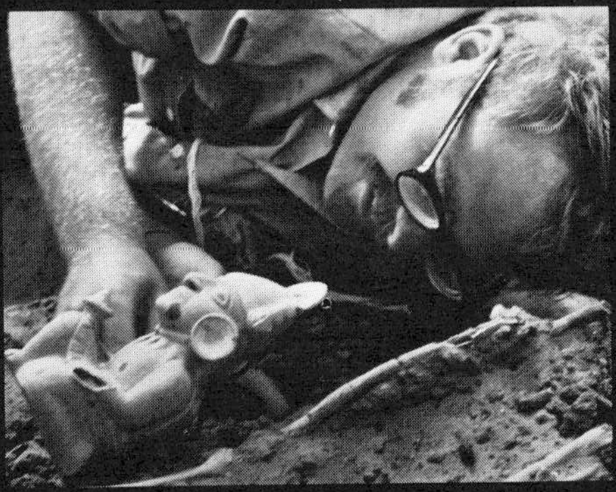

A

The highland Inca site of Machu Picchu.

B

A ceremonial pot from the classic Recuay culture, Peru, circa 20–800 AD.

C

The coastal site of Chan Chan, Peru, a large, fortified urban site.

D

The unearthing of a Moche artifact. Dr. Thomas Pozorski working on a burial site of circa 400 AD.

Their bureaucracy was supported by excellent highways along which the Inca built fortified military posts.

As in Mesopotamia certain elements of kinship structure were built into the Inca system. Unlike Mesopotamia these persisted until the collapse of the Inca empire under the Spanish. The basis of pre-Inca and Inca local social organization was the *ayllu,* an endogamous patrilineal kin group (membership was determined through a male line and marriage occurred within the group). Each ayllu owned its own lands, which were cultivated through cooperative labor. Each had a chief, who had a claim to a percentage of food produced on the group's land. Under the Incas the ayllu was incorporated into state structure and used as a link to subject populations.

The Inca king was both head of state and a sacred person. An Inca calendar was maintained. As in Mesoamerica this was tied to the agricultural cycle and religious observance. Unlike practices in Mesopotamia and the Aztec empire, sacred *and* secular power remained in the hands of the Inca rulers. This difference may be related to the fact that the Inca were not an urban people. Administrative centers such as Cuzco existed, but most of the population lived in small villages scattered across the empire. The only cities that developed in Peru arose during the period of the coastal states, and only some of these were allowed to continue under Inca dominance.

At the time of the Spanish conquest the Inca empire totaled around 6 million people! This population was equal to that of European nation-states. Its rapid fall can be linked to a weakness generated by a recently finished civil war and the ability of the Spanish to mobilize discontent among vassal peoples. Apparently, too, diseases, particularly smallpox and malaria, introduced several years before from Europe took a large toll of people and weakened their resistance to conquest.

Summary

Major landmarks in the early development of technology were the domestication of plants and animals. In many instances domestication, particularly of plants, was accompanied by permanent settlements, trade, and a division of labor based on task specialization. Technological change, village life, and increased population are all associated with the development of social stratification and, under certain environmental conditions, the rise of the state.

Social differentiation begins with rankings based on differences in prestige rather than political power. Frequently economic power is converted into prestige expressed in high rank for a successful individual. In stratified societies individuals with higher social status exercise real power over individuals with lower status. In stratified societies power is economic, social, and political. Class and caste are two forms of stratification. In class-stratified societies one class controls the means of production and access to resources. Castes are occupation-specific groups. Caste members perform certain economic tasks and exchange their own production or services for those of other castes. Castes are also endogamous; marriage is allowed only between members of the same caste group, each of which is also ranked in a hierarchical system.

While nonstate societies are characterized by affiliation through kinship, state societies are characterized by affiliation with a specific territory, which is expressed in loyalty to the state. In nonstate societies legal and political decisions are usually determined within and between kin groups. In state societies such decisions are controlled by a government. In addition, the state may be distinguished from other types of society by the existence of social stratification in which coercive authority is exercised by the government through its powers to tax, to raise an army, and to enforce laws of its own making.

States are frequently associated with urbanism. Urban centers are dense, complex, permanent settlements with large residential populations. They are inhabited by full-time craft and business specialists as well as officials. Urban centers are the focus of religious and symbolic life and the heart of economic activity.

Civilization implies both urbanism and states. Civilizations are characterized by high population density that is usually concentrated in urban centers (there are exceptional cases), a complex division of labor with full-time nonagricultural specialists, social stratification, full-time government officials, extensive trade, a full-time army, a national religion, and an extensive development of the arts and sciences. Most societies defined by anthropologists as civilizations also have writing, although the Inca state-civilization is an exception.

It has been noted that the rise of the state can be linked to such factors as population growth, technological innovations, and changes in social structure. These three key variables are linked in some way to a fourth variable, the environment, which provides the context in which technological and social developments occur. Anthropologists argue over which of these variables causes state development (i.e., which variable is independent). Some favor population growth, which is thought to stimulate technological and social change. Others believe that technological change itself stimulates population growth, which in turn makes social change necessary. Still others believe that instabilities in the social system lead to changes in technology and production as well as population. The latter theory also supposes that population growth is the outcome of productive strategies in which increases in the labor force are a necessity. Finally, there are those who believe that the rise of the state is governed by a complex set of multiple causes involving the four variables listed here. Many who take this latter view also believe that state formation may be caused by different combinations of these variables under different historical and ecological conditions.

More specific theories of state development that involve the variables discussed include the following:

1. Conquest. The military take-over by one people of another is seen as the cause of state development. This theory reasons that the conquering group establishes itself over the vanquished, generating social stratification, with one class governing the other.
2. Trade. The development of trading centers in strategic parts of the world with a concentration of economic power is seen as a stimulus to state formation. But the kind of large-scale trading that produced historically recognized trading states was dependent on the previous existence of trading states. Thus, trade may stimulate the formation of secondary states, but its role in the formation of the first state societies cannot be taken as the only or major cause.
3. Ecological Confinement. This theory assumes that states developed in specific environmental zones characterized by high fertility and limited territory surrounded by deserts or other confining ecological factors. It is based on the notion that high soil fertility and confinement stimulate population growth, with no chances for outmigration. This leads to high population density in a restricted locality, which in turn forces changes in social organization. V.G. Childe, who is associated with this theory, also suggested that the first states had to trade with other ecologically confined societies because of uneven resource distribution.
4. Circumscription, Warfare, and Population Increase. This theory, developed by Robert Carneiro, is an elaboration of the ecological confinement theory of V.G. Childe. When population increases in circumscribed areas, pressure builds up on available resources. New forms of technology and social control become necessary to improve extractive

procedures. Political elites develop that have the power to control production and distribution. Population increase also leads to competition between groups vying for the same resources. This results in warfare, which has a selective effect because those groups with the most effective military organization defeat less effective groups. Carneiro believes that any social and technological innovation directed toward state formation provides an important military advantage. Since the state itself has great power to control production and distribution, it is a likely outcome of the entire process of intensification.

5. Hydraulic Agriculture. This theory, associated with the name Karl Wittfogel, is based on the notion that in certain parts of the world agricultural intensification can only occur with strict control over the distribution of irrigation water. This happens when water is a scarce resource that can only be equitably distributed through the erection of complex irrigation systems including machines for pumping. Under these conditions labor mobilization and water control can only be efficiently achieved through the development of state bureaucracies.

In this chapter we have examined the archeological record concerning the rise of specific states in both the Old and the New World. Examples have been drawn from Mesopotamia, Olmec, Maya, Aztec, and Inca state formation. The factors implicated in this chapter as contributing to the rise of state formation are all seen to have played different but important roles in the development of each of these states, including population growth, social change, technological change, warfare, trade, and irrigation agriculture.

Bibliography

Adams, R. E. W. 1977 — *Prehistoric Mesoamerica.* Boston: Little, Brown. An up-to-date review of data and theory on the archeology of Mesoamerica.

Adams, R. M. 1966 — *The Evolution of Urban Society: Early Mesopotamia and Pre-Hispanic Mexico.* Chicago: Aldine. A comparison of the rise of urban civilization in the Old and New World. Takes a combined ecological and social structural approach.

Carneiro, R. 1970 — A Theory of the Origin of the State. *Science.* 169:733–738. Evolution of the state from a well-known anthropologist who considers the role of war and environmental circumscription to be main elements in the origin of this social form.

Childe V. G. 1951 — *Man Makes Himself.* New York: New American Library. One of the first attempts to put the origin of the state into an evolutionary framework.

Coe, M. D. 1962 — *Mexico.* New York: Praeger. A good but somewhat out-of-date review of Mexican archeology and culture.

Fried, M. 1967 — *The Evolution of Political Society.* New York: Random House. An analysis of political evolution with a discussion of differences between rank and stratification.

Frankfort, H. 1956 — *The Birth of Civilization in the Near East.* New York: Doubleday/Anchor. A classic work comparing the rise of Mesopotamian and Egyptian civilizations.

Millon, R. editor 1973 — *Urbanization at Teotihuacan, Mexico, Vol I: The Teotihuacan Map.* Austin: University of Texas Press. Detailed account of excavations at Teotihuacan.

Rathje, W. L. 1971 — The Origin and Development of Lowland Maya Civilization. *American Antiquity.* 36:275–285.

Sabloff, J. A. and C. C. Lamberg-Karlovsky, editors 1974 — *The Rise and Fall of Civilizations: Modern Archeological Approaches to Ancient Cultures.* Menlo Park, California: Cummings Publishing Co. A fine set of readings that take primarily an ecological approach to the rise and fall of civilizations.

Sanders, W. T., and B. J. Price 1968 — *Mesoamerica: The Evolution of a Civilization.* New York: Random House. Ecological approach to the evolution of civilization in Mesoamerica.

Willey, G. 1971 — *An Introduction to American Archeology* (in two volumes) Englewood Cliffs, New Jersey: Prentice Hall. A general introduction to the archeology of the New World with good material on civilizations and art styles.

White, B. 1977 — *Production and Reproduction in a Javanese Village* (Ph.D. thesis, Columbia University). An analysis of economic influences on demographic trends.

Wittfogel, K. A. 1957 — *Oriental Despotism: A Comparative Study of Total Power.* New Haven: Yale University Press. A classic work relating hydraulic agriculture to the rise of oriental states.

PART 2
CULTURAL ANTHROPOLOGY AND LINGUISTICS

CHAPTER 12

LANGUAGE: THE BASIS OF CULTURE

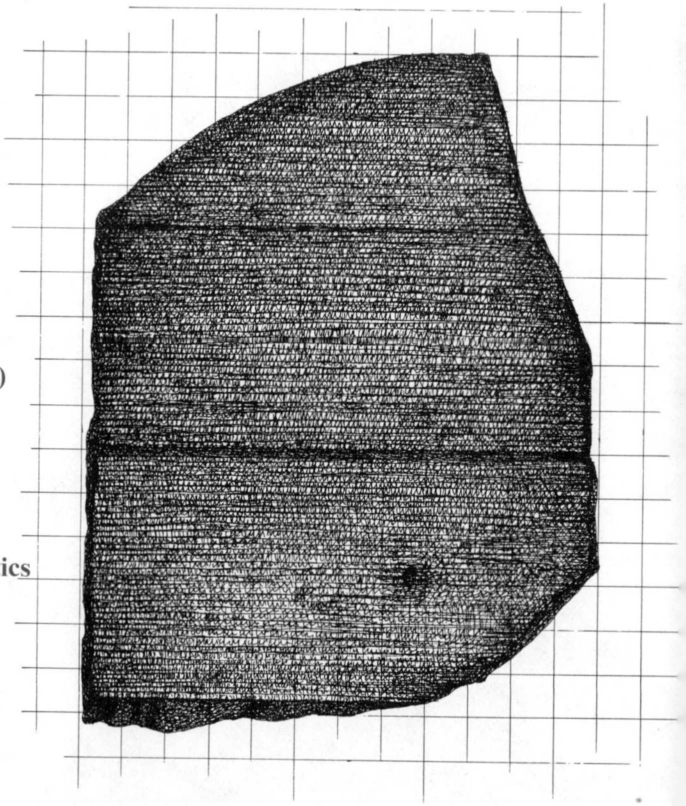

THE EVOLUTION OF LANGUAGE

The evolution of the human species as revealed by the fossil record and the study of living primates points to this basic fact: *culture is the human adaptation.*

Culture is learned, shared, and transmitted from generation to generation within a particular social tradition. It provides the guidelines for thought and action within each such tradition. Culture is based on the ability to use language, the system by which humans express their thoughts and communicate with one another.

Linguistic ability (the capacity to learn and use language) is the result of basic biological features of the human brain. Specific languages are not coded in the brain, but the capacity to learn language (any language) is. The evolution of linguistic ability is the product of brain evolution. Stated another way, the human brain is a *physical* result of the evolutionary process and language is a *behavioral* result. Language as behavior is dependent on the brain but can be studied independently from it as a communications system of great flexibility and complexity.

Essentially there are two ways of looking at the development of language in human behavior. One way is to see language as the refinement and culmination of a long process in the evolution of mammals during which the capacity to learn and use symbols has increased along with the progressive evolution of the nervous system. The other way is to consider language as a totally new capacity limited exclusively to humans. The first view is associated with **learning theory,** particularly the work of the Harvard psychologist B. F. Skinner. Skinner believes that the brain is free of a program for language learning that determines in advance what shape (or grammar) a language may have. This theory implies that grammars (the rules that generate orderly speech patterns) are more or less accidental historical events. For Skinner grammars have developed as language has emerged in the context of social experience.

Noam Chomsky of MIT is the strongest advocate of the theory that language is a strictly human trait. Furthermore, Chomsky believes that a basic universal grammar is precoded in the brains of all normal humans. This universal grammar contains a limited set of rules that are common to all languages. From this it follows that thc particular grammars of specific languages (which are known to differ one from another) are all members of a single family.

The Skinnerian View

If you are a Skinnerian, or if you reject the notion that language is a totally new capacity in humans, then you are likely to interpret the evolution of linguistic behavior as the result of a general increase in learning capacities that occurs with an increase in brain size and complexity.

In other words, according to this theory language is the end product of an accumulation of various forms of communication evolving along with an increasingly efficient nervous system. This theory draws only a minimum distinction between language and other forms of communication. It notes that all communication systems require a **sender,** a **receiver,** a **channel** that carries the **message,** and a **signal** that bears **information** from the sender to the receiver. In human speech, for example, the person who talks is the sender, the signal is sound (carried in the air as sound waves), and the receiver is the hearer. In addition, information is **coded** according to a particular signal system. Our signal system is language, made up of particular sounds arranged in systematic ways. The sender must code the message in words and speak the words in the presence of a hearer. The hearer decodes the words into the message. The latter

B. F. Skinner, one of the leaders of the learning theory school of psychology, who believes that language acquisition is a complex form of learning.

point may sound redundant. *After all, we think and speak in words.* The process of coding and decoding exists, however, even if it is so automatic for us that we do not think about it as we speak.

Organisms communicate with one another by different codes and through different sensory media. Many insects and animals communicate by means of chemical codes. Skunks, for example, signal their presence (defensively) by emitting their characteristic scent. Bears mark their territory by rubbing their backs on trees, and domestic male dogs mark theirs by urinating on particular landmarks in a neighborhood. Chemical signals are generally of long duration. They bear simple messages but the messages persist for an extended period. The male stickleback fish visually communicates its willingness to mate: in the mating season its belly turns red; when it approaches a receptive female it "stands on its head," exposing its signal. Visual signals can be of either long or short duration. Brightly colored male birds signal their sex throughout their lives, while fireflies signal their presence just so long as they are illuminated. Sound signals are *rapidly fading.* They exist only in a moment in time and can be rapidly followed by other signals. Sound, obviously, can form the basis for complex signal systems. Writing is visual and can carry complex messages, but do not forget that writing is a channel for carrying language and language essentially derives from sound.

Charles Hockett, a linguist, has compared language with the communication systems of several species. He lists a series of design features, at least some of which are common to all communication systems. These features tend to accumulate in evolutionary development and only human language contains all of them. In addition, Hockett notes that, while many of the design features are widespread in animal species, they are most fully developed in human speech. His analysis supports the idea of an evolutionary continuum in the emergence of language.

Hockett discusses the following design features:

Productivity. This is the ability to create new messages. If we need a new word to name or describe a new concept, we can make one up with no difficulty. The space age, for example, has seen the rapid invention of a whole new vocabulary. Words and concepts such as "lift-off," "countdown," and "megaton" are **neologisms** (newly developed terms). In Kolongo, the African language spoken by the people I studied, the word for "road" is *motocago,* an obvious borrowing and reworking of words from English used to convey a new concept.

Modern Hebrew, spoken in Israel, is based on an ancient language. In biblical times, obviously, no words existed for a wide range of present-day technological terms. Modern Hebrew makes up for these deficiencies by inventing or borrowing necessary words from other languages. Lacking words for "back axle," Hebrew has borrowed from English . With a slight pronunciation change the term has become *bek-hexel.* A front axle is known as *front bek-hexel!*

Productivity is not unique to human languages. It is a feature of bee communication. By performing a certain kind of dance, a worker bee can signal the location of nectar in an area that has never been visited before. New information can be added to communication by altering the signal.

Human language, however, is much more flexible than any other system. Language can deal with any subject matter. Humans can talk about anything it pleases them to talk about, including things that are made up and have no existence in the real world.

Arbitrariness. Hockett distinguishes between **arbitrary symbols** and **iconic symbols.** When a sign is arbitrary, it bears no similarity to the idea or thing symbolized. There is no inherent relation between the word "house" and the actual physical structure. An iconic symbol, however, shares some quality with the thing symbolized. Thus, he notes, in bee dancing the rate of the dance is inversely proportional to the distance from the hive to the nectar. Most of human language is arbitrary, but so are the call systems of many animals. There is no inherent similarity between the screech of a gibbon and danger, though the gibbon will not utter the call if there is no danger present.

Interchangeability. This term refers to the ability of the receiver of a signal to produce the same signal. Interchangeability is common to many but not all signal systems found in the animal world.

Specialization. When a signal system is independent of other behavioral qualities, it is specialized. Hockett explains this feature by comparing courting behavior in stickleback fish and communication in humans. When sticklebacks are courting, a major signal for the male is the seasonal appearance of the female whose abdomen is distended by roe. The fact that the female is carrying eggs is a signal to

Nonverbal communication.

males to engage with her in courting behavior. Her signal is *dependent* on her actual condition. The signal is therefore a consequence of her actual state of being and is not an independent or specialized part of the communication system alone. When a human calls out that dinner is ready, the family is triggered into coming to the table, but the signal has nothing to do with the caller's state of being. It is rather a specialized feature of the communication system. The stickleback communication, therefore, is unspecialized while the human communication is specialized.

Displacement. When nonhuman animals communicate, they communicate about things directly present in their environment. Monkeys do not emit food or danger signals unless food or danger is present, for in fact when they call they are communicating an internal emotional state triggered by the presence of food or danger. Humans can talk about things that are not present. We can talk about the past, the present, or the future. We can discuss purely hypothetical situations and work out problems before they occur. Bee signals are also displaced, but they are, nonetheless, closely linked to a stimulus.

Duality of Patterning. The basic elements in any language are sounds that by themselves have no meaning. Different sounds, however, allow us to distinguish one word or utterance from another. In addition, sounds are combined, not in an infinite variety of ways, but according to rules that are specific in each language. KPB, for example, is not a sound combination that occurs in English. KOB is such a combination. Meaningful units (words and also parts of words that indicate grammatical categories such as tense or person) are produced by combining the sounds of a language according to its rules. The use of a limited number of meaningless units (sounds) that can be ordered into a large number of combinations that *have* meaning is a powerful and economical mechanism for the generation of complex messages. Thus, language consists of sounds combined according to one set of rules into words and word parts, which are in turn combined into utterances according to a different set of rules. This is what is meant by duality of patterning.

Cultural Transmission. Human language is taught. It is not part of a genetic system. Other animals also learn at least some of their signal systems. Human language is in this regard, therefore, only quantitatively different from some other animal communication systems.

The notion that human language is purely cultural is the major point of contention between learning theory advocates and the followers of Noam Chomsky.

Learning-theory linguists believe that human infants learn to speak by experiencing the act of communication during social interaction with adults. The capacity for language learning is part of our genetic heritage, but the structure of any particular language is completely arbitrary. Language is seen, therefore, as a very complex form of learning.

The Chomskyan View

The second language theory is associated with Noam Chomsky, who states that human language differs *qualitatively* from other forms of communication. In addition, Chomsky believes that differences between human and nonhuman communication go much deeper than the simple addition or elaboration of design features. Instead, he suggests, humans are born with specific brain patterns for language use, and these patterns limit the form that any real spoken language can take. He posits, therefore, a **universal general grammar** coded in the brains of all normal humans.

Chomsky notes that human language learning would be an extraordinary achievement for an organism that was not biologically programmed to accomplish the task. He reminds us that "A normal child acquires this knowledge on relatively slight exposure and without specific training."

The linguist Noam Chomsky, who believes that language-acquisition skills are precoded in the brains of all humans.

Learning theory assumes, says Chomsky, that cognitive structures as complex as language behavior can be learned through experience. This notion as well as the counteridea of a universal grammar is tested through the observation of language acquisition in children. Chomsky uses the following example of simple declarative sentences and their corresponding questions.

(*A*) *"The man is tall." "Is the man tall?"*

"The book is on the table." "Is the book on the table?" From observing these sentences one might derive hypotheses to explain the process by which sentences are formed and transformed. A learning-theory hypothesis would assume that the child processes the sentence from left to right in sequence "until he reaches the first occurrence of the word 'is' . . . he then preposes this occurrence of 'is,' producing the corresponding question . . ."

The hypothesis works for the sentences in question, but it can be proved false by considering some other related sentences. Chomsky uses the following example:

(*B*) *"The man who is tall is in the room." "Is the man who is tall in the room?"*

(*C*) *"The man who is tall is in the room" "Is the man who tall is in the room?"*

While children who are learning to speak make mistakes, Chomsky notes that they never make the kind of mistake seen in sentence (C). This leads him to a different hypothesis:

The child analyzes the declarative sentence into abstract phrases; he then locates the first occurrence of 'is' (*etc.*) *that follows the first noun phrase; he then preposes this occurrence of 'is', forming the corresponding question."*

Hypothesis one (drawn from learning theory) suggests that the speaker is using a "structure-independent rule" that involves an analysis into words in sequential order. Hypothesis two (Chomsky's own) suggests that a "structure-dependent rule" is followed. In the latter case the speaker analyzes the sentence into words *and* phrases which are ordered subparts of the sentence.

Chomsky believes that structure-dependent rules must be programmed in the brain because children are not *trained* to use them in language learning. Thus, "The principle of structure-dependence is not learned, but forms part of the conditions for language learning." Structure-dependent rules are one aspect of universal grammar, which Chomsky defines as "The system of principles, conditions, and rules that are elements or properties of all human languages not merely by accident but by necessity." Necessity in this case means biologically precoded.

Chomsky goes on to state that there is no structure similar to universal grammar in nonhuman animals. Thus, language as opposed to communication is exclusive to the human species. Chomsky is aware that experiments with chimpanzees show that these animals can be trained to use symbols analogous to the words of human language. He says, however, that this communication behavior is not true language. It is not language because chimps do not display the automatic complex grammatical patterns that occur as humans learn to use a particular language. Instead Chomsky sees an analogy between "language learning" in apes and attempts to linguistically retrain humans who have undergone severe brain damage. These individuals have lost the ability to use true language, but they can learn to communicate symbolically. This would sound like quibbling except that the loss of language function often involves disruption of grammatical patterns rather than vocabulary. In addition, it is now known that, while damage to the left hemisphere of the brain (in the so-called "language centers") will disrupt speech as such, damage to the right hemisphere (involved in other forms of symbolic behavior) leads to a kind of colorless speech in which individuals lose the ability to use metaphors. People with right-hemisphere damage are overly literal. They are unable to interpret proverbs, so that a standard phrase like "Too many cooks spoil the broth" might be interpreted as "If you have a lot of people making soup it will not turn out well." Howard Gardner in his book *The Shattered Mind* tells us that even if a right-brain-damaged patient is pushed to give a more fanciful interpretation of this proverb, he or she will be unable to depart from a literal translation. The right-brain-damaged person, therefore, will talk like a computer or perhaps a chimpanzee.

The amazing thing about language in addition to its complexity is its great flexibility. The meanings of words and groups of words shift constantly. Symbols may **denote** (specify) rather limited concepts at the same time as they **connote** (suggest) a wider range of meaning. In poetry, new **metaphors** (figures of speech suggesting an analogy between different objects or ideas) are created, and meaning is both stretched and compressed in the expressive act.

Metaphor is one manifestation of the flexibility of human thought and language. Metaphor is perhaps the most important element in our ability to intuit relationships and shape and reshape elements of consciousness. Because we can extend meanings and create new relationships, we can either enlighten or confuse an audience with our clever use of language.

The existence of flexibility in a communication system coupled to grammar creates both pitfalls and stepping stones for human thought. We are, for example, prone to accept any grammatical sentence as meaningful. If the words are real and the grammar correct, then we assume there must be meaning as well. Thus the sentence "I am here" and the sentence "I am not here" are both grammatical; both contain real symbols and both are logically related to a single real subject. The sentence "I am here" creates no difficulties. The other sentence, however, is a problem for some people. It is empty of meaning, but sounds so much as if it ought to mean something that its acceptance is not out of the question for everyone. It could be used perfectly well in a poem. In fact, poetry is a set of words that fit our grammatical and artistic expectations. The phrases are grammatically real, and because they are presented in an explicitly artistic frame we are more open than usual to the possibilities of extended meaning. Metaphors abound in poetry, and even when they are new and innovative we make an effort to understand them. If we could teach chimpanzees to talk and if we presented them with poetry, I suspect that they, being more direct than humans, would reject poetic expression as gibberish.

Chomsky treats the notion that chimpanzees *almost* speak with derision: "Perhaps some hopelessly confused observer might argue . . . that the distinction between jumping and flying is arbitrary, a matter of degree; people can really fly, just like birds, only less well. Analogous proposals in the case of language seem to me to have no greater force or significance." It should be noted that Chomsky's theory accords well with Holloway's speculations about human brain evolution (Chapter 8).

Criticism of Both Approaches

Jerome Bruner, a developmental psychologist, rejects Skinner's notion that language is an advanced form of learning and Chomsky's notion that language is programmed in advance exclusively in the human brain. Bruner says that there must be a solution to the language problem that lies between the "impossible" (Skinner) and the "miraculous" (Chomsky). Bruner and his associates have studied language acquisition in children and find that many of the constructions that Chomsky believes appear spontaneously in language develop slowly in nonverbal interactions between children and their parents. These observations suggest that language structures are formed in experience, but that the experience is social rather than linguistic. For Bruner and his students language cannot be understood out of its social and developmental context.

LANGUAGE AS A SYSTEM

Language consists of sounds grouped into words and words arranged according to a systematic order into sentences. In more technical terms, language is a system composed of three subsystems: **phonology** (the sound system), **grammar** (the orderly and lawful arrangement of sounds, words, and sentences), and **semantics** (the meaning contained in linguistic expressions). A person cannot speak without knowing the correct sounds of a language and the way these sounds combine to produce words. But knowing words alone does not give a person the competence to speak. Words make no sense unless they are arranged according to rules that **generate** (make possible) proper sentences.

The semantics of a language comes not only from the meaning of individual words but also from the way these words are used in grammatical utterances. Thus in English, a language that is heavily dependent on word order, "Dog bites man" and "Man bites dog" are made up of the same words, but each is a different sentence with a different meaning because the arrangement of the words in the sentence affects the meaning of that sentence.

We all speak to mean, to make sense to ourselves and our hearers. Yet we can make up grammatical sentences with real words that are meaningless. When we do so intentionally, we are playing with language rather than using it for communication. We are violating semantic rules.

The semantic, or meaning, part of language is further complicated by the fact that meaning depends on context. For example, in conversation the words "pair" and "pear" can only be distinguished by their use in a particular sentence. "Would you like your socks?" defines "pair" in the response, "Yes, give me a pair."

The sentence, "Would you like some fruit?" defines "pear" in the response, "Yes, give me a pear."

Meaning is also complicated because words can have both a strict, or denotative, sense and a suggestive, or connotative, sense. Red *denotes* a color, but it can also *connote* a communist or someone who is believed to be a communist. Red also connotes anger, as in the sentence, "His examination grade made him see red." Both denotation and connotation shift with time and usage. Words are constantly expanding and contracting in meaning. This is one reason why language is a highly flexible means of communication.

Flexibility of meaning is a major source of power in language, but the possibility of divorcing speech from a specific context or action also provides great flexibility. We can talk about the present, the past, and the future. We can not only discuss concrete actions or events but also speculate about things that might happen or even invent things that in reality cannot occur. We can, for example, talk about a three-horned unicorn.

Linguistic flexibility derives also from the fact that language is a communications system whereby individuals can produce new sentences never used before that will be understood by those who have never heard them before. What makes this possible is the systematic grouping of a limited number of sounds. There is an infinite number of possible sentences in any language. (There is also an infinite number of nonsentences that lie outside of the rules.) The set of infinitely possible sentences is composed of a small number of finite parts: sounds, groups of sounds (words), and groups of words arranged in grammatical order.

Sounds

The human mouth is capable of producing a wide range of sounds (see Figure 12.1). Every language, however, uses only a limited number of them. *Th* as in "these" or "the" is a common feature of English, but it never occurs in French. Both English and French have *r,* but the English *r* sound is pronounced further forward in the mouth than the French *r.* In English we make a clear distinction between *y* (as in "Yale") and *j* (as in "jail"); a Spanish speaker, in contrast, does not make this distinction and will have difficulty hearing the difference when attempting to speak English. When I did graduate work at Yale University, one of my fellow students who was from Latin America referred to the school as "Jale." The latter, of course, sounded exactly like "jail"! Japanese, who do not distinguish in their own language between *r* and *l,* often say "Ame*l*ican" and "Eng*r*ish." In Kolongo, the language spoken by the Abron of the Ivory Coast, consonant length is very important. In this language the word *nna* means "mother" and the word *na* means "cow." To an English speaker the difference between these two words is difficult to hear. When I did field work among the Abron my first task was to learn the greeting patterns. In the early morning the polite form of greeting when speaking to a woman is "Good morning, mother" ("*Nna gua*"). For a long time I could not understand why Abron who heard me use this greeting broke into gales of laughter. Finally, I realized that I had been saying "*Na gua*" ("Good morning, cow").

Sounds are classified in language according to the ways they are produced. Sounds can be **voiced**—that is the vocal cords can be set into vibration—or they can be **unvoiced.** For example, the only difference between the *p* and *b* sounds in English is that the former is unvoiced and the latter is voiced. Sounds can be either **oral** or **nasal.** In the latter case air is expelled through the nasal passage in addition to the oral passage. Sounds are also controlled by the placement of the tongue and by the use of the lips. The sounds *b, p,* and *m* are **bilabials,** that is, both the upper and lower lips are employed at the same time to produce the sound. On the other hand, f and v are called **labiodentals** because they are pronounced by placing the upper teeth on the lower lip. Other sounds may be produced by placing the tip of the tongue on the ridge above the upper teeth (*n* and *t*) (**alveolar**

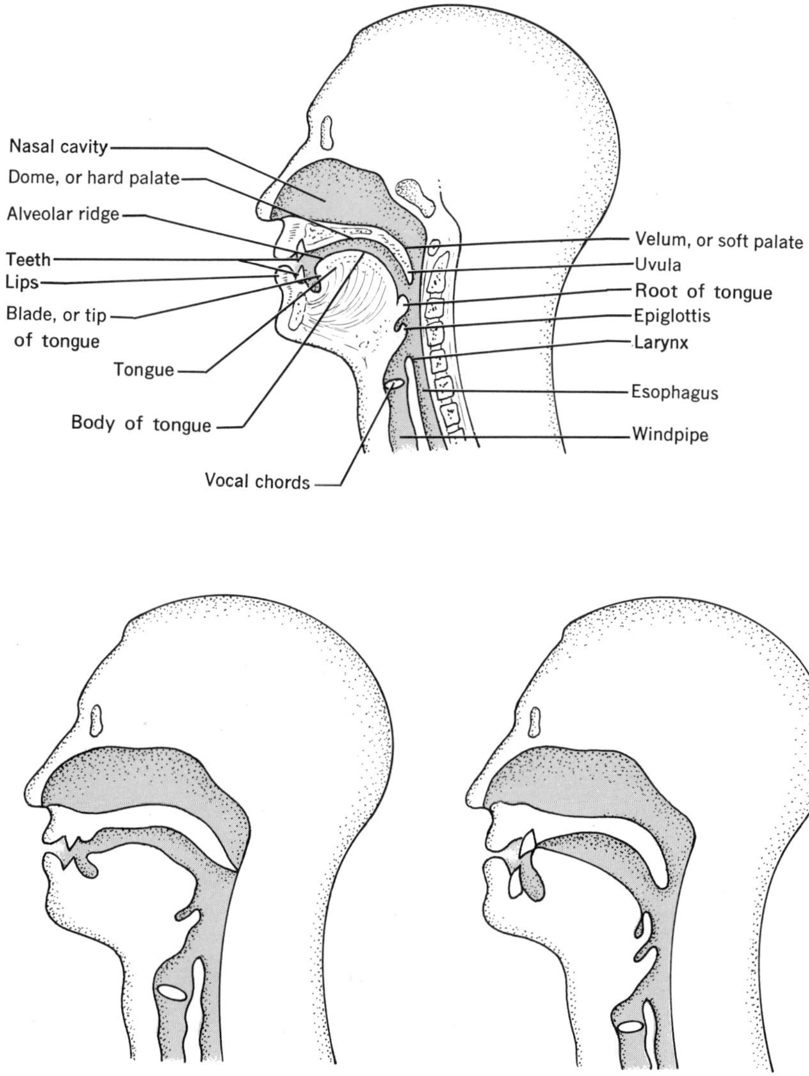

[a] **[t]**

Figure 12.1
The organs of speech. Bottom left shows the articulation when pronouncing [a]. Bottom right shows the articulation when pronouncing [t].

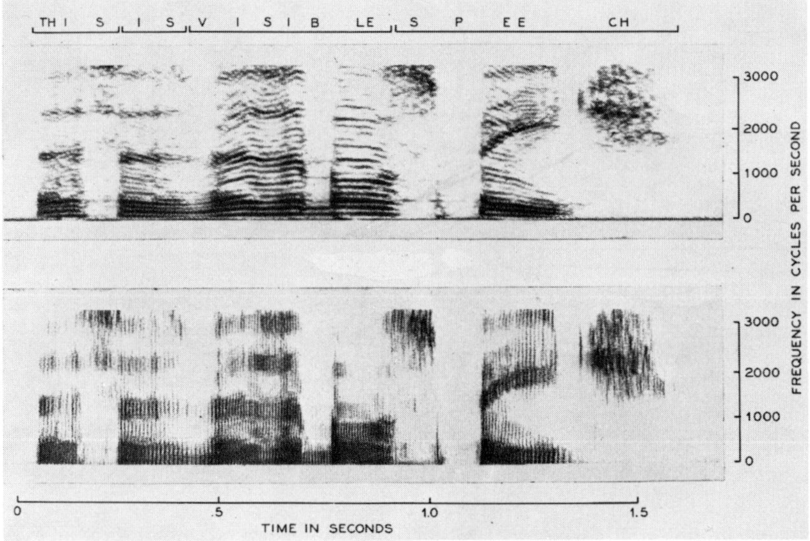

A sound spectrograph of the sentence "This is visible speech." Top: high detail sound. Bottom: low detail sound.

placement) or by placing the back of the tongue on the soft palate (*k* and *g*) (**velar** placement). Some sounds are produced through explosive use of the lips (*b* and *p*). Others are the product of friction (*s, z,* and the *j* of the French *je*); they are called **fricatives.** All languages contain **consonants,** which are produced by obstructing the flow of air through the mouth, and **vowels,** which are produced without any such obstruction.

Many African languages employ **pitch** (low, medium, and high, for example) to distinguish sounds that are otherwise the same. Chinese words are distinguished by what linguists refer to as **tone.** Tones apply to individual sounds within a word and can be rising, falling, level, or a combination of rising and falling. In English, we can distinguish certain sentence meanings by **intonation.** "This is your house?" can be understood by rising intonation as a question, in contrast to the falling intonation of the declarative, "This is your house."

Phonology: Phonetics versus Phonemics. The science of describing and cataloging all the sounds in a language—each individual sound is called a **phone**—is called **phonetics.** The study of phonetics gives us an idea of the range of sounds that occur in any particular language, but it does not tell us how these sounds are arranged as significant units, the building blocks of meaning. The analysis of sound *systems* in language is called **phonology.**

When the difference between two sounds affects meaning, those sounds are said to be linguistically distinctive. Each linguistically distinctive sound in a language is called a **phoneme.*** In English the /p/ in "*p*it" and the /b/ in "*b*it" are separate phonemes because they create distinctive words in the same sound context. In the example the *it* remains constant ("b*it*" and "p*it*"). The /b/ and /p/ are distinctive in the same environment. We can also say that they *contrast* in the same environment.

Often in a language, systematic differences that are not distinctive occur among related sounds. The /p/ in the word "spit" is actually different from the /p/ in the word "pit." In

*In linguistics phonemes are indicated by / /.

order to see this difference (you may not hear it), hold a piece of paper with the bottom hanging loose in front of your mouth and pronounce the two words. If you do it correctly one word will make the paper move away from you while the other will not. The fact that the paper moves in only one case is evidence that the two /*p*/'s are articulated differently. These two /p/'s are *not distinctive* in English (although they might be in some other language). They occur in different environments and are in fact shaped or conditioned by those environments ("s_it" and "_it"). The first /p/ occurs after unvoiced fricative /s/ while the other /p/ is word-initial (it begins the word "pit"). In English these two varieties of the phoneme /p/ never occur in the same context or environment and they never determine meaning. They are, therefore, called **allophones** of the same phoneme. This idea is similar to the genetic concept of alleles. (In genetics two or more forms of the same gene are **alleles** of the same gene.)

English sounds.

CONSONANTS

		Bilabial	Labiodental	Dental	Alveolar	Alveopalatal	Velar	Glottal
Stops	voiceless	p			t		k	
	voiced	b			d		g	
Affricates	voiceless					č		
	voiced					ǰ		
Fricatives								
slit	voiceless		f	**θ**				h
	voiced		v	**ð**				
groove	voiceless				s	š		
	voiced				z	ž		
Lateral	voiced				l			
Nasals	voiced	m			n		η	
Semivowels	voiced	w			r	y		

VOWELS

	Part of the Tongue Involved: Front	Central	Back
High	i ɪ		u ʊ
Mid	e ɛ	ə	o ɔ
Low	æ	ʌ	a

Different languages have different phonemes and different combinations of phonemes. The placement of phonemes may differ as well. Such consonant clusters as *gb, kp,* and *bd* often occur in word-initial position in African languages but not in English. In Kolongo, for instance, the word "*Kp*arese" means "priest" and the word "*gb*awkaw" means "god."

Morphemes. Sounds alone, even phonemes, have no meaning. Meaning arises when sounds occur in particular relationships. The minimal unit of meaning in a language is known as a **morpheme.** A word may be composed of one or more morphemes. "Sam placed Mary's glass on the table," is a sentence composed of words made up of morphemes. "Sam" is a word composed of a single morpheme. "Placed" is a word composed of two morphemes (*place* plus *-ed*). The *-ed* morpheme in this case plays a role in the grammar of the sentence and indicates the past tense of the verb "to place." The word (name) "Mary" plus the *-'s* morpheme indicates a person and possession.

A single morpheme may occur in one or more phonetic forms depending on context. Different forms of the same morpheme are called **allomorphs,** just as different forms of the same phoneme are called allophones. The plural morpheme in English may occur as a *-z,* an *-s,* a *-zes,* or as nothing (in zero form). The plural of "sheep," for example, is "sheep." "Car*z,*" "cat*s,*" "hou*zes,*" "fish(*0*)" all exhibit allomorphs of the plural morpheme in English. Other allomorphs of the plural morpheme exist as well (for example, "mice" is the plural morpheme of "mouse," but moose is the plural of "moose"; "g*ee*se" is the plural of "goose," but "mongoos*es*" is the plural of "mongoose"). A particular sound or combination of sounds may be a morpheme in one context, but in another context the same sound or combination of sounds may either not be a morpheme or be some other morpheme. "There were three Georges in my class" and "This is George's book" have, attached to the name George, different morphemes that sound the same.

Morphemes may be **bound** or **free:** *George* is a free morpheme, *-'s* is a bound form. Free forms can stand alone. Bound forms can only occur attached to other morphemes. Morphemes may consist of a single sound, like the *s* in one plural form in English. They may also occur as a single syllable or even as multiple syllables. Thus, *car* is a morpheme but so are *Massachusetts* and *elephant.*

Morphemes may mark grammatical changes in a word, as of number—single to plural, or of tense—present to past (**inflectional morphemes**); or they may change the part of speech. These are called **derivational morphemes.** In "boy" to "boyish," the *-ish* morpheme converts a noun to an adjective. Verbs can be changed into nouns—for example, "run" to "runn*er*," and so on. The use of morphemes to change parts of speech may be good or poor style depending on the type of transformation employed. To say, "This is poor style*wise*" (noun to adverb) is poor style although it is frequently employed. What makes good or poor style, however, is a matter of taste, usage, and clarity of thought rather than linguistic rules.

Syntax and Grammar

The words "syntax" and "grammar" are often used to mean the same thing: the rules for forming proper sentences in a language. In linguistics, however, **syntax** is reserved for sentence formation while **grammar** is used to cover all aspects of linguistic structure that can be reduced to sets of rules. These aspects include phonological combinations, morphology, and syntax. In theory, at least, a knowledge of the rules of syntax makes it possible for an individual to generate sentences in his or her language. Native speakers of a language can do so, but unfortunately for linguists attempting to analyze a language, the rules used are most certainly unconscious. Attempts by linguists and grammarians to construct grammars for specific languages have always failed to discover real generative rules. The theory or theories of grammar so far developed by linguists have not matched the apparently automatic ability of individuals to speak their own language correctly. This failure is one reason why the linguist Noam Chomsky has been led to assume that there are certain inborn patterns that make it possible for individuals to acquire language and generate successful sentences without a conscious knowledge of syntax. This ability, whatever it might be, must also include semantic (meaning) rules. Although correct syntax can generate proper sentences, these sentences may be meaningless as in "I am not here." In some way, not yet understood, semantics and syntax are linked in the formation of both correct and meaningful sentences.

Semantics

Semantics (the meaning of words and utterances) determines *which* words may be put together in a sentence; syntax, *how* they may be put together. *Semantics includes more than the meaning of individual words.* Language is expressive of such grammatical categories as tense (past, future, present, and each of these in different forms), possession, gender, and subject versus object. Not all languages cut the grammatical pie the same way. Kolongo, for example, has a simple past tense, "*Mi a Gutugu lé la*" ("I went to Gutugu") and a past tense that reflects completed action "*Mi a Gutugu lé mi*" ("I went to Gutugu and have returned"). Some languages lack real past and future tenses. French, on the other hand, has the imperfect—"*Je mangeais*" ("I was eating")—and the *passé composé*—"*J'ai mangé*" ("I ate" or "I have eaten)—both of which exist in English, and the past definite, which is used only in literary expression— "*Je mangeai*" ("I ate"). Because gender exists in Romance languages, certain ideas can be expressed more simply than in English.

Thus, "*une etudiante*" means a female student and "*un etudiant*" a male student. The gender signifies the sex of the student. But gender does not always reveal the sex of the object. "*La personne*" ("the person") is always feminine, even in reference to a male. Thus, "*La personne qui dirige l'ármée et un general*" ("The person who directs the army is a general") uses the feminine *personne* and the masculine *general.*

Gender is a grammatical category that does not really act as a sex marker except in special cases. Thus, while *fille* and *femme* are both feminine, *garçon* and *homme* both masculine, and *cousin* a male cousin, *cousine* a female cousin, the gender of words that do not refer to the sex of individuals varies according to grammatical rules buried in the past history of French down to its roots in Latin. Beard and moustache (*la barbe, la moustache*) are both feminine in French, but the word for the female genital organ (*le vagin*) is masculine!

Languages differ one from another in vocabulary, syntax, and grammar. Some languages have larger vocabularies than others. The ways in which objects of the natural world are classified differ as well. The Eskimo, for example, have many more words for snow than we do. Each of these words marks a different quality of snow, all of which are extremely important to the Eskimo in their environment. We can count as high as we want to while many Indians of lowland South America only have words for the number concepts of "one," "two," and "many." Vocabulary appears to reflect the everyday concerns of individuals within particular cultures.

Grammar and syntax certainly also play a role in the organization of expression, but on a more complex level than vocabulary. For instance, a language may lack a formal past tense, but we cannot assume that it cannot express past action. *This may be the case, but it need not be.* Only an analysis of a language and its use in everday life can tell us.

LANGUAGE AND SOCIETY (SOCIOLINGUISTICS)

The Language-and-Culture Problem

Such differences in the expression and organization of concepts have led some comparative linguists to propose that language actually affects the way in which people perceive their world. The wide range of Eskimo words for snow, a reflection of the cataloging function of language, might allow an individual Eskimo to make more refined judgments than English speakers about a material out of which houses are constructed and upon which people and animals must travel.

The linguists Edward Sapir and Benjamin Lee Whorf suggested that the organization of vocabulary, grammatical categories, and standard metaphor might also play a profound role in the organization of perception and thought. In English, for example, we tend to translate time into metaphors of space ("The day was very long" "We shall do our job in a short time"). Not all cultures translate time in this way. Grammatically, one might suppose a language that does not break time into units such as past, present, and future might express a different vision of events in the life stream. (Note that "life stream" is also a metaphor that reflects the common English relationship between time and space and movement.) Whorf and Sapir went so far as to suggest that language has so profound an effect on culture that it could impede or stimulate different types of philosophical or scientific thinking.

Other anthropologists hold that language follows thought, social action, and environmental adaptation, rather than the reverse. Eskimos have many words for snow because they have invented them out of a need to classify their

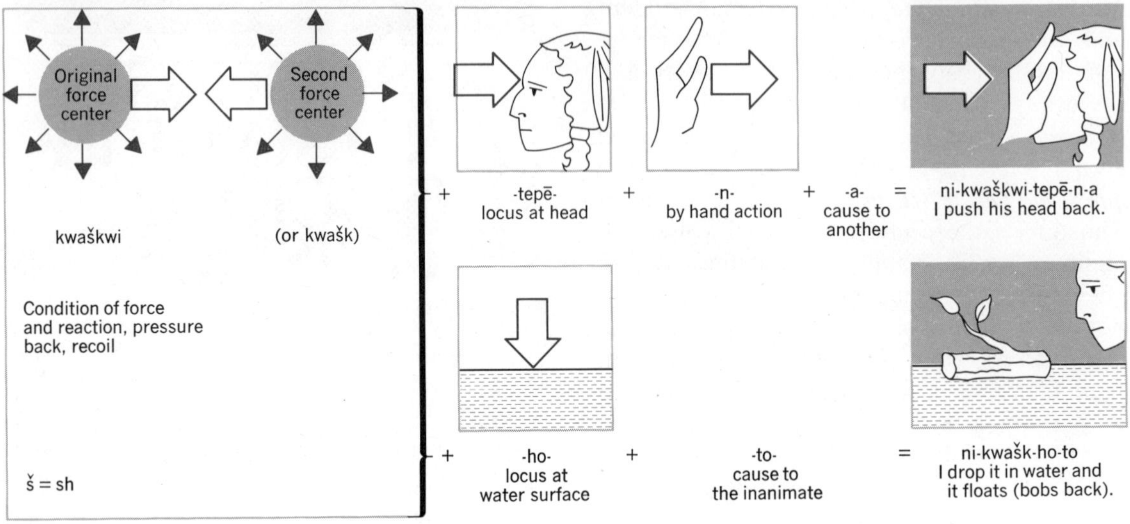

Figure 12.2
Conceptual differences between English and Shawnee. In English the sentence: *I push his head back* and *I drop it in water and it floats* are unlike. In Shawnee the corresponding sentences are very similar. This demonstrates the fact that the classification of events and the analysis of nature follow the same logic. This logic is reflected in the grammar. (Adapted from B.L. Whorf, *Language, Thought, and Reality* (J.B. Carroll, ed.). Cambridge-New York: MIT Wiley, 1956 By permission MIT Press.)

particular technological and environmental system.

The problem of grammatical categories is somewhat more complicated than vocabulary. Different grammars do make it difficult to express the same ideas in translation from one language to another, but this does not mean that the ideas cannot be thought in both languages. In English we can think that someone eats like an animal although we do not have the verb *fressen,* the verb used in German to denote eating for an animal. *Essen* is the German verb that denotes eating for humans. (The same distinction is made in French, *bouffer* and *manger.*) The grammatical category *completed action* exists in Kolongo, but not in English. Yet we have no difficulty in expressing this concept in English when we need to.

Language is, however, a very subtle phenomenon. As the medium of our own thought it is difficult to study objectively. Questions about language and culture lie at the very base of human nature. Studying the mind *with* the mind means that the object of study and the tool used to carry out the study are the same.

Are There Primitive Languages?

That languages differ, even in the size of their vocabularies, does not mean that some languages are more primitive or more "incomplete" than others. Vocabulary words can be borrowed or invented when needed. All languages have grammars that organize linguistic expression. *Anyone who has mastered any language can generate absolutely new sentences that will be understood by competent members of the same language community.* This is the advantage of language as a communications system of high flexibility and relatively low complexity. Remember: the infinite possibilities of linguistic expression are built on a foundation of a limited number of sounds and rules for combining these sounds in words and sentences. No language exists that lacks a complete and ordered set of rules for phonology, syntax, and grammar. Nor is it possible to classify languages as retarded or advanced on the basis of grammatical complexity. The argument that Chinese is more advanced than English because it has a simpler grammar is no better than the argument that English is more advanced than Chinese because it has a more complex grammar. Latin is seen by some as elegant in its complexity and by others as a primitive version of the Romance languages out of which grammatically simpler and more advanced forms developed.

The argument in favor of complexity as a sign of superiority is based on the notion that greater grammatical differentiation allows for greater subtlety of thought and expression. The argument in favor of simplicity rests on the idea that simple grammars have eliminated duplications (redundancy) from the language. But the fact is that all languages are subtle instruments for communication and all languages contain redundancies.

While all human languages differ, all are structured according to rules and all are capable of fully expressing necessary concepts in the culture. There is no truth to the notion that some languages are more advanced or more primitive than others.

Language in Social Context

Language as the basis of culture allows humans to communicate; it also allows us to catalog (organize data), remember, speculate, and believe. These activities are normally carried out in the context of a particular social group that speaks a particular language. Although you can talk to yourself, speaking is a social process learned in a social context.

Language is therefore a social instrument. The basic function of language is to communicate specific messages by means of sounds combined into words emitted in the form of sentences. Because it is a social instrument, however, a linguistic utterance can carry messages that reflect nonlinguistic aspects of culture. The use of different forms of a person's name, for example, can reflect the degree of social distance between speakers. If Mr. Smith greets Mr. Jones as Mr. Jones and Mr. Jones greets Mr. Smith as Mr. Smith, we can form some judgment of their social relationship. They are probably of the same class and know each other in a formal or businesslike way. If, on the other hand, Mr. Smith greets Mr. Jones as Joe, but is himself greeted as Mr. Smith, we can assume he has some form of social superiority. If the two men greet each other as Sam and Joe, they are probably friends, coworkers of equal rank, or both.

Contemporary English has only one form of the singular personal pronoun, "you," but many European languages have two forms—polite and familiar (French: *vous, tu*). The use of these pronouns in conversation can mark the distance between speakers as well as relative social authority. Equals who are socially distant will use the *vous* form in French, as will individuals who are distant but socially unequal (except when the perceived inequality is very marked). But French people will address a child in the familiar *tu* even if they do not know the child. When France had a colonial empire the familiar *tu* form was used with natives.

The head of a business in France may use either the polite or familiar form with his employees. If the enterprise is very large, the *vous* form will probably be used in most cases. If the enterprise is small, the employer will use the *tu* with the workers but will be addressed in the *vous* form. Students or members of labor unions tend to use the *tu* form with one another in order to emphasize solidarity. In the Middle Ages a knight used the *vous* form with his lady and she in turn used the *tu* form with him. This reinforced the *notion* that the knight was the servant of his mistress and would obey her every whim.

There are also class differences that determine how freely a person will use the familiar form in France. Upper-class French people use the *tu* form only under very restricted conditions. People may know each other for many years, be members of the same age and social class, be quite friendly, and yet continue to use the *vous* form among themselves. These same individuals may even use the *vous* form with their servants in order to maintain a wide degree of social distance. In some aristocratic French families children even use the *vous* form when speaking to their parents!

When speaking to God, however, French use the familiar. The custom also occurs in English; the archaic *thou* and *thy* are now used only in religious ceremonies and by the members of the religious community of Friends (Quakers).

Dialects as Social Markers

When societies are divided by class or caste, and sometimes even by sex, members of different subgroups may speak more or less distinct **dialects** of their common language. In a few preliterate societies men and women speak different dialects. In some, members of one sex will understand both dialects while the members of the other understand only their own sex's speech pattern.

In our complex technological civilization, certain professionals may use a set of relatively exotic terms—doctors and lawyers, engineers, philosophers, and, unfortunately, many social scientists. In addition to special (and frequently necessary) professional terms, certain groups develop speech patterns that become unintelligible to the general public. In addition to medical language, members of hospital staffs often speak in abbreviations such as OB, GYN, and DOA. The recent popularity of television pro-

Equals greet each other formally. The late Pope Paul the VI greets the late Patriarch Athenagoras on the steps of Saint Peter's basilica on October 27, 1967.

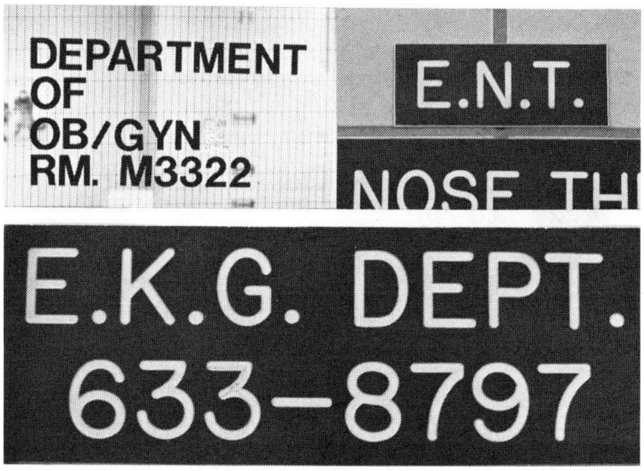

Signs in a hospital are cryptic to nonmedical people. When the letters shown here are substituted for words in conversation, they become part of medical jargon.

grams about the medical profession, some of which took great care to represent accurately the technical aspects of hospital life, have broadened the public's knowledge of these terms. On the other hand, anyone who is not a lawyer and has attempted to read a legal contract or most insurance policies knows how difficult it is to translate from "legalese" into plain English.

In large countries such as the United States, and even in many smaller ones such as England and France, regional dialects of the national language have developed through time. Some have originated in a mixture of a local, ancient language—such as Provençal and Oc in southern France or Gaelic in Scotland—and the national language. Others developed because of geographic isolation. Great Britain, even England alone, is peppered with local dialects that mark one region off from another. Regional accents in the United States are somewhat less complicated, yet Americans from New England, the South, the Middle West, and the West have regional accents. In many cases the regional speech patterns are marked by vocabulary differences as well.

In addition to regional accents social class and ethnic differences can be picked up in speech patterns. The so called "New York accent" is more likely to be heard among working-class New Yorkers than among members of the middle class. Upper-class Scots are more likely to have a standard English accent than a burr. Some people consciously employ their local accent in certain social situations and "standard" speech on other occassions. A Scots accent among Scots can be used as a sign of solidarity like the use of the familiar "you" form among members of the same social group in France.

Many black people in the United States speak a dialect known as Black English. It differs from standard English in its grammar, vocabulary, and pronunciation. Black English is often used as a sign of social solidarity among members of the black community who may or may not speak standard English as well. Those who do speak both dialects may use Black English in one social context and standard English in another. In any case Black English has a set of rules just as standard English has its set of rules. When blacks speak Black English they are not speaking standard English badly, they are instead speaking Black English correctly.

Class and regional dialects often have grammars that differ from the standard grammar of the national language. We have been taught that nonstandard grammatical usage is incorrect or even lacking in rules. Actually, all dialects have regular grammatical rules, even if these differ from the rules taught in the classroom. We may have been taught that "I ain't got none" is a double error because of the use of "ain't" and the *double negative.* For standard English it is correct to say that a double negative makes the sentence positive. Not to have nothing of something means that one must have something of it. But when such a double negative form is used regularly by a social group, it is by no means ambiguous or inverted in meaning. "I ain't got none" in one dialect simply means "I haven't got any" in another dialect.

Since class dialects are often used as social markers, upward-striving individuals may attempt to change their speech pattern. Dialects also change through time. What was once a marker of upper-class speech in New York City is now a marker of the working-class dialect. Thus, at the turn of the century the pronunciation of the words "shirt" and "work" as "shoit" and "woik" were both markers of "aristocratic" speech.

Secret Dialects

American parents of foreign origin often employ their mother tongue in order to keep secrets from their children. Children, on the other hand, teach each other "Pig Latin" or make up secret "languages" to baffle other children or adults. The same pattern exists among criminals who develop a dialect peculiar to their profession. After a while the police and the public become familiar with the terms of the dialect and new forms of slang develop. From the sociological point of view one can say that professionals use **jargon** (the technical vocabulary of their specialty) and people on the fringe of the law use **slang.** Slang is, however, employed by members of various social groups as a means of adding variety to their conversational skills.

Slang may also mark permanent or temporary identity. The drug culture in the United States has made its contribution to the language as have other marginal groups. The entertainment industry has also been responsible for introducing a host of foreign and slang words into the mainstream of the American language.

LANGUAGE CHANGE AND HISTORICAL LINGUISTICS

Languages are in a constant state of change. As technology advances, new terms are invented or borrowed to name and explain the functioning of new items. There are other reasons for change, however. Grammatical systems are never perfect. Phonological and syntactical changes are never-ending processes in which an alteration in one aspect of sound or structure is likely to stimulate adjustments in other parts of the system. One of the earliest documentations of such change in language was that of Jacob Grimm (famous also for the collection of German folk tales he made with his brother). Grimm noted a persistent and regular set of changes that occurred through history in the sound systems of pre-Germanic dialects and which also occur in Germanic languages. These have come to be known as **Grimm's law.** Grimm's law predicts with a high degree of success (there are exceptions) that voiced sounds become voiceless ($d \rightarrow t$), voiceless stops become fricatives ($p \rightarrow f$), and fricatives become voiced stops ($f \rightarrow b$). Thus, the Latin *duo* becomes the English *two,* the Latin *pater* becomes the English *father,* and so on. Vestiges of phonological change in English can be seen in the spelling of such words as dough, tough, and rough. The word for "pocket knife" in French, *canif,* is pronounced *kaneef,* which would be close to "knife" in English if the latter were pronounced the way it looks. (Note also that the English "knife" (*nife*) has a broader meaning than its French cousin; other knives in French are *couteau.*)

When words are borrowed from a foreign language they are eventually shaped according to the grammatical rules of the host language. Thus, the verb "to relax," borrowed by French from English, fits into the standard French conjugation (*Je relaxe, tu relaxes, nous relaxons, vous relaxez, ils relaxent*). The English "pullover sweater" has become *pul* in French, and it is possible to buy a *rosbif du porc* ("roast beef of pork") in France because of a shift in the meaning of roast beef from a cut of meat from a particular animal to a cut of meat from any animal. A shift in the relationship between class status and grammar can be seen in the change from "He looks good, don't he," which can be found in English eighteenth-century novels about the gentry, to "He looks good, doesn't he," which reflects current "correct" usage.

Rosbif du porc and *canif* reflect semantic change that came about during the process of borrowing, but semantic change occurs continually within all languages. The meaning of words (thanks to denotation and connotation and the use of metaphor) is constantly expanding and contracting. In the American form of English, at least, the word "corn," which used to refer to all grain, now refers only to maize. "Meat" used to mean both vegetables and the *flesh* of animals. It was a more general term than "flesh," which was used then to designate what we now call meat. In Middle English the Christ Child used to be referred to as "the silly knave," which came from the German *Selige Knabe* ("holy child"). "Silly knave" in Shakespeare's time meant a not-too-honest, rather stupid person. It is now an archaic expression and is little used. Its evolution in English went from naming a holy person to naming a dishonest person to being dropped from conversational English. The process through which originally positive words or expressions take on a negative or pejorative meaning is called **pejoration.**

Words may also become taboo, sometimes because they are overly sacred and sometimes because they are overly profane. Among Orthodox Jews it is not correct to use the name of the deity. Various **circumlocutions** (substitute terms) have been developed in order to discuss the deity. The same process is found elsewhere. Among the Ainu of northern Japan, the bear is a holy animal and its name cannot be spoken. Substitute terms are developed that describe certain attributes of the bear ("honey-eater," for example), but after a while these become taboo also because of their close psychological and linguistic association with the animal in question. Once the word becomes **reified** (made real) as part of the animal and not merely its signifier, a new term or set of terms has to be substituted. "Honey-eater" has itself become holy!

In the middle of the nineteenth century the United States went through a period of strong linguistic taboos that have only recently begun to break down. Any words suggestive of sex or bodily function were eliminated from polite conversation and literature. H. L. Mencken has documented this process in his interesting and important book, *The American Language.* Mencken tells us that in the middle of the last century such words as "leg" and "chest" could not be pronounced in mixed company. Underwear became "nether garments" and even the leg of a cooked chicken had to be referred to as a "joint." In modern slang, of course, "joint" has come to have a far different meaning. It was deemed incorrect to pronounce the word "female" in the presence of women, and Vassar College, originally named Vassar Female College, had its name changed. Main Hall on the Vassar campus, an imposing Victorian brick structure, used to bear an engraving of the old name. In the late nineteenth century the word "Female" was chiseled out and the marks of this cultural vandalism can still be seen across the face of the building.

As recently as the late 1950s the word "whore" was taboo in newspapers. When the play *Tis Pity She's a Whore* was revived in New York, the advertisements read either *'Tis Pity---* or *'Tis Pity She's a Prostitute!'* The original title bears witness to the linguistic and sociological freedom with which at least certain aspects of sexual mores were treated in early seventeenth-century England. The translation

Main Hall at Vassar College. The word "female" was removed from the central space in the late nineteenth century.

of "whore" into "prostitute" actually changed the intended meaning of the title, since the lady in question did not sell herself to men. The content of much of the drama of that time would have been totally off limits in the Hollywood of the 1930s and '40s.

Linguistic Change and Ethnohistory

According to linguist Morris Swadesh, languages change at relatively the same rates and these rates are measurable. If so, then linguistic change can be used to measure the time two related peoples have been separated from each other. This technique is known as **glottochronology,** or **lexicostatistics.** Swadesh was aware that certain elements of vocabulary were more likely than others to remain stable for long periods of time and to show measurable rates of change. He developed a basic word list (see table) for use in glottochronological studies and first tested it on related languages that had been separated in time for known historical periods. Glottochronological measures are not trusted by everyone and are best used in combination with other dating techniques developed by anthropologists. Yet the discovery by any means that two languages are related, however distantly, provides ethnohistorians with important data concerning the spread and differentiation of cultures. Although British English and American English have been developing as separate dialects for only a short time, there are already several spelling and word differences. In the United States we have "jails," but the English have "gaols," although at present both words are pronounced more or less the same way. In the United States we put things in the "trunk" of a car and fill its tank with "gas." In England people put things in the "boot" and fill the tank with "petrol." We use elevators while the English use "lifts." We live in apartments while the English live in "flats."

Related languages are members of language families. Most languages spoken in Europe (and areas colonized by European nations), Iran, and northern India and Pakistan are members of a large language family known as **Indo-European.** Exceptions in Europe are Finnish, Estonian, and Hungarian, all of which are members of the Finno-Ugric family, and Basque, which has no known related language. Within Indo-European we have smaller groupings of more closely related languages. French, Italian, Spanish, Romanian, Portuguese, and the small regional languages known as Catalan, Provençal, and Romansh are all members of the Romance family. They are all descendants of Latin. The Germanic languages include German, Dutch, English, and the Scandinavian languages.

The Development of Writing

The keeping of records undoubtedly began as people drew pictures of things and events that were important to them. Among traders the first records probably consisted of tallies noting items and amounts traded. The first signs were

a

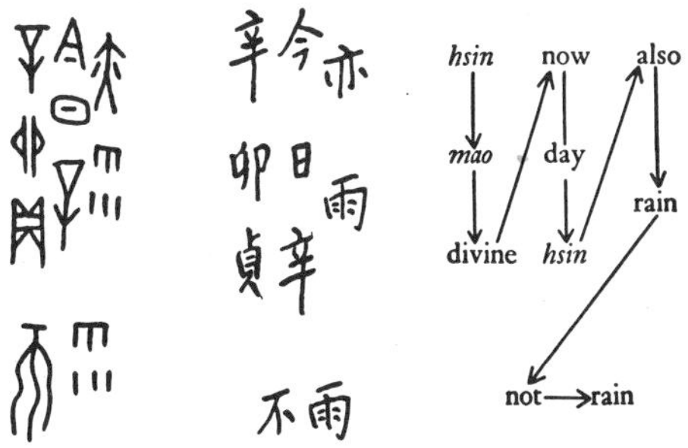

b

c

pictures of real objects. These are known as **pictographs.** As writing systems became more sophisticated, capable of expressing more complex thoughts, some means had to be found to express ideas that could not be directly pictured. The result was **ideographs.** The ancient civilizations in the Middle East all developed ideographic writing systems of great complexity. Other equally complex ideographic systems were devised independently in China and in the New World among the Maya. The Chinese system is still in use. Even though the Chinese speak many dialects, because their writing system is not phonetic (not based on sounds) all Chinese can read the same symbols and texts.

As the writing system developed in ancient Egypt, symbols for sounds were added to the ideographs. This type of mixed system can be found in the records of most Middle Eastern civilizations. The Japanese use a similar system today. Their writing consists of Chinese ideographs, which are nonphonetic, plus a set of symbols that stand for the sounds of syllables. These are used to express such grammatical categories as tense, which does not exist in Chinese and cannot therefore be expressed in ideographs. Such a set of symbols is known as a **syllabary.** The Japanese had to develop this additional system because Chinese is a *noninflecting* language (there are no grammatical markers for verb or noun changes) whereas Japanese has complex inflections.

The **alphabet**—a system of arbitrary signs standing for the phonetic units of a language—

d

Figure 12.3

(a) The development of the alphabetic letter A from an ancient pictograph. In the pictograph the picture of the ox head signifies the animal. The pictograph becomes schematic and more abstract in later forms. In Phoenician the abstract ox head is laid on its side and has taken on a sound value. It stands for the A sound, the first letter of the word for ox. The Roman A is very similar to the letter used for the A sound in Phoenician. The cross bar has been shortened and the letter has been further rotated. Examples of early writing from China, and the Middle East: (b) an oracle bone inscription shown in ancient and modern Chinese with a transliteration and English translation. (c) The earliest example of writing, on a limestone tablet from Kish, circa 3500 BC. (d) left: stone tablet incised with pictographs. right; clay tablet with incised writing, from Nippur, circa 1500 BC.

Swadesh's basic word list.

1. I	35. tail	68. sit
2. thou	36. feather	69. stand
3. we	37. hair	70. give
4. this	38. head	71. say
5. that	39. ear	72. sun
6. who	40. eye	73. moon
7. what	41. nose	74. star
8. not	42. mouth	75. water
9. all	43. tooth	76. rain
10. many	44. tongue	77. stone
11. one	45. claw	78. sand
12. two	46. foot	79. earth
13. big	47. knee	80. cloud
14. long	48. hand	81. smoke
15. small	49. belly	82. fire
16. woman	50. neck	83. ash
17. man	51. breasts	84. burn
18. person	52. heart	85. path
19. fish	53. liver	86. mountain
20. bird	54. drink	87. red
21. dog	55. eat	88. green
22. louse	56. bite	89. yellow
23. tree	57. see	90. white
24. seed	58. hear	91. black
25. leaf	59. know	92. night
26. root	60. sleep	93. hot
27. bark	61. die	94. cold
28. skin	62. kill	95. full
29. flesh	63. swim	96. new
30. blood	64. fly	97. good
31. bone	65. walk	98. round
32. grease	66. come	99. dry
33. egg	67. lie	100. name
34. horn		

was invented only once. It developed in the Middle East among a Semitic-speaking people, sometime between 1500 and 1300 BC. The alphabet is a tremendous advance over other forms of writing. A limited number of simple signs can be used to express any sounds in a language. It is highly flexible and can be learned easily. All known alphabets in the world today are developments from the original invention. As the system was borrowed by different peoples, it underwent considerable change so that today many alphabetic systems appear to be totally different from one another.

LANGUAGE IN ACTION

Translation

Translating from one language to another is always very difficult. For both nonfiction and fiction, the translator must be careful to remain faithful to the sense of the original language. Since each language has its own way of dividing and combining sets of ideas and perceptions, the translator may have to rely on approximations or lengthy explanations. In Kolongo, for example, the verb for "to understand" is *kanga* ("*mi kanga*"—"I understand"). Literally, however, *kanga* means "to hear." Thus, "*Mi kanga Kolongo*" means literally "I hear Kolongo," but a literal translation would be wide of the mark. *Kanga* is like the verb *entendre* in French, which means "to hear" but which may be used as "understood" (*entendu*) or, depending on context, "agreed." The expression in Kolongo *Ho cheri bebe,* is very difficult to translate because it means both "very good" and "very pretty." How it is translated depends on the context in which it is used. The expression *Ho dun* poses even more of a problem. It means "very good" in the sense of eating or drinking something good, but it also means "very sweet." Yet the expression is used for such widely different foods as palm wine (which when properly fermented is neither too sweet nor too sour) and meat. Again, context as well as knowledge of the culture must be the guide for translation, even in such a simple case.

French, like other Romance languages, has two verbs that translate into English as "to know." One, *savoir,* means "to know [by heart]," "to know how [to do something]" ("*je sais nager*"—"I know how to swim") or "to know [about a person or a subject]" ("*deux ou trois choses je sais d'elle*"—"Two or three things I know about her"). *Connaître* means "to know [someone]" ("*je la connais*"—"I know her") or "to be familiar with [a body of knowledge]" (*"je connais l'histoire"*—"I know history"). Even these definitions do not reveal the complexity of meaning involved in these two words and problems involved in their proper use in French—not to mention the problems of translation. As we have already seen, German has two verbs for the English "to eat": *essen,* which applies to humans, and *fressen,* which applies only to animals.

Metaphoric expressions that call forth a set of relationships are often particularly difficult to translate. The translator must search for some equivalent form in the language of translation. Taking certain expressions too literally can lead to poor translations and worse. Even dialects of the same language may contain the same expression with different meanings. In Quebec, *"je suis tout écarté"* means "I am lost," but in literal French and in France, where the expression is not used for "lost," it means "I am all spread out," which denotes very little but has a sexual connotation. When an Englishman wants to visit a woman friend he may very well say, "I'll knock you up," which in England is equivalent to "I'll come up to your apartment." In the United States "I'll call you up" will probably be taken in the sense meant, while "I'll knock you up" is likely to produce unexpected results.

Language is expressive of ideas, but it is also expressive of feelings. A translator must be careful to get the right tone. The French expression *"C'est con"* literally translated would be extremely vulgar in English (the expression contains a taboo word for female genitals). Actually *con* is widely used and carries no particular sexual connotation. Correctly translated, *"c'est con"* would mean "it's foolish" and nothing more. Because the social attitudes towards linguistic usage change through time, one must be careful to consider how an author's linguistic choices might have been received in his or her time. Some four-letter words have lately become so common in American literature that a direct translation into a language spoken by a more prudish culture might carry the wrong affect and misrepresent the author's intentions.

If nonfiction presents considerable difficulties, consider the problem of prose fiction and poetry. Good fiction depends on both narrative and style. The latter is likely to be particularly elusive in translation. And poetry, with its use of sound and sometimes meter and rhyme, presents further difficulties. In many cases it is better for a translator to forget rhyme and meter and concentrate, instead, on the feelings expressed. The rhythms of one language may turn out to be quite boring in another.

So far we have been talking about translation from one language into another. Yet because language is always changing, it is often difficult to understand the full meaning of noncontemporary literature in one's own language, even if grammar and vocabulary have changed relatively little. In some cases Shakespeare's English is our own, but often we have to translate his words (at least mentally) in order to grasp their full connotative range and the feeling expressed. ("Silly knave" is an example of this type.) Anthropologists and folklorists face a particularly difficult task when they attempt to provide a *literary* rather than a *literal* translation from any of the world's folk traditions. Knowledge of both language and culture is of the utmost importance in these cases, but so are considerable skill in writing one's own language and a sensitivity to feelings within the two cultures. Since an oral tradition, perhaps more than a written tradition, is based to a large degree on unspoken cultural conventions, a literal translation that does not include these conventions may leave the reader totally in the dark. Cultural allusions of all sorts are common in myth and folklore. A simple image may invoke a chain of associations that are completely closed to an outsider.

In his book of Australian Aboriginal poetry, *Love Songs of Arnhem Land,* Ronald M. Berndt attempts to deal with the problem of translating poetry from a language and culture remote from the English speaking world. The lines

Mirigin nangal . . . gwaljumngin
gidilaiun

mirigin djalwaljul wadarwul milju
ganidjuman

are translated as

Breasts saw . . . make it move
hands
breasts cold wind with eye
wink
because buttocks move.

These are then given poetic expression in English on the basis of Berndt's understanding of poetic form in English and the emotions expressed in the lines quoted.

We saw their breasts, and their
hands moving . . .
Their breasts in the cold west wind,
as they flutter their eyes at the
men:

Swaying their buttocks . . .

From the latter we get the sense that this is an erotic poem about women seducing men, but many allusions are lost to us and we cannot be sure of the relations between the original lines and the form into which they have been cast by Berndt.

Playing with Language

Children learning to talk can often be overheard chattering to themselves. In the early stages of language learning they repeat sounds over and over; later, word play occurs sometimes with and sometimes without meaning. Children appear to enjoy themselves alone and require neither auditor nor audience. They are playing with sound and with language. Older children and adults play *games* with language. A game is a structured form of playing in which a set of rules determines the limits of play. Word games range from posing riddles and repeating proverbs (both repetition and the invention of new forms are involved) to telling jokes and more formal story telling. Our own culture has such word games as twenty questions and charades, which is partially verbal and partially mimetic. Games of this sort require quick thinking and exercise an individual's ability to think analogically. Riddles and proverbs are also one means of teaching children. Good riddles and proverbs (good in the sense of fitting the particular culture's style and yet creating new analogies and new ways of affirming beliefs) are almost poetic in structure, since, like poetry, they rely for their force partially on metaphor.

Some riddles are meant to be answered. They provide a puzzle that can in fact be solved by finding the right connection of ideas. For example: Q. "How can you do something which is doing nothing?" A. "By fasting." Another type of riddle involves a play on words: Q. "What's black and white and red all over?" A. "A newspaper." This involves the verbal pun that occurs when "red" is substituted for "read." Other riddles have no analogic answer but are rather pure word games that are meant to catch the hearers off guard: Q. "What's big and red and eats rocks?" A. "A big, red rock eater." In West Africa a riddle should work. It should reveal analogies, but they should be completely farfetched or profound enough to fool everyone but the teller. The Sonike of West Africa have the following riddle:

Q. What man kills his children?
What man sells his children?
What man gives his children away?
A. A man who marries a wife of 40 kills his children.
A man who makes love to a slave sells his children.
A man who makes love to another man's wife gives his children away.

Unconscious Use of Linguistic Symbolism and Language

Puns, as we have seen, are word games based on analogies. Two words that sound alike are used in substitute form, producing a joke based purely on the analogy of sounds. More complicated puns may involve both sound and meaning. Puns and other types of "word play" are not always intentional. Sometimes people have two things on their minds at the same time and mix them up, producing a pun or some other "slip of the tongue." The founder of psychoanalysis, Sigmund Freud, saw in these slips a revelation of thoughts coming from the unconscious mind. Psychoanalysts believe that the unconscious has its own "language," which consists of a complex code. This code is not usually available to the conscious mind. When it does "leak out," as in slips of the tongue and in dreams, it must be translated into everyday language before it can be understood. For psychoanalysts, dreams are something like poems in that their meaning is very dense and concentrated. A single symbol or a small set of symbols may stand for a whole range of ideas, feelings, and experiences that are locked within the individual. People undergoing psychoanalysis are asked to recount their dreams to the analyst and then to analyze them through the process of free association. In free association patients are asked to say anything that comes into their minds. Many of the usual restraints of formal language are lifted during free association, and, although phonological and grammatical rules are followed (the patient uses real language), the semantic relationships that flow from the process are freer than the connected speech of everyday life. Free association is a means of using ordinary language to get at another and less understood symbolic system, the unconscious. Linguists and anthropologists are interested in this symbolic system as well as language because it might provide insights into what is thought to be a universal characteristic of symbolic thought in humans. Some anthropologists believe that the unconscious provides the raw material of religious beliefs and of myth. Sometimes the unconscious is inferred by anthropologists from religious and mythic material. Anthropologists resort to inference because few of them are equipped to carry out psychoanalyses in the field, nor do most of them have the time available to devote to this long and complex process. But when belief and myth are used to uncover the unconscious because the unconscious is assumed to generate myth and belief, there is an error of circular reasoning. The assumed relation is taken as true before evidence for it has been demonstrated. Still, the common occurrence of certain symbols and types of symbolic thought in many of the world's peoples does suggest sets of elements that may have their origin in the unconscious. The techniques needed to investigate this particular aspect of symbolism interest most linguistic anthropologists but lie outside of their competence. In most cases, then, they concentrate on the conscious aspects of human communication.

Summary

Culture, the human adaptation, is based on the ability to use language, which is the system whereby humans express their thoughts and communicate with one another. Humans are born with the genetic capacity to learn language, but which language they will learn depends on experience.

There are two ways of looking at language. For some it is the end result of a gradual evolution of intelligence and the ability to communicate. For others it is a totally new capacity exclusive to the human species. The former view is expressed by B. F. Skinner, a psychologist, and Charles Hockett, a linguist; the latter has isolated seven design features that occur in language. Hockett finds that at least some of these features occur in the communication of nonhuman species as well. These are: productivity, the ability to create new messages, arbitrariness, the lack of an inherent relationship between a symbol and the thing or concept it signifies; interchangeability, the ability of a receiver of a signal to reproduce the same signal; specialization, which refers to the fact that language signals are specific to their communication function, (they have no other function, unlike the unspecialized signal that pregnant stickleback females present to their mates *because* their swollen undersides serve to communicate sexual receptivity); displacement, the ability to communicate about things and ideas not present at the time communication takes place; duality of patterning, the use of a small number of meaningless units (sounds) in a wide variety of possible combinations to produce meaningful utterances constructed according to their own rules; and cultural transmission, which refers to the fact that language is not part of a genetic system but is learned.

The notion of cultural transmission suggests that human language is only quantitatively different from some other communication systems in which animals learn at least part of their signals. Thus, the fact that primates other than humans learn signals can be used to argue that the differences between human and nonhuman communication systems are only a matter of degree.

The linguist Noam Chomsky argues that all languages, no matter how different they might be, are based on a universal grammar that is exclusively programmed in the brains of all humans. Chomsky believes that only the concept of universal grammar can explain how children come to utter sentences they have never heard.

The psychologist Jerome Bruner believes that children develop linguistic creativity during the socialization process (growing up in the context of a family).

All languages are systems composed of sounds, and combinations of sounds that can be grouped into words and sentences. Phonology is the study of the sound systems of languages, grammar is concerned with the structure of the various combinations of sounds and groups of sounds into higher order units, and semantics is concerned with meaning.

Languages are flexible systems of communication. They allow individuals to speak about the past and the present, the real and the imaginary. Denotation, the strict meaning of a word, can be altered through connotation, broader extended meanings, and the use of metaphor, the linking of two or more things or concepts into a single idea.

All sound systems are composed of phones, the sounds of a language. Phones can be grouped into phonemes, sets of distinctive sound units (that is, those sounds that actually affect meaning in a particular language). Variations of a single phoneme are called allophones. Sounds, however, taken alone have no meaning. Meaning arises when sounds occur in particular relationships. The minimal unit of meaning in a language is known as a morpheme. Morphemes occur as free forms that can stand alone ("run") and as bound forms that must be tied to other morphemes (-er in "runner"). Variant forms of the same morpheme (the plural forms "cat(-s)" "hous(-es)" ("mice"), etc.) are called allomorphs.

The words syntax and grammar are often used to indicate the same thing, the rules for forming proper sentences in a language. In linguistics grammar refers to any rules of combination, while syntax refers specifically to the rules of sentence formation. Semantics determines which words may be put together in a sentence; syntax, how they may be put together. Semantics is concerned with meaning.

All languages are capable of expressing everything that needs to be expressed in a particular culture. There is no such thing as a primitive language. Some linguists and anthropologists, however, believe that the vocabulary and structure of a language may have some effect on the way in which the world is perceived and therefore how a culture is structured. This theory is associated with two linguists, Benjamin Lee Whorf and Edward Sapir.

The basic function of language is to communicate but it is also a social instrument. The way people talk to each other reflects their position in society, including such variables as sex, race, social class, and the degree of social distance between speakers. Dialects of the same language are often social markers. Black English, for example, may be used intentionally by blacks as a sign of solidarity within the larger American society.

Languages are constantly undergoing change. This fact has been used by linguists to date the length of time two peoples speaking related languages have been separated. This technique is known as glottochronology or lexicostatistics. Developed by the linguist Morris Swadesh, lexicostatistics depends on a basic word list of one hundred words, which is assumed to change at a known rate. These words are collected in two related languages and the differences noted.

The degree of difference yields the date at which the two cultures were separated.

Most languages contain words and expressions borrowed from other languages. When words and expressions are borrowed they are fitted into the structure of the new language. Frequently the meaning of particular words changes through time, and from time to time new words are adopted or created and some old words dropped out. Words become taboo for both religious and sexual reasons. Which words are taboo at any particular time in history is a matter of cultural practice and belief, not linguistic rules.

For these and other reasons translating from one language to another is a difficult process. The translator must attempt to translate the feeling of the word or phrase as well as its literal meaning. While prose is difficult to translate, poetry poses even more problems, since poetic expression is based on complex meanings and allusions. When translating prose or poetry, the translator needs to know a good deal about the culture associated with the language from which the translation is being made.

Language play is also an aspect of linguistic behavior. We see it most frequently in children who play with language as they learn it. Adults also engage in language play, particularly through jokes, puns, and riddles. These test and sharpen the ability of individuals to express themselves in their own language.

The unconscious mind also uses symbols, although these are often closed to us because they are suppressed through psychological mechanisms. Psychoanalysts attempt to get at the unconscious and its symbolism in the process of psychoanalysis. Anthropologists are interested in the unconscious symbol system because it may underlie belief systems and myth.

Bibliography

Chomsky, N. 1957 — *Syntactic Structures.* The Hague: Mouton. The original statement on inherent grammars by the founder of transformational linguistics.

Chomsky, N. 1972 — *Language and Mind,* 2nd edition. New York: Harcourt Brace Jovanovich. A general statement on the theory of transformational grammar as an inborn system.

Chomsky, N. 1975 — *Reflections on Language.* New York: Pantheon. A set of essays for the lay reader dealing with language as an inborn system. Compares learning theory to the structural approach to language.

Hockett, C. F. 1958 — *A Course in Modern Linguistics.* New York: Macmillan. A general introduction to linguistics by a leading linguist.

Labov, W. 1972 — *Language in the Inner City: Studies in the Black English Vernacular.* Philadelphia: The University of Pennsylvania Press. Black English by its major student.

Premack, A. J. and D. Premack 1972 — Teaching Language to an Ape. *Scientific American.* 227:92–99. Report on experiments in chimpanzee language teaching and learning.

Weitz, S. 1974 — *Nonverbal Communication: Readings with Commentary.* New York: Oxford University Press. Articles on communication by means other than language.

Whorf, B. L. 1956 — *Language, Thought, and Reality: Selected Writings of Benjamin Lee Whorf.* Edited by J. B. Carroll. Cambridge, Mass.: MIT Press. Language as a social process by the major proponent of the notion that language shapes culture and perception.

CHAPTER 13
THE NATURE OF CULTURAL ADAPTATION

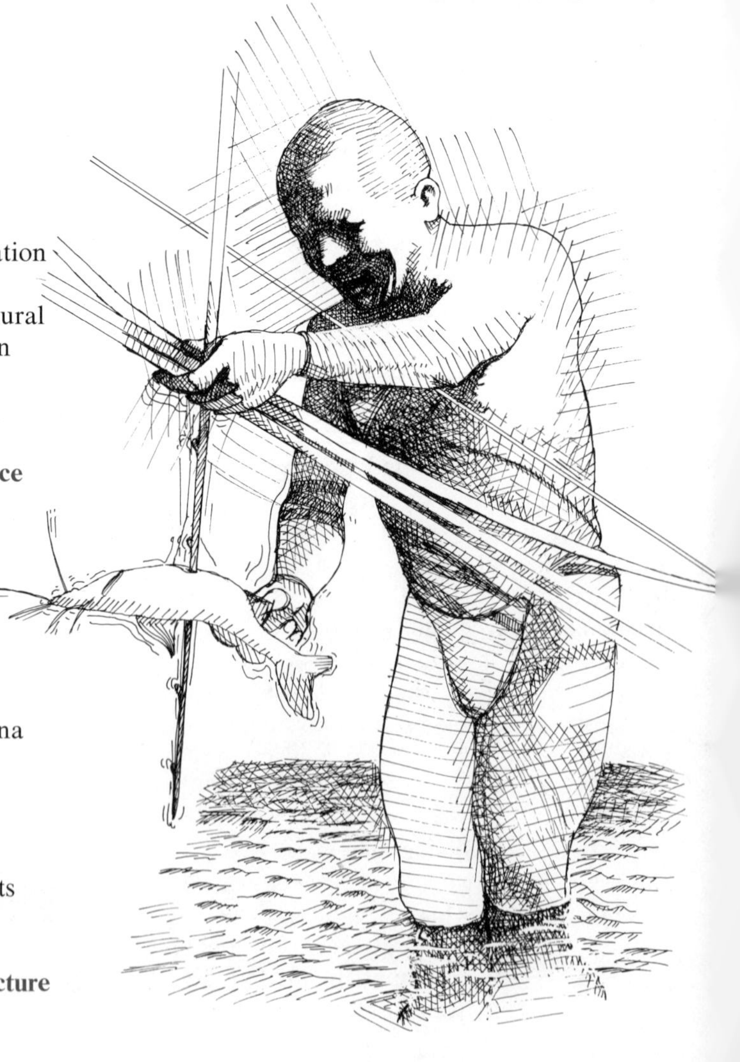

The remainder of this book is concerned with cultural anthropology, the study of living peoples. In general this field is divided into **ethnography** (the collection and publication of data on individual social or ethnic groups) and **ethnology** (the analysis of ethnographic materials in order to make generalizations about culture).

The ethnological perspective of this book is evolutionary and its focus is on adaptation. Humans are animals and as such must accommodate, like all other species, to their environment. Humans must solve biological problems in order to survive, but culture as our major adaptation has itself changed the evolutionary game. The historical development of human societies from the Paleolithic to the present has followed the old biological rules of reproductive survival *plus* a new set of cultural rules that help determine the flow of history. Cultural systems evolve as the result of encounters between societies and their environments *plus* encounters between societies and within societies themselves. Technological solutions to environmental problems change both the environment and the culture. Changes in such aspects of culture as religion or social organization may affect the ways and means by which humans exploit their environment.

DIFFERENCES BETWEEN GENETIC AND CULTURAL ADAPTATION

Adaptation, whether genetic or cultural, occurs when traits (physiological, morphological, and behavioral) are selected by the environment because they confer a selective advantage on those individual organisms that carry them. Genetic and cultural systems differ in significant ways: (1) In cultural systems adaptive behavioral traits are not genetic, rather they are learned and passed from individual to individual as part of tradition. The individuals, therefore, need not share hereditary material. (2) In culture, adaptive behavioral traits may confer an advantage on an entire group even if only some members of that group adopt the behaviors. (We only need a certain number of doctors to treat disease, for example.) (3) Because they are not dependent on genetic mechanisms, new cultural traits may be borrowed by one society from another or they may be invented by individuals within a particular culture. (4) Although species become extinct when the organisms that compose them die out, cultures may disappear when living people abandon their customary way of life. (5) Culture traits may appear as the result of unconscious changes in behavior that are advantageous and are, therefore, selected by the environment. They may also result from accidental discoveries. (The first antibiotics, for example, were discovered when mold spores accidently contaminated a bacterial culture.) In this way some culture change is similar to mutations, which are random changes in genetic material. Culture change, however, may also be the result of conscious planning and intentional innovation and is, therefore, not always dependent on random events. (6) Biological evolution is basically a process in which elements from the environment are converted with increasing efficiency into organisms. In most cultures a good deal of environmental energy is diverted into such activities as religious ceremonialism or the accumulation of prestige marked by differences in wealth. The very existence in human societies of social inequality changes the relationship among individuals in a population and between a population and its environment. (7) As we shall see in the chapters that follow, culture has rules of its own that cannot be predicted from biological rules alone.

Chimpanzee behavior is often very direct and adaptive, whereas humans can sometimes outsmart themselves by thinking too much.

Mind and Culture

The human mind, which is the basis of cultural behavior, is a very special tool. It can produce complicated and elegant solutions to problems, but this is not always so. In discussing the probable eye damage that would result from looking at the sun during a total eclipse, an English doctor said, "Humans are the only idiots that will look at the sun. You can be sure that no other animals would be that foolish." Looking at the sun, of course, is a purely cultural reaction. It is part of the will to know and reflects human consciousness. This consciousness is of genetic origin and has been selected over the course of thousands of years. It has obvious advantages for our species. Nonetheless, consciousness, as expressed through culture, is a two-edged sword. Let us see why.

Worms can learn, even if not very much, and humans, of course, can learn a lot. There are both quantitative and qualitative differences between human learning and learning in other animals. Some species, particularly primates, may learn a great deal, but probably don't think very much, while many humans may not learn much but nonetheless think a great deal. Consider an experiment in which a rat is rewarded about 30 percent of the time when it pushes lever A and about 70 percent of the time when it pushes lever B; if the rewards are randomized between the two levers so the rat can never learn which lever will be rewarded on any one try, the animal will soon learn to maximize its reward by continually choosing the more frequently rewarded lever, in this case B. When humans are presented with the same problem they frequently try to "beat the system" by devising some theory to account for a pattern of rewards that they imagine is nonrandom. The failure results from thinking too much or, of course, not enough. The rat's behavior is more efficient because it *cannot* fall into the "Monte Carlo fallacy." This is the mistaken belief of gamblers that if, in coin tossing, let us say, four heads are thrown in a row, the probability increases of tails appearing next. Actually, every time a coin is thrown, the probability of either a head or a tail is 50 percent. No matter how many times the coin is tossed the probability for heads or tails will remain unchanged. After all, the coin does not know that it has been tossed before.

Metaphor and Theory

Humans are the only animals that are capable of outsmarting themselves. We do so by using two processes that are independent of each other but are both dependent on language. These are *metaphorization* and *theory building*. Metaphorization lies at the heart of both art and science. Metaphoric thinking (discovering new analogies) often provides dazzling insights, but it can also produce faulty conclusions. Theories, too, can lead us astray, particularly when they are logical (and therefore appear to be true) but have not been adequately tested. We can see how both metaphors and theories operate to obscure reality by looking at medical systems in nonindustrial societies.

Most *indigenous* (native) theories of medicine work poorly in the treatment of physical illness. They do work, however, to focus attention on social rifts within society. In general, native therapists use the treatment of disease as the raw material for curing social disorder. Personal illness is viewed as a metaphor for social pathology. The crisis of a disease is linked to a crisis in the social order. Because most patients get well no matter what is done to them, and because curing ceremonies frequently bring conflict into the open and heal it, medical theories that do not work medically tend to persist.

Conscious and Unconscious Adaptation

Even though we sometimes commit the Monte Carlo fallacy or fall into other intellectual traps, correct theories and intelligent observations—coupled to memory and our superior transmission device, language—are powerful tools for adaptation to the environment. Indeed, human adaptation often results from a simple process of conscious problem solving. Theories speed up this process because they point the way directly toward solutions and make it possible to avoid error.

As we have seen, when antibiotics were first discovered, it was through the intelligent analysis of an accident. A mold growing on a petri dish in a laboratory was observed to kill bacteria. After extensive research the active agent in the mold, penicillin, was extracted and antibiotic therapy was born. The discovery of new antibiotics was not dependent on further accidents, however. The development of penicillin stimulated a search for similar substances.

Human adaptation through learning need not be a conscious process, however. A poor theory may lead to good results and good (adaptive) results may reinforce a particular behavior. Furthermore, a theory or an explanation need not occur with every adaptive behavior. An accidental response to the environment may work and thus be rewarded (or selected) directly. There are many behaviors that cannot be explained but nonetheless work.

Both conscious and unconscious trial and error are part of our adaptive equipment. What must have been an unconscious adaptation was the use of lime with maize by early Mexicans. Maize contains the essential amino acid lysine, but only in a form that is nutritionally useless. Lysine is liberated if the maize is prepared with an alkali solution (derived from lime or wood ashes). Most native Mexican recipes for tortillas include lime or ash in the process, and malnutrition due to lysine deficiency is thus avoided.

Another example is found in Korea. Raw fish is an excellent food. It is high in protein and low in fat. It has one disadvantage, however. Raw fish contains an enzyme that destroys thiamine, one of the B vitamins. Cooking is one way of avoiding this problem, for if fish is cooked the enzyme is destroyed. The eating of raw fish is probably a matter of taste; it is a favorite food in Japan and Korea. In Korea it is prepared with garlic, a vegetable rich in sulfur. As it happens, the sulfur compounds in garlic bind the thiamine-destroying enzyme. Thus, raw fish eaten with garlic is just as healthful as cooked fish, unless, of course, the fish harbors a parasite.

Finally, there is an interesting, if not completely clear, relationship between the ability of adult humans to successfully metabolize milk and the cultural practice of herding. All normal newborn human children are capable of digesting milk and its sugar, lactose. In nonherding cultures or those in which adults do not drink milk, most mature individuals cannot tolerate lactose and will get sick if they ingest fresh milk. Where milk is an important adult food item, an apparent biological adjustment has occurred, since lactose tolerance correlates with the cultural practice of herding and the exploitation of milk. Thus, East and West African cattle herders and herders of the desert and mountain regions in the Middle East and India are all lactose-tolerant. On the other hand, the Chinese, who do not use any milk products, show lactose intolerance. In regions where milk products (cheese and yogurt, for example) are consumed by adults but where little fresh milk is drunk, except by young children, lactose intolerance may exist but is bypassed by the cultural practice of eating only those milk products in which fermentation (destroying or converting lactose) has occurred.

Maladaptive Behavior

Not everything humans do is adaptive. Certain maladaptive practices persist because their negative effect is either not understood or mild enough to cause little discomfort. Curiously, other practices persist that cause a great deal of discomfort (various forms of genital mutilation, for example).

There used to be a disease found only among Polish Jewish women that was caused by a small parasite. This parasite occurs in fish used in the Eastern European Jewish specialty *gefilte fish.* In finished form this dish is cooked and the parasite destroyed. During preparation, in order to ascertain whether her fish was properly spiced, the cook would taste it as she added necessary ingredients. The result was a parasitic infection limited to women. This affliction is similar to, if less serious than Kuru, the slow virus disease that infected the women and children of the Foré people of New Guinea. As we saw, Kuru was caused by a virus that attacked the brains of its victims. The practice of endocannibalism coupled to the tasting of undercooked material led to a pattern of infection in which men were excluded. The two methods of food preparation discussed here were both maladaptive, although one was more severely negative than the other.

Limitations on the Concept of Adaptation in Cultural Evolution

Evolutionary thinking, even in biology, is always dangerously close to circular reasoning. If we are tempted to say that an organism, or a population, or a species is well adapted because it survives (because it is there), we are trapped in a circular argument. For this notion can be reversed in the form, "An organism, or a population, or a species is there because it is well adapted." Adaptation becomes the criterion for presence and presence the criterion for adaptation.

In evolutionary biology this problem is overcome by using an independent measure of adaptation, fitness, which can be measured mathematically. If two genetically variant forms occur within a population, we can record their real comparative fertility. This comparison provides an objective measure of selection. In cultural evolution no comparable measure exists. This is not the only problem, however. Culture, as we have seen, is not transmitted genetically. One individual can increase the fertility of his or her group through the innovation and sharing of some adaptive cultural trait. Also, an adaptive trait can be borrowed by one group from another group, even if there are absolutely no genetic links between them.

We cannot compare the fertility of two different groups for an indication of selection unless they are in direct competition and inhabit the same environmental niche. To say, for example, that there are more Chinese in the world than there are Russians or Americans and that, therefore, Chinese culture is better adapted than either Russian or American culture is like saying that microbes are better adapted than both fish and palm trees because there are more microbes in the world than either fish or palm trees. Humans are all members of the same species, but different human populations inhabit different ecological niches, and their adaptation or lack of adaptation in each niche is not comparable.

Cultural Evolution and Energy

One cultural anthropologist, Leslie White, attempted to push evolution into a simple model in which the ability of human groups to extract energy from the environment was the measure of adaptive success. In order to overcome the problem of comparison among units (in this case cultures), White took a chronological view of cultural evolution. He claimed that the history of humankind demonstrates an overall progressive increase in energy extraction. We cannot argue with this conclusion. There is no doubt that a species-wide increase in energy production has occurred progressively since the emergence of culture. We need only to think about the differences between an industrial and a preindustrial economy or the comparative energy consumption of hunters and gatherers on the one hand and the average American on the other. The data of evolution, however, come from a careful examination of local populations as they adapt to specific environmental conditions. White's approach, because it is on such a grand scale, makes it impossible to compare the local adaptation of individual social groups within the context of their particular environments.

General and Specific Evolution

Some of White's students have attempted to overcome this difficulty by distinguishing between what they call *general* and *specific* evolution. General evolution is the *unilinear,* overall process of cultural development on a worldwide scale. Specific evolution is adaptation on the local level. General evolution reflects overall "*progress*" (a dangerous word in science), while specific evolution is supposed to reflect the dynamic encounter between an individual culture and its milieu.

Unfortunately, these two concepts are really not helpful. General evolution is just that: *too general.* It is a truism that through time humans have increased their ability to extract energy from the environment. But measuring energy tells us nothing about the process or about what is involved in producing one particular change and not another. Nor can it predict the direction of change except in the restricted sense that the measure, energy capture, increases through time. Energy capture then serves as both the definition of evolution and its measure. This line of argument is completely circular.

Specific evolution is not much help either, although it is closer to concepts in biological evolution. Specific evolution does, at least, concentrate on individual populations within their environmental contexts. But specific evolution does not provide a successful noncircular measure of evolution any more than general evolution does. In addition, it fails to shed light on those processes that are responsible for both stability and change in adapting systems. In order to find out about them we need rules for generating cultural systems and for transforming the systems under given sets of external conditions.

TECHNOLOGY AND ENVIRONMENT

Although I have warned that the concept of adaptation can be misused in cultural anthropology, we must not ignore the reality that human societies face ecological problems. In order to survive, *all* species must accommodate to their environments. They must extract energy from environmental sources and convert it into organisms. Adaptation involves both physical and behavioral modifications. Anatomy and behavior are logically related to their function. Natural selection shapes organisms by favoring those that are best able to survive in a local environmental niche. Although all species modify their environment in some way and therefore change selection pressures, humans shape the environment more than any other creature. This is one reason why human adaptation cannot be discussed purely in terms of environmental selection. All cultural systems modify natural conditions and are modified by them in complex interactions.

Because culture allows humans to change their relationship with nature, the human species has never become locked into one particular niche. Since the full emergence of *Homo sapiens,* our species has spread throughout the world and has come to occupy every climatic zone and every continent except Antarctica. Human populations have thrived in the lush tropical forests of South America, Southeast Asia, and Africa; in the deserts of Africa, Arabia, and Inner Asia; on the grasslands of East and Central Africa and the plains of North America. Humans occupy the frozen wastelands of the Arctic all the way from the northern tip of Norway eastward across Europe and Siberia to the New World and Greenland. Our species can be found at every altitude from below sea level to almost 20,000 feet.

Survival in each of these environmental zones depends on the cultural exploitation of natural resources and both cultural and biological means of coping with environmental hazards. As warm-blooded mammals we can remain active in a wide range of climates. Clothing and shelter have increased our ability to maintain body temperature under conditions of extreme heat and cold. The evolutionary process has provided us with an immunological system that protects us against many disease organisms. Certain cultural practices serve to isolate populations from disease organisms, and effective treatments for at least some diseases exist in all cultures. Where seasonal food shortages exist, storage methods have been developed to cope with potential famine. Our biological capacity for communication manifested in language and our propensity for cooperation manifested in specific social organizations integrate with productive technology. Our traditions are shaped under the pressures of the environment and culture, and in turn, the traditions feed back into the adaptive process.

Not that humans always treat their environment with respect—far from it. The specter of environmental degradation and misuse has haunted our species from the beginning. The damage used to occur in isolated places and had little effect on even nearby environments. Today misuse of resources and pollution threaten everyone. Industrial power, with its tremendous extraction capacity and its ability to transform natural resources into synthetic products, has unleashed forces that are little understood and that menace the entire world. On the other hand, modern technology is a logical outcome of culture. It is capable of providing benefits on a scale unthought of even 100 years ago. As cultural adaptation has increased, it has also accelerated. Technological change now moves so fast that we have difficulty monitoring it.

THE MAJOR ELEMENTS OF SUBSISTENCE

The procurement of resources differs from culture to culture according to both environmental and technological variables. Hunting in the desert of Australia poses different problems and offers different results from hunting on the ice floes of the Arctic. Soil type, water sources, rainfall, temperature, and altitude affect the types of plants and animals that can be raised in a particular area. Yields depend on both climate and technology. Plants and animals are bred with varying degrees of success to provide food under local conditions. Fertilization and crop rotation are means of maintaining and improving soil conditions and therefore output. How well social groups survive in a particular environment is affected by their level of technology. A principal part of the technology is the particular procurement system employed—hunting and gathering, fishing, horticulture, agriculture, pastoralism, industrialism, or a mixed economy. Within each procurement system strategies vary. Fishing for river-spawning species differs significantly from fishing in the sea; nets, hooks, and poison are fishing techniques used under different conditions.

Technological variables include: available tools, knowledge of the environment and its resources, storage facilities, and methods of preservation. Elements of social organization as well as population size and distribution affect and are affected by environmental and technological variables. The division of labor (who does what according to age, sex, occupational specialization, and class) is a major feature of any productive system.

Hunting and Gathering

The first economy depended on hunting and gathering. The first technology consisted of simple tools such as wooden clubs, stone axes, wooden and stone-tipped spears, stone and bone knives, scrapers, and drills, and tools made of antler. Hunting strategies are still conditioned by the available animals and their habits as well as by the means available to kill them. We have already seen that large herd animals can be hunted with relatively little energy expenditure and that they often provide enough meat to support large populations. The efficient killing of these animals requires the cooperation of many hunters.

Isolated game is killed most efficiently by a few hunters working together. The San of the Kalahari desert in southwestern Africa are very clever hunters. Three to five men leave camp and visit the local water hole or search the surrounding scrublands for traces of animals. When an animal is spotted the hunters attempt to remain downwind from it. They will also strive to keep a cover of tall grass or brush between themselves and their prey. One hunter may move around a small herd in order to drive it toward his companions. Frequently a San will imitate the movement of an animal as he sneaks up on it so that it will not be disturbed by his presence. When he is within range, the hunter will use a bow and small poisoned arrows to make his kill. San poison works slowly and large wounded animals have to be tracked for a day or two before they die. The San are very skilled at tracking and can follow even a weak track over the hard-packed, dry earth of the Kalahari.

While the men hunt the women gather. Armed with digging sticks, they know where to find water-bearing roots that are also rich in carbohydrates. Although the San like to eat meat, their staple is the mongongo nut, a rich oil- and protein-bearing fruit. The nut also is gathered by the women—who, indeed, supply most of the required food.

Where game is varied, hunters have to make strategic choices about what kind of animal to hunt. As Robert K. Dentan has pointed out, these choices will be influenced by the dangerousness of the animal, the amount of edible meat available per animal, whether it is solitary or a herding form, and how easy it is to kill. Whether an animal is dangerous and how easy it is to kill are dependent in part on the prevailing technology. It is, for example, more dangerous and more difficult to kill a bear with a spear than it is to kill it with an arrow or a gun. On the other hand the presence of guns may lead to overhunting and game depletion.

Eric Ross, who has studied hunting in the tropical forest of lowland Peru, has found that hunters concentrate on medium-sized game and avoid large animals. He suggests that this is the most efficient means of extracting food with the least effort. Large animals are rare and solitary in the forest. Hunting them intentionally would be a waste of time. And once captured they are difficult to transport. Thus, size alone is not a good criterion for deciding what will be hunted.

The Basin Plateau Shoshone, a Native American group that used to range widely over the Great Basin in the southwestern United States, relied primarily on gathering for food. Their major source of protein and calories was the piñon nut, a form of pine seed. The rabbit was one of the few animals hunted. Efficient rabbit hunting required the cooperation of the entire group and the use of nets. Hunters, both men and women, were divided into two sections. One section spread out along the length of a long net while the other drove the animals toward it. When the animals became enmeshed in the net they were clubbed to death.

(Left) San women with their children gather vegetable material. (Right) San man with his hunting equipment.

a

b

c

(a) Net fishing in Pakistan. (b) Pole fishing from stilts set in a river in Sri Lanka. (c) Fishing with bow-and-arrow from a dug-out on the Upper Xingu River in the Mato Grosso of Brazil.

Fishing and Marine Resources

Climatic changes at the end of the Paleolithic in Europe led to coastal settlement and the heavy exploitation of marine resources. These resources were both fished and gathered. Shellfish, crabs, and other inshore forms probably made up a large part of the diet. Since little energy is required to gather these resources and because they are plentiful and stable, permanent villages could develop as populations no longer needed to be nomadic.

The Northwest Coast of North America is inhabited by a large number of Native American groups that in the past relied primarily on marine resources for subsistence. Villages existed along the coast and near river mouths, where migrating fish such as salmon would appear, sometimes in great runs. Although famine did occur in years when the salmon run was small, large permanent populations were able to settle in this area.

The inhabitants of the Pacific Islands in Polynesia and Micronesia grow a range of crops and raise pigs, yet they depend on fish as their major protein source—particularly on the smaller coral atolls, where large lagoons surrounded by reefs provide a major breeding ground for edible fish. The reefs also protect the lagoons from the high seas, and fishing within them is safe.

Fishing usually provides a more stable food supply than hunting and gathering. Although most hunting and gathering groups are forced to lead a nomadic existence, fishing peoples often live in permanent settlements. Where marine resources are seasonal, as they are on the Northwest Coast of North America, technological means of preservation and storage may develop.

Many populations that rely on fish for protein inhabit **riverine** (river-system) environments in the lowlands of South America. Fish are trapped in weirs, captured by poisoning dammed-up streams, and speared by individual fishermen. Carbohydrates in these areas are generally obtained through the cultivation of such crops as manioc and bananas. Robert Carneiro, an anthropologist who has done a great deal of field work in this area, has suggested that population density here is dependent on the availability of protein resources. In lowland South America groups that live close to rivers obtain much of their protein from available fish resources, although most also hunt.

Domestication

The development of domestication produced a major change in the relationship between humans and their natural resources. Before domestication most subsistence strategies were based on the availability (both seasonal and numerical) of different edible species. In environmentally marginal areas, the resources were limited in both quantity and variety. In rich environments, however, the variety of potentially exploitable resources was very large while, at least in some cases, the abundance of any particular species was low. In such environments no one element became dominant and a kind of automatic conservation operated. Furthermore, the failure of one or two resources did not generally lead to overall scarcity, since other available resources could be substituted for those that were temporarily absent. A diverse ecology, involving several food sources, is healthy and tends to remain stable.

The development of domestication began a process of differential exploitation in which certain key species in even the most diversified environments came to be the major source of subsistence needs. This development has the advantage of providing large and relatively reliable quantities of food, but it has the disadvantage of making populations dependent on a limited number of species. When, for some reason, these species fail, severe famine can result. In addition, the long-term exploitation of domestic species can lead to a spectacular simplification of the natural environment. The favoring of a few species in great numbers over naturally occurring forms may lead to the extinction of variation. The development of an economy dependent on certain kinds of plants, with a change in subsistence strategy away from balanced nutrition, can lead to a decline in the health of a population. It is also true that many domestic species are more expensive to raise and exploit than wild forms. That is to say, they may drain the environment of necessary elements more rapidly than native plants and animals. It has been suggested, for example, that the harvesting of wild game on the plains of East Africa would be a better means of subsistence than the herding of domestic cattle, which rapidly degrades the environment.

The commercial development of agriculture in capitalist society has led to vast improvements in productive efficiency. Such a practice, however, can be dangerous, for it tends to accelerate all the negative consequences that are the potential results of domestication. **Monocropping** (the exploitation of a single plant species) is often efficient, but it can also lead to rapid soil exhaustion. In addition, monocropping usually has a negative effect on the nutrition of local populations. When available land is given over exclusively, or almost exclusively, to a single crop, it is no longer possible to raise the food required by a local population for a balanced diet.

Early agriculture in both the Middle East and

Nomads herd sheep on the steppes of Central Asia.

the New World was apparently quite diversified. Many species were grown and a balanced diet maintained. The same diversity was apparently true for domestic animals. Herding populations either practiced mixed husbandry and agriculture in sedentary villages or were nomadic and partially dependent on agricultural populations, with whom they traded meat and milk products for grain and other vegetable materials.

Herding and plant domestication are highly variable aspects of culture. Nonetheless, a few generalizations can be made about typical techniques and their implications for cultural development. For both plants and animals the prevalent technology will depend heavily on the species raised, the environment in which they are raised, the techniques used in their exploitation, and the kind of social system characteristic of a particular culture. The intensity of production, for example, may be the result of socioeconomic forces both within and without the society.

Grain versus Root Crops

With the exception of rice, grain crops will not grow well in wet tropical areas. Yet they are hardy and, depending on the species, can withstand different degrees of heat and cold as well as moisture. Wheat, for example, grows over a vast area, ranging from the rather cold parts of northern Europe to the hot South. It can stand drought and heavy rain, but both desert and tropical conditions are too severe. In the dry tropics, wheat is replaced by millet and sorghum. In the wet and cold North of Europe—Scotland, for example—rye, barley, and oats do better than wheat. In the New World, prior to European contact, maize was the only domesticated grass. It does well in a wide range of climates, except where frost occurs very early in the fall and where there are heavy rains throughout the year.

Rice responds perhaps better than any other crop to intensive labor. Wet-rice agriculture is capable of tremendous yields, provided a large labor input is expended in its cultivation. Because it requires a great deal of moisture, a part of its life cycle takes place in paddies, with the roots submerged under water. Rice does well in the warm wet tropics in areas where artificial pools can be maintained and drained when necessary.

Grains as a food source have many advantages. When eaten in whole-grain form they are rich in protein, minerals, and the B-vitamin group. They store well and produce the basis of a rich economy when exchanged for other agricultural and manufactured goods. The rise of civilization in the Middle East was clearly related to the domestication of grain crops and their eventual commercial exploitation.

The damp tropics provide an environment for root-crop cultivation. Each tropical area of the world has its set of root crops. Taro and the yam come from Southeast Asia, where dry (or hill) rice is also grown. The New World yields manioc, also known as cassava, as well as the sweet potato. Africa saw the independent domestication of the yam and the unrelated Guinea yam.

One root crop is native to a cold mountainous area. This is the potato, which was first domesticated in the Andean highlands. Borrowed by Europeans, it rapidly became an important source of carbohydrates in much of the Old World.

Under proper conditions of rainfall, which must be heavy, and tropical heat, root crops produce high yields with relatively little care. Most of them are low in complete proteins, but this drawback is sometimes partially overcome by eating the green leaves of the plants. The sweet potato is probably the best overall food source among root crops, while manioc is the worst. Manioc does have an advantage, however. It grows with little care, in very poor soil, and stores well in the ground. It removes few mineral nutrients from the soil and can, therefore, yield for many years. Manioc occurs in two forms—bitter and sweet. Bitter manioc, which contains a poisonous substance, must be treated before it is edible. After the root is harvested, it is ground or pounded into flour. The flour is soaked with water and pressed. After several washings the poison will be leached out and the flour may be baked or made into cereal or beer.

Root crops produce high yields, but are generally low in protein. Harvesting manioc in Java.

Slash-and-Burn Horticulture

Root crops are generally cultivated by the method known as **slash-and-burn** or **swidden.** A field, usually a forest area, is cut down and burned off. The burning depresses weeds and the ashes serve as fertilizer for the crops that are planted among the stumps. After one or, at most, two crops, the field is rested.

Slash-and-burn cultivation often produces high yields with relatively low labor input. Because the fields must be left in **fallow** (to rest) for a long time, slash-and-burn cultivation requires large tracts of land. When population grows and the fallow period is cut because of increasing land pressure, the cycle may be shortened to the point where grass replaces trees in the fallow period. But grassland is difficult to cultivate with primitive tools and may be taken out of the agricultural cycle altogether. When this occurs, pressure for available land increases even more and the rate of change to grassland may accelerate.

The fertility of tropical soil varies from region to region, but it is often rather poor. Most of the energy and nutrients in a tropical forest are stored in the vegetation, particularly the trees themselves. If these are removed from a field rather than burned on the spot, their nutrients are lost. Continuous cropping on fragile soils may lead to sterility in a short time. If trees are harvested for wood, the forest floor is exposed to harsh rains that wash away the topsoil. In many parts of South America and Africa this process has resulted in **laterization,** the transformation of the land surface into a hard, infertile crust of iron-bearing soil.

Slash-and-burn cultivation does not involve the use of a plow. A simple digging stick, sometimes with an iron point, is the major tool used in both planting and harvesting. This type of cultivation as well as cultivation that depends on the use of the hoe is called **horticulture.** The term **agriculture** is generally reserved for plow cultivation.

Slash-and-Burn Horticulture: The Semai of Malaysia

The Semai live in the mountainous forest region in the interior of Malaysia. The population totals about 13,000 people who live in small settlements widely separated by **climax** and secondary (regrowth) forest. Population density is low, but varies between five per square kilometer to a high of about 25. Their country is cut by fast rivers, and commerce between Semai groups tends to be limited to single river basins. Within each basin local Semai tend to speak the same dialect and frequently intermarry.

The highest mountains in Semai country are between 2500 and 3000 feet. This altitude does little to modify the tropical climate. Rainfall and humidity are high. The year cannot be divided into dry and rainy seasons, although the wettest months are April and October through November, while the driest are February and July.

Men hunt with blowpipes, which shoot small darts covered with a sticky poison. Since contact with Western technology, Semai hunters have also used shotguns. Hunting parties consist of one to three men. Fishing is also an important economic activity; techniques include trapping, fishing with baskets, line fishing, poisoning, spearing, and even catching by hand. Traps supply the major fish resources.

As in so many tropical regions, the soil in Semai land is relatively poor, although it supports a wide range of species. The Semai classify their land on the basis of plant cover, which is itself the result of past farming history. A field a year or two old and still producing some crops is recognized as poor land for replanting. Thick undergrowth marks fields that have been abandoned from two to six years from first planting. These are sometimes partially recleared for small gardens. Forest land with a thick layer of undergrowth is distinguished from climax forest. The first develops from seven to twelve years after gardens are abandoned. The restoration of climax forest takes at least a dozen years. The Semai recognize climax forest land as the most fertile and scrub growth as the least fertile.

No permanent ownership of fields exists among the Semai. Instead, a family has use rights over land they have cleared. Unmarried men help work the fields of the family with whom they eat.

Fields are cleared at the end of the dry season to insure a complete burn and to guarantee that rain will reach the newly planted crops. Women and children begin clearing by cutting the underbrush. Afterwards large trees are cut down by men. Felling a single acre of climax forest takes up to four weeks. Burning can only take place when the felled trees and underbrush are completely dry. The usual drying period is from four to six weeks. Fearing that the rains will come before the drying process is complete, Semai often burn partially dried fields. A second burning is, therefore, often required. After burning, the fields must be left to cool for a few days so that the seeds will not be destroyed by the heat retained in the soil. The heating, however, has an advantage, for it kills weed seeds prior to the planting of crops.

In planting the major crop, hill rice, seed holes are drilled by men with a digging stick, or *dibble.* Women follow them, dropping several rice seeds into each hole. For other crops both dibbling and planting may be done by both sexes. Rice is planted first, followed by maize, manioc, and other minor crops. Once planting is completed the garden receives little care. Burning inhibits weed growth but methods do not exist for the control of insect and animal

Slash-and-burn horticulture among the Semai of Malaysia. (Left) A man tends a burning field. (Right) Women plant.

pests. Exploiting the fact that edible insects and animals are attracted to gardens, the Semai use gardens as convenient hunting grounds.

A vegetable called *amaranth* is the first to be harvested, followed by maize, squash, and finally rice. The rice harvest is well organized and marked by a brief ceremony. Rice harvesting is women's work and is done either with machetes or special rice knives. Harvested grain is laid out on mats near the field. Young men, and sometimes women, tread on the harvested grain in order to free it from the ear. The separated grain is then pounded in a mortar by women. This process separates the grain from the husk. Finally, women winnow the grain by tossing it in a basket. The light chaff blows away while the heavier grains fall back into the basket. The harvest is followed by a village party attended by relatives and neighbors.

The anthropologist who studied the Semai most recently, Robert Knox Dentan, noted an important difference in the agricultural practices of East and West Semai. In the East people resettle every few years when soil depletion forces them to abandon old fields. In the West settlements are more permanent and people rotate their fields around the village every few years. Dentan suggests several reasons for these differences. Many West Semai work for wages and therefore do not clear any land. In the West some low land exists on which it is possible to grow irrigated wet rice, which produces larger yields on permanent fields. In contrast, some of the eastern Semai grow foxtail millet, which produces lower yields than even dry rice and therefore requires extensive land. In the West some Semai grow cash crops. These are tree products, fruit and rubber, all of which grow on relatively permanent plantations that require a long-range labor investment. In sum, the West Semai are more closely linked than the East Semai into the greater-Malay cultural and economic system. The eastern Semai practice a more aboriginal form of slash-and-burn shifting cultivation.

Dry Farmers: The Hopi of Arizona

The Hopi of Arizona live on an arid plateau

6500 feet above sea level. Hopi villages are concentrated settlements (pueblos) built on flat-topped mesas that rise above the surrounding sandy countryside. Game and wild plant food are scarce, but the soil, when properly watered, is fertile. Rainfall, which occurs only in the summer months, sometimes in the form of destructive storms, averages only about 10 inches a year. Frosts are common and the growing season lasts only about three months. Horticulture under these conditions is marginal and requires skillful management. Crops must be planted in carefully chosen sites (near springs and in areas of maximal runoff) to maximize water utilization. Two to three independent fields are planted by each farmer to insure against the damage caused by summer storms. Through the centuries Hopi farmers have developed a series of hardy, deep-rooted, early-maturing crops well adapted to local conditions. Plants include maize, varieties of squash, beans, sunflowers, and pumpkin. Cotton is also grown. May is planting season and the harvest occurs in September. While the Hopi do not irrigate (to do so would be uneconomical in their environment and they lack the necessary technology), they tend their gardens with great care. They lay seeds deep in moist soil zones, weed frequently, and construct windbreaks to minimize dessication and wind damage.

Hopi food resources are supplemented by the collection of wild plants, particularly roots, berries, and seeds. Hunting occurs, but yields are very low. It is more a part of ceremonial life than a subsistence activity. Farm land is owned by kinship groups (clans) and is given to individual families by the clan. Among the Hopi the land as well as the harvests are the property of women, although men do the farm work.

Intensive Agriculture

Slash-and-burn cultivation is relatively **extensive.** Such an economic system works well when population density is low and land abundant. In areas with land scarcity and large populations cultivation practices must change to meet these conditions. One way of increasing crop yields is to increase labor input. The weeding of gardens, for example, reduces competition between crops and plant pests, insuring a better harvest. Irrigation and the application of fertilizer are other methods that can be used to increase productivity. Less land can be used to grow more crops, and large settled populations can be supported.

Intensive agriculture often demands cooperation for the efficient utilization of labor and resources. The control of irrigation water, for example, must be organized in such a way as to result in proper distribution at proper times. If

A Hopi cornfield in the Arizona desert.

waterworks such as dams, dikes, and conduits are necessary, these must be cared for by members of the community involved in production. Individual farmers cannot do this job alone, for the technology necessary to maintain the system extends beyond their own holdings. In China, for example, hydraulic systems were managed by local bureaucracies appointed by central authority. On the island of Bali, which depends on wet-rice agriculture, water resources are controlled and distributed by organizations of local peasants who are the users of water. It is interesting to note in this respect that, in Bali, village affairs are controlled by one group and water by another.

Cultivation Techniques

Cultivation techniques must vary according to the local environment. Fertilization and fallow are unnecessary on the flood plains of great river systems. Rice paddy agriculture requires a good water supply that can be controlled efficiently. Some soils serve best when they are deeply ploughed, others when they are barely scratched—in semi-desert areas, for example, deep ploughing would lead to severe wind erosion of topsoil.

Wet-rice paddy agriculture is a form of labor-intensive farming. Here an Indonesian farmer plants rice seedlings in a prepared paddyfield.

Fertilization and soil renewal also take various forms. The application of green manure, the use of turned-under weeds, is one effective means of maintaining soil fertility. The peasants living on the stony islands off Ireland's western coast use seaweed to fertilize their gardens. One of the most effective and readily available fertilizers is fecal material, both animal and human. Where animal domestication exists along with cultivation, manure is often saved and added to the fields. Manuring is generally associated with high population density and intensive agriculture. (Where population is low, extensive cultivation is the rule.)

The use of human feces (night soil) is generally restricted to areas with very dense populations. Because human feces carry many parasites, their use may produce both **endemic** and **epidemic** disease. Gain must outweigh loss if medically dangerous fecal material is to serve as a basis of intelligent agricultural practice. The practice of applying night soil is, as pointed out, related to population density, but the manner in which it is used varies from culture to culture. In Japan and China, where every scrap of potential fertilizer was jealously collected, the practice almost reached the level of art. Chinese farmers, for instance, constructed attractive outhouses along public roadways to entice passersby. In order to reduce the risk of disease, fecal material was stored for months before it was spread on the fields. The delay was effective because spontaneous combustion, a natural process in manure piles, kills most of the disease organisms.

In contemporary Japan the use of human feces as fertilizer is outlawed. The resource is not lost to the local ecosystem, however. Instead, it is used for the generation of natural gas, which is deodorized in commercial plants and then distributed for household use.

In Java fecal material is not directly employed. It is considered dirty by the predominantly Moslem population. Nonetheless, it has an indirect effect on the fertility of paddies. Human waste accumulates in drainage ditches and open sewers, where it fertilizes large quantities of algae. These in turn are allowed to flow into the rice paddies, where they become a form of green manure.

In India human waste is handled only by *untouchables* and is considered highly polluting from a religious point of view. Nonetheless, in many areas, particularly the densely populated South, individuals defecate in the fields, choosing a different spot each time they need to relieve themselves.

Economic Interdependence

Where adjacent populations practice different types of subsistence, mutually beneficial relationships may develop. People may trade primary products, such as the exchange of meat for grain between herders and agriculturists—but the process may be more subtle. In the south of France near Montpellier, the local ecology is divided between the plain, where grapes are the major crop, and a low limestone plateau where sheep are raised. Most of the sheep milk is used in the fabrication of Roquefort cheese. Until about 20 years ago sheep herding involved **transhumance,** a movement of herders and their flocks between the plain in the winter and the plateau in the summer. In the wintertime sheep were grazed on poor land near areas of grape cultivation. In exchange for the use of their land, grape farmers were given sheep manure for their fields. During the summer months sheep were taken up onto the plateau, where their manure was scattered over the uncultivated scrub and grasslands. The movement away from the plain, however, prevented the degradation of local grassland. Although sheep milk was taken out of the ecosystem by the commercial establishment at Roquefort, the production of milk to be used in cheese making requires that lambs be culled every spring. These lambs supplied a good deal of the locally consumed protein. Lamb skins were sold to nearby urban centers, where they formed the basis of a leather industry. The wool from mature sheep was sold to towns on the plain, where it formed the basis of a textile industry. Until the rather poor-quality wool produced in southern France was replaced by higher-quality Australian wool and synthetic products, these textile factories provided uniforms for the French Army as well as other woolen goods. Each segment of this local economy was complementary to another.

Animal Husbandry

Whether animal husbandry constitutes the major basis of a local economy is related to factors like climate and soil. Except in industrialized countries, animal husbandry as a primary mode of subsistence generally requires some form of population movement. Herding is usually found on poor land that is marginal or impossible for agriculture. Mixed animal husbandry and agriculture are, however, found in almost all environments where agriculture itself is possible. Nomadism may be necessary because of local climatic conditions that make it impossible to maintain large herds without seasonal movement. The efficient exploitation of grassland always requires seasonal movement.

In Swiss valleys short-distance transhumance has been developed into a fine art. Pasture exists on every level from the valley floors (usually above 3000 feet) all the way up to the snow line. The typical Swiss cattle village is located in the valley itself, which is surrounded by sloping pasture. In the spring, cattle are taken up to the first level above the village. This is known as the *mayenne.* They graze in the *mayenne* through May. In June they follow the retreating snow to the low *alpage* where they remain until the end of July. They are then moved up into the high *alpage,* where they graze during August and perhaps the early part of September. The high *alpage* has the poorest grass because it is so near the permanent snow line. Only sheep are found between this area and permanent snow. On the way down in the fall, the cattle usually stay in the *mayenne* again, and in the winter they are kept in the village itself. During the summer months when the cows are in the *alpage,* village hayfields are harvested in order to provide winter feed. Hay may also be harvested in the middle of the summer at the *mayenne* level and stored there for winter use.

Habitation in Swiss cattle country varies with altitude. The range is from substantial villages on the valley floors, to well-built houses in the *mayenne,* to crude but still substantial barns and chalets in the low *alpage.* The high *alpage* rarely has either houses or barns. Instead, cattle are kept close to stone wind-shelters and the herders sleep near them.

Cheese production takes place at each of these levels, for the cows must be milked each day. When the cattle leave the village to go into the *alpage,* they are accompanied by a whole team of men who function as herders and cheese makers. These individuals are hired by local cooperatives and are directed by an assigned head. Production belongs to the cooperative members on a per-share basis.

Recently tourism has become very important to the Swiss economy. Skiing and hiking have invaded valleys that used to be quite isolated. Because skiing is a winter sport and hiking does not usually disturb herding in the *alpage,* particularly when hikers follow existing trails, these new activities have little harmful effect on the traditional economy. A major exception occurs in the *mayenne,* where there is direct competition between the seasonal need of peasants for pasture at that altitude and the desire of tourists and urban Swiss for summer chalets. The *mayenne* is much more profitable in the short run as an area for real estate than for cattle raising, yet the local ecological balance is threatened by the removal of the *mayenne* from the economic cycle. Ecological balance depends on a set of interlocking factors. If one of these is disturbed, an entire system is endangered.

Pastoralism in Arid Environments

Transhumance in Switzerland takes place over a relatively small territory marked primarily by differences in altitude. Seasonal zones exist in vertical layers above a village. In more arid areas herds must be moved over considerable distances in order to insure adequate grass throughout the year. Pastoral nomads on the

Swiss cattle grazing on low pasture in the fall.

Once domestication has occurred species choice is strongly influenced by climatic and other ecological factors. (Left) Reindeer are well adapted to a cold climate and have been domesticated from wild caribou. This large reinder herd is in Swedish Lapland. (Right) Camels are indeed well adapted to a desert environment. Here a camel caravan carries sorghum (a grain crop) across the desert in Sudan.

steppes of Asia, for example, travel many hundreds of miles in the course of a single yearly cycle. Such groups live in tents and travel on horseback. They tend to be warlike and aggressive, at least in part because of their need to have continued access to vast territories for grazing purposes. The pastoral nomad economy is also quite generally dependent on trade. In many cases, for example, cheese and other animal products are exchanged with sedentary farming groups and merchants for grain, salt, and manufactured goods. Access to their trading partners is a necessity for nomads, and they will fight to keep such relationships open.

Species Choice

Although cultural factors other than the economic sometimes intervene to affect preference, one can usually predict accurately what domestic animal will be raised in a particular ecological setting. The more extreme the environmental conditions, the more direct the relationship between animal and ecology. Thus, it is safe to say that camel herding will constitute the major activity in the deserts of Africa and Arabia. The camels will be accompanied by sheep and goats, because both species are hardy and can live on marginal land. The cold highlands of Tibet can only be exploited by yak herding and the far North of Europe by reindeer herding.

The size and density of human populations will also affect the nature of domestication. The pig, which eats garbage and even human feces, is ideal in crowded, wet conditions, from the tropics to cold mountainous regions where they can live on roots and human waste. Cattle demand space and are generally associated with large tracts of grassland and relatively sparse human populations. Cattle, of course, do occur under conditions of high population density. India provides the best example. There they play an important role in the peasant economy, providing traction for plowing, fuel (since cow dung is the major source of flammable material), and protein, mostly in the form of milk products.

Island Subsistence

A major, rather generalized form of subsistence can be found on the islands that dot the Pacific Ocean. These are of two types: low coral atolls with very small land surfaces, and much larger and richer volcanic islands. Volcanic islands range in size from the North and South Islands of New Zealand through some of the larger islands of Hawaii to smaller but still substantial areas such as the group that includes Tahiti. Coral atolls are scattered all over the Pacific, but they occur in greatest number in Micronesia, an area that extends across the Pacific from Okinawa on the west to Wake Island on the east.

Subsistence on all of these islands depends on plant cultivation, minor animal domestication, and fishing. On the coral atolls fishing is the most important source of protein. Even though the land surface of an atoll is very small and populations limited by available space, atolls are blessed with lagoons protected from the open sea by coral reefs. These lagoons are rich in marine resources. Without them survival on these tiny dots of land would be impossible. Cultivation is limited to root crop horticulture and **arboriculture** (raising trees). Breadfruit, a tree crop rich in carbohydrates, and coconuts are found on many islands. Domestic animals are limited to pigs, dogs, and, in some cases, chickens, brought from the Asian mainland by migrant populations. The ecology of the larger volcanic islands is varied and rich and can support large populations exhibiting a complex culture and political structure. Smaller islands have a simpler political and social structure.

ECONOMY, ECOLOGY, AND SOCIAL STRUCTURE

Hunting and gathering populations are small and highly mobile. They possess little and, except for simple personal belongings, do not have private property. The concept of land ownership is absent among such groups. Cooperation in hunting may involve the entire band. Even when this is not the case food is generally shared throughout the group. Fishing folk often settle in permanent villages of considerable size, a reflection of an abundant food base. With domestication we see the beginning of complex property relations. Although land is rarely held *permanently* by kinship groups in horticultural societies, rights to land are granted by custom on the basis of use. Ownership of land and cattle is generally associated with permanent villages but the latter is also found among transhumant pastoralists. Among them ownership of herds is central to the economy and social structure. Frequently, transhumant herders are linked by kinship and trade to sedentary populations. These links form the basis of economic exchange between two different but interdependent economic systems.

Among horticulturalists and agriculturalists the presence of particular types of social organization will depend, in part, on the size and availability of cultivable land in relation to population density.

The rise of full-time specialists, the abandonment of kinship as the basis of most social relations, land ownership, allegiance to a territory, and the development of a class structure can be correlated with high productivity coupled to the rise of urbanism and/or the state.

In general, different types of social organization correlate better with the mode of production than with property ownership. Certain groups may control the production and distribution of economic goods within the population at large as well as trade with other such populations. Elders in Africa, for instance, hold power over younger members of their kinship groups by controlling access to the bride price needed for marriage.

Environment and technology, including the type of resource exploitation and the means used for that exploitation, form an integrated aspect of human adaptation. This is not to say, however, that environment and technology *cause* other aspects of culture in any direct way. The intensification of production may be stimulated by demographic expansion and in turn bring about significant changes in social structure. On the other hand, changes in social structure that are directly linked to production, and even certain aspects of religious belief, can affect both demography and technology.

As we shall see in greater detail in Chapter 24 among the Kachin of Burma the ceremonial cycle and periodic inflations in bride price (money or goods paid in order to obtain a bride from her kin group) create a need for labor intensification that can only be met through population increase. Population in this case apparently responds to an economic need that is itself created by the religious system and the politics of kinship.

Summary

Humans are animals and must, like all other species, accommodate to the environment. But culture as the human adaptation has changed the rules of the evolutionary game. Cultural as well as strictly biological rules determine the flow of human history. Cultural traits do not develop and are not transmitted in the same fashion as biological traits.

Culture is based on the operation of the human mind (our brains exhibit the result of the evolution of the capacity for language and culture). Cultural solutions to problems can be very powerful, but they are not always so. Our very ability to use metaphors and create theories can lead to false solutions, some of which remain popular in spite of their ineffectiveness.

Adaptation can be conscious or unconscious, planned or unplanned. Unconscious behaviors that produce adaptive results can become part of culture through natural selection, just the way that advantageous mutations become part of a gene pool. But not everything humans do is adaptive, at least in the biological sense.

The concept of adaptation in cultural evolution is limited by our inability to find a strict measure. In biology fitness is a mathematical concept linked to adaptation. We have no such measure in cultural anthropology. Because, in a real sense, any culture that survives must be adapted and adaptiveness is evident if a culture survives, we can be led easily into circular reasoning when employing this concept in cultural anthropology.

Leslie White has attempted to measure cultural evolution in terms of the increasing ability of human groups to extract energy from the environment. Although this historical trend is certainly correct, it is so broad that it makes it difficult, if not impossible, to study the process of adaptation in necessary detail. In order to understand cultural evolution we need to know about the specific adaptations of local populations in the context of their specific environments.

In spite of the difficulties that exist with the concept of adaptation in cultural anthropology, we must not ignore the fact that human societies face and solve ecological problems that involve accommodation to the local environment. In many cases this can be studied through the examination of technological systems and their relation to other aspects of culture.

Human subsistence depends on different kinds of extractive techniques (different technologies) through which food is derived from the environment. The major subsistence techniques are: hunting and gathering, fishing, horticulture (cultivation without plows), agriculture (cultivation with plows), and herding of domestic animals. Each of these major subsistence techniques varies according to both cultural and technological variables.

The size of available animals, their numbers, and whether or not they occur in herds will affect hunting techniques. Hunting will also be affected by available tools. Spears are more difficult to use as hunting tools than bows and arrows, bow-and-arrow hunting is made easier by the existence of effective poisons, and guns are more effective than bows and arrows; but the presence of guns may lead to rapid game depletion and food shortages.

The development of domestication produced a major change in the relationship between humans and their natural resources. Humans gain a greater control over food supplies and begin a differential exploitation of key species. This has the advantage of providing large and relatively reliable quantities of food but it has the disadvantage of making populations dependent on a limited number of species. In the modern world this has often led to monocropping, a practice in which a vast territory is planted with a single crop. When all goes well, this is a highly economical and efficient form of agriculture; but it may lead to severe shortages in times of drought and it encourages various insect pests and plant diseases that must be combatted at great expense. In addition, monocropping has severe social and economic consequences for local populations. It may lead to deficiencies in local diets and rural poverty.

Two major forms of carbohydrate food are grains and root crops. Grains do well in temperate climates, are quite high in protein content as well as carbohydrates, and store well. Root crops grow well in the wet tropics (the potato is a highland exception), are low in protein content, and usually do not store well.

Where land is plentiful, slash-and-burn horticulture is a highly productive technique. Forest land is burned and crops are planted in the newly created fields. After one or two growing seasons the fields must be left fallow for several years during which the forest regenerates and fertility is restored. When land becomes scarce and the fallow period is reduced, slash-and-burn horticulture may lead to degradation of the land with decreasing yields.

While slash-and-burn horticulture is extensive (it requires large tracts most of which are in fallow at any given point in time), plow agriculture is often intensive. Intensive agriculture produces high yields due to such techniques as deep plowing, weeding, and fertilization. It often demands high labor input and cooperation.

In many societies the local economy is based on the interdependence of different groups practicing different subsistence techniques. Even among societies that produce surpluses for a market, an interlocking and interdependent exploitation of the local ecology may develop. Such was the case in southern France where sheep herders, grape farmers, leather factories, a wool industry, and local butchers all participated in an economic system dependent on sheep and grapes and a variable environment that had good land for agricultural production and marginal land suitable for grazing.

Which species will be exploited in a local area will depend largely on environmental conditions. Cattle tend to do well where grass is abundant, while sheep and goats can be raised on marginal land with poor cover. Yaks can be raised in the highlands of Tibet where cattle would not survive. The size and density of the human population may also affect species choice and the means by which they are utilized.

The local environmental setting and the technological means by which it is exploited will affect population size and social organization. Hunting and gathering groups are small and highly mobile. They possess little and, except for simple personal belongings, do not have private property. The concept of land ownership is also lacking among such groups. In contrast, fishing and the exploitation of other marine resources allows the development of permanent settlements. Agriculture, in turn, is associated with the concept of property, particularly in land, since permanent fields become valuable. Finally, pastoral nomads, who rely on a wide territory for the successful raising of herd animals, are often warlike.

We must not forget that cultural systems have a strong impact on environments. Not only can overuse lead to environmental degradation, but also cultural factors themselves can affect the development of a technological system and the means by which an environment is utilized. It is the task of cultural anthropology to uncover the rules by which cultural variables interact with environmental variables, and to determine how each influences the other.

Bibliography

Dentan, R. K. 1968 — *The Semai: A Nonviolent People Of Malaya.* New York: Holt, Rinehart and Winston. A mini-ethnography of the Semai, who practice slash-and-burn horticulture in the jungles of Malaysia.

Hardesty, D. L. 1977 — *Ecological Anthropology.* New York: John Wiley and Sons. A general introduction to cultural ecology.

Lee, R., and I. DeVore, editors 1968 — *Man the Hunter.* Chicago: Aldine. Conference papers on the hunting-and-gathering adaptation.

Margalef, D. R. 1968 — *Perspectives in Ecological Theory.* Chicago: The University of Chicago Press. Short, interesting review of ecological theory in biology.

Rappaport, R. A. 1968 — *Pigs for the Ancestors.* New Haven: Yale University Press. A classic attempt to relate environmental adaptation to ritual.

Sahlins, M. and E. Service, editors 1960 — *Evolution and Culture.* Ann Arbor, Mich.: University of Michigan Press. Discussion of general and specific evolution as well as other principles of cultural evolution from an ecological point of view.

Steward, J. H. 1938 — *Basin-Plateau Aboriginal Sociopolitical Groups.* Smithsonian Institution, Bureau of American Ethnology, Bulletin 120. Ecology and social organization of the Basin Plateau Shoshone discussed by a pioneer of cultural ecology.

Vayda, A. P., editor 1969 — *Environment and Cultural Behavior.* New York: Natural History Press. A reader in cultural ecology with many important papers by innovators in the field.

White, L. 1959 — *The Evolution of Culture.* New York: McGraw-Hill. Technological and environmental theory of social evolution.

CHAPTER 14
STUDYING LIVING PEOPLES

The data of ethnology come from the study of living peoples. Anthropologists work in a variety of settings, ranging in size from small villages or groups of villages to large urban centers. The unit of study depends on the problem chosen for investigation. It may be a single individual (often the subject of a life history), a small set of families, the members of a profession, a village, a district, a part of a city, or even an entire urban conglomeration. Some anthropologists have attempted to characterize the culture of an entire nation-state, but this level of analysis rarely depends on traditional methods.

Anthropological data are usually gathered in the **field** (the research setting). It is customary for ethnographers to live with the people they study for an extended period of time, ranging from one to several years. An ethnographer may sometimes be lucky enough to restudy a population years after the original research has been completed. Information collected during field work is used to test hypotheses about culture and behavior as well as to document the life ways of different cultures and subcultures. When this documentation is published it contributes to the growing literature in anthropology. Published work may describe or analyze a culture (as completely as possible), concentrate on a single aspect of behavior, or compare one culture with others. In the latter case the anthropologist's own field data are compared with similar material collected in other cultures.

PREPARING FOR THE FIELD: THE TRAINING OF ANTHROPOLOGISTS

Let us look at field work from the perspective of an anthropological graduate student working toward the Ph.D. An apprentice anthropologist is expected to write a dissertation based on original field work. (A library dissertation is occasionally accepted, but students are generally encouraged to do original research in a foreign setting.) Before embarking on field work, the student must master a large body of scholarly material, beginning with anthropological data and theory. Anthropologists in training must learn what is already known about their discipline. The knowledge of specific cultures comes from reading **ethnographies** (descriptions of particular cultures), and familiarity with theory is gained by reading theoretical statements as well as **ethnological analyses** (the application of theoretical principles to ethnographic materials). With the aid of theory, budding anthropologists can begin to account for both underlying similarities in cultural behavior and cultural differences. Students learn about environmental variables, technological solutions to the problem of survival, the social links that bind members of a social group together, and beliefs about the supernatural. They study contemporary theories of **socialization** (the process of growing up in and learning a culture), the political and legal structures of various cultural systems, production and exchange, and the process of culture change and evolution. The cultures of specific geographic areas are examined in historical and contemporary accounts. Students take courses in statistical analysis, linguistic field methods, and ethnographic techniques.

Anthropology graduate students at Columbia University in a seminar with the author.

These courses constitute the practical side of their training.

Ultimately, the testing of anthropological theory must be based on cross-cultural comparisons in order to find true relationships among variables. Before this goal can be achieved, however, carefully collected materials on single cultures must be gathered. This is the traditional work of the field anthropologist. But no anthropologist can collect and document everything about a culture. The scope of this task is too vast. Field work is selective and based on specific interests. As training proceeds, students are encouraged to concentrate on a problem to focus their field work. The problem may be formalized in a set of hypotheses to be tested under field conditions. The hypotheses are often formulated so as to test alternate theories. For example, some anthropologists are convinced that technology and environment generate the particular forms of such aspects of culture as kinship and religious beliefs. Others are convinced that culture, as a body of symbols, limits and directs solutions to technological and environmental problems. Still others believe that any culture is the complex result of interactions between belief and behavior. (In future chapters I will examine these different approaches.)

Field work may be limited to a single aspect of culture. In her early work Margaret Mead was concerned with sex-role behavior. In her first field study she examined adolescence in Samoa, an island group in Polynesia. Mead found that the transition to adulthood was less stressful in Samoa than in the United States and that this fact could be correlated with the absence of adolescent rebellion and such physiological signs of discomfort as menstrual cramps. She attributed these differences to cultural variables. Later, in New Guinea, she attacked the notion that sex-role behavior is biologically determined. This conviction led to her book *Sex and Temperament,* in which she describes sex-role reversals in several cultures. Mead concluded from these data that "proper" masculine and feminine behaviors are culturally rather than biologically determined.

Once students have defined a problem and a set of hypotheses derived from it, they must work out a methodology for testing the hypothesis. This methodology will guide the collection of data and facilitate the analysis that must follow. The choice of a specific problem helps students to determine the culture they want to work in. Will it be a hunting-and-gathering society or one in which slash-and-burn cultivation is the mode? Will it be a society in which inheritance is patrilineal (through a male line) or matrilineal (through a female line)? Will it be a relatively isolated and stable culture or one in the process of rapid change?

The choice of a problem also affects the methods used for gathering and analyzing data. When this has all been worked out, the doctoral candidate combines the background materials, the statement of the problem with its hypotheses, the methods to be used in gathering and analyzing data, and the significance of the research for the field of anthropology into a **research proposal.** Usually a proposal must be approved by a committee of professors who are charged with directing research. It is also likely to be examined by a university committee on human subjects to be sure that the design respects the rights of **informants** and of the community chosen by the student as a field site. These ethical principles are taken very seriously by professional anthropologists and other behavioral scientists.

Field work is costly, and few students or professional anthropologists can undertake it at their own expense. A budget—including such items as travel costs, fees to informants, living expenses, prices of equipment and medical supplies—is usually worked up, with a justification for each item. The budget is then added to the proposal, which is submitted to granting agencies and foundations, either private or governmental.

Language Competence

When possible, before embarking upon field work an anthropologist becomes competent in the local language. If the language is not offered by the university in which the student is enrolled, then the student may have to go elsewhere for training. There are frequently native speakers with whom the prospective field worker can make private arrangements for language instruction. Often, however, the field language will have to be learned on the spot. For this reason most cultural anthropologists are required to take courses in linguistic field methods. These courses prepare an individual to learn an unrecorded language efficiently through the application of a set of systematic principles.

In this way a student may gain a working knowledge of a language in about three to four months. Of course, much more time is required to achieve fluency, and this goal is reached only by a few individuals. Whether or not it is necessary to be fluent in a language depends on the problem to be investigated. If ritual and symbolism are the topics, linguistic skills are of great importance. If the effects of culture change on traditional agriculture is the subject of study, fluency in the language will be less important.

Further Preparation

When an anthropologist is informed that support will be forthcoming from some agency, the next step is an application for a visa to the country in which the work is to be done. Before clearance is granted, proposals are carefully examined by local social scientists and political officials, who are interested in the benefits and useful knowledge that the research will bring to their own planning efforts.

In addition, anthropologists inform themselves about local health conditions. They obtain necessary immunization shots and purchase medicines. They write letters to individuals in or near the field site who might be helpful, particularly during the initial stages of research. These include other anthropologists, government personnel, and missionaries.

PRINCIPAL METHODS

Participant Observation

The major tool used by cultural anthropologists in the field is themselves. Field work involves an intense personal commitment; during the period of study the researcher must observe and interact on a daily basis with the members of an entire community. This method is known as **participant observation.** It requires living as much as possible like a member of the community and it often demands a sacrifice of privacy that can be threatening. When successfully pursued, it allows the researcher to document the stream of behavioral events as they unfold in the community. When a field worker has been accepted, he or she may become the privileged observer of secret rites and customs not usually open to foreigners.

Integration into a foreign community whose language and custom are different from one's own poses special problems, but it can also be turned to advantage. Many anthropologists have admitted in their writings that, during their first days or even months in the field, they felt like either the village idiot or a helpless infant. The analogy with childhood is apt, for it is the task of the field worker to learn the rules of a culture by living in it. Like children, they make mistakes as they test out notions about correct behavior. As time passes, knowledge grows and integration becomes easier. Correct practice in social situations confirms hypotheses about behavioral rules. In the early days of field work the anthropologist may be the butt of jokes. On the other hand, since most people are kind and indulgent toward children, if the researcher is perceived in this light he or she might well be protected and instructed with great care and patience. A humble attitude and a willingness to learn often contrast the anthropologist to other foreigners and are endearing traits to the local community. As long as an-

(Left) An ethnohistorian collects data in the Ivory Coast. (Right) An anthropological demographer (Nancy Howell) collects data from the !Kung San.

thropologists do not become burdens or dangers to a community, they are often more than tolerated. If local people are employed as assistants and perform such tasks as house building and taking care of daily needs, a field worker may be seen as a distinct economic advantage to the community. The local people may even look forward to the day when the anthropologist can be mobilized to intercede for them with government authorities. This expectation, however, can create serious difficulties, and field workers need to be aware of potential problems.

Participant observation is not a haphazard process. The field worker must keep detailed notes, an accurate record of events as they unfold. These notes must contain information on the particular individuals involved in each particular activity, the time at which the activity has occurred, its duration, and, when possible, its outcome. The notes often include preliminary analyses and further hypotheses to be checked through further observation. Field notes are frequently read and reread by the researcher and their accuracy tested in new situations.

Participant observation is most useful when it is combined with other methods of data gathering. Julian Pitt-Rivers kept three sets of records as he carried out field work in Spain. One contained his notes on general reading and the district in which he did his field work, as well as documents, statistics, and other material he could find on the region. Another record consisted of his field journal annotated with an indication of what was discussed with informants. A third record consisted of data organized by household. This included what land was owned and/or exploited, the occupational activities of each member, and all Pitt-Rivers could discover about their relationships to other members of the community. He recorded all conversations in the vernacular. In addition, a photographic record was kept of farming tools and their use.

Participant observation is essential because it provides information on what people actually do in specific contexts rather than on what they say they do. It allows the field worker to document behavior of which informants themselves are sometimes unaware or which they might distort inadvertently in a description. When direct observations are compared with interviews, revealing contrasts emerge, contrasts between ideal and real patterns of behavior.

Interviews

Not all data are or can be gathered through participant observation. The researcher may want to know about past events or to consider the opinions of individuals about the observational data. People of different ages, sexes, or statuses within a community may have different

MACHIGUENGA TIME ALLOCATION

Excerpts from field notes, June 21, 1973 (explanatory comments in parentheses) - Allen and Orna Johnson

Household 11 - 6:35 am

F. (husband) preparing kapiro (bamboo) for arrowhead
Ev. (first wife) peeling yuca (manioc)
Am. (second wife) warming herself by the fire
H. (son) eating yuca
Man. (daughter) idle
J. (son) eating yuca
D. (son) idle
Av. (daughter) asleep

Household 14 - 6:40 am

M. (husband) fishing at river
R. (wife) eating roasted plantain
E. (son) eating roasted plantain
Jo. (visiting nephew) eating roasted plantain

Household 13 - 6:47 am

C. (husband) intaati hunting shintori (peccary across river)
W. (wife) idle
Mi. (daughter) eating yuca
Mar. (son) eating yuca

Additional notes

After the visit was recorded, M. returned with a large mamori (fish) and gave it to Ev. (his mother-in-law) to prepare. During the meal the children sat in the women's group, but periodically ran over to the men to accept pieces of food.

F. showed us remnants of an arrow broken in shooting at a shintori that got away. Shintori tracks have been seen in the gardens where they have been eating yuca.

A page from the field notes of Professor Allen Johnson. Professor Johnson has developed a technique known as the *random visit.* People are visited at random times during the day and week and their activities noted. A sample of such visits enables the anthropologist to estimate time allocation for various activities performed by members of the community.

STUDYING THE ABRON

For my own first field work I studied the relationship between village hygiene and disease in an Abron village in the Ivory Coast, West Africa. My research took me to Africa in the summer of 1960 and again during the fall, winter, and spring of 1961–62. The following quotes from my book *When the Spider Danced* deal with my first impressions of field work.

When work begins, anthropologists are ignorant of even the most basic rules of behavior. . . .

Looking back, I remember an Abron woman spinning thread. In one hand, she holds an amorphous, loose ball of raw cotton. She pulls and twists at it as the beginning of a coherent thread forms. This is deftly attached to the top of a thin stick weighted at the bottom with a ball of clay, forming a top. The woman spins the top with her free hand and somehow a thread forms around the spindle. As the top spins, she pulls more fiber away from the ball, twisting it with her fingers, letting it wind onto the top. No motion is lost. The thread is even and continuous. The action is mysterious to my own muscular system.

The thread becomes a spider web in my mind. The woman becomes a spider. How can I know a spider? The spider does not learn to spin. This woman was once a little girl. Her mother spent many hours spinning while she watched, until, one day, she tried to spin as her mother did. At first it was difficult. Her mother did not correct her, but let her try again, watch again, try again, until she could do it herself. The movements became natural, and a skill formed that would not be lost until old age took the deftness out of her fingers.

Why does a woman coming back from the water hole with a full basin have leafy branches in the water? Is she going to cook them? I follow her home. She takes the branches out of the basin and throws them aside on the trash heap, which will be swept up later. Must one transport plants of some sort along with water? Women carrying large clay pots or buckets bring water only. Why the difference? Nothing simpler, I'm told. The basins are flat and wide—poor for water transport. As a woman walks, the rhythm of her steps sets up a rhythm in the water. In a deep pot, this

ideas and varying interpretations of the same events. Differences of opinion within a single group are also of interest. In addition, certain members of the community may have esoteric knowledge concerning religious beliefs or the reason behind certain activities. The anthropologist may want to assemble statements on belief systems and collect texts of myths, stories, or even jokes and riddles. All these types of information can be gathered through interviews.

Interviews may be **open-ended** (unstructured and conversational) or **scheduled** (based on a set of specific questions). Both techniques have advantages and disadvantages. Questionnaires are easy to gather and score. Data from responses to the same questions may be easy to analyze, particularly if they are based on a multiple-choice format, in which the respondent is asked is unimportant, the water will not spill; but in the wide and shallow basin, it will soon slosh out. The branches are a simple and effective tool. They break the rhythm of the water and it stays in the basin. . . .

I am white skinned, but after several weeks in the field, I forgot that I did not look like everyone else. Not shaving, I had little cause to use a mirror. As my identity became Abron, I turned black in my imagination. I tried to convert this into physical change by sunbathing. From the Abron point of view, it was probably one of my most idiotic behaviors. Their country is about six degrees north of the equator, and all normal people seek the shade at midday. My African mother, Afua Morofye, concerned for my health and sanity, used to ask me why I lay in the sun. If I wanted to get black, she said, I should eat lots of cayenne pepper. This was not her belief but, rather, her metaphor for my stupidity. Of course, I did not really change much. At the end of field work a villager summed it up well when he said to me, "White man, when you came here you were fat and white; now you are thin and red.". . .

I think that, for the majority of the Abron, I became *their* white man: someone who, for some strange reason, was not like the others, who took a real interest in village affairs, who could be trusted at least partway with what Abron believed. I think that most Abron were amused by my attempts to become Abron. My wearing of Abron dress was, at first, tolerated as a whim. Later, the chief and some of the other notables enjoyed having themselves photographed with me in my toga. In this role, I was the village mascot. My presence broke the boredom of daily existence: I was interesting, just as I found even the most mundane Abron tasks interesting. . . .

How much an anthropologist is really able to integrate himself into a foreign culture, both in his own mind and in the minds of the people he studies, varies from one anthropologist to another and from culture to culture. The task is not self-integration but understanding. This must be translated into scientific discourse, which someday all anthropologists hope will be used to generate a theory of culture and human behavior.

to pick from a set of possible answers. Unless the researcher is very familiar with the culture under study, however, the choices offered may bias the results. Open-ended interviews and discussions about topics of interest to the informants can provide rich, detailed, and undistorted data. But large numbers of such interviews may be difficult for the anthropologist to interpret and analyze.

In conducting interviews, the researcher will want a representative sample of individuals in the community. The results will inform the anthropologist about agreements and disagreements among members of the community and special groups within it. General agreement says something about norms and shared values, while disagreements provide clues to variation in ideas and behaviors.

Mapping and Census-taking

Early in field work, even before the language has been mastered, it is often possible to map a community and take a census. Mapping provides a record of the physical layout of the community, including its use of different resources (gardens, forest land, and fallow fields, for instance, are included in areas to be mapped). Census-taking is one step in the process of becoming familiar with the population under study. It provides demographic data (age and sex distribution, for example) that will be of use during analysis. The map and the census together reveal the locations within the community of specific individuals and groups.

Genealogies

One aspect of census-taking that is of great importance is the making of **genealogies** (sets of relationships through marriage and through blood). Many of the societies studied by anthropologists are kinship based; in such societies social and economic relationships can only be understood in terms of specific sets of kin relations. Genealogies of real individuals reveal the kinship system (see Chapter 15) and increase the value of a general census. They provide data not only on family structure but also on marriage links between families and on other forms of kinship groups. Genealogies are necessary for the understanding of crucial events within the community. Genealogical relationships sometimes provide the order underlying apparently diverse individual actions in social behavior.

Counting

Counting and inventory-taking are crucial aspects of research. The anthropologist's notebook is often full of reports on material culture, including the distribution of particular technological and ritual items. Knowing who owns what and in what quantities, for example, is one important source of data on social structure. In addition, for particular activities it is often of great value to know their frequency, their place of occurrence, and the number and status of participating individuals. Those interested in legal systems will keep track of disputes, noting their frequency, type, and outcome.

Sampling

When data on every individual are impossible to collect, as, for example, in very large communities, **sampling** becomes necessary. A proper sample offers the assurance that a small number of individuals represents the wider

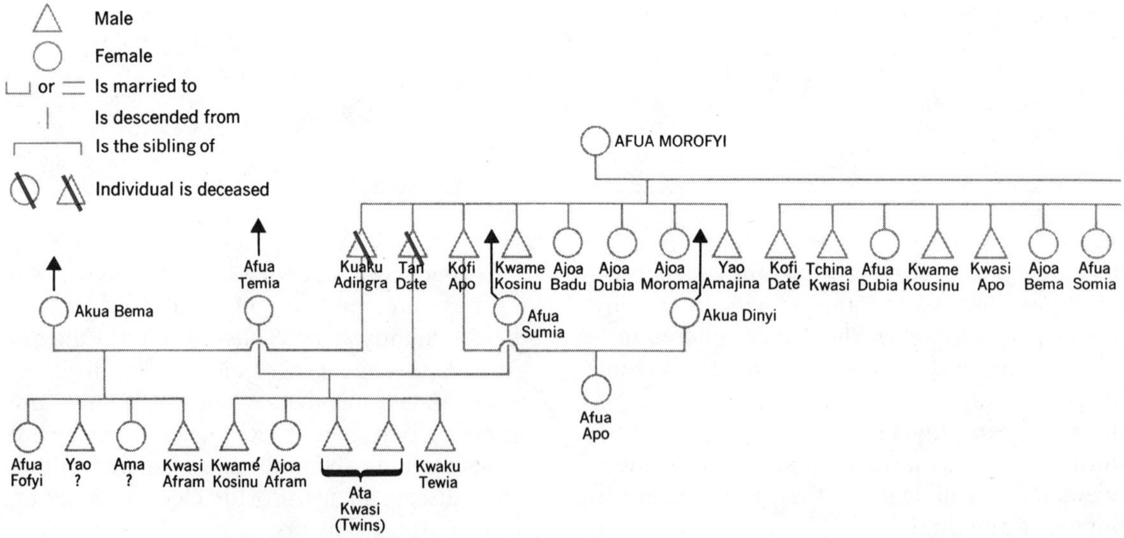

group. Such samples can be drawn from the whole population by choosing subjects at *random.* In a **random sample** every individual member of the group has as good a chance as every other member to be chosen. This procedure reduces prejudice on the part of the researcher, who may, for example, be more comfortable interviewing men than women or who might unconsciously favor one type of person over another. Various methods exist for the drawing of a random sample. If a census has been taken, the name of every community member can be put in a box and a predetermined number can be drawn. There are tables of random numbers that can be used to pick members of the community from a list. Whatever method is chosen, the researcher must also be sure that the sample is large enough to represent the community or the part of the community under study.

Sample size will depend on the size of the community and the assumed representativeness of the sample. In the United States, for example, very small samples (as few as 1500 individuals) can be used with fair success to predict voting behavior for the entire population of a state. In anthropological field work in a traditional small-scale society, any sample smaller than ten percent of the total population will probably be inaccurate. In fact, since the anthropologist often knows little about the culture under investigation, sampling must be done with extreme caution. Voting polls based on miniscule samples work because the individuals chosen are known through long experience to represent the population at large in those characteristics that make specific political predictions possible.

When a population is heterogeneous and information on differences among subgroups is desired, a **stratified sample** will have to be taken. In a stratified sample each segment of the population is treated as a separate unit. Random samples are drawn from each unit and these are analyzed separately for comparative purposes.

It is very difficult for a field worker to use random samples. In many cases it is impossible to gain access to every chosen member of the community. When randomness cannot be achieved and sampling is still necessary, it is important to obtain data on as many individuals as possible. Even then the results may be affected by the absence of a certain category of individual. It is important, therefore, when writing up a field report, to note population size, sample size, and how the sample was chosen.

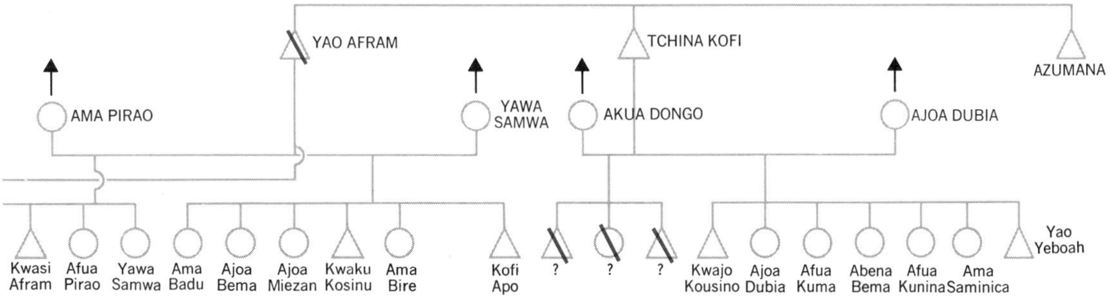

Figure 14.1

A partial genealogy of "my" Abron family, showing the offspring of three brothers: Yao Afram (children from three wives and some grandchildren), Tchina Kofi (children from two wives), and Azumana (no children). The inset shows the meaning of the symbols used to show kinship.

Life Histories

Another useful field method is the **life-history technique,** which requires extensive biographical interviews with one person or a small number of individuals. Life histories provide a time perspective and data on change as it has occurred during the life of the interviewee. The materials recorded are often very rich and can provide unique personal data on a culture as seen through the eyes of a limited number of people. Life histories are, however, difficult and time-consuming to collect. Whether or not they should be used depends on the problem chosen for investigation.

Tests

A wide variety of psychological tests have been used in the field. Many are designed to test perception. Others are used to analyze various aspects of cognition (thinking) and personality. The **TAT** (**Thematic Apperception Test**), for example, consists of a series of drawings (which can be standardized for different cultures) depicting various personal and social situations. The informants are asked to make up stories to go with these pictures. Later they can be analyzed for content and compared to see if any cultural themes emerge. The **Rorschach ink-blot test** is another form of personality test. Some, but by no means all, anthropologists believe that this test is culture-free and can therefore be used to make judgments about personality in different cultures.

Technological Aids

Although anthropologists are their own best tool, modern technology has come to the aid of the discipline. Still photography, cinema, and tape recordings, including videotapes, provide useful records of lasting value. These can be analyzed and reanalyzed long after the anthropologist has returned from the field. Photographic prints, videotapes, and sound recordings can be shown and played for informants in the community being studied. In this way explanations of particular events can be elicited with great care and attention to detail.

ANALYSIS

The anthropological process does not end with field work. Data collected in the field setting must be analyzed and, whenever possible, published. Quantitative data will be subjected to statistical analysis, often with the aid of computer technology. The anthropologist will attempt to make coherent sense out of a wide range of materials collected from many sources. Theoretical ideas will be used in data interpretation and data will be used to test and correct theories.

The testing of hypotheses requires the isolation of **independent** and **dependent variables.** Independent variables are generally equated with cause and dependent variables with effect. A drop in temperature, for example, can cause water to freeze. Temperature is, in this case, the independent variable and the state of water (as gas, liquid, or solid) is the dependent variable. In other situations temperature can be a dependent variable—for example, when the heat of a room is controlled by a thermostat that regulates a heating system.

In anthropology someone might want to test the hypothesis that the presence of initiation ceremonies with genital mutilation for boys is dependent on the strength of ties before initiation between boys and mothers. The reasoning behind such a hypothesis is the idea that in order to fully assume male roles and become members of male society boys must publicly and dramatically be separated from the world of females. Data may then be collected on a range of cultures in which boys and mothers are judged to have particularly close relationships as well as on cultures in which the relationship is relatively distant. Since it may be difficult to judge exactly what is meant by a close or a distant relationship, some measure of this variable must be found. This process is known as making a variable **operational** (defining it in

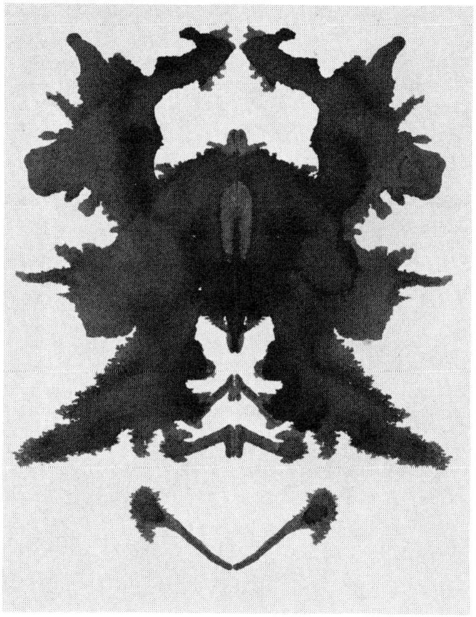

The TAT and Rorschach tests. In order to protect the value of these tests, the illustrations here are not actual examples. (Left) A drawing similar to those used in the TAT test. (Right) An ink-blot similar to those used in the Rorschach test.

such a way that it can be measured). In testing this particular hypothesis, the anthropologist John Whiting used the presence or absence of mother-child households, in which mothers and offspring sleep together, with father usually absent, as the criterion of closeness between sons and mothers. He collected data from published sources on the presence or absence of mother-child households and examined them for the expected relationship between mother-son bonds and the presence of genital mutilation in initiation ceremonies. The results of this search were placed in a fourfold table as follows:

	Initiation and mutilation present	Initiation and mutilation absent
Presence of mother-child households		
Absence of mother-child households		

STUDENTS IN THE FIELD

Three young anthropologists (one graduate student and two recent PhDs at Columbia University) discuss their own field work. Christine Padoch spent 29 months in very difficult terrain among the Iban of Borneo, Eric Ross and his wife Jane spent 19 months among the Achuara in the Amazon Basin of Peru, and Candilario (Candy) Saenz and his wife Barbara spent 19 months among the Tuareg in the Sahara. Christine wrote her thesis on ecological balance, land use, and demography, showing how the Iban adapt to their environment. Eric Ross was interested in the relationships between food resources and taboos. Candilario Saenz studied the social relationships among Tuareg camel herders and a dependent caste of blacksmiths.

The conversation that follows does not deal with technical aspects of field work. Instead, the three anthropologists are asked to discuss the kind of personal problems that are rarely published in formal ethnographies.

Q: I'd like to begin by asking each of you what you most feared about field work before you left.

Candy: I studied a group of nomads. How do you get to know them? Get them to accept you? Get them to let you live with them? It's like going out to meet a bunch of new people; will they like you?

Eric: Well, I think, in a sense, it was the lack of practical preparation; the idea that you've spent most of your time on theoretical issues, and not really knowing the basic ways of taking care of living in a different environment over a long period of time; how to cope with all the practical necessities.

In a perfect relationship between variables we would expect to find the category "genital mutilation present" (the dependent variable) associated *only* with the category "presence of mother-child households." This kind of correlation is rarely found in the testing of hypotheses in the social sciences. When data turn up in all four boxes of the table a statistical test must be applied to see if the correlation is *significant,* that is, to see if the hypothesis is supported by the data. Such tests of significance ask the question: Are the relationships observed due to chance alone *or* to factors other than chance? Note that such findings are expressed as probabilities. In tests of significance the results tell us the probability that the relationship is significant, but they do not prove absolutely that it is. Generally in the social sciences a probability of .05 (five chances out of 100 that the result is due to chance) or lower is used to support a hypothesis of relationship, that is, that the two variables *are* related as suggested. What is actually being tested in these statistical analyses is the **null hypothesis,** which states that there is no relationship among variables other than those due to chance. In science it is necessary to assume first that the null hypothesis is correct. This is the case because it is impossible to prove the nonexistence of something. Instead we attempt to disprove the nonexistence of something, which is the same as demonstrating probable existence. To say that the null hypothesis is rejected is to say that the hypothesis is accepted.

Q: What were some of those problems?

Eric: Well, I think, just living accommodations, how you find a place where you're going to live, how you move around, how you get into an area.

Candy: How to avoid getting ripped off by traders.

Chris: My worries were like Candelario's. After having spent about a total of two months of field work in places before, I thought of myself as an old tropical hand and would have no problems. But there are physical problems. It seems ridiculous that someone going to Borneo did not worry about the physical problems, but I didn't, and, of course, they hit me when I got there.

Q: What were these physical problems?

Chris: I wanted people to love me and answer my questions, and that was what I really worried about. I went there to study agriculture, and the first time I got on top of one of these fields I couldn't get down! It was just physically impossible for me to get down this hill that was covered with wet, sliding slash. I decided it was all over. What was I going to do? Write a letter saying that I was going to study people growing swamp rice? I fell often, just walking around. The Iban are these terrific folks; they thought it was great and they let me go along anywhere. I would fall

Christine Padoch with Ngumbang, an Iban headman.

down five times a day. They would think it was hilarious. They couldn't figure out what was going on.

Q: How did you finally stop falling down?

Chris: Well, I picked a long house [Iban dwelling] that was a little lower down the river where the hills were not quite as steep and . . . I kept falling down. After a while I stopped falling down as much. I stopped falling off logs, but it was always somewhat of a problem.

Candy: Keeping up with people is a problem. I went out one night to look for the goats. These blacksmiths I studied are very poor animal husbandmen, and they would not send anybody out with the goats and sheep. The sheep were supposed to follow the goats, and they would all get lost. We went out to look for them, and I think about ten hours later, at dawn, we came back in. We had been walking all night at a pretty fast clip through stickle-burrs, and I thought I was going to collapse.

Q: Eric, you had a pretty difficult time also?

Eric: Yes, we had problems. I got lost in the jungle twice. That was one of the greatest fears I had. Once the Indians went off on a trip that I thought would be for about half a day. I went off with them, and Jane was expecting me to come back after a short period of time. I got about three miles away into the forest and found out that they were going to be away for about two weeks. I decided that I had to go back. None of them, of course, would take the time to help me go back. They simply pointed in the direction of camp and said that's where you go. Even worse was that, at the beginning of field work, we had planned to study a group other than the one we studied, so that we actually wasted about two months going to a group that ended up not being practical to study. It's a real problem in that kind of environment, the tropical forest, in which it is very difficult to get around.

Q: Is there anything that was a pleasant surprise?

Candy: I think everything that I feared happened! Except the one thing that was nice was this idea of people in the bush versus people in town. I was at a base camp in a small trading village in the edge of the desert, and people there would tell me there are no more nomadic blacksmiths and that the Tuareg were all settled in towns since the drought of 1973. This is the feeling people had who were already in town. When I went out to the bush, I found that people were still there, acting very conservatively, as I was told people used to act in the past. The further I went out in the bush, the more I found people that were very traditional. I found people practicing patterns of behavior that I had heard about.

Chris: Mostly it was pleasant! I was accepted. People answered all my questions. I survived all those times and I found out terrifically interesting things. In totaling it up, there were mostly pleasant surprises. In the beginning, when I came to a long house, it seemed like a very strange place, and somehow I was not quite sure that I was going to make it, that I was going to live there and it was going to seem like life. In the end it all came out. A lot of the problems were not really physical. A lot of it was my intense embarrassment at being totally incompetent at just about anything. I couldn't walk down the path without falling, I couldn't take a bath in the river keeping my sarong up, I couldn't cook a meal over a wood fire, I couldn't talk. That was the worst part of the whole thing. And somehow it all worked out. These things that seemed impossible at the beginning worked out.

Eric: One thing was particularly pleasant. The more acculturated (Westernized) the people that we were in contact with were, particularly the Indians, the less pleasant they were. So it really was the case that the people that we would have the most fear of (who were the most traditional in a head-hunting environment, where there was warfare) were the most pleasant. In the first community we were in, we left a tent with all of our belongings for about two months while we went someplace else. When we came back absolutely everything was there. Nothing had been touched and no one had even gone into the tent. As soon as you find people who have had contact with "civilization," you find that the absence of trust has become a part of life.

Q: How about the methods you were trained to use in the field? Did they work out and were they helpful?

Chris: Well, the first thing is, I always kept thinking that if I'd been really lucky, I would have gone out there to find out about the old days. I really wanted to sit down with one old man who had nothing better to do—and everybody likes to talk about the old days. The idea of doing this quantitative work . . . first, it was so difficult because you had to ask everybody the same questions . . . everyone got so sick and bothered by it. It was as if I did not believe what one person had told me. It was also so terribly tiring. The work that I had laid out for myself should have been done by 20 people with a helicopter. It was absurd to have any graduate student think he's going to go out to a place with the kind of topography and the kind of farming that I found and think he can measure the fields. You read about these terribly precise measurements people do; it's absurd. The amount of precision you can get on any of this stuff is minimal.

Q: Candy, what was the core of your project?

Candy: I was interested in relating social organization among the Tuareg to these blacksmiths. I wanted to study the way work was organized.

Q: Are these blacksmiths a caste?

Candy: Yes, they are. They marry among themselves. They have a monopoly over the blacksmith trade. There are restrictions on marriage into the blacksmith caste. A noble would rather marry a slave than a blacksmith. They had never been studied before, so one of the problems I had was the one that Christine was talking about.

Eric Ross with two Achuara children.

The area I was covering was about 50,000 square miles—that's what it comes down to, you see, it's 250 miles on a side. The nomads were out there and I had to find them. Who were the blacksmiths that were out there? What did they call themselves? Who did they think they were? What was their internal political organization? The structure of their political organization was in the structure of Tuareg society as a whole. I had to do survey expeditions where I would set off, say, a week, and I would have my field assistant get in the Land Rover, and we would go to the native police to find out where they thought the people were camping. We would do a camp a day. People had never seen us before. We had to do it that way. We'd blitz them. We'd come in and catch them by surprise. Sometimes they'd be moving. Sometimes we followed the animal droppings. We'd pick them up to see if they were still moist. We would catch up with these people. They'd stop and we'd say, "We've come to visit you." It was very different from typical field work, and I was not prepared for it at all. I had to have a questionnaire, find the blacksmiths and the nobles among whom they lived, find a noble with some clout, exploit traditional hospitality, and say, "Quick, bring out the mats. You are our host." Except for a couple of times when we were refused, they would bring out the mats and serve tea. We'd call the blacksmith over and have him sit down and ask our questions. On the first visit, which would take most of the day, I'd get, a lot of times, more information than later, when they might get leery and be suspicious. They might ask themselves, "Who is this infidel coming around here to ask these questions?"

Eric: Well, I think the major problem we had was that—unlike, for example, Chris's group and lots of other groups throughout the tropical forest, where there are communities of about 150 people—we were dealing with a very small, dispersed population. There were about ten or eleven people in a community. One of the difficulties was the amount of time you could spend with a particular group before you wore out your welcome. It was extremely difficult to employ any kind of formal techniques in asking people questions. You are dealing with a kind of community where there were only two hunters in the whole village. You'd simply get on people's nerves, and they simply didn't want to tolerate any kind of formal exchange of information. For the kind of information we wanted—getting a lot of detailed data on patterns of warfare and who had killed whom—you would get somebody who was very tired, who had just come back from hunting, and who was the only male present to ask those questions of. We would get him for the duration of a cigarette or two to sit down and talk with us. As long as we would ply him with cigarettes, he would answer questions. We would say, "Who was your relative?" and ask who was related to whom. When he would give us a person's name, we would have to ask how that person died and who was blamed for the death. Was it a shaman [curer and worker of magic]? Was that shaman eventually killed?, etc. People would very quickly get tired of our questioning. The difficulties were then to get in contact with other relatives to check the data. The warfare pattern disperses people and carries them off so that they lose track of relatives midway along in the sequence of information you want.

Q: What about language?

Chris: At the beginning that was the great problem. I had some knowledge of a related language, so I had a little idea of what was going on, but not much. I knew I would learn the language and that it was not an impossible task. I really . . . to me the whole difference is between field work when you can understand what people are saying and the situation in the field before you understand, This is the case even though I had an assistant who stayed with me for two-and-a-half years. For about the first three or five months she was really an interpreter for me. At the beginning, when it was just a matter of getting answers to questions that I could ask, I got information that was somewhat limited. As soon as I could understand what people were saying, whole worlds opened up.

Candy: I had a full-time field assistant who was needed when we came into the camps. In the beginning we used French. I quickly got to the point where I could get genealogies. This is easy to do and you can get the kinship down. It was a year before I really got where I could actually use the language. I finally got where I could sit and talk to people almost freely. I do feel that I got a lot more information then, because when my assistant translated he would leave things out.

Chris: I also noticed how much my assistant edited.

Eric: We found it very difficult. It was literally impossible to find a bilingual informant who knew Achuara and Spanish. For most of the field work we were in the position of having to learn as much of the language as we could. One of the difficulties was, I remember, in recording genealogies—there are a great deal of names used with great frequency passing through the generations. One of the most popular names was *hakao,* which it took us about four months to realize meant "dead!"

Candy: Among the Tuareg you were more accepted if you spoke the language. They felt you were Tuareg . . . I mean you were a person a Tuareg could talk to. This made you less of an outsider really.

Q: If you had it to do over again would you go to the same place or somewhere else?

Chris: If I were going to do it over again, I would go to the same place. Possibly I'd do a few other things. If I were going to do another thing now, I'd pick some place else, not because of any negative feeling but because I've seen hunters and gatherers just being settled down; I've seen people trying to turn into the kind of people I studied. They were being very unsuccessful at it and that fascinates me.

Candy: In the field you are exposed to other people who are very interesting. The sources don't really do justice to what you can find out there. There was a group that used to live among the Tuareg, a group of nomadic potters who kept small herds and dug clay where they settled temporarily. Some of the German ethnographers thought they were remnants of hunters and gatherers, and perhaps they were.

Eric: Well, I think that I would take some logistical considerations more seriously. I would look for a group that is more accessible and also more numerous, certainly. That was really the greatest drawback to our study.

Q: Recently some social scientists, not anthropologists, have suggested that anthropology is about to become extinct because our subject matter is disappearing. What do you think about that?

Candy: Well, it's not really disappearing. It's not that much different from the past. The Tuareg, for example, are not that much different from when they were studied 20 years ago. There have been structural changes and the slaves are nominally free, but the economic factors that caused their labor to be a vital institution are still there. The nobles own the capital. The subject matter of anthropology isn't just traditional peoples anyway. But there are certainly plenty of traditional peoples out there—you just have to go out and look for them.

Candilario Saenz with two Tuareg informants.

Eric: Well, I agree, but I don't think anthropology depends upon the subject matter *per se* anyway. It's a perspective. The Achuara will not be Indians in the traditional sense much longer. They will become peasants and some of them will become urban dwellers. I think that one just has to employ anthropological techniques and perspectives and follow the transformations that will occur and probably have always occurred.

Chris: I agree. I guess the three of us are somewhat atypical in finding more traditional peoples than most anthropologists today. I like to specialize in these things. I'd like to go and study hunters and gatherers—and it's certain that they are not going to be found much longer—but Indonesian peasants are going to stay around for a long time.

Q: How would you feel about working in an urban setting in the United States?

Candy: I had to work in the city as part of my training grant. I found it terribly difficult. When you are far away, you feel justified in going out and bothering a group of people with your presence. They feel a little obligated because you came so far and they answer your questions. Here I was sent a few blocks from Columbia, and people did not see any reason to talk to me. I was taking up their time. They were busy, you know. They were holding down three jobs. Some of them wanted to know if I was an agent of the U.S. Immigration Service. On that basis I think it's easier for me to do field work somewhere else.

Eric: It bothers me that we have tended so long in anthropology to do studies of traditional groups (I feel guilty of this myself) where you can afford to be politically and socially naive. I've spoken to a lot of anthropology students who, if they were going to do a study of a community in Mexico, knew nothing about the political situation of the larger society. I think that if we did more studies in the United States, we'd be forced to cope with all the complexities and be more committed politically and socially to the implications of the work.

Chris: I feel all that. But I enjoy living in tropical places. The beginnings of field work were so difficult, really, that . . . sometimes being intensely lonely . . . the two of you had people with you, and I really was all alone. I used to discuss my deepest feelings with an 18-year-old girl. But in the end, things were so beautiful. They were so interesting. I'm sure that here in New York things are interesting, but I'm not sure they are so pleasant. I wanted to say something else. You know everyone is scared of these people. They are supposed to be horrible and fierce. You go in naive and you have not been taught all these things, but if someone sent me to a dangerous neighborhood in New York, I'd be much more terrified.

Eric: Well, I agree. I think it's precisely the problem—that going to a group that's very far away and is very isolated, with a beautifully different kind of environment, reinforces these romantic susceptibilities that we have.

Q: Chris, did you have any special difficulties or advantages being a woman alone in the field?

Chris: At the very beginning one real problem is the fact that you get protected all the time. I had trouble enough convincing people that I indeed could go to a scary place in the field all by myself, because everyone was trying to protect me. That increased a little more when I was in the field, when everyone saw me fall down so often. Otherwise I think that it went very well, partially because of the nature of the society I was in. Women did indeed have positions of some authority. Sometimes women headed up a household or even a whole long house. I felt that I could find out what was going on with both males and females. If I insisted on it, I could play a man. It was more up to me. It's much harder for a man in the field to play a woman's role.

Summary

Anthropologists work in a variety of settings ranging in size from small villages to large urban centers. Their data are gathered in the field (the research setting) among the people they hope to study. Anthropological information is used to test hypotheses about culture and to document the life ways of different cultures and subcultures.

Anthropological training takes place on the graduate level in universities. Students take a wide range of courses covering theory, what is already known about specific geographical areas, and field methods. When they have decided to study a particular problem and geographical area, they prepare a research proposal that is based on past research, plus a description of the particular contribution the student wishes to make to the discipline. After the proposal is satisfactory to the anthropology department, it is sent to a governmental or private foundation with a request for funding. A copy is also sent to the proper officials of the country in which the research will be undertaken. In general, a research proposal must inform these governments about the methods to be used, the protection of informants' rights, and the potential benefits that the host population can gain from the research.

If a research proposal is funded and is accepted by a host government, the student takes the necessary steps before departing for the field. These include the purchasing of equipment, obtaining necessary visas and travel documents, and innoculations against disease.

Major field techniques include: participant observation, in which a careful record of daily life is kept, interviews, archival research in which local records are studied, photographic and sound recording of important events, measurement of land and gardens, census-taking and the gathering of genealogies. Certain psychological techniques are available for specific research goals. Some of these are used to elicit information on personality types.

Counting and statistical analysis are particularly important aspects of field work. If a community is very large, it may be necessary to interview only a sample of individuals. These samples may be stratified in order to guarantee that different groups are represented. Procedures exist to insure that a sample represents the population under investigation. Subjects are chosen at random in order to avoid bias on the part of the researcher.

In the testing of hypotheses it may be necessary to use statistical techniques to determine whether a particular hypothesis is confirmed or rejected. When these procedures are followed it can be stated with a certain statistically determined probability that a true relationship between variables exists. Such tests are known as tests of significance.

Bibliography

Alland, A. Jr. 1976 — *When the Spider Danced.* New York: Doubleday/Anchor. A personal account of my first field work among the Abron of the Ivory Coast in West Africa.

Bowen, E. S. 1964 — *Return to Laughter: An Anthropological Novel.* New York: Doubleday/Natural History Press. A fictionalized account of real field work by an American woman anthropologist.

Freilich, M. editor 1970 — *Marginal Natives: Anthropologists at Work.* New York: Harper & Row. A selection of essays by anthropologists describing their experiences in the field.

Pelto, P. J. and G. H. Pelto 1978 — *Anthropological Research: The Structure of Inquiry.* New York: Cambridge University Press. Methods and techniques in the context of anthropological and general scientific theory.

CHAPTER 15
MARRIAGE AND KINSHIP

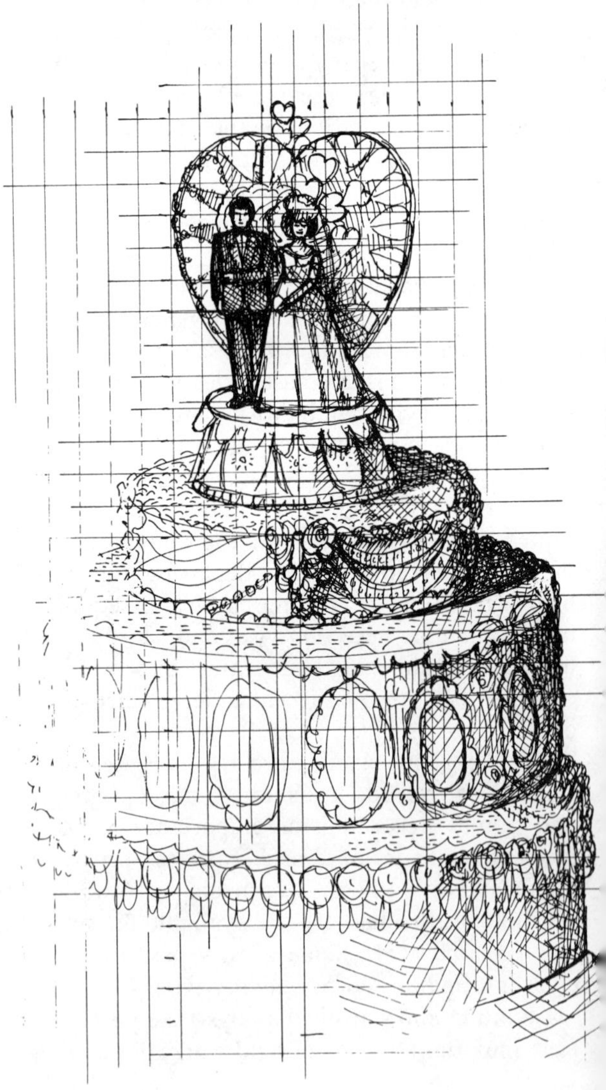

In the animal world mating is commonly temporary. Partners come together for a short period when the female is in heat, mate, and then separate. New partners are taken in each mating season. Even among those primates that live in social groups, unions are not usually permanent. Fidelity to a mate does occur, however, among certain species, particularly birds, and also among some primates. The gibbon has male-female pairs that live together for a lifetime.

In general, mating patterns are closely related to a species' social adaptation and have evolved under the control of genetic mechanisms. Learning, however, molds the behavior of all mammals. Learned responses to environmental variations may, in some cases, lead to modifications of the basic inherent pattern. The relationship between males and females in hamadryas baboons, for example, is the outcome of both genetic and learned patterns that have been selected in the context of a specific environment.

Species differ greatly in the matter of mating between closely related animals. The patterns vary from complete randomness, in which related animals may mate with each other without inhibition, to some degree of selectivity. In certain primate groups, for example, mating with a parent is inhibited. The same pattern is found among some birds.

When reading about the mating patterns of lower animals and humans, we are likely to find the same terms applied to both. Thus, species that mate at random and do not have permanent partners may be referred to as "promiscuous." When mating between offspring and parent is inhibited the term "incest taboo" and "incest avoidance" are often applied. In those rare cases of permanent union within mating pairs, the term **"monogamy"** (*marriage* between a single male and a single female) is sometimes used.

This type of labeling can lead to confusion about mating in animals and marriage in humans. Terms and concepts such as "promiscuity," "incest," "incest taboo," and "monogamy" are all drawn from the cultural order and have no fixed biological definitions. True, the incest taboo is found in all human cultures, but it is defined differently from group to group according to a set of *cultural* conventions. In addition, *mating* between relatives may occur where a taboo forbids *marriage* between them. There are many human societies in which the rules governing sexual relations are more relaxed than, or at least different from, the rules governing marriage. No such distinction can be made in the world of animals. It would be better, therefore, to reserve the term "incest taboo" for restrictions on human marriage and stick with *sexual inhibition* for sexual avoidance among animals. Similarly, terms that apply to marriage systems—such as "monogamy," "polygyny," "polygamy," "polyandry"—and even such concepts as promiscuity should be reserved for discussions of human culture. It is fair to say that humans both mate and marry while other species only mate. One can talk about multiple or single mates or of unique versus open mating systems in animals and thus avoid unnecessary *anthropomorphism* (making animals human) when talking about nonhuman species.

MARRIAGE

Mating among nonhuman animals includes sexual access by definition. In many species it also entails some form of cooperation within the mating pair or between males and females in the larger social group. In many bird species, for example, males as well as females feed and protect their offspring. Among primates, males within the troop may protect both adult females and immature animals of both sexes from predators or the attacks of other troops.

Marriage among humans is far more variable and complicated than mating in the animal world. In our own society marriage is, in part, a social contract between a man and a woman that grants them exclusive sexual access to each other. It gives them the legal right to have children and to raise them in the context of a family. A married couple is also an economic union. One or both of the spouses may work, and even when one does not, there is the expectation that the unemployed member, still usually the wife, will take care of household tasks. Marriage in our society, then, implies three functions: (1) exclusive sexual access, (2) the bearing and raising of children, and (3) economic union. In former times one other function was assumed to be part of the marriage bond. Until recently the male was charged with the protection of his wife. While this responsibility is still expressed in some marriage ceremonies, it is more formal than real in the modern world.

A young American family.

If we examine marriage in the anthropological literature, we find cultures in which one or more of these functions is *not* associated with the marital bond. Eskimo have no notion of exclusive sexual union in marriage and men freely lend their wives to visiting friends. In Polynesia and in many African societies children are raised by a number of relatives and community members. In matrilineal societies (those that trace important social relationships through female lines) economic relations between a wife and husband are sometimes less important than between a woman and her brother. In the Trobriand Islands a male is brought up in the house of his mother's brother, who is responsible for his education. Although divorce is common in contemporary American society, the ideal of marriage as a permanent union remains a part of our ethic. Among the Kanuri of Nigeria divorce is easy and common. Marriages are fragile and easily broken by men, but not by women.

Given all this variation, can anything general be said about marriage? If we exclude modern industrial society (after all, a recent and unprecedented development in human history), the answer is probably yes. The key to the problem lies in understanding that marriage is a social union.

A

B

C

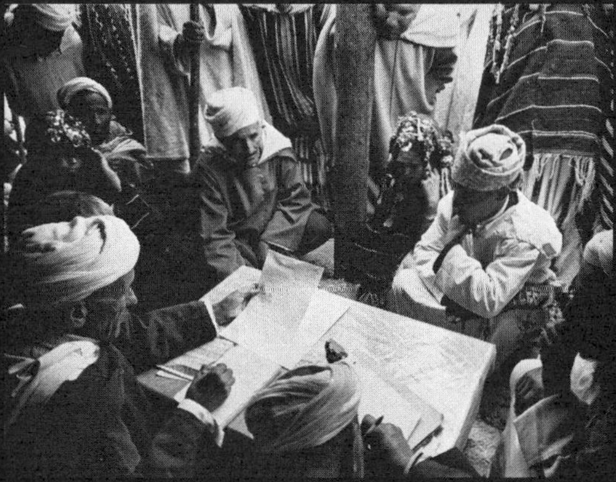

D

E

Weddings around the world.

A

Traditional Japanese.

B

Modern Japanese.

C

Traditional Kwakiutl (Northwest Coast Indian, nineteenth century).

D

Traditional Moroccan.

E

Traditional Indian (Hindu).

THE INCEST TABOO

Anthropologists have long argued over the origin of the incest taboo. Some have suggested that familiarity breeds contempt and that individuals brought up together or parents and their offspring would not wish to mate with each other. The frequency of rape within families, particularly in some social groups, plus the findings of psychoanalysis concerning unconscious incestuous desires among normal individuals, tend to negate this hypothesis. In addition, if people were naturally uninterested in their close relatives there would be no need for a taboo. Finally, while rules against sexual union between close relatives (mothers or fathers with children, and between siblings) are *almost* universal, the application of the incest taboo to other relatives varies widely. In some societies marriage is forbidden with first cousins who are the offspring of mother's sister or father's brother but is preferred with cousins who are the offspring of mother's brother and/or father's sister. Why should one type of cousin be sexually more or less attractive than another?

It has been suggested that the incest taboo is the result of natural selection. Close inbreeding can lead to lowered fertility. Thus, groups with incest taboos would have a selective advantage over groups practicing incest. By the same argument, however, groups that forbid cousin marriage should have an advantage over groups that allow it. There is no evidence that this is so.

According to another explanation of the incest taboo, matings (with or without marriage) within the immediate family or with multiple members of a single family would lead to social disruption. Yet the existence of unions between a man and a set of sisters would tend to disprove this notion as does the union in which a woman is married to a set of brothers, all of whom get along. Apparently, social tensions are largely socially defined.

When the life expectancy of humans was lower than it is today and infant mortality

In American society, beyond the confines of our small immediate families, social relations are regulated by influences other than kinship. We do not usually care whether or not our grocer is an uncle or a cousin. It is the quality of his products, his pricing policy, and perhaps his willingness to give credit that are important. Our daily contacts are largely with individuals whom we know only in one professional capacity or another. A shopkeeper is a shopkeeper and just that. Even our social groups are composed largely of nonkin. We belong to athletic and other clubs, service organizations, churches, and political parties, all of which are based on specific common interests.

These patterns contrast markedly with the societies traditionally studied by anthropologists. In technologically simple, small-scale cultures, social groups are composed of related individuals. The links between them are of two types: genetic, by "blood" (**consanguineal**), and social, by marriage (**affinal**). Age and sex are major attributes in social differentiation, but so are certain culturally defined distinctions. These distinctions relate to economic, political, and ritual roles, all of which are played against a was high, individuals may have been forced by necessity to seek outside of their immediate family for spouses. If a woman had many children, most of whom died, a male of marriageable age might find his mother too old (or dead) and his sisters too young to marry. The same argument would apply to women seeking mates. The general rule under such demographic conditions would be to marry out.

A major way to forge social links between groups would be to contract a marriage between them. If such linkages were advantageous, it would be culturally maladaptive for marriage to occur within the immediate family. Potential marriage partners would be bound to their own families and lost as potential activators of social alliances. The anthropologist E. B. Tylor expressed this theory very succinctly when he said it was a question of "marrying out or being killed off."

Where Incestuous Marriages Are Allowed. Incestuous marriages do occur, if infrequently. Every documented case is related to the maintenance of sacred power. In Egypt and in Peru rulers married their siblings. This practice was justified by the belief that Pharaohs and Incas were the holy descendants of gods. The practice of incest in these cases probably had its own symbolic significance. By marrying their sisters, Pharaohs and Incas reinforced their special status. In a real sense incest marked their place outside of normal society.

Incestuous marriages also occurred in Hawaii among people of high status. The Hawaiians believed that people were born with a certain amount of **mana** (spiritual power). This power was inherited through a male line from a father to his eldest son. People with great mana were the first-born sons of the first-born sons, . . . etc. If the first-born child of a person with great mana were a female, she would be married to her first brother. In this way the line of great mana was continued. In all other cases sibling marriage was forbidden in ancient Hawaii.

backdrop of defined kinship relations. If we do not understand kinship in these societies, we cannot understand anything about their social life. It should be no surprise that in these societies marriage often plays a crucial role in social relationships.

Marriage as Alliance and Exchange

While marriage in contemporary Western societies is largely a matter of personal choice, in traditional societies it involves entire social groups. Whom an individual will marry is the concern of his or her kin and a marriage often involves bargaining among kin, sometimes even to the exclusion of the potential couple. Marriage in these situations is a tie that binds whole groups together. It creates a set of linking obligations based on affinal relations.

Marriage as the establishment and maintenance of social ties between groups can be partially attributed to the incest taboo. The effect of the incest taboo is not only to forbid marriage among certain kin but also to force marriage between groups. Whatever its origin, the incest taboo sets the stage for the formation of social alliances. In fact, incest regulations often vary

△	Male
○	Female
□	Individual regardless of sex
⌴ or =	Is married to
≠	Is divorced from
|	Is descended from
⌐¬	Is the sibling of
●	Female ego whose kinsmen are being shown
▲	Male ego whose kinsmen are being shown
⦸ ⧅	Individual is deceased
F	Father
M	Mother
s	Son
d	Daughter
B	Brother
S	Sister
C	Child (of either sex)
H	Husband
W	Wife

Figure 15.1
Symbols commonly used by anthropologists in the discussion of kinship.

from society to society according to the types of alliances favored. When, for example, kin groups known as lineages are linked in a regular chain of relationships through marriage (such that group A gives women in marriage to group B, and group B gives women in marriage to group C, and group C gives women in marriage to group A—see Figure 15.2a), a closed marriage cycle is formed. This type of system can be created by preferred marriage with mother's brother's daughter and by making other cousins taboo for marriage.

It should be noted that in the example given, the marriage alliance is formed through the indirect exchange of women among linked social groups. A gets its wives from C, C gets its wives from B, and B gets its wives from A. This type of marriage system is known as a **circulating connubium.** Since it involves the linking of a potentially infinite number of social groups through the regular exchange of women, it is also known as **generalized exchange.** Another type of marriage is the direct exchange, back and forth, of wives between two social groups. Group A gives women to group B, and group B gives women back to group A. This is known as **restricted exchange;** and while it creates long-lasting ties, it can only link two groups. Restricted exchange can be generated when two brothers exchange their sisters in marriage (see Figure 15.2b) and the offspring of these marriages continue the custom of exchanging sisters. After one generation, a man in this system will marry a woman who is a *double cross cousin* (see Figure 15.2c). That is, she will be the offspring of father's sister married to mother's brother; thus she will be father's sister's daughter *and* mother's brother's daughter at the same time!

In the view of anthropologist Claude Lévi-Strauss, the central fact of marriage is the exchange of women between social groups. Because men generally occupy positions of power in society, some readers have carelessly assumed that Lévi-Strauss meant to say that men exchange women in marriage. Stated this way, the proposition looks as if it might reflect a sexist bias. Social groups, however, are composed of both men and women, and the exchange of wives between such groups acts for the mutual benefit of all concerned.

Since all cultures have some kind of incest taboo, spouses must come from outside the immediate family and, depending on the system, from outside a defined social group. Women are more likely than men to serve as the links between groups because it is they who actually produce people. In this sense, women have greater "value" than men. In fact, the widespread tendency to treat women as objects may arise in part from their role in marriage exchange. The notion of women as objects should not be exaggerated, however, and it should not be applied across the board to all societies. It may be that the tendency to make the equation "woman = object" is a characteristic of our own culture because we base so many of our own social relations on the exchange of things. Our economic system is depersonalized and depends on competition, whereas exchange in traditional societies is often the occasion for cooperation and the activation of social ties.

A Closer Look at Restricted and Generalized Exchange

Generalized exchange is a means of cementing social bonds among a large number of kinship groups. It occurs primarily in Southeast Asia among such hill peoples as the Kachin of Highland Burma (see Chapter 24). We have examined generalized exchange in one form, that based on mother's brother's daughter marriage. This produces a regular pattern of marriages that flow in

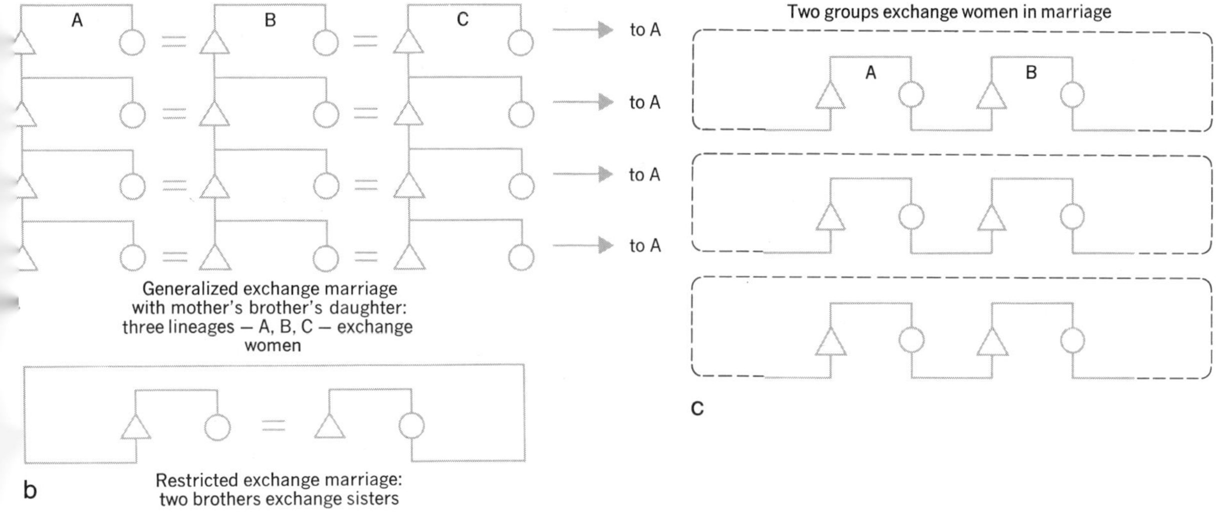

Figure 15.2

Generalized and restricted exchange marriages compared. (a) In the anthropological model shown here, every man is married to his mother's brother's daughter. In real cases group A gives women to group B, group B gives women to group C, and so on. The women that men marry are all considered to be matrilateral cross cousins. (b) Two brothers exchange their sisters in marriage. (c) When this pattern continues into following generations two groups are formed that exchange women between them. In most real cases restricted exchange merely involves the exchange of women between two groups such that women of A are considered to be "sisters" of the men of A and the women of B are considered to be the "sisters" of the men of B. Following the same logic A women are "cousins" to the men of B and B women are "cousins" to the men of A.

the same direction from generation to generation. Group A always gives wives to group B, and group B always gives wives to group C, etc. Another, much rarer, form of generalized exchange exists in which the preferred marriage is with a father's sister's daughter. In this case the flow of marriage partners changes back and forth from generation to generation (see Figure 15.3). If, in generation one, group A gives wives to group B and group B gives wives to group C, in generation two group A will get its wives from group B, and group B will get its wives from group C. The pattern seen in generation one will repeat in generation three and so on every other generation. In technical language, marriage with mother's brother's daughter is known as *matrilateral cross-cousin marriage* and marriage with father's sister's daughter is known as *patrilateral cross-cousin marriage.* Marriage with defined cousins on either side (as found in restricted exchange) is known as *bilateral cross-cousin marriage.* (One's cross cousin is the child of the opposite-sex sibling of one's parent, that is, the child of mother's brother or father's sister. On the other hand, one's *parallel cousin* is the child of the same-sex sibling of one's parent, that is, the child of mother's sister or father's brother.)

It was Lévi-Strauss who first made the distinction between restricted and generalized marriage exchange. Remember: restricted exchange involves marriage between two groups, A and B. Group A consists of men and women who cannot marry each other because they fall in the categories of "brother" and "sister." Group B consists of another such unit. Each group is forced by marriage rules to exchange women with the other. Since marriage between these groups continues through time, all marriage partners are (at least in principle) cousins to each other. Systems of restricted exchange are frequently found among small-scale horticultural groups. They are common in lowland South America, for instance.

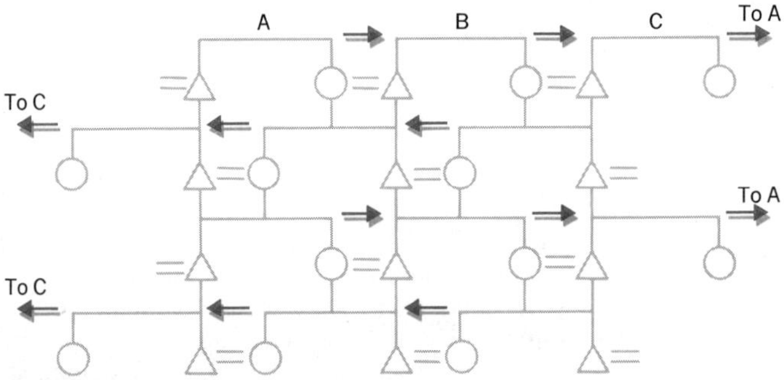

Figure 15.3
Generalized exchange, with father's sister's daughter marriage. In the anthropological model shown here every man is married to his father's sister's daughter. In real cases marriages are between groups, but the fiction of father's sister's daughter marriage is maintained. Note that in the case of generalized exchange with father's sister's daughter marriage, women move in one direction in one generation and in the other direction in the next generation.

Restricted Exchange among the Yanomamö

The Yanomamö live in southern Venezuela and northern Brazil. Their scattered villages have populations ranging in size from 40 to 250, with 80 the general average. According to Napoleon Chagnon, who has published several studies of the Yanomamö, their total population is about 10,000. Yanomamö villages ideally contain two groups of kinsmen. These kin groups are *patrilineal* (membership passes down a line of males), so the offspring of a man are members of his kin group. Such groups are **exogamous,** that is, a marriage partner must come from outside. (If people married within the group, we would say that it was **endogamous.**)

In the ideal case a Yanomamö man will give his sister to a man of another group living in his village, expecting to receive that man's sister as a wife in return. In his study Chagnon gathered data on all marriages among adults in two villages and found that some deviation from the rule actually occurred. Of 52 marriages in one village, 37 were based on sister exchange, four were the result of incestuous union, eight were the result of alliance with other villages or abduction, and three were unexplained. In the other, smaller village seven marriages were of the "correct" type, one was incestuous (in the sense that the mates came from the same exogamous kin group) and nine resulted from alliance or abduction. In the first village, and probably in the second as well, enough marriages were of the ideal type to keep the system of exchange between two lineages (based on the swapping of "sisters") operating.

Elementary and Complex Structures

Lévi-Strauss calls both restricted and generalized exchange *elementary structures* of kinship. In societies with elementary structures the model dictates whom every individual in the society should marry. In *complex structures,* such as our own, we cannot predict whom someone ought to marry because our marriage rules are only negative. The incest taboo continues to *restrict* marriage, but no particular type of marriage with categories of kin is encouraged.

Endogamy and Exogamy

So far we have examined the alliance and exchange function of marriage in which two or more social groups are tied together through marriage. The rule that an individual must marry *out* of his or her social group is called **exogamy.** While all societies are exogamous to some degree (marriage is always outside some defined social unit), rules may also exist that restrict marriage to within certain defined limits. These are rules of **endogamy.**

Some ethnic groups will allow marriage to anyone within the group (except defined classes of relatives) and to some but not all other ethnic groups. The Abron of the Ivory Coast, for example, live in close proximity to the Kolongo, the Agni, the Baoule, and the Lobi. In addition, members of an ethnic group that lives in Upper Volta, the Mossi, often migrate to Abron territory and work for Abron employers. The Abron allow marriage with Kolongo, Agni, and Baoule; they forbid marriage with Lobi and Mossi. Thus one can say that the Abron are endogamous in respect to the Lobi and Mossi but not in respect to the Kolongo, Agni, and Baoule. In many societies endogamous rules apply to an ethnic group and members are forbidden to marry beyond the confines of their own culture.

A particularly pervasive case of endogamy is found in the Indian caste system. **Castes** are ranked, endogamous, economically defined social groups. A wide range of occupational castes exists in India. Members of each caste must take their spouses from within their own group, although sometimes **hypergamy** (upward marriage) is allowed for women. Since Indian society is organized along caste lines, the existence of endogamy would at first glance appear to violate the rule that marriages are alliances among social groups. In fact, kinship relations also play an important part in Indian social structure. In India, as elsewhere, kin groups are united through marriage bonds. It is also an interesting fact that caste relations also act to tie Indian society together. The different castes are economically interdependent and, while they do not exchange women in marriage, they do exchange goods and services.

Bride Price, Bride Service, and Dowry

The exchange aspect of marriage relationships is frequently supported by other forms of exchange or payment associated with marriage contracts. The loss of a woman is a reproductive, economic, and social deprivation for those who give her up. Many societies recognize this loss by requiring the payment of a **bride price** to the woman's social group. This practice is widespread in New Guinea and Africa. In some instances **bride service** is substituted for bride price; the groom may live with the wife's family for several months or even years, performing economically valuable tasks for them on a prearranged basis. On the other hand, there are instances in which a bride takes money or valuables with her into a marriage relationship. This custom, known as **dowry,** is often associated with low status for women and is sometimes seen as a compensation to the husband for the burden he assumes with marriage. In other instances, however, the dowry belongs to the wife and provides her with a certain degree of security if she is not cared for by her husband. In preindustrial Europe the payment of dowry was an important aspect of marriage contracts and was often ruinous for families with many daughters and few sons. Dowry payment, although now outlawed, remains an important element of marriage custom in India.

Postmarital Residence

So far I have discussed marriage in terms of exchange and alliance, but there is also the matter of setting up a household. In marriage individuals move from a **family of orientation** (into which they were born) to a **family of procreation** (in which they raise their own children). The *postmarital residence* (where a couple lives after marriage) is determined by social custom. Although the American pattern is generally **neolocal** (the setting up of an independent household removed to an indetermi-

The presentation of dowry gifts in India among Hindus.

nate degree from the relatives of either the bride or the groom), in other cultures newlyweds often set up housekeeping within or near the already established household of a parent. If the couple goes to live with or near the groom's family the residence is called **virilocal** (the term **patrilocal** is also used). If residence is with or near the bride's household, the residence is called **uxorilocal** (the term **matrilocal** is also used). In some societies a couple will set up housekeeping with or near the husband's mother's brother (his maternal uncle). This pattern is known as **avunculocality.** When the couple has a choice between residence with either the parent of the groom or the parents of the bride, an **ambilocal** rule prevails. Each of these patterns is determined by custom, but exceptions occur in all cultures. The rule serves to establish where people ought to live and reinforces certain aspects of social structure.

SINGLE AND PLURAL SPOUSES

By law, marriage in the United States is **monogamous** (one husband married to one wife). In other parts of the world **polygamy** (plural spouses of either sex) is allowed. In most occurrences of plural marriage it is the man who takes several wives. This arrangement is known as **polygyny.** (Note the difference between *gamy,* spouses of either sex, and *gyny,* female spouses.) In a very few societies a woman is allowed to have more than one husband. This type of marriage is known as **polyandry.** Plural marriage is less common than single marriage even in those societies that sanction it. Having more than one spouse involves a set of obligations that only a few individuals can afford.

Loose Marriage among the Semai of Malaysia

As Americans are finding out, marriage without alliance can be a fragile institution. The fragility is very much evident among the Semai of Malaysia, whom we have already met in Chapter 13. The more traditional eastern Semai have no kin groups and a very weak conception of property. Their villages are small and are moved frequently in response to the require-

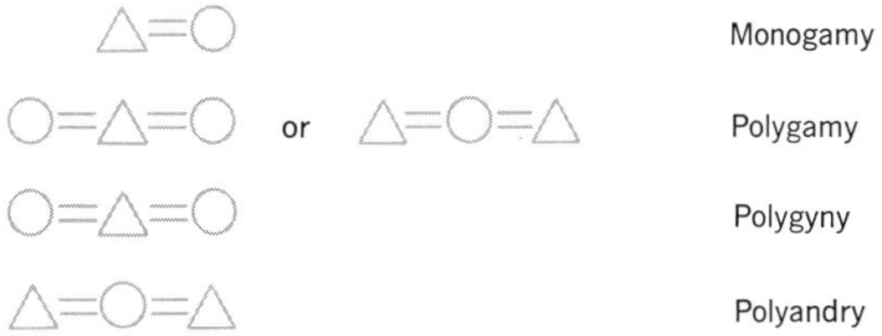

Figure 15.4
The different possible types of marriage.

ments of slash-and-burn horticulture. The western Semai, who have been influenced by Malay culture, live in more permanent settlements and have some substantial private property. Many of them work for wages and some grow cash crops. As we shall see, their marriages are more stable than those of the eastern Semai, reflecting a greater importance of alliance based on kinship.

Among the Semai the incest taboo is extended differently in the eastern and western groups. In the west marriage is forbidden with anyone descended from one's grandparents or great grandparents, that is, first and second cousins. In the east marriage is forbidden with *any* consanguineal kinsman. Paradoxically, the Semai are suspicious of nonkin. Thus, eastern Semai marry individuals who are from among the least trustworthy people around. Even in the west 70 percent of all marriages are with nonkin. The result is a considerable degree of anxiety, which, according to Robert Knox Dentan, is reflected in residence patterns.

Typically, the newlyweds spend a week or two with the wife's family, then a month or so with the husband's family. They may then return to the wife's settlement for a year or two, and so on at gradually increasing intervals, until they finally settle down once and for all.

Furthermore, whichever partner is living among in-laws during the period of shifting residence tends to leave from time to time for visits to kinsmen. Obviously, this *distrust in union* puts a great strain on marriages in general.

In the east marriages are further weakened by the lack of any ceremony that might function to cement the bonds between husband and wife. Couples merely take up residence with each other. Permanent separation is easy and frequent. One partner merely leaves the other, returning to his or her family. The Semai language does not have words for either marriage or divorce. Yet affectional ties do develop between individuals. The longer a couple stays together, the more likely it is that their union will last. The only exception arises when a man takes another wife. In this event his first wife may leave him. The looseness of Semai marriage (if "marriage" is the right word) is further confirmed by the fact that women as well as men can have multiple spouses. Among the Semai monogamy, polygyny, and polyandry all exist side by side. These different types of union are not, however, the result of marriage rules, but rather of the casual attitude the Semai have toward marriage as an institution.

A traditional Bakhtiari man (Iran) with his three wives and children.

The more acculturated west Semai have borrowed many features of the Malay wedding ceremony. Among them marriage is an event marked by public display and a sense of transition in the status of the marriage partners. During the ceremony the couple is lectured about their responsibilities to each other as well as toward their in-laws. They are told that they must treat their in-laws with deference, should not quarrel with them, talk about sex, or indulge in any form of horseplay. They are also instructed not to complain to their blood kin in cases of marital disputes. The formalization of the marriage is reinforced by the public payment of money to the family of the bride by the family of the groom. Part of the money is kept by the bride herself. This payment symbolizes the transfer of the woman from her own family to the family of her husband. She must henceforth rely on his kin for emotional support. He in turn must accept her kin as "family." Because a man's family has invested in his marriage (through bride payment), he must treat his wife with respect. Otherwise his kin will lose the right to reclaim the money if they divorce.

Western Semai marriages are more stable than eastern Semai marriages. In the west the marital union involves a linking of more than just the married couple. It is probably no accident that this shift in the meaning and stability of marriages has occurred in the context of increasing importance of property.

Sororal Marriage, the Sororate, and the Levirate

Different versions of each form of plural marriage exist. In some societies a man may marry several wives, but he may not take them from the same family. In others he may marry two or more sisters. In the practice of polyandry women often marry a man and one or more of his brothers, although a few cases of polyandrous marriage can be found in which husbands come from different families. Among the Abron of the Ivory Coast marriage to sisters is forbidden, although polygyny is permitted and occurs among older rich men. The King of the Abron provides an exception to the taboo on marriage to sisters. It is, in fact, considered lucky for the Abron King to marry twin sisters.

The custom that allows marriage between a man and a group of sisters is known as **sororal** polygyny. Sororal polygyny should not be confused with the sororate, a special form of monogamous union. Monogamous societies exist in which both wives and/or husbands are encouraged to marry the brother or sister of their deceased spouse. Marriage of a man with the sister of his deceased wife is known as the **sororate.** The marriage of a woman with the brother of her deceased husband is known as the **levirate.** This custom is described in the Old Testament and was practiced by the ancient Hebrews. It is also common in many parts of Africa. Both the levirate and sororate are means of continuing marriage ties between families after the death of a spouse. This supports the idea that marriage is an alliance between social groups.

Among the Nuer of East Africa a widow takes a new husband from among her deceased husband's male relatives or she may take a lover who is unrelated to her dead husband. In either case any children resulting from the union are considered to be offspring of the dead husband and therefore belong to his social group. This event is described by the Nuer as a ghost marriage, since the original husband is considered to father children after his death. The Nuer also permit female-female marriages. Here again it is a social tie that is reinforced. The female husband does not have sexual relations with *her wife,* but she does serve as the legal father of any offspring that result from unions between her wife and men of the village who act as lovers. These men will be the biological fathers of the children (their *genitors*), but the female husband will be their legally recognized father (their *pater*). Female-female unions are another case of social alliances between social groups, for such marriages are contracted for that purpose.

Among the Nyakyusa of East Africa, studied by the English anthropologist Monica Wilson, a marriage can legally persist even after the death of the two original spouses. If the wife dies the husband will often marry one of her sisters. If subsequently the husband dies, the new wife may marry one of his brothers!

MARRIAGE RULES AND ECONOMIC RELATIONS

It should be clear that in traditional societies marriage is much more than just a union between two individuals. Whom one is to marry, the stability of the marriage (even after death), and where the newly married couple will live are all part of the social fabric. Marriages are social and economic unions that tie groups together. Variations in marriage and residence among and within cultures can be used to illustrate the complex relationships among these social customs, environmental adaptation, and economics.

A Tibetan Case

Tibetan pastoral nomads, studied by Robert B. Ekvall, live under extremely harsh conditions. Where Ekvall did field work, the winter temperature never rises above 0°F. Summers, on the other hand, can be hot and the weather is always variable.

One day's experience early in July near the upper knee of the Yellow River at about 12,000 feet altitude, 34 degrees north, is a good illustration of the diurnal change in temperatures. During our noon halt we ate in burning heat—heat waves danced across the plain—and although it probably was less than 80°F in the shade, it certainly was much over 100°F in the sun. Shortly after we started to travel in the early afternoon, the sky clouded over and a violent thunderstorm swept across our route. Rain changed to hail, pelting us with such force that it was with difficulty we kept our pack animals on the trail, and by the time we made camp, it had become a blinding snowstorm. At dawn the next morning, the tent ropes were frozen stiff and over 4 inches of snow lay on the ground. By midafternoon, it had melted in the bright sunshine and the day promised to be hot.

The only animal that can do well under these extreme conditions of weather and altitude is the yak, and, indeed, the Tibetan herding economy depends on it. The economy also requires cooperation between the sexes. Although the society is patrilineal and patrilocal, women have great autonomy and power.

Livestock is controlled by the tenthold, a family group of varying composition occupying a tent. The oldest active male in this group is responsible for decisions concerning the economic management of the herd, but he does not own it. His decisions may be challenged by other members of the tenthold, particularly by the senior wife, who is mistress of the tent.

Family organization fluctuates between extended and nuclear organization. Disputes between the wives of different sons of a founding male often lead to a break-up of an extended family tent, for the women do not like to share authority. Marriage may be monogamous, polygynous, or polyandrous. Each type of marriage can be directly linked to socioeconomic conditions.

The most common pattern is monogamy, because most men do not have the wealth to support more than one wife. Patrilocal polygynous marriages do occur among older men of wealth and power. In these polygynous unions each wife usually lives in her own tent and the husband presides over two or more tentholds. This multitent arrangement is rare but quite stable. It tends to endure because the unit is economically strong. A certain amount of economic power is required to establish such a household, and once it is established it tends to preserve wealth.

A special form of matrilocal polygynous marriage to a mother and her daughter occurs under the following circumstances. Although tents are generally patrilocal and the society patrilineal, when a family has only daughters, a surrogate son may be brought in. Residence for him is, of course, matrilocal. The man drops his affiliation with his own patrilineage and is adopted into the patrilineage of his father-in-law. If his father-in-law dies early, he may marry his wife's mother.

Polyandry is also associated with economic conditions. When two brothers decide not to divide a family herd because it will reduce their wealth, they may agree to share one wife to avoid the conflict that would arise if two wives lived together in the same tenthold. These marriages are unstable for economic reasons and one brother is likely to establish his own tent in a monogamous union when he can afford to do so.

Ekvall points out that these variations in family structure and marriage are based on economic rather than on sexual needs. He notes that there is a great deal of sexual license both before and after marriage. As a consequence, the importance of sexual satisfaction within the family is reduced. Management of the tent, on the other hand, depends on a smooth partnership between members of the opposite sex, so marriage is an *economic* union of great importance. The Tibetan experience is instructive because various types of marriage exist in the same culture and can be correlated with differing socioeconomic conditions. The concept of marriage as economic union is reinforced.

Summary

It is important to distinguish between marriage and mating. Mating is the sexual union between animals that leads to the production of offspring. Marriage is a social union between two or more humans. While mating is exclusively sexual, marriage has educational, social, and economic functions as well. Marriage is defined differently in different societies. The only thing it has in common everywhere is the fact that it is a social union.

In American society, beyond the confines of our small immediate families, social relations are regulated by influences other than kinship. Our daily contacts are with individuals we know only in one professional context or another. Even groups of friends are composed largely of nonrelatives. When we belong to groups they are usually based on specific common interests such as athletics, religion, politics, or charity.

In traditional societies kin relations are of great importance. Kinship links among individuals are of two types: consanguineal (blood relations) and affinal (relations through mar-

Tibetan nomads camped outside a fortified village.

riage). Most economic, social, political, and religious activities in traditional societies take place among groups of kin.

While marriage in Western society is largely a matter of personal choice, in traditional societies it involves entire social groups. Marriage provides an occasion for the formation or strengthening of alliances among different kin groups. The existence of the incest taboo in human societies, whatever its origin, forces individuals to marry outside of their group.

Claude Lévi-Strauss has examined different kinds of marriage systems. He divides them into elementary and complex structures. Elementary structures define both whom an individual should marry and whom an individual should not. Complex structures continue to forbid marriage with certain categories of people but do not have positive rules according to which individuals choose their mates. Lévi-Strauss suggests that elementary marriage structures are common in traditional societies. These he divides into systems of restricted and generalized exchange. Restricted exchange occurs between two social groups and can be generated by cousin marriage that is the result of sister exchange. Generalized exchange is also based on cousin marriage, but it is capable of uniting a large number of social units. This is accomplished by allowing marriage with only mother's brother's daughter or, in some cases, with father's sister's daughter. Such a system produces a circulating connubium, in which groups regularly give women to other groups and receive women in turn.

While all individuals must marry beyond the confines of some defined group, social rules may exist that restrict marriage to *within* a group as well. Outmarriage is known as exogamy; inmarriage as endogamy. The immediate family is (with special exceptions) exogamous. Castes (ranked occupational groups) are endogamous. Castes are a major element in Indian social structure. Kinship relations, however, are not absent in Indian society. Kin groups in India are exogamous. Castes are complementary to kin groups since, although they are endogamic, exchange of goods and services takes place among them and all occupy strategic places in the total fabric of Indian society.

The economic nature of marriage is further supported by the existence of bride price, bride service, and dowry. Bride price and bride service reflect obligations on the part of a groom's kin group toward his wife's. Both are compensations for the loss of a woman to her own social unit. Dowry is a sum of money or a collection of valuable goods that a woman brings to her marriage. Dowry is associated in most cases with low status for women and reinforces the notion that she will be a burden to her husband. In other cases dowry is kept by the wife and serves as insurance for her and her children in case of divorce or the death of her husband.

Marriage involves not only exchange and alliance but also the physical movement of spouses according to residential rules. Individuals are born into a family of orientation; when they get married they form a family of procreation. Residence may be neolocal (the couple sets up an independent household in an area of their choice), virilocal (near or with the groom's family), uxorilocal (near or with the family of the bride), or avunculocal (near or with the brother of the groom's mother).

Marriages may be monogamous (a single spouse) or polygamous (plural spouses). More than one wife at one time is called polygyny and more than one husband at a time is called polyandry. Marriage to a group of sisters is known as sororal polygyny. This should be distinguished from the sororate, in which a man marries the sister of his deceased wife. The marriage of a woman to her deceased husband's brother is known as the levirate. The permanence of the marriage bond and its function as a link between spouses' social groups is affirmed by customs in which the death of the spouse does not break the original marriage bond. Among the Nuer of the Sudan a dead husband continues to "father" children when his former wife has sexual relations with his brothers or nonrelated lovers. Among the Nyakyusa of East Africa a marriage bond may even survive the death of both husband and wife. If a man dies his wife marries his brother and if at a later time the wife dies her new husband will marry one of her sisters.

The kind of marriage that exists in a society and the type of alliance formed through marriage is closely related to the social and economic systems. Flexibility in marriage rules among the Tibetan nomads, for example, can be correlated with specific kinds of economic ties and the amount of riches available to particular groups of kin.

Bibliography

Bohannan, P. and J. Middleton, editors 1968 — *Marriage, Family, and Residence.* New York: Natural History Press. A collection of articles on marriage, family, and household.

Dentan, R.K. 1968 — *The Semai: A Nonviolent People Of Malaya.* New York: Holt, Rinehart, and Winston. Data on marriage among slash-and-burn horticulturalists in the interior of Malaysia.

Ekvall, R. B. 1968 — *Fields on the Hoof: Nexus of Tibetan Nomadic Pastoralism.* New York: Holt, Rinehart, and Winston. Account of Tibetan nomad ecology and social structure with data on marriage forms.

Freud, S. 1950 — *Totem and Taboo.* Translated by James Strachey. London: Routledge and Kegan Paul. Freud's theory of the origin of the incest taboo and totemism.

Lévi-Strauss, C. 1969 — *The Elementary Structures of Kinship.* Boston: Beacon Press. Theory of marriage as exchange between social groups.

Morgan, L. H. 1963 — *Ancient Society.* Cleveland: World Publishing. Marriage in the context of cultural evolution and kin groups by one of the earliest American anthropologists. This book, originally published in 1877, had a strong influence on Marx and Engels and led to their *Origin of the Family, Private Property, and the State.*

CHAPTER 16

FAMILY, KINSHIP, AND KIN GROUPS

FAMILY UNITS

The composition of nonhuman primate troops is species-specific and relatively invariable. Although the environment does play a role in the composition and structure of some primate social units, variation between species is far more distinctive than variation within species. Among humans, in contrast, the family unit and other more extensive kinship groups vary significantly from culture to culture. In traditional societies kinship is the primary social glue and organizing principle, but the particulars of kinship differ enormously. In modern industrial society kinship is of greatly reduced significance in holding the social order together. Documenting and understanding this variation are major tasks for anthropologists.

Although children must be reared by adults, what a family consists of is highly variable, reflecting, in its many forms, aspects of economic and social life that are unrelated to child care. **Nuclear families** (the type most familiar to us—see Figure 16.1) consist of a husband and wife with their children. This is the common pattern in middle-class America. It is also found among the Eskimo; for them, as in our culture, the independent family functions as the main economic unit.

Although anthropologists once thought that the nuclear family in some form (alone or embedded in one of the larger units to be discussed below) was universal, comparative research has changed their thinking. Among the Nayars of India, for example, a woman goes through a formal marriage ceremony during her childhood but never lives with her "husband." Instead, she has a series of affairs with visiting lovers who make no contribution to the basic, female-centered economic unit. In fact, the tenuous status of the lover keeps him from exerting economic power over the female-dominated group. On many of the islands that dot the Caribbean a large number of families are **matrifocal,** consisting of a mother and her children (Figure 16.2). While a percentage of nuclear families does exist, men frequently circulate through the community, establishing relationships of different duration with several women. On some of these islands, where unemployment is common, men are away from home, often on other islands, for long periods of time. Labor migration and economic instability play an important role in this kind of family organization.

The Abron of the Ivory Coast, among whom I worked, have separate households for men and women. Although fatherhood and motherhood are both recognized, and parents share certain economic tasks, emotional ties tend to be strongest in one's unisexual household. In addition, the socialization of children is shaped by the mold of residence and family structure. Girls are raised primarily by their mothers.

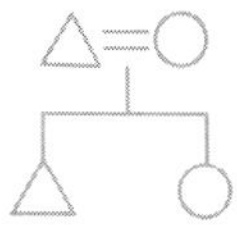

Figure 16.1
A nuclear family with two children.

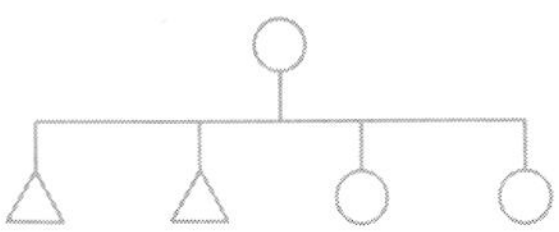

Figure 16.2
A matrifocal family, showing a woman and her four offspring.

Men and women live apart in many parts of the world. The round house in the center of this picture is a women's residence while the rectangular house to the right is a men's house. Gimi village, Eastern Highlands Province, Papua-New Guinea.

Boys begin their lives in their mother's house, but soon after they are weaned they move to their father's all-male household.

Extended Families

Frequently in Europe and elsewhere, particularly among farming populations, the family group consists of an old couple, their eldest son, his wife, and their children. This **stem family** (see Figure 16.3) reflects a pattern of economic cooperation and land ownership in which title flows down a single line from fathers to their eldest sons.

Joint families (brothers living in the same household with their wives and offspring, often with the brothers' parents—see Figure 16.4) are common in China and other areas where cooperative labor and the sharing of common resources within the family favor a large household.

The Family and Domestic Cycles

The membership of any family changes

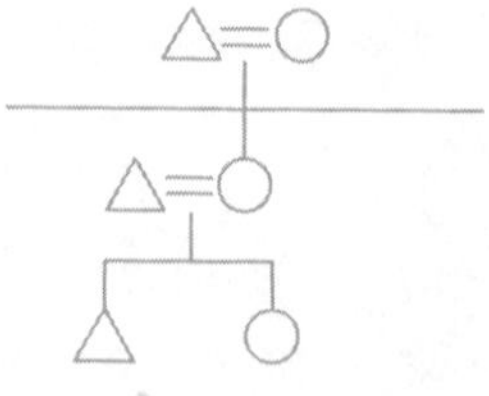

Figure 16.3

A stem family of three generations. Note that one son of a couple with his wife and children are included in the same household.

through time. As humans grow up, they move away from their family of orientation, the household in which they were born, to a family of procreation, the family in which they will raise their own children. Where the nuclear family is the pattern, as in our own society, this change represents a real shift in basic social and spatial relationships. Where the family of procreation is not residentially removed from the family of orientation, as among extended families, new social relationships have to be worked out in the context of the original structure.

Most families go through a set of regular changes. In the United States young couples tend to establish independent households in which they raise a relatively small number of children. During the child-raising stage the woman may not work (although this pattern is now highly variable). Because she has few children, generally close together in age, the American woman who enters the work force after child-bearing does so at a relatively early age. When children become adults they leave their parents behind to form new nuclear households. Older American couples often live alone, sometimes quite far from their children. Particularly in the middle class, many older people (married, divorced, widowed, and unmarried) move into "retirement" communities. Their main social contacts in such communities are restricted to people in their own age category.

In most of the world exclusive of the United States, the aged live with or near their children or other significant kin. They maintain frequent

Women socializing in an American retirement home. Although these people may be visited from time to time by their relatives, they have little social contact with members of younger generations.

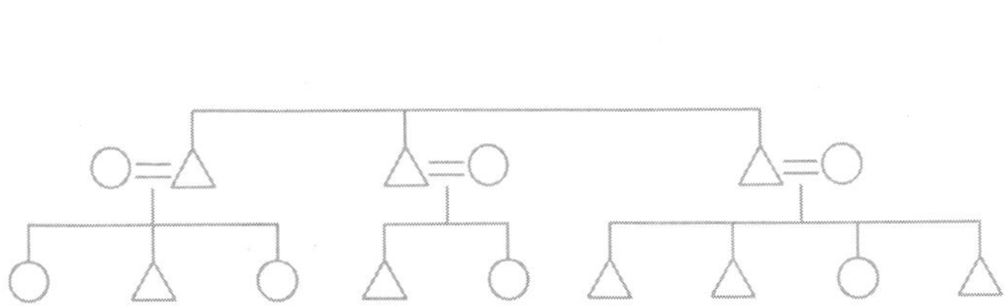

Figure 16.4
A joint family showing three brothers living together with their wives and children.

contact with individuals of all ages and their lives are less isolated.

In societies with virilocal residence the maturation of sons in or near their father's household may lead to disputes over property. Grown sons may wish to exert their authority as they move toward the age of leadership. These disputes can become so severe that a son or sons will move out of the parental domain and found new households, thus starting a new cycle that will eventually develop into new extended families.

Since the presence of close relatives provides an economic advantage in societies that require cheap, cooperative labor, large joint families may be able to accumulate considerable wealth. As long as the household can remain united the family can maintain economic power and, sometimes, political influence as well. If, however, the family fragments, or its members decline in numbers, it may sink into poverty. Thus, the economic status of families, particularly in peasant societies with joint family structure, may wax and wane as the domestic cycle runs its course.

KINDREDS

At birth a child automatically acquires a set of relatives on both the father's and mother's side. These make up a **kindred** (Figure 16.5). Although kindreds exist everywhere (people always recognize a set of relatives wider than their immediate family), they are not fixed entities with a definite set of members, since every individual (except unmarried brothers and sisters) belongs to a unique kindred. You and your cousin might agree that you both belong to the same kindred, but if the two of you sat down to make separate lists of kindred members, your lists would differ in part. Therefore, they rarely function as social groups.

The Jewish family circle was an attempt to keep kindred affiliations alive in the context of American society. These individuals are members of the Kurzweil family circle as it existed in the 1950s. The circle includes people related to one another by blood and through marriage. Because a kindred has no definite boundaries, a great deal of individual choice is involved in membership. After marriage a couple could decide to belong to the family circle of either or both of the spouses.

DESCENT

In many parts of the world the role of kinship in social life is complicated and enriched by the existence of descent groups. Membership in such groups is determined by principles that eliminate the overlapping, indefinite affiliation and the dual loyalties that occur in kindreds. Every member of a descent group claims his or her descent from the same ancestor. Thus, while kindred membership is determined on the basis of whom an individual counts as his or her relatives, descent group membership is always reckoned downward from a fixed point in a genealogy, from an ancestor. Descent can be traced **ambilaterally,** through *either* sex, or **unilineally,** through only male or female links. If, for example, descent is determined ambilaterally, individuals can claim membership in a descent group through either of their parents. If descent is unilineal, membership can only be traced through a line of males or females (father's father's father or mother's mother's mother, for example). When either sex can be used for tracing membership, the resulting groups are **cognatic.** If male or female links are used exclusively, the resulting groups are **unilineal.**

Cognatic Groups

We have already met one set of cognatic relatives, the kindred, and seen that they do not constitute a fixed social unit. Many small-scale hunting-and-gathering societies are **bilateral** in structure. When necessary, individuals can mobilize allies from among kindred relatives. Such societies have no fixed descent groups. Large stable populations, on the other hand, tend to divide themselves into social units with clear boundaries. Although unilineal descent is the easiest way to create such groups, they can also be created by adding certain residence requirements to ambilaterality. In this type of system an individual has the right to choose membership in any of a number of groups with which they have kinship ties through either males or females. Once the choice has been made, the individual takes up residence with that group. Residence activates membership, which then becomes permanent. Once the choice has been made and membership established, the individual gives up his or her claims to membership in other such groups. Cognatic groups of this type, which are based on ambilateral descent *and* residence choice, are known in anthropology as **ramages.** Ramage organization is widespread in Polynesia, where it appears to function as an

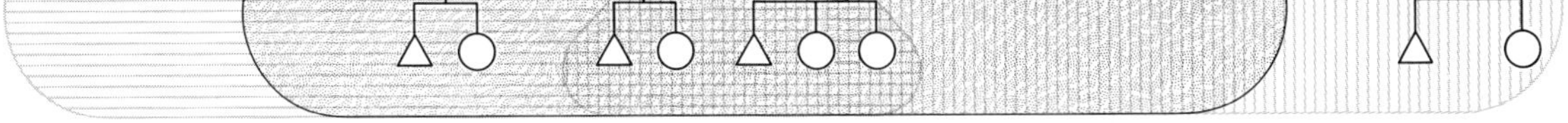

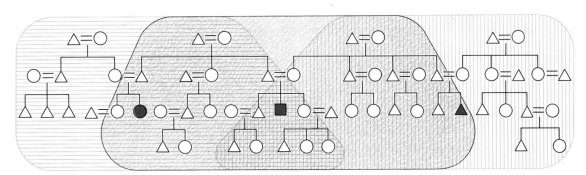

Figure 16.5
Overlapping kindreds of three individuals (indicated by solid color). Note that while everyone on the chart is related to everyone else, no single individual counts the same relatives in his or her kindred.

COGNATIC DESCENT AMONG THE MAORI

The Maori are a Polynesian people inhabiting both the North and South Islands of New Zealand. In former times the Maori were divided into localized tribes, each of which was headed by a chief. Each tribe was in turn segmented into cognatic descent groups known as *hapu.* Single *hapu* were often localized in villages, although large villages might contain more than one *hapu. Hapu* were named after a founding ancestor, usually male.

The Maori *hapu* was not an exclusively exogamous group, and people sometimes married within their own *hapu.* This practice created multiple links among members. *Hapu* membership was fixed when an individual settled down and established permanent residence. The bias was toward virilocality, but uxorilocality also occurred. When father and mother were from different kin groups, their children were considered to be members of both *hapu.*

Among the Maori, as in much of Polynesia, rank (as expressed in *mana,* or sacred power) descended through a line of oldest sons. *Hapu* chiefs were the eldest sons of the eldest sons through several generations of the founding chief. *Hapu* themselves were ranked against one another, however, so that individuals could raise their status by activating links to those highly ranked *hapu* to which they could establish a descent relationship. Descent through the female line could be used in this way to enhance rank.

adaptation to land scarcity. These cognatic descent groups provide individuals with a wide choice of group membership. What choice is finally made in each instance is probably linked to the best available land at a particular time. Ramages provide a flexible means of distributing individuals over a limited cultivable area and at the same time maintain a kinship-based social organization.

Unilineality

Compared to cognatic groups, a far simpler, but less flexible way of forming a closed kin group is to trace descent exclusively through male *or* female links. Descent through a line of males is known as **patrilineality,** and kin groups based on this principle are **patrilineal.** Such groups include all individuals, male or female, related by blood traced through men, back to a real or assumed founding ancestor.

Patrilineal kin groups are the most common type of unilineal group. They are found on the steppes of Asia and among many of Africa's cattle people. Herding is a male-dominated activity and many pastoral nomads are also warlike. These two patterns tend to favor patrilineality, which is associated with male dominance in the economic and political spheres. An ethnic group whose economy is based largely on intensive agriculture (wet rice farming, for example) is usually patrilineal, as are societies in which major economic resources are in the hands of men. These factors suggest again that patrilineality is associated with male control over production.

Kin groups that trace descent through the female line are **matrilineal.** Such groups include all individuals, male and female, related by blood traced through women, back to a real or assumed founding ancestor. One must be careful not to confuse matrilineality with **matriarchy,** which refers to political rule by females. There are many matrilineal societies in the world (although they are much less common than patrilineal societies), but there is no sound evidence that true matriarchies ever existed. This does not mean, however, that women never occupy important political positions. They can and do in many societies.

Matrilineal organization is associated with horticultural societies. It is found, among other areas, in America among the Iroquois and the Pueblos of the Southwest, and in African ethnic groups distributed across the southern part of the continent. It generally occurs when food production is dominated by women, yet many societies of this type are patrilineal. The anthropologists Carol and Melvin Ember have examined data from a large number of societies and have found that patrilineality predominates in horticultural societies where local warfare is also present. Thus, in Highland New Guinea, where local small-scale wars are a constant feature of life, groups are patrilineal and patrilocal. (The general term for unilineal kin groups that trace membership to a founding ancestor is **lineage.**)

It should be noted that, in general, unilineal descent of a particular type is strongly associated with residence. Patrilineal kin groups correlate well with patrilocal residence and matrilineal kin groups are found in association with matrilocal and avunculocal residence.

Of course, not all societies are unilineal. Cognatic descent groups exist in many parts of the world, and there are societies with no descent groups at all. In each case there are strong relationships between descent (or its absence), the environment, the economy, whether or not warfare is present, politics, and ideology.

The General Function of Lineal Kin Groups. Lineal kinship groups provide a means of organizing society into subunits, each of which has a set of rights and duties associated with membership. Such groups are found in many societies of intermediate size that lack centralized political authority. Rare among hunting-and-gathering societies, lineal kin groups are common among cultivators and herders.

Such groups are said to be *corporate* when they function as legal, economic, social, and, frequently, ritual bodies. Members of corporate kin groups often control land together and share the fruits of their combined labor. Many of the groups worship founding ancestors and control the social behavior of members. Finally, many corporate descent groups are held together by links between the living and the dead. Religious activity in societies with descent groups often includes worship of deceased ancestors who, it is believed, continue to take an active interest in lineage affairs.

Segmentary Lineage Organization Among The Tiv

The Tiv of Nigeria represent the "ideal" type of lineage organization. According to Paul Bohannan, who wrote the major study of Tiv society, in 1952 their population totaled about 800,000. The Tiv live on a plain cut by the Benu and Katsina Ala Rivers. The country is covered with high grass and widely scattered trees. The climate is tropical with distinct dry and wet seasons. Tiv economy is agricultural with three major subsistence crops: millet, sorghum, and yams. These grains and starchy tubers are prepared as gruel and served with a sauce of oil, meat, and green vegetables. A man who is a member of a Tiv community has the right to exploit a sufficient amount of land belonging to his community. He does not own the land but he has the right to use it.

Tiv social organization is based on the *segmentary lineage principle* (Figure 16.6). It is a lineage *system* that, to quote Bohannan, "comes into being when several lineages are grouped to form a single social unit." Tiv lineages are organized by citing genealogical relationships (tracing relationships) among individuals and lineage segments. The entire Tiv society can trace its descent through genealogical links to a single founding ancestor. Thus all Tiv belong to a single major lineage. This lineage is broken down into segments by tracing descent from closer relatives in the genealogical chain. The Tiv lineage system forms a hierarchy of segments that run from the minimal lineage (a set of brothers and their children linked upward to their common father) through a wide range of

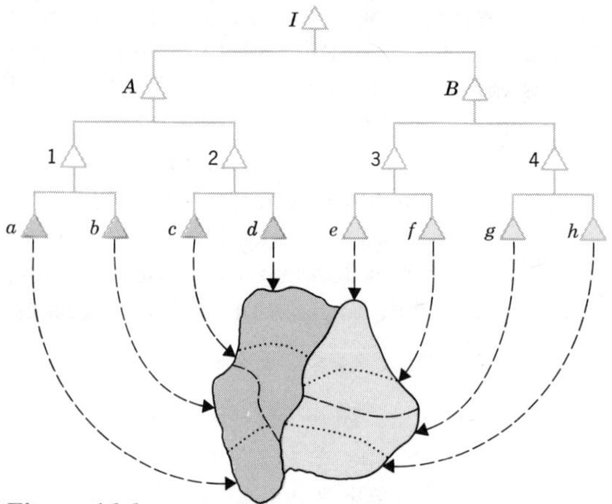

Figure 16.6
Tiv segmentary lineage organization. In the Tiv case genealogical and spatial relationships are harmonious, that is, members of the same lineage segment occupy the same territory. (From P. Bohannan, 1954, the International African Institute.)

intermediate lineages all the way up to Tiv society as a whole. Each level of this segmentary hierarchy corresponds to a territory. Tiv lineages are strictly patrilineal. Since they are also territorial it follows that residence is patrilocal. When a woman marries, she leaves her home lineage and goes to live among the lineage mates of her husband.

The lineage system among the Tiv is territorial and political. It acts to control law and warfare throughout the society. The Tiv have no chiefs. Instead, shifting alliances among small lineage segments are constantly in the process of responding to local political and social conditions. As the anthropologist Marshall Sahlins has pointed out, segmentary organization that is linked, as it is among the Tiv, to territorial units is a highly adaptive and flexible mechanism, particularly under conditions of territorial expansion. Local disputes between small segments tend to remain bounded by the checks and balances exhibited by the relative political equality among segments. On the other hand, segments can unite to fight a common enemy.

Intralineage Marriage among the Bedouins

The Bedouins of the Arabian peninsula have a system of property holding and marriage that keeps wealth within the confines of a patrilineage. The Bedouins are patrilineal and patrilocal. Their economy is based on the herding of camels, goats, and sheep. This is primarily a male activity, and women are generally restricted to the immediate household. Patrilineal organization is so strong that preferred marriage for a man is with a parallel cousin of one's own lineage (the daughter of father's brother). Such a marriage rule is rare in the rest of the world. In this instance it works to keep property, primarily in the form of herd animals, within a patrilineage. This marriage also forces the group in on itself, generating strong loyalties within and hostility without. For the Bedouins loyalty to place is translated into a particularly strong loyalty to the lineage group, which, because the Bedouins are nomads, moves across the landscape.

Lineages and Clans

A patrilineal (or **agnatic**) corporate kin group that traces its descent from an assumed *real* ancestor is known as a **patrilineage.** Its matrilineal counterpart is known as a **matrilineage** (Figure 16.7). Several such groups related to each other through more distant links, usually a fictional ancestor, may form a **clan.** Thus, the clan has a longer genealogical depth and encompasses a greater number of individuals than a lineage. The term clan is normally restricted in anthropological terminology to units that are recognizably different from lineages. Thus, clan is *not* used by Bohannan in his description of the Tiv, although the major Tiv lineage has about 800,000 members. Usually it is correct to say that clans are much larger and less well-organized social groups than lineages, but the Tiv case casts some doubt on this as a general rule. The distinction is most useful when the anthropologist can determine that such groups

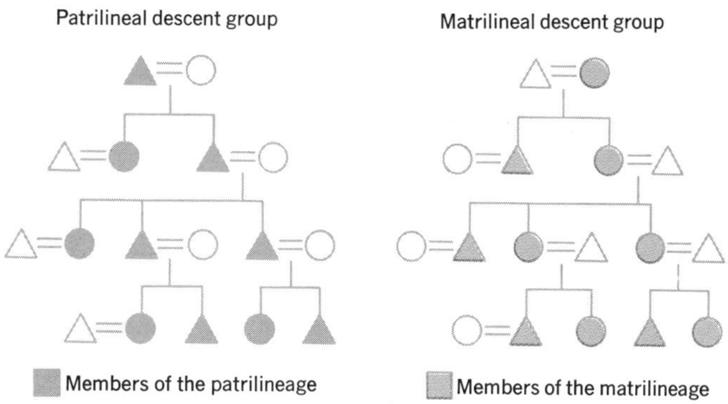

Figure 16.7
Lineage organization. (left) patrilineage; (right) matrilineage.

Kinship affiliation is often represented symbolically. (a) A Scottsman with the symbols of his clan. (b) A Thunderbird pole from the Kwakiutl people of the Northwest Coast of North America. Such poles were erected by kinship groups and often contained genealogical information as well as religious symbolism.

are recognized by members of the society or when different rules can be ascribed to membership in lineages on the one hand and clans on the other. In some cases, for example, the rights and duties of lineage members are strictly defined while clan membership is governed more by emotional ties than by rights and obligations. Lineages are generally exogamous groups; the clan in many instances is not.

Moieties and Phratries

The complexities of unilineal social organization are not exhausted with the distinction between clan and lineage. Some societies, particularly in lowland South America and Australia, are divided into two large kinship groups. These may or may not be divided into lineages or clans. Such a *dual* division is known as **moiety organization.** The word *moiety,* borrowed from French, simply means *half.* In many cases moieties are ritual groups. During ceremonial periods each moiety has its special role to play in religious performances. In addition many, but not all moieties are exogamous. When they are, each moiety provides spouses for the other. This is an example of restricted exchange.

Another frequently used term for social units is **phratry.** The phratry is a generally loose confederation of clans that recognize common kin ties. One can think of lineages nested into clans, and clans nested into phratries, just so long as it is realized that not all lineage societies have clans and not all clan societies have phratries. Moreover not all clan societies have lineages.

Double Descent

Since the evolution of *Homo sapiens,* humans have spread all over the globe and have come to occupy a wide range of environments. A look at diverse technological systems reveals that these many environments are exploited in different ways. Social, historical, and ecological factors all shape the kind of inheritance of valuables, succession to office, and descent found in any particular society. These factors also shape and are shaped by the type of social system present. It should be no surprise, therefore, that cognatic and single unilineal descent are not the only means of ordering units within society.

Among the hunting-and-gathering Australian Aborigines, for example, there are groups in which two different sets of moieties exist. One set is patrilineal and the other matrilineal. In these systems individuals inherit different moiety membership from *each* parent. In other words an individual will belong to one of two possible *patrimoieties* and one of two possible *matrimoieties.* Such a system is known as **double descent** (Figure 16.8). People affiliate unilineally with a patrilineal group, but also unilineally with a matrilineal group. In a moiety system with double descent there are four divisions in the society. These are patrimoieties A and B, and matrimoieties C and D. The society is divided into four units because each individual within it must be either AC, AD, BC, or BD. Double descent is not limited to moiety organization and can be found in lineage-based societies as well.

Double Descent: The Yako of Nigeria

The Yako live in large permanent settlements of up to 11,000 individuals. Patrilineages are localized, with small segments sharing a common dwelling. A cluster of family compounds

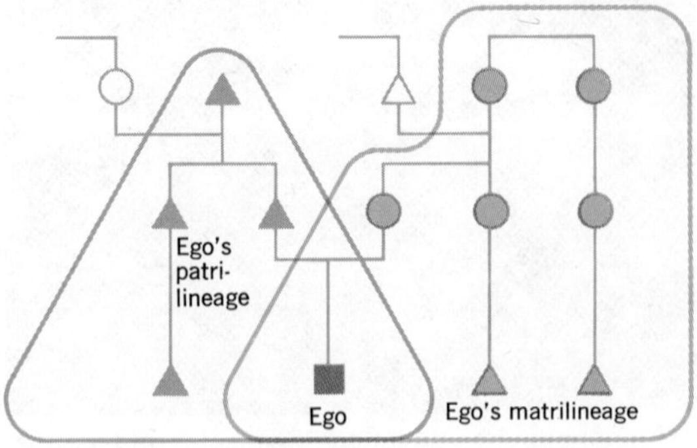

Figure 16.8
Double descent, showing an ego's patrilineage and matrilineage.

makes up a larger lineage group. This unit has title to land ownership. Several such units are grouped into neighborhoods and constitute a clan. As among the Tiv all of these segments are patrilocal as well as patrilineal. A man takes his wife or wives from other districts.

Matrilineal descent is also acknowledged among the Yako. All Yako belong to their mother's matrilineage. While the patrilineage is a land-based group dealing with the ownership of fixed property, production, and the associated ceremonies, the matrilineage is responsible for movable property, death payments, certain legal obligations of the membership, and ceremonies associated with fertility. Each individual's place in Yako society is determined by membership in both patrilineal and matrilineal groups.

MODELS AND REAL BEHAVIOR

Social structure is an abstraction that anthropologists build up from data. In the construction of such categories as matri- or patrimoiety, lineage, or clan, we can easily forget that real behavior may only approximate the anthropologist's model. Social structure serves to effectively organize a society for survival in the world. As an adaptive mechanism it need not bind individuals into rigid categories that could inhibit rather than enhance adaptation. Individuals do not always act according to their own or the anthropologist's rules.

Since many kin-oriented societies are often also preliterate, documents to prove a particular set of relationships are often lacking. Genealogies and other aspects of kinship must be remembered, and memory can be selective. Individuals and groups can make claims on the system that have no basis in easily established fact. These claims can often be justified through such social customs as the giving of feasts. Claims of this type may be accepted by others if their own self-interest is reflected in them in some way. Sometimes competing claims form the basis of disputes that are only resolved through violence.

Social Fictions

All societies, including our own, have useful fictions that can be used to validate social claims. Adoption, for instance, is a form of fictive kinship that is accepted as real by our legal institutions. Almost all documented cultures have means through which individuals can be incorporated into a kinship network even though no real blood or marriage ties exist. In our own culture we can adopt children and

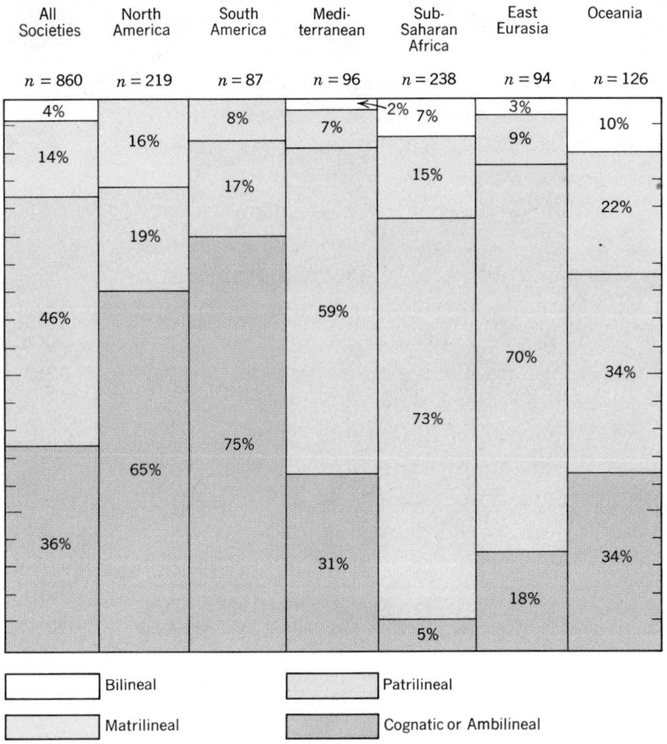

Figure 16.9

The relative frequencies of four types of social organization. Double descent is not shown since it is rare except in Australia. (Adapted from E. Bourguignon and L. Greenbaum, *Diversity and Homogeneity in World Societies.* New Haven: HRAF Press, 1973.)

incorporate them into our immediate families. In rare instances adults are also incorporated in this way. There are no legal barriers to the adoption of adults, but there are few reasons in our own culture for it to occur. In other societies adult adoption may serve an important social function, as might other forms of fictive kinship such as the establishment of blood brotherhoods.

A nonkinship legal fiction that has had great power in American society is the equation of corporations with individuals under the protection of the Fourteenth Amendment to the Constitution. Corporations, like individuals, have the right to declare bankruptcy, and when they do so individual stockholders are protected from liability. Many historians have pointed out that the rapid industrialization of the United States was greatly facilitated by the legal fiction of corporate identity and its protection under the Constitution. Social fictions are probably a universal means of justifying contradictions in what are supposed to be coherent rule systems. They are accepted as true because they reduce the many strains that emerge between the ideal and the real in social life.

DIAGRAMING KIN RELATIONS

Before we plunge into the maze of kinship terminology, you should play with the following strings of kin terms and their accompanying diagrams.

ego = I, or the person whose kinship is being traced; F = father; M = mother; U = uncle; A = aunt; GF = grandfather; GM = grandmother; B = brother; S = sister; C = cousin; s = son; d = daughter; ne = nephew; ni = niece; gs = grandson; gd = granddaughter; gch = grandchild.

1. My father's father is my grandfather.

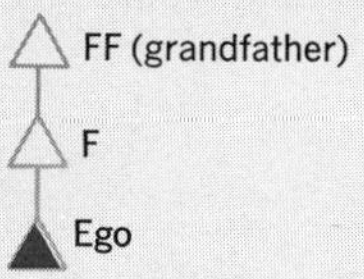

2. My father's father is my *lineal* relative. My relation to him is *direct.*

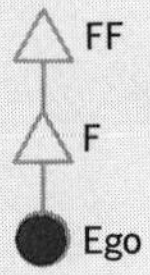

3. My mother's father's mother is my great grandmother. My relation to her is direct. She is my lineal relative.

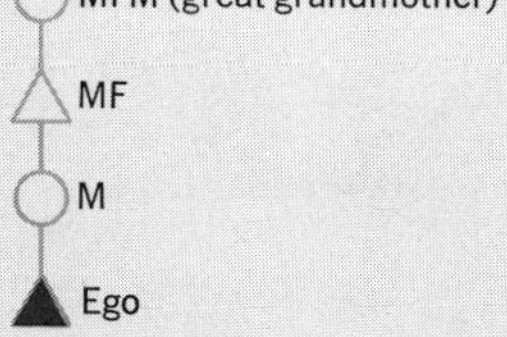

4. My mother's brother's daughter is my cousin. My relation to her is *indirect. It is traced through a linking relative,* in this case *either* my mother's father or my

mother's mother. My cousin is a *collateral* relative.

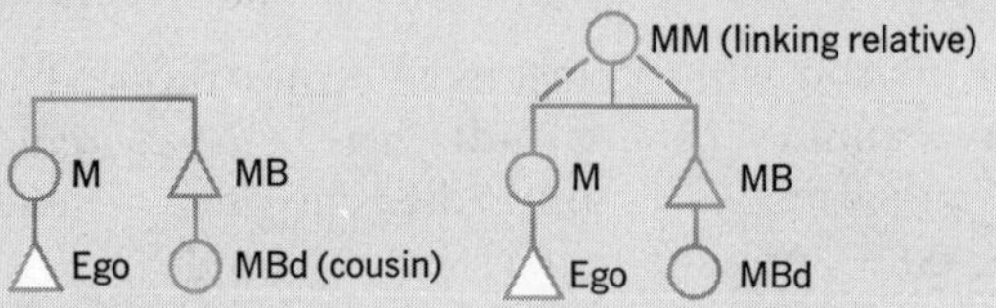

5. My brother and sister are also collateral relatives. The linking relatives between us are our mother and father. Brothers and sisters are collateral relatives but they are closer to me than cousins because there are fewer links between us.

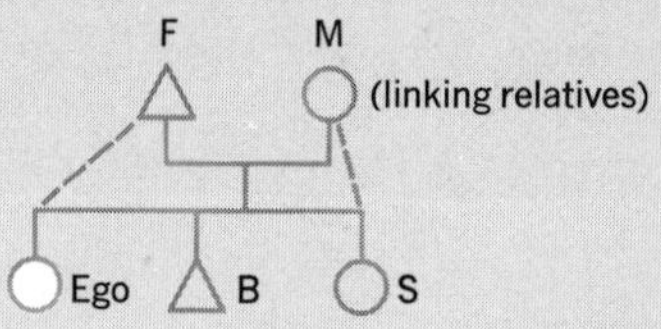

6. My mother's father's sister's son's daughter *or* son (MFSsd/s) is my second cousin.

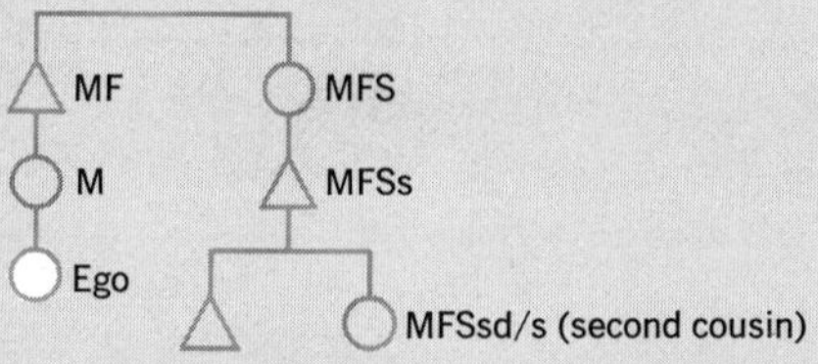

7. My FFBds/d is also my second cousin.

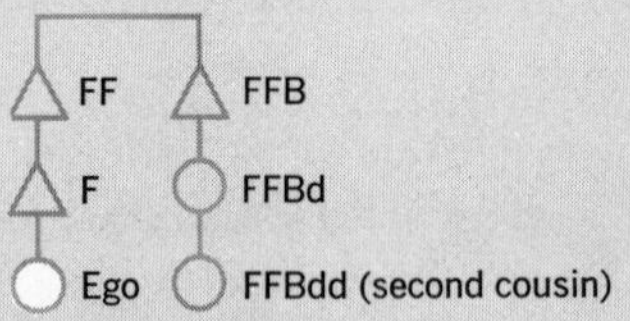

8. My FMMFBddss/d is my fourth cousin.

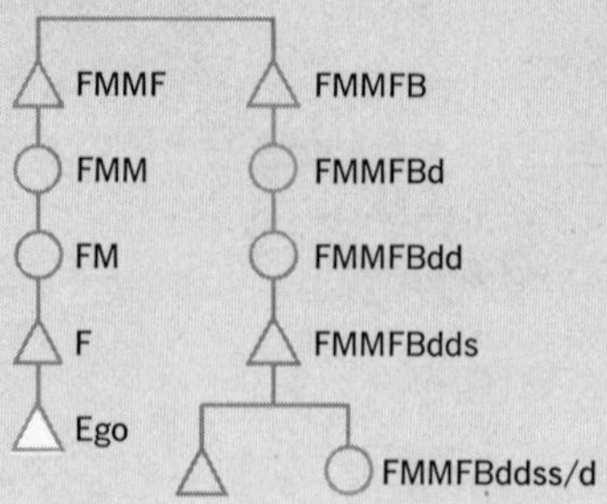

9. My FFMSsd is in generation plus-one while my FFMSsdds is in generation minus-one.

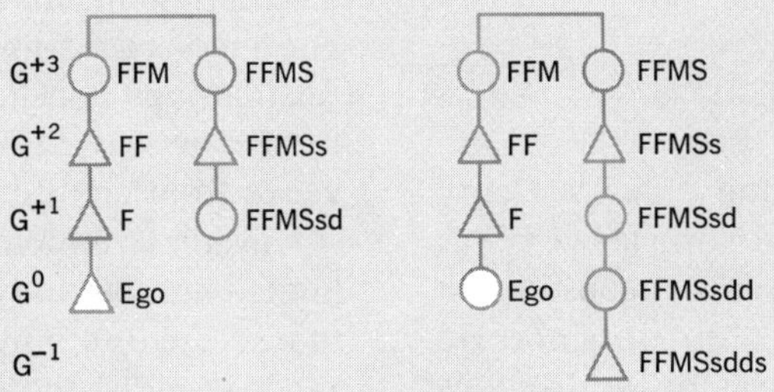

10. My FMMFBssdd is a fourth cousin. One linking relative between us is FMMFM. The other is FMMFF.

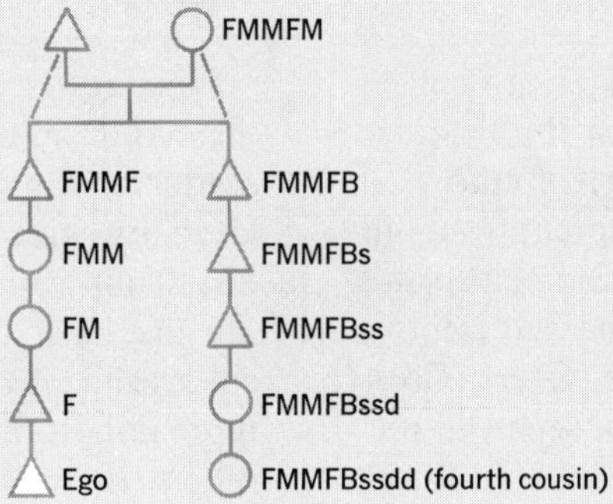

11. An ego's lineal, collateral, and affinal (relatives by marriage) kin.

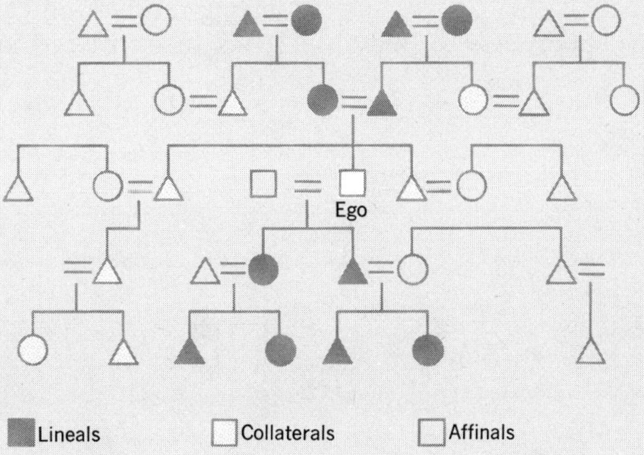

KINSHIP TERMINOLOGY

In the late nineteenth century Lewis Henry Morgan, a Rochester, New York lawyer, was charged with the task of writing a constitution for his fraternal group, the Gordian Knot. He decided to base it on the laws of the Iroquois Federation. A group of Iroquois lived near Rochester, and so he embarked on what was to become one of the earliest field studies of social organization.

One of the things Morgan did was to collect kinship terminology; that is, what the Iroquois called their different relatives. He found that the Iroquois kinship system is different from our own. Among these Native Americans a person's parallel cousins are called by the same terms that are applied to brothers and sisters. Cross cousins, on the other hand, are a separate recognized category (Figure 16.10). In addition, mother and mother's sister are called by a single term, and father and father's brother are also called by a single term.

Later, Morgan had the opportunity to study another Native American society, with a language unrelated to Iroquois. Although the actual words for kinsmen were different, the system used was identical to that of the Iroquois. Still later, Morgan discovered another type of kinship system. His work showed that, although kinship is based to some degree on biological relationships, kinship systems as such are cultural. The way in which people categorize kin varies from culture to culture.

Kinship terminologies can be classified into a limited number of types, each of which appears to be related to other features of social organization. Among those factors that appear to affect kinship terminology are residence patterns, marriage rules, and descent systems.

Categories of Kinship

Kinship terms are systematic and are based on certain potential distinctions that can be made among kinsmen. Generation, sex, collaterality, bifurcation (the cross versus parallel distinction), and the elder-younger distinction are the most common criteria of consanguineal kinship. In some systems the sex of ego is more important than the sex of the kinsmen. In others the sex of linking kinsmen (which forms the basis of bifurcation) separates categories. There are also systems in which the death of a linking relative will change a whole set of kin terms. In any case all kinship systems consist of

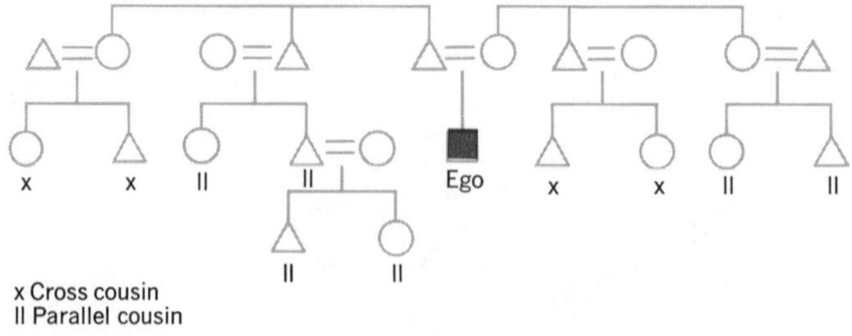

Figure 16.10

Cross versus parallel cousins. Cross cousins are the children of the opposite-sex siblings of one's parents. Parallel cousins are the offspring of the same-sex siblings of one's parents.

categories that can be used to lump biologically different relatives under a single term and to distinguish members of one set from another. Different systems rely on different criteria.

In discussing kinship terms I shall use English words in quotation marks to refer to kin called by the same term. In each case the word used will be borrowed from the English term applied to ego's closest kinsmen. Thus, when I refer to father and father's brother in the Iroquois system I will use the term "father" or the abbreviation "F" for both kinsmen. You should note, however, that the Iroquois do not call their fraternal uncles "father," but rather apply a single kinship term to both their biological father and their paternal uncles.

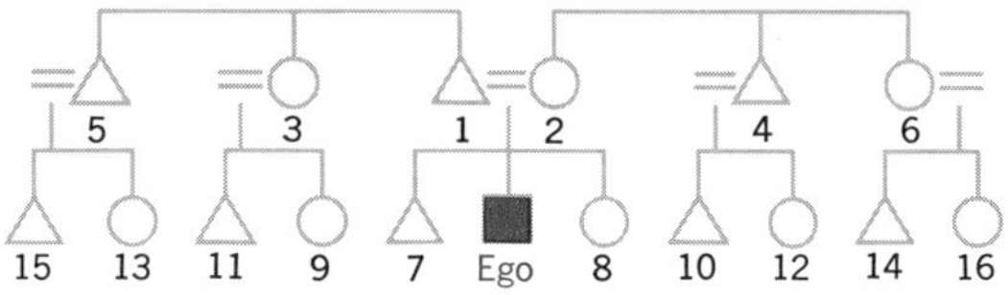

Figure 16.11
Sudanese terminology. Every relative is referred to by a different term, as indicated by the numbers.

Sudanese Terminology

In **Sudanese** terminology, a very rare form of kinship classification, every type of relative is referred to by a different term and no types are lumped (Figure 16.11). In our system in contrast to the Sudanese system, for example, we merge father's brother's children, father's sister's children, mother's brother's children, and mother's sister's children under the same term- "cousin." Of course, we also merge other kin, such as father's brother and mother's brother as "uncle."

Bifurcate-Merging Systems: Iroquois Terminology

Figure 16.12 presents a typical **Iroquois** (or **bifurcate-merging) system.** The term *bifurcate merging* is used because parallel cousins (father's brother's children and mother's sister's children) are merged with one's own brother and sister, while cross cousins (father's sister's children and mother's brother's children) are distinguished. In addition, other cross and parallel relatives are distinguished. Thus, mother and mother's sister, who are parallel relatives, are grouped under one term, as are the male parallel relatives, father and father's brother. The cross relatives—father's sister and mother's brother—are given a separate category which I would label "uncle" and "aunt." In the generation below a male ego, any children of individuals that ego calls "brother" are referred to by the same term that ego applies to his own children. With a female ego the children of any individual that ego calls "sister" will be called by the same term that ego applies to her own children. A male ego's sister's children or a female ego's brother's children will be cross relatives and a special term will mark this distinction. A male ego's relationship to his own

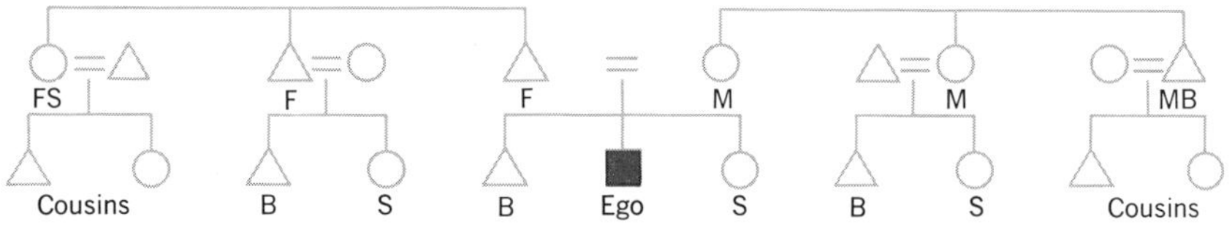

Figure 16.12
Iroquois terminology showing the cross-parallel distinction in ego's and ego's parent's generations.

sister's children is equivalent to ego's own relationship to his mother's brother. He is, after all, the mother's brother to his sister's children.

The Iroquois, after whom the system is named, are not, of course, the only group with this terminology. They do, however, provide a good example of the type of social organization that is associated with this system. They have a moiety organization and bilateral cross-cousin marriage; that is, preferred marriage is with a cross cousin. In addition, they are matrilineal. Moiety organization is associated with bilateral cross-cousin marriage and individuals in ego's moiety will be referred to as "brother" and "sister" while members of the opposite moiety will be referred to as "cousins."

Descriptive Versus Classificatory Systems: Eskimo Terminology

Morgan noticed that, among all the systems he collected, only one kept all direct lineal relatives separate terminologically. All other systems merged some lineal relatives with collaterals. A **collateral** relative is any relative that is not related directly to ego as an ancestor or descendant. Father, father's father; son, son's son; mother, mother's mother, etc. are lineal relatives. Uncles, cousins, brothers, and sisters are all collateral relatives. The system that separates all collaterals from all lineal relatives is known as **Eskimo** kinship terminology (Figure 16.13). It is found in various forms among Eskimo groups and among ourselves!

The Eskimo system recognizes distinctions between kinsmen based on *sex* (father versus mother, uncle versus aunt, son versus daughter, etc.), *generation* (mother versus grandmother, father versus son, etc.), and differences in *collaterality* (son versus nephew, daughter versus niece, brother versus cousin, mother versus aunt, etc.). The Iroquois system also recognizes age and sex, but does not, as I have already noted, distinguish between different degrees of collaterality. Thus, father, a lineal (and therefore a collateral of degree zero) is lumped with father's brother (who is a collateral of degree one) in the same kinship term. Brothers and sisters (who are collateral-degree-one relatives) are lumped with parallel cousins, who are degree-two relatives, and separated from cross cousins, who are also degree-two collateral relatives.

Morgan called systems that separate lineal and collateral relatives *descriptive kinship terminologies.* He called systems that merge lineals and collaterals in any way *classificatory kinship terminologies.* Descriptive systems are rare among the world's peoples. They are associated with social systems in which the independent nuclear family is the major productive and social unit. This is the case among Eskimo hunters as well as modern Americans.

Crow and Omaha Terminology

Many of the world's kinship systems recognize generation as a general criterion for distinguishing one kinsman from another. Not all of them do, however. There are two major exceptions that are mirror images of each other. These are known as **Crow** and **Omaha** systems (Figures 16.14 and 16.15). Both are associated with corporate lineage organization, but the Crow system is found almost exclusively among matrilineal peoples and the Omaha system is found almost exclusively among patrilineal groups.

The main feature of Crow and Omaha systems is the suppression (or better, the skewing) of generation distinctions among the offspring of mother's brother and father's sister. In the Crow system the mother's brother's children (who are in ego's generation) are called by the same terms that a male ego applies to his own children. Thus they are reduced from generation zero (ego's own generation) to generation minus-one (the generation below ego). On the other hand, father's sister's children are terminologically equivalent to ego's own parents or father's sister and her husband. Although they are also in generation zero, they are kept in generation plus-one.

In the Omaha system reverse skewing occurs. Mother's brother's offspring are kept in generation one above ego and father's sister's children

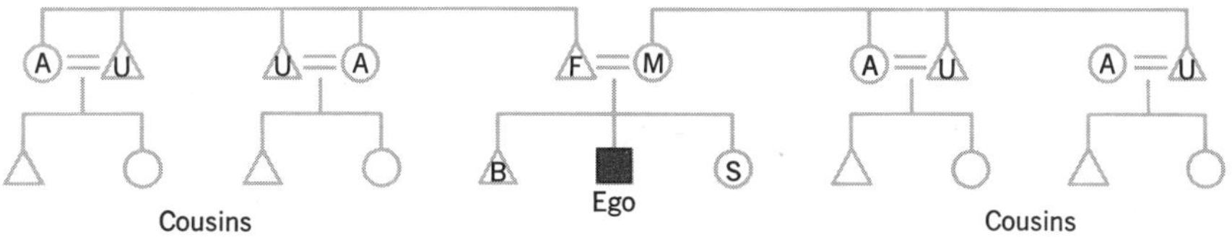

Figure 16.13

Eskimo terminology showing the separation of lineal and collateral relatives. (This is also the American kinship system.)

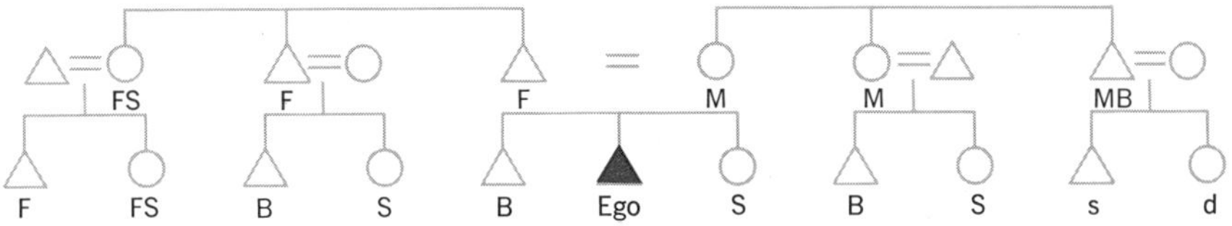

Figure 16.14

Crow terminology for a male ego. Note the skewing of generations for mother's brother's offspring and father's sister's offspring.

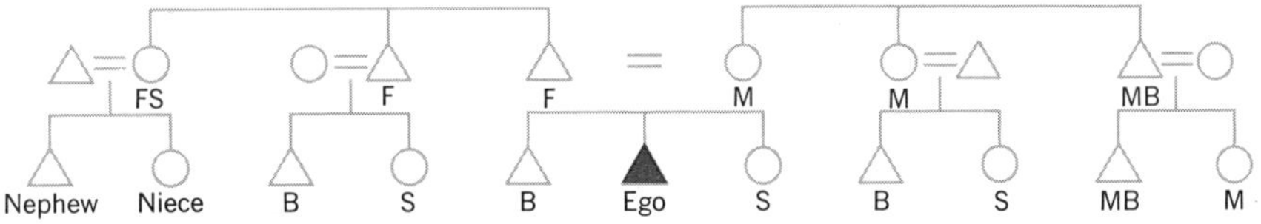

Figure 16.15

Omaha terminology for a male ego. Note the skewing of generations for father's sister's offspring and mother's brother's offspring. Omaha terminology is a mirror image of Crow terminology.

are dropped one generation below ego, making them equivalent to ego's own children or ego's nephew and niece.

Crow and Omaha Terminology and Lineages. We can look at Crow and Omaha systems another way. In the Crow system the members of ego's own matrilineage are divided by a large number of kinship terms. Other members of ego's kindred (those who belong to ego's father's matrilineage) are lumped into only a few categories. In the Omaha system, as usual, the reverse occurs. The members of ego's own patrilineage have a large number of kinship terms applied to them while the members of ego's mother's patrilineage tend to be lumped together.

Variations in Crow and Omaha Systems. In actual practice Crow and Omaha systems vary in complexity and the degree to which distinctions are made between

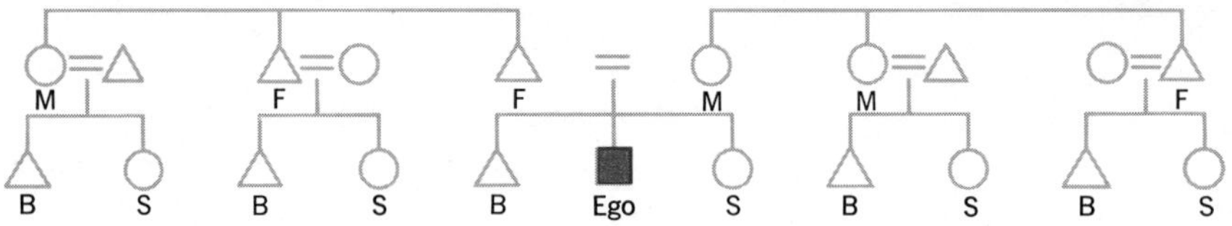

Figure 16.16

Hawaiian terminology showing the merging of lineals and collaterals in each generation. The only distinctions shown here are those of sex and generation. It should be noted, however, that Hawaiian terminology often involves the use of elder-younger distinctions.

relatives. Some of these systems appear to recognize parallel and cross distinctions (bifurcation) among certain kin while others do not. The Abron, who have a Crow system, distinguish between mother's brother and father's brother. Mother's brother is given an "uncle" term while father's brother (a parallel relative, remember) is merged with father. On father's side there are two alternate terms for father's sister. One of these shows no cross-parallel distinction. Instead, father's sister is called by the same term as one's own mother (*nna*). The alternate term (*sewa*), on the other hand, is equivalent to "aunt" and recognizes her cross status.

Hawaiian Terminology

Not all kinship systems are so complex. Let us turn to one that is much simpler, the **Hawaiian** system (Figure 16.16), which is widely distributed in Polynesia. In the Hawaiian system major distinctions are made only on the basis of generation and sex. Members of any one generation are merged into two categories: males and females. Thus, all members of generation plus-two are given terms equivalent to "grandmother" and "grandfather." All of ego's relatives in his or her own generation are given terms equivalent to "brother" and "sister." All of ego's relatives in generation minus-one are terminologically equivalent to ego's "sons" and "daughters."

Elder-Younger Distinctions. There is a further wrinkle in Hawaiian systems, however. Polynesian societies are very conscious of seniority. Thus a whole series of terms ("elder father" vs. "younger father," "elder mother" vs. "younger mother," for example) that reflect relative age status in each generation is part of the Hawaiian system.

Elder-younger distinctions are recognized elsewhere in the world. Many African societies, the Abron among them, take seniority very seriously within the context of the family and also the lineage. Their kinship system contains general terms for brother and sister (*heko* and *eyeko*) and elder-younger terms that can be applied to any sibling regardless of sex. Thus, *hano* means elder sibling of either sex, and *velo* means younger sibling of either sex.

AFFINAL KINSHIP

Kinship systems may also contain terms for affinal relatives. When societies distinguish affinal from consanguineal kin they are, of course, activating another of many potential contrasts (affinal versus consanguineal). In English we use only the term "in-law" plus consanguineal kin terms to indicate different affinal relatives. The number of these relatives in our own system is quite small. We recognize son- and daughter-in-law, father- and mother-in-law, and brother- and sister-in-law.

Although the French kinship system is similar to the American, it does display differences in both consanguineal and affinal kin terms. Thus, *cousin* is a male cousin while *cousine* is a female cousin. This difference is rooted in the gender distinctions of the French language. On the affinal side, instead of a term equivalent to in-law plus relative, the French attach the words *beau* and *belle* to the words for father, brother, mother, and sister (*beau père, beau frère, belle mère, belle sœur*). This usage is again in keeping with requirements of gender and the agreement between nouns and adjectives in French. On the other hand, special terms exist for son-in-law, *genre,* and daughter-in-law, *bru.* While the American system has separate terms for both spouses (husband and wife), French and other European languages borrow the word for woman (*femme* in French, *frau* in German) and add an appropriate pronoun (*ma femme*—"my wife," *sa femme*—"his wife") to indicate a wife. In French a husband is *mari.* A term for spouse does exist in both masculine and feminine forms (*époux, épouse*).

The differences between the American and French kinship systems are due, in great measure, to linguistic patterns. Other differences, in kinship systems in general, as we have seen, are due to correlations between terminology and the social system. Kinship systems are linguistic and the differences among various kin terms are semantic. The underlying basis for most kinship systems as semantic systems will rest on both social conditions *and* the structure of the language. The categories used to distinguish kin will, in most cases, be strongly influenced by social structure at large, but the system will also have to conform to linguistic principles.

Kinship terminology is part of a culture's cognitive structure. It is both social and semantic. As a reflection of real behavior, it faces outward toward social interaction. As a reflection of logical order, it faces inward towards the organization of thought.

Summary

Human family units are highly variable. The nuclear family (a husband and wife with their children) is the type most familiar to middle-class Americans, but there are many others. There are cultures in which husbands and wives live in separate houses. In many of these cases women live with their young male children and their daughters while men live with their sons as soon as the latter can leave their mother's care. Families may be of the extended type. The stem family consists of an old couple living with their eldest son, his wife, and their children. The joint family consists of a group of brothers and their spouses and children living together with or without their own parents. Both kinds of extended family are associated with the economics of family life.

Individuals are born into a family of orientation. Marriage creates a family of procreation. This is part of a phenomenon known as the *domestic cycle,* the series of changes in a family's structure that take place through time.

An individual's relatives on both sides form what is known as a *kindred.* All individuals except siblings have different kindreds, although the kindreds of close relatives overlap to a considerable degree. In traditional societies, where kinship plays a major role in social life, an individual may appeal to members of his or her kindred in times of need.

In many parts of the world, however, the role of kinship is complicated by the existence of descent groups. These are units with a definite bounded membership. Every member of a descent group claims to be able to trace membership back to the same ancestor. While kindreds consist of that group of people to whom an individual is related, descent groups are based on the principle of common descent from an ancestor.

Descent can be traced ambilaterally (through either the mother's or the father's line of kin) or unilineally (from father through a male line, or from mother through a female line). When descent is traced ambilaterally, the resulting group is cognatic. When descent is traced unilineally, the resulting group is unilineal.

Cognatic descent groups with fixed boundaries exist, but in order to avoid ambiguous membership (like that of the kindred), affiliation is often based on more than descent. In general, cognatic groups are based on descent and residence.

When individuals can activate links from either the mother's or the father's line in order to establish themselves in a residential cognatic descent group, the resulting group is a ramage. Ramages are found in many Polynesian societies.

A far simpler but less flexible way of forming a closed kin group is to trace descent exclusively through male or female links. When the links are male, the group is patrilineal. When the links are female, the group is matrilineal. Groups that trace descent from a common ancestor through males are patrilineages, and those that trace descent through females are matrilineages. The general term for these groups is *lineage.* The kind of descent group found in a society, as well as the absence of such groups, is related to environment, technology, other features of social organization, and ideology. In most instances descent and residence are *harmonious;* that is, matrilocal and avunculocal societies usually have matrilineages, and patrilocal societies have patrilineages.

Lineages may be grouped into clans. In general, clans are groups in which the members claim descent from a common ancestor but cannot demonstrate it. The links between clan members may be much less formal than the links between lineage members. While most lineages are exogamous, not all clans are. A group of clans may be grouped into a still more inclusive set of kin known as a *phratry.*

Some societies are organized into halves, moieties, which may or may not contain lineages and clans. In many cases each moiety has different ritual functions and most are also exogamous. When the latter is true, one moiety in the society exchanges spouses with the other.

Descent can also be double. This is the case when individuals inherit membership in one group from their fathers and in another group from their mothers. Among some Australian Aborigines, everyone is a member of a patrimoiety and a matrimoiety. These societies are divided into four units, resulting from the combination of two patrimoieties and two matrimoieties.

Means exist in many societies for manipulating the facts of social life. Since kinship is important in traditional societies, it should not be surprising to discover that one means of manipulating the system involves the creation of fictive kinship links among individuals. One form of fictive kinship is adoption. Individuals who are unrelated to a family or kin group can be legally adopted into that group. Such a means of incorporation is widespread and continues to function in American society.

Everywhere in the world people have labels which are used to define kin relationships. These constitute kinship terminologies. Kinship terminologies are systematic and are based on certain recognized distinctions that can be made among relatives. Generation, sex, collaterality, bifurcation, age, and the elder-younger distinction are the most commonly found criteria used to form kinship categories. Kinship systems can be classified into a limited number of types. In Sudanese systems each type of relative is given a separate term. There is no merging of relatives. In the Iroquois, or bifurcate-merging, terminology a distinction is made between cross and parallel relatives such that parallel cousins are assimilated into the classes "brother" and "sister" while cross cousins are classified as "cousins." Similarily father's brother and mother's sister are included in the classes "father" and "mother" while father's sister and mother's brother are "aunt" and "uncle."

The Eskimo system, which is also the American kinship system, separates lineal and collateral relatives. The terms "father," "mother," "son," "daughter," etc. are limited to lineal relatives, those who form a direct line of relationship.

In Crow and Omaha systems generation is not a major factor in creating categories. The Crow system is associated with the presence of matrilineages and the Omaha system is associated with patrilineages. Structurally they are the mirror images of each other. In Omaha, for example, father's sister's daughter is equal to ego's own daughter and in the Crow system mother's brother's daughter is equal to ego's own daughter.

In the Hawaiian system collaterals are merged with lineals but there is no bifurcation. Thus all of ego's relatives in the parental generation will be called either "father" or "mother." Similarly, all cousins will be called "brother" or "sister." The Hawaiian system, however, does make a distinction between elder and younger siblings and the birth order of all other relatives.

Kinship terminology is part of a culture's cognitive system. It is semantic (it has meaning) and it is social.

Bibliography

Bohannan, P. 1965 — The Tiv of Nigeria. In *Peoples of Africa,* edited by J. L. Gibbs, Jr. New York: Holt, Rinehart and Winston. More on Tiv ethnography, particularly social structure.

Buchler, I. R., and H. A. Selby 1968 — *Kinship and Social Organization: An Introduction to Theory and Method.* New York: Macmillan. An advanced book that takes a systematic approach to kinship, particularly kinship terminology.

Davenport, W. 1959 — Nonunilineal Descent and Descent Groups. *American Anthropologist.* 61:557–572. One of the first papers to examine cognatic descent.

Forde, C. D. 1950 — Double Descent Among the Yako. In *African Systems of Kinship and Marriage,* edited by A. R. Radcliffe-Brown and C. D. Forde. London: Oxford University Press. Discussion of double descent in a lineage-based society.

Fortes, M. 1953 — The Structure of Unilineal Descent Groups. *American Anthropologist* 55:17–41. The classic paper on unilineal descent.

Gough, K. 1959 — The Nayars and the Definition of Marriage. *Journal of the Royal Anthropological Institute.* 89:23–24. Paper on the absent spouse pattern among the Nayars.

Keesing, R. M. 1975 — *Kinship and Social Structure* New York: Holt, Rinehart and Winston. One of the best short introductions to the subject.

Murdock, G. P. 1949 — *Social Structure.* New York: Macmillan. Systems of classification, plus statistical tests of theories connecting kinship and social organization to psychological variables.

Schneider, D. M. 1968 — *American Kinship: A Cultural Account.* Englewood Cliffs, New Jersey: Prentice-Hall. An anthropologist looks at American kinship as a symbolic system.

CHAPTER 17
CROSS-CUTTING TIES

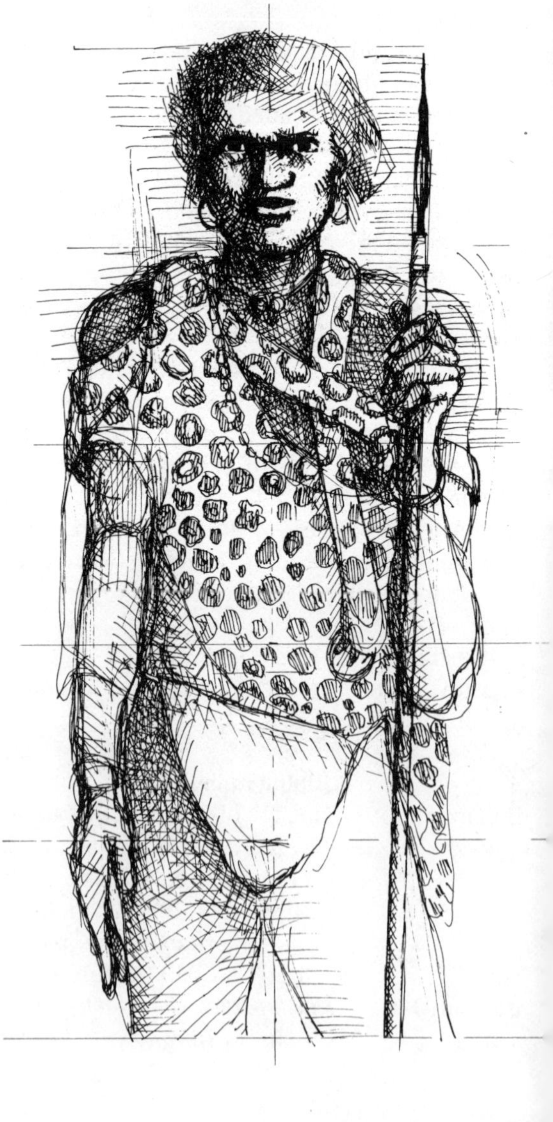

BEYOND KINSHIP: HORIZONTAL TIES

Social systems based on unilineal or cognatic descent and lacking some form of central political authority are subject to easy fragmentation. Politically they are fragile conglomerations, often unable to organize beyond the local level. The tendency to fragment may not be maladaptive under all circumstances, however. Anthropologist Marshall Sahlins has observed that segmentary lineage organization in Africa provides a powerful means for expansion. Under the pressure of population growth, when there is no land shortage, the segmentation of lineages allows groups to split away from the main body and establish themselves in a new territory. When lineages are threatened from the outside by superior military strength, they can activate their old ties with other segments whose members will come to their aid.

Societies organized according to descent groups have a set of vertical divisions. But cross-cutting horizontal divisions may also exist. Because they cut across loyalties based on descent, these divisions can serve to unify rather than further divide a social system. Among the organizing principles that can function in this way are *ritual interdependence, religious leadership, territorial affiliation, the elder-younger distinction, castes, and secret societies.*

Ritual Interdependence

The two divisions of a moiety organization are both competitive and cooperative. Each moiety is potentially a separate political entity that may express hostility toward its counterpart. Such hostility and competitiveness are often reduced to symbolic expression (athletic events, for example) and take place in a ritual context. Thus, whatever aggressions might develop between the members of each moiety are muted or at least channeled into a tension-reducing activity. Interdependence is enhanced in the symbolic realm when both moieties must cooperate in the performance of certain key rituals. While symbolic aggression may be acted out during these performances, the ritual itself cannot be successful without the full participation of both groups. Where moieties are exogamous, each needs the other for the exchange of spouses. The in-law relationship itself may be two-edged, since it unites the groups through kinship, but affinal relationships often create their own set of tensions. Thus, on the social level moieties are true divisions, yet on the ritual level they may act together for the good of all. In many societies that lack moieties but do have lineages and/or clans, these social units may also function together in the performance of ritual.

Religious Leadership

Among some typical lineage-based societies certain religious authorities act for the entire social group. They may even settle disputes between lineages. The Nuer of the Sudan, studied by E. E. Evans-Pritchard, are split into segments based partially on territory, but ultimately on lineages. Evans-Pritchard notes that the smaller the local group, the more cohesive it is. Conversely, solidarity decreases among increasingly distant units.

> *It might be assumed, therefore, that there is always greater opposition between two groups than between the segments of either and that the segments are held together, as it were, by this external pressure, but we cannot admit that this view accords with the facts, because greater hostility appears to be felt between villages, groups of villages, . . . than between larger tribal sections and between tribes.*

Evans-Pritchard goes on to suggest that, paradoxically, Nuer society is held together by the set of mutual oppositions that exist between its many parts. This odd pattern is particularly evident in the occurrence of feuding.

The feud is a political institution, being an approved and regulated mode of behavior between communities within a tribe. The balanced opposition between tribal segments and their complementary tendencies towards fission and fusion . . . is evident in the institution of the feud which, on the one hand, gives expression to the hostility by occasional and violent action that serves to keep the sections apart and, on the other hand, by the means provided for settlement, prevents opposition developing into complete fission. The means of settlement is the leopard-skin chief. . . .

The leopard-skin chief is a sacred person without political authority, but as a ritual specialist he can exert some political control over feuding groups. He need not be obeyed, but if he acts wisely his decisions are generally accepted by the interested parties.

It was clear from the way in which my informants described the whole procedure that the chief gave his final decision as an opinion couched in persuasive language and not as a judgement delivered with authority. Moreover, whilst the sacredness of the chief and the influences of the elders carry weight, the verdict is only accepted because both parties agree to it. . . .

If the leopard-skin chief did not exist in Nuer society, he would have to be invented. The politics of kinship, based as it is on potentially hostile segments, provides no means for maintaining social order. The leopard-skin chief, a ritual specialist and not a chief in the political sense of the term, provides the forum for the settlement of disputes. It is his wisdom, manifested in his ritual knowledge, that allows him to function politically.

A Nuer leopard-skin chief. Although he has no real power he uses his religious authority and prestige to mediate disputes.

Territorial Affiliation

Although nonstate societies do not recognize national territory as an organizing principle, territorial allegiance may emerge under certain conditions. If descent and postmarital residence are in harmony (if, for example, a society is both patrilineal and patrilocal), any local group is likely to define itself by both kinship and territory. The territorial affiliation may be reinforced by identification with sacred places that either serve the local group or are under their protection.

When a society is divided into several villages, members of the same lineage may live in different and sometimes distant places. Local loyalty may surface under some conditions, while kinship affiliations may be activated under other conditions. Where several lineages or parts of lineages occupy the same territory, local loyalty may be an important force in social organization. In societies with a harmonious relationship between descent and residence, group loyalty is strengthened by both village *and* lineage affiliation.

Matrilineal organization is relatively unstable; it is found primarily in agricultural societies where women perform much of the labor and have considerable economic power. The instability develops because even in matrilineal societies men hold the majority of political offices. If residence is patrilocal, women of the matrilineage move away. If it is matrilocal, a woman will have conflicting loyalties to her husband and to her brothers, who are the active members of her matrilineage. Frequently, matrilineality and matrilocality occur in a large village where several matrilineages occupy different neighborhoods. Men leave the immediate proximity of their matrilineages, but do not reside far away. They are thus able to maintain an active role in the affairs of their own lineages.

The Hopi Indians of the southwestern United States are matrilineal and matrilocal. The pueblo itself is a concentrated settlement made up of several clans. Agriculture is the major economic activity. Women are at the center both economically and politically, while men occupy most of the ritual roles. Men have little power in their wives' households. A woman may divorce her husband by simply putting his shoes outside the door. Men are tied into the system through their important place in ceremonial life. They occupy most religious offices. Ritual, particularly in relation to agriculture and the magical control over rainfall, is vital to these people who live under very arid conditions. Economic pursuits are closely linked to ritual performance, and religious groups are of great importance to the entire community.

The Mundurucu of the Brazilian lowlands, studied by Yolanda and Robert Murphy, are patrilineal but matrilocal. Mundurucu ideology is strongly male-oriented and the men believe that they dominate society. Women, however, are the mistresses of their own houses. Men sleep and spend much of their time in a communal men's house. Because they leave their own social group at marriage, men from scattered locations must deal with a set of united women. Daily life is at least equally controlled by women.

Taos Pueblo (New Mexico), ca. 1935. The people of Taos, like the Hopi and other pueblo peoples, have a strong attachment to place as well as to a kinship group.

The Elder-Younger Distinction and Age Grades

I have already noted in several contexts that the criterion for the division of labor in simple, small-scale societies is limited to differences in sex and age. Age groups always provide a potential basis for horizontal loyalty, as well as for the establishment of real status differences.

Elder-younger distinctions are found in many cultures. Frequently these are not institutionalized, but appear in the comportment of individuals. That is, younger people are expected to defer to their elders. In some African societies, particularly among the cattle peoples of East Africa, however, age groups have become an aspect of organized social life. Individuals, usually only boys, are born into an **age set.** This age set consists of all (male) children born within a limited period (let us say a span of five years). Each age set takes a name and every member is seen as part of a group that will move through a system of changing responsibilities. In other words, each age set will pass through a series of stages or **grades.** When a set occupies a particu-

Among the Masai, a cattle people of Kenya, youths of one age grade are responsible for cattle herding.

lar grade, its members are expected to perform certain specified tasks. Among cattle peoples, in the first age grade with responsibility the members assume care of the herds. The next age grade may require military service, while a later grade may involve some low degree of political authority. The next stage may yield elder status and greater power, and the last may lead to retirement from active participation in the life of the social group. As each age *set* moves up into a new age *grade,* it is replaced by a younger age set. In age-graded societies loyalty to one's own age set may, and frequently does, cross-cut ties to one's lineage.

The Nyakyusa of Tanzania, studied by Monica Wilson, present an extreme example of age-grade organization. Among the Nyakyusa a village is not inhabited by a group of kinsmen but rather by a group of age mates with their wives and young children. The Nyakyusa are patrilineal and patrilocal. But in this society such a statement means only that wives come to live in the age village of their husband, not that a man's village consists of his patrilineal relatives. In fact, members of any one patrilineage are scattered through the territory.

The age-village starts when a number of herd-boys, about 10 or 11 years old, build together at the edge of their fathers' village. . . .

A boy's village starts quite small with, perhaps, not more than ten or a dozen members, but it grows as young boys from the fathers' village, or from other men's villages in the neighborhood become old enough to join it. When the original members are fifteen or sixteen years old the village is usually closed to any further ten-year-olds, who must then start a new village on their own. . . .

The boys who thus establish a village continue to live together through life. When they marry they bring their wives to the village and, when the last of them die, the village dies.

A shadow (or parody) of age-grade organization exists in the institution of class-year membership at colleges and universities. Freshmen may be forced to wear beanies or other identifying clothes and seniors may be granted privileges not extended to the members of other classes. In addition, particular age sets may be marked for life by their year of graduation.

Members of these sets may be invited back to the campus for special ceremonies at specific times according to a fixed cycle.

Castes

A true caste system, *as system,* pervading every level of society, only exists in India. Castes are stratified and endogamous occupational groups. In India if you are a weaver you must be a member of a weaver caste, if you cut hair you must be a member of a barber caste. This does not mean that every member of a weaver caste weaves or that every member of a barber caste cuts hair. There are certain other occupations open to members of each caste, usually some form of agricultural activity. People are born into castes and remain members of their castes for life. Individuals born into groups that perform "polluting" activities, such as cleaning latrines, are not even considered to be members of caste society. They are outcastes and are referred to as "untouchables," since no caste member is supposed to have any physical contact with them.

Because occupation is based on cast membership, the caste system creates an economic interdependence that cuts across the vertical lineage distinctions that also exist in Indian society. Lineages are united through ties of marriage. Because they are exogamous, mates must be sought in other lineages. Castes, however, are endogamous; members must marry within the group. Thus, marriage ties unite separate lineages within each caste while caste organization unites the entire society through a system of interlocking economic ties.

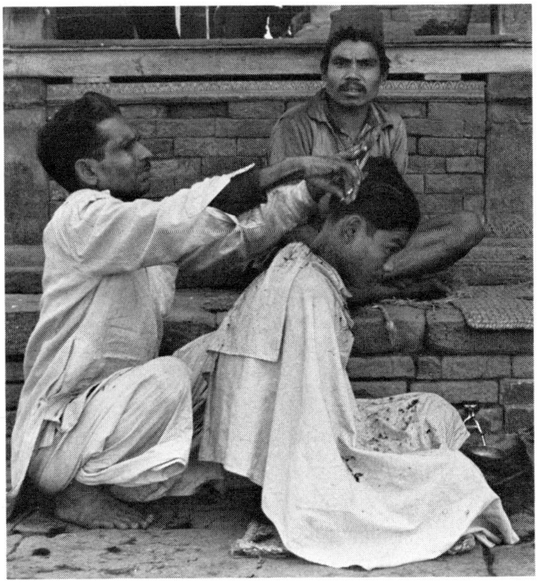

A member of the barber caste cuts hair in India.

Since independence India has attempted to do away with the system of occupational castes and has outlawed the principle of untouchability. While many untouchables have entered public service and some have risen to high rank, the status of outcaste is still prevalent in rural India among the vast peasant population.

Indian society is pervaded by its caste system, but there are other societies with some endogamous occupational castes. African societies living on the southern fringe of the Sahara Desert often have castes of ironsmiths who are segregated from the rest of society and who marry among themselves. These ironsmiths are usually a despised group and might best be described as outcastes, since they occupy the same position as untouchables in India.

In Japan there is a group known as *Burakumin* who live in isolated communities and have little contact with the mainstream of Japanese society. These individuals are the descendants of butchers and meat handlers who lived during a period of Buddhist piety. Strict Buddhists are vegetarians. In less tolerant times Japanese Buddhists looked down on anyone who had anything to do with the killing of animals and the preparation of meat. These individuals became a caste. In present-day Japan laws exist to help Burakumin integrate into the mainstream. So far, however, prejudice against the *Burakumin* remains strong and there is little intermarriage between them and other Japanese.

Japan is a modern industrial nation-state, and little would change if the *Burakumin* were absorbed through intermarriage. Although India is also an independent nation well on the way to industrialization, it is still primarily a peasant culture. If castes were eliminated from the social structure of rural India, the entire fabric of Indian society would change significantly.

Secret Societies

In parts of West Africa, particularly in Liberia, the Ivory Coast, Sierra Leone, and the Republic of Guinea, a network of secret societies existed—and in some places continues to exist—that cut across not only village and lineage boundaries, but sometimes across the boundaries of ethnic groups. There are both men's and women's societies. These groups have a policing function and exert considerable political-legal control over the populations among whom they are organized. Membership in these societies is not secret and they are so named because each has special rituals known only to initiates. Early missionary accounts of these groups, particularly of the *Poro* societies of Liberia, distorted their purpose and pictured them as bloodthirsty cults. Nothing could be farther from the truth.

As with leopard-skin chiefs, secret societies draw much of their power from ritual functions. Many are charged primarily with the initiation of adolescents into adult status. K.L. Little, who has worked among the Mende in Sierra Leone and Liberia, lists the following principal secret societies and their functions: the *Poro,* who initiate young boys; the *Sande,* who regulate women's affairs; the *Humoi,* who are charged with the regulation of sexual conduct among both sexes; the *Njayei,* who are concerned with agricultural fertility and the treatment of certain diseases; and the *Wunde,* who provide military training.

Each of these societies has an educational function that it fulfills during its initiation rites. The Poro and the Sande particularly function as teachers, educating the young in the customs and ethnic lore of the region.

Little describes the structure of these institutions and compares them to the medieval church in Europe.

A Poro ceremony. The costumed and masked Gbetu represents a mountain spirit controlled by men of the Poro society. The Gbetu is accompanied by its speaker, horn-blower and flag-bearer, all characters in this aspect of Poro ritual.

In terms of their institutional personnel and apparatus of hereditary officials, masked spirits, rituals, etc., the secret societies are an embodiment of and a means of canalizing supernatural power. . . . Like the medieval church, they lay down various rules of conduct, proscribe certain forms of behavior, and are the sole agency capable of remitting certain sins. On the other hand, both their control over supernatural power and their regulation of lay conduct and behavior is, to some extent, departmental, and even a matter of specialization. That is to say, particular fields of the cultural life and their regulation tend to fall within exclusive province of specific societies. The combined effect, however, is to produce a general pattern of life influenced very largely by secret society activity and function.

It should be clear by now that kinship-based societies do not necessarily lack mechanisms of integration that tie its members into the wider social fabric. Only the least differentiated and smallest-scale societies lack at least one of the institutions discussed here. They are small enough to maintain social integration without special means.

Summary

Social systems based on descent, lacking some form of central political authority, are subject to easy fragmentation. Sometimes such fragility is adaptive because it allows individual groups to expand over a wide territory. Frequently institutions exist in descent-based societies that function to create some kind of horizontal tie that can hold a loose federation of lineages or clans together. These institutions differ widely in the principles of organization. They include:

1. Ritual interdependence, which is frequently found in association with moiety organization.
2. Religious leadership, in which a priest figure also acts as a chief and can use sacred authority to influence political decisions. The leopard-skin chief among the Nuer of the Sudan is one such figure. While the leopard-skin chief cannot enforce his judicial and political decisions, he has a good knowledge of social reality and can influence politics through force of argument and the respect in which he is held.
3. Territorial affiliation, in which there is a sense of place based on common residence and membership in the social group.
4. Age grades, in which a group of men whose membership cuts across lineage lines moves together into different status positions. Age grades are common in East Africa among cattle-herding peoples. Different grades are associated with such rights and duties as herding, military activity, government, and elder status with an advisory function.
5. Castes are endogamous occupational groups. When an entire social system is based on caste organization, the society is held together by economic interdependence. In India, the only full-scale caste society known, lineages within castes are united through marriage while castes are united through the economic system.
6. Secret societies, common in West Africa, serve an educational and political function. In Liberia and Guinea as well as parts of the Ivory Coast several secret societies for men or women exist that cut across village, and in some cases, even ethnic divisions. Membership in these societies is known. What makes them secret is the ritual associated with each, ritual that is open only to initiates.

Bibliography

Evans-Pritchard, E. E. 1940 — *The Nuer.* Oxford: Oxford University Press. A classic ethnography discussing lineage structure, law, age grades, and the role of religious "chiefs" in the life of an African cattle people.

Hammond, D. 1972 — *Associations.* Reading, Mass: Addison-Wesley Modular Publications, 14. An article on cross-cutting associations and age groups.

Little, K. L. 1960 — The Role of the Secret Society in Cultural Specialization. In *Cultures and Societies of Africa.* Edited by S. and P. Ottenberg. New York: Random House. Examination of the role of male and female secret societies in West Africa.

Murphy, Y. and Murphy, R. 1974 — *Women of the Forest.* New York: Columbia University Press. An examination of women's power in a patrilineal but matrilocal society.

Wilson, M. 1960 — Nyakyusa Age-Villages. In *Cultures and Societies of Africa.* Edited by S. and P. Ottenberg. New York: Random House. The institution of age sets pushed to its ultimate expression and analyzed from the point of view of social structure.

CHAPTER 18

ECONOMIC ANTHROPOLOGY

Economics is concerned with human activities and social relations related to the *production* and *distribution* of *goods* and *services.*

In the United States we live in a capitalist society in which the profit motive contributes to a high degree of productivity and shapes much of our social life. In our system one goal of production is the creation of a surplus for reinvestment. This reinvestment leads to economic growth. The capitalist system is based on a market economy in which money plays an important role. Money can be used to pay for anything the market has to offer. It is an "all-purpose" medium of exchange. Money can be "made" through the placing of interest-bearing loans (investment), the rental of land or other forms of property, and profit from the sale of goods. Workers are paid a wage in money for their productive activities and use that wage to pay for necessary goods and services.

The traditional societies studied by anthropologists frequently have economic systems that differ markedly from our own. Except when they are locked into a national or international market these societies produce primarily for subsistence needs. Although some surplus may be produced, it is not the major goal of economic activity. When surplus is produced, it is often converted into prestige or used to mount elaborate religious ceremonies. In any case the goal of surplus production is not reinvestment for a profit. Many traditional societies either lack money altogether or have a medium of exchange that can be used for only limited types of transactions. In order to better understand some of these differences, let us compare a related set of economic activities in our own and in a traditional African society.

BUYING AND SELLING FOOD IN THE UNITED STATES AND A GHANAIAN VILLAGE

When Mr. and Mrs. Pennypicker go to the supermarket on Friday night, they stock up on a wide variety of food for the week. Which supermarket they choose depends on its distance from their house, the quality and variety of its products, and its pricing policy. As moneywise shoppers, the Pennypickers have compared prices in their local papers and clipped discount coupons published in order to entice them into a particular store. Taking a shopping cart, the Pennypickers systematically go down each aisle of the store taking products from the shelves. Each section of the store has special items such as frozen foods, soups, bread, dairy products, meat, and so on. Many of the items are packaged in brightly colored boxes or cans marked with brand names. Prices are stamped on each item and generally vary by brand. In most cases the supermarket offers its own brand at a price slightly lower than that of other companies. When they have finished their rounds, the Pennypickers wait on line at a checkout counter where a clerk totals their purchases on a cash register and bags their food for them. This clerk is the first store employee they have any contact with during their evening's shopping. When the groceries are totalled Mr. Pennypicker, who sells insurance for a large company, pays the bill by check, written on an account that is maintained by his monthly pay.

American supermarkets are complex business ventures run for a profit. African traditional markets are ways of conveniently exchanging small amounts of produce.

Most likely the supermarket in which the Pennypickers shop is owned by a large corporation. The chain has branch stores in many states and its own product-distribution system. It sells its own products, as well as the products of other companies, in large quantities. It employs a vast number of workers, but consumers themselves provide some of the labor required for shopping by pushing self-service carts as they make their rounds in the store. This self-service aspect of supermarket shopping reduces costs for the market owners. For these reasons supermarkets are able to sell their products at prices often considerably lower than those found in small, family-owned, neighborhood stores. Supermarket sales, in fact, now account for most of the grocery business in the United States.

Supermarkets are run specifically to make a profit for a large number of investors, who may never even visit a branch store. The corporation is run by a board of directors whose duty is to insure profits, but most local decisions are made by managers who specialize in such tasks as sales, pricing, buying, and corporation finance. It is these managers who are responsible for marketing and production. Corporation executives are at the head of a chain of command that may include regional directors, store managers, section managers, and such service personnel as butchers, wrappers, and checkout clerks. Although these individuals are all employees of the company, only the executive and managerial positions carry decision-making power.

Every Friday at dawn during the harvest season, Kousia Date, an Ashanti woman, goes to her lineage's gardens and picks a few surplus yams. Her kinship group has granted her the right to a certain quantity of their communal supply. She puts her yams into a large flat basin and, carrying a small stool, walks five miles to a village market. This market is open only on Friday, but it is part of a system of similar village markets open one day a week on a rotating basis. For a few pennies in local currency Kousia Date is allowed to set herself up in a section of the market reserved for yam traders with small amounts of produce. Everyone in her section is a woman and everyone charges the same price for a standard number and size of yams. Competition is fierce, but it consists of enticing verbal invitations to shop rather than aggressive pricing policy. Kousia Date will probably sell her yams to customers who know her well—other market women, friends, and kin. As she sits before her produce, she will have animated conversations with adjacent women and individuals in the passing crowd who stop to gossip and exchange information. If she is lucky, she will have sold her yams by late morning. If, at the end of the market day, she has some left, she will take them home to be cooked for the evening meal. Assuming that she is successful, she will take the money received for the yams and spend it on a few necessary items. She might buy some dried fish and a few vegetables to be used in the sauce that is served with the staple food, boiled and pounded yams. She might also buy some fuel for her lantern, or a piece of cloth to be made into a dress or wrap-around. In any case, when she returns home she will probably have spent most of the money she took in from the sale of yams.

Ghana is a "third world" country in transition. Traditional and modern economic systems exist side by side. The same market in which Kousia Date has carried out her small transactions will contain permanent trading stores that, although not as large and as well-stocked as American supermarkets, are run for a profit. They may even be branches of large trading companies. Markets in Ghana are also frequented by women who are the traditional cloth traders. Some of these are wealthy business people who live in large houses complete with servants and drive large European or American cars. Although they specialize in one product their often-realized goal is profit.

The activities just described are **production, distribution,** and **consumption.** These constitute the major elements of economic behavior. Other aspects of economics, including **labor, ownership, wages,** and **money,** have also been touched upon. We have seen how activities and customs that bear the same labels differ in two societies, one modern and the other traditional. We shall now take a deeper look at economic activities and customs to see whether or not these differences are central or superficial to an understanding of economic anthropology.

OWNERSHIP

In the United States and other capitalist countries private ownership is the basis of the economic system. Laws exist for the protection of private property, ranging from guarantees that it cannot be arbitrarily taken away to rules governing loss and bankruptcy. Individuals or corporations who own property are free to sell or rent it.

The land on which Kousia Date plants her yam garden is farmed by herself and other members of her matrilineage. They do not own it, nor do they rent it from anyone. Instead, they have *proprietary* (use) rights over it. These rights continue as long as it is farmed. If it is abandoned, title reverts to the village community. Even the village cannot sell it, however. Land is held in "trust" for those kin groups that make up the village population.

In hunting-and-gathering societies, where farming is not practiced, use rights are rarely divided among separate kin groups. Instead, the entire band is free to hunt and gather over an established territory. Such bands may also have title to water resources within their territory. In many cases hunting and water rights are associated with the notion that the people of a certain band "belong" to the land. This idea is an inversion of our Western view that land belongs to individuals.

Like hunters and gatherers, herders rarely divide their territory among kin groups. Nomadic communities as a whole may have rights over a wide area, across which they move their herds with seasonal changes in climate and vegetation. The stock that is raised, however, will in most cases belong to individuals or families rather than to the community or even to large kin groups. Thus, although lineages almost always exist in herding cultures, they often function as political and religious rather than as property-holding units.

A rather curious kind of property relationship existed until recently on the Aubrac plateau in central France. Cattle were owned, as private property, by individuals living in the nearby valleys. Grazing land on the plateau was owned by local peasants, again on an individual basis. During the winter cattle were kept and foddered in barns by their valley owners. In the spring the Aubrac peasants descended as a group into the valley and, according to contracts established over many generations, rented cattle from specific owners. The movement of cows into high pasture, where they spent the spring and summer months, was a festive occasion. The animals were decked in flowers for the migration. As they moved toward the high country, the music of their bells could be heard for miles around. During the pasturing season cows were milked each day by their peasant renters, who made the milk into Cantal cheese, later sold to local wholesalers. In the fall, before the snows, the cows were returned to their owners for winter feeding and shelter. The system of divided ownership, cows on the one hand and warm-season grazing land on the other, provided a form of economic integration between the people of two ecological zones.

PRODUCTION

The elements of production are work, access to resources, and access to the technological means of performing work. In addition, production may involve such facilities as transportation and storage.

Kousia Date works her garden with tools made by her husband. These are simple but efficient. After the yam harvest the tubers are stored on lineage property in large racks constructed out of natural materials by lineage members. The major aspect of production in Kousia Date's garden is labor; investment in costly technology is absent although tubers for planting are sometimes bought and the metal parts of the iron hoes and digging sticks she uses for cultivation are purchased in the local markets. When Kousia Date is not using her tools, they may be borrowed by a lineage mate or a friend in the village. This is not an unusual practice in traditional societies. Tools are often owned by individuals, but they are freely loaned when needed by others. Such tools, which are usually cheap and simple, are manufactured locally by either the users, the user's relatives, or specialists who sell them at low prices.

The supermarket in which the Pennypickers do their shopping is part of a highly mechanized system. Food is grown on large farms with the aid of motorized equipment. It is packaged in factories equipped with complex assembly lines, and it is transported in a fleet of heavy trailer trucks. The store itself is a large and expensive building equipped with such technological wonders as frozen food bins and computerized cash registers. The entire profit structure of the store is based on high volume, which itself depends on a large initial investment.

In technologically advanced societies, where factory production is the major economic mode, tools, equipment, and working space are specialized and expensive. The majority of the labor force must work for those who can afford to invest in complex machinery and large factories.

The Mode of Production and Work

All societies have distinctive patterns of controlling production and distribution. These patterns constitute **the mode of production.** In addition, technology and the way in which work is organized are part of the mode of production, as are the social relations that attach to any aspect of economic life. Societies that share the same technologies may have different modes of production if the **social relations of production** are different. A society that depends on slave labor, for example, has a different mode of production from one in which labor is paid for in wages. Production in any society is part of social organization.

African women tending their farm in Zaire. Such farming is labor intensive and involves little capital investment. Farms in the United States are often large and highly mechanized. They require relatively low labor input per production unit, but a high capital investment.

The Organization of Work

Work patterns depend on production goals (how much and when people wish to produce), the prevailing division of labor, existing technology, and environmental factors. We have already seen that in hunting-and-gathering societies the division of labor is based primarily on sex and age. Generally speaking, mature men hunt and women (sometimes with the aid of their children) gather. In horticultural and agricultural societies work patterns are highly variable, although men often perform most of the tasks requiring great strength.

Kousia Date's garden is cleared by the men of her lineage. They also plant the yams at the beginning of the rainy season. She plants other vegetable crops and is responsible for weeding. As the yam vines grow, the men return to the fields and tie them to poles, which they have cut and set in the fields. When mature, the yams are harvested by men and women working together. They are stored in yam racks constructed by men, and carried to the village, when needed, by women.

Yam gardening for the Ashanti is a subsistence activity. The majority of yams have been grown for eating by those who planted them, and there are no yam plantations dependent on hired labor. Time allocation (when and how long people work) as well as the intensity of work are governed by the needs of those who participate directly in the production process. In addition, yam cultivation is an individual activity. It does not require team work. Although it is customary for a group of men to plant at the same time, they do so for social reasons rather than for the requirements of the labor process. The organization of work in this case is quite open. When things are done depends on the seasons. Who does what is a matter of a simple division of labor between men and women. Except during the harvest season cooperation is minimal and unnecessary.

Cooperative labor, is, however, often an obligatory aspect of economic activity. The Mbuti of the Ituri Forest in Zaire hunt with the aid of nets. These are individually owned, but a successful hunt can only take place through cooperation. The game snared by the Mbuti is swift and agile. A man hunting alone would be unable, in most cases, to take full advantage of his individual skill. It is only when a line of nets is spread across an animal's path that the group is sure to capture it. We have seen that the hunting of large herd animals may also require group participation. This was the pattern on the plains of North America before the horse became a major feature of hunting technology. Activities such as house- or boat-building may be more efficient (and more fun) if they involve group participation. The construction of large irrigation works, the damming of streams, and the building of defensive fortifications demand cooperative labor as well as planning.

Net hunting among the Mbuti of Zaire requires cooperative labor among a group of male hunters.

Craft specialization and social differentiation, as in the development of castes or economic classes, create a division of labor. Yet the individuals performing different roles in society contribute to the overall integration of an economic, social, and political organization. Castes in India are craft- or task-specific. Members of each caste participate in only one aspect of economic life, but each specialization is a part of a total system. Although members of different castes are not allowed to marry, all castes are allied through economic and ritual ties.

Work schedules depend on such environmental variables as seasonal availability of resources and climate. In horticultural societies without irrigation systems, planting must occur near the beginning of the rainy season. Where slash-and-burn cultivation is practiced, trees and underbrush must be cut and burned before the rains begin. Planting usually takes place soon afterwards to forestall erosion of the bare soil. Harvest periods, of course, are determined by the rates at which different plants mature. Weeding patterns vary according to the amount and quality of the harvest desired. In traditional cultures the work rhythm is determined by individual and local group needs. These are usually linked rather closely to subsistence requirements.

In technologically advanced industrial society work patterns are controlled by the market place. Both employment and unemployment depend on the state of the economy. Lack of demand in one major industry affects the entire system. Production takes place on a large scale and involves hired labor. Workers own neither the tools they use nor the products they make. They have nothing to sell but their labor. For this they receive wages.

The Social Relations of Production

As we have already seen, in traditional societies kinship is the basis of the economic system. Work takes place in the familiar context of daily life, along with recreation, politics, and religious

Although industrial production accounts for most manufacturing in modern capitalist countries, craft industries still persist on a small scale. In many cases such handmade products are more pleasing than machine-made goods. Umbrella making in Japan. Weaving in the United States.

worship. All of these articulate with kinship. In these societies the social relations of production can only be understood in the context of specific types of kin group activity.

Kousia Date's garden is farmed by herself and her lineage mates. Her kin group does not hire people to work for it, and it alone owns the products of its labor. The tools Kousia Date uses in her work either belong to her or to kin and friends. As we have seen, these tools are either purchased locally at low prices or are manufactured by their users from readily available materials.

Lineages among the Ashanti, Kousia Date's ethnic group, are allied through marriage. Bride price exists and is quite expensive. Without the help of his lineage mates, a young man is unable to marry. This custom gives lineage authorities considerable power over their younger members. Not only can they influence the selection of a wife—thus controlling the alliances made by a lineage—they can also coerce their younger members to work for them in a variety of tasks, including wage labor outside the local economic system. The relations of production are based on lineage control over land, work, and access to marriage payments as well as a basic inequality between lineage elders and younger members.

To return to our own economic system, before the rise of industrial capitalism in Europe, small-scale craftspeople worked in family shops that were usually located in their homes. As the factory system emerged, these individuals were gradually pushed out of business. In most cases they were forced to enter the labor market as unskilled, or at best, semiskilled workers. Enclosure laws (the taking away of common pasture land) in the agricultural sector of the economy drove many peasants into the city, where they too became factory workers.

In modern capitalist society the relations of production are based on a class structure in which one class owns the means of production and the other works as free labor. When the majority of individuals in a society do not have access to land and/or tools, they may be forced by circumstance to work for others. Capital accumulation (saving for investment) is difficult for wage earners. Movement from one class into another, although it does occur, is therefore rare. How frequently it occurs depends on such factors as the ability of the economy to expand, the openness of the prevailing educational system, and the development of a managerial class. Large modern corporations are frequently run by *technocrats,* specially trained managers, some of whom have moved into executive positions from the ranks of the working class.

On the productive side we must not forget that capitalism unleashed a tremendous technological revolution that eventually transformed material life in the richer countries. Profit became the major goal of the capitalist class and the means of achieving success. The range and availability of products increased to an extraordinary degree. Items that were unimaginable or available only to the rich became commonplace and cheap. As capitalism developed, it became more and more dependent on consumption and, in many cases, waste. New markets are necessary for expansion, and these can only be created by raising the standard of living *and* by creating demand. The dynamic nature of capitalism, which has had both positive and negative consequences, can be traced directly to the profit motive. This is the major driving force of the "free enterprise" system. It changes the focus of labor from subsistence to the creation of products that will be sold to make further profits. The relationships that exist among workers and between workers and employers are a special feature of the capitalist system. When we compare traditional societies and our own economics, we can see that capitalism's social forms are in no way universal.

EXCHANGE

Exchange is a fundamental aspect of human social life. It is a natural consequence of the division of labor that exists in some form in all societies. Yet exchange is characteristically different in different types of society. For exchange relationships are essentially social relationships that extend beyond narrow economic patterns. In fact, it is only in some parts of modern society that purely economic concerns dominate exchange.

Many anthropologists divide exchange relationships into three broad categories: **reciprocity, redistribution,** and **market exchange.** We shall now examine each of these in turn.

Reciprocity

Egalitarian societies, without centralized political authority, do not display great differences of wealth. Some people may have somewhat more in material goods than others, but property does not tend to accumulate in the hands of any one individual or group. Nonetheless, such societies are not made up of autonomous individuals. Cooperation and exchange are basic to the social fabric. Such cooperation and exchange are based on **reciprocity.** What is given and what is taken tend to be about equal. In one circumstance an individual may take from another. Later the roles will be reversed. No one keeps track of exchange systematically, but a sense of balance is maintained. Reciprocal exchange has an obvious adaptive function, since it helps distribute necessary goods to those in need. Yet it often occurs in ritual or trivial transfers as well, as if the exchange itself were more important than what is actually exchanged. The act reinforces social cohesion. Furthermore, because the items exchanged are of equal value, reciprocal exchange serves to maintain and reinforce the egalitarian ideology of the society.

Reciprocity is not exclusive to egalitarian

societies, however. It functions among friends and relatives in our own culture when gifts are exchanged. These are often of equal value, but need not be, and are offered at such special occasions as birthdays and Christmas. Sometimes reciprocity is delayed. At marriages, for example, gifts flow only toward the new couple, but they, as part of a social group, will give marriage gifts to others in their turn. Exchange of this type is known as **generalized reciprocity.** It is characterized by voluntariness and lack of demand for absolute equality in the exchange process.

In some groups equal return *is* implied directly in the exchange process. This pattern, called **balanced reciprocity,** occurs frequently as a form of labor exchange in horticultural societies. It often takes the form of cooperation in such activities as planting and harvesting. Balanced reciprocity used to occur in the social life of rural America in such events as barn raisings, the lending of farm machinery, and cooperative harvests.

Exchange does not occur only among kin, friends, and allies. Enemies and competitors often enter into various kinds of reciprocal relationships. Each may try to gain the upper hand at the expense of the other. In highland New Guinea ethnic groups that trade with each other are often also potential enemies. Exchange among these groups in times of peace involves goods and even women. Although they may be united by affinal ties, such groups are rivals. One trades with the other in the hope that it will gain an advantage in the trading relationship. This type of exchange is known as **negative reciprocity.**

Gift giving at certain major holidays is a form of generalized reciprocity that has continued to function in our own highly stratified society.

Redistribution

Redistribution is a mode of exchange in which goods, usually the products of the hunt or harvest, flow upward to a "**big man**" or to an hereditary chief and are then redistributed by him downward to members of the social group at large. Big men are individuals who have managed to gain prestige through hard work and the clever manipulation of economic activity, particularly the borrowing and loaning of goods from and to kin.

Redistribution is associated with societies that display rank differences without the emergence of true stratification *and* with those stratified societies in which kinship continues to occupy an important place in the political system. Redistribution is a means by which goods are converted into rank based on prestige *or* a means of reinforcing existing rank. In both cases the "giving" of goods through redistribution is the mechanism that provides prestige. Thus, in redistributive societies neither big men nor chiefs retain more than a small portion of what they receive. The rest is returned via redistribution to group members. If a society is organized into kin groups, goods may be given to the leader of each kin group by his followers and be passed on by these leaders to the chief. Redistribution in turn will be made to individuals via the leaders of each group.

In the New Guinea highlands, where hereditary chiefs do not exist, big men emerge in the political system when certain individuals are able to manipulate their kin and trading partners to their own advantage. An emerging big man will increase his stock of pigs through a careful husbanding of resources and clever trades. These goods are eventually converted into prestige through the giving of large and elaborate feasts that return the goods to those who gave them in the first place. When an individual has become a big man, goods will more easily flow toward him, and the process of maintaining prestige is a bit easier than gaining it. But because big men emerge in a competitive situation (many men compete for the few big man positions), rank, once gained, may be lost to another. Big men cannot rest on their laurels until they retire from active political-economic life.

Redistribution frequently occurs in the context of ritual. Harvest ceremonies are particularly common occasions for redistribution. These ceremonies provide a ritual context for economic activity and act to reinforce political and social ties within the framework of religious life.

Redistribution on Ponape. The inhabitants of Ponape, a Micronesian island in the Eastern Carolines, in spite of a century of contact with Europeans and Japanese, retain redistribution as a major feature of ceremonial life. Even though a money economy now predominates on Ponape, large redistributive feasts continue to occur. These provide occasions for reinforcing the prestige of existing chiefs as well as for creating new chiefs. Ceremonial feasting is associated with four traditional products: pigs, pit breadfruit, kava, and yams. (Pit breadfruit is a starchy tree crop that has been stored for years in leaf-lined pits. It is distinguished from ordinary breadfruit, the major subsistence crop on Ponape, because the latter is always eaten fresh during its harvest season. Kava is a slightly intoxicating but nonalcoholic drink prepared from the pounded roots of a type of pepper plant.) With the introduction of a money economy, Ponapeans now eat a great deal of rice, canned fish, and canned meat. Although these sometimes play a role at feasts and enter into redistribution, they are not central to the ceremonial aspect of feasting.

Feasts occur from September to December during the yam harvest. The season begins with two particularly large feasts given *for* district chiefs. In precontact times these feasts were required obligations for commoners and served to establish their rights to cultivate land. Hosts at these feasts must provide kava and at least one pig. The prestige gained at a feast by a host is related to the amount of kava served and the number of pigs roasted and distributed. Yams and pit breadfruit are provided by the members of the host's kin group. Each household head contributes a yam, as well as other food, when such feasts are given. Prestige is attained on the basis of the size, shape, and variety of the yams and the age of the pit breadfruit. Absolute quantity is not a factor, however. Prize yams are grown in secret places and take more than one growing season to mature. They are classified by their size and the number of men that are needed to carry them—yams can attain weights as high as 220 pounds. In addition to growing large yams, individuals engaged in prestige competition attempt—also in secret—to develop new varieties. The new varieties are "unveiled" with much excitement at feasts.

Individuals are not supposed to show their pride at success in growing new varieties or producing the largest yams, but each chief watches to see which men consistently bring the largest and most interesting yams to feasts. These men are eventually chosen to fill vacant titles or, if they already have titles, to be promoted to higher rank.

Redistribution among the Ashanti. The Ashanti political system is complicated by the fact that, although it is based on state organization, kinship continues to play a major role on the local level. The Ashanti state is headed by a King and a Queen Mother and is divided into royal and commoner lineages. Both the lineage system and the political hierarchy enter into the structure of redistributive activities that take place in the context of ritual. Typical of this pattern is the yam

Large yams being brought to a redistributive feast in the village of Awak on the island of Ponape.

A pile of taro and other goods waiting to be distributed by a host at a wedding, Fiji.

harvest that takes place every year in the month of October. During the ceremony agricultural products as well as domestic animals (chickens, goats, and sheep) are given to lineage chiefs by their followers. These in turn are presented to village chiefs and ultimately to the King. These gifts are sorted out and divided by each authority and given back to the people through their lineages. The animals are slaughtered and the meat cut up into small portions that can be widely distributed. Yams too are given to everyone, even those who were too poor to contribute to the King. These cannot be eaten until the King, and, later, village chiefs have tasted them as the first products of the new harvest. Such events are known in anthropology as *first-fruit ceremonies.* The tasting of first fruit signifies that a taboo (ceremonial restriction) on the eating of new yams has been lifted. The King's and his chiefs' prestige is therefore linked to the well-being of the entire society and is displayed through a religious rite involving redistribution.

Who Gains from Redistribution? It would appear that in nonstratified redistributive societies the chief is chief in name only. He obviously has neither the desire nor the power to retain the "gifts" that are presented to him by his followers. Since reciprocity works so well in egalitarian societies, we are forced to ask why redistribution might take place at all?

Chiefs and big men do have a function in these societies. Although disputes are usually settled through compromise and agreement, chiefs and big men serve as the focus of discussion. Their authority is respected. After all, chiefs and big men are at the center of much

A Bella Coola (British Columbia) house displaying a sign commemorating a potlatch.

ritual and much gift giving, and it is by virtue of redistribution that they are the source of plenty. These economic and ritual functions reinforce the position of chief or big man not as a power but rather as a point of reference around which disputing factions may gather.

In many redistributive societies chiefs and big men play on each other and their followers to increase prestige. In New Guinea big men compete as hotly as corporations that manufacture toothpaste. In these noncapitalist societies financial gain is not the reward, nor is profit reinvested in order to increase it. Instead, a big man manipulates goods to gain more prestige than his adversary.

The Potlatch. Redistribution in its most exaggerated form occurred until recently on the Northwest Coast of North America. There, at the close of the nineteenth and the beginning of the twentieth century, *fighting with property* became a drama played out by the rich and powerful. These displays of power, called **potlatches,** were marked by competitive feasting and redistribution as well as the ceremonial and public destruction of goods. (I will give a detailed examination of the potlatch in Chapter 24.) The potlatch was a game-ceremony played to celebrate some major event, such as the death of an important lineage member or the accession to office of an individual. It occasioned the coming together of rival groups, each headed by its kinship leader or chief. The host offered his guests a spectacular meal and lavished gifts upon them. These ranged from blankets and baskets to enormous quantities of food, particularly dried fish. At the height of the potlatch the host would impress his audience by giving away a mass of food and luxuries and also destroying goods before their eyes. The items destroyed included: mountains of blankets, coppers (large decorated flat-sheets cut into distinctive patterns and made from unsmelted native copper nuggets found in the area and used as a form of money); and even whole canoes, sometimes filled with food. A potlatch must have been watched quite nervously by the invited chiefs and notables in whose honor the feast was arranged. After a certain period of time, often only a year, it would be the duty of one of them to provide a reciprocal feast for the host and the host's group. Each feast had to be more lavish than the previous one. Each part of the cycle increased the quantity of gifts that were either redistributed or destroyed. Thus, a host could only gather enough materials for a potlatch by borrowing from his followers and allies.

In addition to creating or reinforcing prestige, the potlatch undoubtedly increased the social distance between notables and their followers. This distinction became so marked that some anthropologists have referred to Northwest Coast cultures as class societies. In my opinion, the term class should be reserved for those cultures in which the means of production are controlled by a particular group within society. Northwest Coast chiefs manipulated people and borrowed from them but as with all chiefs their role was based on persuasion rather than true power, economic or otherwise.

Early accounts show that prior to European contact the potlatch was less exaggerated than the great waste-feasts described. As the area became flooded with consumer goods and money gained through trade or wage labor, the ante in each potlatch increased. The spectacular potlatch with its extremes of property destruction were the outcome of a new affluence that appeared without a marked increase in real consumption or investment for growth.

The Kula: a Game Played for Fun—and Profit? One of the first great field workers in anthropology was Bronislaw Malinowski. At the time of the First World War he spent six years in the Trobriand Islands north of New Guinea, where he discovered a unique trading network known as the **Kula.** The Kula is a form of exchange among individuals inhabiting the Trobriands and other nearby islands. Articles of two kinds constantly circulate through trade in opposite directions around the circle of islands. Long necklaces of red shell, called *soulava,* move clockwise around the circuit, while bracelets of white shell, called *mwali,* move counterclockwise (see Figure 18.1). Each of these items meets articles of the other class as it moves around the trade network and is exchanged for them. Every movement of the *soulava* and *mwali* and every detail of the transactions involved in their trade are regulated by traditional rules and conventions. Indeed, many acts of the Kula are accompanied by elaborate magical rituals and public ceremonies.

The Kula trade is limited on every island to a small number of men. None of these traders ever keeps a Kula item in his possession for more than a limited time. One trade does not finish the Kula relationship. Once a man is involved in the Kula he remains involved in it. A trading partnership is a life-long affair.

Malinowski notes that the ceremonial exchange of *soulava* and *mwali* is the main function of the Kula. Nonetheless, a great deal of ordinary economic activity accompanies these exchanges. The Kula is also associated with the building of large sea-going canoes used in Kula trade, important funeral ceremonies, and a set of taboos. A clever and important Kula trader can enhance his prestige by trading for and holding, if only for a limited time, an important *soulava* or *mwali.*

The Kula shares certain features with vertical redistribution systems, in which real goods are given back to the people by their chief, and with the potlatch. In all three practices the individuals who occupy the key roles in distribution gain prestige by playing those roles. The Kula can be

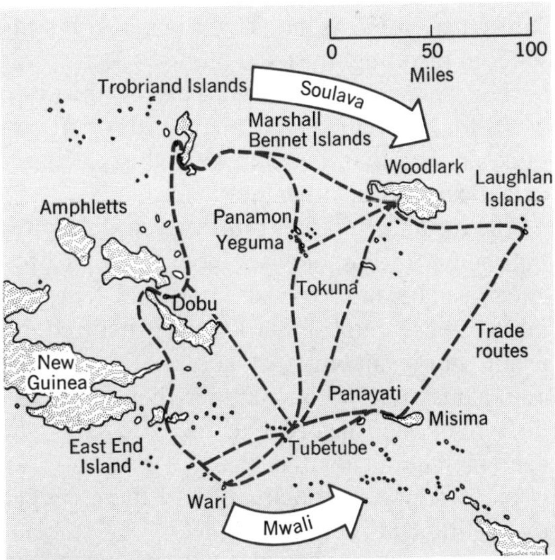

Figure 18.1
Map of the Kula trade showing the circulation of *soulava* and *mwali.*

seen as a means of encouraging and regulating real economic trade among a set of often hostile islands, and/or as a means of creating big men in the context of Melanesian culture. It must also be seen, however, as a game involving a complex strategy and a wide-ranging set of players who have nothing to gain from their winnings but the fun of having played well and their accumulated reputations for having done so. Hostility and enjoyment both play a role in the potlatch and the Kula, but in the Kula the element of pure enjoyment must have been more important than the hostile feelings generated between rivals.

The Market

In speaking of the market we must be careful to distinguish between markets that function merely as a convenience for the exchange of goods, like Kousia Date's, and markets that function for profit. Markets of the former type exist and have existed in many parts of the world. In them trade consists of exchanges made between individuals for items of like value, sometimes through the direct barter of real goods and sometimes with the use of money as a medium of exchange. Someone might come to the market with a few pennies (or some other form of money) and leave with a chicken or some yams. The chicken- or yam-seller in turn might use the money just received to buy something else. Markets of this type serve for the selling and buying of small surpluses rather than the commercial exploitation of agricultural or other products.

The capitalist market functions so differently that some anthropologists have used its presence to mark one type of society off from another. The capitalist market is structured for profit. Large amounts of goods are sold and merchants attempt to maximize their gain. Profit is reinvested in order to increase sales and each merchant's relative share of trading. Price is set by supply and demand and there is open competition in the marketplace.

MONEY

Prior to the invention of money, items could only be exchanged through barter. This was clumsy and inconvenient. If, for example, a person had peas and wanted a chicken, he or she had to find someone with a chicken who wanted peas. Where a medium of exchange exists, the peas can be sold to anyone who wants them and the money can then be used to buy a chicken from a chicken seller.

Many different items can be used as money. These may be natural or artificial. In the Pacific and parts of Africa, for example, cowrie shells are used, while in other areas items as diverse as bird feathers, iron bars, or even salt do just as well. In order to function as money an item must have a precise value (which establishes how much of it is necessary for a certain purchase). This value is usually based on the difficulty involved in making or extracting it. All the items mentioned above, for example, are relatively hard to come by, either because they are rare locally or because their production is the result of a slow and difficult process. Salt, for example, is unlikely to be used as money among peoples who have easy access to it. In highland New Guinea salt must be manufactured from plant material. Salt extraction is performed by specialists and is arduous. For this reason it is unlikely that the supply of available salt will rise beyond a certain relatively stable level at any point in time. Thus, salt can serve as a safe medium of exchange. Its value in relation to the objects for which it is exchanged will remain stable. The introduction of large quantities of commercial salt would produce an inflation since the value of salt would fall in relation to other exchange items.

Frequently money in traditional societies cannot be used to obtain every good or service there is to obtain. Rather it functions only in special kinds of exchange. Such units of exchange are known as **special-purpose money.** Special-purpose money may be used only for such restricted commerce as the buying of ceremonial items or for the payment of bride price.

The kind of money we use is called **all-purpose money.** It is good for virtually all kinds of exchange, without restriction. It may seem paradoxical that much of our money is made from paper, an easily acquired and "cheap" item. The value of paper money, however, is determined by the control over its supply exercised by the government. When a government prints a great deal of money, it becomes cheap—that is, it buys less. When, on the other hand, money is in short supply, its value increases and it can buy more. In this sense paper money is no different from salt as a medium of exchange in the New Guinea highlands.

In capitalist society all-purpose money can be used to make more money by lending it out. In fact, the capitalist type of market economy cannot exist without money in the form of *capital.* Capital is money invested in order to make a profit. There is no reason, except the profit motive, for a large corporation to own such unrelated businesses as a car rental service, factories that produce communications equipment, and a large commercial bakery. Yet these are only some of the companies owned by International Telephone and Telegraph. In precapitalist societies money, when it exists, is never used in this way. It is not capital but merely a convenient means of exchange.

TRADITIONAL VS. MODERN SOCIETIES

I have already noted that economic activity in modern nation-states, whether they be capitalist or "socialist," is driven by the circulation of capital, creating social relations that revolve specifically around production and distribution. Thus, modern life is played primarily on an economic stage. A market mentality tends to dominate our view of the world and we think in terms of supply and demand, profit and loss. Modern economists have even invented an "economic man," a creature of pure sense and rationality who is constantly maximizing his (or her) gain. In our system each economic transaction is ideally decided on the basis of self-interest. The entire system is regulated, at least in theory, by a free market, and profit is the motive of exchange. The majority of traditional societies studied by anthropologists treat exchange differently. Their social systems are not dominated by economics, but rather by kinship. A person may trade with a kinsman rather than with a stranger because it is socially correct to do so, even if the transaction is unprofitable in our sense of the term. Comparative economics, which takes an anthropological view, teaches us that there is no one type of exchange system and that what we call economics operates differently in different societies. All societies have production, distribution, exchange, and consumption, but the ways in which these relate to the fabric of social life differ. Economics exists everywhere, because everywhere societies exist people must solve a range of adaptive problems that come down to a basic fact: to live, humans must eat. The way in which this basic fact integrates with other aspects of culture, however, is highly variable. A full understanding of the human adaptation blooms when we see how culture operates as a mediator in the relationships between humankind and nature. Economic anthropology teaches us that our own culture's view of human productive activity is special and limited to a particular historical period and a particular type of economic system.

Summary

Economics is concerned with those human activities and social relations that involve the production and distribution of goods and services. There are major differences between the economic systems of traditional and capitalist societies. Although production, distribution, and consumption are aspects of economic life everywhere, each of these factors is organized differently in modern and traditional systems. Traditional societies produce primarily to meet subsistence needs. When surplus production occurs, it is usually channeled into such noneconomic activities as politics or religion. Social relations are based on kinship and exchange usually involving some kind of reciprocity. Capitalism depends on a market where profit is the major motive. Economic relations are impersonal and based on the concepts of profit and loss. Private property is a major factor in capitalism and many laws protect it.

The elements of production are work, access to resources, and access to the technological means of performing work. Here again, many differences exist between traditional and capitalist societies. In traditional societies tools are simple and either owned by individuals or kin groups. When some items must be purchased, they are cheap and easily accessible. The major aspect of production is usually labor, and people generally work for themselves or their kin groups. In capitalist society the means of production—tools and other aspects of technology—are usually controlled by owners, who hire laborers to work in large business enterprises. Tools, equipment, and working space are specialized and expensive.

The mode of production of a society consists of the way in which work is performed and the social relations that revolve around production and distribution. The way in which people work is determined by prevailing technology and such environmental factors as climate and seasonality of resources. In traditional societies, at least, the labor process is closely tied to the environmental and technological requirements of the prevailing economy. Time allocation (when and how long people work) and work rhythms are governed by the needs of those who participate directly in the production process. In technologically advanced industrial society work patterns are controlled by the market place. Both employment and unemployment depend on the state of the economy.

Major differences exist between traditional and capitalist societies in the way in which social relations are tied to economics. In traditional societies production is kinship based. Where kin groups are present, elders may exert pressure on younger members to produce. The social relations of production are based on lineage control over land, work, and access to bride price. In capitalist society the social relations of production are based on a class structure in which one class owns the means of production and the other works as free labor.

Exchange is a fundamental aspect of human social life. It is the natural consequence of the division of labor that is found in some form in all societies. Yet exchange is characteristically different in different types of society. Many anthropologists divide exchange relations into three categories: reciprocity, redistribution, and market exchange. Reciprocity is characteristic of egalitarian societies without both centralized political authority and great differences in wealth. It may be generalized, balanced, or negative. Generalized reciprocity is that form of exchange in which the movement of goods and services among individuals and groups is informal. Although the value of exchanged items balances out over time, goods may flow in one direction at one point in time and in another at a later point in time with no absolute equivalence. Balanced reciprocity implies equal return directly in the exchange process. Balanced reciprocity often involves labor exchange in such cooperative activities as planting and harvesting. Negative reciprocity occurs when enemies or potentially hostile groups enter into exchange relations. In cases of negative reciprocity one individual or group may attempt to gain the upper hand at the expense of another.

Redistribution is a mode of exchange in which goods flow upward to a big man or to an hereditary chief and are then redistributed by them downward to members of the social group at large. Redistribution is associated with societies that display rank differences without true stratification *and* stratified societies in which kinship continues to occupy an important place in the political system. Redistribution is often a means for converting goods into rank based on prestige or a means of reinforcing existing rank.

The market is a place for the exchange of goods. In speaking of the market we must distinguish between markets that function *merely* as a convenient place for the exchange of goods and the capitalist market that functions for profit. Markets of the former type exist and have existed in many parts of the world, but the capitalist market functions so differently that some anthropologists have used its presence to mark one type of society off from another. In the capitalist market large amounts of goods are sold and purchasers as well as merchants attempt to maximize their gain. Profit is reinvested in order to increase sales and the merchant's share of trading. Price is set by supply and demand on the basis of open competition between sellers.

Exchange relations can be facilitated by the use of money as a medium of exchange. Any agreed-upon item can be used as money, but those that maintain a relatively constant value are generally favored. The value of the exchange medium will depend on its supply in the local system. Items that remain in relatively constant supply and that are not common function well as money. In traditional societies money may not be usable in all transactions. Its use may be limited to such activities as the payment of bride price or the costs of ceremonies. When the function of money is limited in this way, it is known as special-purpose money. All-purpose money, on the other hand, is a full medium of exchange and can be used in any economic transaction.

In the capitalist system money is also capital; it can be used to make more money through investment.

Bibliography

Burling, R. 1962	Maximization Theories and the Study of Economic Anthropology. *American Anthropologist* 64:802–821. A discussion of economic anthropology from the point of view of scarce means and unlimited ends.
Codere, H. S. 1950	*Fighting with Property.* Monograph 18 of the American Ethnological Society. Discussion of the potlatch as competition.
Dalton, G., editor 1967	*Tribal and Peasant Economies.* Garden City, New York: The Natural History Press. Production and distribution in cross-cultural perspective.
Malinowski, B. 1961 (1922)	*Argonauts of the Western Pacific.* New York: Dutton. A classic of ethnography and a description of Trobriand production as well as the Kula trade.
Mauss, M. 1954	*The Gift: Forms and Functions of Exchange in Archaic Society.* New York: The Free Press. Exchange viewed as the motor of society by a founder of French anthropology.
Sahlins, M. D. 1972	*Stone Age Economics.* Chicago: Aldine. A semi-Marxist approach to anthropological economics also influenced by French structuralism.

CHAPTER 19
SOCIAL CONTROL: CONSCIENCE, POLITICS, LAW

CONSCIENCE

Social control, *the regulation of behavior within and between social groups,* has three aspects: the *individual,* the *political,* and the *legal.* The individual aspect is the operation of conscience, the desire by members of a society to conform to its norms and rules. The political aspect concerns the development and enforcement of public policy. The legal aspect concerns rules of conduct and their application, including means for settling disputes. Both law and politics are characterized by rules, decisions, and their application to behavior.

Most normal people are brought up to believe that they should behave according to accepted custom. They develop patriotic feelings about their social unit or nation and loyalty to their family and friends. They also conform because they fear the internal feelings of guilt and shame. Those who fear guilt are directed by a personal desire to behave correctly. They do so in private as well as in public. Those who wish to avoid shame may conform in public, but not in private, since shame is stimulated by the public notice of improper behavior.

Socialization among the Semai and the Yanomamö

The Semai of Malaysia and the Yanomamö of southern Venezuela are, as we have seen, slash-and-burn horticulturalists. The Semai plant hill rice while the staple crop of the Yanomamö is the banana or plantain. Both occupy a tropical forest environment and depend on hunting for a major part of their protein supply. The Semai are known for their exceptional nonviolence whereas the Yanomamö are among the most war-like people described in the anthropological literature. Semai nonviolence is clearly linked to their social and political system. But Yanomamö aggressiveness has created a considerable degree of controversy. Some observers attribute it to political structure and a shortage of women created by female infanticide. Others believe that it can be linked to protein scarcity and the consequent need to expand hunting territories. I will not examine these hypotheses here. Instead, we will look at the ways in which children in these two cultures learn appropriate behavioral roles. This learning process, or **socialization,** leads, in each case, to typical adult behavior: nonviolence among the Semai and aggressiveness among the Yanomamö.

The Semai. Food sharing is a major feature of Semai culture. It takes the form of *generalized reciprocity* (discussed more fully in Chapter 18), a type of exchange characterized by giving without account keeping. This ethic is so strong among the Semai that a person who calculated the worth of a gift would be guilty of violating a taboo (*punan*). The imperative to share is so strong in this culture that individuals are expected always to give what food they can afford to others. Food exchange is similar to the kind of marriage system known as generalized exchange. It produces a network of interlocking relationships among a wide group of individuals. Among the Semai all individuals give gifts of food to others, but any particular gift is *not* reciprocated directly by the person who has received it. R. K. Dentan explains this system as follows:

For example, A shares a pig with B, C, D, and others; B shares a python with A, C, D, and others; C shares a deer with A, B, D, and others. Some people give less to A than A gives them; others give more. In the long run A gets back from the group of people with whom he shares roughly the equivalent of what he has given to them.

Semai children are taught that to make people unhappy, particularly by frustrating their desires, will lead to immediate physical injury. The injury occurs not to those who frustrate others but to those who have been frustrated. As they grow up, Semai children learn that to insult or to deny requests to someone is *punan* (behavior or thought that will bring misfortune to another). The Semai have the strong ethical notion that injury to others is wrong. They characterize themselves as a nonviolent people. This self-image is so important that an individual Semai will not say that anger is bad, but rather that the Semai do not feel anger. When these norms are violated, as they sometimes are, the behavior is denied. This strong nonviolent ideology reinforces the notion of what is *punan,* which in turn supports the entire exchange system.

Semai children are given a great deal of freedom. If children are asked to do things they do not want to do, they simply say "I don't want to." Children are never forced to comply with requests made to them by adults. This freedom raises the question of how such children can be taught their culture, but a moment's reflection allows us to realize that not forcing compliance reinforces the norms of noncoercion and nonviolence. To force a child to do something would be *punan,* and the Semai are more consistent in applying their cultural rules than many Americans are. Noncoercion, then, implies a kind of passive learning that grows out of the application of adult norms to children. Children also learn their culture through active participation and play. Dentan documents a game that allows aggressive feelings to be expressed but that promotes nonviolence. Between the ages of two and ten children of both sexes flail at each other with long sticks. This activity is accompanied by dramatically aggressive posturing. The sticks, however, never find their mark. Instead, they freeze a few inches away from their target.

Semai parents are not always patient with the naughty behavior of their children. If a child has not learned to avoid certain improper activities, particularly those that are physically dangerous, parents will yell at them. Occasionally they even threaten to hit children, although such threats are never carried out. More frequently parents attempt to scare an errant child by crying out "fear fear." Children are sometimes warned that if they do not behave, strangers will get them. They are also told that misbehavior can lead directly to natural calamities. In fact, the Semai have a special word for such a cause-and-effect relationship. Children learn early to associate thunderstorms, feared by all Semai, with anger. In this way they come to internalize social rules and to fear their own aggressive impulses.

Semai children playing at stick fighting. Semai children never hit each other with these sticks.

Semai children are never punished for their own aggressive actions. Thus no model exists in adult behavior for aggressive acts that can be copied in later life by growing children. When children fight, adults immediately separate them and take them away from the scene of action. As they grow, Semai children learn that *punan* is the major breach of the social and natural order. *Punan* is dangerous to everyone.

The Yanomamö. Yanomamö men beat their wives frequently and warfare is a constant feature of life. Insults flow freely within a Yanomamö village. Individuals are quick to take offence at the actions and insulting words of others. Violence is particularly a male prerogative. Boys learn early to imitate their fathers, among whom patience is not a virtue. Like Semai children those of the Yanomamö learn a great deal of their culture passively by watching and later imitating adult behavior. The adult behavior that stands as a model for them, however, is very different from that seen by Semai children.

Yanomamö children learn that danger exists in the world, but they do not learn to fear it. Danger is a product of human and supernatural forces. It is unleashed by one's enemies and must be counteracted. Supernatural power rests with shamans, who are men. Women and children are not allowed to participate in rituals, which include the taking of hallucinogenic drugs.

Children of both sexes spend a good deal of time with their mothers, but boys are indulged by their fathers from an early age. They are encouraged to be fierce and are rarely punished even when they aggress against their own parents or sisters. Not only is aggression condoned, but individuals learn to respond to it with counteraggressive acts of physical violence. Compare Napoleon Chagnon's description of club fighting among the Yanomamö with Dentan's analysis of stick fighting among the Semai. The Semai learn not to hit each other, while Yanomamö children witness anger turn rapidly into acts of violence.

Most duels start between two men, usually after one of them has been caught . . . trysting with the other's wife. The enraged husband challenges his opponent to strike him on the head with a club. He holds his own club vertically, leans against it and exposes his head for his opponent to strike. After he has sustained a blow on the head, he can then deliver one on the culprit's skull. But as soon as the blood starts to flow, almost everybody rips a pole out of the house frame and joins in the fighting. . . .

Needless to say, the tops of most men's heads are covered with long, ugly scars of which their bearers are immensely proud.

Yanomamö men are highly aggressive and often engage in bloody club fights.

Conscience and Conformity. For the Semai it is bad to hurt anyone. Individuals are constantly on guard concerning their own behavior toward others. Rather than fear others, they fear their own *punan.* Among the Yanomamö aggression is common, and everyone is on guard against the aggressive acts of practically everyone else. In one case social control is internalized, in the other it is externalized and expressed directly. Of course, the Yanomamö are not always fighting each other. There are alliances based on sister-exchange marriage and others between villages, but these alliances are fragile. People are trained to expect the worst from their fellows and to protect their own interests.

Conscience is a basic means of social control in all societies, but its expression in behavior varies according to the established norms of culture and individual variation in the strength of commitment to these norms. In most traditional societies the socialization of children is more uniform than in our own. Under these conditions we can expect more conformity to internalized feelings about correct behavior. In addition, traditional societies are also small in scale. In most of them everyone knows everyone else. This naturally leads to a more personalized set of social relationships than exists in American culture. We interact with a large number of people whom we do not know personally. Under these circumstances plain self-interest is likely to play a major role in our dealings with others. I do not mean to suggest, however, that Americans lack real ethical feelings in their interactions with others. Social norms and social conscience *are* learned in the context of the home and school. The strength of commitment to these values differs by social circumstances, however, as do their overall contents. Although most Americans actually do conform to the norms of their society by choice rather than by coercion, breaches of ethical standards are also quite common and can be found in all segments and classes. In addition, in modern Western society people often apply their ethics to some but not all situations. Thus, in real situations they tend to particularize their behavior rather than to act uniformly on the basis of norms that are supposed to be applied universally.

Ideal and Real Norms and Rules

In all societies people may sense the difference between *ideal* and *real* rules or norms. Ideal norms and rules concern the way people ought to behave but may not, while real rules and norms are enforced and apply widely throughout a culture.

Rule systems are in constant flux and change. Often, when enough people violate some custom, it ceases to guide behavior. In contrast, an unacceptable custom may eventually become accepted. In our own system, with its codified and published laws, changes in attitude and behavior may render a law dead. Dead laws remain on the books but are never applied. In many instances laws may be reinterpreted according to contemporary morality. When this happens, the wording of a law does not change but its application does.

LAW AND POLITICS

In American society it is fairly easy to distinguish between law and politics, between legal and political decisions. Our Constitution provides a clear separation of powers among the various branches of government. This separation has been upheld since the early days of the Supreme Court. Public policy is determined by Congress and administered by the President. The application of law falls to legal authorities: the police for enforcement and the courts for interpretation and judgment.

A possible confusion arises from the broad use of the word *law* in our legal-political system. Congress passes bills that become law. Some of these are directly concerned with individual behavior, while others are concerned with such governmental and therefore political matters as welfare, education, and the support of military forces. Both types, however, affect public policy. Congressional and presidential action are political. The interpretation of this action—decisions about its legality in the framework of the Constitution and in the light of past interpretations—rests with the courts.

Among the Ashanti of Ghana there is no such separation of powers. The Ashanti King is the supreme legal, political, and religious officer of the Ashanti state. He makes and interprets the law, but in doing so, of course, he follows custom. To deviate too widely from custom would be to court rebellion. Whereas in our system law is vested in the Constitution, law among the Ashanti is maintained by religious belief. The charter of the Ashanti King comes from the religious sphere. It provides a justification for the use of power, which is exercised by officers of the state.

In all societies law and public policy are both enforced by authority, which may be embodied

Many societies have formal means for making legal and political decisions. A Masai council in Kenya, and the United States House of Representatives in session.

in individuals or in a group acting as a whole. The application of authority may be expressed as *persuasion, coercion,* or *punishment.* Punishment may be physical or psychological. Psychological punishment frequently takes the form of social ostracism. In kinship-based societies ostracism may be tantamount to a death sentence. Clearly law and politics are intimately linked. In order to analyze their roles in culture, however, we must make an artificial separation between them.

SOCIAL INTEGRATION AND POLITICAL ORGANIZATION

In even the most technologically simple cultures, characterized by small numbers and frequent face-to-face interactions, decisions must be made about economic, social, and ritual behavior. If group hunting is to occur, if the camp must be moved, if puberty ceremonies are to take place, people must agree to participate cooperatively.

In more complex societies the lines of authority must be clearly drawn and political position within the total group assured. Large populations are cumbersome. They require special political institutions in order to insure cohesive action when necessary.

In the broad sense cultures can be divided into two major types: those *with* and those *without* centralized political authority. Cultures without some form of headship (known technically as **acephalus** societies) consist of a socially cohesive group of individuals united by ties of kinship and/or residence. This is the usual pattern among nomadic hunters and gatherers who live in small, mobile units. Larger but still acephalus cultures consist of several kin groups living together in the same permanent village. This pattern is frequent among agricultural peoples. Allegiance may be divided between the village as a whole and one's own kin group.

Centralized political authority is associated with both kinship and state societies. In the former, compromises must occur between the principle of kinship and the principle of centralization. In state societies, as we have already seen, kinship no longer forms the basis of major social relations. Loyalty has shifted away from ties between related individuals to ties with the state as a territorial-national entity. The state functions to maintain social order.

Consensus

Acephalus societies are often "ruled" by consensus. Individuals meet as equals to discuss possible action. Frequently the advice of one person is considered more readily than the advice of another. In hunting, for example, the most skilled hunter may command authority. Generally, however, this authority is limited to the activity in which the individual excels. Coercive power does not exist and the expert will be followed by others out of respect. Often the advice of a **shaman** (or curer) is sought concerning a wide range of activities. The supernatural gifts possessed by shamans establish their power. Interestingly, this power may result in ambivalent feelings and hostility. In many lowland South American cultures shamans are frequently suspected of witchcraft. If several deaths occur locally a shaman may be blamed and killed. The killing of a shaman under these circumstances is a political act and serves to restore harmony to the village.

Politics in Segmentary Societies

Lineage-based societies are politically flexible. Collective action can take place on any level depending on social need. Disputes between segments are often mediated by the elders of the next-highest unit. As in nonlineage societies shamans and other religious specialists may play political roles that transcend the limits of any particular lineage boundary. We have also seen how certain forms of horizontal social organization (castes, age grades, secret societies) can operate as a form of political integration in acephalus societies.

Recognized Chiefs

Many small- and intermediate-scale societies, particularly those that practice animal husbandry or cultivate land, have local leaders. Such individuals are often referred to by anthropologists as *chiefs.* Many of these "chiefs" have little real power, although they can function as the center of political discussion and compromise. Chieftanship of this sort is often hereditary, and succession to office may be unilineal. Among the matrilineal Iroquois, women of rank elected male chiefs. Among the Pueblo, several hereditary chiefs with different functions held office within the village. Some of these chiefs were war leaders, some led hunts, and others fulfilled ceremonial roles. As we shall see later, chieftanship tended to become solidified and institutionalized under colonial administrations.

According to Robert Lowie, a student of Native American cultures, chiefs in North America varied greatly in power and authority. Many were appointed by a council of elders. Sometimes they could designate their own successors. On the plains groups of "soldiers" or "police" appointed by chiefs functioned to control such activities as communal hunting. In principle these "police" acted under the direction of a chief or the council that had appointed them, but frequently they were quite autonomous in their actions. These groups had the authority to restrain braves from warring at inopportune times, to supervise migrations, and to control crowds at major ceremonies. Among the Cheyenne a council appointed one of five military clubs to direct migrations and hunts. Once such groups were appointed, chiefs exerted little control over them. Each club had its own chief, however, and this individual did wield considerable power over the membership.

Central Authority

Central political authority with coercive power can exist with or without the state. When power extends beyond an individual village to a larger territory and when kinship and territory function together as major forms of integration, the term **chiefdom** is often used. In Africa large empires developed between the ninth and seventeenth centuries. These were ruled by individuals with real political authority. Some anthropologists refer to these empires as African *states* or *kingdoms* and to their rulers as kings.

(Left) A high chief in Fiji receives a cup of sacred kava from a server who shows deference by the manner in which he serves. (Right) An African chief with his ceremonial umbrella, which serves as a sign of office.

Others call them *chiefdoms* in order to distinguish between European states in which kinship no longer functioned as an essential element in the political sphere and African "states" where kinship continued to play an important role in the organization of political power. Kings were often drawn from senior lineages and local politics was often played out within and among lineages.

The Abron State or Chiefdom

As in many other African states, kingship among the Abron is an overlay on lineage organization. Certain matrilineages have come to be isolated as royal or noble lineages. Although distinguished from lineages of commoners, these lineages continue to segment through time. According to tradition, shortly after the Abron arrival in the Ivory Coast from Ghana the royal line split into two factions. These factions settled in the villages of Zanzan and Yakasse. After considerable dispute over who should rule, the leaders of Zanzan and Yakasse agreed to alternate royal authority. On the death of a king, a ranking member of the royal line in the currently nonruling village would take up the kingship. As time passed and the Abron population increased, the number of royal lines grew from two to four, and finally, several years before I did my field work, to five. Each of these royal lines now resides in different villages and each in turn expects to take up the kingship on the basis of the agreed-upon rotation.

The power of the Abron kingship does not exist in the person of the ruler. Instead, it is fixed in a "golden" stool, which circulates with accession to power. A King without the stool cannot reign. An incident that occurred during my own field work will illustrate how this operates.

In 1960 the Abron King was Kwame Adingra, the son of the previous King. Since the Abron are matrilineal, his succession violated the rules. In addition, Adingra inhabited the wrong village. According to Abron custom the stool should have passed on from Adingra's father to the royal lineage head in the village of Herebo, a man named Kofi Yeboa. But Adingra was able to take power with the help of the French colonial authorities, who favored him because he and his father had responded to Charles DeGaulle's call to arms against the Germans in 1940.

Throughout Adingra's reign many Abron expressed dissatisfaction with the illegality that had brought him to power. This discontent was particularly apparent in other royal villages. Chiefs of the royal lineages resented Adingra's power and feared that they too could be bypassed in royal succession.

In the fall of 1961 a group of young men from the royal village of Tabgne made off with the stool from Amamvi, Adingra's village.

Then the police stepped in. The stool was taken to Bondoukou, the local administrative center, and put into a jail cell. The government of the newly independent Ivory Coast used the incident to exert its own authority over the King. The government declared that it would decide where the stool (and the kingship that went with it) should reside. As long as the stool remained in Bondoukou, Adingra could not reign. The stool was not merely the sign of office, but the office itself.

In January 1963 Adingra was killed in an automobile accident on the way back from Bondoukou. The stool was immediately "liberated" and passed to Kofi Yeboa, its rightful guardian. Every Abron I spoke to during my trip to the Ivory Coast in 1973 expressed satisfaction that Yeboa was the new King and that the principles of matrilineal succession and circulation of the kingship had been restored.

African chiefdoms or states share certain features with European feudalism of the Middle Ages. In large African empires the king ruled over a set of local chiefs similar to barons. These in turn ruled over still lesser chiefs, all the way down to the local village. Among the Hausa of Nigeria each "baron" was considered a slave of the King. Each was responsible for collecting taxes. After he took a share of the revenues, it was his duty to pass the rest on to the King. Local leaders also came to the King's assistance in times of war, supplying men for the royal army. These "barons" were often appointed by the King to assure support on the local level. This assurance was particularly important when standing armies were uncommon and communications between the capital and the provinces were often difficult.

States

The major features of state organization were discussed in Chapter 11. Let me remind you that in the formation of a state national-territorial allegiance replaces kinship as the binding force in political relations. States are also characterized by the presence of full-time economic specialists, social relations that are based on economics rather than kinship, centralized political authority, legal codes under which crimes are acts against the state, taxes, and a standing army. Heads of states, whether kings, dictators, or presidents, are assisted by an established bureaucracy and other officials. These may include hereditary, elected, and appointed officeholders.

POLITICAL ORGANIZATION AND SOCIAL EVOLUTION

Cultures have been ranked by some anthropologists on the basis of their political solidarity, on the assumption that the ranking reflects evolutionary development. The usual rank order goes: patrilocal bands, tribes, chiefdoms, and states.

Patrilocal Bands

Patrilocal bands are associated with small-scale hunting-and-gathering societies. They are flexible nomadic groups that range over a home territory. The major features of patrilocal-band social structure are exogamy and patrilocal (virilocal) residence. Most bands are bilateral in kinship reckoning (although double descent occurs among Australian groups). Political, social, and economic decisions are made by the group as a whole, but the advice of respected individuals is often followed. Such individuals lead specific activities such as hunting. The adaptive function of patrilocality is assumed to rest in the importance of keeping together males familiar from birth with the same territory in hunting, sharing game, and in warfare. Bilaterality is vital among small groups for it allows individuals to muster support from both matrilateral and patrilateral kin, thus increasing the range of potential aid from relatives in what is a very small pool of individuals.

Composite Bands

Elman Service has noted that band-level social organization also includes what are called *composite bands* such as those found among Algonkian-speaking Native Americans in Canada. Composite bands are composed, as the name suggests, of loose social groups with informal residence rules. Since these bands appear to be less highly structured than patrilocal bands, Service suggests that they are the result of disorganization rather than progressive evolution. They are a specific adaptation to the near destruction of "original" band structure that tends to occur after contact with European or other colonizers. Depopulation is seen as a major cause of their formation. Composite bands, then, are not a stage in sociopolitical evolution, but rather the result of collapse in the face of colonial domination.

Tribes

Elman Service has also noted that tribes are similar to a large collection of bands, but that their residential segments as well as the ties that bind these segments together are significantly different. Tribes are wider social units than bands. They are united by such cross-cutting ties as age grades, secret societies, and dispersed segmentary lineages. The activation of these ties allows segments of a tribe larger than a local unit to operate together in activities like important ceremonials and warfare. Under precolonial conditions centralized political authority does not exist in tribes, but both local groups and cross-cutting segments may have appointed or hereditary chiefs. Although the coercive power of such chiefs is usually limited, they often have considerable authority among their followers. Tribalism may have emerged with the development of domestication, which is associated with a stronger sense of territory and control of natural resources than is found in band organization. Tribal organization provides a greater defensive solidarity than band organization.

Morton Fried, who has published several articles and a book on tribes, agrees with Service's characterization of tribal organization, but he believes that tribes are the outcome of contact between different ethnic groups when one has greater military power than the other. Fried suggests that tribal formation is either a defensive adaptation to superior military power or a creation of colonial authorities. When rulers of expanding colonial empires need to deal effectively with native populations, they sign treaties with appointed "chiefs" in order to solidify control over what would otherwise be populations with diffuse authority.

According to Fried, therefore, tribes are adaptive in two contradictory ways, depending on historical circumstances. They may represent a tightening of organization in the face of outside power *or* they may be created by that power in order to take control over a loosely organized native population. In the latter case tribalism is an adaptation for the colonizers rather than for the colonized.

Chiefdoms

The next level of political organization is that of the chiefdom. This form of organization is marked by real political authority and the emergence of specialized political office. Chiefdoms are associated with high productive capacity and economic redistribution through which the chief is able to solidify his political power. As we have seen, ritual also adds to the chief's power when he is seen as the link between the ancestors and/or the gods on the one hand and his followers on the other.

Chiefdoms range in size and complexity from small-scale nomadic pastoral societies to large pastoral and agricultural groups. They have been found on the resource-rich islands of Polynesia and on the Northwest Coast of North America, where stable marine resources supported large sedentary populations in relative affluence.

WAR

Regardless of political level, traditional societies, like modern nation states, generally have relations with other groups. Trade and warfare, to be discussed next, are both aspects of intergroup relations. We have seen how the Kula ring links several ethnic groups into an economic and ceremonial network. In New Guinea intergroup ceremonies are a common feature of social life. They occur among groups that both trade and war with each other. Such ceremonies reinforce trade links, signal the end of hostilities, and help to maintain peace. We have also seen how other forms of cross-cutting ties such as age grades and secret societies bind local political units into wider political networks. In general, however, the traditional societies studied by anthropologists are relatively independent units. Alliances are often a matter of immediate necessity and may crumble under the pressure of divisive forces.

War *is armed aggression by one group against another.* As such it is a political act. In this sense warfare is just as social an activity as reciprocity and, in fact, often occurs among groups that trade with one another in times of peace.

There are three major explanations for warfare in the anthropological literature. The first explains warfare as the expression of innate aggressive tendencies in the human species. The second interprets warfare as a cultural process that is ecologically adaptive. The third treats war as a strictly cultural phenomenon that cannot be explained in terms of ecological adaptation. According to this approach war is the expression of political, social, and religious forces.

War as Innate Aggression

War must not be confused with aggression, even if aggressive acts, both individual and collective, occur in war. Warfare may provide an appropriate cultural setting for aggression,

War was, until recently, common among and between ethnic groups in the New Guinea highlands. Many warriors participate in this formal battle among the Dani of Irian Jaya (formerly Western or Dutch New Guinea), but few individuals will be killed.

but it is a social activity with a wide set of motivations, *one* of which *may* be aggression. All kinds of behavior occur during warfare. There is cooperation between soldiers and between soldiers and civilians. There are acts of bravery, of which the motives may range from anger and aggression to altruism and even cowardice. Except under extreme circumstances in which anger and aggression fuel heroic acts, war is a calculated activity in which coolheadedness is valued over impulsive action. War as a social pattern develops in specific historical and cultural circumstances and has nothing to do with the supposed genetic bellicosity of particular biological groups.

War as Nongenetic Adaptation

The anthropologists Andrew P. Vayda and Marvin Harris have been associated with the second position—that war as a cultural behavior is ecologically adaptive. Their explanations are, however, very different. Vayda sees war as a means of redistributing populations over scarce land. This serves in turn to regulate economic, social, and even psychological variables, since high population density is associated with poverty, social disorganization, and psychological stress. To take a psychological example, Vayda suggests that crowding increases aggressive encounters. Eventually such encounters within and between groups lead to an outbreak of war. The outcome of the warfare is a redistribution of population. Vayda summarizes his position as follows:

(1) a diminishing per capita food supply and increasing intragroup competition for resources generate intense domestic frustrations and other in-group tensions; (2) when these tensions reach a certain level, release is sought in warfare with an enemy group; (3) a result of the warfare is reduction of the pressure of people upon the land, either because of heavy battle mortality or because of the victorious group taking its defeated and dispersed enemy's territory; (4) the reduced pressure on the land means that the diminution of per capita food supply and the increase of intra-group competition over resources are arrested and that domestic frustrations and other in-group tensions can be kept within tolerable limits.

Marvin Harris's approach to an explanation of warfare is more complicated than that of Vayda. His basic contention is that technological-environmental conditions often require some kind of population-regulating mechanism. This mechanism operates against natural population growth and consequent ecological degradation. Overhunting, overgrazing, and overcropping to feed ever-increasing numbers are quite clearly maladaptive strategies that must be overcome if a population is to live in harmony with its environment. War, then, is a major form of population control, but the control is indirect rather than direct. Harris realizes that the number of deaths in warfare, particularly in nonwestern societies, is often low and has little effect on demographic patterns. A much more effective means of population control (one that is documented for several cultures) is infanticide. Female infanticide is more effective than male infanticide because it is the number of women in a population that determines the potential for population growth. Women, however, are recognized as valuable in most societies. We have already seen how the role of women in marriage exchange provides one form of social cohesion. In addition, female labor occupies an indispensable place in the economies of many cultures. For female infanticide to occur, women must be devalued.

Harris and William T. Divale have approached this problem in a paper entitled *Population, Warfare, and the Male Supremacist Complex*. The authors argue that the most effective way to devalue women is to increase the value of men. Warfare and aggression do this effectively. Every group that has war must nourish and cherish the male members. Under conditions of scarcity girls may then be sacrificed for the good of the group. In parts of the world where certain food resources are scarce (Amazonia, for example, where the authors assert that protein is in short supply), the population–warfare female–infanticide complex is reinforced by the existence of a created scarcity of marriageable women. Female infanticide makes females scarce within the group. Men must then raid other groups in order to capture wives. Aggression becomes a necessary part of a wide-ranging ecological adjustment. When natural resources are scarce, it makes more sense to let other groups raise potential wives. These can be captured when they have reached maturity.

Appealing as this theory is, it suffers from a paradoxical conception of adaptation. If people need to control their population, they are likely to know it. Eskimo, for example, practice both female infanticide and **geronticide** (the killing of old people). They do not enjoy either practice but realize their necessity under extreme environmental conditions. The function of women as reproducers is consciously known everywhere. Since birth control is relatively ineffective in nonwestern societies, and because abstinence is a rare practice, infanticide is a likely choice when population regulation is deemed necessary.

Of course, not all populations recognize that increasing population can lead to environmental degradation. Under conditions of natural population growth, such groups will increase until environmental degradation does take place. Several choices then remain available: migration, technological change, the imposition of some form of population control, or warfare to expand the home territory.

The term "natural" population growth may be misleading, however. Many populations remain relatively stable with birth and death rates closely matched. The recent population explosion is the result of a decrease in death rates and sometimes an increase in birth rates as well. Birth rates may go up when a population is forced to produce more than it needs for its own subsistence. This often occurs under colonial domination.

We have already seen in Chapter 11 how economic expansion may be dependent on population increase when expansion itself depends on increased labor. As we shall see later, social processes may affect demographic patterns, stimulating population growth under some conditions and inhibiting it in others.

In biology the only noncircular measure we have of adaptation is selective fertility. Such a statistic is based on successful reproduction and is at odds with population control. To say that a culture that limits population is well adapted is to fall into the circular argument, "What is there is adapted, what is adapted is there." Adaptation, at least in the biological sense, should imply that those groups that increase energy extraction and convert energy into population are better adapted than those than maintain population at a steady state. Cultural adaptation may have different rules and require different measures from those of biological adaptation. This is, in fact, my own point of view, but if it is correct we cannot rely on the biological model to explain cultural evolution.

Let us now look at two cases. In one, warfare is intimately linked to social-political structure. In the other, it appears as part of the economic system. These cases are offered as a caution against both the genetic and the ecological models of war discussed above.

Akwe-Shavante. David Maybury-Lewis has written a deeply moving account of his work among the Akwe-Shavante of lowland South America. He has also published a long monograph describing both the social and political structure of Akwe-Shavante society. The Shavante are a war-like, fractious people. To an outsider much of their behavior seems both arbitrary and highly aggressive.

Shavante society is composed of precariously balanced factions. The social structure is rife with tensions that arise, at least in part, from conflicts between consanguineal kinship affiliation and marriage ties. This conflict is embedded in a moiety system and is amplified by a complex ritual and symbolic system. Although war is frequent and reprisals for alleged attacks of sorcery common, Shavante do not attack without cause. If, as the dictionary tells us, aggression is unprovoked attack, no Shavante is aggressive. Political life consists of juggling factions to maintain an uneasy peace, and it is only when the balance of power in any group appears to be in jeopardy that fighting occurs.

On the psychological level, however, the Shavante *are* aggressive. The Shavante believe in and fear sorcery. This is a common manifestation of projected aggression. Projection in this case means that if one has certain feelings that are not acceptable to one's self, they are pushed out of consciousness. Later they emerge as a belief that someone or something else has those feelings. Thus, for the Shavante sorcerers are evil people who act aggressively against others. The Shavante believe that sorcery must be combatted—not magically, but through physical reprisal. Such reprisals are never taken by individuals. Rather they are group actions, political acts that always fit the pattern of factional disequilibrium. When one faction in a group appears to be gaining the upper hand in daily life, members of the other faction may accuse a member of the first faction of sorcery and collectively kill him. In so doing, they believe that they are acting in their own defense, although psychologically the act may be seen as aggressive. On the political level this behavior acts to restore balance within the group.

War and Trade in New Guinea. New Guinea highland cultures are characterized by high population density supported by horticulture, pig raising, and a series of extended trading networks through which practical and ceremonial goods circulate. Social organization is fluid and relatively egalitarian. We have already seen how the economic system functions through redistribution and the emergence of big men who play political roles. I must now add that warfare is a common feature of these cultures.

The region is characterized by diverse ethnic groups tightly packed into narrow mountain valleys. These groups form shifting alliances, of greater and lesser permanence, against enemies. The basic social pattern in these cultures consists of repetitive warfare and economic as well as ritual exchange. Curiously both exchange *and* warfare contribute to solidarity and dissension. Ethnic groups vary in size and, depending on their historical fortunes, expand and contract in both population numbers and territory. Jockeying for position in an unstable and hostile social environment, groups form alliances of varying duration. Warfare demands allies for both offense and defense. Warfare, of course, also requires enemies. The exchange of goods in stable ecological and social situations usually implies at least temporary peace and the strengthening of social bonds within and across groups. For highland New Guinea this description is only partly true.

New Guinea trade is, in part, a complicated game of gift giving, in which donors expect a return of goods with interest from trading partners. Failure to reciprocate with interest leads to social disgrace. Successful players, on the other hand, become big men and, as such, command considerable authority in their social groups. Success in trading depends on the support of blood kin and affines. Both types of relative contribute to the accumulation of goods to be donated and traded. Success also depends on the formation of intelligent strategies in which control of goods is carefully monitored by the big man. He must decide when to give and to whom within the confines of other big men's desires and the rules of the game. He must manipulate trading with a range of more and less important partners and decide how long he can delay giving away a large herd of donated pigs without depleting his and his group's resources. Rather than control production, big men control distribution and use this control as a means of increasing their prestige in the community. Trading in these situations provides competition between individuals and groups. The competition produces hostility between groups tied to different big men. Exchange plays a role in the formation and maintenance of alliances, but at the same time contributes to intergroup tension, which can flare into overt disputes and warfare.

War as the Expression of Cultural Forces

Among the Shavante who have little trade, the political game revolves around factions. In highland New Guinea, with its larger and more sedentary populations, trade plays an important role in both muting and stimulating violence. Warfare *may* have the effect of dispersing populations or redistributing land. It *may* serve various psychological needs and regulate a set of ecological variables as Vayda has suggested. But even though this may be an outcome of warfare in many cases, the *causes* of war appear to lie more in cultural and political than ecological relations.

Tribal and Modern Warfare

Before we leave the subject of warfare, I must point out that modern warfare and even tribal warfare as we know it may have very little to do with war among small, relatively isolated traditional societies. The intensity of modern warfare is almost never seen in the kind of armed intergroup encounters described by anthropologists. Most are simply raids with little mortality on either side. While conquest is sometimes the goal of war, winners frequently do not invade or take over their enemies' territory.

Writing on the subject of war, Elman R. Service notes a difference between modern war and the fighting of "primitives." For them, battles, for example, are frequently between individuals. When the struggle escalates to include groups, fighting remains unorganized and individualized. Service separates true aboriginal wars from warfare after contact with civilization. He notes (as have several authors before him) that the Iroquois, who provide a famous case of military and political organization, united in the face of a specific colonial situation. Located between the English and the French and having exhausted their own fur resources in the previous Dutch colonial period, the Iroquois desperately attempted to maintain control over the fur trade. After failing to negotiate economic treaties with the Algonkian groups to the north and west, they finally went to war, but only as a last resort. Aided by their English allies they pushed westward, conquering many less well-organized ethnic groups. The basis of their power was the confederacy of five and then six previously independent "tribes." The alliance, never more than a rather shaky affair, did provide considerable military unity. One probable reason for Iroquois warfare was French pressure on the Algonkian. Since the Iroquois traded with the English and the Algonkian with the French, each European power urged "its Indians" to continue hostile relations.

The push of Americans westward had a similar effect. Group warfare developed among the inhabitants of the Great Basin after the introduction of the horse and the increasing encroachment by whites on natural resources. Service tells us:

The turmoil caused by variations in the acquisition of the horse and then the gun in the Western states caused the same hide-and-seek tactics as in the East earlier and resulted in the same polarity of fragmentation vs. *confederation. In the northern, or Plateau, part of the Shoshonean area the first to acquire the horse and to confederate into large war-making bodies were those known generically to the trappers and explorers as Snakes, while their victims were usually called Diggers. . . . The Snakes and later the intruding Blackfoot and Piegan were clearly the cause of the Digger's poverty and fragmentation.*

North America is not the only area in which this process occurred. In fact, it happened worldwide. Service points out that in Africa the slave trade caused widespread disruption in areas far from the actual slaving centers. Contact with Europeans, first for trade and later under colonial exploitation, led to the formation of a series of native conquest states in East and South Africa. Each of these states became a military power in the Western sense of the term.

This material demonstrates that it is dangerous to talk about warfare in traditional societies in the same terms as warfare among nation states. Furthermore, we must be careful to distinguish between small-scale traditional warfare among societies relatively untouched by colonialism and warfare generated by the colonial situation itself.

LAW

Law *is an aspect of social control that operates through rules of conduct and their application to behavior.* In our own culture laws are codified and enforced in the name of the state. An array of functionaries—legislators, judges, administrators, the police—acts to pass, define, administrate, and enforce the law. The input from individual citizens comes through the vote, peaceful protest, legal tests of laws in our court system, and sometimes from violent action. The American Revolution was a final protest against a series of laws deemed unjust by the colonists.

In nonstate societies the situation is quite different. We have already seen how political decisions are often reached through consensus, if not by the entire group then by a significant segment of it. This segment quite often consists of elders, a status open in time to almost everyone. Disputes of a legal nature are also frequently solved by consensus. Remember that wrongs (torts) in these societies are usually seen as acts against an individual or at most against an individual and his or her group. It is rare that these wrongs are taken as crimes against the body politic. Torts may be settled between individuals or between their separate groups, or they may be mediated by authorities that span social units. Thus, in lineage societies disputes between two segments may be adjudicated by the leaders of the next highest segment. Or, as already pointed out, they may be resolved by negotiation in the presence of a religious leader such as the Nuer Leopard-Skin Chief.

Society-wide legal authority somewhat akin to our police does exist in some noncentralized political systems. This power is often limited to punishing specific types of social transgression—for example, among the multiple secret societies found in West Africa.

Law among the Kapauku

The Kapauku are horticulturalists who live in the broad highland valleys of Irian Jaya (formerly Dutch New Guinea). Their population totals about 45,000 individuals. First contact with Europeans occurred about 1938, but a permanent government outpost was not established until after the Second World War in 1946.

The Kapauku are farmers who produce a considerable surplus. The sweet potato is the major crop, while pigs provide an important source of animal protein as well as the major economic asset. Since humans and pigs both eat sweet potatoes, the plant is crucial to the entire subsistence economy. All agricultural land is owned individually, and there is a great deal of variation in the amount held by any one person. The size of a farm depends on the number of dependents who can be mobilized to help farm it, the owner's wealth, and certain of his personal characteristics.

As in much of highland New Guinea, pig breeding is central to the political system. High prestige and status—which translate into legal and political power—come from the accumulation and subsequent redistribution of wealth. Thus the Kapauku are a redistributive society, one with particularly high productivity.

According to Leopold Pospisil, the Kapauku ethnographer, the Kapauku have true money in the form of cowrie shells and two types of necklaces. This money can be used not only for the purchase of goods and land, but also to pay for wage labor. Since shell money is not produced locally, it must be obtained in trade with lowland people. Its supply is, therefore, small and, according to Pospisil, relatively fixed in quantity. Prices are set largely on the basis of supply and demand. Both trading and production are oriented toward profit, which, as we have seen, is translated into prestige and power.

These characteristics have led Pospisil to suggest that the Kapauku are primitive "capitalists." He has been criticized by many anthropologists, however, for ignoring important differences in the social relations of production between the Kapauku and capitalist economies. Land among the Kapauku, for example, is actually held by sublineages. Private title *only* exists within the territory of these groups. Furthermore, all sublineage members have access to land so that an alienated working class has not emerged. Since redistribution forms the basis of political power, true capitalist accumulation does not occur. Thus, while there are real differences in wealth among individuals, a class structure has not emerged.

Kapauku ethnography is particularly rich in the presentation and analysis of legal material. Trained as a lawyer as well as an anthropologist, Pospisil has made a major contribution to our understanding of legal systems in traditional societies. Pospisil collected a large number of legal cases that he examined in the context of Kapauku political and social organization.

Kapauku social organization is basically segmentary. There are groups of varying inclusiveness from the level of confederacies down through lineages, sublineages, households, and families. Legal systems corresponding to each level exist. These differ in the content of specific laws and in the use of sanctions against particular offences. The head of a Kapauku household cannot, for example, sentence someone to death. In addition, offences of different kinds are punished by the authorities of different levels. Breaches of etiquette, verbal insults, and quarreling are punished by family heads. Crimes such as treason and desertion in war are tried by the head of the entire confederacy.

Pospisil was struck by the secular character of Kapauku law. Of 121 rules he extracted from the legal system, only 14 had anything to do with the supernatural. These 14 concerned the breaking of taboo or the use of magic against others. Of the 176 cases he reported Pospisil found only seven that dealt with offences against the supernatural. The majority (70) of the legal rules regulated economic behavior; 91 of the 176 cases dealt with economic violations.

According to Pospisil the Kapauku have categories of law covering the following types of offences: *offences against persons,* including murder, attempted murder, manslaughter by accident, battery, attempted suicide, sorcery, the violation of taboo, lying, sexual offences;

offences against rights in things, including ownership of land, trapping and hunting laws, ownership of movable property, theft, destruction of property, and inheritance. The Kapauku also have laws that serve to regulate a wide range of economic activity, including sales, barter, pig breeding, land lease, credit, loans, labor, gifts, and the forcible seizure of property. In addition, a special category of law covers offences against and by authorities. Finally, the Kapauku recognize offences against society as a whole.

Social Control in Egalitarian Societies

I have saved the simplest, most egalitarian societies for last in my discussion of law. Some of these have unique mechanisms for handling disputes or the breach of custom. Among the Mbuti of the Ituri Forest in Zaire neither chiefs nor shamans exist. Nor do the Mbuti believe in witchcraft and sorcery. Yet disputes do often break out in the small camps inhabited by individual Mbuti bands. Social structure is so fluid in these groups that if dissension continues without resolution one of the offended parties will leave with his or her spouse and join another camp. Since Mbuti bands are exogamous, individuals and their families have little difficulty finding some relatives among whom they may establish a new residence.

Sometimes a Mbuti will transgress the norms of society without offending any particular individual. Such action constitutes a breach of custom. If the behavior persists and is sufficiently abrasive to the members of a camp, it will be singled out and parodied by a "clown." Clowns are not appointed and they do not accede to office through hereditary succession. Instead they emerge, if you will, from among the members of the egalitarian band on the basis of their skill. A good clown is perceptive to the norms of Mbuti culture and is a talented mime. When a person behaves improperly, he or she will be mocked by the clown before the entire group. Such a performance is usually sufficient to embarrass the offender and inhibit the deviant behavior.

Among the widely dispersed Eskimo another means of social control exists that bears a faint resemblance to clowning. When two Eskimo get into a dispute, usually about women, they may fight. The strongest makes his point at the expense of the weakest. There are instances, however, when the fighting takes on a symbolic rather than an overtly violent nature. Eskimo groups are known for a kind of public combat known as the *shame song.* In these oratorical contests two adversaries get up and sing about each other in public in a series of stanzas improvised on the spot by each singer. The contest is decided by the assembled group on the basis of the skill with which a singer hits the mark against his opponent's words. Once the contest is over and the audience has rendered its judgment, the decision is final and must be accepted.

In many societies an individual may be accused of engaging in illegal or antisocial supernatural behavior. Such accusations are common in Africa, parts of lowland South America, and Asia. Even shamans are not immune from suspicion. In fact, shamans are often highly suspect precisely because they have greater access than ordinary people to the spirit world. In some cases the accused are quietly killed after the group has decided to get rid of them. Frequently, however, they may be forced to submit to an *ordeal,* such as taking a poisonous substance. According to belief, if the accused is guilty death will result, if innocent the poison is vomited up and the individual lives. Ordeals of this type are not unknown in our own culture. Well into the seventeenth century, Europeans, including American colonists in New England, believed in witchcraft. Accused witches were often tortured until they confessed and repented. Many were also forced to submit to lethal ordeals. In general, their guilt was assumed in advance. Such a system of beliefs tended to reinforce the behavioral code. Deviants feared the accusation of witchcraft and its attendant results.

Summary

No society can exist without some form of social control based on conformity to rules of behavior. Social control has three aspects: the individual, the political, and the legal. Most normal individuals are brought up to behave according to the accepted custom and both shame and guilt reinforce conformity to social norms.

In all societies people sense the difference between ideal and real rules or norms. Ideal rules and norms concern the way people ought to behave but may not, while real rules and norms are generally obeyed.

Law and politics are two aspects of social control. Political decisions are made by authorities, be they chiefs or presidents, and affect public policy. Politics touches on such social relations as trade and commerce, warfare, and taxes. Laws are codified rules of behavior that apply to all members of a designated group; for example, all citizens or such special groups as doctors in the practice of their profession.

In all societies law and public policy are enforced by authority embodied in individuals or in a group acting as a whole. The application of authority may be expressed as persuasion, coercion, or punishment.

In even the simplest cultures decisions must be made about economic, social, and ritual behavior. All social activity requires that individuals agree to participate cooperatively. In complex societies, which are characterized by large populations and a detailed division of labor, the lines of authority must be clearly drawn. In the broad sense cultures can be divided into two major types: those with and those without centralized political authority. Cultures without some form of headship (acephalus societies) consist of socially cohesive groups of individuals united by ties of kinship and/or residence. Centralized political authority can be found in both kinship-based and state societies. With the full emergence of the state, kinship no longer plays a political role and the state functions to maintain social order.

Collective action in lineage-based society is taken by the segments concerned. Such groups are politically flexible. Collective action can take place on any level depending on social need. Disputes between segments are often mediated by the elders of the next highest unit.

Many small- and intermediate-scale societies, particularly those that practice some form of animal husbandry or horticulture, have local leaders often referred to as chiefs. These chiefs vary greatly in power and authority. In most cases they use persuasion rather than coercion to enforce the social order.

Central political authority with real coercive power can exist with or without the state. In Africa, for example, large empires developed between the ninth and seventeenth centuries. While kin groups remained important on the local level, these empires were ruled by chiefs or kings with real political authority.

Cultures have been ranked by some anthropologists on the basis of their political complexity, on the assumption that such ranking reflects evolutionary development. The usual rank order goes: *patrilocal bands, tribes, chiefdoms,* and *states.* Morton Fried has questioned the validity of one of these levels, the tribe, stating that tribal organization under the authority of chiefs is the result of colonialism.

War is armed aggression by one group against another. As such it is a political act. There are three explanations of warfare in the anthropological literature: war as the expression of innate aggression, war as a cultural process that is ecologically adaptive, and war as a cultural phenomenon that need not be adaptive. The genetic hypothesis is probably wrong because war can be only partially linked to individual aggression. Furthermore, there is little evidence that even individual aggression is instinctive. War may indeed function adaptively in many situations, producing a redistribution of populations over crowded territory or providing a group with increased access to resources, but in some situations war is probably best understood in a political or even religious context.

War as we know it has little to do with what is called *war* among small-scale traditional societies. The intensity of modern warfare, with high rates of killing, is almost never seen in the kind of armed intergroup encounters described by anthropologists.

Law is an aspect of social control that operates through rules of conduct and their application to behavior. In our own culture laws are codified and enforced in the name of the state. In nonstate societies disputes of a legal nature are frequently solved by consensus. Wrongs (torts) in these societies are usually seen as acts against an individual or at most against an individual and his or her group. Rarely are these taken as crimes against the body politic.

Coercive legal and political power do not exist in egalitarian societies. Nonetheless, mechanisms of social control do exist in such groups. Among the Mbuti of the Ituri Forest, for example, unofficial clowns mock individuals who breach social custom. This performance is usually sufficient to embarrass the offender and inhibit the deviant behavior.

Mocking takes another form among the Eskimo. When two Eskimo get into a dispute, usually over women, they may fight. There are many instances in which this fighting takes on a symbolic rather than an overtly violent nature. In such cases Eskimo engage in a dual with shaming songs. The two disputing individuals get up and sing about each other in public. The one who makes up the best songs is judged by the community to have won the dispute.

In many societies a person suspected of having committed a serious crime is subjected to an ordeal. This may involve the taking of a poisonous substance or, as in cases of witchcraft accusations in Europe during the Middle Ages, dunking in a lake or river. In the case of ordeal it is assumed that an innocent individual will survive and the guilty succumb. Such a system of beliefs reinforces the behavioral code.

Bibliography

Bohannan, P. editor 1967 — *Law and Warfare: Studies in the Anthropology of Conflict.* Garden City: Natural History Press. Articles on conflict, law, and war.

Chagnon, N. 1977 — *Yanomamö: The Fierce People.* New York: Holt, Rinehart, and Winston. Study of a warlike people in the jungles of South America.

Fried, M. 1967 — *The Evolution of Political Society: An Essay in Political Anthropology.* New York: Random House. An introduction to political anthropology from a contemporary cultural evolutionist.

Fried, M. 1975 — *The Notion of Tribe.* Menlo Park, California: Cummings. Discusses the ambiguity in the term *tribe* and the possible colonial origins of tribes.

Divale, W. T. and M. Harris. 1976 — Population, Warfare, and the Male Supremacist Complex. *American Anthropologist* 78:521–538. An attempt to correlate warfare with population pressure and female infanticide.

Maybury-Lewis, D. H. P. 1967 — *Akwe-Shavante Society.* Oxford: Clarendon Press. Discussion of aggression and social structure in lowland South America.

Pospisil, L. 1958 — Kapauku Papuans and Their Law. *Yale University Publications in Anthropology.* 54. A detailed discussion of law and legal cases among the Kapauku of Irian Jaya.

Service, E. R. 1962 — *Primitive Social Organization: An Evolutionary Perspective.* New York: Random House. A stages approach to the evolution of political structure.

Vayda, A. P. 1968 — Hypotheses about Functions of War. In War: *The Anthropology of Armed Conflict and Aggression.* Edited by Fried et al. Garden City: Natural History Press. War viewed functionally from the perspective of human ecology.

CHAPTER 20

RELIGION AND THE SUPER-NATURAL

Theories of Religion
Stages in the Development of Religious Belief
Religion as a Projection of the Group
Religion as the Projection of Conscience
Supernatural Beliefs and Practical Problems: Magic
Religion as an Ecological Regulator
Religion and Social Control
Symbolism in Religion
Religion as the Solution to Conceptual Problems
The Roots of Religious Thought
The Building Blocks of Religion
Ritual
Ritual Space
Types of Ritual
Sacrifice
The Cast of Characters in Religious Belief
Witches
Sacred Restrictions: Taboo
Mana
Abron Religion
Beliefs
Rituals
Syncretism as a Viable Religion: Nativism

A great deal of human thought and action is directed toward the **supernatural,** *that which is empirically unknowable and is believed to exist beyond the visible universe.* The belief in supernatural entities and principles rests on faith (an inner sense of truth) rather than science. It can be reinforced, however, by the interpretation of ordinary phenomena according to preconceived, often logical, systems. Knowledge of the real world may be used to bolster science and religion at the same time. The difference between the two depends on how evidence is gathered and evaluated. Scientific hypotheses are phrased in such a way that they are *falsifiable.* They are open to empirical test. Religious questions such as "Does God exist?" cannot be answered "yes" or "no" according to empirical criteria. Answers are either accepted or rejected on the basis of faith.

Supernatural beliefs may be individual or collective. **Religion** consists of *a set of collective beliefs and practices concerning the supernatural.* This does not mean that individual variations in religious belief do not exist. They probably do in every religion, but adherents are convinced that they share belief in the major elements of the system. This idea is reinforced by participation in common rituals. When people worship together, they share in the outward manifestation of inward beliefs.

THEORIES OF RELIGION

Stages in the Development of Religious Belief

Early anthropologists, many of whom practiced Western religions, assumed that religious systems evolve like social systems in a particular order. Since they tended to equate evolution with progress, they saw religious development as a progressive movement toward truth. Phrased in religious terms, they saw revealed truth emerging slowly as human culture evolved toward higher and, therefore, better forms. This conviction led them to construct schemes of *unilineal* development. In general, these schemes began with **animism,** the belief that everything in nature (humans, animals, plants, and even such objects as rocks, rivers, and mountains) contains personified, conscious spirits or souls. One of the founders of anthropology, E. B. Tylor, suggested that animistic beliefs, and indeed all religion, originated in attempts made by members of "primitive" cultures to explain their dreams and other psychological phenomena.

While animism describes much of the thought behind so called "primitive" religions, some early scholars noted that other concepts existed in these belief systems as well. R. R. Marett pointed out that more abstract, impersonal powers, such as mana, were also part of many religious systems. The term **animatism** was coined to cover these beliefs.

The next assumed stage in the evolution of religious thought was **polytheism.** Polytheism marks a shift from animism and animatism to a belief in multiple gods identified with, but not equal to, natural forms. Gods of the forest, mountains, and sea fit this category. The ancient Greeks had such gods, but in addition they associated supernatural entities with such phenomena as Death and his brother Sleep. Even

Part of the Greek pantheon depicted on a sixth-century BC pot. From left to right: an old man, Dionysos and Athena seated, and Hermes.

such emotions as Hate and such concepts as Beauty were associated with individual gods in the Greek system.

The final stage in religious development, it was thought, came with the emergence of **monotheism,** the belief in a single god, or God, as among Christians, Jews, and Moslems. Monotheism is generally also associated with a strong and codified morality or ethic. The emergence of this ethic was taken as proof of the superior nature of monotheistic religion.

These evolutionary schemes were all based on the notion that monotheism *is* revealed truth. All ignore a great deal of evidence (some of which, at least, was available at the time) that each type of belief can be found in most, if not all, religious systems. Rather than represent stages, these ideas may represent universal tendencies inherent in religious thinking.

It was Andrew Lang who first pointed out that, along with animistic beliefs, West Africans had a concept of a high god. This god, remote from the natural world, had created the universe and everything in it. Lesser gods, associated with local animals, plants, and natural features of the landscape, could be called upon to intercede for humans with the high god.

Ancient Greek culture, long considered a sophisticated form of civilization and the basis of much of our own modern philosophy, was both animatistic and polytheistic. Such beliefs may not be an official part of Christian, Jewish, or Moslem tradition, but they persist in many forms among believers. Fate, for example, is often seen as a force apart from God. Many religious and "nonreligious" people hold superstitions that are nonofficial supernatural beliefs.

Lang used his discovery of an African high god as "proof" of God's existence. He believed that religious truth was a characteristic of human understanding. His evidence was accepted as support for the concept of psychic unity among all people. It also tended to confirm a nonevolutionary approach to religious systems. This evidence should not be used too hastily against an evolutionary interpretation of religious beliefs, however. While a unilineal scheme is obviously wrong, religion may still play a very important adaptive role in the life of any human group. In fact, most theories about religion in anthropology attempt to demonstrate its positive, and therefore adaptive, function in social life. Some of these theories can be framed in specifically evolutionary terms.

Religion as a Projection of the Group

The French sociologist Émile Durkheim is associated with the idea that belief systems in culture are a projection or representation of the group. Durkheim was particularly interested in the religion of Australian Aborigines. He noted that a major feature of Aboriginal religion was the unifying force it exerted on social life. Durkheim saw religion as the first means adopted by humans to order the universe and themselves into a coherent social whole. He defined religion as follows:

A

B

C

D

Religion often finds its expression in art. In some cases religious belief is depicted, in other cases religious art has an instrumental function—as an icon or as a magical item.

A

The Annunciation, by Rogier van der Weyden, depicts an event sacred to Christians.

B

Christ, from the Cathedral of Monreale (Italy).

C

The great Buddha at Kamakura, Japan.

D

(Left) Baoule ancestor figure (Ivory Coast, West Africa). (Right) an Ikenga or protective figure, Ibo (Nigeria).

E

Aztec rain god, Tlaloc.

E

A religion is a unified system of beliefs and practices relative to sacred things, that is to say, things set apart and forbidden—beliefs and practices which unite into one single moral community called a Church, all those who adhere to them. . . .

Durkheim was a functionalist. That is, he believed that society as a collective entity consists of connected parts, all of which contribute to the smooth functioning of the whole. He viewed funerals, for example, as a means of saving the group in a moment of crisis. Durkheim reasoned that the death of another is supremely frightening to individuals because it reminds us of our own mortality. The presence of death creates a strong urge to flee. Such flight could lead to the fragmentation of the social group. The funeral ceremony acts as a centripetal (unifying) force, tying people together in a strong ceremonial context when they are naturally most likely to separate.

In his readings on Australian religion Durkheim was struck by the identification of social segments such as moieties and clans with natural entities. These he called **totems,** although the word comes from Ojibwa, a Native American language. Totems in Australia included such animals as kangaroos and dingo dogs, various plants, and even such features of the environment as mountains and watercourses. The majority of emblems used by native Australians were animals and plants. Durkheim noted that, of 204 kinds of totems collected by Spencer and Gillen in the late nineteenth century, 188 were animals or plants. Inanimate objects included the boomerang, cold weather, darkness, fire, lightning, the moon, red ochre, resin, salt water, the evening star, a stone, the sun, water, the whirlwind, the wind, and hailstones.

Durkheim thought that all totemic groups are exogamous and are, therefore, linked to other groups by marriage. This practice creates an interlocking society of which subgroups are an integral part. Durkheim believed another characteristic of totemic groups to be the observance of a taboo on eating their own totem.

If totemism is the identification of social groups with certain entities, usually chosen from the natural order, then it is indeed widespread among traditional cultures. Not all totems are taboo, however, and not all totemic groups are exogamous. In fact, there are some groups that can be defined as totemic that forbid marriage with nonmembers.

Many social scientists since Durkheim have been attracted by the phenomenon of totemism and the taboos believed to be associated with it. Sigmund Freud developed a theory of the incest taboo based on the identification of the father with the forbidden totemic animal. According to Freud, the sons of the primal group (the first society) rebelled against their father, killed and ate him, and took his women (the father's wives and their own sisters). This act, born of hatred and frustration due to the father's exclusive access to women, evoked strong guilt in the sons, who also loved and respected their father and leader. Since he could not be brought back to life, he was symbolically recreated in the taking on of a sacred emblem. Henceforth it was to stand for the group and could not be killed or eaten. At the same time the sons instituted the incest taboo: Women of their own group were no longer available to them sexually. They had to marry out—and society was born.

Claude Lévi-Strauss suggests that totems are a conceptual device for classifying social groups by means of natural emblems. He suggests that animals are frequently chosen because they "are good to think," not because they are good to eat. What he means by this cryptic statement is that identification of human groups with natural groups can provide an excellent conceptual model for social life. When totemism includes exogamy, it reflects a basic difference between human social groups and natural groups of animals. In the natural world bears can only breed with bears, and wolves with wolves. In the world of culture social rules determine that bears must marry wolves and wolves bears. Thus, in using natural symbols totemic groups with a rule of exogamy make a symbolic statement about the difference between nature and culture. Breeding between members of the same species is part of the natural order. The incest taboo and exogamy are part of the cultural order. In identifying with animals in this way humans actually are making a symbolic separation between the realms of nature and culture, between animals and humans.

Religion as the Projection of Conscience

The founder of psychoanalysis, Sigmund Freud, believed that religion was the projection in social form of individual conscience. Freud saw the human being as conflict-ridden. Individual instinctual forces seek outlets in personal gratification. Individual conscience develops along with the successful identification of the growing child with the parents. Maturity comes with the *introjection* (taking into one's self) of parental authority and discipline. Freud saw culture as the force that restrains individual instinctual impulses and religion as that part of culture that embodies the conscience. Religion is the outward projection of inner life, particularly the part of inner life that is concerned with ethical behavior. This aspect of Freud's overall theory of culture appears in two books: *The Future of an Illusion* (dealing specifically with religion) and *Civilization and its Discontents* (dealing with culture at large). In the latter book Freud claims that culture emerges when individuals set their immediate gratifications aside. When this is possible, social life with its restraints on natural strivings becomes possible.

The psychoanalyst Carl Jung, one of Freud's students who later broke with him, also saw religion as a kind of projective system. But Jung had a more mystical bent than Freud. He believed that religion is not the projection of a socially derived conscience, but rather the projection of consciousness itself.

Durkheim contrasts with both Freud and Jung because in his theory religion is an aspect of the social whole and could not exist without it. Durkheim rejected psychological explanations of social phenomena. His scientific motto was "Social facts shall only be derived from social facts." Both Freud and Jung, on the other hand, saw religion as individual psychology writ large. In this way they were able to jump from insights concerning individual psychological problems to speculation about social control and "social pathology."

Supernatural Beliefs and Practical Problems: Magic

The English anthropologist Bronislaw Malinowski, along with many other early anthropologists, attempted to differentiate magic and religion. Magic in his view is related to immediate practical ends; it is in a sense an aspect of technology. When people want something difficult to obtain, they engage in some magical action and hope to be rewarded. Religion, on the other hand, was seen as being more "noble." Religious beliefs concern the whole cosmos and God or gods. A person can appeal to a god for aid, even though there is no way to insure that the god will respond positively. In fact, many religions have stories similar to the tale of Job, in which God brings down misery on his people in order to test their faith. Magic is part of the supernatural, but it is more secular than religion. Magical acts often involve "self-help." Malinowski suggested that practical activity without recourse to magic occurs in daily life when no danger is present and success is relatively assured. In more risky situations, he hypothesized, magic will be used along with physical technology.

Several different types of magic have been noted by anthropologists. Sir James Frazer was one of the first to attempt a typology and explanation of magical acts. He distinguished between *imitative* and *contagious* magic. Imitative magic is based on what Frazer called the *law of similarity.* This law assumes that things which resemble each other are the same. Thus, if you stick pins into a doll that represents a real person, that person will get sick. A dance in which game animals are imitated as victims of the hunt may also serve as imitative magic if the dancers believe that the imitative hunt will provide real success. Contagious magic is based on the *law of contact.* It assumes that things which have once been in contact will always be in contact. Thus, harm can be done magically to someone by performing operations on bits of his or her hair, nail parings, clothes, or other things associated with the person. Frazer grouped both of these types of magic under the *law of sympathy,* which assumes that things act on each other at a distance through a "secret sympathy."

Magical acts can also be grouped into positive and negative (or white and black) magic according to whether the operation works for the good of all or is harmful to someone. Defense against harmful magic can be thought of as countermagic. Many cultures have formulas for the repulsion of black magic. In these cases the magical act may turn against its perpetrator.

Actually, it is difficult, if not impossible, to separate magic and religion. Both are aspects of supernatural belief, and usually the aspects merge. A belief in magic often rests on religious principles, while religious ceremonies often contain behaviors that would be difficult to separate from what Malinowski called magic. Many rituals take place specifically to insure the success of a particular project—war or trade, for example. In these rituals a god or gods may be appealed to while certain acts with an allegedly pragmatic (useful) value are performed. Moslem peoples in Black Africa, for example, believe that illness can be cured by writing Koranic scripture in ink on a special board, washing the message with water into a cup, and drinking the liquid. One could say that this is a magical application of religious belief, but the distinction appears forced.

An even clearer example of the difficulty involved in analytically separating religion and magic is found in fertility ceremonies practiced by a wide range of horticultural and agricultural peoples. Although these ceremonies often contain supplications to the gods for help and protection of newly planted fields, they also contain instrumental acts believed to guarantee, say, adequate rainfall.

When shamans attempt to cure sick patients, they often consult with the gods using a variety of means, including trance and divination. Many diseases are attributed to spirits angered by some social conflict within the kin group or village. The cure may require the establishment of social harmony through mediation.

In examining these complex and multifaceted rituals how are we to determine which elements in them are magic and which are religion? If we were to succeed in making such separations, in what sense would they be useful in increasing our understanding of the phenomena in question? In most cases the attempt to separate instrumental acts from supplication—that is, magic from religion—is an unnecessary and unwarranted imposition on the data.

Religion as an Ecological Regulator

Roy Rappaport has suggested that religion may operate as a regulator in the management of resources. He has attempted to connect pig husbandry among the Maring of New Guinea to warfare and rituals during which many pigs are slaughtered and their meat distributed. Rappaport notes that, although individual Maring are not aware of it, these rituals serve to keep the pig population within reasonable limits. They take place when the pig population grows too large for efficient exploitation of other subsistence means, particularly such crops as sweet potatoes. When the system works well, pigs eat damaged and surplus root crops and thus convert carbohydrates and low-grade protein into high-grade protein with little cost. When there are too many pigs, the animals begin to compete with humans for basic agricultural products. In addition, large pig herds are difficult to manage. Animals get away from their owners and frequently invade gardens. This can lead to hostile encounters between pig owners and those whose gardens have been damaged.

Rappaport has also pointed out that intergroup rituals serve in information exchange so that rival groups receive signals about their relative strengths and weaknesses and can make strategic decisions on the basis of them. This provides an unconscious means for regulating the distribution of populations in a limited territory when such groups practice frequent warfare. Information transmitted in the context of ritual performances may be accepted as true even by hostile parties because of the sacred nature of the event. Participants do not question the truth of supernatural events. Secular messages sent and received during ritual are not questioned because they occur in and are part of the ritual process.

Religion and Social Control

The last chapter discussed the role of religious leaders in social control, including the areas of politics and law. In both state and nonstate political systems priests and shamans may exert a secular influence on group members. The relationship between religion and power is most apparent in *theocratic* states, in which priests are rulers. In egalitarian societies religious specialists may be the only individuals capable of mediating disputes.

Shamanism among the Netsilik Eskimo. The Netsilik Eskimo are hunters and gatherers who live on the Arctic coast of the Northwest Territories of Canada. They follow a seasonal migration pattern—sealing on the ice in the winter, fishing for char with stone weirs in the summer, and hunting caribou in the fall.

The major feature of overall social organization among the Netsilik is the *ilagiit,* a bilateral kindred that includes between 30 and 50 individuals scattered across several camps. Marriage partners are chosen by preference from this group. The patrilocal extended family forms the basis of the local social group. Members cooperate in daily activities and provide mutual aid in case of difficulties. This group is headed by an elder, who serves as the leader of the hunt.

The only cultural specialist of any sort in the Netsilik camp is the shaman, who deals with a range of religious matters, such as curing disease, controlling the weather, and even finding lost objects. Shamans (*angatkoks*) are individuals who respond to a divine call. An already established shaman observes the behavior of boys to see if any are likely candidates. After a boy is chosen, he becomes an apprentice; he lives first in the household of an elderly *angatkok* and later in a separate igloo, where he is taught shamanistic techniques and obtains special paraphernalia from his parents. After training is completed, he receives a protective spirit from his teacher. At first he practices with the older man, but eventually he sets up on his own.

The Netsilik believe in a large number of supernatural beings, most of which are dangerous to humans. Shamans are aided by only one class of spirits, called *tunraqs.* These they acquire as gifts from other shamans or because a spirit wishes to attach itself to one of them. Evil spirits include the ghosts of men who died in bed believing that they had been killed by magic. *Tupiliqs* are another category of evil spirits. They are round in shape and filled with blood. *Tupiliqs* are capable of causing illness. Potentially the most dangerous of all evil spirits are the *tunraqs* themselves. When a shaman sends one of his helper *tunraqs* on a mission and it is unable to succeed, it becomes a reverse spirit, a *tunraq kigdloretto,* literally a "bloodthirsty being who even turns against his own master." These spirits have to be brought under control by other shamans.

According to Asen Balikci, the ethnographer of the Netsilik, powerful links exist between shamanism and the basic religious beliefs of the Netsilik. In fact, religion is integrated around the person of the shaman, who is considered to have a particularly strong soul. He has the power to strengthen another person's soul or steal it, causing sickness and death. In addition, shamans are in touch with the major Eskimo deities and they are the primary source of myth. Shamans are considered to be generally good by other Netsilik. People who are helped by shaman are grateful, but they also fear the shaman's power. It is, for example, considered

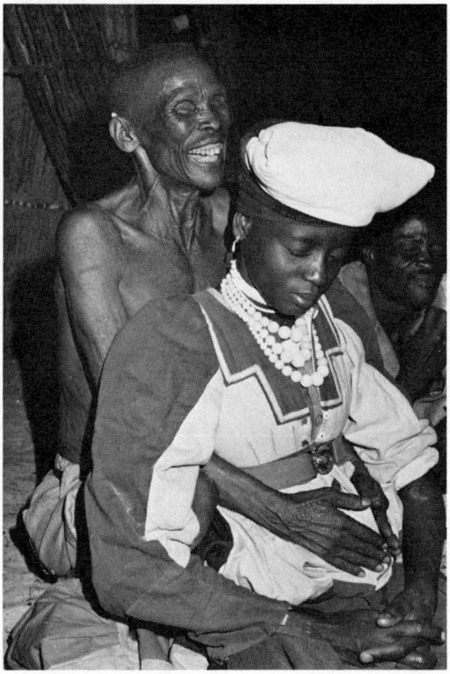

Shamans, sacred individuals who have direct contact with the supernatural, exist in many cultures. Shamans frequently perform healing ceremonies and have for this reason sometimes been called medicine-men, an appellation that is doubly wrong since women are frequently shamans. (Left) A Herero shaman (South Africa) works to cure a patient. (Right) A Sia (Native American) shaman performs a curing ceremony for a sick boy.

quite dangerous to make a shaman angry, but if an *angatkok* engages in evil acts, he is killed by the community.

The shaman has important social functions within Netsilik society. He is also a mediator between the people and their environment. Shamans are called upon to control environmental threats, individual and group crises, and interpersonal relations. In addition, the shaman himself manipulates his position in order to increase his prestige among the people.

While shamans function to reveal sources of tension and thus aid in relaxing it, they also contribute to the generation of anxiety within the group. The possibility that they can use their powers for aggressive ends is a constant factor in the emergence of suspicion and hostility. According to Balikci, "The individual lived in an atmosphere of suspicion and fear, dreading both the attacks of his camp fellows and the spirits who might initiate an evil action of their own volition. This action contributed to the isolation of the individual from society. . . ."

This hostility is directed mostly at nonrelatives. It therefore has an effect on the marriage system of the Netsilik, who, unlike most Eskimo groups, have a high frequency of cousin marriage. Marriage within the family to a cousin is considered safer than marriage to a nonrelative, but intrafamily marriage, in turn, contributes to the isolation of one Netsilik group from another. This isolation then increases potential hostility and suspicion between social units.

The very fact that shamans have the only

power positions in what is a basically egalitarian society probably contributes to the ambivalence with which they are treated. The source of their power is unknowable by ordinary people and therefore perhaps even more frightening than secular political power. This pattern of ambivalence, trust, and mistrust, with its consequences of social cohesion on the one hand and hostility on the other, is a common feature of other societies in which shamans are the only religious and political specialists. In the Amazon Basin, far away from the wilds of northern Canada, shamans are central figures in religious performances, the cure of disease, and, at least indirectly, politics. Among many of the more warlike groups in lowland South America, the life expectancy of shamans is very low. They can expect to be murdered by members of their own group when their magic apparently fails them and they can be punished for "causing" misfortune.

Symbolism in Religion

Symbolism is a major element in all religious belief and ritual. Symbols make real and concrete a range of abstract and difficult concepts. Sometimes they bring together elements that are logically paradoxical. The mystery of three-in-one embedded in the Christian Trinity is a good example of this kind of relationship, one that is manifested materially in the act of crossing one's self in the name of the Father, the Son, and the Holy Ghost.

In religion and art the *affective* (emotional) power of symbols may come from their effect on psychological processes. Humans appear to be "moved" by the power of certain culturally defined metaphors and other kinds of linguistic and symbolic connections between disparate elements. Victor Turner, an anthropologist, has suggested that ritual symbols are powerful because they are *polyvocalic* (that is, they have many voices), thus providing a wide set of connections between elements and creating a conceptual unity among them. The color red, for example, may represent death (bleeding to death), life (through its relation to menstruation and therefore female fertility), and danger (because bleeding is dangerous) all at the same time. These referents may be aroused by painting a statue of a devil red. The elements are then combined with the ideas of evil, power, and other cultural associations with the devil. These connections unify culturally important concepts in emotionally charged packages.

Symbols may be united in narratives and myths to provide explanations of the origin of the universe and the place of humans within it. The use of symbols in this way provides coherence in a world that is often frightening and incoherent to individuals.

Religion as the Solution to Conceptual Problems

I began this chapter with the statement that a great deal of human thought is directed toward the supernatural, which I defined as that aspect of belief that concerns what is empirically unknowable. It should be no surprise, therefore, that religion, as institutionalized supernatural belief, is concerned with human problems that have no empirical solutions. Among these are the ultimate reasons for existence, death, the possibility of an afterlife, the justification of moral and ethical behavior, and an overall explanation of the universe, including such problems as causality and the existence of evil and misfortune.

Almost all religious systems confront these questions in one way or another. There are two reasons for this. (1) Answers to these questions are often unknowable in any sense other than the religious. (2) Answers to these questions are often stated in relation to what *ought* to be rather than what *is*. Science, as powerful as it is, cannot deal with many of these problems, specifically because it cannot make judgments about values. Although science can be used to decide whether or not a particular course of action will lead to specific ends, including ethical ends, it cannot decide which ends or values are correct in some absolute sense. This is not to say that scientists do not or should not have values, only that science cannot tell us which values are correct and which are wrong.

Most of the world's myths deal with such problems as the reasons behind the existence of death and evil. Many myths also provide guidelines for ethical behavior. When these myths are acted out in the performance of religious ritual they provide a powerful link between belief and practice. The Catholic Mass, for example, which involves a repetition of the Passion of Christ, allows the faithful to share materially in a key event of vast symbolic and ethical importance.

Dogon Cosmology and Ritual. The Dogon live on the arid plains and hillsides of the southern fringe of the Sahel (the region south of the Sahara Desert) in Mali. They are an agricultural people who occupy large cliff villages, similar to pueblos, perched over their fields that dot the plains below. Dogon cosmology is complex and highly organized. As a description of the universe, it rivals any of the great philosophical-religious systems of the world, and only a small part of it can be presented here. This cosmology is dramatized in a body of rituals performed by the Dogon at specified occasions.

The primal germ of life is symbolized among the Dogon by the smallest domesticated plant seed, that of *fonio,* an African dry-country grain. In the beginning, when time began to flow, this seed, which had up to then lain dormant, quickened like the developing fetus in a pregnant woman. Eventually it burst forth, expanding to reach the outer limits of the universe. The expansion took place in a spiral path. According to Marcel Griaule and Germaine Dieterlen, who spent many years in the study of Dogon cosmology, this spiral movement has two related symbolic meanings. It represents the conservation of matter (matter neither increases nor decreases) and the perpetual alternation of opposites. These pairs include: right and left, high and low, male and female, odd and even. Life, for the Dogon, is generally dependent on paired forces (frequently expressed as twins) that can produce unity only in combination.

The beginning of the universe took place in an ovoid, the *egg of the world* (also the *fonio* seed). The germs of things, already differentiated, lay within this egg. As they expanded, these germs developed into seven segments of increasing length. These segments plus the original *fonio* seed signify the seeds of the eight basic cultivable plants. These eight seeds are also contained in the clavicles of every human being. They represent the bonds between humans and the crops on which they depend.

Inside the core of the first seed was an oblong plate divided into four sections. Each section, controlled by one of the four elements (earth, air, fire, and water), contained certain of the 24 categories into which the universe is classified. In the spiral movement of creation each segment of the plate turned on itself and flung the signs into space. Each sign came to rest on the thing it signified. This juncture converted potential being into real being; that is, only when things are united with their symbols do they become actualized. To put it another way, there

A Dogon village (Mali, West Africa) perched on a cliff face.

is no meaning without language and no language until symbols are assigned to their referents. Thus, the Dogon have a rather sophisticated view of the symbolic process.

Universal expansion and differentiation are also symbolized in the contemporary world by a star named *fonio* (after the first seed). It rotates around the brightest star in the sky (Sirius, or the Dog Star to us). The Dogon believe that *fonio* is the smallest and heaviest of all the stars in the universe. As it moves in orbit around Sirius, it upholds all creation in space. Its orbit is also used to determine the Dogon calendar, thus linking it materially to human life.

As we have seen, these events took place within an enormous egg. This egg also contained *Nommo,* the son of *Amma* (God the creator). Here Dogon cosmology becomes very complex, because *Nommo* is actually divided into eight parts. The egg of the world was originally divided into twin placentas, each of which was supposed to contain twin *Nommo.* This gives us four *Nommo* (two in each twin placenta). Each of these twins contained two spiritual principles of opposite sex; each was therefore a pair, so that we end up with eight. Taken all together, the eight *Nommo* as one represent unity. As four sets of paired gods they represent the pervasive duality in Dogon thought.

In Dogon cosmology, as in the cosmology of most peoples, God is seen as the reflection of perfection. The myth, therefore, needs to explain the disorder and imperfection of the contemporary world. In many myths this disorder and imperfection flow from a mistake or rash action that occurs during the process of creation itself. The Dogon adopt this explanation and present it in a beautifully organized symbolic way.

In one of the placentas the male *Nommo* did not await the end of the normal gestation period. Instead, he emerged prematurely and, in so doing, tore a fragment of his placenta from the egg. This fragment fell through space and became the first Earth. This Earth had only a male soul and was, therefore, incomplete and imperfect. It was this imperfection that gave rise to impurity. *Yurugu,* the egg-breaker, realizing that he needed the help of his female double to restore order, returned to heaven seeking the rest of his placenta. But his female twin soul had already been given by *Amma* to the remaining couple in the other part of the egg. *Yurugu's* female counterpart was put in charge of the rest of the egg. From that time on *Yurugu* has been on a fruitless quest for his female twin, whom he cannot retrieve. *Yurugu* returned to Earth and procreated incestuously with the Earth, his own placenta (who is also, as inconsistent as this might seem, his own mother). The creatures she gave birth to were monsters because they were incomplete, lacking, as they did, *Yurugu's* correct other half.

Amma then decided to send the *Nommo* of the other portion of the egg to Earth. They came on a gigantic arch. Two *Nommo* of the sky stood at the center of this arch. The *Nommo* who were to become the ancestors of humankind stood at the four cardinal points. The arch itself was a new undefiled Earth. Its appearance coincided with the coming of light into the universe, which until then had been dark. Rain fell and purified the Earth and made it fertile. The eight seeds were planted by the *Nommo* and gave forth plants, animals, and humans.

The sin of *Yurugu* could not be expunged. The Dogon believe that his actions, which represent imperfection and incompleteness, created death. Today the dry, uncultivated, uninhabited parts of the Earth belong to *Yurugu,* while the other "true" *Nommo* represent fertility, life, and culture.

For the Dogon the human being represents both the Earth's beginning and the existing universe. Humans encapsulate time. All people contain two souls of opposite sex—one dwelling in the body and the other in the sky or water. Blood is associated symbolically with the eight seeds, which are distributed evenly across the collar bones. The order in which these seeds occur, however, depends on a person's sex and place in the Dogon social system.

Humans are also conceived of as the seeds of the universe and the result of its expansion.

Dogon masked dancers performing one of their many rituals. Dogon art (dance, carving, painting, and oral literature) is widely known and appreciated. For the Dogon it is an essential element in religious performance.

Thus, every individual is a microcosm of existence. The vibrations of the original seed gave rise in turn to the various organs of the body. The first and sixth vibrations gave rise to the legs, the second and fifth vibrations produced the arms, the third and fourth produced the head, while the seventh vibration gave rise to the sex organs.

Dogon cosmology is linked closely to social organization. Harmony in the universe depends on harmony in social relations. Each human being, after all, is the universe and all humans taken together are also the universe. Disorder among the seeds within a person creates an outward manifestation of social disorder. This can spread from the individual to his or her kin and finally to the entire social group. This disorder must be halted. Thus, individual sickness or antisocial acts are taken as a threat to religious and social harmony. Peace and unity can only be restored through the performance of proper ceremonies. Dogon ceremonies themselves reenact the process of creation and allow for the manifestation of belief in concrete acts.

THE ROOTS OF RELIGIOUS THOUGHT

E. B. Tylor believed that religious ideas came from dreams. Freud thought that religion was the result of conflict between an individual's basic biological drives and the need to live in society, as well as a projection outward of family conflicts. Jung suggested that religion was the manifestation of the collective unconscious. Many psychologists and anthropologists take the view that it is in some way a projection of basic mental patterns played against the need to make sense out of the universe. Religious individuals believe that religious inspiration comes directly from the supernatural; while it may have to be sought after, religious knowledge is revealed truth.

These ideas are not necessarily contradictory. To hold that religion is based on the mind and its structure does not necessarily dictate either acceptance or rejection of the supernatural origins of mental structures. Here again, we are faced with the difference between science and faith. Even though difficult to prove or disprove, ideas about religion as a product of mental patterns can be empirically investigated. How these patterns got into the mind may be a question of faith.

Certainly we can agree that religious thought requires consciousness and that consciousness implies some awareness of mortality. People are aware of the stream of time. They know that the world existed before and believe that it will go on existing after their own death. All humans must face the fact of death and attempt to come to terms with it. Consciousness begins early in life as the growing infant becomes aware of the world and begins to differentiate itself from others, to engage in self-definition. As individuals develop toward adulthood, they must cope with questions about their own being and their place in the world. It is perfectly natural that questions concerning self and others are then extended outward. People begin to define their own social groups in relation to other social groups. They probe humanness and its relationship to the rest of nature. Indeed, a common dichotomy found in the cosmologies of traditional societies is the distinction between culture and nature: Humans are frequently seen as both part of the natural order and standing apart from it. It is not only anthropologists who have recognized culture as the mark of humanity. Many traditional myths, like those of the Dogon, attempt to account for the origin not only of the human species, but also of culture and language.

This sequence of development supports the idea of interaction between basic mental patterns and human experience with the outside world. In other words, **psychic unity** (the modes by which all humans perceive and organize experience) plus the facts of existence combine to shape religious thought and practice. Widespread similarities among religions throughout the world can be attributed to the common building blocks of religious thought. Differences can be attributed to variations in historical circumstances and environmental patterns. We would expect to find rain gods where water was an important and unreliable resource; a corn god among hunters and gatherers would be a surprise indeed. Yet we are not surprised to find that corn gods, water spirits, and rain gods all share common elements within the context of different religions.

THE BUILDING BLOCKS OF RELIGION

Religion is founded on belief *and* practice. Belief may be supported and transmitted by formal and informal means. A great deal of religion is taught to children by their parents in the form of moral training or as myth. Generally, however, people learn and maintain their religion through participation in ritual. Certain rituals, particularly puberty rites, entail formal learning. Among Jews, for example, the Bar and Bat Mitzvah for boys and girls at the age of 13 comes after a special period of preparation. First Communion among Christians also requires the learning of religious principles. Puberty rites are widespread in nonwestern societies. During these initiation ceremonies boys and girls, usually in separate groups, are taught the proper form of adult behavior as well as the secrets of supernatural life.

Ritual

In **ritual,** beliefs are acted out. A ritual may vary from a reaffirmation of shared religious feelings to active participation in a supernatural event. For a Catholic to participate in the Mass is to relive the Passion of Christ. For all Christians Communion provides intimate contact with God. Spirit possession is common in many parts of the world, particularly in the American South, Africa, lowland South America, and Southeast Asia. During possessive states a god or spirit is thought to actually take over the body. In some instances possession occurs among both participants and religious functionaries, in other cases it is reserved for a priest or priests.

Spirit Possession in Trenganu, Malaysia. Spirit possession is a major feature of curing ceremonies in Trenganu prov-

A

B

C

Rituals involve the acting out of belief.

A

Funeral of a child, Tibet.

B

Baptism, U.S.

C

Pueblo Sun Dance.

D

Fire walking in Fiji (such ceremonies reinforce belief through the witnessing of a miraculous act. The ability of the fire walkers to perform without being burned is evidence for the truth of the belief system).

E

Secular ceremony in the Shetland Islands off the Coast of Scotland. Although no longer religious, this ceremony—which is, in part, a celebration of the past—affirms historical belief and the solidarity of the community of participants.

F

The initiation of a Shavante boy by an old man.

G

Young Senufu girls go off at dawn for their puberty

D E

F

G

ince in Malaysia. A sick person engages a shaman (*bomoh*) to diagnose and treat his or her illness. The *bomoh,* working with a group of musicians, goes into trance and is possessed by a series of spirits (*hantu*) who provide information about the illness and the steps necessary for a cure. In many cases people become ill because they have been unable to follow their inborn talents and desires. Among Trenganu Malays these impulses are known as *angen* (wind). When I visited one of my graduate students, Carol Laderman, there, in 1966, she was in the midst of a study of childbirth, health, and disease. During my stay we attended a curing session for a man seriously ill with asthma. Formerly this man had been a skilled performer of *silat* (a Southeast Asian form of self-defense done to music) and was also a *wayan kulat dalang* (shadow-puppet performer).

Because of his age he had abandoned both pursuits. During the ceremony the *bomoh* went into trance in order to let the spirits speak through him. The *hantu* said that the patient could only get well if his *angen* for *silat* and shadow puppetry could be expressed. After the diagnoses the cure began as the sick man himself went into trance and acted out both a silat and a *wayan kulit* performance. The next day when we visited his house, he was already breathing easily. The cure had taken effect. Since asthma often has a psychological cause, it is not surprising that the ceremony could produce such spectacular results.

Ritual Space

Rituals frequently occur in specially demarcated areas. These may range from part of a dwelling space otherwise used for secular activities to specially built and consecrated buildings such as churches, mosques, and synagogs. A consecration ritual may be necessary before a space can be used for religious purposes. Conversely, a ritual area may have to be deconsecrated before it can be turned back to secular use. There are no universally applicable rules about this. The curing ceremony that I witnessed in Malaysia took place in the ill man's house. On the other hand, possession in many cultures can only occur at a shrine or other sacred setting. In our own culture we may pray anywhere, but the social part of our religious life is usually performed in a special place set aside for that purpose.

Types of Ritual

Rituals can be divided into two major categories: **calendrical rites** and **life-crisis rites.** The former follow a fixed schedule. They may occur frequently—Sunday or Saturday services, for example—or they may mark a special annual event such as Christmas or Passover. Calendrical ceremonies may last for only one day (Easter Sunday) or for an extended period (Passover, Lent, or the Moslem month of Ramadan, a sacred month of fasting). The type of event commemorated during a calendrical ritual varies widely. Among the most common are: the birth of a sacred person, the first harvest at the end of the planting season (first-fruit ceremonies), the celebration of some historical or mythical event, the change of seasons (particularly the coming of the planting season or the harvest), and a major supernatural occurrence.

Life-crisis rites signal a transition in the life of an individual or group. Such events as birth, puberty, marriage, and death can be marked. Puberty ceremonies and funerals are among the most widespread life-crisis rites, but marriage in many societies is not marked religiously. In some cultures the birth of a child is not celebrated, but giving it a name is an important ritual occasion. Name-giving (and name-taking) relate to achieving a *social* position within the community.

Many rituals simply occur when the need arises. Disease, for instance, is frequently treated in a ritual context. If people fear witches, special ceremonies take place when the danger is considered most acute. Special ceremonies may be required before embarking on a hunt, a trading expedition, or war. Safe return after perilous activity also provides the occasion for ritual.

Ceremonies may be public or private. They may be restricted to initiated individuals or encompass the entire social group. They may be exclusive according to sex, age, or some other social category. Often during a ritual a myth or part of a myth is acted out. The performance may occur in a theatrical setting complete with costumes and masks, dancing or music, or it may simply be a retelling to a congregation of worshippers.

Sacrifice

Many rituals are marked by the performance of sacrifice, in which some kind of offering is made to supernatural entities, usually a god, gods, or the ancestors. A sacrifice may be real or symbolic. An animal may be killed and its body left to rot or, after its blood has been shed in a sacred place, the meat may be distributed to members of the congregation. The ancient Greeks broiled meat on the altar, believing that the gods took sustenance from the smoke. The cooked meat was eaten by the worshippers. In many parts of West Africa eggs are placed on an altar for several days. After a specific time period has elapsed, the eggs are removed and eaten by their owner. It is believed that the gods eat only the spirits of the eggs and that they can be consumed by humans after the sacrificial period is over. On the island of Bali various food items, including fruit and rice cakes, are offered in combination with flowers and small palm-leaf sculptures. These are placed on an altar and then immediately taken home, where the food is eaten. The decorative parts of the sacrifice are thrown out unceremoniously. Another form of offering occurs in Bali, where the gods are believed to inhabit the sacred mountain of Agung. During temple festivals the gods are enticed down from the mountaintop by dance and music performances by the faithful.

THE CAST OF CHARACTERS IN RELIGIOUS BELIEF

Religion concerns the supernatural, and people can connect with it through beliefs and rituals. But all societies have felt the need for religious specialists to manage, interpret, and intercede. Specialists include such actors as shaman, priest, and minister. Priests can intercede directly with the supernatural whereas ministers do not have special access to the gods. Priests and shamans may be assisted in performing their religious function by secular individuals.

The supernatural world itself is often inhabited by a wide range of creatures from devils to deities. Among nonwestern peoples, particularly those not associated with the monotheistic religions, a large pantheon of gods may be worshiped. Evil and misfortune may be attributed to a devil or some other type of malevolent spirit. Some types of misfortune are attributed to special causes.

Many of the world's peoples believe in ghosts and many worship the spirits of dead ancestors. In general (there are exceptions), **ghosts** are defined as dead who are somehow misplaced. Their state may be due to the manner in which they died or the lack of a proper funeral ceremony. Some ghosts are the spirits of people who committed evil acts during their lives. Ancestral spirits, on the other hand, usually inhabit a special place. This may be a heaven (or hell) or some real or mythical part of the world. Ancestral spirits can be as dangerous to the living as ghosts, but they usually vent their anger against the living only when some special obligation such as sacrifice has been neglected.

Belief systems often include a wide assortment of other creatures that were once living humans. The belief in vampires is widespread, and in some cultures sorcerers are supposed to be capable of raising the dead and using them for evil purposes. Some living people may also take on supernatural powers. They may be changed into animals with supernatural attributes for a variety of reasons and a variety of causes. In European folklore someone becomes a wolf person (a *lycanthrope*) when bitten by another lycanthrope.

Frequently, minor spirits such as goblins and gremlins fill out the supernatural world. These are usually held responsible for small troubles and may be interpreted as annoying rather than dangerous. Sometimes these creatures even turn out to be helpful. In general, they are believed shy and are only seen fleetingly.

Witches

A major category of supernatural creature is that of the *witch* (*warlock* is a term sometimes applied to male witches). Witches are humans with supernatural powers. They may be born with these powers or learn them through initiation. In many cultures (including our own until recently) witches are believed to fly, change themselves into animals, and become invisible: they are associated with certain animals known as *familiars.* Witches are distinguished from *sorcerers* by many anthropologists on the basis of power and its origin. Sorcerers learn a special technology that can be used to produce supernatural effects. Their gifts are acquired rather than inherited, and they use learned magical techniques for their ends. Although sorcerers may perform only beneficial acts, in many cultures they occupy a position opposite to that of shamans. In these cases they engage in evil rather than beneficial commerce with the supernatural.

In some societies only sorcerers can employ "black" magic against others. There are other societies, however, in which any individual can learn to use magic for good or evil ends. Hostile magical acts include such practices as: *pointing* some magical object at an intended victim with the goal of causing disease or death; *object intrusion,* in which pins or other sharp objects are stuck into a representation of the victim; and the magical *manipulation* of something that was once a part of the victim, such as fecal material, hair, or fingernails. Sometimes an intended victim can be tricked into touching or using some object that has been treated in a magical way.

Sacred Restrictions: Taboo

All societies forbid access to certain things and proscribe certain behaviors. Marriage is not allowed between some types of kin, a range of plants and animals may not be eaten, certain places may not be visited, or special forms of social behavior may be allowed only to individuals with specific statuses. When such restrictions are related to religious belief, they are called **taboos.** The word taboo is borrowed from the terminology of Polynesian religion.

Not all cultural prohibitions are taboos, however. Avoidance may occur for social or practical reasons that are purely secular in nature. In our own culture people allergic to poison ivy avoid contact with it. People are taught to recognize this plant and to understand its possible harmful effects. The same is true of poisonous mushrooms. On a more trivial level, it is considered impolite to burp in public or for men to wear hats indoors. Among hunting and gathering populations certain animals are not killed because they are either too dangerous or too difficult to capture. The presence or absence of certain domesticated plants and animals in a culture may be related to both practical resource management strategies *and* religious belief. It cannot be decided in advance whether or not a real taboo exists under such circumstances.

There are basically two types of taboo. In *total-avoidance taboos,* an object is never touched or a potential food never eaten. In *partial taboos,* restrictions apply to certain times of the year or particular uses. Certain foods, for example, are often taboo until a harvest ceremony. In many parts of the world special categories of people cannot eat designated foods such as organ meat (liver, heart, brains). These nourishing and easily digestible parts are sometimes reserved for the old or the very young. In India beef is forbidden to caste Hindus, but the animal serves as a source of traction, its dung is used for fuel, and its milk constitutes a major source of protein. Beef is taboo, but the use of cows is not.

Mana

Another concept carrying a Polynesian label is *mana.* Mana is a supernatural power; a sacred quality that resides in people, acts, and things. Individuals of high status in Polynesian societies have a great deal of mana while lesser individuals have less mana. In some societies it is a good thing to come upon some object charged with mana, since it will bring good luck to its taker. In other societies mana can be dangerous. It is an entity that evokes ambivalent feelings, probably because power in the abstract and supernatural sense can be frightening as well as useful. In Polynesia mana was dangerous to low-status individuals; a commoner who even accidently touched a chief risked death from the power of the chief's mana. Objects highly charged with mana were taboo to all or some categories of people.

ABRON RELIGION

Beliefs

The Abron religious system has many of the features outlined in this chapter. Like most West Africans the Abron believe in a high god who created the universe and who serves as the deity for all humanity. In addition, the Abron share a god, Tano, with the rest of the Akan people. (The Akans are a linguistically and culturally related set of ethnic groups originating in what is now Ghana.) Tano is associated with a river in Ghana. Every year priests of the temple of Tano in Abron territory make a pilgrimage to the river Tano and take some of its water back to the Tano shrine in the Ivory Coast, the home land of the Abron. Tano is the spirit of the river and the protector of all Akan peoples. Under Tano are a series of lesser gods known as *gbawkaw.* These may be natural objects such as trees, mountains, or other special geographic features, or manufactured images ranging from small anthropomorphic sculptured figures to resin-covered bottles decorated with cowrie shells. *Gbawkaw* may be regional, village, lineage, or even personal deities. In this respect the Abron religious hierarchy is a projection onto the supernatural of secular political authority.

The King of the Abron is the leading religious functionary. He is responsible for presiding over the major Abron ceremony, the Yam Festival (*Odiwera*) that occurs in the fall of each year. The Yam Festival is a first-fruit ceremony and marks the end of food shortages that occur in the dry season. As such, it is a time for general rejoicing and a symbol of renewal similar to our own May-day celebrations. The association of the King with the major food staple and a great feast reinforces loyalties to Abron authority. After the King has celebrated the yam harvest in his capital, local yam festivals occur in each Abron village. There the village chief takes the place of the King as the presiding authority.

The Yam Festival is a redistributive feast. Large quantities of yams and other foods, particularly meat, are "given" to the royal stool. In reality they are placed before the stool for a few days in order that their "souls" may be taken in sacrifice. After this they are given back to the people and the feasting begins in earnest.

Aside from the King and Abron chiefs, priests are the major religious figures. Priests may be either male or female. They conduct ceremonies, practice divination in order to predict the future or the cause of some misfortune, treat illness, and care for local *gbawkaw.* Priests, *kparesogo,* are also charged with protecting people from witches, *deresogo. Deresogo* are mortals possessing hereditary evil powers. Like European witches they fly, change themselves into animals, and can kill their enemies by supernatural means. No Abron admits to being a witch, and all Abron believe in their existence.

The Abron also have sorcerers, as they have been defined in this chapter. Sorcerers, *sogo,* are trained, they use magical techniques for their ends, and they are capable of both beneficial and evil actions. Unlike witches, *sogo* really exist. Many are Moslem Abron who claim to know and use magical powers. They are sometimes consulted in cases of illness but are more likely to be appealed to for love potions. Most Abron feel rather ambivalent about *sogo,* both fearing and respecting them. Sometimes they are accused of causing disease, but they may also be sought out in times of need. Needless to say, no *sogo* ever admits to having participated in black magic. Instead, they claim to have medical and magical knowledge that is used for the benefit of their clients.

Although the Abron do not directly worship the earth, they believe that it is sacred. The land must be respected, for it nourishes all life. Anyone who farms on the Abron day of rest will be punished for desecrating the earth. This punishment takes the form of illness, death, or madness.

In addition to deities and witches, the Abron supernatural world is inhabited by ancestor spirits and ghosts. The ancestors are venerated and the ghosts are mildly feared. Each lineage has its ancestral stools. When someone dies, a part of the soul goes into the stool, where it is believed to reside; another part goes to heaven, where it waits to be reborn in an infant. Sometimes, because of some misfortune, a person becomes a ghost. When this happens, villagers may become the victims of pranks. In order to prevent a ghost from returning to the village, a corpse is turned rapidly several times before it is buried. This, it is believed, will make it dizzy. It will lose its sense of orientation and be unable to find its way back to the village.

The open bush is inhabited by bush devils, *bonzam,* rather nasty creatures that Christian Abron associate with the biblical Devil. When people wander off the beaten track they may be surprised by *bonzam* and either driven mad or killed. *Bonzam* are often used to account for the disappearance of someone. The forests and rivers of Abron country are inhabited by spirits know as *gina.* The best translation of this term is probably "goblin." *Gina* are rather harmless, although they go out of their way to fool people and play pranks on them.

While minor illness and misfortune may be due to natural causes, serious illness is usually attributed to some supernatural power. General epidemics are believed to be caused by the high god or by Tano. Sudden deaths in a village are often taken as evidence of witchcraft. Serious illness, on the other hand, may be attributed to the ancestors signaling their displeasure at some social transgression. Ancestors may also kill victims when they are lonely in heaven and desire company. The best way to insure one's self against this kind of misfortune is to sacrifice to the ancestors on their special day.

The Abron believe in malevolent magic. An individual may harm another by hiring a *sogo* to cast a spell on an enemy or by practicing object intrusion. A small doll is fashioned in the image of the intended victim and sharp objects are stuck into it. But there are preventive techniques against this type of attack that turn it back on its perpetrator.

Rituals

The Abron celebrate both calendrical and life-crisis rites. In addition to the Yam Festival, which comes in the fall, the Abron take a day of rest one day a week and celebrate their ancestors every 42 days. The spirits of dead priests are also honored on a 42-day cycle, but this ceremony takes place on a Friday while secular ancestors are honored on a Wednesday. The birth of a baby is not marked, probably because the child's entrance into Abron society is only tentative; infant mortality is very high. After a week, however, it is assumed that the baby has come to stay and so is named. Naming is a formal event participated in by lineage members and, in small villages, by the entire population. Marriage is also celebrated in a rather complex ritual and, according to some of my informants, puberty is marked for both boys and girls. Since I was unable to see any puberty ceremonies and because people were unwilling to talk about them (some even denied that they occur), I have no really sure data on their existence or the form that they might take.

The really major ritual in the life stream of individuals is, perhaps somewhat ironically, their funeral. Funerals mark the transition between the secular and sacred realms. They establish a continuing link between living Abron and their ancestors. Since ancestral spirits are the keepers of the land, they are very important to all living Abron. They command great respect and in turn assure a bountiful life.

Abron religion reflects both sacred and secular aspects of belief. Deities are hierarchically arranged in a pattern that recalls Abron political structure. Political leadership is tied to ritual and manifested in the context of economic redistribution. Agricultural practices and respect for the land as a source of bounty are reinforced by the sacred nature of Mother Earth. Social control is exercised by ancestors and an abundant pantheon of greater and lesser gods. Evil is attributed to witches and bush devils—the one mortal, the other supernatural. Ceremonial life marks important individual transitions and reinforces respect for leaders. Finally, religious ceremonies focus on both types of political loyalty: that which is oriented towards the Abron nation and that which is oriented toward kinship organization.

Recently some Abron have converted to Christianity and others to Islam. So far, these conversions have been few in number and have not disrupted the fabric of Abron ethical and religious life. The adoption of Islam is least disruptive because it has no effect on residence and marriage rules. Christian converts, on the other hand, are encouraged to break the accepted duolocal residence pattern, and men are expected to remain monogamous. If the Abron King were to convert to either Christianity or Islam, it would have a serious effect on ceremonial and political life. Kingship is tied to the sacred stool, and the stool itself embodies much of Abron belief. On the other hand, the Abron are quite eclectic (they borrow ideas freely from other cultures) and often incorporate alien customs into their social system without difficulty. As in other parts of Africa, it is likely that a religious **syncretism** (a union of disparate beliefs and practices) will develop in which borrowed elements will give rise to a new religious tradition. Both Islam and Christianity in Black Africa have already evolved toward such modified forms.

SYNCRETISM AS A VIABLE RELIGION: NATIVISM

Syncretistic religions (constructed from ideas borrowed from different religions) exist in parts of the world other than Africa. Javanese religion is a combination of Islam, Hinduism, and older, more native forms of belief. In many peasant cultures around the world the national religion exists only in modified form on the local level. The Catholicism of an Irish or Italian peasant living far from the city, for example, may combine elements of prechristian belief with established church doctrine. Catholicism itself accommodated to older religions by adopting and changing formerly Jewish or pagan holidays into Christian celebrations. Halloween (the evening before All Saints' Day) is a thinly disguised prechristian celebration. In the same vein, beginning at the end of the nineteenth century, Native Americans began to incorporate Christian ideas into their own religions and to borrow certain beliefs and ritual practices from one another.

Frequently a syncretistic religion takes on the form of a **revivalistic** or **revitalization** movement, in which an attempt is made to recapture old values or eliminate a foreign political domination. This is the source of the *Ghost Dance,* a ritual that developed among Native Americans on the Great Plains of the United States at the end of the nineteenth century, and the *peyote religion* that spread from group to group early in this century. The Ghost Dance was a religious-political movement in which a basic ritual was converted into a magical and secular protest against white rule. Misunderstood and seen as a danger by the United States government, it was banned. Peyotism, which combines elements borrowed from Southwestern Indian traditions and Christianity, is more passive, although it has served as one basis of pan-Native-American unity. Since its practices include the taking of a hallucinogenic drug, peyote, this church was once banned in several states. More recently it has been accepted, and the taking of peyote is tolerated in the context of ritual.

Revivalistic or revitalization movements need not borrow elements from an introduced religion. Instead, they frequently advocate a return to a pure form of past ritual and belief. Usually, however, a close look at historical data shows that the revitalized form of native religion contains new elements that attract and unify members around a religious-political doctrine.

Sometimes revivalism actually promotes rejection of native culture, even when its ideology is anticolonial. **Cargo cults** in Melanesia (New Guinea and its surrounding islands) exemplify such rejection. Cargo cults call for the destruction of native material culture and even the acceptance of white goods in the form of air and sea cargo but not of white rule. In general, cargo cults destroy large quantities of indigenous goods in the expectation that supernatural powers will overturn colonial authority and provide the native population with the products of Western consumer society. This will arrive as cargo sent by the gods.

The doctrine of uniting a people against political and religious domination by colonizers is known as **nativism.** Movements in this vein call for a return to old values or adoption of local autonomy, with the acceptance of "positive" aspects of the colonial experience. Although such movements are often religious in content and tone, they may also be secular. The Irish revolution against British colonial domination was basically secular, although religious conflict obviously played a role in mustering loyalty to the Irish cause. The State of Israel presents a similar case. Although many Jews worked for the foundation of a Jewish state on religious grounds, the Zionist movement was and is basically secular. Biblical prophecy was converted to a political stand in the face of discrimination in Europe before World War Two.

The foundation of communes in the United States, which have a history that goes back well into the nineteenth century, has often been based on both religious principles and the desire to recapture or revitalize "old" values. In the late 1960s and into the 1970s communes based on revivalistic Western and Eastern religions were founded in many parts of the country.

Whatever its origins, religion in its many forms is a universal aspect of human culture. It provides a central ideology and point of commitment for the faithful and is a major unifying force within a social group made up of believers. As a marker of identity for different cultures and social groups, religion has also been used to justify patriotic resistance to oppressors as well as intolerance and hostility to nonbelievers.

Summary

The supernatural concerns beliefs about what is empirically unknowable because it exists beyond the visible universe. Religion consists of a set of collective beliefs and practices concerning the supernatural.

Early anthropologists attempted to place the development of religious systems into an evolutionary order and identified this evolution with progress. Early religions were associated with animism, the belief that everything in nature contains conscious spirits. E. B. Tylor suggested that animism had its origin in the attempts of "primitive" people to explain their dreams and other psychological phenomena. While agreeing with Tylor that animism was an important element in primitive religion, R. R. Marett pointed out that abstract, impersonal powers also existed. He referred to a belief in such abstract powers as animatism. Evolutionists suggested that animism and animatism give way in the progressive development of religion to polytheism, a belief in multiple gods, identified with but not equal to natural forms. The final stage in religious thought was the emergence of monotheism, a belief in a single god as among Christians, Jews, and Moslems. Monotheism is also associated with a strong morality or ethic.

Andrew Lang pointed out that in Africa, at least, the concept of a high god existed along with animistic beliefs. Many of the world's religions show a combination of animistic, animatistic, polytheistic, and sometimes even monotheistic beliefs. Hindus, for example, believe that their many deities are actually the expression in different forms of a single high god.

There are many anthropological theories concerning both the origin and function of religion in culture. The French sociologist Émile Durkheim is associated with the idea that belief systems are a projection (or expression) of the social group. He defined religion as a system of beliefs and practices relative to sacred things that unite individuals into a church. Religious systems united the social group into a harmonious whole. Durkheim noted that kin groups frequently identified themselves with natural entities, or totems. Totems include such elements as plants and animals or even geographic features like streams or mountains. Sigmund Freud suggested that totemic groups, all of which he took to be exogamous, were founded on the incest taboo and an identification of the totemic symbol with an original clan father. Claude Lévi-Strauss suggested that totems are a conceptual device for classifying social groups by means of natural emblems.

Freud believed that religion was a projection in social form of individual conscience. Religion, for Freud, was a collective representation of conflicts and their resolution that develop in the context of individual families. Carl Jung also saw religion as a projective system, but of consciousness itself. Durkheim contrasts with both Freud and Jung because he rejected psychological explanations of social phenomena. Religion for him was a collective representation of the social group.

Bronislaw Malinowski was concerned with the pragmatic aspects of magic and drew a distinction between magic and religion. While religion concerned the whole cosmos and supernatural realm, magic was used for practical ends. Malinowski further suggested that practical activity without recourse to magic occurs in daily life when no danger or difficulty is present and success is relatively assured. Only in less sure situations will magic be resorted to.

Sir James Frazer drew a distinction between imitative and contagious magic. The former depends on the law of similarity (like things are in important ways the same) and the latter on the law of contact (things that have once been in contact remain in contact). For Frazer both forms of magic could be related in a more abstract sense to the law of sympathy (things act on each other at a distance through a secret sympathy).

While Malinowski's and Frazer's discussions of magic are useful, actually it is difficult if not impossible to draw an absolute distinction between magic and religion. Magical acts are often based on religious belief and religious practices often contain what Malinowski would call magical acts.

Roy Rappaport has suggested that rituals (religious ceremonies) function as regulators of ecological variables. He points out that pig festivals in New Guinea occur when the pig population begins to outrun locally available resources. Pig ceremonies act to restore a balance between human and pig populations.

Most anthropologists agree that, whatever its other functions, religion acts as a strong force for social control. In egalitarian societies priests or shamans may be the only individuals who can act to restore order in cases of conflict.

Symbolism is a major feature of all religious belief. Symbols make real and concrete a range of abstract and difficult concepts. Many symbols are polyvocalic—that is, they provide a wide set of connections among elements, creating a conceptual unity among them. Symbols may be united in narrative and myth to provide explanations of the origin of the universe and the place of humans within it.

Religion is founded on belief *and* practice. People generally learn and maintain their religion through participation in ritual. Ritual involves the acting out of beliefs.

Rituals may be divided into two major types, calendrical rites and life-crisis rites. The former occur at fixed times and celebrate such events as the first harvest, the death of a founding ancestor, or some other noteworthy secular or sacred event that has become incorporated into religious belief. Life-crisis rites occur at single points in the life history of an individual—birth, marriage, and death, for example.

The religious world is inhabited by a cast of characters both natural and supernatural. Gods, ghosts, ancestors, devils, and spirits are among the supernatural entities encountered in belief systems. In addition to these, most religious systems include human specialists who deal with religious matters. These include priests, ministers, shamans, and curers. The belief in witches is common among the world's peoples. Witches are both natural (they are living humans) and supernatural (they have gifts that allow them to act in supernatural ways).

All societies forbid access to certain things and proscribe certain behaviors. Some of these proscriptions are secular. In American culture, for example, it is not considered polite to burp in public or for men to wear hats indoors. Other restrictions are based on religious belief. Violations of these restrictions, known as taboos, may lead to punishment by religious authorities and/or supernatural powers. Some things and behaviors may be totally taboo—that is, they may never be touched or used or done. Other taboos are partial. They may obtain for specific times of the year or apply only to certain persons within society. In many cultures certain foods may be eaten only after a harvest ceremony has taken place. Specific items of food are often taboo to one or the other sex or to people of certain ages or social categories.

Mana, or sacred power, is related to taboo in the sense that individuals with great mana must not be touched by individuals with less mana.

Many religious systems, particularly in the modern world, are syncretistic; that is, they contain elements borrowed from many religions. Recent converts to Christianity in the Third World often retain elements of their original religion and incorporate them into their new belief systems. Christianity itself incorporates beliefs from prechristian times.

Religion is often used by oppressed peoples as a means of protesting or overturning a secular political system. Nativistic or revivalistic movements attempt to revive old values as a protest against a social or political order. Such movements are themselves often syncretistic. Cargo cults, which developed in Melanesia after World War II, centered on the belief of native peoples that if they destroyed objects of their own culture, the gods would remove them from colonial authority and replace their old things with cargo—Western material objects.

Bibliography

Balikci, A. 1967 — Shamanistic Behavior Among the Netsilik Eskimos. In *Magic, Witchcraft, and Curing.* Edited by J. Middleton. Garden City: Natural History Press. The role of the shaman in social control and curing.

Douglas, M. 1966 — *Purity and Danger.* Middlesex: Penguin. Study of pollution concepts and taboos from an English structuralist point of view.

Durkheim, E. 1961 — *The Elementary Forms of the Religious Life.* New York: Collier Books. Religion as projection of the group. This book is by the founder of French anthropology and sociology.

Frazer, J. G. 1911–1915 — *The Golden Bough: A Study of Magic and Religion.* London: Macmillan. One of the first comparative studies of religion. A mammoth if somewhat wrong-headed attempt at synthesis and theory-building.

Freud, S. 1950 — *Totem and Taboo.* London: Routledge and Kegan Paul Ltd. Freud's interpretation of the notion of taboo and incest regulation.

Griaule, M. 1954 — The Dogon of French Sudan. In *African Worlds.* Edited by D. Forde. Oxford: Oxford University Press. Data on a fascinating African cosmological system.

Harris, M. 1974 — *Cows, Pigs, Wars, and Witches.* New York: Random House. A theory of taboo as functional from the leading cultural materialist.

Lévi-Strauss, C. 1963 — *Totemism.* Translated by R. Needham. Boston: Beacon Press. Structural explanation of totemism as a system of classification.

Mair, L. 1969 — *Witchcraft.* New York: McGraw Hill. Witchcraft viewed in the context of social structure.

Malinowski, B. 1948 — *Magic, Science, and Religion and Other Essays.* Boston: Beacon Press. Introduces distinction between magic, science, and religion from a British functionalist.

Middleton, J. 1967 — *Gods and Rituals: Readings in Religious Beliefs and Practices.* Garden City: Natural History Press. A good set of articles on the subject.

Norbeck, E. 1961 — *Religion in Primitive Society.* New York: Harper and Row. An introduction to theory and data in the anthropology of religion.

Rappaport, R. A. 1968 — *Pigs for the Ancestors.* New Haven: Yale University Press. Ritual regulation of protein in the form of pigs in Highland New Guinea.

Tylor, E. B. 1873 — *Primitive Culture: Researches into the Development of Mythology, Philosophy, Religion, Language, Art, and Custom.* A classic work by a founder of English anthropology. Material on beliefs and a definition of religion are offered.

CHAPTER 21
THE ARTS

As the expressive and symbolic aspects of human behavior, language and art are twin offspring of culture. Because they are both communication systems and because language is often used in art, just as art is often used to carry a linguistic message, it is easy to think of art as a form of language. We have already seen why language occupies a central place in the evolution and adaptation of *Homo sapiens,* a social species with high intelligence. But if language functions so well as our major form of communication, and if art is indeed in some sense linguistic, why should art exist at all, much less occur in one form or another in all cultures? One answer to this question is that, while the *purpose* of language is to communicate, art has no purpose apart from itself. The philosopher Immanuel Kant, who held to this view, said that art was "purposeful purposelessness." The poet Archibald MacLeish said, in a similar vein, that "a poem should not mean but be." Another, slightly different answer to our question about art is that, while art and language are both communication systems, what they communicate is different. The primary message of art is aesthetic rather than linguistic. I define art as *play with form, the purpose of which is to produce an aesthetically successful object or performance.* By aesthetically successful I mean that art arouses and satisfies a specifically aesthetic emotion in humans; the object or performance produces aesthetic pleasure. Although we do not normally get pleasure from a sad experience, we can get pleasure from a sad poem because the poem arouses pleasure—not because it is sad, but because it deals aesthetically with sadness.

The point of these statements about art is that while language is a medium through which a message is communicated, art *as art* communicates only itself (it arouses the aesthetic emotion); whatever else it communicates is an extra-artistic message.

The discussion so far suggests strongly that "art for art's sake" is a valid concept, yet this is a Western idea. Even a word for *art* does not exist in all languages, and there are many cultures in which what we would call art *always* has a specific nonartistic function. Perhaps the major difference between the art of traditional cultures and that of the contemporary Western world can be found in the tenuous connections between art and life in our own culture. In modern Western society it may be true that "art imitates life" or that "life imitates art," but we can say these things precisely because the two categories are maintained as separate entities. In traditional societies art reverberates *through* life. It appears embedded in the mainstream of culture as a major feature of belief and ritual. It serves to make real and immediate the world of the supernatural. Yet recent anthropological research also shows that purely aesthetic standards *do* exist in all cultures. If questioned properly, people will make purely artistic value judgments about what we in the West would call art.

Since we lack historical documents for traditional societies, and because much of our knowledge of the art from these cultures is known only from collections torn from their contexts, it is useful to examine the place of aesthetics in religious art from mediaeval Europe, a society for which written records do exist.

Mediaeval society was, like many of the cultures studied by anthropologists, quite conservative. Religion played a major role in the life of the people and, although one can speak of European culture, local and regional styles in religious art were pronounced. The art historian Meyer Schapiro has written widely on the art of this period. One of his articles, *On the Aesthetic Attitude in Romanesque Art,* sheds a good deal of light on the question of purely aesthetic standards in an art that was created for strictly religious purposes. Schapiro tried "to show that by the eleventh and twelfth centuries there had emerged in western Europe within church art a new sphere of artistic creation, without religious content and imbued with values of spontaneity, individual fantasy, delight in color and movement, and the expression of feeling that anticipate modern art."

The remains of the Abbey Church Of Cluny. Largely destroyed after the French Revolution, Cluny was the largest church ever built in the Romanesque style and a major center for religious art.

Schapiro rejects the notion that mediaeval art was simply secular art used for religious purposes, but rather argues that, given its religious purpose, the artists who created it dealt in their work with aesthetic problems. Schapiro notes that Saint Bernard wrote a severe critique of the art of Cluny (a religious order) specifically because he realized its essentially nonreligious and, therefore, in his opinion, frivolous nature. In part, Saint Bernard said the following:

In short, so many and so marvellous are the varieties of shapes on every hand, that we are more tempted to read in the marble than in our books, and to spend the whole day wondering at these things rather than in meditating the law of God. For God's sake, if men are not ashamed of these follies, why at least do they not shrink from their expense?

In addition to what are essentially negative comments by Saint Bernard, Schapiro adds a set of positive judgments about mediaeval art by its contemporaries. He tells us that, far from considering this art only as the bearer of a religious message, people of the time deeply appreciated it for its originality and artistic skill.

There is, no doubt, a strong current of aestheticism in the culture of the twelfth century, flowing through different fields, the plastic arts no less than the Latin and vernacular poetry. It affects the forms of religious life in ritual, costume, and music, as well as church building and decoration.

Twelfth-century critics were even conscious and appreciative of native arts that preceded their own period, including pagan Roman art. As early as the eleventh century artists were beginning to copy details of ornament borrowed from classical sources. During this time a distinction was made between the worth of such art as art and its religiously unacceptable aspects.

To put this material in anthropological perspective it should be pointed out that in Africa, at least, and no doubt elsewhere, a great deal of religious borrowing has frequently occurred among ethnic groups, partially on the basis of art styles in different types of masks and cult figures. It is the physical presence and formal impact of these sculptures that encourages the incorporation of associated rituals into the religious practice of a society.

THE ARTS IN WORLD CULTURE

Art of some type exists in every culture, but not every art form is universally distributed. Oral traditions (myths, epics, tales) are probably found most widely, followed by dance and music. Minor visual art (decorated useful objects, for example) is also widely distributed. Important painted and sculpted objects are more restricted in distribution. In our own culture we make a distinction between *ritual,* which usually takes place in a sacred place like a church, and *theatre,* which is generally secular. If we hold to this separation, then theatre is common only in the West and the literate cultures of Asia. If, on the other hand, we recognize the similarities in form between ritual and theatre we can say that theatre and ritual *as performance* are widespread.

Oral Literature

Oral literature in the form of myth, prose, and poetry is found almost everywhere. **Myth,** defined strictly as a religious account of the origins of humans and the supernatural, is distributed in a wide arc from Europe all the way across Asia and into the New World to the tip of South America. Evidence that North Asiatic mythology diffused into the New World lies in similarities between Siberian tales and the myths of Native Americans. Origin myths are also found in Australia. In addition, *legends* dealing with the historical past are common in European folklore and in Africa. These legends are often told in the form of epic poetry, with or without rhyme. One major European legend, *Beowulf,* is taken as the foundation of North European literature. Another set of legends, the *Iliad* and the *Odyssey,* marks the beginning of ancient Greek literature. Both *Beowulf* and the *Iliad-Odyssey,* in fact, contain elements of myth and legend, showing that these are not easily separated categories.

Not all oral literature is as weighty as myth and legend. Just-so tales that "explain" elements of culture and nature, such as the origin of the elephant's trunk or how the leopard got its spots, are found everywhere. They are told for enjoyment, often with great animation, and are not necessarily meant to be believed.

The telling of myths, legends, and tales, as well as the recitation of poetry, is an important activity in nonliterate cultures (see Box on Navajo poetry.) It is an activity that provides both recreation and instruction. In Africa the skilled teller of tales gains prestige from the exercise of a highly respected talent.

Dance

Dance, with and without music, is a common feature of culture, occurring in both secular and ritual contexts. Mimetic dances, which imitate some task such as planting or the movement of

Young Aboure (Ivory Coast) boys listen to a traditional myth told by an elder. This is one way they learn the traditions of their ethnic group.

hunted animals, are frequently encountered by anthropologists. The !Kung San of the Kalahari Desert, for instance, are skilled mimes. They frequently imitate animals *during* the hunt in order to approach game unnoticed. After a successful hunt !Kung San often pass the night miming the entire expedition for the appreciation of their camp fellows. In other cultures more serious dances may occur before hunting in order to insure success. The Ingalik, a Native American group living in interior Alaska, have a 16-day ceremonial called the Animal Dance. The Animal Dance, which combines elements of mime, dance, and other forms of theatre, is performed to insure the fertility of animals hunted by the Ingalik. Many parts of this ceremony are quite sexual in nature, while others parody human misbehavior. This combination of parody and a focus on human sexuality is probably related to fertility in general on the one hand and to social control on the other. A certain degree of sexual license is allowed during part of the Animal Dance ceremony, but improper sexual behavior is marked out for ridicule.

Dance is also a common part of initiation rites. The Baruya of highland New Guinea have a puberty ceremony for boys that lasts six weeks. After a special hut is constructed by the men and women of several villages, the boys are isolated from their mothers. Sons and mothers will not have social contact until the boys reach full manhood. The ceremony itself takes place mostly at night within the confines of the hut where the boys are dressed by their male relatives. Dancing is a principal activity in these rites.

Dance may also celebrate the successful completion of some action. Victory and harvest dances are well known from many parts of the world.

Curing ceremonies, which exist all over the world, frequently include dancing. Navajo cures, for example, known for their spectacular sand-paintings, do so.

Divination often occurs in trances, and trances are often brought on by dance. Abron

Navajo Poetry

Song from the Mountain Chant:

The voice that beautifies the land!
The voice above,
The voice of the thunder,
Among the dark clouds
again and again it sounds,
The voice that beautifies the land.

The voice that beautifies the land!
The voice below,
The voice of the grasshopper,
Among the flowers and grasses
Again and again it sounds,
The voice that beautifies the land.

Song from the Mountain Chant:

Maid Who Becomes a Bear
Sought the gods and found them,
On the summits of the mountains
Sought the gods and found them,
Truly with my sacrifice
Sought the gods and found them.
Somebody doubts it, so I have heard.

Holy Young Woman
Sought the gods and found them,
On the summits of the clouds
Sought the gods and found them,
Truly with my sacrifice
Sought the gods and found them.
Somebody doubts it, so I have heard.

Matthews, Washington 1897
Navaho Legends. Published for the American Folk-Lore Society by G. E. Stechert & Co.: New York.

White House (a ruin in Canyon de Chelly) prayer, taught to Dawn Boy by Hastshehogan (House God) in one of the myths of the Night Chant.

I.

1. *In Kininaekai. (White House.)*
2. *In the house made of dawn.*
3. *In the story made of dawn.*
4. *On the trail of dawn.*
5. *O, Talking God!*
6. *His feet, my feet, restore.*
7. *His limbs, my limbs, restore.*
8. *His body, my body, restore.*
9. *His mind, my mind, restore.*
10. *His voice, my voice, restore.*
11. *His plumes, my plumes, restore.*
12. *With beauty before him, with beauty before me.*
13. *With beauty behind him, with beauty behind me.*
14. *With beauty above him, with beauty above me.*
15. *With beauty below him, with beauty below me.*
16. *With beauty around him, with beauty around me.*
17. *With pollen beautiful in his voice, with pollen beautiful in my voice.*
18. *It is finished in beauty.*
19. *It is finished in beauty.*

II.

1. *In Kininaekai.*
2. *In the house of evening light.*
3. *From the story made of evening light.*
4. *On the trail of evening light.*
5. *O, House God! (1907:29)*

(The rest as in I., except that lines 12 and 13 are transposed.)

The poem is in two parts because the White House ruin is painted white (the color of the East and dawn) only on the upper story, the lower story being the natural yellow (color of the West and twilight) of yellow sandstone. Matthews says in a footnote (pg. 29), "The Navahoes do not think this the result of a mere whim, but that it is intentional and symbolic. White is the color of the east in Navaho symbolism, and they suppose the upper story was sacred to Hastsheyalti, or Talking God, who was a god of dawn and of the east. Yellow is the symbolic color of the west, and they suppose the lower story belonged to Hastshehogan, or House God, who was a god of the west and of the evening twilight."

Matthews, Washington 1907
Navaho Myths, Prayers and Songs, with Texts and Translations. Pliny Earle Goddard (ed.), University of California Publications in American Archaeology and Ethnology, vol. 5, no. 2, September: 21–63.

priests, for instance, often enter a trance state during major ceremonies in which they are charged with foretelling the future. Once during my own field work, an Abron woman priest danced in a trance state for several hours. During that time she was possessed by a *gbawkaw* (god) who talked through her. The *gbawkaw* warned that an epidemic was about to strike the village and told the people how to prevent it by performing another ritual on the following day.

People also dance for particular gods. Dancing may be a regular part of ritual. Many Pentecostal churches in the United States forbid secular dancing but incorporate it into their own services. Social dancing is considered a sin by these groups, but dancing for God is not only sanctioned, it is required.

Of course, not all dance is religious or even serious. One way to express joy is to dance. In our own culture people do not often just get up and dance, but most Abron will, particularly if someone is playing music. Social dancing is found all over Africa as part of expressive culture. In the United States social dancing is more structured. People go out to dance, and dancing often has a relationship to courting behavior. It occurs formally at "dances" and informally at parties. People on dates frequently go out to dance in establishments providing music and drinks. To go dancing is to go out for pleasure. It is one feature of Western and, lately, Asian leisure culture. Of course, there is another aspect of dance in Western and Asian culture—dance as performance. Professional dancing of many types is seen in theatres and on television. It is a completely secular art form requiring highly trained personnel and a devoted audience. Dance in this sense is a far cry from the participation one finds in religious ceremonies around the world. Its origin, however, is undoubtedly linked to former religious and popular expression.

Music

Music is perhaps the easiest art form to practice alone, simply for the pleasure involved. Even today lonely shepherds in Europe play simple flutes to pass the time as they guard their flocks. The human voice itself is an instrument. Music is another aspect of the human being's inventive capacities; sung and whistled melodies can be created in infinite variety whenever an individual is moved to make them.

Music performance can also be, of course, a group phenomenon. Choral and orchestral music are found in many cultures, particularly as an aspect of ritual. In many cases specific types of musical performance and special compositions are closely associated with individual rituals. The Mbuti of the Ituri Forest in Zaire associate music with social harmony, and their major ritual, the *Molimo,* involves group singing accompanied by sacred flutes. Musical groups composed of skilled performers exist in many cultures. These may play for both sacred and secular occasions.

Music consists of two major aspects, *tonality* and *rhythm.* Different musical traditions have emphasized each in different degrees. Tonality is most highly developed in Western music, with its wide range of instruments. Rhythm is particularly complex in African and Indian music, although complex melody can be found in both as well. Rhythm is enhanced in those regions by a wide range of percussion instruments. These include hollow drums with skin heads over each opening, tambourines with a single head, plank and log drums, rattles, scrapers, bells, and gongs of various types. African drummers usually perform in groups, with each drummer contributing his own rhythmic line to the elaborate polyrhythms that make up the major musical focus. Indian drumming is quite complex, but a single drummer is the rule. He works on a variable tone drum and hits different parts of the head and rim to produce different tones and timbres.

In addition to the percussion group, musical instruments include winds and strings. These are both widely distributed in the Old World, including Africa. Flutes of various sorts are found practically everywhere. The haunting music of Peruvian Indians is based primarily on a variety of flutes, including the pan pipes. Reed instruments are also common, although I know of none in the New World. Double-reed oboe-like instruments are found all over Eurasia and Africa. While many of these are blown directly, bagpipes of various types also occur. The latter are most common in Great Britain, Ireland, and the countries around the Mediterranean Sea. Most bagpipes have at least two

A

B

C

D

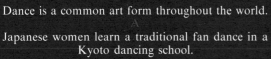

E

Dance is a common art form throughout the world.

A

Japanese women learn a traditional fan dance in a Kyoto dancing school.

B

A traditional men's dance, New Delhi, India.

C

Traditional Scottish dance.

D

Traditional Cuna (Panama) dance of welcome.

E

Modern theatrical dance in the United States.

A

B

C

D

A variety of musical instruments are played by the world's peoples.

A

A !Kung San man plays a bow. The bow is plucked with the thumb and the tone is controlled by the placement of the lips on the bowstring.

B

A Nepalese villager plays a traditional horn.

C

Tibetan monks announce prayer time by playing decorated conch-shell horns.

D

Traditional Japanese string, percussion, and wind instruments played at a hollyhock festival in Kyoto.

E

A Kenyan plays the drum at a dance festival.

sound-emitting segments, one of which produces variable notes when holes are covered and uncovered with the fingers. The other pipe or set of pipes is called a drone. It adds a constant background tone to the music. The bagpipe player blows into a tube that is attached to an air sac. It is this sac that provides the wind for the instrument. Because the sac can be kept inflated the drone need not be interrupted for breath. In addition to reed and flute-like instruments, horns of various types are also found throughout the Old World.

Strings of two types occur. The most common are guitar-like and are played by strumming or plucking. In Africa large gourds are often used as the sounding boards for harp-like strings. Instruments in which a bow is drawn along a string or strings are less common than plucking instruments. Where they occur they add a distinctive type of tone and timbre to the range of possible musical sounds.

Visual Art

Visual art—particularly painted and unpainted sculpture—is widely distributed. West Africa from Cape Verde to Angola is justly famous for a wide variety of sculptural styles. Most common are masks and figurines, but carved doors and house posts are also found. Sometimes these sculptures are painted with a single color, often a shiny black, but *polychrome* (multicolored) examples also occur.

Stone and metal sculpture are widespread across Asia, but wood carving is found as well. One of the most developed carving styles, including highly decorated and complex polychrome designs, comes from the Northwest Coast of North America. In that region such groups as the Tlingit, Tsimshian, Haida, Bela Coola, and Kwakiutl produced a dizzying array of useful and ceremonial objects ranging from spoons to house posts. No other area of the Americas has such a highly developed wood carving style or the variety of objects, although the Iroquois in the East, some Western Eskimo groups and Southwestern Puebloans did make fine painted masks and some statues.

Mesoamerica and highland South America are the New World domains of stone and pottery sculpture. The Aztec and Maya and the cultures that preceded them produced an amazing array of sculpted figures, ranging from realistic to highly stylized forms. Some of these include whole scenes from daily life peopled with cleverly sculpted figures. Pre-Inca and Inca civilizations in the Andes and coastal Peru are also noted for both stone and clay work. Clay was used primarily for pots. This, however, did not limit the artists' ability to express a wide range of animal and human forms, which appear on these pots in painted and sculpted form. The Moché culture of Peru developed a style of realistic and satirical pot design ranging from portraits to what might now be classed as pornography. Weaving was also highly developed as an art form in the Andean highlands.

Metal casting, often in gold and silver but also in bronze, is found in ancient Europe, all over Asia, in parts of Africa (although silver is not used in the latter area), and in the art of pre-Columbian civilizations in the New World.

Three extremely important areas for visual art occur in Southeast Asia and the Pacific. These are Indonesia, Papua and New Guinea, and the smaller Pacific islands, particularly Polynesia. Indonesia is now primarily Moslem, but in the past pagan and Hindu influences helped inspire several art styles in architecture, painting, carving, sculpting, and weaving. Among the non-Moslem, non-Hindu cultures where art was highly developed are the Batak of Sumatra, the Dyak of Borneo, the Nias Islanders, and the Mininkabao of Sumatra.

Although many styles occur in New Guinea, most appear to be of common origin. Finely carved and painted masks, figurines, shields, house posts, and hooks used for hanging objects safely away from rats are found in great abundance along the Sepik River and along the Papuan Gulf, in what is now the Republic of Papua and New Guinea. Another important group of carving peoples is found in the lowland Asmat area of West Irian, the Indonesian part of New Guinea.

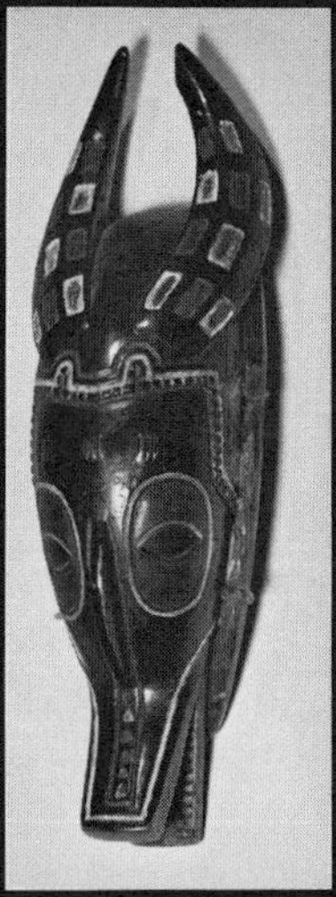

A

B

C

D

E

The styles of visual art are extremely variable by area and through time.

A

Wooden, painted mask, Guru (Ivory Coast, early 20th century).

B

Painting, *The Education of the Virgin,* by the 17th-century French painter Georges de La Tour.

C

Painting, *Giovanni Arnolfini and His Bride,* by the 15th-century Flemish painter Jan Van Eyck.

D

Wooden ceremonial bowl from Santa Cruz, Solomon Islands.

E

Clay figures from precolumbian Mexico.

A

B

C

D

E

Many cultures can be distinguished by their traditional architecture.

A

A mosque in Djenne, Mali. This structure is made of wood and sun-dried clay.

B

The sacred Ajanta Cave in India.

C

The inner courtyard of the main pagoda at Rangoon, Burma.

D

A mosque in a Senufu (northern Ivory Coast) village.

E

Granaries (foreground) and houses (background) in Labbezanga village, Mali.

The large islands off the coast of New Guinea are also known for fine carving and straw weaving. The styles of these cultures are too numerous to mention here. Further away from the large land masses, Polynesian culture developed its own art styles, marked by finely carved and incised wood sculptures, baskets of various types, and feathered cloaks. The Maori of New Zealand developed a highly baroque style in which no space was left undecorated. Maori houses are masterpieces of fine carving, with elaborate scroll designs cut into the walls and posts.

Architecture

A house or temple is often more than just a home or place of worship. Buildings provide surfaces and interiors for decoration, and their forms alone can go well beyond simple function. Many years ago the Museum of Modern Art in New York had a photography show called *Architecture Without Architects.* In that exhibit houses and other structures from cultures all over the world were offered as examples of aesthetic building. All types of construction materials were included, ranging from mud to grass to stone.

Among traditional cultures the more spectacular feats of architecture include those of the Pueblo Indians of the Southwest of the United States, who built large "apartment houses" out of stucco and mud bricks; the cliff dwellings of the Dogon of Mali, discussed in the last chapter; the large frame houses of various Indonesian and New Guinea peoples, often with elaborately carved and painted fronts; the large single dwellings of lowland South American Indian groups; and, of course, the elaborate stone temple architecture of the ancient civilizations of the Old and New World.

THE ROLE OF THE ARTIST IN SOCIETY

Art is, of course, produced by persons skilled in different degrees in the various media. In numerous cultures art is created by many individuals for their own use and the use of others. Art production may range from the casual decoration of personal belongings to the fabrication of masterworks for secular or ceremonial use. While skilled artists are relatively rare in our own culture, they are common in others. In Bali, for example, practically every adult and many children produce art of high quality, ranging from dance and music to carving and painting. Given the narrow distribution of artistic talent in our own culture and its wide distribution in Bali, little can be said about the *inherent* range of artistic ability among humans. The differences, however, are most likely due to the place of art in each culture as well as the degree to which Balinese and Americans are encouraged to engage in aesthetic activity. In Bali artistic production has traditionally been a part of religious observance, and more recently it has become a major feature of a growing tourist industry.

In our own society professional artists produce a commodity subject to the rules of supply and demand as well as prevailing taste. The commercial value of professional art is maintained through the mechanism of scarcity. Only a few artists succeed and their work is highly valued.

In most traditional societies the artist is an individual recognized for his or her talents but nonetheless only a part-time specialist. There are few cultures in which artists work their skills full-time, and indeed they may not even be paid for their work. Frequently an artist is also a shaman, and creative activity is performed in conjunction with religious ceremonies. A mask may be carved, a song sung, or a dance danced in the context of a specific ritual by the leader of that ritual. Sometimes the artist is considered an outsider or a person with dangerous supernatural power to be revered and feared at the same time.

The Role of the Mask-Maker in Secret Societies and Myth in Liberia

Warren L. d'Azevedo has studied the role of the carver among the Gola of Liberia. The Gola are one of the ethnic groups that participate in the widespread network of secret societies found in Liberia, Guinea, and the western Ivory Coast.

The great public ceremonies in this area dramatize the founding of the Sande and Poro societies. According to the foundation myth, in the beginning was the Sande. Women were the keepers of all ritual objects and were responsible for the performance of ceremonies. While men ruled in the secular sphere, women had power over the supernatural. Peace reigned over the land. Then a period of terrible wars struck, during which the men found out that they could not trust women with military secrets. They discovered that a woman is loyal only to her own kin and to the Sande society. It was this fact that led to the founding of Poro, the men's society. It was decided that each society would take its turn at control of the country. The Poro would reign for four years and the Sande for three in perpetual rotation.

Balinese children begin to learn art at an early age. Here a young boy apprenticed to a master carver learns to work in stone. The carvings will be used as temple decorations.

Each society has special and exclusive spheres of knowledge. Men claim that they do not know the content of Sande ritual and women disclaim any curiosity about the Poro. This mutual exclusiveness creates a necessity to have intermediaries between the men's and women's societies. These intermediaries, older men and women, are called *zo; Mazo* in the Sande and *Dazo* in the Poro. These individuals are considered old enough to have passed out of the age at which exclusive involvement in either the Poro or Sande is considered necessary. Both *Mazo* and *Dazo* are individuals who know a good deal about the society that is the counterpart of their own.

The woodcarvers who make masks for these secret societies occupy a unique place in the social-ritual system. Most important is their role in the making of masks used by the Sande in the public ceremonies, as well as their relationships with Sande women. These men, who are not considered to be among the *zonya* (plural of *zo*), participate intimately in the affairs of the women's society. As soon as an individual carver has participated in the production of Sande or Poro masks that have been used in public ritual, his status in society changes markedly. The objects he makes are not considered the products of human hands but are instead the visible forms of supernatural beings. The better his skill at making a mask, the greater the public illusion

A zo gbe (sacred character of the Sande society). Zo gbe masks are the work of the most prestigious Gola carvers.

that the mask is the result of sacred intervention. At the same time the artist's fame, if not publicly acknowledged, grows among those charged with the regulation of sacred affairs. When a mask must be carved, the concerned *zonya* will attempt to obtain the services of a well-known master carver whose fame depends on his objective skill *plus* the success in ritual performance that his masks have had. Among the Gola and related people judgment about good masks is based on a combination of aesthetic and practical principles.

Most professional carvers profess intensive devotion to their skill. At the same time they are proud and vain. The community considers them to be both irresponsible and untrustworthy. They yearn for admiration and seek crowds. This deviant aspect of their personalities is considered to be a threat to their own families, and women fear that carvers can produce infertility among female relatives.

When a mask must be carved the *zonya* have to enter into negotiations with a carver. During the work period he must be fed and cared for. Sometimes a carver works in total isolation, but sometimes he demands that women be brought for his sexual gratification. The women in their turn will attempt to direct the work and influence the carver's use of certain techniques and styles. When the work is finally complete, the carver affirms his symbolic ownership of the mask by informing the women that he can destroy it at any time and instructing them in rules associated with caring for it. The special relationship between the carver and the owners of the mask is a permanent one. He enjoys special privileges. Members of the group and the carver refer to each other as lovers, and the carver can expect sexual favors from the women. The relationship of the carver to his mask is so intense that many men who carve see themselves as mothers of the objects they have created. d'Azevedo quotes one carver's sensation of watching his mask come to life in the context of ceremony.

I see the thing I have made coming out of the woman's bush. It is now a proud man jina *with plenty of women running after him. It is not possible to see anything more wonderful in this world. His face is shining, he looks this way and that, and all the people wonder about this beautiful and terrible thing. To me, it is like what I see when I am dreaming. I say to myself, this is what my* neme *has brought into my mind. I say, I have made this. How can a man make such a thing? It is a fearful thing I can do. No other man can do it unless he has the right knowledge. No woman can do it. I feel that I have borne children.*

d'Azevedo points out that the carver of sacred objects in these societies is both the creator and interpreter of symbolic effects. His work embodies the principles of both male and female orientations to life. It is the carver's own vision that unites them in an expression of the sacred. It is his power that allows for the expression of sacred ideas in the life of ritual.

THE FUNCTIONS OF ART

Art *as art* arouses emotional feelings in receptive individuals. In this way it commands attention. This attention-getting quality of art has been converted in many cultures into unconscious and conscious extra-artistic functions. Art in this way becomes useful beyond the purely aesthetic sphere.

Art as a Social Marker

Art may be used to define a group in relation to other groups. A particular culture may consciously exploit its own set of symbols and its style to serve as a marker of the group. Individuals, for example, may be recognized as members of a particular society by the way they decorate themselves, their style of dress, or even their characteristic hair style. Until recently, rural Europeans of different countries could be told apart by their dress. In France regional costumes were common until the end of the nineteenth century and persisted in rural areas until the Second World War. Different Indian ethnic groups in the Americas could be identified by characteristic dress and sometimes by face painting as well.

Similarly, within any one culture art may serve to demarcate particular subgroups divided by caste, class, age, grade, sex, or status. Clothing and ornament are the most common means of achieving this end, but decoration on dwellings is also common. The wealthy in many societies may even accumulate art as a sign of status. In some cultures high-status individuals commission artists to work specially for them. In West Africa, for example, kings often had court artists at their disposal who were charged with the creation of objects that could be owned only by members of the royal family.

Kilenge Big Men and Art. The anthropologist Philip Dark has described the relationship between art and the status of big men among the Kilenge of New Britain, Papua-New Guinea. Art among the Kilenge is used primarily in rituals, during which costumes, masks, music, and dance all play an important role. Each Kilenge village is divided into two exogamous patri-groups called *pidgeon.* One *pidgeon* is considered "big" and the other "small." Each is headed by a big man or lord, called *natavolo* in the local language. The position of *natavolo* is hereditary. The primary function of art among the Kilenge is to enhance the prestige of big men. Each *pidgeon* has its own crest and a set of designs that are its exclusive property. Many of the important masks used in ceremony are said to belong to the big man of the *pidgeon.* The artists who produce Kilenge art work for the *pidgeon* in the service of the big man. Although an artist is recognized as the individual who carves and paints a mask

Well-made and well-designed jewelry, particularly when it is made of precious materials, functions as both personal decoration and as a status marker.

or other object, he is not considered its maker. Instead, this honor goes to the big man whom the artist serves. Dark notes that he himself commissioned the making of an hour-glass drum by a local carver. When the piece was finished, he was praised for it. At another occasion a chief borrowed some ink and paper from Dark in order to do some drawings concerning ghosts. The next day the chief returned with some designs and a drawing of a witch. Later Dark found out that their actual execution was the work of a village artist. Among the most spectacular art forms found among the Kilenge are elaborate outrigger canoes, with painted sterns and bows and elaborately carved paddles, and masks used in ceremonies. The most striking of the masks, the *bukumo,* is some 12 feet in diameter. It is constructed on a wooden frame that fits on the head of the dancer. The frame is decorated with hornbill and eagle feathers, which are formed into a huge half circle. Both sides of this half circle are covered with painted coconut fiber. The *bukumo* ceremony requires a great feast, and much food must be collected by the sponsor before it can take place. The mask itself performs at the ceremony (*sing-sing*), celebrating the circumcision or ear-piercing of a big man's son.

Art as Communication

Although art is not language, it can be used as the vehicle for communication. Art may symbolize a wide variety of things. If, for example, it marks social divisions within society, such as Kilenge *pidgeons,* it functions to communicate these differences. A society-wide art style communicates a degree of social unity.

In American society the multimillion-dollar advertising industry depends on the communicative function of art, which is manipulated to sell a wide variety of products. Much of advertising is based on psychological studies that probe the unconscious effect of certain colors and key symbols on the target public. Ads are made that appeal to specific segments of the population such as women, teenagers, men, the working class, or the middle class. The art itself attracts the eye; it arrests our attention. In this way, it makes us receptive to any message that it may carry. Music is often used to advertise products. Although advertising jingles have texts and are, therefore, partially linguistic, we come to associate certain tunes with certain products, even when we do not remember the words that go with the melody.

Art and religion are often closely linked. Art makes real a system of beliefs and communicates these beliefs in aesthetic form. Religious art can function as *narrative*—it can tell a story—as, for example, in the stained glass windows of European cathedrals. Art often functions as "text" for nonliterate populations. While religious art may merely *symbolize* a religious idea or entity, it can also *embody* an idea or entity. A statue may *represent* a god, it may be a *place of residence* for a god, or it may be the *material form* of a god. The emotional impact and communication function of art in these different cases will differ according to the beliefs associated with the art object.

Art as Information

Art can be the medium for the storage of knowledge in societies that either lack writing or have a large nonliterate population. Such knowledge can be sacred or secular. Church windows and stone carvings on churches in the Middle Ages, masks and figurines, as well as symbolic decorations on holy objects, can all function as sacred texts. Chinese writing began as sacred symbols scratched into bone used for divination. These pictures were abstracted and developed into the ideographs of later Chinese writing. House posts in the villages of Northwest Coast Indians served as signs of wealth and power, but they also contained information concerning family and clan histories as well as symbolic representations of relationships between humans and their animal "relatives."

When an art object is *itself* sacred, it becomes part of sacred information. That is to say, rather than just representing a god or ancestor it becomes a manifestation of that god or ancestor. What would normally be an intangible supernatural element becomes real and concrete. A picture of a saint in Roman Catholicism is only a representation and is not itself a holy object. For Orthodox Christians, however, an icon is more than a picture. It is sacred.

Among the Dogon of Mali statues of Nommo and carvings of sacred snakes are kept in sanctified caves until such time as they will be used in ceremonial performances. These objects embody the power of the things they represent. Among the Hopi and other Pueblo Indians Kachina masks worn during ceremonies bring the Indian gods to life. Children believe, and women are supposed to believe, that the masked dancers are the Kachina themselves. The male dancers who wear the masks know, of course, that they only represent the gods. Yet the masks themselves must be treated with great respect. The men believe that, if they have sexual relations during the ceremonial period or break other taboos, the masks will punish them by sticking to their faces.

Art is a form of play in which children are able to learn about the organization of space and the use of color and to engage in fantasy experiences. In our culture it is also frequently a pleasurable social activity.

Art as Experience and Preparation for Experience

Art's ability to arouse strong emotional feelings in receptive individuals gives it the potential to carry more than a neutral message. We have already noted that we can "enjoy" a sad poem although we are not likely to seek out a sad experience in our real lives. The emotional response to art and the fact that the artistic experience is only make-believe allows us to tolerate in art what we might reject in real life. Yet the make-believe experience of sadness as well as a wide range of other emotions allows us to experience what might otherwise be painful feelings in a harmless or even therapeutic way. For those individuals who produce art, particularly those who do it only for the pleasure of the experience, artistic activity is a means of manipulating space, color, and objects in relation to conceptual and intellectual ideas. Copying from nature can sharpen one's perceptions of actual scenery and make one acutely aware of the environment. Dealing with abstract designs heightens a sense of spatial relations and balance, while the creation of sacred objects in the realm of art can bring an individual into close personal contact with the supernatural. In many societies the carver of masks is also a shaman. Only a holy person can create holy objects, and the creation of holy objects reinforces the sacred status of the person who makes them.

Art as Game Playing

The production of art involves playing with form. Although art may have real and serious consequences for artists and public alike, there is also a game element in artistic production and appreciation. This play aspect is tied to the purely innovative side of artistic behavior. Such play allows individuals to experiment with their own emotions in a context of fantasy. The overt consequences of this emotional play are minimal since the activity does not involve real everyday experience. This fantasy-play aspect of art is true for both artists and those who appreciate their art. For while the artist plays at making art the observer plays at interpreting it.

In experimenting with materials and techniques the artist is freed of the obligation to produce something useful. Paradoxically, this very freedom from useful (or instrumental) activity may lead to the discovery of some new process or product. A toy, a game, or some new way of doing art may serve as the basis for the discovery of some new technique or object. Archeological evidence suggests, for example, that the wheel first appeared on small toys and was only later transferred to such practical objects as carts. Indeed, the only evidence of the wheel in the New World is found on small toy clay animals. Perhaps if Europeans had not interrupted the development of New World culture, the wheel would have been adapted to useful objects as it had been in the Old World. Archeological evidence from many parts of the world also shows that certain techniques, such as the use of metals and glazing in the preparation of pottery, may have first developed as decoration rather than for practical purposes. The artist and the potter apparently experimented with form, but through this experimentation produced innovations that had wide practical consequences.

Some anthropologists, among them John Roberts, have suggested that game playing in general provides a chance for individuals to master cultural problems. Since games are not generally serious occasions (excluding professional sports and games played in the context of religious rituals), harmless experimentation can take place without dangerous or unpleasant consequences. O. K. Moore, a sociologist, has categorized artistic activity as one form of game playing in which individuals learn to master techniques and form.

Jack Fischer, an anthropologist, has investigated the relationship between a society's social system and the complexity of its art style. Fischer found that if a society is highly stratified its art is likely to be asymmetrical and complex. Conversely, if the society is egalitarian its art is likely to be symmetrical and relatively simple (simple in this case relates to the degree of elaboration in design elements). These results touch on several of the points already made in this section. The relationship between art style and social organization suggests that art can, perhaps in very subtle ways, function as a code that describes the society in which it is produced. Experiencing such art (as an aspect of play) may prepare individuals to live in their particular societies.

Art and Ideology

The arts of a particular culture may reflect prevailing ideology. As such, they can be an overall expression of a commonly held belief system. The performance of ritual—a communal act involving music, dance, incantations, and the wearing of masks and costumes—allows a community to express its common beliefs through common action. The artistic elements in ritual reinforce the special nature of the event and isolate it from the ordinary. Such isolation gives it special value and connects it firmly to the supernatural.

In modern times we have had vivid examples of the relationship between art and ideology on the *secular* level in Nazi Germany and the Soviet Union. The Nazis rejected modern art as degenerate and also banned the playing of music written by so-called "inferior people." The music of Jewish composers was not played in Germany during the Nazi reign. German composers, on the other hand, were elevated to the status of semisacred figures and exploited for their propaganda value. Apparently the makers of Nazi propaganda realized the emotional value of some modern art, however, because many of their own efforts in such mass art as political posters used modern expressionistic techniques.

Russian art under Stalin was even more conservative in some senses than German art under Hitler. While the Russians never banned the playing of foreign composers and never suggested that "degenerate" art was the product of inferior peoples, they did condemn all forms of modern art as "bourgeois formalism." Russian composers were censored for writing music that was not "immediately understandable" by the masses, and Russian painting in that period can best be described as romantic realism.

Art used to foster an ideology. A Nazi propaganda poster from 1938. Although the Nazis condemned expressionistic art as degenerate, they used it in their own propaganda.

Art and Consumption

In capitalist society art has become a means of making money. While many artists struggle to make a living and a few practice their profession in order to become rich, the market tends to dominate public taste. In visual art dealers and collectors alike exploit the market by investing in works they believe will rise in value. Museums, often dependent on donors who are themselves collectors, frequently set the market trend; lending a piece for a major show enhances its value for future sale. In this climate money is spent to buy art, but the art is bought as a commodity to be sold at a later date to make more money. Such a process can be alienating for those artists who are committed to the notion of self-expression and who are uninterested in what will sell on the art market.

Classical music and the serious compositions of modern composers depend on a rather small public and donations from private and government agencies. The same is true of dance, both modern and ballet. Only a few composers and dance companies can work full-time at their art. In the United States the teaching profession, often at the university level, provides a means of support for many musicians, composers, and dancers.

Popular music, on the other hand, *is* big business, particularly through the sale of records and the personal appearance of "stars" on TV and in theatres around the country. Pop music, like visual art, is very much in the hands of the market, which through advertising campaigns often sets trends and "makes stars."

In our own society, then, art must be partially understood in terms of the economic system that dominates so much of our lives. Although the individual artist may struggle for self-expression and be true to his or her art, what does and does not get sold may have more to do with profit than with aesthetics.

Although art exists everywhere and everywhere it exists it has an aesthetic function, it can easily be tied to other aspects of culture. These range from the sacred to the secular. Its ability to stimulate an emotional response in sensitive individuals makes it a likely means for the transmission of cultural ideas and values.

Summary

Most authorities agree that art and language are the human species' two major means of communication. While it is clear that language communicates linguistic messages, it is not clear what art communicates. Because art sometimes uses language (as in poetry and prose) and because nonverbal art can carry a linguistic message (as in pictorial advertising), it is easy to confuse artistic and linguistic communication. Yet there is something special about art that distinguishes it from language. Art arouses an emotional response in receptive individuals. This response is *aesthetic;* that is, it is an emotional reaction specific to art.

I have defined art as *play with form, the purpose of which is to produce an aesthetically successful object or performance.* The object or performance produces (that is, communicates) aesthetic pleasure. This definition separates the aesthetic (artistic) element in art from whatever nonartistic functional aim it may have. Although there are languages in which no word appears for "art" in general, all societies have some form of what we call art in the West. In addition, anthropological studies have shown that people in cultures other than our own do make purely aesthetic judgments about the artistic quality of particular works. An examination of written records from medieval Europe shows that although the purpose of church art was religious, aesthetics (questions of artistic style and form) played a major role in its planning and execution.

Art of some type exists in every culture, but not every art form is universally distributed. Different regions of the world are rich in specific artistic media, such as sculpture in West Africa and the Northwest Coast of North America, and myth (oral literature) in Europe, Asia, Australia, and the New World.

Artistic activity—particularly dance, singing, and other forms of performance—is frequently associated with religious rituals. In addition, a great deal of visual art (painting and sculpture) is made specifically for religious purposes. Not all art, however, is religious, or even serious. Song and dance can be simple pastimes or group amusements and many practical objects are decorated to provide pleasure for their owner.

Art is produced by individuals skilled in different degrees in different media. It may be produced by the many or the few, it may be simple and easy to produce, or complex and difficult, the domain of the specialist. In most traditional societies full-time artists are absent, but in many only some individuals are considered skilled enough to produce art for others or for the use of the social group. Frequently the artist is also a shaman, and his or her artistic activity is considered to be one manifestation of sacred powers. Among the Gola of Liberia the carver of masks used by the Sande (women's secret society) has a very special status within the culture. He has the right to make unusual demands upon Sande women and feels that his work is the result of personal skill and divine intervention. In a real sense the carver of Sande masks is the mother of the mask, and he feels as if he gives birth to his creations. In contrast, the carver and mask-maker among the Kilenge of New Britain is seen only as the person who actually produces an object; its real maker and the person who gets credit for its creation is a big man. In Kilenge society art work produced by one person brings prestige to another, the person who commissions the art.

Because art can arouse emotional feelings in receptive individuals, it commands attention. This attention-getting quality of art can be exploited for a number of purposes. Art may be used to define a group in relation to other groups or to differentiate different categories of individuals within a social unit. Individual statuses may be marked by dress, decorations, or even hair style. Art may also be used to mark status within the group. The prestige of Kilenge big men, for example, is enhanced by art work commissioned by them.

Although strictly speaking art is not linguistic, visual and dramatic art may be used to carry a linguistic message. Religions around the world make use of art to communicate both religious feelings *and* doctrine. This same capacity to communicate has been exploited in the secular realm by advertising in American culture. Although advertising jingles contain words and therefore are directly linguistic, we come to associate certain tunes with products even if we do not remember the words that go with the melody. In a related way art can store information for cultures that lack writing. Thus, church windows in medieval Europe illustrated the Bible stories heard in church. When an art object is sacred, it can convey sacred information and make the supernatural real and immediate. An icon is more than a picture of a saint and a Hopi Kachina mask is more than just a mask. In both cases the objects have supernatural powers and are themselves sacred.

Because art is capable of arousing emotions in a play-like context, we can tolerate in art what we might reject in real life. This experience may indeed prepare us to deal with emotional conflict when it is unavoidable. In addition, the fact that the production and appreciation of art is a play-like activity allows us to experiment freely with such things and ideas as spatial relations and balance. Visual art can make one more conscious of the environment. The innovative aspect of art play may lead to practical discoveries in the sphere of technology.

Art may be used to support a prevailing ideology. Nazi Germany made much of what it called degenerate art, condemning it as the product of inferior peoples. At the same time an attempt was made to substitute German art as the visible sign of the Nazi ideology. In many cases German propaganda art used some of the emotionally charged techniques of the very modern art it criticized and banned. Soviet art under Stalin condemned Western art, calling it bourgeois and formalistic. In the Stalin period official Russian art followed a docrine of romantic realism.

Bibliography

Alland, A., Jr. 1977 — *The Artistic Animal: An Inquiry into the Biological Roots of Art.* Garden City: Doubleday/Anchor. An attempt to find the roots of creativity and artistic behavior in human evolution, with a discussion of art and structuralism.

Boas, F. 1955 — *Primitive Art.* New York: Dover Books. A classic on art, with an attempt to refute the notion that art styles follow universal principles of development.

Forge, A., editor 1973 — *Primitive Art and Society.* Oxford: Oxford University Press. A good collection of papers relating art to social behavior.

Lévi-Strauss, C. 1966 — *The Savage Mind.* Chicago: University of Chicago Press. Discussion of art in the context of structuralism in Chapter One.

Merriam, A. P. 1964 — *The Anthropology of Music.* Evanston, Ill.: Northwestern University Press. The use and function of music in culture.

Otten, C. M. 1971 — *Anthropology and Art: Readings In Cross-Cultural Aesthetics.* Garden City: Natural History Press. An excellent collection of articles treating art and culture from a variety of perspectives.

CHAPTER 22 PSYCHOLOGICAL ANTHROPOLOGY

FREUDIAN ANTHRO-POLOGY

Since its beginning anthropology has had two main focuses of study: cultural behavior and human nature. The latter interest has been pursued within the subdiscipline known as psychological or (more recently) cognitive anthropology. There are several distinct theoretical and methodological approaches within this field. Some, like *structuralism* and *Freudian anthropology,* probe for mental patterns common to all humans. Another approach, known as *ethnosemantics,* or *emics,* attempts to derive rules that govern thought and perception in specific cultures.

Sigmund Freud, the founder of **psychoanalysis,** is also the father of psychological anthropology. Freud attempted to construct a theory to account for the underlying basis of human behavior and cognition in all cultures. This theory was built on the analysis of biological drives and unconscious symbolic thought as they operate in the context of culture. Although he spent his life studying and treating neurotic patients, three of his published works attempt to show that the same patterns that operate in neurotics operate in normal individuals as well. These were *The Psychopathology of Everyday Life, The Interpretation of Dreams,* and *Jokes and their Relation to the Unconscious.* Freud was primarily interested in universal patterns, in what anthropologists now call psychic unity. In my opinion it is unfortunate that much of his contribution in this respect has been deflected by his anthropological disciples in the United States who have emphasized cultural differences. Many of these individuals have abandoned Freud's search for the universal. In its place they have emphasized the role of culture in generating different psychological patterns.

Freudian Theory

The Unconscious. When Freud began his therapeutic work, he used hypnosis. Under hypnosis his patients recounted "events" in their lives that had been "forgotten." In each case they told about having witnessed a "primal scene" during infancy. This scene consisted of the sexual act, often performed by the child's parents or family servants. Eventually, Freud abandoned hypnosis for the technique known as *free association,* in which patients lie down on a couch and speak about anything that comes into their minds. Free association and another technique, the recounting and analysis of dreams, have the same effects as hypnosis. Patients remember things about themselves that are normally forgotten. Under these new therapeutic conditions the primal scene continued to appear. Eventually Freud realized that this scene, rather than having actually been witnessed, was usually a fantasy constructed in the imagination. Once he understood this, Freud interpreted the primal scene as a symbolic expression of conflicts within the patients themselves.

What patients revealed to Freud was clearly not part of conscious memory. Nor did the speech patterns of free association and dreams follow the ordinary patterns of everyday language and experience. Instead, they were full of complex symbolism and appeared to have a grammatical form different from language. Freud came to believe that he had discovered another part of the mind. He called this deeper part (which controls the individual's emotional life) the **unconscious.**

According to Freudian theory, experiences and thoughts that have been pushed out of the conscious mind because they produce painful conflicts do not disappear. Although the person is unaware of them, they exert a strong influence on behavior and can produce neurotic symptoms. The only way to cure these symptoms is to deal with their cause. The analytic process consists of bringing unconscious material into consciousness so that the patient can resolve deep conflicts.

Freud's notion of the unconscious involves two concepts, both of which are important to anthropology. The first is that *what we know and experience* (what our sense and our senses tell us) *may not be a true or full reflection of reality.* An inner sense of truth may exist that generates surface "reality." The second concept is that *the unconscious is a biological fact.* Freud believed he had discovered a universal, genetically based mechanism that underlies all human behavior. He had developed a theory of psychic unity. This universal base interacts with culture and individual experience to produce the variations we see in human behavior.

Sexuality and Gratification: Id, Ego, and Superego. The human being, like all animals, has a number of drives or biological needs such as hunger, thirst, self-preservation, and sex. Normal social life in the context of the family and larger social groups guarantees food and protection. These drives are satisfied through cultural mechanisms and little conflict develops under normal conditions. Sex is another matter.

In working with his patients, Freud discovered that sexual feelings appear early. It was his discovery of "infantile sexuality" that caused Freud to be rejected by scholars and public alike. This very rejection fits in well with Freud's assertion that sexuality comes into conflict with family life and culture. The family provides an infant with food and shelter. Parents minister to the needs of their children, but they do not allow infantile sexual behavior to be expressed fully because it would tend to produce conflicts within the family unit. Culture therefore suppresses sexual desires until they can be expressed in adult life through socially accepted means. Freud discovered that sexual feelings in childhood underlie emerging psychological problems. It is the sexual part of our biological life that comes into conflict with culture. To be human we must express our inner feelings, but we must also live in culture. It is this universal and basic conflict that produces psychological problems.

Sigmund Freud, the founder of psychoanalysis.

Because humans are animals that must grow up in the context of social groups, individual desires *must* be "civilized" so that group harmony can be maintained. Because humans think, use language, and have culture, the civilizing process is largely involved with the symbolic.

These ideas led Freud to construct a theory of personality composed of three "parts." The part of personality that is most rooted in biological needs and is therefore least civilized Freud called the **id.** Id feelings demand immediate gratification. They are selfish and uncompromising. The id is governed by the **pleasure principle,** which simply means that it pursues pleasure. Humans must, however, learn to put off id desires or channel them into socially harmless or even useful activity. In order to accomplish this a child must incorporate the standards of his or her culture into the developing personality. In this process id feelings do not disappear, but they are tamed. Freud called the process of dealing with reality that must occur in all cultures the development of the **ego.** The ego is the integrated personality that results when id feelings are properly channeled and under the control of cultural forces.

A healthy ego is not controlled solely from the outside, however. Freud believed that culture had to be taken into one's self, that is, incorporated into the personality. The child comes to identify with the parents and adopts their values. This incorporation is experienced as *conscience.* Conscience is an inner feeling of right and wrong that directs behavior. Freud labeled this inner feeling the **superego.** The superego acts to control id feelings so that the integrated personality, the ego, can function in a free and healthy way.

The healthy ego, then, is the result of a synthesis between id drives and the control of the superego. When the id has not been tamed or when the superego exerts too strong or unreasonable control, mental illness can result.

The Oedipus Complex. Mental illness was seen by Freud as a process developing out of an *unavoidable* conflict between selfish ever-present, individual, biological drives and one's place in the family. If the conflict is unavoidable, however, how could anyone grow up to be a healthy, normal human? How could ego development proceed in the context of culture and family life? Freud saw the family as the source of both conflict *and* resolution. The basic confrontation between sexual feelings and ego development must be worked out during the socialization process in the family unit. Freud presented this part of his theory in terms of the *Oedipus myth* (see Box) and called the psychological problem that resulted from intrafamilial sexual conflicts the **Oedipus complex.** The details of this complex lie at the base of the most controversial part of Freud's theories.

Soon after birth, and well before the development of language, an infant experiences the mother as a source of gratification that comes from nurturant behavior such as feeding and general comforting. The gratification occurs in

THE OEDIPUS MYTH

Laius, the King of Thebes, is told by an oracle that his son Oedipus will kill him when he grows up. Oedipus is abandoned in the country to die, but is found by a peasant couple who give the child to Polybus, King of Corinth. Oedipus is raised as the son of Polybus. When he grows up, Oedipus learns from the oracle at Delphi that he will kill his father and marry his mother. He vows never to return to Corinth and travels to Thebes. On the way he kills a man on the road who will not yield to his chariot. When he comes to the gates of Thebes, he solves a riddle posed by a great sphinx terrorizing the city. "What has one voice and yet is four-footed in the morning, two-footed in midday, and three-footed in the evening?" The answer is a human: an infant crawls on all fours, an adult walks on two feet, and an old person leans on a staff. Oedipus's solution to the riddle causes the sphinx to kill herself and frees the city from a curse. Oedipus is crowned King and marries the recently widowed queen. Years later, after they have four children, a great plague falls on Corinth. Oedipus vows to end it. He is told by the oracle that he must find and banish a man who has killed his father and taken his mother as a wife. Gradually, Oedipus discovers that he is guilty of this double crime. The man whom he killed on the road was his father, Laius, and his wife is Jocasta, the woman who bore him. Jocasta kills herself, and Oedipus, in anguish over these acts, puts out his eyes and banishes himself from Thebes.

the intimate contact between the body of the mother and the infant. The infant is cuddled and wrapped in clean, soft, warm clothes. It is picked up and fondled when it cries. As the source of gratification the mother becomes highly desirable to the infant. Shortly after birth the infant begins to explore its own body. Eventually it finds its genitals and discovers a source of pleasure. This pleasure can be achieved alone, but it is readily identified with that other source of pleasure, the nurturant mother. Feelings of sexual desire are soon associated with maternal contact. Both maternal contact and sexual stimulation have a strong dual effect on the developing child. They produce gratification *and* they reduce general anxiety. This growing relationship of dependence on the mother produces a strong desire for her exclusive attentions. In metaphorical terms the child wants to possess the mother. (This is as true for girls as for boys according to Freud.) A little later a new discovery is made. A boy, already aware that he has a penis, discovers that his father also has one. He also notices that the father is an object of attention for the mother. Since the penis is associated with gratification and because the father "competes" for attention with the child, the conflict takes on a strongly sexual connotation.

Eventually boys discover that girls lack the penis. This leads to a fear of castration—the "castration complex"—in which the boy believes he will be castrated by his father to end the competition between them. At the same time boys come to identify with their fathers. Like themselves, they have penises and, like themselves, they possess the mother. The mixture of identification and competition plus the fear of castration leads to the Oedipus complex, which consists of a feeling of hostility toward the father and a strong wish to have exclusive possession of the mother. The normal resolution of the Oedipus complex occurs when the boy gives up his desire to "possess" the mother and replaces hostility toward the father with strong identification.

What about girls? Freud believed that females develop the same feelings toward both parents as boys do. That is, they wish to get rid of the father and possess the mother. The discovery by a girl that she lacks a penis leads to strong envy. The resolution of a girl's Oedipus complex is seen as more complicated and less complete than that of boys. Girls cannot automatically or naturally transfer "love" for their mothers to other females as can boys. Instead they have to develop an identification with their mothers and then transfer their sexual feelings for her to the opposite sex.

The concepts of castration anxiety, penis envy, and the difficulty females are supposed to experience in resolving the Oedipus complex have led to major criticisms of Freud's theory. Many, but by no means all, feminists have labeled Freudian psychology as sexist. But if we remember that this aspect of Freud's theory is both biological *and* cultural, it is possible to remove whatever sexist aspect it might have.

Freud and Anthropology

Freud's theories have had a tremendous impact on anthropological theory and practice. The impact has been both direct—from Freud's own work—and indirect—from interpretations of his work, including criticisms by anthropologists. I have already noted that Freudian psychology provides anthropology with a way of giving substance to psychic unity. It also sets the stage for theory building that rejects the primacy of conscious thought in behavior. Freud's concept of the unconscious opens up a vast field for the analysis of such diverse aspects of culture as myth, kinship, and religion. Freud himself began these explorations in those few books in which he dealt specifically with anthropological problems. These were *Totem and Taboo, The Future of an Illusion,* and *Civilization and its Discontents.*

Freudian Anthropologists: Personality and Culture

The introduction of Freudian theory directly into anthropology came about in the 1930s. Geza Roheim, a strict Freudian, was the first psychoanalyst to do field work. He attempted to demonstrate the universality of Freudian theory through the investigation of "primitive" cultures. American Neofreudians, on the other hand, rapidly departed from the orthodox position taken by Roheim.

The first moves in this direction were inspired by such psychoanalysts as Karen Horney and Erich Fromm. While they accepted the notion of the unconscious, they rejected Freud's universalistic biological orientation. Freud's theory was converted from one that explained universal human patterns to one that explained personality differences on the basis of cultural variables.

Among the theoretical constructs brought into question by Neofreudians was the Oedipus complex. Doubts about the universality of the Oedipus complex were partially confirmed by the work of Bronislaw Malinowski in the Trobriand Islands. Trained as an anthropologist, Malinowski believed that the Oedipus complex would not appear in a matrilineal society. Matrilineality in many cases implies a particular kind of family structure in which fathers play only a minor role in the socialization of their children. This role is performed instead by mother's brother, and it is from him that a male eventually inherits. In addition, postmarital residence in many matrilineal societies is avunculocal. Malinowski's original hypothesis was that the Oedipus complex would not appear at all under these conditions. After his field work he modified this view. The complex did appear but in a different form. Malinowski discovered that typical Oedipal feelings continued to occur in boys, but ambivalence and hostility were directed at the mother's brother rather than at the biological father.

Roheim never accepted Malinowski's findings. He claimed that Malinowski was unable to uncover deeply buried invariant Oedipal feelings because he lacked psychoanalytic training. Malinowski's revision of Oedipal theory won the day among anthropologists, however. His arguments were logical and based on a real field experience. Just as important was the fact that they fit the theoretical expectations of those who saw culture as the major determinant of human behavior.

A new school of anthropology was born out of this particular kind of cross-cultural psychological approach. Two of Franz Boas's students, Ruth Benedict and Margaret Mead, became the guiding lights of psychological anthropology. Each in her own way sought to show how culture shaped personality within the context of Freud's basic discoveries.

Benedict is most famous for her widely read book *Patterns of Culture.* In that work she extended Freud's analogy between individual personality and culture. She described basic psychological patterns in three societies and then categorized the cultures in terms of these patterns. The societies chosen were the Kwakiutl of the Northwest Coast of North America, studied for several years by Boas himself, the Dobuans, an island population near the Trobriands in Melanesia, and the Zuñi, a pueblo group studied by several anthropologists. There

Ruth Fulton Benedict, an early pioneer of the culture-and-personality school, was also a cultural relativist.

were three major points in *Patterns of Culture.* The first was that cultures are coherent wholes that reflect a unified psychological structure and world view. The second was that each culture can be described as a personality type. Finally, Benedict questioned the notion of normality. She suggested that what was "normal" in one culture might in fact be abnormal in another. This aspect of her theory was borrowed from Boas and his students, who, in their attempt to remain objective scientists in the face of often exotic anthropological data, took a position of **cultural relativism.** Cultural relativism holds that an understanding of alien cultures can only come about when anthropologists suspend their value judgments and analyze data on their own terms. Cultural relativism demands description rather than prescription. Extended to psychological principles and taken literally, cultural relativism can push one into the position that no such thing as psychopathology exists in the general sense. Relativism can also lead to the view that abnormality is merely any deviation away from the norms of a culture, no matter what those norms may be. Thus, if everyone in a culture were schizophrenic, that condition would be normal. Nonaffected individuals would be (in this sense at least) abnormal. It is not difficult to fall into this trap if one begins with the assumption that behavioral norms in a culture are an expression of individual personality. Thus, if people behave suspiciously and one labels this behavior *paranoid,* then every "normal" person in the culture is "paranoid."

In *Patterns of Culture* Benedict characterizes each of three cultures according to specific psychological principles. The Zuñi are described as passive and "Apollonian."* They resolve conflict through avoidance or consensus. Their rituals are stoic and the extremes of emotional expression are avoided in interpersonal relations. The Zuñi are contrasted to the Kwakiutl, whom Benedict called "Dionysian." Their rituals are violent and extreme. They have emotional rites, including the fierce competition of the potlatch. While the Zuñi are peace-loving, the Kwakiutl are warlike. While the Zuñi are egalitarian, the Kwakiutl are ranked. The Zuñi live for moderation. The Kwakiutl live for the joy of excess. Between these two cultures Benedict put the Dobuans, whom she characterized as paranoid. Dobuans have a strong belief in witchcraft and mistrust one another.

The man who did the major ethnography on Dobu, Reo Fortune, described Dobuans as nasty and crafty people. Reading his book *The Sorcerers of Dobu,* one realizes instantly that he did not like them very much. This point of view is reinforced by Malinowski in the introduction he wrote for Fortune's book. Yet if we turn to Malinowski's own major work, *Argonauts of the Western Pacific,* we get a different picture. All we need do is compare the following quotes, the first from Malinowski's introduction and the second from *Argonauts,* to see what dangers lurk in shallow "psychologizing" about an anthropologist's subject population.

The district of Dobu is, as it were, shrouded in a cloud of superstitious fear for all its neighbours. The very name of Sewatupa, the mythological centre of all sorcery, witchcraft, and evil things that befall man, strikes terror into the heart of Trobrianders and Amphlett islander alike. Dr. Fortune was as impressed as I was by the difference in this respect between the Trobriand Islands and the koya, *the mountainous southern archipelago. The Trobrianders, frightened enough by sorcery and witchcraft at home, become yet more panic-stricken as they sail south. The Dobuans, on the contrary, seem to breathe more freely in the healthy atmosphere of the Trobriands—healthy because deprived of really dangerous, pernicious, or aggressive magic.* (Introduction to Sorcerers of Dobu.)

In personal appearance, the Dobuans have a very distinct physique, which differentiates them

*Benedict borrowed the terms Apollonian and Dionysian from Oswald Spengler's work *The Decline of the West.* Apollonian refers to the rational and stoic in culture, Dionysian to the intuitive and emotional.

sharply from the Southern Massim and from the Trobrianders; very dark skinned, small of stature, with big heads and rounded shoulders, they give a strange, almost gnome-like impression on a first encounter. In their manner, and their tribal character, there is something definitely pleasant, honest and open—an impression which long acquaintance with them confirms and strengthens. They are the general favorites of the whites, form the best and most reliable servants, and traders who have resided long among them compare them favorably with other natives. (From Argonauts of the Western Pacific.)

Quotations of this sort can only cast doubt on the validity of psychological analyses in anthropology, for they appear to be impressionistic and subjective if not downright inaccurate. One major problem in Benedict's work was that except in the case of the pueblos she relied completely on the work of others. If that work had at least been psychological in nature, such comparisons might have been possible, but the data she used were not really comparable.

Margaret Mead was less interested in describing the personality of a culture than in studying the effect culture has on the shaping of personality. Her early work in Polynesia and New Guinea involved the testing of several notions about male and female behavior. Her major concern was questioning the accepted idea that the behavior of men *as* men and women *as* women is natural and biologically determined. If this is the case then one should find the same patterns in all cultures. Men should be aggressive and dominating, women shy and submissive. In her field work Mead did find that men's and women's roles and behaviors differ from each other, but the expected universal patterns did not occur. Among the Mountain Arapesh the men act much the way the stereotypic woman is supposed (or was supposed) to act in our culture, while the women were ambitious and aggressive. The differences between Arapesh men and women and between all Arapesh and typical Americans were attributed by Mead to culture. She attempted to show that the human personality was flexible and open. At the same time Mead did not abandon Freud's schema in which early child experience is thought to shape the developing personality and during which sexual conflicts develop. Because she concentrated only on cultural differences, however, Mead tended to lose sight of what Freud suggested were universal aspects of human personality, particularly the rules Freud believed governed the unconscious.

Margaret Mead, also a pioneer of the culture-and-personality school. Mead was one of the most versatile anthropologists. Her contributions to the field go well beyond psychological anthropology. Mead was also an intrepid field worker, who carried out research in many parts of the Pacific, and a popularizer of anthropology for the lay public.

I do not wish to fault Mead's work. She was one of the first anthropologists to wed what was then the new psychology to anthropology. She was a pioneer among those who probed for the cultural factors that foster personality differences in different cultural settings.

In the 1950s the growing field of personality and culture fell into a chicken-and-egg debate over whether personality caused culture or culture caused personality. Some participants were willing fence-sitters who declared that the development of personality and culture was a cyclical process. Each had an effect on the other. Most of Freud's hypotheses about human nature were lost in the process.

The study of personality and culture had its major impact on anthropology in the years between the end of the Second World War and the end of the 1950s. During that time such important figures as Cora Dubois and Abram Kardiner investigated the role of culture in the formation of both personality and such institutions as religion and medicine. Kardiner proposed that *basic personality structure* is generated by behaviors associated with child training and that the formed personality in turn gives rise to derivative institutions (he called them *secondary institutions*). These institutions are seen as expressions in culture of the personality type that is formed by the institutions associated with child rearing. These he called *primary institutions.* Thus, the belief systems of culture, its myths, its rituals, and its religion are projections of basic personality. Secondary institutions are a cultural means of dealing with and reinforcing a cultural pattern that was generated in the first place by child training.

The most recent trend in Neofreudian anthropology has been the cross-cultural testing of certain psychological principles. The most notable of these tests have been carried out by John Whiting and various associates. Whiting has correlated a whole set of dependent variables, but principally genital mutilation (circumcision, for example) and other forms of male initiation, with the strength of the bond occurring between mothers and their male infants. This study indicates that intensive puberty rites, with traumatic operations, occur in societies where the mother-child relationship has been very close and intimate. The highest correlations between these two variables, for example, were found in societies with mother-child households, in which the mother lives with her children separate from her husband. Whiting reasoned that such arrangements produce strong bonds between mother and son as well as a strong psychological identification by the son with the mother and therefore with females. In order to separate boys from the world of women and integrate them into the adult male realm, the cultural institution of complex and severe initiation rites has developed in these societies.

Culture at a Distance and Cross-Cultural Research

During the Second World War American anthropologists were cut off from their subject populations. This deprivation had an important side effect on two types of personality-and-culture studies and gave rise to a new kind of literature in anthropology. At Yale University anthropologists turned their attention to already published sources and attempted to make them more readily available for comparative analysis. To this end the Cross-Cultural Survey was established. (The Cross-Cultural Survey was later expanded and institutionalized under the name Human Relations Area Files, or HRAF.) The guiding hand behind this endeavor was George Peter Murdock. The area files consist of reprinted pages of ethnographic sources coded with numbers on their margins for particular categories. If a page contains six such categories six copies are made, and one of each is filed under the appropriate number. A researcher interested in gambling, for example, need only go to the file drawer marked 777. There all data on gambling from several hundred ethnographies will be found in one place. This method of tabulation enables anthropologists to speed up data accumulation from a sample of cultures. In the 1960s Murdock, who had moved to the University of Pittsburgh, and his associates published the *Ethnoatlas,* which contains a shorthand code tabulating a wide range of cultural facts from several hundred societies. While these materials are used for many types of cross-cultural study, they have been most heavily exploited by those interested in psychological anthropology.

Although Murdock himself is not a member of the personality-and-culture school, his investigations of social structure have a strong psychological cast. In one of his major works, *Social Structure,* he correlated types of kinship system with such social factors as residence patterns and descent. The theoretical foundation of Murdock's *Social Structure* is borrowed from learning theory, a nonFreudian form of psychological explanation. Murdock hypothesized, for example, that kinship terminology is determined by similarities in social interaction and role playing between primary kin (mothers and fathers, siblings, children) and such more distant secondary kin as cousins or uncles and aunts. Thus, if mother and her sister play similar roles toward ego, they are likely to be called by the same term. The same would be true for father and father's brother. In addition, if one called one's own mother and her sister by the same term (as in the Iroquois system), one is likely to refer to mother's sister's children as one's brothers and sisters. This is indeed the case in Iroquois systems, in which parallel cousins are called siblings by ego. The psychological principle on which all of this is based is called **stimulus generalization:** entities that share significant attributes will be grouped under the same category.

During the war a Neofreudian approach to culture continued at Columbia University, where the students of Franz Boas began the study of culture at a distance. Margaret Mead and Rhoda Metraux were among the first to turn from the study of "primitive" cultures to more complex societies. Their work in this field is known as "national character" research. National character studies were attempts to relate cultural factors to personality and vice versa on the scale of whole nations. Research tended to focus on relationships between child training and adult personality as reflected in the culture at large. Methods included interviews with immigrants to America and analyses of published documents and films. The most notable books to come out of this work were *The Chrysanthemum and the Sword* by Ruth Benedict, an analysis of Japanese character, and two works by Geoffrey Gorer, one on Russian personality and the other dealing with American character.

These books were criticized on many grounds. In general, national character studies lacked historical perspective and took a simplistic, single-factor approach to adult personality. Gorer, for example, related adult Russian personality (which he characterized as rigid) to the practice of swaddling infants.

Studies of national character suffer from poor controls over the quality of the data gathered and a rather naive and mechanical approach to theory. The inferring of national character from interviews with refugees can be criticized on the grounds that refugee populations do not represent an objective sample of the population of the country under study. The use of literature and other aspects of intellectual culture to analyze national character is open to the criticism that books and films are produced by only a small and urban segment of the population. The counterargument that successful works of art represent popular taste is not thoroughly convincing since the media are capable of manipulating the public and its taste.

Freudian theory itself has come in for much criticism in anthropology. Some reject it because it is difficult to test directly. Behaviorists reject it because it involves theoretical concepts that are not directly observable and testable. These concepts include the unconscious and the tripartite division of the personality into id, ego, and superego. The Oedipus complex has come under attack not only from behaviorists, but also from those who see in it a culture-bound **(ethnocentric)** and sexist bias.

ETHNO-SEMANTICS

We have already examined one aspect of ethnosemantics in our discussion of kinship terminology. Using linguistic models, **ethnosemanticists** analyze the way in which native informants order and categorize various aspects of their universe. In the case of kinship systems, for example, this type of analysis would be used to determine the rules that generate a set of kin terms. We saw that in our own kinship system such categories as "blood" kin versus affinal kin, generation, the degree of collaterality, and sex operate in defining kin terms. The rules that determine particular kinship categories can be presented as formulas. Cousin, for example, in the American kinship system can be defined as any individual of either sex in ego's own generation who is related to ego through two links to a common ancestor (father's father or mother, or mother's father or mother).

The Logic Behind Ethnosemantics

All classification systems are guided by conscious or unconscious logic. This logic determines which features are used in classification. Collaterality versus lineality enters into the logic of our kinship system, but plays no part in the Iroquois system. Sex of kin is relevant in our system when distinguishing between uncles and aunts, but not for defining cousins.

The analysis of semantic domains has included plant and animal classifications, disease categories, and various aspects of technology. The goal of such analysis is the understanding of those rules that govern a particular system of classification.

Recognized contrasts and similarities must necessarily underlie all systems of classification. Which differences and similarities are recognized varies by culture. We, for example, do not classify male and female mallard ducks as separate species even though their coloring is very different. We know from observation that the two mallard types are determined by sexual rather than species differences. We classify duck-billed platypuses as mammals even though they lay eggs. We do so because they nurse their young and have other major characteristics that we use in defining mammals. We also recognize that in our system of classification platypuses are very peculiar mammals. Thus, we isolate them within the class Mammalia by the designation *monotremata* (egg-laying mammal). Our system of classification is not based on observation alone. It reflects and is influenced by the modern theory of evolution. A different theory might well have led to a different system. If, for example, egg-laying versus live birth were the only criterion that was used to separate birds from mammals, we would put the hapless platypus in the bird class.

Ethnosemantics, also known as ethnoscience, depends on the verbal responses of informants for its data. The informants are asked a series of questions concerning a particular cultural domain, say, animal taxonomy. Since classification rules are often unconscious, interviews must be structured to reveal the underlying logic. The clearest method for eliciting such data comes from linguistics. A linguist working with an unrecorded language begins an analysis by determining the phonemes and morphemes of that language. Phonemic analysis begins with *minimal pairs.* An informant is asked, for example, if the combination of sounds *bin* and *pin* are the same or different. If the informant responds "same," |b| and |p| are not separate phonemes in that particular language. If the response is "different" then |b| and |p| are separate phonemes. Although this is the easiest way to do a phonemic analysis, it can also be carried out by analyzing a text. Since allophones of the same phoneme are shaped by context, we can group them by searching for consistent relationships between sound variants and their place in the text.

Many classification systems can be ordered

by levels of inclusiveness. In seeking such order, the anthropologist must find out what units fit a given level of the system. We might, for example, wish to understand the way in which dogs are classified by professional dog-handlers. The entire class "dog" is derived from its standing as a mammal, a carnivore, *and* a *canid.* Within the grouping *canid,* the domestic dog contrasts with such wild species as foxes and wolves. The entire set of domestic dogs is then divided into major groups. These include: sporting dogs, hounds, terriers, working dogs, toys, nonsporting dogs, and a mixed group of breeds that are not yet part of the accepted system.

One of these major groups is subdivided into lesser units. The sporting dogs are divided into pointers, retrievers, setters, and spaniels. The other major groups are composed of breeds. Some breeds have subclassifications while others do not. Thus, fox terriers are divided into smooth and wirehaired types. Dachshunds are separated by hair form (wire, short, and long) and by size.

Because work in ethnosemantics resembles phonemic analysis, it has come to be known as **emics.** The overall goal of emic analysis is the understanding of culture as a set of psychological rule systems. That is, emics attempt to determine how thought in a specific culture is governed by conscious and unconscious rules. In addition to probing traditional systems of classification, emic analysis has been applied to such cultural domains as kinship, law, religion, and rules that govern behavior in various social situations.

Critique of Emic Analysis

Some anthropologists have pointed out that actual behavior is only vaguely rule-determined (rules are guidelines for action but do not fully determine action). A true understanding of culture, they argue, can only come from the observation and analysis of real behavior. Some go so far as to say that rules exist *after the fact* to justify what people do. According to this group, known as **cultural materialists,** what people do consciously or unconsciously is determined in large measure by the real circumstances of their lives. Many rules are, therefore, an artifact or result of behavior. Materialists favor **etic** analyses, that is, those that are based on data from behavioral observation (etic derives from phon*etic*).

Materialists also tend to mistrust emics because they feel they represent an attempt to get inside the heads of informants. They find it difficult to believe that it is possible to really discover what goes on in the head of another human being, much less a member of a foreign culture.

Emics are also criticized on methodological grounds. This criticism centers on the way in which emic data are collected and analyzed. In early emic studies only a single informant was used. Such an approach is reasonable in linguistic analysis because language must communicate specific messages to be effective. It is, therefore, a widely shared system with relatively low variability. Once anthropologists leave the realm of language, however, they enter much more ambiguous fields. Materialists rightly point out that rule systems and other cognitive domains are often highly variable.

More recent work in emic analysis *has* used multiple informants and has probed the complexities of variable systems as well as the "rules" behind rule breaking. On the other hand, emic analysis does, in most cases, continue to ignore relationships between emic categories and real behavior. This is justified, however, by the claim that ethnosemantics, like most linguistics, is concerned specifically with codes rather than their application to behavior.

To the claim that, in trying to get inside the informant's head the anthropologist abandons analysis and theory to the informant, the emic analyst replies that informants are only relied upon for certain kinds of data. Both the questions and the subsequent analysis come from the anthropologist and both are guided by anthropological rather than native theory. In linguistics it is the linguist who determines what the phonemes of a language are, not the informant. Most native speakers are, in fact, unaware of the phonemic system of their language. In emic analysis it is the analyst who applies a theory and a method in order to determine what the traditional thought system is.

There is one final criticism of emic analysis that has been saved for last because of its importance. An emic analysis, specifically because it comes from the head of the anthropologist, may be logical and coherent, but *still* not accurately capture the logic of the traditional system it purports to analyze. A great deal of ink has been spilled, for example, over the logic of kinship systems in various cultures, including our own. Yet it is very difficult to determine whether or not an emic analysis (no matter how logical) has produced the same rules that are used by informants to generate the system. The only major claim that emic analysis can make, therefore, is that it has ordered data formally in such a way as to make elements of the system predictable. The logic of our analysis works to generate elements of the system, but we cannot be sure that it is the same as the logic used by members of the culture.

Finally, emic analysis makes no claims to the discovery of cross-cultural laws. On the other hand, the comparison of different emic systems from different cultures might yield interesting regularities. Brent Berlin and Paul Kay have collected and analyzed basic color terms from a wide range of cultures. They found that the maximum number of basic color terms (terms like red, yellow, black, but not like ultramarine, pink, or light-blue) that can be found in any culture is 11. In addition, the number of such terms found correlates well with cultural complexity. This suggests an evolutionary relationship between an emic category (color terminology) and sociocultural development. This suggestion is reinforced by the data that show the 11 possible color terms appearing in a regular order. When only two terms are present in a language, these will be black and white. When three terms occur red is the added category. After red comes blue, and so on.

STRUCTURALISM

While ethnosemantics (emics) attempts to uncover the internal logic of specific traditional systems, the goal of structuralism is to uncover panhuman mental patterns. Structuralists search for the logic of psychic unity. Structuralism is based on a scientific paradigm (that is, model or pattern) that contrasts with **positivism.** Positivism has been the major paradigm in social science and remains so in most of the English-speaking world. It will be necessary, therefore, to take some time to contrast the two approaches.

Positivism has its roots in eighteenth-century philosophy. It begins with the proposition that experience is the only source of knowledge. Understanding must come *exclusively* through *empirical* (experimental and observational) science. Positivism has its own psychological theory about how we organize sense data. Individuals come to know the world as they experience it. Each encounter between ourselves and nature allows us to become familiar with normal patterns that exist in nature. Our theories and expectations (predictions in science) are built out of these patterns as we discover them.

In psychology the positivist point of view is taken by those who reject the existence of biologically determined, precoded means of perceiving and behaving. Positivism thus provides the basis for learning theories which hold that both lower animals and humans are empty slates ready to record environmental clues. In anthropology positivism underlies the position of cultural materialists, who tend to mistrust data that do not come from observable behavioral patterns. All positivists see the external environment as the causal agent responsible for the development of perception and behavior.

Structuralism—as practiced by Freud in psychology, Noam Chomsky in linguistics, and

Claude Lévi-Strauss in anthropology—postulates the existence of innate **schema** (patterns). These schema are specifically human and have evolved as a special feature of the human brain.

Structuralism owes its major philosophical debt to Immanuel Kant, who believed that the reality discovered by each human results from an interaction between external stimuli perceived by the individual and innate structures of the mind. It is these structures that shape the perceptive field. They make it coherent. If these structures did not exist, sense data would be an unorganized blaze of incoming stimuli.

Animals as well as humans must have perceptual structures. The difference between animal and human structures is the *mind,* in which organized experience is subject to complex cognitive manipulation. For a structuralist the mind is an organizing, active force in determining how perceptions are patterned and how experience is cataloged for both recall and action. According to this theory data are layed down and used according to predetermined organizational principles.

In an article comparing positivism and structuralism in the human sciences the molecular biologist Gunther S. Stent said the following:

Probably the best known pioneer of structuralism is Sigmund Freud, to whom we owe the fundamental insight that human behavior is governed not so much by the events of which we are consciously aware in our minds or which we can observe in the behavior of others, but rather by the deep structures of the subconscious which are generally hidden from both subjective and objective view. The nature of these covert deep structures can only be inferred indirectly by analysis of the overt surface structures.

The overt surface structures referred to by Stent are the facts of daily life, including certain glimpses into the unconscious mind. The latter are revealed through slips of the tongue, neurotic behavior, and dreams.

Stent goes on to point out that structuralist theory cannot be verified the way theories in physics can be verified, that is, through empirical tests. They are merely "plausible" explanations. Not that structuralists are anti-empirical or opposed to experimentation. All structuralists work outward from a theory to data with the hope that theory will predict real behavior. They realize, however, that structures themselves (the unconscious mind and its "grammar") are not subject to *direct* test or experience. Instead, they are models made up by scientists to account in a logical way for mental and behavioral patterns. It is hoped that these plausible models are *isomorphic* (equivalent or congruent) with the way the mind really works, but we cannot *directly* know the human mind.

Models of what have come to be called **deep structures** (a term borrowed from the linguistics of Noam Chomsky) are used to understand what we can never directly see or know. These models are applied to human behavior as explanations of the mental operations that underlie it.

Structuralism in Anthropology

We have already examined Freudian theory. Let us now look at structuralism in anthropology. The founder of anthropological structuralism is the French scholar Claude Lévi-Strauss. Lévi-Strauss has spent his life attempting to probe the depths of human nature and uncover its underlying logic.

Lévi-Strauss begins with the idea, accepted by most anthropologists, that human culture, as opposed to animal behavior, depends on complex symbolic activity. He goes on to point out that a major, perhaps *the* major, feature of social life is exchange. Humans exchange symbols when they communicate, they exchange objects and services in economic activity and gift giving, and they exchange people in marriage. The incest taboo occupies a central place in Lévi-Strauss's theory. The prohibition of incest is a cultural and symbolic act that generates exchange behavior and, at the same time, functions as a coded statement about human society in relation to the natural world. Incest is animal-like, whereas marriage is a human cultural institution. As symbol-making animals, humans

Claude Levi-Strauss, the founder of structuralist anthropology and the best-known French anthropologist.

create statements about their relationship to nature through practical cultural acts which stand for (symbolize) the dichotomy between the human and nonhuman worlds. As an affirmation of our special place, of our worth, so to speak, we exaggerate and mark off our separation from nature by emphasizing particular cultural symbols. The incest taboo is one of these, as is the wearing of clothes. So are physical mutilation, circumcision, for example, and scarification of the body. Still another example is found in eating practices—the cooking of food, the order in which we eat different foods, and the people with whom we eat. All these cultural behaviors mark us off from the "natural" world. Cooking changes natural products into a cultural item, food, to be consumed by humans rather than animals. Clothing is worn by humans while animals go naked. Facial and body painting as well as scarification transform our *natural* bodies in a *cultural* way. Thus, according to Lévi-Strauss humans have a very strong tendency to symbolize their cultural selves with cultural means.

The nature-culture dichotomy is one of many binary contrasts that Lévi-Strauss believes humans use to classify experience and themselves. The mind is coded to work in terms of opposites. The meaning of one term can only be defined in relation to another or a set of contrasting terms. This idea is borrowed from modern linguistics, and Lévi-Strauss acknowledges his debt to that discipline. Lévi-Strauss believes that a grammar of relationships and rules for transformations are structured in the brain, but not specific symbols. The fact, for example, that nature and culture appear frequently as major oppositional symbolic elements in such cultural products as myths and rituals is the result of common human experience. Lévi-Strauss's task is to determine the laws of structural grammar. In this respect structuralism is similar to ethnosemantics. It differs from ethnosemantics, however, in that it searches for cross-cultural regularities in human thought and is not interested exclusively in the details of any one classification or mythic system. While ethnosemantics attempts to demonstrate how a single culture classifies one domain (dogs, for example), structuralism looks for the roots of all classification systems as well as the rules according to which they transform.

But Lévi-Strauss is also a philosopher and is interested in the human condition as a philosophical problem. He believes that the nature-culture dichotomy appears with almost universal frequency because it is a shorthand statement about our special place in the universe. Nature and culture become the symbols of our universal struggle for meaning. According to Lévi-Strauss humans see the nature-culture dichotomy as both a contradiction (we are cultured but also a part of nature) and as an affirmation of human as opposed to animal nature. The distinction, however, creates dissonance with the idea of oneness within the universe that is so often a part of belief systems. Lévi-Strauss notes that humans frequently attempt to resolve this dissonance by reducing the contradiction or contrast between elements in opposition. This effort is particularly evident in myth, where certain creatures function as *mediators;* their role is to reduce or resolve fundamental oppositions. The animals used as mediators in these myths are usually themselves difficult to classify. They occupy ambiguous positions in the classification system because they share characteristics with animals that otherwise fit into separate and clear-cut categories. Thus, the pangolin, a mammal with scales like a fish, is a likely choice for the role of mediator. Such animals can be used to bridge the separation between opposed categories; mammals are warm-blooded land animals, fish are cold-blooded water animals; mammals have fur or hair, fish have scales; yet pangolins are mammals with scales rather than hair or fur.

If classification systems and myths are based on oppositions and contradictions, they are, by implication, structures. That is, every element in such systems is related to every other element so that a change in one will lead to a systematic or predictable change in another. In his analyses, therefore, Lévi-Strauss has attempted to uncover a wide range of transformations that take place within myths and among related myths. He does this to determine the rules of transformations.

In four long volumes Lévi-Strauss has traced transformations in the mythology of the indigenous populations of North and South America. Myths in South America use cooking as the marker of culture. In North America, where climate dictates the wearing of clothes, clothing, particularly the hiding of sexual organs, replaces cooking as the key symbol of culture. In each region the particular units, the symbols used in myth, change. Common animals, for example, are adopted into the stories. As myth diffuses from one geographical region to another, local animals replace less familiar ones. What does not change is the basic structure of the myth itself, that is, the basic relationships among elements.

Criticisms of Structuralism

Structuralism has been criticised on many grounds. Among the most important are the following:

1. By creating entitities (structures) that are not directly open to empirical test, structuralist hypotheses cannot be falsified (proved untrue). Positivists claim that hypothetical structures are excess baggage and are unnecessary for an understanding of sense data.

Structuralists reply that sense data can never be understood without a theory that accounts for underlying mechanisms. Lévi-Strauss himself has used the analogy of watch and clock faces from several factories representing several styles. A thorough classification and analysis of these faces could never lead to an understanding of how watches work. In order to achieve such understanding, it is necessary to take the watch apart and examine its internal mechanism. When it comes to mental operations, we cannot take the machine apart. A brain dissection cannot reveal how the mind works. Instead, the scientist must construct a plausible model of mental function and use it to test hypotheses about real behavior. Structuralists *have* demonstrated empirically that myths from many parts of the world tend to fall into regular patterns. In addition, they have been able to show relationships between the deep structures of myths when the surface structures have been so different that the underlying similarities were originally unperceivable.

2. Although some scholars are ready to admit that the structures uncovered by Lévi-Strauss and his followers are real, the critics charge that they are too simple and few in number to be used in *generating* myth. If Lévi-Strauss is searching for a "grammar" of the mind or a grammar of myth, he has failed to provide one that is rich enough to be of value.

This criticism is both fair and unfair. It is fair to say that Lévi-Strauss's grammar cannot really generate myth the way grammar is supposed to generate meaningful sentences in a language. He has discovered a set of principles but is far from a full understanding of the way in which codes operate to generate myth. It is unfair, however, to use this accusation against Lévi-Strauss without noting that linguistic grammars at the present state of knowledge also fall far short of their goal. No grammar has yet been constructed that can generate all possible real sentences in a particular language and distinguish between meaningful and unmeaningful sentences.

3. Structuralism has been criticized because it deals with data in a totally nonhistorical way. Lévi-Strauss does not deal with change and does not investigate the relationships, if any, between structures and historical factors. In addition, critics of structuralism have been quick to point out that Lévi-Strauss deals with the mind and not with real behavior.

These accusations are partially true, but their factual basis is not denied by Lévi-Strauss. He believes that, in order to uncover mental structures, external events and history must be held constant. Once structures are understood, however, they can be studied in relation to changing historical circumstances. While Lévi-Strauss has not himself used structuralism in this way, some of his followers have. As for his concentration on the mind at the expense of behavior, there is no argument at all. Lévi-Strauss and other structuralists freely admit that the subject of their investigation is mental structures and therefore human nature.

4. Some critics have complained that the structures Lévi-Strauss claims to uncover in the data are really in *his* mind. Materialists, for example, say that it is really impossible to get inside someone else's mind and that Lévi-Strauss presents us with a grand projection of his own mental patterns.

This criticism is really misplaced. All structuralists realize that the structures they "discover" are in their own minds rather than in the minds of the informants. First of all, structures are never elements of consciousness. Native informants are not aware of them. Second, a structural analysis consists of *constructs* made up by the scientist to account for the data and to describe a system. The test of these constructs consists in determining whether they explain the data fully and whether they can be used to predict change in systems. In structuralism change consists of transformations of the structural order. Many, but by no means all, anthropologists feel that structuralism has been able to uncover a great deal of basic information on universal mental patterns and that these patterns can be used to analyze data ranging from kinship to purely symbolic activity.

To criticize structuralism for using mental constructs is to demand that it play the scientific game according to positivist rules. It in no way means that structuralists play their own game badly. Mental constructs are an old device and occupy an important place in such hard sciences as physics. No one has ever seen gravity, and while we might feel its effects when apples fall on our heads, the effect is not the same thing as the construct itself. An apple falling and a myth transforming from one version to another according to orderly but unconscious rules are both data that can be used as evidence for the theory and its basic constructs.

THE DEVELOPMENTAL LEARNING THEORY OF JEAN PIAGET

There is an alternative approach both to positivism and to structuralism—the developmental psychology of the Swiss psychologist Jean Piaget. Piaget is interested in how children come to understand and deal logically with what they perceive and experience. His experiments have focused on the development of logic as a child goes through the maturation process. Piaget believes that very little of the emergent mental patterns are genetic. Rather, he sees them as the inevitable outcome of a series of encounters between basic mental equipment and experience. For Piaget the development of environmental manipulation according to logical and correct principles follows a particular order. That is to say, certain types of discovery about the world must precede others. Psychological maturation results from experience and feedback from events to the mind. The growing child learns to control and understand the environment through a process of *assimilation* (taking in) and *accommodation* (learning to cope).

Piaget recognizes that human learning is a complex process and that it does not consist of a mere difference in degree from the learning of lower animals. He also recognizes that logical manipulations (at least those of a complex nature) are a human capability. He has offered experimental evidence to show that logical operations (such as the understanding of the "conservation of matter") occur before rather than after or along with linguistic understanding of these principles. Thus, for example, when a very young child is shown two water containers, one short and thick and the other tall and thin, and when water is poured from the first into the second in front of the child, he or she will say that there is more water in the tall, thin container then there was in the short, thick one. As children mature, they come to realize that water poured from one container into another will not increase or decrease in amount even if the height of the water changes. This is the "conservation of matter" principle.

Recent experiments have shown that not all logical operations occur in the sequences predicted by Piaget. In addition, even the idea that they occur in necessary sequences has been called into question. It appears that children make certain discoveries about the world quite early in development, forget them, and then find them again in the context of new experiences.

Whether Piaget's original developmental sequences turn out to be correct, he was one of the first psychologists to focus on the development of mental operations. As such he was among the pioneers in the study of psychic unity and its foundations. At the present time his methods and theories are being tested by anthropologists to see if they apply in different cultures and even among our primate relatives.

The Swiss psychologist Jean Piaget working with children. Piaget is a major figure in developmental and cognitive psychology.

Summary

Psychological anthropology attempts to discover the roots of human nature, to find the cultural reasons for personality differences in different societies, and to test hypotheses about perception and thought in different cultures.

Freud was the father of psychological anthropology. He constructed a theory to account for certain mental and behavioral patterns that he believed were operational in all cultures. While Freud treated neurotics, his theories apply to normal people as well. They are concerned particularly with the rules that govern unconscious thought, the development of neurotic behavior on the basis of certain key family conflicts, and the emergence of the complete personality. The latter is based on a synthesis between id (biological) drives, the developing conscience (the superego, derived from parental models), and the ego, or self. The human being is everywhere faced with a set of conflicts between id drives for immediate satisfaction and the need to delay pleasure in the context of society. The existence of culture and social life are necessary for human life, but culture is in direct conflict with the developing individual. Within each family the child wishes to possess its mother and get rid of its father. At the same time the father is feared and loved as well. Freud referred to this conflict as the Oedipus complex. He believed that it was the inevitable and universal outcome of family life combined with infantile sexual feelings, particularly toward the mother.

The introduction of Freudian theory directly into anthropology occurred in the 1930s. Geza Roheim, a strict Freudian, was the first psychoanalyst to do field work. He studied Australian Aborigines and attempted to demonstrate the universality of the Oedipus complex. In the United States a group of analysts, led by Karen Horney and Erich Fromm, developed what has come to be known as Neofreudianism. Neofreudianism abandons Freud's orientation toward a biological explanation of unconscious processes and substitutes cultural explanations. Neofreudians accept the unconscious but believe that neurosis and conflict are based on cultural variables rather than fixed biological principles. The anthropologist Bronislaw Malinowski attempted to disprove the existence of the Oedipus complex in a matrilineal society (the Trobriand Islands) but found instead that cultural factors merely changed its focus. In the Trobriands young children displayed the complex in relation to their maternal uncles rather than their fathers.

The two most famous figures in psychological anthropology and the founders of the so-called "culture-and-personality" school were Ruth Benedict and Margaret Mead. Benedict is particularly well known for her book *Patterns of Culture,* in which she attempted to demonstrate that the members of different cultures had characteristic personality types and that cultures themselves could be characterized in terms of personality. Benedict compared the Kwakiutl, the Zuñi, and the natives of Dobu, an island near the Trobriands. She suggested that the Kwakiutl were highly emotional, the Zuñi stoic, and the Dobuans paranoid. The fact that very different personality norms could be discerned in each of the three cultures led Benedict to question the notion of normalcy. For her what was normal in one culture might be abnormal in another and vice versa. This theory is an aspect of cultural relativism, which advocates that the norms of any particular culture be examined only in the context of that culture rather than on the basis of some absolute value system.

Margaret Mead had a long and varied career in anthropology. Her early culture-and-personality work concentrated on the testing of hypotheses about sexuality and the cultural basis of male and female roles. Mead attempted to demonstrate that typical male and female behavior was culture-specific rather than biologically determined.

More recent work in culture and personality has tended to focus on the cross-cultural testing of specific psychological hypotheses. Foremost among the researchers in this area is John

Whiting, who has examined the relation between initiation and personality development and has also tested a range of hypotheses relating child training to personality and such cultural elements as medical beliefs.

During the Second World War anthropologists were cut off from their subject populations. At Yale University an effort was put into coding studies published from many cultures so that they could easily be used for cross-cultural comparisons. This resulted in the Cross-Cultural Survey, which later became the Human Relations Area Files. Many of the early studies employing data from these files were psychological in nature.

In the same period at Columbia, Margaret Mead and her associates began to study culture at a distance. Using interviews with refugees and published material as well as films, students of culture at a distance attempted to analyze the relationship between cultural systems and personality. Culture-at-a-distance studies focused on such complex cultures as Russia and Japan and thus turned some anthropologists toward modern society and away from traditional societies.

Ethnosemantics and structuralism are branches of psychological anthropology that do not deal with personality. Ethnosemantics is a systematic attempt to uncover the rules that govern classification systems within specific cultures. Ethnosemantics has also focused on anthropological methodology, particularly on how data are gathered and analyzed. In general, it has been strongly influenced by the work of modern linguists, particularly those who describe and analyze unwritten languages.

Structuralists are concerned with how the human mind works. They believe that a universal grammar of relationships underlies all types of classification systems and such cultural products as myths. This grammar is based on binary oppositions which are united in structures in such a way that a change in one element of the system will produce an orderly change in the other elements. Through the analysis of myth, classification systems, kinship, and even such behaviors as cooking and body painting, structuralists attempt to extract universal rules of mental process.

Both ethnosemantics and structuralism concentrate on what have come to be known as emic phenomena. This term, which contrasts with etic, refers to the mental aspect of cultural data. Etic analysis concentrates on real behavior and emic analysis on what informants say or think.

Ethnosemantics has been criticized because in the past it tended to rely on information gathered from a single informant and because, at least from the point of view of cultural materialism, it is impossible to get inside people's heads and find out what they really think. Structuralism has been criticized because it also deals with mental rather than behavioral patterns, because it often uses constructs that are not *directly* open to empirical test, and because it has not (yet) produced a grammar of mental processes than can be used to generate or predict real cultural phenomena.

A major point of confusion exists in at least some of the criticisms of both ethnosemantics and structuralism. Informants, whether they provide the anthropologist with information by such activities as making canoes or telling a story, are acting as a source of data, not an explanation of that data or a method of analysis. The analysis and the method used to derive it are in the hands of the anthropologist. The theory an anthropologist constructs to explain both thought and behavior is in the anthropologist's and not the informant's head.

While ethnosemantics sees culture as the major variable in the construction of classification systems, and while structuralists seek universal biologically based laws that they believe underlie all classification systems, psychologists influenced by Jean Piaget believe that logic develops out of an inevitable sequence of experiences that occur as all children grow up in the world. Development is a slow process of discovery, combined with a very few genetic capacities that underlie it.

Bibliography

Barnouw, V. 1963 *Culture and Personality.* Homewood, Ill.: Dorsey Press. Three views of personality set within the perspective of anthropology.

Benedict, R. F. 1946 (1934) *Patterns of Culture.* New York: Penguin Books. Cultural relativism applied to the concept of abnormality with an attempt to describe the personalities of three cultures.

Benedict, R. F. 1946 *The Chrysanthemum and the Sword.* Boston: Houghton Mifflin. Japanese personality and culture studied from a distance. One of the culture-at-a-distance studies undertaken during the years of World War II.

D'Andrade, R. G. 1973 Cultural Constructions of Reality. In *Cultural Illness and Health: Essays in Human Adaptation.* Edited by L. Nader and T. W. Maretski. Washington, D.C.: The American Anthropological Association. Emic cognitive anthropology applied to the perception of reality.

Fortune, R. 1932 *Sorcerers of Dobu.* London: Routledge and Kegan Paul Ltd. Ethnography of Dobu suggesting that Dobuan culture is paranoid.

Freud, S. 1962 *Civilization and its Discontents.* New York: W. W. Norton. The relationship between individual drives and the development of civilization.

Freud, S. 1950 *Totem and Taboo.* New York: W. W. Norton. Origin of the incest taboo and totemism according to Freud.

Freud, S. 1976 *The Future of an Illusion.* New York: W. W. Norton. The origins of religion in psychological projection.

Freud, S. 1965 *The Psychopathology of Everyday Life.* New York: W. W. Norton. Freud's basic discoveries applied to the behavior and thought of normal individuals.

Freud, S. 1960 *Jokes and Their Relation to The Unconscious.* New York: W. W. Norton. Another demonstration that Freud's basic discoveries could be applied to normal life.

Gorer, G. and J. Rickman 1949 *The People of Great Russia: A Psychological Study.* London: Cresset. Study of Russian personality and culture from a distance.

Lévi-Strauss, C. 1963 *Structural Anthropology.* New York: Basic Books. Several articles that introduce the reader to the many facets of structural anthropology.

Lévi-Strauss, C. 1966 *The Savage Mind.* Chicago: University of Chicago Press. An introduction to structuralism with a great deal of material on classification systems and their internal logic.

Lévi-Strauss, C. 1969–73 *Les Mythologiques.* (four volumes) Paris: Plon. Structural study of myth in South and North America. The major work by Lévi-Strauss. Two volumes translated.

Malinowski, B. 1961 *Argonauts of the Western Pacific.* New York: Dutton. Mentions Dobu in first chapter.

Mead, M. 1928 *Coming of Age in Samoa.* New York: William Morrow. First culture-and-personality study. Adolescence in Samoa compared to United States.

Mead, M. 1935 *Sex and Temperament in Three Primitive Societies.* New

York: William Morrow. Cultural variations in sexual roles in three New Guinea cultures.

Mead, M. 1949 — *Male and Female.* New York: William Morrow. Mead generalizes from her studies of sexual behavior in traditional societies and applies these to modern culture.

Piaget, J. 1968 — *Genetic Epistemology.* New York: Columbia University Press. A good outline of Piaget's theories concerning the development of cognition.

Romney, A. K. and P. Epling. 1958 — A Simplified Model of Kariera Kinship. *American Anthropologist* 60:59–74. An application of emic cognitive anthropology to a classic problem in kinship analysis.

Stent, G. 1975 — Limits to the Scientific Understanding of Man. *Science.* 187:1052–1057. Discussion of positivism and structuralism and their relation to social science.

Wallace, A. F. C. 1970 — *Culture and Personality,* 2nd edition. New York: Random House. An excellent introduction to modern culture-and-personality studies from a leader in the field. The book considers the role of certain environmental factors in personality.

Whiting, J. W. M. 1964 — The Effects of Climate on Certain Cultural Practices. In *Explorations in Cultural Anthropology.* Edited by W. Goodenough. New York: McGraw-Hill. Relates residence, mother-child bonding, climate, and the intensity of initiation ceremonies, particularly at adolescence.

Whiting, J. W. M. and Child, I. 1953 — *Child Training and Personality: A Cross Cultural Study.* New Haven: Yale University Press. Relates a series of child-training variables to disease diagnosis and treatment as well as to personality.

CHAPTER 23

ETHNOGRAPHY INTO ETHNOLOGY I: THEORY

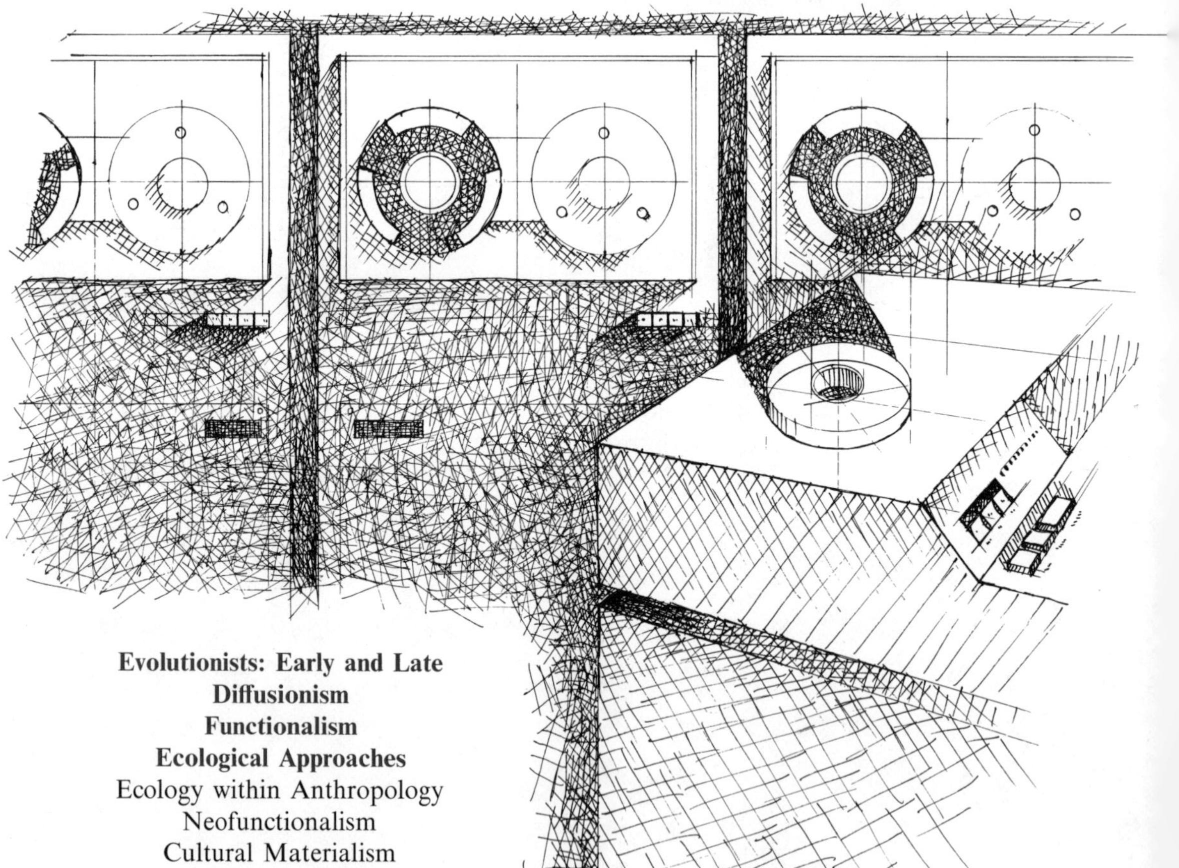

Evolutionists: Early and Late
Diffusionism
Functionalism
Ecological Approaches
Ecology within Anthropology
Neofunctionalism
Cultural Materialism
Marxist Approaches
Structuralism
General Problems in the Study of Cultural Adaptation

We have now examined the institutions found in all human societies. Kinship, technology, politics, economics, and socialization are all part of culture. All exist within a historical and geographical framework (the environment, past and present), and all interact with that framework as cultures change through time.

Although most contemporary anthropologists tend to focus on one aspect of the discipline (politics, kinship, religion, ecology, for example), all attempt to gain an integrated view of the cultures they study in the field. Institutions in the abstract do not add up to a culture in reality. In the chapters you have just read, it has been impossible to keep a clear separation between such aspects of culture as religion and politics, or politics and kinship. Yet in teaching anthropology and in learning it, we must begin with a narrow focus. The time has now come to put things together, to look at a few case studies as examples of anthropological analysis. Before we can take this final step, however, we need to review the current status of theory in anthropology.

When an anthropologist takes ethnographic data and converts it into an ethnological analysis, the analysis will be colored in advance by the chosen way of looking at the data. As I have pointed out before, there is no such thing as objective observation. If this is so for the collection of data, it is even more true of analysis. What anthropologists see and what insights they draw from data are influenced by their particular theoretical visions.

In what follows I will examine the major schools of anthropology. These will be discussed both historically and in relation to their place in contemporary anthropology. It should be noted that anthropology is far from being a unified discipline in which most scholars agree on major theoretical issues. On the contrary, anthropology is divided into many schools, each with its own theory and approach to data.

EVOLUTIONISTS: EARLY AND LATE

Cultural evolutionism has had a long and distinguished history in anthropology. We have already met several principal evolutionists and their theories in the chapters on archeology. Evolutionists can be roughly divided into three schools: unilinear, multilinear, and ecological.

Unilinear evolutionists, the best known of whom are Lewis H. Morgan and V. G. Childe, view human cultural development as a single line of progress in definite stages from a state of simple technology and social organization to a state of complex technology and social organization. Correlations are suggested between various technological levels and such aspects of culture as family organization, social structure, kinship, religion, and political organization. One of the early insights provided by evolutionists was the notion that a great transformation in culture occurred with the rise of states. In the state a whole new set of social relations developed. These included a reduction in the importance of kinship, the development of contractual relations between individuals based on their economic specializations as well as their place in an emergent class structure, loyalty to the territorially defined nation rather than to a kinship-based unit, and the emergence of full-time political leaders who embodied the state and its laws.

Multilinear evolutionists believe that different environmental conditions lead to different adaptational patterns. For them the evolutionary process in culture has followed a set of paths each dependent on a different interaction between technology and local environmental conditions. Similar conditions lead to similar developmental paths. The major figure in multilinear evolution was Julian Steward. Steward was concerned with culture-environment relations and called his approach **cultural ecology.** Despite his emphasis on the environment, he saw an aspect of culture as the major variable in evolution. Steward noted that the effect of the environment on culture was mediated by the organization of work. If two different environments could best be exploited by the same work patterns, then parallel cultural developments would follow in each. This idea was tested by Robert Murphy and Steward in an influential article, *Tappers and Trappers: Parallel Processes in Acculturation,* that examined parallel systems of social organization among fur-trappers in the forests of North America and rubber-tappers in lowland South America. In both cases economic efficiency required work units made up of single individuals who had to cover a wide territory as they extracted resources from the environment.

Ecological evolutionists (human ecologists) follow a Darwinian model of culture change. They, including the neofunctionalists to be discussed below, concentrate on the close relationships that develop between a human population and its immediate physical environment. Ecological evolutionists are interested in the effect of demographic patterns on environment and vice versa, as well as the relationship between these variables and technology. Some take a micro-level approach and look at local interaction patterns in order to describe the processes involved in short-term stability and change. Others follow a developmental model and collect data on long-term change, arranging them into universal *or* multilineal sequences. Those who take a micro approach are interested in adaptation *per se.* They attempt to tease out fine-grain adjustments between contemporary behavior and the environment. The developmentalists, many of whom are archeologists, tend to be progress-oriented. They see cultural evolution as the result of an orderly process of accumulation. If one were to draw a parallel between the micro and developmental approaches to cultural evolution on the one hand and work in biological evolution on the other, one could say that the micro approach, like much of population genetics, studies fluctuations in living populations in relation to their environment at a single point in time while the developmentalists work like paleontologists, creating an ordered sequence of development through time. Both approaches are ecological in that they are concerned with the relationships between the environment and culture. The adaptational significance of eating garlic with raw fish noted in Chapter 16 is a good example of the micro approach. The sequence of cultural development from hunting and gathering to settled agriculture to the rise of the state set in the context of specific environments—river valleys, for example—is a good illustration of the developmental approach.

DIFFUSIONISM

It was noted long ago that not all cultural traits are invented by the people among whom they are found. Where there is contact between social groups, borrowing frequently occurs. The use of tobacco, which originated in the New World, was carried to Europe by early explorers and moved rapidly from there to the rest of the world. The borrowing of traits across the boundaries of culture is known as **diffusion.**

Intellectual as well as material traits diffuse. Islam began in the Middle East and rapidly spread westward across Africa and into Spain and eastward all the way into Southeast Asia. Christianity, which also began in the Middle East, spread across Africa and northward into Europe.

During the period when cultural evolutionism was popular among a large percentage of anthropologists, extreme diffusionism was offered as an alternative explanation for similarities found among distant cultures. Diffusionists believed that humans were basically uninventive and that the existence of similar traits could only be explained as the result of borrowing rather than similar pathways of evolution. One school, headed by G. E. Smith and W. R. Rivers, held that all aspects of "high" culture originated in ancient Egypt and diffused outward from there to the rest of the world, wherever its elements are found. Most early diffusionists coupled the idea of borrowing with migration. In their view people moved outward from a center (often Egypt) in waves to populate the rest of the world. Each wave carried a more sophisticated level of culture.

Diffusion is a fact, but so is invention. Similar cultural traits, both material and mental, have developed independently at different times and in different places. Furthermore, to say that a trait has diffused tells us little about the process involved in its integration into a host culture. Is it used the same way? Does it have the same meaning? How and why have its form and functions changed within the context of specific cultures?

Just after the Second World War the idea of the drive-in movie diffused to Japan. But at the time individual Japanese could not afford to own cars. Model Volkswagen "beetles" without engines were constructed and set in the "drive-in" lots. Individuals would arrive on foot, buy their tickets, and pick a mock car in which to sit. These drive-in movie houses were clearly the result of diffusion from the United States, but the most interesting thing about them was their transformation in the context of Japanese culture.

FUNCTIONALISM

Historically there have been two major functionalist schools. One of these was founded by A. R. Radcliffe-Brown and the other by Bronislaw Malinowski. Both schools viewed human society as an integrated and functioning whole and both were based on an organic (biological) analogy—but the analogies were applied differently.

Malinowski saw the human condition as one in which a set of basic biological needs had to be fulfilled. These needs (such as hunger, thirst, sex, sleep) he called *primary drives.* These drives are converted in the context of culture into *secondary drives.* Secondary drives determine how basic needs are met. For example, although hunger, a primary drive, occurs among all humans, what people desire to eat, a secondary drive, and what they avoid are determined by what foods are acceptable and unacceptable as determined by culture. Thus Hindus avoid beef while American and French people generally relish it. Pork is taboo for Jews and a treat for Chinese. Malinowski saw cultural institutions as mechanisms for the satisfaction of these drives. He saw culture as a set of institutions that make the human adaptation possible. He and his followers spent a good deal of their research efforts studying how social institutions function to serve social and biological needs. His view of magic gives some clues to the way in which he understood the concept of function. He saw magic as a particular aspect of technology applied under special conditions. Taking fishing as an example, he pointed out that the natives of the Trobriand Islands had a set of technological devices for fishing such as boats, nets, hooks, and line. These were used without magic when fishing was safe and relatively sure, as within the confines of the protective reef surrounding an island. Under more dangerous conditions, when the catch was less sure, the islanders added special fishing magic to their equipment. Magic helped to guarantee the success of fishing and the safety of the fisherman.

Radcliffe-Brown had a similar notion about culture. He saw it as an adaptive device, the means for coping with environmental and social problems. But while Malinowski tended to reduce function to biological and psychological factors, Radcliffe-Brown insisted that culture is superorganic—that is, exists in its own right. The function of cultural traits, he argued, cannot be explained through recourse to drives. Instead, one has to show how a series of related institutions or parts of institutions function to maintain a culture. Radcliffe-Brown asked such questions as: Why do joking relationships exist between certain categories of kin? What is the reason for the special social relationship that exists between a male and his mother's brother in so many societies? In addition, he warned against the use of what he called "conjectural history" in anthropology. He did not trust oral records, realizing that such data could be manipulated by informants to justify their own self-interest. He did not say, as some have suggested, that historical records should not be used when they are available and verifiable. He did, however, emphasize the **synchronic** analysis of culture, insisting that institutions could best be understood in terms of their overall function at a particular point in time.

Functionalists of both schools downplayed history as an important part of anthropology. In addition, they tended to focus on social systems and ritual. Little work was done by functionalists on material culture or ecology, which were less important to them than social relationships.

Because Radcliffe-Brown and to some extent Malinowski and his followers saw cultures as unique, integrated wholes, they were suspicious of comparative studies. The same trait might appear in different cultures but have an entirely different origin and function. Comparisons therefore are dangerous and often lead to false conclusions. This restriction on anthropological research and theory makes cross-cultural study practically impossible. If we are to have a truly comparative science, say the critics of functionalism, we must abandon this particularistic view.

Functionalism has been criticized by a number of philosophers of science on the grounds that its reliance on an organic analogy is open to question. One can talk of the function of the liver within an organism because organisms are finite, bounded entities made up of parts that *must* work together if the entire system is to function. It has never been demonstrated that societies or cultures are equivalent to living creatures in this respect. Another criticism concerns causality. Functional explanations are *likely* descriptions about the way in which particular institutions function. They do not, however, explain why a particular kind of institution exists. Anxiety, for example, may be reduced by projecting hostility onto witches, but this could also be accomplished by projecting it onto goblins. Psychologists have noted a whole range of anxiety-reducing mechanisms in cultural behavior. But functional explanations cannot explain why one such mechanism exists rather than another, functionally equivalent one.

Finally, the assertion that society is a functioning whole suggests that conflicts, social disruption, and change are all indications of social pathology. Such a view has implications for any research that is oriented toward the analysis of change. It is antievolutionary, and has also been accused of being politically naive. In some, but by no means all, cases the struggles of native peoples for self-determination was labeled as a symptom of social pathology by early functionalists.

A school referred to as "neofunctionalism" has developed within the ecological movement in anthropology. This school, led by A. P. Vayda, has attempted to avoid the problem of causality by carefully defining certain aspects of culture as self-regulating systems. Neofunctionalists are strongly influenced by *cybernetics,*— they apply to culture the concept of self-regulation (feedback), which is also applied to such mechanical systems as thermostats and such biological systems as temperature-regulation in warm-blooded animals.

Negative feedback helps a system to remain stable in the face of environmental fluctuations. The system can remain stable when information about the environment is fed into it and used to make adjustments. If a thermostat is set for 70°, it will turn the heat on when the temperature drops below that figure. A thermostat can do this because it contains a metal bar that is heat-sensitive and moves through expansion and contraction in response to heat. When the air surrounding the thermostat falls below its setting, the bar contracts and sets on a switch that controls a furnace. When the temperature goes beyond the setting, the bar expands and turns off the furnace. It has been suggested that, in an analogous way, certain cultural practices, particularly religious ceremonies, occur in response to quantitative changes in environmental variables and act to bring human-environmental relations into harmony. If a system can be shown to be self-regulating, then one can not only describe it but predict how it will function under a set of stated conditions. Neofunctionalism is discussed more fully under ecological approaches.

ECOLOGICAL APPROACHES

Ecology is *the set of relations among organisms and their environment.* Ecological systems are assumed to have evolved as environmental pressures (both inorganic and organic) have shaped each member of the biological community. An ecologist within the discipline of biology might study a lake or desert as a biological community. The analysis would include the cataloging of species present; their frequency and specific distribution within the overall geographic space; interactions among these species, including their places in the food chain; an analysis of climatological and chemical factors that affect species distribution and numbers; and the flow of energy within the defined ecological system.

The key concepts of ecologists within biology are *energy, information, integration,* and *succession.* Every biological system requires **energy** for its operation and the maintenance of its organization. Organization depends on **information** in various forms. Reproduction, for example, requires the correct transfer of information from generation to generation in the form of the genetic code. If ecologists are correct in assuming that environmental adaptation demands the accommodation of species within a biological community to one another as well as to the physical environment, then information in some form must also be passed among the species present in any particular environment. This information is conceived of as feedback, in the form of selection pressures on each species within the system. Thus, for example, any change in the system—such as the introduction of a new species—will lead to adjustments in that system.

The concept of **integration** assumes that organisms, populations, and communities are organized as dynamic biological systems. Organisms maintain themselves through sets of homeostatic (stability-preserving) processes. Ecologists assume that this is also true on the level of populations and biological communities. What happens on one level of the food chain will affect the levels above it. When the population of a predator increases, the population of its prey will decline. Such a decline will in turn lead to an eventual decline in the predator population as its food resource becomes scarce. The reduction in predators will then allow an increase in prey, and a cycle of population growth and decline will be set up in the species concerned. Such cycling may have an effect on other species within the system as well.

No ecological system is completely stable, however. Systems change through time, frequently in an orderly and predictable way. Orderly change is known as **succession.** If a forest is cut down or destroyed by fire, for example, and the environment is left to regenerate itself, a predictable set of plants and animals will occupy the space successively until the environment reaches what is known as its climax. In theory, the climax is stable, but it too, is subject to change due to factors like a shift in climate, the introduction of new species, or such natural disasters as flood, fire, and windstorm. Human beings, of course, often disturb a climax zone, producing an entirely new set of ecological conditions.

Ecology within Anthropology

Within the discipline of anthropology ecology has been approached from three directions (at the end of this chapter I will point out a fourth approach that is now emerging). These are *cultural ecology, ethnoscience,* and *human ecology.*

Cultural ecology was the name given to multilinear evolution by Julian Steward. Remember that Steward was concerned with the different paths that cultural evolution takes in the context of different technological and environmental conditions. His major concern, however, was the organization of work in the context of specific environments—and how these work patterns affected other aspects of culture—rather than a detailed analysis of human populations as parts of natural ecological systems. Steward concentrated on the ways in which human populations were controlled and distributed by a combination of environmental and technological factors. Harsh environments and low-level technology were seen as restricting factors on both population size and concentration.

Ethnoscientists take an emic approach. They concentrate on the ways in which human populations perceive and classify their environments. They attempt to analyze native systems of classification in order to understand the environment as a cultural phenomenon. One justification for this approach is that humans can only utilize what they are aware of. The method of exploitation will be conditioned by the way in which such knowledge is organized. Adaptation, therefore, can only be understood as a specifically cultural accommodation to *knowledge* of the environment. In general, ethnoscientists see each culture as a unique system, and although some of them believe that generalizations about adaptation may eventually emerge, their work is often limited to narrow linguistic aspects of specific cultures. Ethnoscientists have tended to study areas like disease classification or plant and animal categories. Some ethnoscientists have compared native systems with Western scientific classification to see what differences and overlaps occur. Such studies procede from the assumption that overlaps will reflect "natural" order, that is to say, an order inherent in nature. Contrast this view to the structuralist position that overlaps between different systems of classification reflect a mental order, an order inherent in the mind. Structuralists hold that whatever exists "out there" (in some objective sense) is only knowable through the mind. The mind is assumed to work in specific ways as a filter and organizer of information. Cross-cultural regularities in systems of classification, then, are taken as evidence of identical mental processes.

Human ecology draws its approach most directly from biology. Human ecologists view human groups as biological populations, each living in an ecological niche, interacting with the environment. It is the task of human ecologists to study in detail the ways in which populations have adapted to their specific environments. Many human ecologists have used the principle of negative feedback long applied by biologists to living systems.

Neofunctionalism

The use of negative feedback to explain cultural stability has led to the development of **neofunctionalism,** which is based on the study of systems, in particular human ecological systems. This approach attempts to establish laws that govern the process of cultural adaptation. Unlike the functionalism of Malinowski or Radcliffe-Brown, neofunctionalism does not pretend to explain the reason for the existence of particular cultural traits. Recognizing that functional analyses in social science cannot provide adequate causal explanations, neofunctionalists simply attempt to describe a feedback system in a culture and then explain the way it works. Such systems are assumed to maintain themselves in a steady state, that is, they maintain their integrity in the face of environmental fluctuation. Neofunctionalists assume that certain aspects of cultural behavior such as ritual can be explained in terms of self-regulation. They attempt to define a system in order to understand what variables act to maintain others within certain limits. The system to be maintained may be the niche within which the population lives, or the size of the population, or some other biocultural aspect of the population in question. Predictions about the operation of feedback are open to empirical test and can be used to verify the existence of the hypothetical system.

Neofunctionalists have used the potlatch as an example of self-regulation. We shall examine this argument in detail in the next chapter; here it will be sufficient to say that the neofunctionalist explanation of the potlatch correlates the feasts and redistributions that are integral to it with times of famine and scarcity in an environment subject to wide variation in resource availability. According to neofunctionalists potlatches are given by villages which are rich in food at a particular time. The invited come from those villages that are poor in food. The entire system (as it operates through time) serves to distribute variable resources evenly across a widely distributed population.

Similarly, neofunctionalists have explained large pig feasts in New Guinea as a mechanism for the regulation of pig populations so that they do not come into direct competition for resources with human populations. Pig raising is essential for many New Guinea peoples. Men with large pig herds gain prestige, and pigs are a major item of trade. They also constitute an efficient way of converting low-grade vegetable protein into high-grade animal protein. The culture thus contains a contradiction. Men wish to retain pigs because they are a source of prestige, but they are also valuable food, and can become a nuisance when there are too many of them. Pigs in New Guinea can become too much of a good thing. Since people are loath to kill pigs, however, there must be a cultural mechanism that triggers pig killing and therefore acts to regulate the system. Neofunctionalists argue that ceremonial pig feasts operate to regulate the pig population. These feasts, they maintain, occur when the pig population begins to threaten the ecological balance between humans and pigs. This explanation argues that New Guinea peoples do not consciously realize that pig-killing ceremonies occur when the ecological balance is in danger. Nor do they realize that the ceremonies act to restore the system to equilibrium. All of this is an unconscious process triggered when the pig population reaches a certain size. Information about the environment, in this case the pig population, is fed back into the culture and sets off a ceremonial cycle. This is supposed to be true also of the potlatch. People do not potlatch because they are aware of scarcity in certain parts of their territory, but rather for such cultural reasons as the elevation of a youth to adulthood. Neofunctionalists would claim that ceremonies are unconsciously triggered at specific times of ecological need.

Neofunctionalists argue that pig feasts in New Guinea and potlatching on the Northwest Coast provide a cultural means for adaptive behavior when it is advantageous for the population at large. An underlying assumption of neofunctionalism is that unconscious mechanisms (such as those that underlie these rituals) have the advantage of serving a population as an adaptive mechanism when the conscious choice of individuals might be maladaptive. In New Guinea individual men wish to maintain large pig herds. On the Northwest Coast individual chiefs may wish to increase their stock of resources. In both cases culture takes precedence over individual desire. Thus, if the neofunctionalists are correct, these rituals act like a thermostat. They regulate a system and keep it going.

Positive feedback is equally adaptive but it accounts for change rather than stability in systems. Positive feedback occurs when the environment rewards a change. In genetics, for example, we know that a positive mutation, one that is favored during the selection process, becomes more abundant. By the same reasoning, if the consequences of a new cultural behavior are positive, if it increases the survival chances of the population, it will tend to become part of culture. A change need not evolve as the result of conscious choices. But populations that respond to positive feedback will replace populations that do not respond. The spread of agriculture and domestic animals is an example of this kind of change. Domestication has economic and demographic advantages. Populations that shift to these production strategies tend to grow at faster rates than populations that do not adopt them. Hunters and gatherers are pushed back into the more inaccessible parts of the environment or into productively marginal areas in which agriculture and animal domestication are unlikely to work. At the present time the few remaining hunting and gathering populations are rapidly disappearing.

While neofunctionalist explanations are appealing, particularly because they appear to have scientific rigor, accurate measurements of the cases they offer do not exist. Thus, while their explanations of the potlatch and New Guinea pig feasting are attractive, we cannot be sure they are correct. Potlatches still occur on the Northwest Coast and pig feasts are still a feature of life among many New Guinea peoples, but the conditions under which they *may* have served as adaptive mechanisms have long since disappeared. In addition, neofunctionalist explanations require very precise measurements over a relatively long time period. To date no anthropologist has been able to provide the kind of data necessary to fully support the neofunctionalist argument.

Cultural Materialism

Cultural materialists are closely allied to the evolutionary ecological school of anthropology. They contend that demographic, environmental, economic, and technological factors are responsible for cultural change and evolution. Such aspects of culture as politics, religion, and art are seen as the result of these factors. In the words of cultural materialists the techno-environmental "base" determines the ideological "superstructure." Cultural materialists separate what they call *emic* and *etic* aspects of culture. They concentrate on the etic, which consists of actual behavior and its effects on the development and operation of culture. They have asked such questions as why cows are sacred in India and why pork is taboo among Orthodox Jews. Cases of taboo are chosen as test cases by cultural materialists because anthropologists and others have traditionally given them ideological, or emic, explanations.

The sacred cow is a particularly favored case. It has been assumed by many to be a totally dysfunctional custom maintained by religious belief, bringing hardship to a population stressed by protein shortages as well as general malnutrition. Marvin Harris, in a widely discussed paper, argued that the taboo on eating cows among Indian Hindus provides many ecological benefits. Kept alive, but not particularly well cared for, the cow in India, an energy-poor country, is a major source of fuel (cow dung is burned). In addition, cows provide a major source of traction (they are used to pull plows) and are an important source of protein through milk production. Harris also points out that cows are raised on marginal land. Thus, they compete only slightly with humans for calories in a calorie-poor land. Finally, he points out that although caste Hindus do not eat beef, cows are, in fact, eventually eaten by outcastes and Moslems. A close look at cattle management in India shows that a religious custom that on the surface appears strange and maladaptive has a positive function within the overall Indian ecological system.

For the taboo on pigs among Jews and Moslems a different sort of argument is advanced. Cows are not eaten in India but are exploited in other ways. The pig was originally avoided by Semites because it is an ecologically expensive and destructive animal to raise in the fragile and overexploited Middle Eastern environment. According to Harris the pig taboo evolved as a response to environmental conditions. Overgrazing and general lack of adequate rainfall, combined with increasing population, made pig raising unprofitable and perhaps even dangerous. In addition, he notes that, while pork is a favored meat among many peoples, it is one of the few herd animals that cannot be exploited for milk. Pigs, he says, are also difficult to raise in a hot dry climate because they do not sweat and are subject to heat stress.

Certainly some cultural materialist analyses demonstrate that apparently illogical and maladaptive traits can provide benefits for populations practicing them. Cultural materialism provides an important lesson for those who assume that customs different from their own, which have no readily apparent explanation, are somehow strange, maladaptive, backward, or "superstitious." Cultural materialism, on the other hand, cannot account for the *origin* of cultural traits, particularly such aspects of ideology as taboos. It suffers from the same defects as all functionalist explanations: it cannot tell us why one solution is favored over another.

Cultural materialists attempt to overcome this objection by taking a historical perspective. This approach adds another dimension to functionalism, which under the influence of its British founders was particularly static and even antievolutionary. If one can demonstrate a correlation between the development of a culture trait and a particular ecological change, or the spread of a particular trait as an adaptively superior mode of coping with environmental problems, the case for a materialist explanation is strengthened. Thus, Harris argues that pigs were raised by Semitic peoples until natural and culturally induced environmental change reduced their value to that of a serious risk. Unfortunately, at the present time the archeological evidence for this hypothesis is, to say the least, ambiguous. The case is, in fact, not proven. In addition, there are compelling arguments for an ideological explanation of the pork taboo. The strongest of these is that taboo results from a set of complex political and social factors. Food taboos in many parts of the world are a cultural statement about self and group identity. Over and over again anthropologists find cases in which the motto "food makes the person" holds true. This works in two ways. People define themselves by what they eat and do not eat. They also define others this way. If the only reason for not raising pigs in the Middle East were ecological, good resource management would dictate the substitution of such animals as camels, goats, and sheep for pigs. But resource management does not require a taboo, which is a strong religious statement. Taboo goes beyond simple avoidance for practical reasons of some particular resource to a religious affirmation. Yaks are the preferred animal in highland Tibet because they do well there. Reindeer are raised by Lapps because Lapland's harsh environment would make cattle raising a very risky business. Yet Tibetans and Lapps do not taboo other types of herd animals. They know about them but also know better then to try to raise them. Taboos are religious imperatives. They require more than ecological explanation. People are generally not so foolish as to raise animals in an environment that is unsuitable for them, but this does not require a taboo.

We cannot assume that conscious and/or unconscious adaptation to environments always occur. Human beings often exploit their niches with no regard for the future. Natural resources may be wasted or misused until they are exhausted. When this happens, new forms of exploitation must be found if a particular environment is not to become inhospitable for humans. Resource management does occur, but not always, and not always well. One major problem that human groups have faced in this regard is what is known as the *tragedy of the commons.* The phrase refers to the selfish exploitation of a resource that is potentially available to everyone. Ocean fish are a good example. The world's fisheries once appeared to be an inexhaustable resource, exploited by fleets from many countries. Restriction of fishing by one conscientious country alone makes no sense in terms of conservation. It merely means that the country will get less fish while some other country's fishermen will get more, since under this type of global exploitation each fisherman attempts to maximize his own catch with no regard for the eventual disappearance of the fish population. The only effective control in this case would be an international agreement respected and enforced by all parties. Such agreements are difficult to achieve because marine resources are the major means of meeting the nutritional requirements of certain countries. A recent attempt to limit whale hunting (the exploitation of a marine mammal resource) has come up against the strong resistance of the Japanese and Russians who have a greater need than other countries with fishing fleets to use whale meat along with fish as a major protein source. Even the widespread awareness of this problem has not led to its solution.

MARXIST APPROACHES

Cultural materialists identify themselves strongly with a Marxist approach that stresses economic relations. Many anthropologists who consider themselves Marxists in one form or another, however, strongly disagree with cultural materialists. A Marxist approach to society need not imply a mere economic determinism, nor need it assume that one part of culture always causes some other part. All Marxists study production, but they study it in relation to those social forms involved in the control and distribution of what is produced. In addition, many Marxists concern themselves with the ideology of production, control, and distribution. Thus, they distinguish between societies in which surplus is reinvested for further profit and societies in which surplus is used for the construction of monuments or the mounting of complex and costly religious ceremonies. They recognize the difference between money as capital (a medium for investment) and as a mere convenience in the process of exchanging goods and services. Anthropologists with a Marxist orientation attempt to determine the mode of production in a society by analyzing the prevailing technology, the way in which work is organized, and the complex of social relationships that revolve about the productive process. In addition, they attempt to analyze the way in which goods are used in the economy as well as the culture at large.

Marxist anthropologists (cultural materialists aside) have been critical of ecologists. They feel that ecological anthropology has failed to account for the tremendous effect culture has on environment. They have criticized the view that population growth is the result of a natural process and point out that many populations use effective forms of population control and have used them for centuries. Recent evidence, for example, shows that female infanticide has been a widespread practice in Europe for several centuries. Marxists have suggested that population increase, particularly overpopulation, is a cultural response to particular socioeconomic circumstances in which children are necessary in order to keep the productive process going. Marxists see productive capacities as a function of complex interactions between social groups, with the environment playing only a secondary role as a control mechanism. Thus, they are wary of any theory such as neofunctionalism that suggests a mechanism operating to keep environmental exploitation below the breaking point. Production is not the result of environmental accommodation but rather the result of social relationships and a particular type of economic ideology. These scholars recognize that environmental limitations exist, but the limitations only set outer limits on the system. They can be altered or overcome when a shift occurs in productive strategies or socioeconomic relationships.

STRUCTURALISM

I have discussed structuralism as an approach to science and as a means of analyzing culture as a mental process. Although undesirable as both theory and method among positivist-oriented anthropologists, structuralism has had a strong impact on European anthropology. More recently it has begun to influence American anthropologists as well. Structuralism has had its greatest success in the analysis of kinship, mythology, and ritual. Symbolic anthropology, which focuses on art, myth, oral literature, dance, and ritual, has become very popular. Many of its practitioners use some form of structural analysis in interpreting their data. In most cases structuralism treats data in a nonhistorical way. It is, therefore, like functionalism, open to the criticism that it ignores process, including historical contacts and internal change. Structuralism has borrowed its orientation from linguistics, particularly the theories of the Swiss linguist Ferdinand de Saussure. De

POSITIVISM VERSUS STRUCTURALISM

There are two major conflicting orientations (or paradigms) in anthropology today: These are *positivism* and *structuralism.* Be forewarned, however, that in order to simplify current theory I have lumped together some points of view that are frequently separated. Cultural materialists and ethnosemanticists will find each other to be very strange bedfellows indeed. Nonetheless, although I recognize that materialists and semanticists study different things, they share an approach to science that contrasts markedly with that of the various schools of structuralism.

Positivists put their basic trust in observable empirical data. They are *not* antitheory, rather they attempt to *induce* theory from observable phenomena. Positivism has little if any use for constructs that themselves are not open to *direct* observation and test. Positivism, particularly in behavioral science, takes the strong view that culture is a *purely* learned phenomenon. Positivists believe that all humans are born as *tabulae rasae* (empty slates) upon which experience writes the rules of behavior.

In anthropology many positivists believe that the environment acts as a selective agent. It rewards correct (correct is called *adaptive*) behavior and punishes incorrect or maladaptive behavior. Some positivists, particularly those associated with the school of anthropology known as cultural materialism, distrust the concept of "mind" as it applies to behavior. They believe either that mind is irrelevant to an understanding of real behavior or that science can only answer questions about behavior when behavior is separated from the concept of mind. On the other hand, those positivists interested in cognitive anthropology (ethnosemanticists, for example), interpret culture as a code system—a learned pattern of thought that is, of course, produced by the mind. But these scholars, although they deal in their research with mental processes, avoid the concept of mind and concentrate instead on thought as the output of a learned cultural system.

Structuralists, in contrast, make active use of constructs that cannot be tested directly. They mistrust sense data taken alone as much as positivists mistrust intangible constructs. Structuralists view behavior as the product or outcome of mind. For structuralists, understanding behavior depends on the construction of abstract models. Put another way, behavior is seen only as an output of a machine. These outputs provide clues to what lies behind behavior, its cause. Without some theoretical notion about how the machine operates, pure observation never leads to real insights.

Since structuralism is concerned with the mind, it is important to understand where structuralists believe scientific constructs are located. Some critics have accused them of literally trying to get inside the heads of their informants. The models created by structuralists to account for order in behavior are made up in their *own* heads. They are intellectual exercises undertaken by scientists that allow them to test a set of abstract ideas against sense data and its organization. Rather than distrust the concept of mind (as an abstraction), they depend on it. Models of the mind are central to all structural theories in the behavioral sciences—even of Marxists, who have been accused by some of being purely economic determinists.

Structuralists and some positivists are interested in change, but in different ways. Structuralists believe that change consists of transformations governed by the rules of culture (internalized in the mind) interacting with external variables (or to use a more accurate term, *parameters*). To some structuralists change implies adaptation to external circumstances. Some might even call such change evolution. Others view cultural change, at least in traditional societies, as circular and superficial. Even though traditional societies differ one from another, and although all change through time, these differences and changes are seen as minor variations on a theme. It should be pointed out, however, that the latter view, although frequently ascribed to structuralists, is actually quite rare. When it does occur, it is usually in the context of structuralism as a philosophical view of history rather than as a scientific theory and method of analysis.

The positivist position on change is difficult to outline. Some, for purely strategic reasons, avoid discussing it. Others base their anthropological theory on the notion that a healthy culture is stable. For these, change equals some kind of social pathology. Still other positivists follow an evolutionist tradition. They see change *primarily* as the result of selection. Humans do things in different ways for a number of reasons, and what they do is then subject to environmental selection. Evolutionists by definition take a historical, or at least temporal, approach. They do not deny that previous conditions both within a culture and its environment affect the next step in evolutionary development. One group of evolutionists, cultural materialists, do not see *mental patterns* or structures as generating or restricting change. For them it is ultimately not what people think (consciously or unconsciously) that counts but, rather, what they do in real situations. Marxist anthropologists see change as the result of historical processes in which social relations related to the economic system are the major variables. History is driven by contradictions inherent in productive activities and their related social relations.

Saussure noted that in analysing language one can take *either* a synchronic or diachronic approach. He was aware that languages change through time and that such change can and should be studied. But he pointed out that a sound system or grammar can only be understood as a stable system. To understand transformations through time, one must first understand synchronic rules. These rules can only be determined if the system is studied at one point in time.

Structuralists are interested in systems and their transformations. In fact, the demonstration that systems change according to rules provides the evidence that structural theory works. To date most structuralists have investigated transformations by studying different versions of the same or related myths or kinship systems as they are distributed through space. Lévi-Strauss, the best-known structuralist in anthropology, has, for example, undertaken a massive comparative study of the mythology of North and South America. He traces a set of common elements arranged in different patterns. These patterns are transformed according to stated rules as one moves from one version to another across the boundaries of culture. Space is substituted for time in the investigation of structural rules. The rationale is that anthropologists rarely have access to versions of a myth that can be put into a historical sequence.

Transformations through time, however, are also subject to structural analyses. A French classicist, Marcel Détienne, working with Greek mythology was able to analyze historical change in a series of related myths. Because he knows the language and literature of ancient Greece well, and because historical documents exist, Détienne was able to relate structural transformations to ethnographic facts, including political change. Put in historical context, the transformations of Greek myths and their associated rituals show both a connection to external historical events and a regularity that demonstrates their internal systematic structure.

GENERAL PROBLEMS IN THE STUDY OF CULTURAL ADAPTATION

Several problems exist within anthropological theories concerned with cultural adaptation. (1) Functional explanations reveal neither cause nor a systematic understanding of process, although neofunctionalism deals with the latter problem. (2) Since the mere presence of a culture implies adaptation on some level (what is there is adapted and what is adapted is there), adaptation tells us little about origins or the reasons why a particular behavioral system functions at any particular level of efficiency. (3) While adaptation in purely biological systems can be measured in terms of reproductive success, reproductive success alone explains very little in cultural evolution. One reason is that within cultural systems not all environmental energy is converted into organisms. As soon as social inequality in any form develops, energy tends to be diverted to maintain such inequality. The fruits of labor are no longer distributed evenly. (4) Many anthropologists forget that the theory of evolution is a theory about process and therefore a theory about *how* evolution occurs rather than a theory about *what* will evolve. Even within biology, evolutionary theory cannot predict what the next stage in evolution will be. Unfortunately, cultural process is poorly understood. Recently (as we shall see in the ethnographic examples to follow) structuralism has begun to provide clues to the internal aspect of cultural change and evolution by uncovering rules governing culture as a system. These rules can be used to predict how individual cultures will change under different sets of external conditions. Structural analysis combined with a historical-ecological perspective may provide anthropology with means for understanding both internal adaptation (the adjustment of the system "to itself") and external adaptation (the adjustment of the system to changes in the environment). The claim is that structuralism can tell us something about the uniqueness of human nature and how this nature interacts with historical and environmental forces. We can only accomplish this task, however, when several threads of anthropological theory are brought together. Analysis must rest on good historical reconstruction, structural analysis of the cultural system as such, consideration of function, and a close look at relations of culture and environment.

Summary

The relationship between data and theory in anthropology is complex. Data are generally collected with some theoretical view in mind and theory is, of course, influenced by data. When an anthropologist takes ethnographic (field) data and converts it into an ethnological analysis (an explanation of cultural forms), the analysis will be colored in advance by the chosen way of looking at the data. There is no such thing as objective observation.

The major schools of anthropology that have developed since the nineteenth century are evolutionism (unilineal and multilineal), diffusionism, functionalism, neofunctionalism, human ecology, cultural materialism, ethnosemantics (discussed in Chapter 22), Marxism, and structuralism.

Unilineal evolutionists tend to view human cultural development as progress from a state of simple technology and social organization to one of complex technology and social organization. Although few today would accept unilineal evolution as a viable approach to cultural development, theorists of this school made an important contribution to anthropological theory when they noted the great transformation that occurred with the shift from kinship-based societies to state formations.

Unilineal evolution has been replaced in large measure by various multilineal approaches that relate the specifics of cultural development to interaction between major environmental and cultural variables. The major figure in multilinear evolutionary theory is Julian Steward, who related environmental variables, technology, and the organization of work to the development of social institutions. Steward called his approach cultural ecology.

More recently cultural evolutionists have taken an ecological approach that is close to ecology in biology. Some study the fine-grain adaptations of human populations in specific environments and through short time runs, while others, mainly archeologists, study the long-term development of major cultural areas.

In the early days of anthropology evolutionists were opposed by, among others, diffusionists of various types. Diffusionists were concerned primarily with the role played by borrowing in the development of culture. Diffusionists believed that humans are basically uninventive and that the existence of similar traits in different parts of the world should be explained on the basis of borrowing rather than parallel evolution. One school of diffusionism, associated with G. E. Smith and W. R. Rivers, held that all aspects of "high" culture originated in ancient Egypt and diffused outward from there to the rest of the world.

Functionalism is associated with two major figures in anthropology—A. R. Radcliffe-Brown and Bronislaw Malinowski. Malinowski saw culture as the human species' way of solving basic biopsychological needs. Primary drives (such as hunger) were converted into secondary drives (their specific cultural expression as, for example, hunger for beef). These culturally shaped secondary drives were satisfied through cultural mechanisms. Radcliffe-Brown was not particularly interested in the relationships between individual needs and culture. Instead, he focused on culture as a set of integrated and therefore functioning institutions. Culture traits were explained in relation to their function as parts of a whole.

Functionalism, because it tends to view cultures as integrated and stable, is unable to explain change. In fact, some functionalists view change as dysfunctional or even pathological. Functionalism has also been criticized on the grounds that the organic analogy on which it is based does not apply to culture. One can talk of the function of the liver within an organism because organisms are finite, bounded entities made up of parts that must work together if the entire system is to function. It has never been demonstrated that societies or cultures are equivalent to living organisms in this respect. In addition, functionalism cannot tell us how a particular culture trait arose nor why it rather than another equally "functional" trait is part of a cultural system.

Neofunctionalism, associated with A. P. Vayda, attempts to overcome the shortcomings of functionalism by studying cultures as systems in interaction with key elements in their environments. Neofunctionalism makes no claims about explaining cause but rather focuses on how a system operates. Employing the concept of feedback, neofunctionalists attempt to describe a system and those mechanisms that regulate it. They attempt to predict what features of environmental variation will trigger specific cultural reactions that operate in the system to keep it stable.

Neofunctionalism is one of the several ecological approaches in anthropology. Julian Steward's cultural ecology is another, and ethnoscience still another. Ethnoscientists, who take an emic approach to culture, collect data on native classification systems and analyze the basic logic underlying them. In this way they hope to understand how cultural knowledge about the environment is organized. Ethnoscientists believe that adaptation can only be understood as a specifically cultural accommodation to information organized according to linguistic rules.

Cultural materialism is closely allied to the various evolutionary schools in anthropology. Materialists, the best known of whom is Marvin Harris, contend that demographic, environmental, economic, and technological factors are responsible for culture change and evolution. Other aspects of culture—such as religion, politics and law, art, and social organization—are seen as the result of these four basic causal elements. Cultural materialists separate what they call etic and emic aspects of culture. Etics concern real behavior and emics what people think. For materialists etic data are more important than emic data, because, in their opinion, it is real behavior that counts in the operation and development of culture. Cultural materialists have been accused of falling into the functionalist trap; that is, they cannot explain the origin of any culture trait and cannot be sure that their essentially functional explanation is correct. They attempt to overcome this objection by taking a historical-developmental approach to data. So far, however, their historical arguments have been rather unconvincing.

While cultural materialists identify themselves with a Marxist approach to anthropology, many anthropologists who consider themselves Marxists strongly disagree with them. For these a Marxist approach to anthropology need not imply a mere economic determinism, nor need it assume that one part of culture always causes some other part. All Marxists study production, but they often study it in relation to those social forms involved in the control and distribution of what is produced. Those Marxist anthropologists who are not cultural materialists have been critical of the various schools of ecology. They feel that ecologists have failed to account for the tremendous effect culture has on the environment and have criticized the view that population growth is the result of a natural process. For Marxists production is not the result of environmental accommodation but rather the result of social relationships and a particular type of economic ideology.

Structuralism has been particularly influential among European anthropologists. It has had its greatest success in the analysis of kinship, mythology, and ritual. Structuralism treats data in a nonhistorical way. It is, therefore, like functionalism, open to the criticism that it ignores process. Structuralists, however, are not interested in process. Instead, they focus on human nature defined as *mind.* Although they recognize cultural differences and attribute them to various historical and social processes, they are interested in that which is common to all humans everywhere and throughout history. Their task is to explain psychic unity.

All anthropologists agree that culture is the human adaptation, yet several problems emerge when various adaptational models are used to analyze or explain cultural behavior. (1) Functional explanations cannot explain cause. (2) The very presence of a particular culture or trait implies adaptation. Therefore the notion of adaptation tells us little about the origin of a trait or why it and not some other trait exists in a system. (3) While we have a noncircular measure of adaptation in biology (reproductive success), we have no similar measure in cultural anthropology. (4) The theory of evolution is a theory about process (how evolution occurs) and not a theory about what will evolve. Evolutionary theory is appealing because it has been so successful in biology, but it has still to prove itself in cultural anthropology. Recently structuralism has offered clues for an understanding of the internal aspect of culture change and evolution. It does this by uncovering rules governing cultural systems that can be used to predict how change will occur under different sets of external conditions. Structuralism, however, is a highly controversial topic in anthropology and its role in evolutionary studies has yet to be assessed.

Bibliography

Bloch, M. editor 1975 — *Marxist Analyses and Social Anthropology.* New York: John Wiley. A group of essays that approach Marxist anthropology from different perspectives.

Godelier, M. 1977 — *Perspectives in Marxist Anthropology.* Cambridge: Cambridge University Press. Structural Marxism from one of its leading proponents.

Harris, M. 1968 — *The Rise of Anthropological Theory.* New York: Crowell. The history of anthropology viewed from the perspective of cultural materialism.

Malinowski, B. 1954 — *The Science of Culture and Other Essays.* Garden City: Anchor Books. Functionalism based on biopsychological drives and their cultural solutions.

Morgan, L. H. 1877 — *Ancient Society.* New York: Henry Holt and Co. Grand scheme of social evolution by a student of North American Indians.

Radcliffe-Brown, A. R. 1952 — *Structure and Function in Primitive Society.* Glencoe, Ill: The Free Press. Essays on one form of functionalism in which society is viewed as an integrated whole.

Steward, J. H. 1955 — *Theory of Culture Change.* Urbana, Ill.: University of Illinois Press. Multilinear evolution and cultural ecology from their founder.

Vayda, A. P. and R. Rappaport 1968 — Ecology, Cultural and Noncultural. In *Introduction to Cultural Anthropology.* Edited by J. A. Clifton. Boston: Houghton Mifflin. A summary statement of neofunctionalist ecology with a criticism of ecological studies by Steward on the one hand and ethnoscientists on the other.

CHAPTER 24
ETHNOGRAPHY INTO ETHNOLOGY II: DATA ANALYSIS

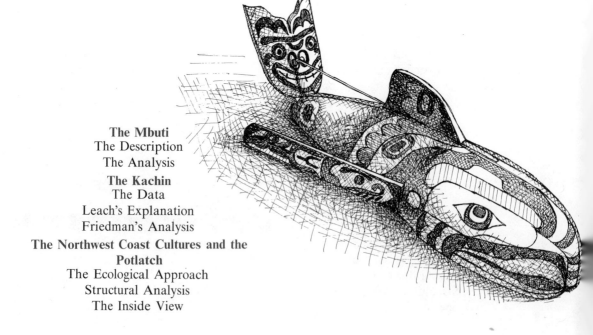

THE MBUTI

The material in this chapter has been drawn from contemporary anthropology to illustrate how anthropological theory is applied to data and how data are used to construct theory. The first example deals with a single culture (the Mbuti) and a single point of view. The data for this point of view, however, come from one author and the theory from two others. The second and third examples (the Kachin and potlatch exchange on the Northwest Coast of North America) have been chosen specifically because they have created a great deal of argument within the discipline. These studies illustrate how controversies within anthropology can develop when different theories and approaches are applied to the same data.

No society exists without cultural rules and none exists in a "state of nature." The "noble savage" is the creation of eighteenth-century European philosophy. The romance of precultural humans living in perfect harmony with nature is a pseudoscientific retelling of Adam and Eve before the fall. It is, perhaps, a projection of desire for a presumed lost innocence in a world of war, famine, and social unrest.

If anthropologists have now abandoned the search for the noble savage, they are nevertheless touched when people are found who live in relative harmony with one another and the environment. It is for this reason that we are drawn to the Mbuti who inhabit the Ituri Forest in Zaire in central Africa.

The Description

The Mbuti (formerly known as the pygmies) are hunters and gatherers who depend on the forest for their livelihood. Their relationship with the forest is reciprocal, for their culture has beneficial effects on the local ecology in the following way. The Mbuti are proud hunters. Indeed, in order to prove his manhood a Mbuti youth must kill an elephant single-handed, armed only with a spear. Because bark is a favorite food of elephants, their overabundance threatens the fabric of the tropical forest environment. Mbuti hunting thus controls the elephant population and preserves an ecological balance among flora and fauna.

The Mbuti themselves disturb the local environment in only limited ways. They lack domestic animals (except dogs), practice no agriculture, live in small bands, and are forced by the limits of their subsistence techniques to move frequently. Such movement is necessary because the tropical forest is a **generalized ecological zone.** That is, the richness of the tropical forest consists in the number of species present over a wide territory. The tropics, although lush, are generally poor in the number of any one particular species in a given limited space. Environments of this type can be contrasted to **specialized ecological zones,** in which a few species predominate but occur in great numbers. Grasslands, tundra, and semideserts are zones of the latter type. Hunters and gatherers who live in generalized environments must move frequently as they temporarily deplete resources around an impermanent settlement. It makes no sense to stay within one small geographic zone until all or most of the exploitable animals and plants have been used up. A growing scarcity of game and other resources eventually increases the work load beyond reasonable proportions. It is easier to move on than to stay put. For this reason hunters and gatherers rarely damage or deplete a single zone. Left to itself the territory surrounding an abandoned camp will replenish in time. In this sense the Mbuti are not conscious ecologists. The conservation of natural resources is the outcome of their economic patterns and desire for a tolerable work load.

What is particularly unusual and attractive about the Mbuti is their relative nonviolence. They have no wars, no black magic, no witchcraft, no chiefs, and little disharmony. These traits contrast the Mbuti with cultures marked by strife and competition. The Mbuti are not "noble savages," however. Petty bickering is common in their communities. They are no less human than we, but their culture contains practices that dampen conflict. When individual Mbuti are dissatisfied with their fellows, they pack up and move to another social group, where they will usually be accepted without any social initiation. If an individual Mbuti acts contrary to the rules of Mbuti culture, he or she will be teased by an individual who adopts the role of clown. Social pressure maintains equality, and equality is the major aspect of Mbuti social structure.

We are indebted to the Anglo-American anthropologist Colin Turnbull for a sensitive and comprehensive picture of Mbuti life and to the French anthropologists Maurice Godelier and Jacques Barrau for an analysis of his rich data. In addition to reading the accounts of Turnbull and others on the Mbuti, Godelier and Barrau corresponded with Turnbull for many months asking him specific questions. This procedure allowed them to sharpen their analysis. The theoretical approach taken by Godelier and Barrau combines ecological and structuralist thinking. I will turn to their analysis later, after describing key aspects of Mbuti life, as revealed by Turnbull.

Archeological data indicate that people like the Mbuti were probably the original inhabitants of most of tropical Africa. With the development of plant and animal domestication, individual hunting-and-gathering groups retreated into the central forest. When confronted by agriculturalists or herders in great numbers, they had no choice but to retreat or become absorbed by another cultural system. At the present time, the Mbuti and related people live in close contact with small villages of settled Bantu-speaking horticulturalists. The latter may be remnants of former herding peoples who were themselves displaced by politically stronger cultures. Because they are few in number and because their mode of subsistence differs completely from that of the hunters and gatherers, these small-scale horticulturalists can live in close proximity to them without disrupting local environmental conditions. Further, because their culture is based on cultivation and permanent village settlement and because the Mbuti are hunters, a satisfying symbiotic (mutally dependent) relationship has grown up between villagers and Mbuti. This relationship is one of considerable historical depth. No group like the Mbuti speaks its original language. Instead, each has adopted the Bantu language of the population with which it is associated. On the other hand, these Bantu peoples recognize the hunter-gatherers' prior claims to the land.

According to Turnbull, the quality of relationship between Mbuti and villager is defined differently by each group. Villagers think of the Mbuti as their slaves (or at least dependent serfs); the Mbuti see the villagers as a sometimes annoying convenience. The symbiosis consists of an economic exchange in which the Mbuti provide meat and sometimes work to the villagers, who reciprocate with grains, bananas, salt, and iron. The Mbuti steal frequently from the villagers, break promises concerning exchange, and generally mock the villagers' culture. Since villagers fear the forest and the Mbuti fear neither forest nor village, any time a Mbuti group feels put upon by their village "overlords," they fade into the jungle where they take up independent existence.

Mbuti (in the background) and Bantu exchange produce and game in a Bantu village.

According to Turnbull, villagers view the Mbuti as uncultured savages. The Mbuti are convinced in turn that villagers are buffoons. In Turnbull's account a Mbuti always gets the upper hand in relation to the villagers. For the Mbuti, they are objects, another aspect of the environment to be used or ignored as the Mbuti see fit. Since Turnbull lived primarily with the Mbuti and because it is obvious that they own his sympathies, a final judgment concerning Mbuti-villager relations must await further study. There is no doubt, however, that the relationship is unequal. Mbuti hold at least some trump cards because their turf, the forest, is for cultural reasons off limits to the villagers.

The Mbuti hunt with three tools: nets up to 100 feet in length, bows and arrows, and lances. While all Mbuti groups use bows and arrows, net hunting is restricted to one particular ecological zone in the deep forest. Some groups hunt preponderantly with nets, others exclusively with bows and arrows, others with lances. As is so often the case among hunting-and-gathering populations, men hunt and women gather. Among net hunters, however, the cooperation of women and children is particularly necessary—they drive game toward a group of men holding a line of nets. Among the Mbuti cooperation is intense. Aside from hunting, relatively few tasks are one-sex oriented. Men will even readily collect vegetable food when they find it as they move through the forest.

A Mbuti house in the forest. These temporary structures are well suited to the nomadic life practiced by the Mbuti.

Although Mbuti bands must remain small, they cannot survive below a certain number. Net hunting, for instance, cannot remain efficient with fewer than six or seven families. Although social groups are not particularly stable, the requirement of minimal size produces communities consisting of seven to 30 hunters with their families. During the course of any one year a community may lose and pick up several members. Once a year, during the honey season, the bands break up for a short period. After the honey has been collected, they join together again.

Migration of particular hunting bands generally takes place on a monthly basis. Groups move within the confines of a larger home territory, the boundaries of which are known and respected by other bands. Interpenetration does occur, however. When one group hunts on another's territory, the trespassers share some of their game with the home band.

Kinship terminology is of the Hawaiian type. Ego calls all members of his or her generation "brother" or "sister." The generation above ego takes parental terms and the generation below ego is referred to with terms applied to one's own offspring. Bands are exogamous and marriages are preferred with groups beyond the band's immediate vicinity. The marriage rule involves "sister" exchange but excludes alliances with one's mother's and father's mother's bands. Since all related females in one's own generation are referred to as "sister," it should not be surprising that marriage rarely involves the exchange of real, biological sisters. When a man wishes to marry, he must find among his own relatives a suitable woman (a "sister") whom he can "give" as a wife to his future brother-in-law. Since all partners in the marriage-exchange system must agree, it sometimes takes considerable statesmanship to produce a successful pairing of two willing couples.

Mbuti society is marked by an absence of institutional political authority. Elders are looked up to and consulted in matters concerning the hunt and migrations to new camps. The only status that can be defined as political, in even a loose sense, is the clown. The role of clown is played by one or several members of the band who are gifted with a keen sense of humor. Clowns act as a means of social control, particularly when band members become too boastful. A man who praises his own hunting, for example, will be tolerated for a time without comment. Eventually, however, the boaster will be teased into silence. Individual Mbuti do not humble themselves before their campmates, but contentiousness is not tolerated for very long.

Mbuti religion has a single major focus—the forest. The forest is mother, father, sister, brother, and friend to all Mbuti. The forest is the source of all provisions. When people seriously offend Mbuti custom, the forest is called upon to punish them. When harm comes to an individual, when sickness strikes a village, it is because the forest is sleeping. Although the Bantu believe in witchcraft, Mbuti have neither sorcery nor witchcraft. In their view illness is not to be treated by acting against some evil force. Instead, the forest must be awakened from its sleep.

The forest is the Mbuti universe. It is an all-encompassing entity. In normal situations the forest is harmonious. Birds sing, small animals chatter in the trees. The Mbuti contrast this peaceful murmuring to both a silent and an overly noisy forest. Each of these indicates a threat to natural order and hence danger. This notion is translated into human terms. Peaceful interaction within the camp indicates harmony, silence betrays a sulking hostility, and shouting implies dissension within the ranks of the band. Silence and noise alike are resented by the forest. They are both symbol and symptom of evil.

The Mbuti have few ceremonies. Their young men are initiated into manhood along with Bantu village children. According to Turnbull villagers encourage the initiation in order to affirm the Mbuti's slave status. The ceremony is thought by the villagers to establish unbreakable links between them and Mbuti initiates. The rites are long and rigorous, with physical deprivation and hardship. Turnbull discovered, however, that these rites are systematically subverted by the Mbuti. Within the confines of the initiation house, as soon as villagers turn their backs, Mbuti men comfort their boys and mock the sacred symbols that are central to the transition from boyhood to manhood. Turnbull suggests that the Mbuti submit to these rites only to prove they are as brave and as hardy as any villager. As real rites of passage, they are meaningless to the Mbuti.

Girls, however, are initiated by the Mbuti themselves. The ceremonies take place within the sacred confines of the forest, away from the prying eyes of villagers. This rite, known as the *elima,* marks girls' first menstruation and their coming of age as women. It involves temporary residence in a special hut where eligible girls are allowed to live with friends of their choice. These include both initiated and uninitiated girls. Within this hut, girls are taught the ways of motherhood by old women. In addition, they learn the songs sung by adult women. According to Turnbull special *elima* songs are sung by the girls to the boys who cluster around the initiation hut, hoping for a chance to get a look at one of the inmates.

The Mbuti, unlike many other peoples, do not equate menstruation with evil. Menstrual blood does not symbolize uncleanliness. Blood in other contexts can symbolize death, but in puberty ceremonies it is recognized as a sign of life and fertility. The coming of menses, therefore, is greeted with joy rather than apprehension.

The *elima* is an occasion for the "presentation" of eligible girls to their potential mates.

Mbuti girls prepare for the *elima* ceremony.

Among the Mbuti this custom takes the form of rather aggressive displays of "affection" during which girls seek out favored males. Turnbull reports that he himself was once chased for a half-mile through the forest. Although it is considered cowardly to run, a male, once caught, is obliged to visit the *elima* house that night.

Turnbull suggests that the *elima* actually functions as a puberty rite for both girls and boys during which males have to prove their manhood. Even after a boy has been invited to the *elima* house, he must battle his way in past a ferocious band of women. In addition, before marriage, an event that often follows closely on the *elima,* a boy must prove his prowess as a hunter by killing a large game animal. The symbolic and *real* aggression displayed by the girls during the *elima* reinforces their relatively equal status in Mbuti society. The equality of women is also reflected in myth and in the Mbuti crisis rite, the *molimo* ceremony.

The *molimo* occurs in two forms: the *grand molimo,* a funeral ceremony, and the *small molimo.* The latter is performed during times of tension or trouble in the village. The purpose of the *molimo* is to awaken the forest. It is a rite that demands full participation from all adult males in a camp. The *molimo* itself is an object, a long horn usually of bamboo. It can, however, be made of any tube-like structure including, for example, discarded drain pipes. It is the *molimo* that is sacred, not the material out of which it is made. The *molimo* is hidden deep in the forest, where it sleeps until it is called upon to perform. During the long nights of the ceremony the *molimo* carried by a group of men, emerges from the forest. The *molimo* horn provides a counter-voice to singing performed by the men of the camp. When it enters a camp it may become violent. Sometimes it attacks the roofs of houses, particularly of those who have transgressed Mbuti rules of behavior. At dawn it retreats to its resting place.

The ceremony is a *coming together* rather than an organized rite with a series of complicated and stereotyped ritual actions. Hunting and gathering activity is intensified during the course of the ceremony, for the *molimo* in one sense is a celebration of the bounty of the forest. Every day during the ceremonial period, which can last a month or more, young boys collect food and firewood from everyone in the camp. Since the *molimo* relates to the well-being of the entire community, everyone must make a contribution, and *molimo* gifts are often copious. In the evening women and children shut themselves in their huts, while the adult males gather around the *molimo* fire to sing. The *molimo* basket, full of offerings, is hung nearby, to be eaten after the singing. Singing is an important aspect of the *molimo* because it is a *gentle* means of awakening the forest. When the forest sleeps, remember, harm can come to the Mbuti.

Turnbull had the occasion to witness a *molimo* far from the village settlements. There it took its full course. To Turnbull's surprise, the women, who during most of the ceremony had not participated, played a very special role.

After a while the men started singing again; but gently and then with a shock I realized that the women were singing as well, the sacred songs of the molimo. And they were not just joining in, they were leading the singing. Songs that I had thought only the men knew and were allowed to sing—all of a sudden the women were showing that they not only knew them but could sing them with just as much intensity.

During this phase, an old woman danced before the *molimo* fire and scattered it, kicking embers into the circle of male participants. The men responded by gathering the embers, replacing them in the hearth. They danced violently as the *molimo* fire was restored to life. This interaction between the sexes occurred three times. Each time the fire was put out by the woman, it was brought to life again by the men. Finally the woman abandoned her attempt to scatter the fire and retreated to her hut. Turnbull thinks that female participation in the *molimo* is a symbolic reenactment of a myth in which the *molimo* once belonged to women and was stolen by men.

The role of women in the *molimo* became even clearer toward the end of the ceremony, when the old woman reappeared, this time alone. She entered the circle of men with a long roll of twine. She passed among the men and knotted a loop around each man's neck until they were all tied together.

Moke spoke. . . . He said, "This woman has tied us up. She has bound the men, bound the hunt, and bound the molimo. We can do nothing." Then Manyalibo said that we had to admit we had been bound, and that we should give the woman something as a token of our defeat, then she would let us go. A certain quantity of food and cigarettes was agreed upon, and the old woman solemnly went among us again, untying each man.

After this act, which appears to symbolize the submission of the men, the ceremony is brought to an end. The *molimo* makes its last appearance in the camp. It is preceded by two young men swinging firebrands high in the air. The *molimo* horn in the hands of its bearers is "excited" to a frenzy. Turnbull witnessed the final climax of a ceremony in a Bantu village. There the *molimo* horn invaded the settlement and ran amok among the houses of the villagers. It tore leaves from roofs and banged into walls. This vandalism may have been done expressly to reinforce the villagers' fear and dislike of the forest. After raiding the village the horn returned to the *molimo* fire circle and scattered the embers. The circle of men attempted to restore the fire. The *molimo* persisted, however, and eventually the men joined it.

All except a few of the elders followed it on its last tour of the camp, slow and majestic, tramping out the fire of life until there was only one glowing ember left.

According to Turnbull this aspect of the *molimo* ceremony is an acknowledgement of the gift of fire from the forest. It also symbolizes the right of the forest to take it away from them.

The Analysis

Taking Turnbull's data Godelier and Barrau

attempt to explain Mbuti culture in terms of production and reproduction. They analyze the net-hunting Mbuti in relation to a hunting-and-gathering technology in a generalized ecological system. Godelier, who has published separately on the Mbuti, abstracts a limited set of constraints (limiting elements) within the culture that operate in combination with the local ecology to maintain Mbuti society in a state of equilibrium. For Godelier the constraints are determined by *the conditions of production.* Nonetheless, he sees religion as fundamental in maintaining the basic equilibrium of the system. For Godelier, as we shall see, religion among the Mbuti is more than a mere justification of an existing system. Rather, it functions to drive the system, to make it work. The constraints are three in number:

1. *Dispersion.* Mbuti ecology and technology require that group size be limited and that bands move over a considerable territory.
2. *Cooperation.* This is a necessary outcome of the hunting process, particularly among net hunters, who cannot as individuals successfully harvest game.
3. *Fluidity or nonclosure of the group.* Bands are in a constant state of flux. People move from group to group, producing a frequent variation in social composition.

According to Godelier these three constraints form a system. Each affects the others. Constraint number two, for example, is affected by constraint number one, because the size of the group must be maintained for effective hunting. It can be neither too large nor too small. Constraint number three affects constraint number two because flux constantly modifies the size and composition of the band. If the social relations within a band were to deteriorate to the point where desertion occurred on a large scale, the life of remaining band members would be jeopardized. On the other hand, openness or flux allows bands to reconstitute themselves when depleted by sickness or minor social disturbances. Under these conditions certain bands may disappear or be absorbed by other bands, but the overall health of Mbuti society is maintained.

Godelier notes that the three constraints are harmonious with a Hawaiian kinship system. A division of labor based on sex and age alone, along with a need to establish equivalent social relations from one band to the next, creates social categories of kin based only on sex and generation. Such kin terms as uncle or aunt (as well as their reciprocals, niece and nephew) make no sense within the context of Mbuti culture. Among kinship systems the Hawaiian is the simplest. The Mbuti have no ranking either within the social structure or the kinship system. Nor do the Mbuti have kin groups of any sort.

The Mbuti practice "sister"-exchange marriage, a system often found in association with moieties. Sister-exchange marriage, in fact, provides the classic case of restricted exchange as defined by Lévi-Strauss and cited in Chapter 15. The Mbuti, of course, do not have moieties. Mbuti marriage exchange contains a further rule that inhibits the development of exclusive marital relations between two bands. Individual males cannot take wives from within the band of their mother's or their father's mother's bands. This rule forces all bands to form marital alliances with a wide range of like social units. Among the Mbuti, however, marriage is the concern of nuclear families and not of bands. Thus the marriage rules together with the focus on ties between nuclear families reinforces both fluidity and dispersion. There is one aspect of marriage that touches directly on band composition. This concerns marital residence. After marriage the new couple may reside either uxorilocally or virilocally. Choice of residence is very important to band economy, for it is only at marriage that a young man is given a net by his mother and her brother. The new husband then begins to participate as a full adult in productive activities. In general, then, marriage rules and the fact that individual bands can exert only minor control over members (constraint number three) inhibit the formation of unilineal kin groups such as lineages.

Turning to political structure, Godelier points

out that equality of status, as well as the systematic rejection of violence, is in keeping with the entire productive system. If a man tries to impose himself on the group, he is subject to ridicule. Such nonviolent action restores group equilibrium (constraint number two). The cooperative nature of Mbuti groups is always voluntary, however. The loose organization of the band can lead to schism (constraint number three: fluidity), and if too much pressure is put on individuals, they will quit their group. Although capital punishment is rare among the Mbuti, its occurrence in two specific situations acts to reinforce cooperation. An individual is killed only (1) if he falls asleep during the *molimo* (a serious breach of unity both in the group and between the group and the forest) and (2) if he casts his net in front of the other hunters (thus endangering the integration so necessary during hunting).

War is absent among the Mbuti. If it were to occur, suggests Godelier, it would lead to the establishment of rigid territorial boundaries between Mbuti groups. That development would be incompatible with all three constraints. Incompatibility with constraints is also the reason why there is no witchcraft. Witchcraft or sorcery would produce suspicion within and among groups. Suspicion, in turn, would lead inevitably to frequent ruptures and the eventual solidification of boundaries between bands.

In sum, Mbuti politics guarantees that no authority can accumulate within the fluid and open social structure. Big men cannot emerge and social equality is maintained.

The entire structure is supported by Mbuti religion, itself a major part of the social system. We must remember that for the Mbuti the forest represents the totality of existence. The forest isolates and protects bands. It provides game and honey. The Mbuti cannot live without the forest. So strong is this tie that when the forest sleeps the Mbuti are put in immediate peril.

The ceremony of the *molimo* brings about an intensification of hunting activity as well as the participation of men and women in dancing and singing. It binds the group to itself. The *molimo* horn has a double aspect: it is the voice of the forest but it is also the sum of human voices united in communion with the forest. For this reason to *not* hunt together or to *not* sing together (to cast one's net in front of the others or to fall asleep during the *molimo*) are equivalent crimes. Both acts break the fabric of cooperation and the necessary unity of the band.

According to Godelier the forest represents a supralocal reality—it defines the outer limits of the Mbuti universe. It is within this universe that the Mbuti maintain their society. The forest sums up the totality of conditions (material as well as social) that govern Mbuti society. In Mbuti myth and belief it is not hunters who trap game in their nets, but the forest that gives to hunters a certain amount of game to trap in their nets. Godelier concludes that Mbuti supernatural beliefs are a representation of the conditions of production and reproduction in Mbuti society. Since the *molimo* ceremony is an intense form of social practice, it plays a central role in maintaining Mbuti culture:

> *During the* molimo, *hunting is practiced in a manner that is much more intense than during the ordinary season. As a result the amount of game taken is increased many fold. With the greater intensity of hunting and the resultant greater abundance of game to share, cooperation and reciprocity are intensified and tensions in the interior of groups are reduced to a minimum. The dances and songs imply both the participation of all and the union of all with the group. Thus, the material, political, social, ideological, emotional and aesthetic aspects of Mbuti religious practice enlarge and exalt all the positive aspects of social relations. They reduce to a minimum (but do not destroy) all the contradictions contained in the heart of Mbuti social relations. . . . Religious practice is both a material practice and a political practice. It is situated at the heart of the productive process as well as the processes implied in the continuation of Mbuti life and culture from generation to generation.*

THE KACHIN

Southeast Asia is marked by great diversity of ethnic groups, particularly in the interior mountainous regions where so-called "tribal" peoples are able to maintain a certain degree of autonomy in spite of surrounding nation-states. For the most part plain and river-valley peoples are attached to a national culture: Chinese, Burmese, Thai, or Vietnamese. But the hills abound in separate, loosely organized local populations differing from one another in language or culture or sometimes in both.

In general, the valleys are densely populated. Wet-rice agriculture in permanent terraces supports large populations. The valley peasants live in contact with urban centers where civilization flourishes.

The hill people, in contrast, are only tenuously connected to the urban areas. They grow hill, or dry, rice in a system of shifting cultivation. Their population density is low. Trade between hills and valleys, hinterlands and coastal cities provides connections among these various populations. Warfare—associated with the expansion and decline of states—has also affected the degree of contact between state centers and local groups.

Anthropologists have been aware for some time that it is difficult to place secure labels on many of the South Asian ethnic groups. Linguistic boundaries cannot be used because in many cases people speaking the same language (if at times different dialects) differ culturally. Cultural boundaries are difficult to establish as well, since populations practicing the same general cultural forms may have different types of political and social structure. Finally, groups with similar social and political structure may differ according to such customs as form of dress, house type, and religious beliefs. Regions of this complexion raise many interesting questions for anthropologists who wish to find order in apparent chaos.

One of the first scholars to approach this problem was the English anthropologist Edmund Leach. His book, *Political Systems of Highland Burma* has become a classic of anthropological analysis and documentation. Recently, however, Leach's interpretation has come under attack from an anthropologist named Jonathan Friedman. It is this controversy that we shall now examine. Ethnographic data drawn primarily from Leach's work will be presented first, followed by Leach's ethnological interpretation and, finally, the Leach-Friedman controversy.

The Data

Leach's work focuses on the Kachin area of highland Burma. The populations inhabiting this geographical zone speak a number of dif-

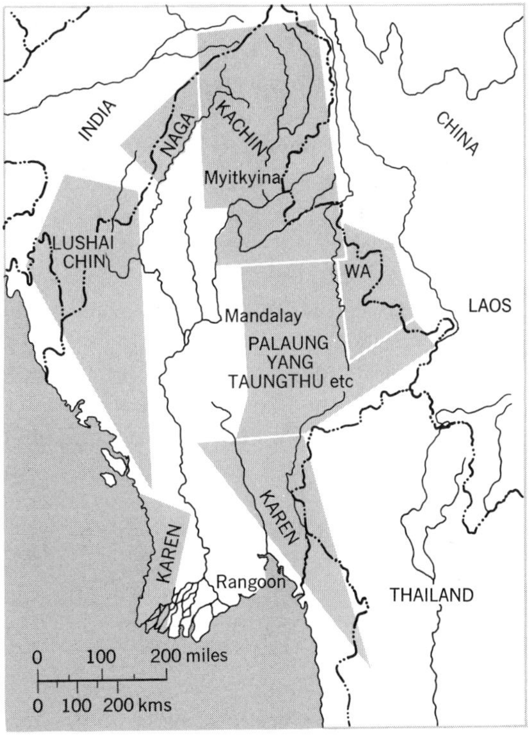

Figure 24.1
Distribution of ethnic groups in Burma.

ferent languages and dialects. There are also wide divergences in culture. In order to provide his readers with some preliminary sense of organization, Leach divides the whole of these populations into Shan and Kachin. In general, these subdivisions can be distinguished on the basis of geographical settlement, economy, and social structure. The Shan live in valleys, practice wet-rice agriculture, and are organized into states of varying size and power. The Kachin are hill-dwelling, dry-rice, slash-and-burn horticulturalists. Generally they lack a state organization. Kachin social organization is, however, quite variable. Leach divides it into two types. Some Kachin live in small local units with no significant ranking and no real chiefs. This type of organization is called *gumlao* social structure. Other Kachin groups are hierarchically organized. Chiefly power ranges from control over a few local villages to control over a ministate of significant size. This type of organization is called *gumsa* social structure. A curious feature of Kachin social organization is the unstability of both *gumlao* and *gumsa* structures. *Gumlao* organization tends to develop into *gumsa* organization, and *gumsa* organization in turn tends to fall apart and return to the *gumlao* form.

Leach took on the task of explaining the two types of Kachin organization as well as the cycling process that occurs between them. He begins by analyzing differences in local ecology, dividing the Kachin highlands into three basic ecological zones.

Zone A is a typical monsoon (wet tropical) forest country. Rainfall and climate favor forest restoration after the temporary abandonment of horticultural sites. The Kachin of this area realize that cultivated plots should be used for one year and then left fallow for 12 to 15 years. When this fallow period is respected, deforestation does not occur. Kachin villages in this area are small and widely scattered. Leach notes that within zone A, historical factors, such as local wars or external administrative interference, have led to the concentration of some populations and a reduction of the 12-year minimum fallow. As a consequence forest restoration is impaired and overall fertility is lowered. The Kachin themselves are aware of the dangers of such misuse of land and reduce fallow only when local land scarcity forces them to do so.

Zone B (grassland) lies outside of the monsoon forest area. Both rainfall and temperature are much lower. In zone B cleared land is unlikely to return to forest even when abandoned for long periods. Although rice is the preferred crop, people in many areas are forced to rely on such cereal substitutes as maize, buckwheat, millet, wheat, and barley. In zone B cereal crops of any type may be so unproductive that populations favor cash crops that can be traded with other groups for food stocks. Cash crops are typically tea, opium poppy, and *hwang lien,* a Chinese medicinal plant. The poor quality of zone B forces groups into trade linkages with local valley populations. Trade often leads to permanent political as well as economic ties between uplands and lowlands.

Zone C is intermediate between A and B. Forest and grassland are interspersed, depending on exposure to prevailing wind and resulting rain patterns. The Kachin of Zone C practice both monsoon and grassland horticulture. In addition, where possible, they practice wet-rice agriculture on elaborate terraces. Hill terracing is associated with high population density and permanent communities. According to Leach the real advantage of these hill-terrace systems is military and political rather than economic, for they lie close to trade routes on an east-west line from Yünnan (in China) into Burma. High density and stable settlements provide the organization and manpower for control over the trade routes. Leach notes that both *gumsa* and *gumlao* types of social organization can be found throughout zone A. Zone B can be subdivided into three sections, two *gumsa,* the third *gumlao.* Zone C is *gumlao.*

Social Organization. All Kachin have patrilineal descent. Marriage is preferred with a mother's brother's daughter (matrilateral cross-cousin marriage). When this type of marriage occurs among a series of lineages, a set of regular exchange relationships is established between wife-givers and wife-takers. Lévi-Strauss was the first to note that in this type of *generalized exchange* wife-givers have higher status than wife-takers, since the latter are indebted to the former. In Kachin terms lineages that give wives are *mayu* to lineages that take wives. Wife-takers are *dama* to wife-givers. Anthropologists, therefore, refer to this particular case of wife-giving and -taking as a *mayu-dama* relationship. In the abstract anthropological model of generalized exchange with matrilateral cross-cousin marriage a group of lineages form a closed loop. A gives wives to B, B gives wives to C, etc., and C gives wives to A. This would mean that members of lineage A have higher status than members of lineage B, members of lineage B higher status than members of linege C, and members of lineage C higher status than members of lineage A. This is, of course, paradoxical, since members of lineage C should have the lowest status of all three lineages. In real cases of generalized exhange of this type the marriage loop is *never* closed and involves many more than three lineages. The large number of lineages engaged in this kind of exchange marriage attempt to establish their position in a hierarchy by giving women in marriage to a number of other lineages to which their women are "mother's brother's daughters."

Property Ownership and Authority. Under the *gumsa* system the chief "owns" his domain, but only in the sense that he has final authority over it. He has no right to dispose of it as if it were his own. In fact, more obligations than rights accrue to a man who is chief. Nonmovable property, land, and houses cannot be sold or given away. The land itself may be farmed on a use basis, but such use is not ownership.

While a chief may have a great deal to say about the disposition of "his" land, he is conceived of merely as its guardian in his role of senior member of his lineage. In the *gumsa* system a chief may have authority over a whole series of junior lineages. In the *gumlao* system authority (in a weaker sense) is limited to the single lineage over which the headman presides. In the *gumsa* system a chiefly class emerges to rule over commoners and slaves, while under the *gumlao* system all lineages are equal and there are no class distinctions.

Chiefs and village heads rule or own the land, but they do not have rights over what is produced on it. Individual members of a lineage have the right to use land. An individual can either rent or sell his right to permanent tenancy.

A curious feature of *gumsa* organization is that it is *both* segmentary (based on lineages) and class-stratified. You might guess that it is also unstable, since segmentary organization implies equality and stratification by definition is based on inequality of status. In theory, rank in the *gumsa* system depends on one's birth. It is, according to Leach, thought of as fully dependent on lineage membership. One is either born into a royal lineage or one is not.

Rank among *gumsa* Kachin is in many ways similar to caste in India. Marriage is endogamous by rank (but lineage exogamous) and a series of ritual obligations mark the relationships between groups of unequal status. A major sign of caste-like status is the flow of gifts from inferiors to superiors. The ceremonial aspect of such gift-giving becomes apparent when you realize that little economic advantage accrues to the receiver. Receiving a gift puts one in debt to the giver. It is for this reason that chiefs must in the end give away more than they receive. As is usually the case, the outcome of such a redistributive system is increased prestige for the chief. He receives only in order to pay back with interest! Among the Kachin the repayment of gifts often takes the form of ritual sacrifice to the gods. Goods which are sacrificed are taken out of the system and do not recirculate.

In his description of rank, Leach is careful to distinguish between a rather rigid model of inherited rank that reflects how the Kachin describe their system and the facts of real behavior. Kachin society is actually quite fluid, and individuals along with their lineages may lose or gain rank. The practices that allow for this fluidity are the same as those that validate a chief's power in the first place, the giving of gifts and feasts. Because kinship links are complex, and because Kachin society clings to a segmentary model, a commoner lineage can easily claim high rank through the manipulation of genealogies. These claims can then be dramatically reinforced by giving lavish feasts. Prestige for the chief and his kin group is established through the generous fulfillment of ritual obligations. Thus, economic goods flow through the system in order to establish or maintain social rank through ritual activity. Clearly, their production, social structure, and ritual are closely tied.

Kachin Religion. Kachin religion is based primarily on ancestor worship. It also reflects the ranking system. The gods (*nats*) are also ancestors. They are arranged in a religious hierarchy that is an exact duplicate of Kachin social structure. There are chiefly *nats*, aristocrats, commoners, and slaves. Furthermore, ceremonial rules require that one must approach the greater *nats* by way of lesser *nats*. Only chiefs can make sacrifices to chiefly *nats*. This privilege allows chiefs to hold a monopoly over a major ritual and reinforces the flow of gifts to them from members of lower-status lineages. The giving of gifts to chiefs thus becomes a ritual as well as a social obligation. When chiefs redistribute goods in the context of religious ritual, they gain prestige and assure the well-being of the entire society.

Leach's Explanation

Even mere ethnographic description has its explanatory elements. As we have seen, the instability in Kachin social structure arises from the difference between a rigid ideology of status (based upon social castes) and a more flexible system of behavior (playing the redistributive game to gain status). In addition, Leach points out quite clearly that rank and segmentation are major contradictory elements in Kachin social life. What needs to be explained is the apparent cycling among Kachin groups as they move from *gumlao* to *gumsa* organization and back again.

Leach sees the entire highland Burma area as a single social unit in constant flux. He accounts for the rise of *gumsa* organization on the basis of two major principles—one psychological and the other cultural. He assumes that all humans have a drive for power. Given the opportunity, individuals will attempt to rise above their peers. Prestige and rank are the outcome of this psychological drive. The particular form that this drive takes is shaped by cultural factors. In this case the Shan state stands as a model for the Kachin. In addition, the development of Kachin *gumsa* organization is affected by ecological and historical factors. These include population density, trade, and warfare patterns. Leach assumes that the ecological conditions in zones A, B, and C are stable. *Gumsa* develops in the tropical forest zones where the constant break-up of the local group is necessary. This break-up occurs because slash-and-burn horticulture only works with long fallow periods and therefore relatively small and widely scattered human settlements. Local dispersion is unfavorable for the development of large-scale, stable state formations. But, says Leach, the area *is* rich enough for political experimentation.

In *gumlao* ideology there are no chiefs and all lineages have the same rank. Thus there is theoretically no difference between a *mayu* (wife-giving lineage) and a *dama* (wife-taking lineage). Leach notes, however, that *gumlao* groups do adopt stratification that is apparently based on the ranking of lineages.

These factors are used to explain the cycling upward from *gumlao* to *gumsa*. But what about the reverse process? Leach claims that the weakness of the *gumsa* system lies in the attempt on the part of chiefs to obliterate the segmentary principle. The successful chief, he says, is always ready to deny links of kinship with his followers. He tends to convert kinsmen into subjects. Whenever they can, Kachin chiefs model their behavior on that of Shan princes.

The basic difference between a Shan state and Kachin society is that the Shan are loyal to place rather than to kin. This transition from kinship-based social organization to regional political unity never fully evolves in Kachin *gumsa.* It always retains its kin-oriented *mayu-dama* relationships. Thus, while the *gumlao* tends to breed stratification, particularly from the *mayu-dama* relationship, the *gumsa* breeds rebellion from absolute rule.

> Gumsa *organization was . . . I insist, a kind of imitation of the Shan political order. There is nothing very mysterious about this. In our own age we are familiar with the phenomenon of subject colonial peoples who, in achieving independence, carry on with a political system imitated and modified from that of their former rulers. . . .*

Leach does not believe that rebellions can occur in the context of Kachin society alone. Rather they result from aftereffects of a weakening of Shan power in a particular geographic area.

> *So long as the Shan system flourished, the* gumsa *system could flourish too, but in a subordinate status. In such conditions we should not expect* gumlao *rebellions. Difficulties would only arise when external factors led to a decay of Shan power. It is then that Kachin chiefs would get the chance to assume powers close to that of a* Saopha (*Shan Prince*) *and it is only then that a* gumlao *revolt is likely to ensue.*

Note that the causal chain here runs a complicated course from *gumlao* to *gumsa* organization *via* a psychological drive for power, tropical forest horticulture, and the existing model of the Shan state. *Gumsa* organization emerges as a relatively stable form of intermediate social organization. It retains an element of stratification and is, at least partially, dependent on the Shan state. When the Shan state weakens, the *gumsa* chiefs attempt to solidify their own power by breaking out of the kinship-lineage system. It is at this point that the segmentary elements in Kachin society come to the fore, and rebellion follows. Rebellion restores the Kachin system to a *gumlao* social organization.

Gumlao rebellions are not the mere result of historical factors, however. They are led by real men who share certain special characteristics. The *gumlao* rebel is himself a chief who refuses to accept the status differences imposed by the *mayu-dama* relationship. Thus, as the *gumsa* chief attempts to cut away from the kin-oriented status system, he cuts the ground away from under himself. His rivals of lower status refuse the tribute due him, because tribute depends specifically on the mechanisms of the segmentary kinship system.

> Gumlao *revolt emerges at precisely that point in the political cycle at which the* gumsa *chiefs themselves have been led to infringe the formal rules of their system.*

> *The mythical archetype of the* gumlao *leader is that of a minor aristocrat of ambition and ability who might himself have been a chief if the accident of birth had not dictated otherwise. The myth is the description of the real man.*

Friedman's Analysis

By placing the Shan and Kachin in a wider framework of Asian political systems Friedman sets out to explain not only the cycling of *gumsa* and *gumlao* but also other forms of political organization in South and Central Asia. He rejects a psychological explanation of *gumsa* development.

Friedman attempts to show how various types of social organization are the result of transformations of one basic structure. These transformations occur in an orderly fashion because the system consists of a set of connected parts, like gears in a machine. A change in one will change the others in a predicted direction. In Friedman's own words "social evolution is the outcome of processes that are inherent in social forms."

Friedman focuses on the relationships that exist in Kachin society among kinship, religion, and productive activities. He uses Leach's data as a point of departure but places them in a different theoretical framework.

Friedman sees population growth and decline as responsive to a series of social pressures, particularly labor needs. The need for labor is itself a product of social and economic activities. Not all societies produce and/or consume to the same degree or at the same rates, and not all productive systems require high labor input. Friedman rejects Leach's contention that zones A,B, and C in the Kachin area are natural areas. Instead, he sees them as the outcome of a particular social process that has favored the reduction of fallow and an increased need for labor.

In fact, one of the transformations we shall discuss consists precisely in violating the optimal limits of forest regeneration resulting in ecological degradation, a gradual succession to secondary forest and grassland. Leach's so-called "ecological zones" are not natural zones but rather the result of the progressive over-intensification of a basically extensive technology, a phenomenon which is more closely linked to increasing population density than to any other factor.

It is important to note that Friedman does not assume that increased population (mouths to feed) produces greater labor needs. Instead, it is greater labor needs that produce an increase in mouths to feed, at least in areas in which production can only be increased by increasing labor. The key to Leach's environmental zones is the degree to which the social system has generated different intensities of production in each area.

Friedman turns first to the egalitarian *gumlao* form. The *gumlao* unit (the largest social group that recognizes a set of loose political and social ties) consists of several hamlets of ten or more houses each that form a village cluster. The local lineage is the main economic unit. It contains four or five households that are linked together in religious worship at a common altar.

The major element linking villages together is belief in common descent from a single founding ancestor. This ancestor is also the *nat,* or territorial spirit. All local lineages as well as their *nats* are linked by the segmentary lineage principle.

Friedman agrees with Leach that demographic growth leads directly to territorial expansion. Under the requirements of slash-and-burn horticulture, expanding populations must disperse outward in order to maintain overall low population density. The actual size of any one local group, however, is not determined by technology and environment alone. In fact, Friedman criticizes those anthropologists who claim that cooperative units are technologically determined. He says that this notion results from a confusion between the facts of cooperation and the social form that it takes. The technology of slash-and-burn horticulture requires certain tasks, but the nature of the groups performing these tasks is *not* technologically determined. An examination of different *ethnic* subdivisions in the Kachin hill area reveals differences in the size and composition of the work groups.

Both Friedman and Leach accept the importance of generalized-exchange marriage among the Kachin. Matrilateral cross-cousin marriage creates a system that leads to a constant renewal of alliances between wife-giving and wife-taking lineages. Generalized exchange can be also used to create new alliances when wives are exchanged with new partners (lineages).

The *mayu-dama* relationship, in which wife-givers have higher status than those to whom they give wives, pre-establishes the conditions for ranking and the emergence of a hierarchical social structure. This potential ranking does not always emerge, however, because differences in social status are not admitted among *gumlao* Kachin. Because they have an ideology of equality they tend to supress rank differences. A small number of lineages marrying in a circle generally maintain low bride price for all groups. The *mayu-dama* system can only be converted into true ranking when differences in bride price occur among lineages. What needs to be explained is how this shift from potential to actual ranking occurs. According to Friedman the solution lies in religious practice, particularly feasting, for it is feasting that links production to social differentiation.

A local lineage producing substantial surplus food can offer a feast to its community. During these feasts the hosts represent the entire community before the spirits of fertility and prosperity. The feasts bring prestige to the host lineage, prestige that can be converted into relative rank in the context of wife-giving and wife-taking lineages. What happens is that a feast-giving lineage can increase the bride price it demands from its *dama* (wife-takers). Thus, "surplus that is converted into prestige generates affinal (in-law) ranking."

The functioning of this system transforms the egalitarian marriage circles into a political and economic hierarchy of wife-givers and wife-takers.

So far, I have shown Friedman's explanation of the development of ranking but not of the emergence of the *gumsa* system. For although marriage, coupled to ceremonial life, can generate rank, it does not, in and of itself, generate chiefdoms and an aristocracy. An analysis of *gumsa* requires a further look at religion.

The *nats,* remember, are distant ancestors. Society cannot operate without their help. The relations between the living and the *nats* contain the roots of a new social relation, in the following ways. As among the Mbuti, surplus among the Kachin is not defined as the product of intensified human labor, but rather as the work of the gods. Community feasts are necessary because they increase the wealth of the entire group. Hereditary chiefs emerge as the result of feasting activity. This is the sequence of events:

1. A wealthy lineage head can give feasts only because he has good harvests.
2. Good harvests are the result of sacrifice to the *nats* and the resultant action of the *nats* in favor of the successful farmer.
3. The success of the wealthy man is, therefore, due to his influence with the spirits.
4. Since the spirits are ancestors, success can be related to closeness of genealogical relationship with them.
5. The successful man, therefore, has claim to close genealogical relationship with the spirits.
6. The lineage head claims that his lineage is the same as that of the local spirit. His *nat* becomes the territorial deity.

You can see how important this process is by examining the differences between ritual in *gumsa* and *gumlao* systems. Among the *gumlao* Kachin, community ritual takes place at the village altar. All the gods belong to the community.

Among *gumsa* Kachin two of the major spirits are found in the house of the chief. Only he can make sacrifices to these spirits and, therefore, only he can guarantee the well-being of his group. The *gumsa* chief owes his sovereignty to his descent from the *mung nat,* the territorial spirit.

Alliance and exchange relations among the Kachin are horizontal, but they take place among segments that are potentially different according to rank. Religious feasts involve vertical relations and lead to the development of affinal and, finally, segmentary rank in which chiefly lineages emerge.

In *gumlao* society the community sacrifices to its gods; in *gumsa* society the community supports the living descendants of the gods, who in turn act as intermediaries between their subjects and the gods. Much of the tribute paid to the chief is returned to the community in the form of redistributive feasts, but some of it can be used as bride price for elaborate chiefly marriages.

Expansion and Constriction. In the Kachin economy the development of stratification tends toward the emergence of the state, complete with social classes. This development occurs in the context of rapid population and territorial expansion. The Kachin economy in its *gumsa* phase operates with an increasing demand for surplus, which is converted into prestige and rank. Since Kachin economy is labor-oriented (labor-intensive) rather than investment-oriented (capital-intensive), the demand for greater surplus requires a greater amount of labor. Large families, therefore, have a positive value. In addition to having many children, Kachin chiefs enslave large numbers of inhabitants from surrounding areas. Since there is little technological change (slash-and-burn remains the major form of production) territorial expansion must occur if the rising population is to be absorbed. Friedman points out that with a fallow cycle of 12 years, territorial expansion must occur at a rate at least 13 times faster than the rate of increase in the labor force. If expansion were blocked, the fallow cycle would have to be shortened and environmental degradation would result. Constant expansion, however, makes political control difficult. Furthermore, because the *gumsa* system maintains strong segmentary aspects, central authority is unlikely to develop.

In order to keep the system operational, a greater and greater amount of labor must be put into lower-yielding land. Production per individual falls but demand (based on the number of mouths that need feeding and inflated bride price) rises. Eventually the system collapses under its own weight. The demands placed upon individuals lead to open rebellion. The upshot is a return to the *gumlao* system, a result of a conflict between a type of social organization that demands ever-increasing production and a set of technological, environmental, and demographic constraints.

All lineages in the *gumsa* organization are connected to one another by virtue of the *mayu-dama* network. Any increase in bride price at the top levels produces an increase at all levels. The more the chief accumulates, the greater the inflation at other levels of society. Eventually, the majority of lineages find it impossible to meet their debt obligations. According to Friedman, the situation becomes critical at the point where the chief starts to accumulate an inflated portion of a decreasing surplus. It then becomes literally impossible for most people to meet the requirement of debt payments. Friedman agrees with Leach that the center of discontent in the *gumlao* rebellion is likely to be on the level of petty aristocrats. It is these individuals who have most to lose. Unlike Leach, however, Friedman does not link the *gumsa* collapse to the fall of a related Shan state. If we were to follow Leach, we would assume that rebellion againt a *gumsa* chief would produce a change in power but not necessarily a collapse and return to *gumlao* equality. Friedman's explanation provides the reason for the system's total collapse. From the point of view of petty chiefs and commoners, the rebellion is necessary. It eliminates crushing debts as well as growing despotism.

Friedman notes a superficial resemblance between this cycle of economic-political development and economic depression in our own economic system. In our system, however, surplus is converted into capital for further investment while in the *gumsa* system it is converted into relative rank. Our depression results in the devaluation of property. The rebellion against *gumsa* authority and a return to *gumlao* organization results in a devaluation of social status.

Once the *gumlao* system is restored, the conditions for a return to *gumsa* organization are reestablished. The rebellion, with its consequent political breakdown, leads to population dispersion. This allows the forest to regenerate. A return to *gumlao* structure recreates the conditions we started with. The original contradictions reappear and the cycle begins again with the movement towards *gumsa* organization and so on.

THE NORTHWEST COAST CULTURES AND THE POTLATCH

Sometime during the precolumbian period a unique and highly complex set of related cultures developed along the Northwest Coast of North America. These peoples, now partially westernized, practiced hunting, gathering, and fishing. Marine animals were the major source of food, and of these salmon were the most important. In order to spawn, salmon make periodic runs from the sea into upland rivers. There they were caught in large numbers and dried for future use. Other species of migratory and nonmigratory fish, sea mammals, and some land mammals such as deer and mountain goat provided secondary food resources. Women gathered clams and other shellfish in tidal pools, fished some of the in-shore species of fish, and collected plant food, particularly berries. The richness of food resources, plus the annual return of salmon and other spawning fish to the same river channels, permitted the development of large permanent villages.

The Northwest Coast, running from northern Washington State to Alaska (below the habitat of the southernmost Eskimo population), is warmed by the Japan current. Rainfall is high and fog is common. The mild wet climate favors the growth of large exploitable evergreen forests. In former times wood was used for cooking and in the construction of an assortment of articles ranging from kitchen utensils and bowls to large canoes and houses. Easily carved and resistant to rot, this wood provided the major medium for a flourishing ceremonial art. Masks, house posts, "totem poles," boxes, and trunks were all made of wood. Most were carved and many were painted as well. Some of the finest examples of non-Western art come from this area. Famous among collectors is the carving of the Tlingit, Tsimshian, Haida, Nootka, Bela Coola, and Kwakiutl.

With local variations, these and other less well-known ethnic groups shared a common culture, including a mode of subsistence, religion, art, and certain features of social structure, particularly political organization. On the other hand, these groups differed markedly in language. Even today the Tlingit and Haida in the North speak different languages, both of which are apparently related to the Athabascan spoken among inland Indians in Alaska, in western Canada, and in the Southwest of the United States by the Navajo. The Tsimshian speak a language included in another family known to linguists as Penutian. Further to the south, one finds a linguistic group known as Salishan.

Social organization on the Northwest Coast was also quite diverse. Groups in the north

A Northwest Coast Indian village at Alert Bay, Victoria, British Columbia. The building in the foreground is the village schoolhouse.

were matrilineal. Towards the south there was a transition to patrilineality. Bilaterality (or some form of ambilineality) was found among the Kwakiutl, who also practiced double descent. In the latter group individuals could inherit certain names and rituals through the male line and another set through the female line. Political organization was relatively loose among all groups. Basic social units were composed of extended families or lineages. In some areas these units were grouped into alliances, and some alliances were grouped into shifting confederacies. The north is characterized by a system of rank and chieftainship that was for the most part hereditary. The rank and status system of these peoples is still a debated point within anthropology. According to some authorities rank in the south was looser and depended on wealth. It is known that each social unit had a great deal of political and economic independence. Lineages or extended families held title to their own economic resources such as fishing areas and hunting territories. In addition, all groups held slaves. These were either war captives or people who had fallen into debt. They had no rights and at their master's death were sometimes killed.

Moieties were frequent in Northwest Coast societies. In general they had complementary ritual functions and participated in ceremonies stressing links between the world of humans, the supernatural, and animals.

Ceremonies were of several types. Although many had a secular as well as a sacred content, all emphasized the role of the supernatural in the everyday life of the people. Major rituals were held in the winter, but social need or illness could lead to ceremonial performances at any time. Shamans who performed as priests and as curers occupied an important place in the culture.

In their heyday Northwest Coast ceremonies were among the most spectacular found anywhere. They even rivaled technically complex theater productions in our own culture. Special props were common and the ceremonial space was equipped with secret doors and traps for the sudden appearance and disappearance of supernatural characters. Costumes and masks were very elaborate. Many masks were compound in form—a hinged outer face could be opened by hidden strings to reveal an inner mask representing another character. Some of these compound masks contained three separate faces.

The attention of the general public to the peoples of the Northwest Coast was heightened not only by their art but by a particular custom—the potlatch, which was described in a book that is probably the best-known work in anthropology. I refer to *Patterns of Culture* by Ruth Benedict (discussed in Chapter 22). One of the three "tribes" she analyzes is the Kwakiutl. From an anthropological point of view, the Kwakiutl are one of the most thoroughly studied populations. Franz Boas, the father of American anthropology, spent a good deal of his life engaged in the collection and analysis of Kwakiutl data. When he was not in the field, Boas maintained an active correspondence with a literate and intelligent informant, George Hunt. With the aid of Hunt, he published a long series of books and articles dealing with many aspects of Kwakiutl culture. Benedict herself did no work among the Kwakiutl, but as a student of Boas she was intimately familiar with his published and unpublished material.

Patterns of Culture, as we saw, is primarily a "psychoanalysis" of three cultures, each of which, according to the author, displays a different type of personality. The Kwakiutl are described as aggressive and competitive. In describing the Kwakiutl, Benedict focused on the potlatch, a ceremonial feast during which a great deal of property is given by the host to his assembled guests.

The potlatch is a redistributive feast. What drew Benedict's attention to it, however, was what she saw as its exaggerated character. The potlatch, as she described it, was a major dramatic event in the life of the Kwakiutl. The redistributive function of the potlatch apparently occurred in the context of a contest between competing big men who used it to enhance their power. Helen Codere, another anthropologist who has published on the Kwakiutl, referred to the potlatch as "fighting with property." During a potlatch, involving powerful individuals, gifts flowed from host to guests with the proviso that the guest's chief would soon reciprocate with interest sometimes as high as 100 percent. In order to prove his greatness the host also destroyed mounds of material goods such as blankets and ritual objects known as coppers. Literally gallons of fish oil would be poured on the ceremonial fire. Guests were actually made to feel the heat of their host's generosity.

Early readers of these accounts wondered at the bountiful nature of an environment that could support such "waste." For many, the potlatch seemed to reflect an unquenchable desire to consume. It was not long before Northwest Coast peoples were compared to those Americans who exhibit their economic success through conspicuous consumption. Among more cautious interpreters the potlatch was taken as the perfect model of redistribution. If the potlatch was unusual, it was because the system was overheated by the bounty of nature.

Not all anthropologists agreed that the potlatch was as wasteful and spectacular as Benedict described it. Those familiar with the history of the Northwest Coast pointed out that the great destructive competitions so impressive to white observers came well after the introduction of Western trade goods. Since the native populations lived outside of the capitalist system, a sudden increase in affluence was absorbed not through reinvestment but through increasingly elaborate ceremonies. The potlatch as described by Benedict was, according to the critics, a last and exaggerated phase of a more normal redistributive system. In its late phase, the potlatch was a distorted travesty of a former functional custom. It could be taken as the result of incomplete and dysfunctional Westernization in which a native custom lived on beyond its time.

Argument over the potlatch has recently escalated. There are those who even question whether or not it *ever* existed as such in precontact times. Because of this controversy I will examine various theories and interpretations of the potlatch, rather than describe a single Northwest Coast culture. We have seen two such interpretations: one is psychological; the other views the potlatch as a distorted form of redistribution brought about through historical events of culture contact. As we shall see below, even a purely economic analysis can be approached from different points of view. In addition, I will discuss an ecological explanation and examine one that attempts to understand the ceremonial aspect of Kwakiutl life from the native point of view. The latter analysis is published in an eloquent book, *The Mouth of Heaven,* by Irving Goldman. Goldman's analysis attempts to understand beliefs and events from the perspective of those experiencing them. For an anthropologist with this orientation such an understanding provides a rich insight not only into the workings of another system but also into ourselves. Such an analysis of ethnographic material allows us to "experience" one version of the human condition and therefore to widen our understanding of the human condition in general.

The Ecological Approach

An ecological approach to the potlatch has been taken by A. P. Vayda, W. Suttles, and S. Piddocke. The most complete presentation of this point of view has been presented by Piddocke in his article, "The Potlatch System of the Southern Kwakiutl." Piddocke's arguments will be followed here. He believes that the potlatch functioned to optimize resource distribution in an area known for intermittent periods of *localized* famine. He is in agreement with those who believe that a description of the potlatch in its last phase is of little value. Piddocke suggests that the later form of potlatching can be deduced from his model of the original form when historical processes are included. He presents the following propositions:

1. Although the Kwakiutl have been described as living in an area of high surplus produc-

tion and enjoying superior storage methods, the description applies only to the Kwakiutl and their environment as a whole. The local village was subject to scarcity of food and dependent on other villages in time of need. Implicit in this first hypothesis is the notion that hunting-and-gathering economies, no matter how strong their resource base, are subject to natural variations in abundance. It also assumes that the concept of a *good harvest year* cannot apply to the territory of an entire ethnic group. In any given season some villages will do well and others will do poorly.

2. The potlatch in its original form was held exclusively by chiefs or headmen of the various localized kin groups (*numayms*) that made up the winter-village groups. Potlatches were thus a series of exchanges of food and wealth between such groups. These exchanges functioned to counter variations in productivity and maintain a basic subsistence level for the entire population.
3. In the potlatch food could be exchanged for wealth objects, and these could be exchanged for increased prestige.
4. The desire for prestige and the existing rivalry between chiefs was the motor of the system. It motivated potlatching and maintained overall survival. Note the assumption that the relationship between potlatching and survival is maintained by an *unconscious* mechanism. The cultural practice that guarantees continued economic well-being is not consciously constructed or manipulated by individual Kwakiutl. This idea is one of the major tenets of ecological anthropology. It assumes that system-maintaining mechanisms operate as cybernetic (feedback) systems on the cultural rather than the individual level.

Piddocke reviews the subsistence base and economic activities of the Kwakiutl. He lists the following resources: salmon, salmon spawn, herring, herring spawn, eulachen or candlefish, halibut, cod, perch, flounder, kelpfish, devilfish, sea slugs, barnacles, winkles, seals, porpoises, occasional beach-stranded whales, mountain goats, elderberries, salal berries, wild currants, huckleberries, salmonberries, viburnum berries, dogwood berries, gooseberries, crab apples, clover roots, cinquefoil roots, sea milkwort, bracken roots, fern roots, erythronium roots, lupine roots, wild carrots, lily bulbs, eel grass, and some sea weeds. Although these are seasonal resources, many were stored for winter use. This variety suggests abundance, but Piddocke points out that the distribution of each of these edibles was limited and subject to seasonal variation. He cites evidence that the Kwakiutl fought intensely over rights to both hunting and fishing grounds as well as gathering sites. Trespassing was a serious offense and often led to conflict. According to Boas, wars were waged to take the land away from people.

In addition, Piddocke cites evidence of frequent local famine and scarcity. It might also be noted that a well-known Tsimshian myth analyzed by Lévi-Strauss begins during a famine and concerns two women who leave their village in search of food.

Piddocke lays great stress on the contention that the potlatch was an affair between chiefs. In fact, he notes that the position of chief was described by the Kwakiutl themselves as the office of giving potlatches. One of the major historical changes that occurred during the contact period was the "democratization" of potlatch giving. By the time Boas was in the field potlatching was not an exclusive prerogative of chiefs. Most students of Kwakiutl culture agree that this change was due to the introduction of European trade goods, which raised by many fold the amount of disposable wealth available in the area. In addition, the contact period saw a significant decline in population, which led to a large number of unfilled positions within each tribal group.

The weak link in Piddocke's argument is that he offers absolutely no data on *when* potlatches were held. If, as he suggests, the potlatch served to redistribute scarce resources, they must have occurred primarily in time of need. Such information does not exist. Lacking proof, Piddocke argues that potlatches occurred frequently and *could have* functioned as suggested. Although Piddocke himself separates the potlatch from certain other ceremonies, it is likely that his own list contains many events that were, in fact, not potlatches. No doubt the peculiar nature of ceremonial exchange among the Indians of the Northwest Coast, particularly during the post-contact period, plus the extension of the label "potlatch" by anthropologists to practically every ceremony, made it seem as if it were the driving force of Northwest Coast society. Thus, Piddocke could read the ethnographic material on the Kwakiutl and say with assurance:

> *The potlatch had no one essential function but several. It distributed food and wealth. It validated changes in social status. It converted the wealth given by the host into prestige for the host and rank for his* numaym, *and so provided motivation for keeping up the cycle of exchanges.* The potlatch was, in fact, the linch-pin of the entire system. (*emphasis mine*)

Structural Analysis

A radically different view of the potlatch has been offered by Abraham Rosman and Paula Rubel in their book, *Feasting with Mine Enemy.* In addition to Boas's work, they consulted every scrap of evidence they could find concerning actual potlatches. They paid particular attention to when potlatches were held and the social categories of people invited to them. Rosman and Rubel's major anthropological interest is exchange. Their research goal is to order a set of variations on a theme: *the exchange of goods, services, and marriage partners in different cultures.* In this work they have been strongly influenced by Claude Lévi-Strauss, who, as we have already seen, has concentrated a good deal of effort on marriage exchange. Rosman and Rubel approach the potlatch in much the same way as Lévi-Strauss approaches marriage. In their analysis of the potlatch they assume that the manner in which goods are exchanged reflects the same social-structural relations as marriage. They also assume that the structural transformations described by Lévi-Strauss for different kinds of marriage occur in ceremonial exchange as well.

A similarity exists between the Rosman-Rubel analysis of the potlatch and Friedman's analysis of the Kachin. The total system, of which the potlatch is a part, can only be understood when examined in a comparative framework. The potlatch is reported from many groups on the Northwest Coast. These groups differ, as we have seen, in the degree and kind of ranking and in descent rules. Rosman and Rubel wanted to see what relationships existed between these structural variations and the particulars of the potlatch within each specific social setting. Their book analyzes exchange and ceremonial life among the Tsimshian, the Tlingit and Haida, the Nootka, the Bella Coola, and the Kwakiutl. When these data are compared, a structural pattern emerges.

Briefly, Rosman and Rubel found a direct relationship between the type of marriage system in each society, and who the guests and hosts at a potlatch were. In each case an examination of potlatch participants shows that this ceremony reinforced these exhange systems. Thus, the potlatch and marriage appear to be different sides of the same social coin: *exchange* in the context of rank. Among the groups in the North, where ranking was strongly hereditary, marriage (as among the Kachin) was with mother's brother's daughter. Remember that this type of marriage contains an incipient form of ranking in the relationship between wife-givers and wife-takers. The potlatch among these groups reinforced the rank system. Hosts and guests came from sets of two lineages, wife-givers and wife-takers traditionally linked by marriage. Among the geographically central groups, which were relatively egalitarian, the preferred form of marriage was with father's sister's daughter. This type of cousin marriage does not generate ranking among wife-givers and -takers. Rosman and Rubel found that potlatching in this area reinforced relative equality since hosts and guests consisted of sets of three linked wife-giving and -taking lineages. Finally, among the Kwakiutl they noted a complex marriage system that correlates well with a relatively open rank system. Among the Kwakiutl the potlatch was used as a means of generating rank. Hosts and guests came from intermarrying lineages, but these were not part of a regular system of wife-giving and -taking.

The Inside View

Irving Goldman among others objects to the position that anthropological analysis can proceed without concern for the native point of view. He wants to know specifically how natives conceive of their culture from the inside. Only with that basic knowledge can understanding be transferred to outsiders, including anthropologists. In approaching Kwakiutl society, Goldman does not focus on the potlatch but on ceremony and religious belief in general. Rather than explain Kwakiutl ceremonies in terms of social, ecological, or psychological function, he wishes to understand their meaning as a philosophical system. As far as he is concerned, they have an important meaning in and of themselves. Their only context is the philosophical-religious context. This orientation leads Goldman to concentrate on the great winter ceremonial that began in the month of November and marked a transformation of the entire Kwakiutl community from a "human to spirit conclave." During this period, the social organization of the local group was altered. Lineage houses became ceremonial centers and nobility became shamans. Holders of titles were divided into two complementary ritual groups. These were the *seals,* who consorted with spirits, and the *sparrows,* who managed the ceremony.

In his analysis of Kwakiutl society, Goldman asserts that rank was *not* attained through competition. Ceremonial life reflected and reinforced rank, but its true meaning lay elsewhere. He also objects strongly to the notion that the potlatch was an interest-bearing investment of property. He agrees that property was *associated* with rank but not in the way suggested by Boas and others.

A Kwakiutl father publicly gives away his copper in honor of his son. Potlatching and gift giving frequently occurred when a person's status was ceremonially changed.

The misunderstanding of Kwakiutl ideals about matters we label as "exchange," "property," "wealth," and "rank," arises from an uncritical application of a European model of status relations to a totally different system of meaning.

Goldman emphasizes that the Kwakiutl conceived of property as representing lives and not inanimate things. Value was seen as a quality of things and not a quantity. It symbolized supernatural powers and personal force. The distribution and exchange of property in the context of ritual was a materialization (making real) of circulation of certain spiritual forces *within as well as between* social groups. Property had a unifying rather than a divisive effect on social relations. As Rosman and Rubel put it, a great chief needed great competitors. Chiefs were competitors *only in a symbolic sense.* Objects used in the potlatch not only had power but they had meaning. They represented life and its force. To exchange property was to enter into communion with the forces of life.

Exchange was a vast metaphor for the forces of the universe. It was set in motion by changes in the natural order ranging from seasonal changes (the coming of winter, the salmon runs) to stages in the lives of individuals as they moved from birth to death.

To reinforce his interpretation of exchange in the context of Kwakiutl ceremony, Goldman notes that, in the strict sense, the term "potlatch" has no valid place in the vocabulary of anthropologists writing about the Kwakiutl. It is local jargon and is not even a Kwakiutl word. When "potlatch" is used in place of different Kwakiutl terms for property distribution, it leads naturally to the abuses noted not only by Goldman but also by the other authors we have examined in this chapter. Going back to Boas's notes, Goldman found that George Hunt rarely used the term "potlatch" in his own translations of Kwakiutl texts. In his publications Boas altered such expressions as "he gave away" to "he gave a potlatch."

If the term potlatch kept its meaning in the Chinook jargon, from which it is borrowed, Goldman would not object to its use. But it has, he says, been distorted in the anthropological literature. In Chinook "potlatch" refers specifically to gifts. For anthropologists it became an institution in and of itself. Goldman points out that in precontact times there never were such events as potlatches. Gift-giving (potlatch) occurred only in the context of specific rituals. Goldman's objection to the term is not an academic quibble. When the potlatch is defined as an institution, the exchanges that took place during Kwakiutl ceremonies become the reason for these ceremonies. This interpretation totally inverts their meaning. Exchange took place in the context of ceremonies and not vice versa.

Goldman does not deny that antagonism was a feature of Kwakiutl ceremony, but he objects to the idea that ceremonies reflected particular antagonisms between individuals or groups. Antagonistic displays were dramatic events meant to symbolize the perpetual struggle of natural forces. For the Kwakiutl strength in opposition to weakness was a major point of dramatic departure. In ritual events such as the

Masked dancers in the Kwakiutl cannibal ceremony. This and other ceremonies were marked by dramatic action, the use of complex masks, and music and dance.

potlatch this theme was played out, and, as the ceremony unfolded, weakness gave way to strength. This transformation, however, occurred only in a cycle of never-ending struggle. In the real world and in the ritual cycle:

Life and death, vigor and illness, victor and victim, killer and killed, devourer and devoured are permanently bound in restless opposition. The pattern of opposition is permanent, but the figures change in position constantly, yielding and then regaining cyclical ascendancy.

Beyond the human world the Kwakiutl universe was divided into four realms: animals, trees, supernatural beings, and the sky. Together these constituted existence. Separately they reflected diversity. The four became one when they coexisted. The inherent *separateness* of each realm had to be overcome through ceremonial interaction. The boundaries of each natural division were crossed for the purpose of acquiring powers. Among the Kwakiutl supernatural powers were *not* an aspect of rank and they were *not* inherited. *Rank,* says Goldman, was *fixed; power* was *acquired.* Thus what so many took for rivalry over rank were actually demonstrations of power. One did not, however, acquire power by demonstrating it. Ceremonies were not competitions, but rather shows of force, generally supernatural force. Not that rank and power were unrelated. That would be unthinkable in a redistributive society. After all, prestige comes from giving away, and giving away is *one* manifestation of power. The highest chiefs among the Kwakiutl had a heritage of power and the best chances of enhancing it through marriage. Therefore, according to Goldman, rank and power were interrelated, so that chiefs acquired power and those who acquired power were said to become chiefs.

Goldman summarizes Kwakiutl cosmology as follows:

Kwakiutl thought, which is as critically self-conscious as our own, seeks its reality in the natural world—in the life of animals and plants, in seasonal periodicities, in the growth and life cycle of individuals, in sensory phenomena, in the continuity of species, in the regularities of transformations, in the hierarchies of weakness and strength, in antagonisms and friendships, in gender, in birth and death, in the complexities of life renewal. The Kwakiutl have represented all natural phenomena as interconnected in obedience to preordained law. They have also allowed for will, for human agency, and they have not ignored the unpredictable, the indeterminate, and the apparently chaotic in life.

In Goldman's view (which has received criticism from some experts on Northwest Coast culture), Kwakiutl life was dominated by religion. Although he recognizes reciprocity as a feature of Kwakiutl ceremonialism, he feels that economic motives cannot explain the inner meaning of actions which, on the surface, might appear to be related largely to exchange. For Goldman the exchange relations embedded in Northwest Coast ceremonialism are a vast metaphor for the eternal flux of nature and the flow of time.

In this chapter we have seen that anthropology is much more than mere description. Ethnography takes its place in the science of human behavior as it is transformed into ethnological analysis. The interpretation of data depends on the interpreter's theoretical orientation. The "facts" of kinship, of exchange, of ecology, of politics take on different meanings in the light of different theories. Nonetheless, I think it is fair to say that all anthropologists agree that the institutions described in separate chapters of this book operate together and interpenetrate in the life of a culture. Kinship, economic and political relations, the dominant technology, the environment in which a society is embedded, religious beliefs—these taken together form a cultural web, a set of fragile connections that must be constantly renewed. In each culture this web has a specific architecture; anthropologists call it a structure. All agree that the structure of culture has dynamic properties, that it changes through time and that the change has a degree of order. To understand a single culture, or culture in general, we need to know more about the architecture and the dynamics of this structure. It is in the search for understanding that each anthropologist is guided by his or her particular theoretical orientation. It is here that the arguments within the field are focused. And, finally, it is here that the solutions will have to be found.

Summary

In this chapter we have discussed how anthropologists analyze ethnographic data and attempt to explain cultural variation. The cases chosen have included the Mbuti, a hunting and gathering group living in the tropical forest of Zaire in central Africa; the Kachin, rice-growers who live in the highlands of central Burma; and the Indians of the Northwest Coast of North America, a number of ethnic groups whose economy depended largely on fish.

The analysis of the Mbuti focused on their stable culture and the close relationship between their religion and their economic system. The Mbuti rely on the forest for their well-being and have deified it. Cooperation is the hallmark of their culture. According to Maurice Godelier Mbuti culture is an integrated system held together by three constraints, each acting on the others to maintain stability. These constraints are: (1) Dispersion—group size must be limited and bands must move over a wide territory. (2) Cooperation, particularly in net hunting, which would be disrupted by any display of personal ambitions. (3) Fluidity or nonclosure of the group, which produces frequent variation of social composition within any one group.

The analysis of the Kachin focused on the differing interpretations of two anthropologists, Edmund Leach and Jonathan Friedman. Both attempt to explain two sociopolitical variations that occur among Kachin peoples as well as their instability. These variations are known as the *gumlao* and *gumsa* systems. The *gumlao* system is egalitarian while the *gumsa* system is stratified. *Gumlao* systems tend to develop into *gumsa* systems through time, but the *gumsa* is itself unstable. It eventually crumbles and returns to the *gumlao* form of social organization.

Leach explains this variation largely on psychological grounds. He notes that the *gumsa* form is a weak imitation of neighboring Shan states. Although the Kachin evolve toward state formation, their environment is not rich enough to sustain such development. In addition, the dispersion of populations necessary in a slash-and-burn economy is unfavorable for large-scale state formation. The movement towards *gumsa* occurs because, in Leach's view, all humans have a drive for power. Given the opportunity, individuals will attempt to rise above their peers. Prestige and power are the outcome of this psychological drive. The form that this drive takes in any particular culture is shaped by cultural and historical factors.

Leach explains that the return to *gumlao* organization is due to an inherent instability in the *gumsa* system. Its weakness lies in the attempt on the part of chiefs to obliterate segmentary kinship principles based on lineages joined together through marriage. The successful chief, he says, is always ready to deny links of kinship with his followers. The chief tends to convert kinsmen into subjects. Whenever they can, Kachin chiefs model their behavior on that of Shan princes, but the Shan are loyal to place (typical of states) rather than kin. The change from kinship-based social organization to regional political unity never fully occurs among the Kachin, who retain their kin-oriented system. This system is held together by mother's-brother's-daughter marriage, which links lineages as wife-givers and wife-takers (the *mayu-dama* relationship). For Leach the causal chain from *gumlao* to *gumsa* and back again operates as follows: *gumlao* evolves into *gumsa* via a psychological drive for power, and the existing model of political power, the Shan state. *Gumsa* organization emerges as a relatively stable form of intermediate social organization. It retains an element of stratification and is, at least partially, dependent on the Shan state. When the Shan state weakens, the *gumsa* chiefs attempt to solidify their own power by breaking out of the kinship-lineage system. It is at this point that the segmentary elements of Kachin society reassert themselves, and rebellion follows.

Friedman argues that political systems cannot be derived from psychological principles and attempts to explain Kachin social organization on the basis of the *mayu-dama* relationship in which wife-givers have higher status than wife-takers. This operates in combination with the religious system in which lineage chiefs sacrifice to the ancestors (*nats*). Friedman's analysis is both structural and economic. He sees a potential for *gumsa* development inherent in the structural implications of mother's-brother's-daughter marriage. This potential is realized when bride payments and sacrifice to the nats become expensive and wife-takers emerge as commoners and wife-givers as an elite. As stratification develops, the elite groups can demand higher and higher bride prices for their women. This leads to increased productivity in a system that depends on labor rather than capital investment. The only way to increase productivity under these circumstances is through population increase. The Kachin economy in its *gumsa* phase operates with an increasing demand for surplus, which is converted into prestige and rank. In addition to having many children, Kachin chiefs enslave large numbers of inhabitants from surrounding areas. In order to keep the system operating, a greater and greater amount of labor must be put into lower-yielding land. Production per individual falls, but demand (based on the number of mouths that need feeding as well as inflated bride price) rises. Eventually, the system collapses under its own weight. The demands placed on individuals lead to open rebellion. The final result is a return to the *gumlao* system.

The last example in this chapter deals with the analysis of the ceremonial feast known as the potlatch. The potlatch, found among a number of ethnic groups inhabiting the Northwest Coast of North America, has excited the attention of anthropologists for many years. The potlatch was a spectacular redistributive feast during which, at least after acquisition of European trade goods, a great deal of property was destroyed. Ruth Benedict compared the potlatch to conspicuous consumption in the United States in that rank was often displayed through the possession of expensive belongings. The potlatch was seen by Benedict as a great competition between big men, with each trying to outdo the other. At any given potlatch the host would give extravagant gifts to an invited rival chief and his followers and destroy vast quantities of goods. The guest's chief was, according to Benedict, obliged to repeat the performance, acting as host to the chief who had potlatched for him. Each time a potlatch occurred, the host had to repay his rival with interest as high as 100 percent. If a chief could not meet his obligations to a rival he lost all his prestige.

Stewart Piddocke argues that the interpretation of the potlatch offered by Benedict applies, if at all, only to the late phase of Northwest culture. Examining the Northwest Coast environment and economy, Piddocke concludes that, although it was an area rich in resources, these resources were unevenly distributed in any given year. Such a situation led to local famines. These could be overcome through some sort of interarea redistribution system, in which naturally favored villages could supply food to unfavored villages. Piddocke suggests that the potlatch functioned as just such a redistributive mechanism.

Abraham Rosman and Paula Rubel take a different view of the potlatch. For them, it functioned as a redistribution system, not in an ecological but in a *social* sense, by materializing particular kinds of exchange relations linking social groups. Interethnic differences in the potlatch are the important variables for Rosman and Rubel. They found that differences in marriage preference and marriage exchange could be related successfully to significant differences in social structure, and that these in turn correlated well with variations in the potlatch.

Irving Goldman objects to the potlatch as a category. He notes that potlatching, when it did occur, was part of a ceremony, but *not* its major focus. For him it is wrong to interpret any

Northwest Coast ritual in economic terms. Taking an inside view and attempting to explain Northwest Coast ritual as an aspect of a coherent ideological system, Goldman sees the exchange of property as a metaphor for the circulation of spiritual forces. Unlike Benedict, Goldman feels that the antagonisms displayed in the potlatch as a feature of ceremonialism dramatized the perpetual struggle of forces in the world of nature.

The purpose of this chapter has been to show that anthropology is more than pure description and that *ethnography* takes its place in the science of human behavior as it is transformed into *ethnological* analysis. The interpretation of data depends on the interpreter's theoretical orientation. The "facts" of kinship, of exchange, of ecology, of politics take on different meanings in the light of different theories. While anthropologists continue to argue theory among themselves, all agree that the institutions of society form a cultural web, a set of fragile connections that must be constantly renewed. In each culture this web has a specific structure and this structure has dynamic qualities. It changes through time in an order that is, at least partially, predictable. Anthropological theory attempts to arrive at successful generalizations about this structure.

Bibliography

Benedict, R. F. 1946 (1934) — *Patterns of Culture.* New York: Penguin Books. Discussion of the potlatch in terms of conspicuous consumption, with a psychological explanation of potlatch behavior.

Codere, H. 1950 — *Fighting with Property.* American Ethnological Society Monograph 18. Potlatch viewed as competition.

Friedman, J. 1975 — Tribes, States, and Transformations. In *Marxist Analyses and Social Anthropology.* Edited by M. Bloch. New York: John Wiley and Sons. A structural-Marxist view of Kachin society.

Godelier, M. 1977 — *Perspectives in Marxist Anthropology.* Cambridge: Cambridge Univ. Press. Discussion of Mbuti social structure based on Turnbull's materials.

Goldman, I. 1975 — *The Mouth of Heaven: An Introduction to Kwakiutl Religious Thought.* New York: Wiley-Interscience. An attempt to reconstruct Kwakiutl religious thought from the point of view of the Kwakiutl.

Leach, E. 1954 — *Political Systems of Highland Burma.* Cambridge, Mass: Harvard University Press. Pioneer ethnography and analysis of Kachin society in the context of highland Burma culture and society.

Piddocke, S. 1969 — The Potlatch System of the Southern Kwakiutl. In *Environment and Cultural Behavior.* Edited by A. P. Vayda. Garden City: Natural History Press. Ecological explanation of the potlatch in precontact times.

Rosman, A. and P. Rubel 1971 — *Feasting with Mine Enemy.* New York: Columbia University Press. A structural analysis of the potlatch in several Northwest Coast societies.

Turnbull, C. 1961 — *The Forest People.* New York: Simon and Schuster. Humanistic monograph on the Mbuti.

PART 3

ANTHROPOLOGY AND THE MODERN WORLD

CHAPTER 25

CULTURE CHANGE, ACCULTURATION, APPLIED ANTHROPOLOGY

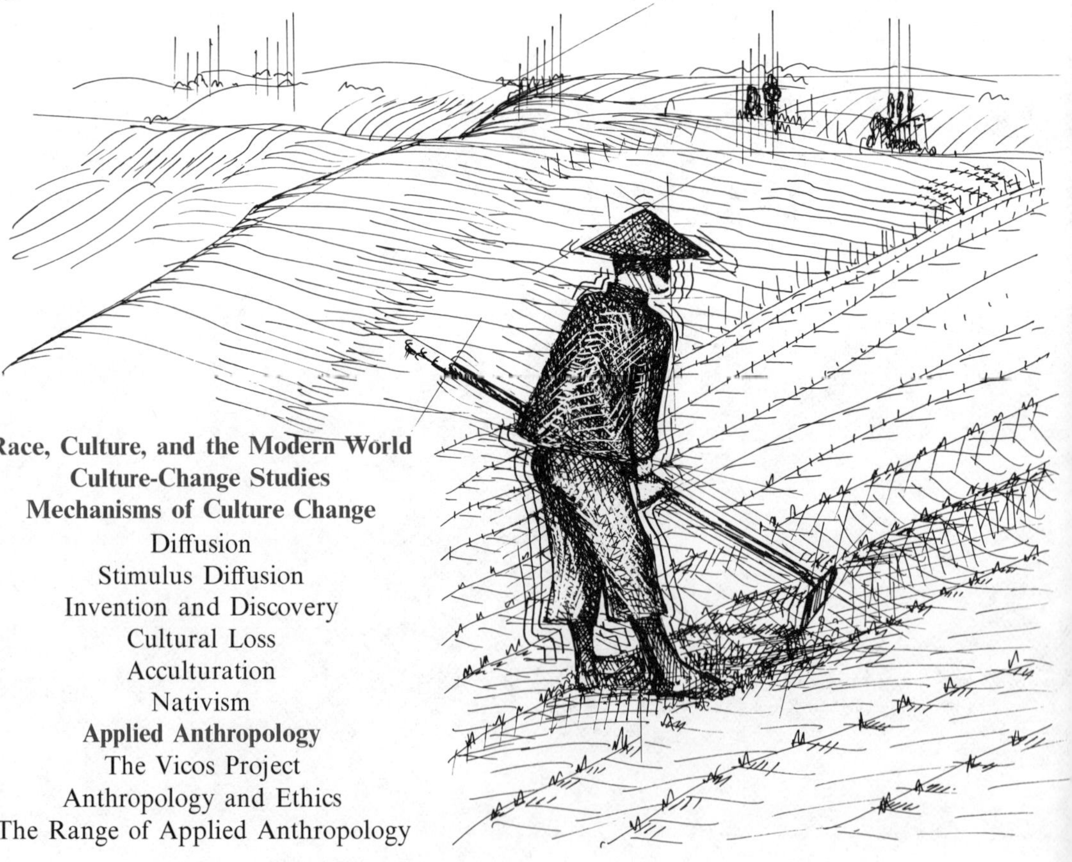

It did not take anthropologists to discover that the world can be divided into rich and poor nations and that within any country rich and poor exist side by side. In the early days of Western colonialism Europeans were convinced they were out to civilize the world. Their goal was to bring the fruits of culture to the backward of the earth. The premise that European civilization was superior in moral standards as well as in technological know-how had to be supported by a theory, however. In addition, the persistence of differences in wealth had to be justified. With the rise of colonialism two sets of explanations became popular among Europeans. One explanation was biological; the other was cultural. Both served to justify the *status quo*. The biological argument was based on the **Social Darwinist** principle that the most fit survived and flourished, and that, by virtue of their superior nature, were destined to rule. As a corollary to the biological argument, it was suggested that climate had an effect on behavior. Peoples living in temperate zones were said to have more will power and energy than those inhabiting the tropics. Generally the argument had an even more racist tone. Indeed, among the most conservative Europeans, the task of civilizing colonial peoples was seen as hopeless. These populations were to remain wards to the West forever.

More liberal thinkers adopted a cultural argument: "inferior" peoples could be brought up to Western standards through a slow process of training and remedial education. While colonial powers exploited their subject populations economically, many local officials truly believed in their civilizing mission. The "white man's burden" was for them a reality to be taken seriously. Whether or not a genetic argument was employed, most agreed in the superiority (racial or cultural) of the West. It was against this background of value judgments that anthropology emerged.

RACE, CULTURE, AND THE MODERN WORLD

In general the profession, particularly in the United States, has actively been hostile to racist arguments. This hostility is due, in part, to the central place of the culture concept in modern anthropology. Behavioral differences among societies are attributed to culture and not to race. In the United States a liberal philosophy stressing equality and individual freedom has also mitigated against a racist view.

The concept of cultural relativism, dictating that each culture should be judged only on its own terms and not on the basis of absolute values, is squarely opposed to the idea that some cultures are superior to others. Thus, cultural relativism leads anthropologists to reject the notion that European culture is superior to other cultures. But, the culture concept taken alone can lead to other misunderstandings concerning the roots of inequality. Some anthropologists assume that such problems as social disorganization and poverty are a form of "social pathology" due to imperfections within particular cultures. Although the cause of such disorganization might be attributed to colonialism or some other form of contact between cultures, its perpetuation is given a cultural explanation. The clearest example of this has been the contention that the poor exhibit what has come to be called a "culture of poverty" and that this culture of poverty is responsible for a range of maladaptive behaviors found among the poor. We shall examine the culture of poverty in the next chapter. It is brought up here to illustrate the fact that, when the concept of culture is used too freely, it can obscure economic and political factors that play a role in all forms of domination and inequality.

Thus, the concept of culture is open to the same misuse as the concept of race. This is very much the case when ideological explanations such as "the poor are poor because the culture of poverty breeds laziness" are accepted uncritically as fact. The contemporary world is a web of interlocking nations and social units of various sorts, ranging from castes and classes to linguistic and ethnic groups. All are tied together into a worldwide system of resource exploitation, trade, distribution, and even pollution. Different degrees of wealth and power, different aspirations, and different potentials for the realization of these aspirations create a constantly changing set of dynamic problems. The solution to these problems is of the utmost importance for our very survival.

Can anthropology help solve any of the problems posed by living in the modern world? Although it has provided many concepts that can be profitably used to understand both historical process and contemporary behavior, it sometimes looks old-fashioned and out of date. As a discipline anthropology has tended to focus on one particular kind of society—small-scale, non-Western cultures. These were once thought to be isolated, self-contained units, each with its own unique cultural system. It is doubtful, however, that any such system ever existed. Certainly none have existed for at least the past several hundred years. Even the most remote parts of the world have been penetrated by elements of culture that had their origin far away. This is not a new phenomenon. Artifacts from ancient China are found all the way into New Guinea and on the Northwest Coast of North America! In Central and South America diffusion from independent centers of civilization into the less technologically sophisticated hinterlands occurred early. Western culture itself is the result of local developments *and* borrowing from Asia and Africa. Contemporary anthropology is aware of these problems and is now actively engaged in the study of culture change and modern society.

CULTURE-CHANGE STUDIES

With the end of westward expansion in the United States at the close of the nineteenth century, American anthropology began to document the vanishing cultures of the subjugated Native American populations. This trend continued well into the 1930s and in many cases involved "*salvage*" anthropology. That is, a disappearing culture was reconstructed on the basis of work with one or at most a few old people. Often cooperation between anthropologist and informant developed into a long-term and intense relationship. Franz Boas worked closely with the Kwakiutl George Hunt, who supplied important data on his culture for many years.

The process of reconstruction led to a fiction known as the **ethnographic present:** cultures were described in the present tense as they had been before contact. But the use of the present tense in ethnographies produced a sense of timelessness and stability that is far from the truth. Archeological data and history have amply demonstrated that culture change is a perpetual, if variable, process. In spite of this reality, field workers, in their zeal to recapture the past, often ignored the actual present. Ethnographies rarely described how informants lived and interacted with their fellows as well as with Western culture.

In the 1930s some anthropologists, particularly in the United States, began to study culture change and the historical process that occurs when two societies come into contact. At first this research was strangely old-fashioned, perhaps because it was dependent upon preexisting theories within anthropology. Later it began to develop its own methods and concepts.

MECHANISMS OF CULTURE CHANGE

As I have already pointed out, much of the evidence for culture change came originally from history and archeology. The mechanisms of change were delimited and their relative importance debated well before ethnographic field work became a major aspect of anthropology. These mechanisms are few in number. They include *diffusion* and *stimulus diffusion, invention* and *discovery,* and *cultural loss.*

Diffusion

Cultural traits are often "borrowed" by one society from another. The process by which borrowing occurs is called **diffusion.** Material traits and ideas both diffuse. Thus gunpowder was invented in China and brought to Europe by Marco Polo, and Hinduism originated in India and diffused from there to Southeast Asia. Diffusion can occur rapidly or slowly. The attraction of a particular culture trait may be felt immediately or it may be resisted for a long time. The use of tobacco spread completely around the world in less than 100 years. Islam and Christianity spread rapidly to many parts of the world in the 200 to 400 years after their origins (see Figure 25.1). In contrast, many traditional societies continue to block the efforts of Islamic or Christian missionaries although missionaries have been present among them for centuries. Pueblo groups in the United States, for instance, have been particularly resistant to change. While they have adopted some aspects of Christian belief, much of their original religion and ceremonial life is still intact.

Unless culture change is forced on a people, they can and do exert both conscious and unconscious choice. At the end of the nineteenth century Japan adopted the capitalist mode of production very rapidly but retained many aspects of traditional Japanese culture. The Ponapeans of Micronesia have adopted a money economy but have maintained the traditional system of ceremonial exchange. As a result there are parallel economies in Ponape. Certain crops are grown for subsistence while others are reserved for ritual. But in addition, because many Ponapeans work for wages, food items such as canned fish and rice can be bought in stores.

Even when traits diffuse, they may change their form or their function or both. Catholicism in Mexico has adopted many elements of preconquest native belief, which have been integrated into the religion, producing a synthesis. (Such blending is known as **syncretism.**) Japan provides an example in another sphere. Manufacturing techniques are based on the modern

Japan has been highly industrialized since the end of the 19th century and is today a modern capitalist country. Traditional and Western culture exist side by side in modern Japan.

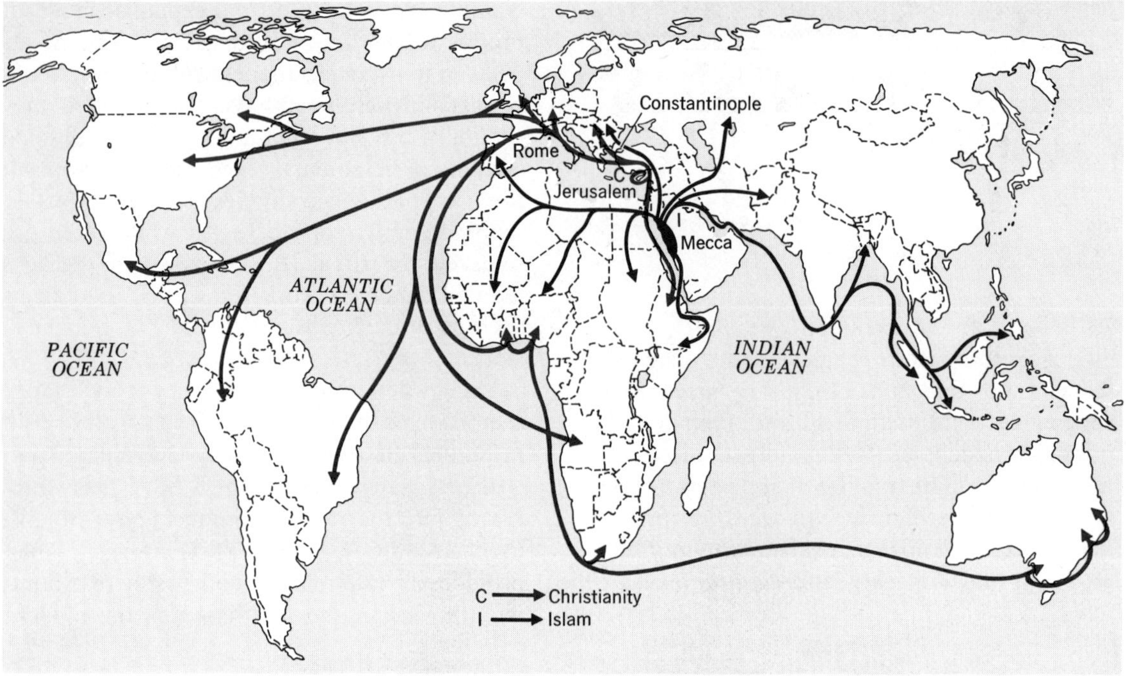

Figure 25.1
The diffusion of Christianity and Islam throughout the world.

factory system, yet the factory system in Japan retains features of traditional Japanese social organization. These have provided Japanese capitalism with its own highly successful dynamic. In preindustrial Japan personal loyalty was focused, in many cases, on traditional but non-kinship-based corporate groups. A sense of teamwork permeated such groups. This identification has been translated in a new context into intense worker loyalty to companies. Companies, in turn, provide job security for life, housing and medical care of high quality, and excellent retirement plans. Although Japanese companies are hierarchically organized, traditional elements of social organization are exploited to foster a sense of teamwork. Thus, workers and executives often exercise, party, and even vacation together. A janitor is made to feel just as important as the company president. His role in the smooth operation of what is seen as a "social organism" is rewarded symbolically and materially with a traditional yearly bonus.

Even mundane items of material culture can diffuse intact and yet change their function completely. A simple set of three linked tools known as a *chatelaine* diffused centuries ago from China to Europe. Originally the chatelaine was used to clean nails and ears. In Europe the identical form has been functionally transformed into a handy pipe tool. One element is used to scrape the pipe bowl, another serves to open clogged holes, while the third is used to pack tobacco into the bowl.

Diffusion may be inhibited or blocked by either the host or the exporting culture. In Islamic countries conversion to Christianity or any other religion is often outlawed. Cultures possessing technological advantages frequently attempt to maintain a monopoly over them. A new weapon, for instance, may be closely guarded as a state secret. Other items may be traded but their method of manufacture kept secret. In the modern world patent rights allow inventors and companies to keep new products and techniques in their ownership for limited periods.

Before patent laws and other forms of protection were developed, however, desirable items were often smuggled from one nation to another in order to break monopolies. Silkworms were taken out of China hidden in bamboo tubes; in Europe they became the basis of a silk industry no longer dependent on China for finished cloth.

Stimulus Diffusion

Monopolies were also broken by technological innovations. While the Chinese exported porcelain willingly to Europe, they kept its manufacturing technique a closely guarded secret. French pottery manufacturers actively searched for their own method of porcelain production and, after much experimentation with different types of clay and firing techniques, succeeded. The Chinese monopoly was broken and European porcelain production flourished.

In the early years of the United States a brilliant but illiterate Cherokee named Sequoyah developed a writing system for his own language. It was based on the idea that symbols could be used to indicate the sounds of a language. Sequoyah had seen English in written form and understood how it was used, but he could not read it. The **syllabary** system he developed borrowed some letters from the English alphabet, but he also devised new signs.

Although both the invention of porcelain in Europe and the development of a writing system for the Cherokee required innovation, both were *stimulated* by the prior knowledge that such cultural elements existed. In both cases innovators were guided by previous ideas. This process is known as **stimulus diffusion.**

How Common is Diffusion?

Although debates over the frequency of diffusion raged in the early days of anthropology, we now realize that the event is very common. It has been estimated that about ninety percent of all culture traits found in a particular society are the result of diffusion. Culture is truly the result of sharing among peoples. Printing and gunpowder are Chinese, as are noodles and fine pottery. Glass was invented in Egypt, rubber comes from Central and South America, and the Irish potato is Peruvian! Maize, squash, and beans are New World crops, while coffee was first domesticated in Africa.

Invention and Discovery

Invention and discovery have played a role in human adaptation ever since culture emerged as the human adaptation and the first tools were made. There is little difference between them, for both require the recognition that certain materials and ideas can be used culturally. One can *discover* that a certain plant is edible or that fire changes meat in a desirable manner. One can consciously set out to *invent* a tool or a technique for the manufacture of a specific item. But both discovery and invention yield new knowledge to a cultural system. This knowledge can be practical or theoretical, real or imaginary: the development of a new religious system is as much an invention as the development of a new tool; mathematics is theoretical, but it has practical applications; and music requires technical mastery but has no *direct* practical applications.

Some invention is based on the unconscious accumulation of knowledge and some is the direct outcome of conscious search. The tremendous explosion of knowledge and technological mastery of the last 200 years has been a very unusual experience in human history. Up to the Industrial Revolution change was relatively slow. Now industrial capitalism is based, in part, on the introduction of new manufacturing techniques and new products for the highly competitive marketplace. Thus, the rapid increase in invention and discovery that marks modern Western society is very much the result of a particular cultural process.

Cultural Loss

Not all cultural traits are retained. New ideas and techniques often replace previous cultural forms. The horse and buggy are now rare on the roads of America. Local arts and crafts in traditional cultures around the world are rapidly giving way to manufactured goods. As a result the ideas and skills that go into the making of such arts and crafts disappear with them. As we shall see below, cultural loss can have severe, unanticipated consequences in a social system.

Frequently when traditional societies adopt new religions, for example, they abandon and therefore lose important facets of their original culture. Islam, for example, discourages any visual art in human form. Similarly, many Protestant missionaries in Africa discouraged all local forms of visual art and dancing. Culture contact has often produced population loss, which in turn has affected local social organization. In many parts of the world including Africa, North and South America, and the Pacific kinship organization has been severely affected by population decrease.

The fact that cultural loss can have negative consequences is becoming apparent in our own society. The current obsolescence of our rail system can be traced directly to an increase in automobile and airplane travel, both of which were once considered to be a blessing of modern technology. The ongoing energy crisis, however, is putting pressure on a rapidly deteriorating public transportation system and forcing us to rethink some of our priorities.

Acculturation

Some early anthropologists studying American Indians eventually became concerned with contemporary relations between Native Americans and whites. Frequently, anthropologists were the only outside witnesses to abuses and mismanagement on the part of government officials and others who had dealings with local groups. They also witnessed discrimination against Native Americans and a great deal of social disorganization on the reservations. Such observations and a general growing concern of researchers for native peoples led to the development of two new subfields of anthropology. These were acculturation studies and applied anthropology. **Acculturation** is the process whereby the people of one culture take on the characteristics of another culture. They become *acculturated.* Sometimes this is a gradual and voluntary process, but often it involves coercion. Until recently, for example, reservation children were taken off to boarding schools where they were not allowed to speak their own languages.

One of the shortcomings of many, but certainly not all, acculturation studies (which we will meet again when I discuss the culture of poverty) is the tendency to look at traditional native cultures as closed systems. Although anthropologists are aware that acculturation depends on interaction, some neglect the dynamics of cultural contact and the ways in which culture change is often imposed from the outside. Frequently the source is found in economic relations.

Tappers and Trappers. "Tappers and Trappers: Parallel Processes in Acculturation" by Robert F. Murphy and Julian Steward examines how the exploitation of natural resources for trade with whites led to parallel shifts in social structure among two populations living in different environmental zones and practicing two different types of subsistence activities. One population, the Mundurucú, are tropical horticulturalists and live in Brazil. The other population is the Northern Algonkian Montaignais living in the boreal forests of eastern Canada. In precontact times the Algonkians were hunters and gatherers.

Before economic relations were established with whites, the Mundurucú lived in villages consisting of a men's house and women's houses. Residence was matrilocal by village, but the population was divided into patrilineal clans and moieties. The men of a village engaged in cooperative hunting and cleared gardens together. The women of each household were responsible for the cultivation of family plots. Warfare and headhunting were common, and chiefs functioned as war leaders.

First contact consisted of economic relations with traders who were interested primarily in wild rubber, which had to be gathered from widely dispersed trees. Rubber tapping is an individual activity. In order to deal effectively with collectors, traders established relationships with chiefs who could act as intermediaries. Eventually, chiefs became appointees of traders. The authority of traditional chiefs was then undermined and warfare ceased. Trade led to an influx of manufactured goods and a reduction in locally produced crafts. As the latter disappeared the Mundurucú became increasingly dependent on this exchange.

As the process of acculturation continued, increases in rubber production began to interfere with traditional food production (by both hunting and horticulture) and village life. Individual tappers began to deal directly with traders, and chiefs became intermediaries with Indian agents and missionaries. These factors led to a breakdown of cooperation and the end of the men's house. Villages were still held together by weak ties of kinship, but tension manifested in the form of sorcery and sexual rivalry produced a tendency for residential dispersion. Finally, local leadership could no longer function as an integrative mechanism. Individual trade in rubber led to the abandonment of kinship obligations, and families spread out along the rivers where the rubber grew and could be easily collected by traders.

Like all Northern Algonkians the Montagnais were originally nomadic hunters of large migratory animals. The effective economic and social group consisted of multifamily winter hunting groups that were nominally patrilocal. Individual families frequently shifted from one group to another. Although winter groups were sometimes required to split into smaller units by scarcity, the Montagnais preferred to live in larger social units since collective hunting was the most effective means of taking larger animals. The sharing of game among members of the social group was necessary for survival because individual families suffered periodically from poor luck.

A Brazilian worker taps rubber in the forest.

In the summer months the Montagnais grouped themselves into somewhat larger units. During this period they fished in lakes and rivers and hunted caribou. These summer bands, which inhabited loosely defined territories, had no formal organization and no chiefs.

As among the Mundurucú, an influx of trade goods led to the gradual replacement of native crafts. This trend produced economic dependence, and trapping became a major activity. Under these conditions trapping for the fur trade increasingly interfered with subsistence hunting, and winter provisions had to be purchased. Unlike hunting, trapping could be most efficiently pursued individually. This fact, plus the emerging pattern of individual economic relations with traders, weakened traditional social patterns. Eventually the nuclear family became the only viable social unit, and trapping territories became fixed and individually owned.

Although the new resources exploited by the Mundurucú and the Montagnais differed (in one case rubber and in the other fur-bearing animals), they were both most easily exploited by individuals working alone. Both resources were rather thinly dispersed through the environment, so collective labor was not efficient. The end result of both contact situations was a dependence on manufactured goods and a fragmentation of the original pattern of social organization.

Nativism

Indigenous populations rarely accept the threat of cultural (and frequently physical) annihilation. Resistance may be passive or active. In the West of the United States Native Americans continued physical resistance to white expansion until it became painfully obvious that such resistance could only lead to their own extinction. Even then nativistic movements, based on religious revelation, led to sporadic attempts at violent rebellion. **Nativism** is an attempt to maintain, or restore, native culture. It may produce violent action, as in the otherwise different Irish and Israeli attempts to establish independent homelands, or it may be founded on passive resistance to established authority. It may be based on religious or secular ideas.

The Ghost Dance Religion. The Ghost Dance religion was a nativistic movement among Indians of the West that spread rapidly at the end of the nineteenth century. It began in the Great Basin of the Southwest, where a prophet named Wodziwob predicted a great cataclysm in which the whites would disappear, leaving behind their material goods. At the same time the ancestors would return on a great train and restore all the land to the Indians. The elements here are the same as those found later in the cargo cults of the Pacific region.

In 1889 Wovoka, the son of one of Wodziwob's assistants, reported a vision in which the ancestors returned during the performance of a ceremony which in his dream was called the "Ghost Dance." This revitalization movement appeared as the last desperate resistance to white expansion was taking place among the Sioux. Although Wovoka's message was not overtly political and he did not himself call for violent action, the movement was converted by the Sioux into a militant call to resistance. The following is an English translation of a Sioux text now in the Bureau of Ethnology archives.

The persons in the ghost dancing are all joined hands. A man stands and then a woman, so in that way forming a very large circle. They dance around in the circle in a continuous time until some of them become so tired and overtired that they became crazy and finally drop as though dead, with foams in mouth all wet by perspiration. All the men and women made holy shirts and dresses they wear in dance. The persons dropped in dance would all lie in great dust the dancing make. They paint the white muslins they made holy shirts and dresses out of with blue across the back, and alongside of this is a line of yellow paint. They also paint in the front part of the shirts and dresses. A picture of an eagle is made on the back of all the shirts and dresses. On the shoulders and on the sleeves they tied eagle feathers. They said that the bullets will not go through these shirts and dresses, so they all have these dresses for war. Their enemies weapons will not go through these dresses. The ghost dancers all have to wear eagle feather on head. With this feather any man would be crazy if fan with this feather. In the ghost dance no person is allow to wear anything made of any metal, except the gun made of metal is carry by some of the dancers. When they come from ghosts or after recovery from crazyness, they brought meat from the ghosts or from the supposed messiah. They also brought water, fire, and wind with which to kill all the whites or Indians who will help the chief of the whites. They made sweat house and made holes in the middle of the sweat house where they say the water will come out of these holes. Before they begin to dance they all raise their hand toward the northwest and cry in supplication to the messiah and then begin the dance with the song, Rte misunkala ceya omani-ye.

The Ghost Dance, which began as a peaceful movement, served to strengthen Sioux resist-

Part of the Ghost Dance performed at the end of the 19th century by Arapaho.

ance against white encroachment on their territory and culture. This resistance eventually led to the terrible confrontation at Wounded Knee in which many women and children were massacred by government troops. James Mooney, who studied and documented the Ghost Dance for the Bureau of American Ethnology, said the following of Wounded Knee:

On New Year's day of 1891, three days after the battle, a detachment of troops was sent out to Wounded Knee to gather up and bury the Indian dead and to bring in the wounded who might be still alive on the field. In the meantime there had been a heavy snowstorm, culminating in a blizzard. The bodies of the slaughtered men, women, and children were found lying about the snow, frozen stiff and covered with blood. Almost all the dead warriors were found lying near where the fight began, . . . but the bodies of the women and children were found scattered along for 2 miles from the scene of the encounter, showing that they had been killed while trying to escape. A number of women and children were found still alive, but badly wounded or frozen, or both, and most of them died after being brought in. Four babies were found alive under the snow, wrapped in shawls and lying beside their dead mothers, whose last thought had been of them.

Today there are new stirrings among Native Americans. Since the 1960s several attempts have been made to unite all Indians in a broad-based Native American movement. The preservation of Indian culture in all its variety is one aspect of this movement. Another aspect has been the development of a series of land-claim cases, particularly against state and local governments in the eastern United States. Some of these have been successful, others not. In general, the chances of winning such a case rest on the ability of the Indian group to demonstrate that it constitutes a cultural entity showing continuity with the past. The nature of these trials tends to further encourage nativism among the populations concerned. In many cases anthropologists have been called in as expert witnesses to offer testimony about the validity of a particular Indian group's claims to being a genuine cultural entity with historical title to land. Expert testimony of this type is one way anthropologists can help solve longstanding disputes between ethnic groups on the one hand and government on the other. This is not the only way anthropologists actively engage themselves in problems concerning the modern world, however. Some anthropologists specialize in what has come to be known as applied anthropology.

APPLIED ANTHRO-POLOGY

In theory **applied anthropology** enmeshes the anthropologist in the planning and implementation of programs designed to help native populations adapt to a changing world. Most anthropologists have the interests of the local population in mind when they engage themselves in this type of work. In fact, the American Anthropological Association's Statement on Ethics specifically states that the anthropologist's first duty is to the individuals and groups he or she studies. Nonetheless, if they do not have a clear vision of what is involved, applied anthropologists may fail in this obligation. If a program is planned by outsiders with no input from the individuals concerned, it may either fail or lead to severe disruption. Yet if anthropologists work closely with local people in designing a program suited to their needs, they may run into the resistance of local or national governments. Conflict often occurs between insiders and outsiders; the anthropologist may be caught in the middle.

It is not unusual that a program advertised as aid may actually serve the interests of outsiders, ranging from private companies to various governmental agencies. Some applied anthropologists in fact, are hired by special interest groups in order to help them exploit a natural resource. A mining company may, for example, hire an anthropologist in order to gain access to land or to hire local labor. This effort need not harm the native population, provided attention is paid to the effects of economic change on the local ecology, subsistence systems, and social organization. Frequently, however, local interests will clash with the interests of developers. Applied anthropologists caught in these situations may find themselves in the uncomfortable position

Applied anthropologists have helped introduce alternate energy sources in different parts of the world, particularly those that are energy poor. Here we see Central Asian nomadic hunters in Asiatic Russia preparing lunch with a solar cooker. These people roam the desert and hunt with the aid of golden eagles.

of supporting a *status quo* or change inimical to the interests of a native group.

The Vicos Project

In 1952 a group of Cornell University anthropologists under the direction of Allen Holmberg leased a hacienda (plantation) with about 2000 Indian peons (serfs bound to the land) in Vicos, Peru. Located in the highlands, Vicos was an extremely poor and backward community. The best land was reserved for commercial crops that benefited only the hacienda owners, and the Indians were left with the poor soils of the mountain slopes on which to cultivate their subsistence crops. Sanitary, public health, and educational facilities were lacking in Vicos. In cooperation with the Peruvian Indian Service, the Cornell anthropologists introduced a program of planned change at Vicos that was to last for ten years. The goal of the project was to improve social and economic conditions on the hacienda through the active participation of the inhabitants themselves. The role of the anthropologist in the experiment was to aid in the implementation of locally made decisions. Change was introduced slowly and discussed at "seminars" consisting of the inhabitants of Vicos. One of the first innovations was a high-yield potato variety. This was chosen because the potato is the traditional subsistence crop in the area and because an improved species could provide a material base for economic advancement. The Vicos Project was founded from the beginning on the double notion that only self-help could work in the long run and that real material success was necessary to provide the basis for social change. The high-yield potato served a major self-perceived need of the community.

On the traditional hacienda any profits made belonged to the landlord and were drained from the community. At Vicos these were reinvested. Agricultural techniques slowly improved along with sanitary conditions in the village. Eventually, a school was built with local labor and accumulated capital. The school represented a positive change in the peons' attitude toward

House construction at Vicos. Self-help and cooperation have made this a successful community.

the possible rewards of education.

At the end of a ten-year period the people of Vicos had accumulated enough capital to buy their own lease and take control of their future. The experiment also provided them with the confidence and the expertise to run their own lives. This progress was not met without resistance, however. The success of the Vicos Project led to rebellious incidents in neighboring haciendas. In 1960 three Indians were killed when they attempted to take control of their land. Fearing wide-scale disruption, local landowners and business people attempted to block the Vicos purchase in the courts. It was only after the intervention of a government agency under pressure from the Cornell group that the people of Vicos could buy their hacienda for a fair price. Vicos became an independent community in July of 1962. Since then land reforms and redistributions have been instituted by the Peruvian government itself, but the record is a spotty one due to a continuing struggle between peasants and landowners in the country at large.

The Vicos Project, nonetheless, proved that self-help and self-education were viable means for economic progress among an extremely deprived segment of the population. As conditions at Vicos improved, local prejudice against natives by Peruvians of Spanish extraction decreased. This is the same kind of result that can be seen in those urban communities in the United States where slum dwellers have been helped to improve their own neighborhoods through small subsidies under the condition that they provide their own labor. These projects, involving what has come to be known as "sweat equity," tend to restore local pride and a sense of community among the poor and economically deprived. This, in turn, leads to a wider acceptance by society at large.

Anthropology and Ethics

Although the situation is now changing, anthropologists are not often called upon to offer their opinions concerning modern social problems, and few take part in programs of planned change around the world. In part this is so because anthropology is primarily an academic discipline. In addition, many governments believe that anthropologists study "primitives" rather than emerging or developing nations. Some believe that anthropologists have a stake in keeping the *status quo* alive in order to preserve "primitive" populations for study. Where would anthropology be, it is argued, if its subject matter were to disappear? Although some anthropologists are romantics of this type, few would consciously stand in the way of change and fewer would be able to do so even if they had the chance. We are a relatively powerless profession. Finally, many anthropologists are wary of getting involved in programs because they fear the negative results that might ensue. For many of these scholars involvement in planned change means playing God without benefit of the supernatural powers attributed to deities. Practical experience with applied anthropology has often proved to be less than rewarding for all concerned parties. In many cases anthropologists are hired to make suggestions that are neatly filed away but never consulted, much less used. In other instances some advice is taken, but not enough of it to make a coherent program for change work.

The role played by some anthropologists in the recent war in Southeast Asia made many of their colleagues wary of cooperation with government. Hired, for example, to relocate peasants outside of battle zones, anthropologists soon found that the people they had intended to shield from danger were subjected to terrible living conditions in relocation camps. In the eyes of the military the relocations were necessary to deprive rebel troops of food and other supplies that had been provided by local populations. In addition, removing local people provided free-fire zones where bombing could occur on an unrestricted basis. Once the people were resettled, the military displayed little concern for those they had displaced. Anthropologists in Vietnam were also employed by the military to convince local ethnic populations (the hill people), who had always been hostile to the central government, to work for, rather than against, this government and its military efforts. At one point during the Vietnam war the *New York Times* reported that the CIA considered one anthropologist to be worth ten soldiers. Eventually, many potential clients of applied anthropologists in other countries came to assume that the CIA lurked behind every anthropologist, even those engaged in what has been termed pure research.

At the height of the Vietnam war the American Anthropological Association created a committee on ethics to deal with some of these problems. The committee was charged with creating a set of guidelines for the profession and acting as a review agency to consider grievances against alleged misconduct. The Association of Applied Anthropology has its own set of ethical guidelines, and all applied anthropologists are morally, if not legally, obliged to follow both sets of rules. At the very least, these guidelines were created to sensitize anthropologists to the multiple obligations they have to the populations they study. In addition, as an official statement of the anthropological community, these guidelines inform others about the self-imposed standards under which most professionals are bound to operate. The ethics committee also advises anthropologists when they are caught in the midst of conflicting loyalties that may affect their responsibility to the scholarly community, as well as the people they study. Thus, although anthropologists are urged to protect anonymity when community members so desire, they are informed that such anonymity is difficult to maintain. Informants should, therefore, not be misled by promises that will be difficult to keep in the small world of professional anthropology where everyone knows everyone else and their research locations are not difficult to guess.

The Range of Applied Anthropology

Applied anthropologists have worked in the following capacities. (1) They function as advisors to governments and government agencies. As advisors they may help in the planning of change, such as the development of new industries, techniques of land management, and the improvement of agricultural practices. In addition, they may investigate epidemiological problems and help raise the health standard of the population in question. (2) They may be hired by an ethnic group to help with such legal matters as land claims, the codification of native law, or the organization of pressure groups to lobby for governmental action. (3) Anthropologists may be attached to such UN organizations as WHO (World Health Organization) or FAO (Food and Agricultural Organization) to help in research and application of specific programs aimed at improving the health and economic status of Third World nations. (4) Applied urban anthropologists may work in neighborhoods in order to mobilize individuals for social action, community health projects, or political action.

In addition, basic research in published form may lead to reform by calling attention to problems or injustices within a community. Thus, anthropologists who choose to study politically topical aspects of some culture or subculture may make an indirect contribution to the amelioration of some aspect of its social life. James Spradley, who has concentrated his efforts on various aspects of American society, studied drunks in Seattle, Washington. He found that drunks and "bums" in the community were systematically exploited by the police for private purposes such as lawn mowing and car washing. The usual practice was to arrest harmless but vulnerable individuals and impose short jail terms on them. They were then released to spend their time working in assigned tasks. When this violation of civil rights was publicized in the press, it was stopped.

Modern American society does not lack social problems. Among the most pressing areas in which an anthropological input can be made are: welfare, education, mental illness (cause and treatment), public health and epidemiology, hospital services, aging, poverty, minority relations, energy (use and conservation), ecology, population, and the politics of economic growth. Often the presentation of facts will serve to raise public consciousness to action. The ethical problems that lurk in manipulating public opinion can be avoided if the anthropologist serves as a catalyst, raising awareness, but leaving the decision-making process in the hands of the local community. Although this kind of applied work sometimes receives government support, when it does it is often looked upon with suspicion, because government authorities too often wish to control the direction of change within a community. There is frequently an attempt, on the part of centralized agencies, to *coopt* (take over) grass-roots movements.

Applied anthropology of this type is not always done by anthropologists. Some of the most interesting examples are provided by community leaders and spontaneous grass-roots movements as well as the innovative action of youths who are inspired to serve their communities. In the United States such motivation is often given official support in such agencies as VISTA; even in these a struggle often develops between official policy and the workers' perceptions of local needs.

Summary

In the early days of Western colonialism Europeans were convinced that they were out to civilize the world. The notion that Europeans were superior to colonized peoples was supported by two theories, one biological and the other cultural. The biological theory held that Europeans were racially superior to subject peoples and that this would always be so. The cultural theory held that for historical, and in some cases, climatological reasons European culture was more advanced than the cultures of subject peoples. The mission of Europeans was to bring enlightenment to the colonial world.

Anthropology as a discipline has, in general, been hostile to racist arguments. Behavioral differences among societies are attributed to culture and not to race. In addition, the doctrine of cultural relativism, which is very strong in anthropology, dictates that cultures should be judged on their own terms and not on the basis of some set of absolute values. On the other hand, when looking at poverty and other forms of social inequality, some anthropologists have misused the concept of culture by attributing these problems or their perpetuation to "cultural pathologies" within the disadvantaged subgroup rather than to its relationship with the larger society.

The fact that anthropology established itself as a discipline specializing in the study of small-scale non-Western cultures led it away from a view of the world as a web of interlocking nations and social units tied together into a worldwide system of resource exploitation, trade, distribution, and even pollution.

In its early days American anthropology tended to concentrate on Indian cultures. The vanishing cultures of Native Americans were documented through work done with single informants. This trend, known as "salvage" anthropology, led to a fiction known as the "ethnographic present," in which cultures were described in the present tense as they had been before contact. The use of the present tense in ethnographies produced a sense of timelessness and stability that is far from the truth. In the late 1930s and early '40s some anthropologists began to study culture change and the historical process that occurs when two cultures come into contact. The major mechanisms of culture change defined during this period were: diffusion, the borrowing of traits by one culture from another; stimulus diffusion, the invention of a trait based on a borrowed idea; invention and discovery, independent innovation by a particular culture; and cultural loss, the abandonment of a culture trait. Later, as studies of change became more sophisticated , the concept of acculturation (the general process of change that takes place as the culture of a dominant group comes to replace the culture of a subordinate group) became important.

As anthropologists focused their attention on change, they soon discovered that many cultures resisted the various pressures put upon them to adopt the culture of a dominant group. Nativism, the attempt to maintain or restore native culture, is a widespread phenomenon, occurring in many forms and among many peoples. The Ghost Dance religion that swept the western United States at the end of the nineteenth century was one such nativistic or revivalistic movement. For a time it brought hope to a number of Native American groups that white oppression would cease and their old ways flourish once again.

The most recent involvement of anthropologists with change is found in applied anthropology, in which the researcher participates actively in the planning and implementation of change. In theory applied anthropologists are ethically bound to keep the interests of the culture they are working with uppermost. In practice this is often difficult because of conflicts between native populations and the governments responsible for their well-being. Conflict may also occur when anthropologists are hired to help private corporations develop resources in territories occupied by "primitive" or peasant cultures.

One of the most successful applied anthropology projects took place at Vicos in Peru during the 1950s. A group of Cornell anthropologists led by Allan Holmberg, working in cooperation with the Peruvian Indian Service, leased the hacienda of Vicos. The Vicos Project was successful because its goals were realistic and tied to economic reality, and because the inhabitants of the hacienda had a hand in every step of the planning process. The role of the anthropologist was to guide and not to dictate. Resistance to the success of the Vicos Project came from landowners and business people who felt that the ability of the Indian peasants to determine their own futures was a threat to their established dominance over the local economy. It was only when the Peruvian government stepped in to allow the hacienda members to buy their land at a fair price that the future of Vicos was assured.

During the Vietnam war American anthropologists became particularly conscious of ethical issues within the profession. A committee on ethics was established by the American Anthropological Association to issue guidelines for ethical conduct in the field and to deal with cases of unethical behavior. The formation of this committee has strengthened the ability of the profession to deal with ethical issues and protect the rights of informants.

Today applied anthropology is a growing and wide-ranging field. Applied anthropologists work as advisors to government agencies as well as ethnic groups that feel they need the expert advise the anthropologists can give them.

Bibliography

Foster, G. 1969 — *Applied Anthropology.* Boston: Little Brown. Theory and application of anthropology to problems in the modern world, particularly the Third World.

Murphy, R. F. and J. H. Steward 1968 (1956) — Tappers and Trappers: Parallel Processes in Acculturation. In *Theory in Anthropology.* Edited by R. O. Manners and D. Kaplan. Chicago: Aldine. 393–408. Parallel cultural change in two different environments on the basis of parallel shifts in the organization of work.

Mooney, J. 1892–3 — The Ghost Dance Religion and the Sioux Outbreak of 1890. *14th Annual Report of the Bureau of Ethnology.* Washington, D.C.: Government Printing Office. Classic account of nativistic movement among Native Americans.

Holmberg, A. 1965 — The Changing Values and Institutions of Vicos in the Context of National Development. *American Behavioral Scientist* 8: 3–8. An analysis of the Vicos Project by one of its directors.

CHAPTER 26
LOOKING AT THE MODERN WORLD

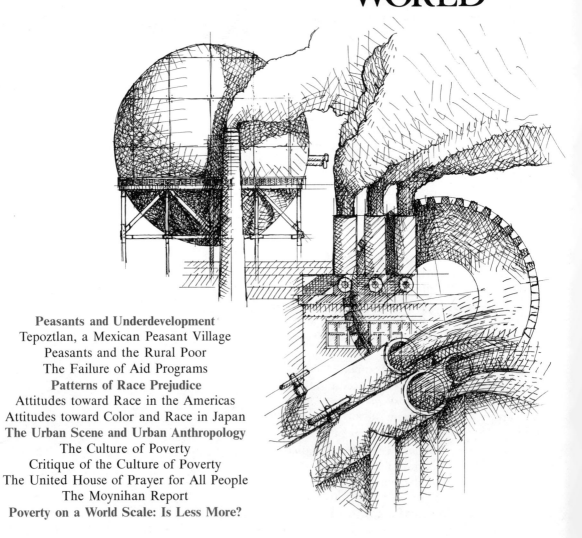

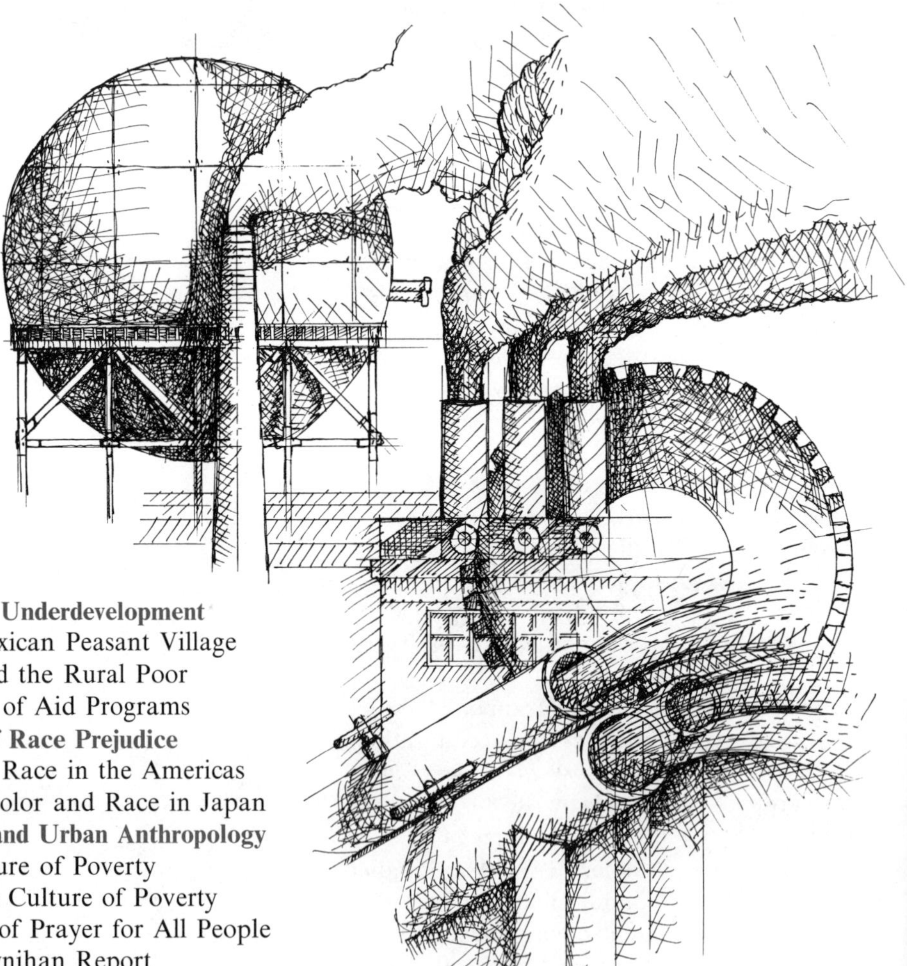

PEASANTS AND UNDER-DEVELOPMENT

The majority of people alive today are not members of the kinds of societies studied in the past by anthropologists. Instead they are segments of national cultures; either small-scale agriculturalists, known as peasants, or urban dwellers. Any comparative science of human behavior, which is what anthropology hopes it is, must take these people into account. In recent years many anthropologists have turned their attention to both urban and rural populations, particularly in what have come to be known as "Third World" countries, most of which are former colonies of European powers. The methods and goals of anthropology have been adapted to new areas without losing sight of the unique comparative nature of the discipline.

In this chapter we shall range over a variety of topics that cover the role of anthropology in the modern world. These are: peasants, the rural poor, and urban populations. The discussion will deal with problems arising out of under-development *and* development, the dislocations felt almost everywhere as the human species as a whole responds to rapid change, and an unequal distribution of the world's resources. Such inequality is a major cause of racism and sexism, both of which continue to serve as major divisive forces in contemporary life. Anthropologists deal with these problems in two ways. They provide scientific information for the public and planners alike so that intelligent and informed choices can be made in national and international policy, and they engage themselves in the planning process as applied anthropologists.

According to Eric Wolf, an expert on peasant societies, **peasants** are: ". . .*rural cultivators whose surpluses are transferred to a dominant group of rulers that uses the surpluses both to underwrite its own standard of living and to distribute the remainder to groups in society that do not farm. . . .*" Peasants, in short, are poor farmers who are economically dominated by a ruling class.

Peasants are often described as backward, antiprogressive, ignorant, and sometimes even downright stupid. Even Karl Marx, who saw the revolutionary vanguard in the working class, took a very negative view of peasants.

> *10 December 1848 was the day of the* Peasant Insurrection. *Only from this day does the February of the French peasants date. The symbol that expressed their entry into the revolutionary movement. Clumsily cunning, knavishly naive, doltishly sublime, a calculated superstition, a pathetic burlesque, a cleverly stupid anachronism, a world historic piece of buffoonery and an undecipherable hieroglyphic for the understanding of the civilized—this symbol bore the unmistakable physiognomy of the class that represents barbarism within civilization.*

At first glance peasant ideology and behavior tend to confirm this view. Most peasant societies are technologically backward and most peasants are extremely conservative. Some peasant groups appear, on the surface at least, to accept their poverty. On the other hand, it is a fact of history that the successful socialist revolutions of the twentieth century (with the possible exception of the Russian Revolution) have been peasant wars against a repressive land-owning

(Left) Peasants in Northern Italy harvest wheat. (Right) A peasant woman gathering dried weeds outside her home in a village along the shores of Lake Titicaca, Peru.

class. The recent history of China, Cuba, and Vietnam provide evidence that peasants can be organized to change their lot.

A close look at peasant societies shows that they are complex systems that respond through time to historical forces. One of the frequent major assets in peasant studies is the existence of such historical documents as birth, death, and marriage records, as well as land titles showing both ownership and property sales over a long period of time. When these are used in combination with field work, an excellent picture of peasant life under changing circumstances can be drawn. Of equal importance to the anthropological analysis of change is the existence of the *restudy,* in which a previously researched site is visited again several years after the initial study. One of the very first restudies was that undertaken by Oscar Lewis at Tepoztlan near Mexico city.

Tepoztlan, a Mexican Peasant Village

Tepoztlan was first studied by Robert Redfield in 1940. Oscar Lewis studied it again in 1947. The village is located in the Mexican highlands about 60 miles south of Mexico City. Tepoztlan is the administrative center for eight villages grouped in an administrative category known as a *municipio.* When it was last studied, it contained 662 house sites, which were separated for the most part by gardens and corrals. In 1940 the population was 3230. By 1947 it had risen to well over 4000. In the description that follows, data from the 1947 study will be used. Since Lewis went to Tepoztlan specifically to *re*study the village, a great deal of comparative material appears in his analysis.

About one half of the village population was bilingual in Spanish and Nahuatl (the indigenous language of the region); only five spoke Nahuatl alone. The latter tongue was devalued socially, particularly by young people in the village, many of whom were ashamed to speak it in public. Parents frequently used Nahuatl as a private language, and many children came to associate it with quarreling and scolding. Although Spanish was used by more and more people over the years, literacy did not increase much over the 1940 level of 42 percent.

Tepoztlan was not an isolated community. In

addition to being a small administrative center, it was connected to the rest of Mexico by a highway and by a rail system that was used primarily to transport commercial products to Mexico City. Passenger traffic was handled by a bus service. The village also had a few telephones, and mail service had existed since 1927.

Tepoztlan contained three types of house. These were the flimsy *jacal* (constructed of corn stalks with a thatched roof and earthen floor) and the adobe house, both of which are basically Indian, and the more substantial dwellings, located in the center of the village, that showed a Spanish influence. Only five percent of the houses were *jacales.* Although only the very poor lived in *jacales,* the wealthy could be found in both Spanish-type and adobe houses. They turned to adobe because during the Mexican Revolution many houses of the rich were destroyed by rebellious peasants. After that time a considerable number of wealthy people attempted to hide their riches by living in dwellings with simple exteriors.

Most dwellings in Tepoztlan, rich or poor, lacked sanitary facilities of any kind. Indeed, only one private house and two tourist homes had flush toilets. A few houses located in the center had piped water. For the rest the water supply had to be obtained at village fountains. Furnishings reflected a combination of traditional and modern culture. It was, for example, not uncommon to find a portable radio and a traditional cooking hearth in the same house.

The basic diet of the people of Tepoztlan consisted of corn, beans, and chili pepper. The amount of other foods consumed by any family depended on their economic status, the season, and their personal preferences. Corn was the major food and ranged from 10 percent to 70 percent of a family's diet.

The economy of Tepoztlan was based on household production, and the population could be divided into peasant farmers, artisans, and merchants. The village depended on trade with nearby regions for such basic dietary elements as salt, sugar, rice, and chile. In addition, it obtained cloth, agricultural tools, and other manufactured goods from urban centers. It had no pottery manufacturing, no weaving, and no basketmaking.

Tepoztlan was land-poor. Only 15 percent of the land was cultivable by plow and oxen and an additional 10 percent by slash and burn. Even if land had been distributed equally

The central fountain at Tepoztlan, Mexico.

among the peasants, there would have been only one-and-a-half acres of farm land and about eight acres of forest and grazing land per capita. In order to survive economically, then, the average Tepoztecan had to find nonagricultural sources of income during the year.

According to Lewis, Tepoztlan economy was based on an adaptive mixture of traditional and modern concepts of ownership and labor patterns. Well-developed standards of private property existed as well as a strong sense of individualism. There was a relatively wide range in wealth and a highly developed system of marketing and trade. Capital was invested for a profit and wage labor existed. However, there was a relative lack of capital, no credit institutions, and people feared to display their wealth except on ritual occasions. Religion and ritual continued to play an important role in production as it does in all simple societies.

The division of labor was largely traditional, particularly between the sexes. Men were expected to support their families, while women's work centered around the household and the care of children. Women's work was, however, less rigidly defined than men's. Women, particularly widows, could engage in men's work without criticism, but men could almost never do women's work. Ninety percent of employed adults were engaged in agriculture, but several other occupations existed in the village. Among these were teachers, masons, bakers, curers and midwives, and rope-makers. These were followed in frequency by butchers, barbers, corn merchants, charcoal-makers, tile- and brick-makers, and employees of the bus company. Less numerous still were shoemakers, carpenters, ironworkers, musicians and other ritual specialists, firework-makers, mask-makers, silver workers, millers, druggists, chauffeurs, and plumbers. The distribution illustrates that Tepoztlan society was divided occupationally between traditional crafts and a modern economic system.

Three kinds of land tenure existed in the village. About 80 percent of the land was communal. This was controlled by the *municipio* and was not divided into plots. Less than five percent of the land was part of the *ejido* system designed to redistribute land to poor peasants. *Ejido* land used for plow agriculture was divided into separate plots assigned to villagers according to eligibility determined by national law. The rest of the land in Tepoztlan was privately held and was primarily used for plow agriculture. All three types of land were worked individually rather than collectively.

Lewis suggests that three themes pervaded the social structure of Tepoztlan. The first was a *strong in-group feeling* among the members of a particular social unit. These units included, in order of increasing magnitude, the family, the neighborhood, the village itself, and the *municipio.* Feelings of solidarity were graded, becoming weaker from the family to the larger units. The second principal theme ran somewhat counter to the first. This was the feeling of *nucleation,* or greatest loyalty to the center. Tepoztecans felt superior to the people of surrounding villages. This conviction was materially reinforced by their better economic position. They had a high standard of living and better educational facilities in comparison with outlying areas.

The third theme was the principle of **familism** (the individual's primary loyalty was to the nuclear family). Close kinship remained the basis of social relations in Tepoztlan. Indeed, any social relations an individual had with nonkin were played out against a background of suspicion. Lewis notes that the nuclear-family loyalty of Tepoztlan can only be understood in terms of historical process. It was, he says, a defensive reaction to the disorganizing effects of the Spanish conquest, which destroyed the ancient Indian clan system. At the time of the conquest, clan land was transferred to the village government. Since such communal lands have persisted and since most villagers did not have private land holdings, the extended family did not have the opportunity to develop into a corporate land-holding group. Only the nuclear family has a corporate structure.

Lewis concluded that the structure of Tepoztlan was based on the interaction between two opposing elements. One was the collective tradition based on Indian culture. This was manifested in the persistence of communal land and collective labor. The other element was the result of Spanish domination and acculturation. This resulted in individualism and what Lewis calls "isolating familism."

From the above it should be clear that Tepoztlan can only be understood in historical perspective. Peasant culture in general is the historical result of interactions between local, somewhat traditional populations and a national economy. Although most peasant societies share certain characteristics, all are the result of unique historical circumstances.

By the time of the Spanish conquest Tepoztlan was part of the Aztec empire and reflected all the complexities of state organization. It was a stratified society with a few lords and ruling families. Interestingly, in contrast to the contemporary village, during the Aztec period Tepoztlan's economy was quite diverse. In addition to corn growing, manufacturing of various sorts existed. Two other plants—cotton and maguey—provided the basis for local weaving and rope-making industries. Other occupations included lime production and paper making. In addition the people produced honey, sugar, files, nails, needles, and pulque (an alcoholic drink).

Tepoztlan was conquered by Cortez in 1521. It was granted to him in a Spanish decree of 1529. Before conquest the village had been quite spread out. The Spanish concentrated the villagers in order to control them. But the postconquest period was highly disruptive and the overall population dropped from a high of about 15,000. The major causes of decline were deaths from epidemics, flight to avoid taxes, and deaths of workers in the mines of Taxco and Cuautla.

The first years after independence (1821) saw little change in the village. The first great change came with the reforms instituted by Benito Juarez in 1857. At that time church and state were separated and church lands were confiscated. These were distributed among a small number of villagers who became the new local aristocracy. These *caciques* controlled local government and turned the economic system to their benefit. They forbade the planting of communal lands in order to assure themselves a cheap labor supply. The majority of the population at this time was poor and many people went hungry.

In 1911 Tepoztlan liberated itself from the rule of the *caciques.* This came a year before Emiliano Zapata called for revolt in Morelos. During the ensuing Mexican Revolution Tepoztlan was the scene of invasions by rebel and government troops. It was a time of great suffering. Cattle were killed and crops were appropriated by whatever army was present. Women were raped and taken as hostages and large parts of the village were burned. Most of the villagers' sympathies were with the Revolution, but only a few of them understood the political ideals of the movement. Most, in fact, attempted to remain neutral and joined the fighting only under duress. The ablest village leaders meanwhile killed one another in a struggle for power.

After the Revolution, in the period from 1920 to the time of Redfield's and Lewis's studies, Tepoztecan society was transformed. The *caciques* had lost their power and prestige, and the communal lands of the *municipio* became available again to villagers. In 1929 the village received additional land under the government reform program. Lewis described the political atmosphere in the period after the Revolution as intense, dramatic, and often tragic. Political interest was focused around such issues as the preservation of the forests and other commercial resources. The issue of the forests arose because initially work was scarce and people began cutting down the local trees for charcoal production. As a result the village became divided into two factions. One, which was composed mainly of ex-Zapatistas (followers of Zapata), was conservationist; the other, led by sons of former *caciques,* favored exploitation of the resources. These factions later came to be known as the Bolsheviki and the Centrales. Their struggle continued throughout the twenties and thirties and was often quite bloody.

Lewis summarized change in Tepoztlan by noting a series of important economic and social factors that gradually brought the village into the mainstream of Mexican life. These included the granting of *ejido* lands to landless farmers, the building of corn mills, a new road, and the expansion of school facilities. These changes led to a rapid increase in population, an improvement in health services, and a marked rise in the standard of living as well as the aspirations of local people. A class of small landholders developed, new economic specializations appeared, and the use of Nahuatl decreased.

Peasants and the Rural Poor

Not all peasants have fared as well as the Tepoztecans. Economic exploitation of small landholders is a feature of modern life in many poor countries controlled by small elites.

Even when peasants are landowners, they often lack control or even influence over such crucial economic factors as supply and demand. In many cases they live in the most backward parts of their countries and have little access to modern conveniences, ranging from uncontaminated water and basic medical services to consumer products that reduce individual drudgery.

Many peasants are sharecroppers who work for absentee landlords. Because they often live on marginal (economically poor) land and because in most cases landlords are uninterested in increasing production through capital investment, any increase in output depends on labor input. That is to say, it is hard work, often backbreaking work, lacking such amenities as fertilizer and mechanical farming equipment that produce greater output.

Not all the rural poor are peasants, of course. In countries where landownership is in the hands of small elites, we find both peasant sharecropping and large estates in which *hired laborers* work as field hands for low wages. Because political power is in the hands of the elite who suppress any attempt on the part of agricultural workers to organize, those workers remain among the lowest paid in the national economy. Furthermore, since agricultural centers are in backward areas, generally far from the cities, workers are denied access to hospitals and good schools. It is not in the interest of landowners to educate peasants and agricultural workers. For education might lead to migration and better jobs—and worse, from the owner's point of view—to unionization.

Agriculture in the Third World is often highly dependent on the international market for a limited range of crops. Sugar, peanuts, and cocoa, for example, constitute the major exports of such industrially backward countries as Cuba, Senegal, and Ghana. The economies of the poor countries rise and fall with international pricing fluctuations. In order to gain convertible currencies, however, these nations are forced to raise cash crops. In many of them land that was originally used to raise a wide range of subsistence products is converted to a monocropping system. Cropping of this type leads to a decrease in nutritional standards in the local population, for farmers are forced to use a major part of their incomes to buy food they formerly raised for themselves. Monocropping is also dangerous for the local ecology, since the conversion from a highly diversified ecology to a simple one can have disastrous effects on the local ecosystem. Large tracts of the same agricultural product increase the danger of plant disease and make the local economy highly vulnerable to the effects of crop failure.

Although much of the poverty of the Third World has been attributed to rising population, it is probable that population increase is itself the *result and not the cause* of such poverty. In areas where capital investment is low or absent and agricultural production flows out of the region, the only way the peasants or laborers can keep their families alive is to increase the labor force. In such poor areas of the world, the cost of having children is low and their labor is valued. Children, indeed, are one of the few valuable assets that a family has. With schooling at a minimum, children can begin to make a direct economic contribution to the family as early as five years of age. Boys and girls can work in the fields, and girls can free their mothers for agriculture by taking care of the household and younger siblings.

The poverty of peasants in the Third World becomes understandable only in light of the national and world economy. This point of view has been developed by A. Gunder Frank in a series of economic studies of the Third World. It is Frank's contention that underdevelopment is no accident of history or geography. It results from systematic exploitation; he calls this *the development of underdevelopment.* His thesis is that the poor regions of the world were and are dependent on the major industrial nations for manufactured goods and that colonialism leads to the draining of resources and wealth from dominated areas. Frank explains the reasons why labor-intensive rather than capital-intensive production developed in Latin America.

Because of commerce and foreign capital, the economic and political interests of the mining, agricultural, and commercial bourgeoisie were never directed toward internal economic development. The relations of production and the class structure of the latifundia [*great plantations*] *and of mining and its economic and social "hinterlands" developed in response to the predatory needs of the overseas and the Latin American metropolis. They were not the result of the transfer, in the sixteenth century, of Iberian feudal institutions to the New World as is so often and so erroneously alleged.*

If this analysis helps us to understand the poverty of rural Third World people, what about their apparent unwillingness to accept change, except in those cases when they rebel totally against traditional authority? A look at the dynamics of the total system provides the necessary clues.

It is a common practice among the landholding class to increase rents if workers at their end increase productivity. Thus, improvements made by peasants or workers are usually drained off by landholders. This was true in the South of the United States, where sharecropping was, until recently, a major aspect of agricultural production. It is still true in much of the Third World. Where land and houses are rented from a landowner, capital improvements may lead to a direct increase in rent charged.

When monocropping becomes the rule, peasants and agricultural laborers lose any leverage they might have on the economic system. In addition, their nutrition and health suffer from the absence of proper food. Locked on an economic treadmill, the worker can do little to change the social and economic situation.

The Failure of Aid Programs

Planned change has been a popular idea since the end of World War II. It has come on the coattails of independence and "rising expectations" in the Third World; at the same time the dependence of the rich nations on the labor of the poor nations has decreased. In the power struggle between the East and the West, rich nations on both sides, each acting in its own self-interest, have increased their aid to the world's poor. Yet poverty continues to plague the Third World.

There are many reasons for this persistent condition. First of all, and most simply, much of the aid destined for the poor never reaches them. There is so much corruption in many of the poor countries that only the rich benefit from economic aid. When aid is distributed to the poor, it comes by way of the rich, who frequently claim to have made the relief possible. Aid thus serves to further increase the dependence of the poor on those with power.

In many cases the local situation is poorly understood by government agencies and even planners, and change is frequently imposed on people without their consent. Sometimes peasants are willing to experiment with new techniques, as long as they are provided free, but when support is withdrawn, the innovations may be abandoned. The explanation may be that indigenous techniques are less costly, and peasants must be wary of costs for reasons already discussed. Anthropologists have documented many cases of this type and have aided in designing projects that avoid these pitfalls.

Not only do they often maintain imbalances, but frequently aid programs increase imbalances between rich and poor. This is precisely what happened in many parts of the world with the introduction of "miracle" rice and wheat, the so-called **Green Revolution.** These grains are the outcome of genetic engineering whereby plant specialists exploit the ability of some variants to produce greatly enlarged fruiting bodies. In biological terms, these plants are freaks. They are short and quick-growing, and have fewer energy-absorbing leaves. They provide a definite advantage for agricultural production. But as freaks, such plants are dependent on tender loving care. They need to be enriched with chemical fertilizers and protected from insect pests with expensive insecticides. They tend to be far more vulnerable to disease than more hardy but less productive species. (When I was in Bali on a research trip, Balinese farmers told me that their miracle rice was attacked by a parasite that had never bothered the rice crop in the past.) Thus, the introduction of miracle grain demands capital intensification. Only rich farmers can afford to make the change. The change itself leads to increased unemployment.

Another instance of the failure of aid has been documented by the anthropologist Glenn Petersen, who worked on the island of Ponape in the United States trust territory of Micronesia. Ponape is one of the larger and more fertile islands in a vast group that extends across much of the Pacific between Hawaii and the Philippines. Indigenous crops on the island provided Ponapeans with an adequate supply of calories, and fishing supplied adequate protein. Ponapeans are efficient farmers, when they want to be, and produce yams weighing over 200 pounds. These are used as prestige items in the many ceremonial feasts that take place. In precontact times Ponape was a product-rich island without a money economy. After contact an array of consumer demands developed, ranging from canned food (a prestige item) to manufactured clothes, automobiles, films, and other products of modern technology. None of these are produced on Ponape (it is too small for all but the most modest industrial development) and must be bought with money. The obvious solution for the island's new economic demands is commercial agriculture of some type. For a time aid programs focused on this possibility. Ponape has had some modest success with plantations of black and white pepper. Indeed, Ponapean pepper is already known as among the best in the world. The acceptance of pepper and other commercial agricultural crops has generally failed, however, in the face of, and in spite of, Ponapean willingness to produce ceremonial crops. Officials generally ascribe the commercial failure to laziness and backwardness. There is no cash shortage on the island, however. For the Ponapean situation is not one of poverty so much as of affluence, but affluence of a special type. The United States government has an important strategic interest in Ponape and the rest of Micronesia. These islands cover the central Pacific, and the American government does not want to see the region fall under the influence of other foreign powers. At the present time the Ponapean economy is supported by a large number of government jobs, available to most people who want to work. The cash flow into the island from the mainland is large enough to discourage officially supported commercial agriculture. In addition, those individuals who have grown new agricultural products have been disappointed by fluctuations in the market price of their products, the frequent unavailability of necessary fertilizer, and the hazards of unreliable transportation. In short, they have come to mistrust the economic effects of a system dependent on forces beyond their control. As long as other income alternatives exist, Ponapeans are wise to stick to them.

PATTERNS OF RACE PREJUDICE

Economic exploitation is often justified on the basis of race or sex. Yet racism and sexism are frequently analyzed apart from the economic system in which they are embedded. Many historians, for example, have noted that slavery as an institution was more brutal and pervasive in North America than in South America. They go on to attribute these differences to variations in racial attitudes held by Anglo-Saxons on the one hand and Latins on the other.

Attitudes toward Race in the Americas

The anthropologist Marvin Harris has analyzed race prejudice in the Americas in its original historical and economic context. He concludes that material conditions are the major factor in the persistence of specific behavior and attitudes towards race.

Harris begins his argument by noting the reasons why black Africans were preferred as slaves over Native Americans by colonists in both North and South America. In his view Africans were preadapted by their own cultural experience to field labor. In addition, Africans were less susceptible to European diseases than the recently contacted Amerindians. It is well known that such diseases as smallpox and measles killed millions of the native population in the early days of colonization.

Looking at South America, Harris describes racial patterns in Brazil at the beginning of the colonial period. He notes that whites and blacks, as distinct groups, never existed there. Instead, one finds a continuum ranging from "black" at one end to "white" at the other. The Brazilian conception of race consists of a multifaceted system rather than the dual distinction found in the United States. Harris relates the dichotomy in the United States to the concept of **hypodescent,** a means of determining racial membership. In the United States anyone descended from a black ancestor, no matter how remote, was classified as black. Since blacks were socially inferior, black descent moved an individual downward (hypodescent) on the social scale. This practice was not employed in South America. There racial classification was based on minute differences of physical appearance as well as an individual's educational and social standing.

An important point made by Harris is that the Brazilian classification system is open and ambiguous. Individuals find it difficult to define

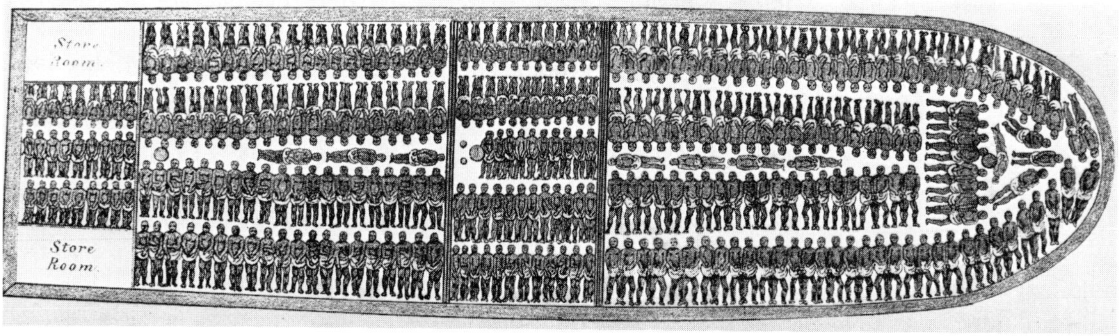

Slaves were brought by slavers from Africa to the New World packed into the holds of ships. During the crossing many died from lack of food, disease, and heat prostration.

Slaves planting sweet potatoes on the James Hopkinson plantation in 1862, Edisto Island, South Carolina.

racial terms. Forty percent of a representative sample of Brazilians ranked *moreno claro* as a lighter type than *mulato claro* (both are considered relatively light categories) while 60 percent reversed this order. Individuals may also change their evaluation of someone's racial classification at different times and in different circumstances. In order to test this ambiguity, Harris showed a sample of 100 Brazilians a set of photographs in which the individuals portrayed varied in hair shade, hair texture, nose and lip width, and skin tone. He asked them to assign the faces to categories of their own choosing. These 100 subjects produced 40 different racial types! The highest percentage of agreement among subjects for the racial type of any one picture was only 70 percent and this was for *branco* (white). The lowest percentage of agreement was 18 percent for *sarara,* a mixed type.

In Brazil an individual can change his or her racial classification through a change in status and life style. Passing from one racial classification to another does not depend on phenotypic characteristics. Nor need one "pass" in secret from one group to another. An individual's "color" will be perceived differently according to his or her standing in the community.

Many have used this somewhat open system to argue that racial prejudice is absent in Brazilian society. Harris warns us that this, in fact, is not the case. He points out that a stereotype of black exists that is quite unflattering. Blacks are considered by many to be innately inferior in the qualities of intelligence, honesty, and dependability. In addition, aesthetic judgments are made about race, with whites favored over blacks, even among those who define themselves as black. What is interesting and curious about these stereotypes is that they do *not* show themselves in actual behavior.

What people say they will or will not do with respect to pretos *and* mulatos *does not issue into actual behavior. Indeed, extremely prejudiced Brazilians have been observed to behave with marked defference toward representatives of the very types whom they allege to be most inferior. Racial prejudice in Brazil, in other words, is not accompanied by systematic racial segregation and discrimination. Before two individuals can decide how they ought to behave toward each other they must know more than merely that one is dark-*

skinned and the other light. A Brazilian is never merely a "white man" or a "colored man"; he is a rich, well educated white man, or a poor, uneducated white man, . . . etc. . . . The outcome of this qualification of race by education and economics determines one's class identity. It is one's class and not one's race which determines the adoption of subordinate and superordinate attitudes between specific individuals in face-to-face relations. . . . Color is one of the criteria of class identity; but it is not the only criterion. . . .

Harris goes on to discuss the reasons behind this type of classification. He rejects the notion that it is due to the past attitudes of Latin slaveholders. An examination of slaveholding records in both North and South America shows that "law and reality had equally small resemblances to each other." The Anglo-Saxon record is not as bleak as defenders of Latin racial attitudes might pretend. New Englanders abolished slavery in their part of the United States long before it was abolished in many parts of Latin America. For Harris, "Understanding of the differences in the status of free 'non-whites' in the plantation world can only emerge when one forthrightly inquires why a system which blurred the distinction between Negro and white was materially advantageous to one set of planters, while it was the opposite to another."

Harris argues that when the New World was settled by the Portuguese and Spanish, there was such a severe manpower shortage in the home countries that it was difficult to populate the colonies. The New World was then flooded with African slaves whose labor was necessary for the economic success of the growing plantations. On the other hand, immigration to the English colonies was massive, and slaves were brought in rather late in history. Harris cites population statistics from Virginia to demonstrate that not until the second half of the eighteenth century did blacks exceed 25 percent of the population. In Brazil the ratio of whites to blacks was the opposite. In 1819 there were almost as many mestizos (mixed people), free and slave, as whites. Because there were so few whites in their colonies, the Portuguese were forced to create a class of free half-castes. These individuals occupied necessary roles that placed them between the slaves and the white masters. According to Harris, there were certain economic and military functions which slaves could not be trusted to perform and for which there were no available whites. This situation was most acute in the realm of military and police duties. Thus, the half-castes were often used to fight Indians. They were also of great importance in the growing cattle industry. Slaves could not be trusted out in cattle ranges, and immigrants from Portugal felt that work of that sort was beneath their dignity. In addition, Harris suggests that the bulk of agriculturists who supplied food for the one-crop plantations may have been "aged and infirm manumitted [freed] slaves, and favorite Negro concubines who with their mulatto offspring had been set up with a bit of marginal land."

The same activities that could only be performed in Latin America by a free, racially mixed population were performed in North America by free whites, many of whom had originally come to the New World as indentured servants. After their terms of service, these individuals were able to buy land and begin farming.

Racial hostility in the United States was the result of direct competition between whites and blacks on the lower levels of economic activity. In fact, hostility between poor whites and blacks was encouraged by the white ruling class. Thus, racism in the United States developed out of this historical background.

I agree strongly with Harris that individual historical instances of racism—and, I would add, sexism—have their roots in particular historical and social circumstances. It is no accident, for example, that many English people believe IQ is intimately linked to biological differences in class membership, whereas many Americans believe that IQ differences have a racial basis. Class, rather than race, has been a major aspect of the English social system. Social and historical facts, however, do not explain the readiness with which humans everywhere are apt to use *biological* markers to explain *social* inferiority. This tendency, which transforms *cultural* differences into *natural* differences, may be related to a set of fundamental distinctions that humans use to classify themselves and others. The structuralists, including Sigmund Freud and Claude Lévi-Strauss, have pointed out that such oppositions as self–other, my group–other group, nature–culture, occur frequently as individuals and groups attempt to sort out and classify the natural world. Apparently, it is psychologically important for humans to establish boundaries around themselves in an ongoing quest for identity.

The very fact that we organize symbols into sets of opposing categories and that we tend to reach self-identity through contrast with others may provide the psychological basis for the emergence of racism and sexism. The forms that these take will, of course, be determined by particular historical circumstances.

Attitudes toward Color and Race in Japan

Racism is not at all limited to the Western world. Instances of prejudice can be found in any country that has had experience with foreigners in great numbers and for which historical records exist. Even local differences in culture or historical circumstance can lead to racist attitudes. In addition, strongly held cultural stereotypes can affect the way in which people define themselves and others to a surprising degree. Japan, a country that was isolated from foreign contact for many centuries, provides two interesting examples of local prejudice. In the first case, we shall see how strongly held notions about color led to self-hatred among some Japanese once they became aware of light-skinned Europeans. In the second case, we shall see how a genetically Japanese but culturally defined subgroup came to be "inferior" within the mainstream of Japanese life.

A Japanese sociologist, Hiroshi Wagatsuma, has traced the history of Japanese attitudes toward whites and blacks. He has shown how these attitudes have tended to shape Japanese feelings of self-esteem. He informs us that, long before the Japanese had any contact with either whites or blacks, they placed a high value on white skin. The color black was associated with filth and evil. Japanese saw themselves as white. The word *shiori* (white) was used to describe the ideal Japanese type. Although some individuals were described as "brown," the term "yellow" was never used.

In the early days of Imperial Japan, ladies used white powder on their faces. Long, smooth, black hair was also valued, while kinky or wavy hair was considered ugly and animal-like. This concept of beauty continued up to modern times. So concerned were upper-class Japanese with whiteness that they avoided exposure to the sun. The concept of masculine beauty was a bit more complicated. Whiteness and the life of leisure were contrasted with darkness and the life of the warrior, or samurai. So Japanese distinguished between beautiful men who had white skin and attractive men who were dark-skinned, masculine, and dependable.

When European traders came to Japan, they were never characterized as white. Japanese prints show Europeans as ruddy or brown, occasionally as grey. Japanese women placed near Europeans in these early pictures are always depicted as white. The features of Europeans that most impressed the Japanese artists were height, hair color, general hairiness, big noses, and the European eye.

At the time of Commodore Matthew Perry's voyage to Japan in the middle of the nineteenth century, both American and Japanese men were depicted as white, but Americans were distinguished by their hairiness, particularly their beards. At the same time Japanese women were shown as whiter than both Japanese and American men. In 1860 the Japanese government sent a trade expedition to the United States. Among the visitors were a group of 63 warriors, some of whom recorded their impressions of American women. One wrote: "The women's skin was white and they were charming in their gala dresses . . . but their hair was red and their eyes looked like dogs' eyes which was quite

Early in the contact period between Japan and Europe, Japanese artists depicted Europeans as darker than Japanese and with semi-oriental features. (Left) Harbor scene showing Europeans and Japanese, Edo (Tokyo) 17th century. (Right) Matthew Galbraith Perry as depicted by a Japanese artist (circa 1854).

disheartening. . . . Occasionally I saw women with black hair and black eyes. They must have been of some Asian race and naturally they looked more attractive and beautiful."

By the late 1920s wavy hair had become an acceptable feature of feminine beauty. American motion pictures had a very strong influence on Japanese aesthetics and some women began to alter their physical characteristics to mimic the Western phenotype. Some had the bridge of the nose altered by plastic surgery and even the eyes were modified in this way.

As you might imagine, the Japanese self-image suffered along with the desire to transform physical appearance. The white skin of European women has become an obsession for some Japanese. Beautiful Japanese women are still imagined as white, but when they are compared with Europeans their darker skin becomes apparent. At the same time, some Japanese have come to associate a range of Caucasian features with virility. These include height, large hands and feet, and a hairy body. It is interesting to note in this respect that many Japanese associate white features with characteristics whites themselves associate with blacks.

Wagatsuma cites Japanese informants concerning skin color. One mother said, "My daughter is very 'white' among the Japanese. Looking at her face, I often say to myself how white she is. As a mother I feel happy. But when I see her among Caucasian children in a nursery school, alas, my daughter is *yellow* indeed."

Japanese culture is a complicated mixture of traditional and modern elements. Although many Western-oriented Japanese attempt to look European, conservative Japanese maintain a preference for native phenotypic characters. For them the oriental eye, a small low nose, straight black hair, and traditional dress all carry a positive value and reflect "beauty."

Except for the Ainu, who live far in the north on Hokkaido Island, there are no native non-oriental ethnic groups in Japan. There is, however, as we saw in Chapter 17, an outcaste group known as the Burakumin or Eta. These people, the descendants of a butcher caste, are genetically Japanese, yet they are seen as a group apart with its own set of racial characters. Folk beliefs about the Burakumin attribute their origin to either an aboriginal Japanese population or to such foreign areas and peoples as Korea and Philippine pygmies. The Burakumin are segregated and live in small groups on the outskirts of towns.

A whole series of dubious physical and behavioral characteristics are attributed to the Burakumin. The Burakumin are supposed to have a reddish tinge in eye color, to have more prominent cheek bones than Japanese, to have a non-Mongolian eye, to be excessively short, and to have short necks. They are also said to eat meat, which proper Japanese are supposed to despise. The popularity of steak houses in Japan since the end of the Second World War will probably put an end to this notion.

In folk tales the Burakumin are described as dirty and diseased and able to walk barefoot through dirt without having it adhere to their feet. In addition, as is so common with racial prejudice, they are thought to have abnormal sexual and excretory organs. Some Japanese also believe that the Burakumin have one rib missing.

The Burakumin have been thoroughly studied by Western physical anthropologists. In addition to being measured for external phenotypic characteristics, they have had blood group frequencies and other genetic traits investigated. Although there are some slight differences in gene frequency, as would be expected in any isolate population, the Burakumin cannot be distinguished from other Japanese by physical features alone.

THE URBAN SCENE AND URBAN ANTHROPOLOGY

Much of the world's population is crowded into urban centers. Urbanization is occurring everywhere at increasing rates. Because anthropology has tended to focus on small-scale, traditional societies, the discipline has generally ignored the urban scene. Recently this attitude has changed and many cultural anthropologists now specialize in the subfield of **urban anthropology.** This is not yet a unified field. Some urban anthropologists are concerned with the development of urban centers in different parts of the world at different times in history. These individuals join with archeologists in studying the dynamics of urbanization. Other urban anthropologists are interested in urban dwellers as subgroups of a wider national culture. Already they have corrected the notion fostered by many sociologists that such aspects of social structure as kinship play no role in the dynamics of urban society. Comparative studies in urban anthropology demonstrate that generalities about urban social organization are premature and dangerous. In Africa, for example, wide kinship networks continue to shape patterns of social interaction within cities.

In the United States cities provide a vast laboratory for the study of social class and ethnic diversity in the context of a centralized industrial system.

As you will see below, some of the early urban studies were naive. The concept of culture was applied to urban subgroups as if they were traditional isolate societies separate from their national setting. Clearly, urban dwellers are not typical anthropological populations, and they must be studied and analyzed with new techniques, according to theories that put them into their appropriate context.

The Culture of Poverty

In the 1950s some anthropologists turned toward the study of the urban poor, most of them focusing on the United States and Latin America. Cities in the United States, particularly on the East Coast, which were the traditional starting place for immigrants from abroad and from American rural regions, provided a rich ground for research. In Latin America urban centers have been the targets of internal migrations from poor rural areas. Indian and mestizo peasants, with a cultural background often different from that of city dwellers, occupy the slums and squatter settlements of many Latin American cities. They form the bulk of the urban poor in Latin America.

The best known of the early students of urban poverty is the anthropologist Oscar Lewis, who published a series of books in the 1950s and '60s. These were based on taped interviews with a small number of informants in only a few families. Lewis realized that this method violated the rules of statistical sampling. He felt, however, that what was lost in representativeness could be gained from an in-depth analysis of the life histories of real people. In fact, Lewis produced a body of unique documents that were deeply moving. Instead of the cold statistics and abstract view of human life found in so many sociological and anthropological studies, Lewis presented his readers with real people caught in the web of poverty. Lewis's original study focused on the Mexican family. This was later followed by an investigation of family life in the Puerto Rican slums and New York City.

It was from this work that Lewis developed the concept of "the culture of poverty." His idea is that poor people (reacting to their social position) develop a set of unique cultural characteristics that become *self-perpetuating.* If so,

Slums are common in the urban areas of the world. (Left) Rich and poor live side by side in Caracas, Venezuela. (Right) New York City has many poor neighborhoods.

then the poor become the victims not only of economics but of their own culture. Lewis himself described the culture of poverty as an adaptation and reaction of the poor to their marginal position in capitalistic society. Lewis characterizes the poor as follows: They are fearful of society at large; they are hostile to political authority and hate the police; most are not members of an organized church and rarely participate in elections; they lack coherent social organization. The poor live in the present. They take gratification when they can. Thus, saving for the future is unlikely, as is placing a value on education as a way out of poverty. These negative values operate against the adoption of behaviors that might allow individuals to escape from a slum existence.

Critique of the Culture of Poverty

Some of the characteristics attributed to the poor are by no means exclusive to the lower class. Hostility to political authority is a characteristic the poor share with many members of the middle class. Their fear of the police is often justified, since they are the frequent victims of police brutality. Blacks in the urban ghetto, for instance, are more likely to be shot at if they are seen running near the scene of a crime than whites are. While middle-class people can usually expect to receive bail and fair trials, the poor are often incarcerated for months before their cases come before judges. Then they are often represented by incompetent lawyers and face stiffer sentences than members of the middle class. At the very least, there is a severe discrepancy between punishment for crimes committed by middle-class and lower-class Americans.

It is true that the poor live on the economic margins of society because they are unable to share in some of the economic benefits that are common in the middle class. It is also true, almost by definition, that many poor people cannot save money, but this is the result of their economic position rather than their culture. Nor are they able to participate in the "credit-card society," since access to this means of living above one's head is the exclusive privilege of the affluent. There is an old joke about an American millionaire who came to the United States from Europe to make his fortune. "When I came here I was a failure," he was reported to have said; "I only had a dime. Now I am a success because I am ten million dollars in debt." There is more truth than meets the eye in this story. People who owe small amounts of money in the United States are often hounded by collection agencies. Large borrowers, however, are often treated kindly by banks that are nervous about the recovery of their large investment.

Living in the *present* is frequently the only possibility for those who cannot accumulate a nest egg for the future. Nonetheless, there is evidence that the poor do plan and carry out concerted action that is future-oriented. Anthony Leeds has studied several squatter settlements in Latin America. These consist in most cases of illegally constructed houses. The rule in many countries in Latin America is that if a person can put a roof on a structure during the night without attracting the attention of the police, the authorities have no right to evict the tenant or remove the house. To build such a dwelling in so short a time, an individual must secretly accumulate building materials, muster a work force, and build with great haste. All of this takes forethought and organization. Leeds also found that, as these settlements develop, a social structure evolves in them that is both unique and complicated. Because these communities lie outside the usual pattern of legal authority, their structure is often invisible to the middle class, including middle-class social scientists!

The poor have many ways of dealing with society at large. These vary with circumstance and cultural background. My own first research consisted of an extended study of a black urban church. Although the members of this church were mostly urban poor, they exhibited few of the qualities outlined by Lewis as characterizing the culture of poverty. When this church is viewed in the context of society at large, its development can be seen as an organized if unconscious adaptive reaction to tough social conditions.

The United House of Prayer for All People

Store-front Pentecostal churches dot the urban black ghetto. The sects are usually limited to the small number of followers of a particular minister who has founded his or her own variation on a general theme. The theme is drawn from a fundamentalist interpretation of the New Testament and the conviction that the last days, "the final judgment," are upon us. In many cases the leaders of these sects present themselves as prophets as well as ministers. Sometimes, they claim to have supernatural powers.

The United House of Prayer for All People of the Church on the Rock of the Apostolic Faith (the complete name of the sect under discussion) was founded in 1921 by C. E. (Sweet Daddy) Grace, a Portuguese-black immigrant from the Cape Verde Islands off the coast of West Africa. Grace settled in New Bedford, Massachusetts, a city with a large Portuguese immigrant population. Many in New Bedford were from Cape Verde and the local population was mixed. His first church (House of Prayer) was constructed in Wareham, a suburb of New Bedford. People (particularly blacks, but some whites) were attracted to the sect by the story that Grace had raised his sister from the dead.

Growth in New England was slow and Grace moved to the South, where he rapidly developed a substantial following. As his reputation as a miracle worker and curer grew, the sect spread northward. This growth was also facilitated by the great lower-class black migrations to the urban centers of the Northeast that were taking place at the same time. In New York City Grace opened a church in Brooklyn in 1930 and one in Manhattan in 1938. The first church in New England during this period was built in 1956. After that congregations were established in Stamford, Hartford, and Bridgeport (all in Connecticut), all cities with substantial black populations. Sometime during this period Grace also established himself in Detroit, but the sect had little success in Chicago. A Los Angeles branch was also founded, but the majority of Grace's followers came from the South and Northeast.

"Sweet Daddy Grace." Charles E. Grascas photographed with members of the Grace Army in 1934.

During the Depression and the Second World War the Church grew into a large organization. At one point Grace claimed over one million members, but several thousand is a more likely guess. Compared to other storefront churches, however, Grace was certainly successful. In most cases congregations were able to construct distinctive church buildings, and businesses associated with the sect grew into rather large enterprises.

The theology of the United House of Prayer is similar to that of other Pentecostal churches that emphasize doom and salvation. Salvation in this instance, however, can only come to the faithful through the intercession of the prophet Daddy Grace, who is accepted by the faithful as the spirit of Jesus incarnate. The Church grants the unique gift of salvation to those members who live according to prescribed doctrine, which includes rules against smoking, drinking, dancing, and adultery. Salvation is manifested through the Holy Ghost, which enters the body of the faithful during church services. To receive the Holy Ghost is the major goal of all church members. This great event takes the form of a trance state, during which a member loses control over the body, dances for God, and speaks in "foreign" tongues. Speaking in tongues, which is mentioned in the Old Testament, is an expression of ecstatic religious fervor. Possession of this type, which is common in Christian and many other sects, gives objective proof to the members that they are on a righteous path and reinforces the sacred beliefs associated with the sect.

According to Church doctrine, Daddy Grace was God's last prophet, sent by the Almighty from the Holy Land to the United States. Just as the spirit of God entered into the mortal body of Jesus Christ, it entered into the mortal body of Daddy Grace. Grace thus carried God's message in the final days of Earth. He claimed, indeed, that when he died the world would come to an end. His funeral in New Bedford, which I attended, was, as you might imagine, an emotionally charged affair, heightened by the fact that Grace gave his own funeral oration on a tape he had recorded some months before. The doomsday aspect of Grace's prophesy faded away a few months after his death in 1969, and the new bishop who originally intended, or so he claimed, to be nothing more than a secular leader, eventually took over Grace's claim to supernatural powers. He soon began to call himself Daddy Grace, adding his own last name.

The Church is planted firmly on the rock of Christianity. The prophet replaces neither God nor Jesus. The leader is, however, the equal of Jesus, his modern counterpart. He is the purveyor of God's word, and exercises some of God's power, particularly the ability to cure disease. The faithful regard Daddy Grace as healer, savior, and teacher. The common hymns of the black revivalistic church such as "Calling Jesus" and "Jesus on the Mainline, Ask Him What You Want" are changed to "Calling Daddy" and "Daddy's on the Mainline, Ask Him What You Want."

Although the Church does not limit itself to blacks (it is after all the United House of Prayer for All People), Grace's success was primarily among blacks and he himself was highly conscious of this fact. A light "black" with a prominent, narrow nose, he passed himself off as a "white man come to lead the colored people." This aspect of church doctrine was to fade along with a certain white paternalism that existed even in the civil rights movement. Daddy Grace's "whiteness" was exploited by himself and his ministers, who constantly reminded the faithful that it was Daddy as a white man and not the American government who raised them from their inferior social position. Members were fond of a hymn with the words "Lincoln talked about it but Daddy made it true." Grace also said that he had put Franklin D. Roosevelt in the White House and had also been responsible for his removal. The death of FDR in office was taken as a validation of the latter claim. It was even mentioned in sermons as one of Grace's miracles. Several unsuccessful court cases against Grace and the Church, primarily for nonpayment of taxes, were taken by members as victories over Southern whites by a black organization. The fact that the Church's tax-free status was protected by the Constitution was rarely mentioned.

During my study in the early 1960s the Church took no direct political stands, although its attitude toward FDR shows that he was a popular figure—as he was among many blacks. While politics was avoided, patriotic symbols were incorporated into the religious symbolism of the Church. And although the membership was effectively cut off from the wider community of blacks by their identification with the Church and its intense activity, they saw themselves linked to the outside world through the white man, Grace himself. All the church buildings, constructed by independent congregations, are painted red, white, and blue, giving them an American as well as Christian symbolism. Within the context of the church, blacks are equal to whites. Members are insulated, at least during services, from the pains of prejudice and are accepted by Grace, the benevolent white man. Since the faithful spend up to seven nights a week in church, they pour out their hopes in a constant environment of brotherhood and sisterhood. Outside they are subject to ridicule because of their membership in a "strange" sect, but this is taken as a test of faith and does not weaken the righteous, who return with renewed vigor to the bosom of safety for the gift of salvation.

The name "Sweet Daddy Grace" is a happy composite of three key symbols. The word "grace" is constantly manipulated. Bible passages mentioning a state of grace are taken as indications of the church's unique position among the many revivalistic sects found in the black ghetto. Members are constantly reminded that, in order to be saved, it is necessary to attain a state of grace. Those who are saved are therefore saved through grace (and by Grace).

"Daddy" was the father symbol, and even after his death members continue to act out their parts as his children. When alive, he chided them as children and constantly reminded them of their dependence on him. There was no questioning of the father, and no accounting of his activities, from the financial to the sexual, was permitted.

"Sweet" has a special meaning in the language of black culture. Not only does it reflect the benign nature of the leader, but it has sexual connotations as well. This does not mean that the sect lacks a moral doctrine. As we have already seen, members must live "clean" to remain in a state of grace and rigid rules are layed down by the doctrine of the church.

Sect doctrine is bolstered by a series of key slogans that help to validate the organization and its practices. God is said to have created the earth and man the world. This dichotomy of earth and world is equated with good and evil; the idea is extended so that the United House of Prayer is said to be the only church of God on *earth.* All other churches are "churches of the world," that is, created by humans. They are logically worldly and therefore inherently evil. They preach false doctrine and tempt the weak in spirit. They exist to trap the weak in spirit and lead them away from "Grace."

Members of the Church are enjoined to "go higher" to seek the spirit that dwells in the "House of the Lord." This spirit is the Holy Ghost, who enters into the bodies of those who live clean. But "going higher" is also equated with money collection, so that when members are told to "press on" or to "seek the heights," they receive a double image of holiness and a large bank account for the church. Every year a national convention and baptism is held; during that period the church that has collected the most money for the national organization is feted by the Bishop. Because baptism occurs along with the grand collection of the year, a major sacrament of the church is linked to financial affairs.

The dollar bill is overtly used as a key symbol of the Church. When Daddy Grace visited the local churches, he was presented with elaborate symbolic gifts, usually covered with money. This practice has continued with the new Bishop. At various times these are enormous crosses, keys to the city, hearts, and floral wreaths. The money lends a certain substance to these gifts. During services, attended by the Bishop, members show their loyalty to him by running up to his "throne," at the front of the altar, and pressing dollar bills into his hand. A special part of major services involves what is called "program." At this time individual members and groups entertain the congregation by singing and reciting prayers. During programs the Bishop beckons from his seat for dollar bills, which he then presents to the performers. Although a good deal of the money collected in church finds its way into the leader's pocket, much of it is returned to the membership in the form of food, clothing, and subsidized rent.

In many ways Daddy Grace was the "big man" involved in a redistributive network. The poor membership could do nothing with their individual meager funds, but invested in a block by Grace they could be used for the benefit of everyone. Even Grace's personal possessions added to the glory of every individual member. Included in Grace's personal property, in addition to several "castles," was the "Eldorado," known at one time as New York's tallest apartment building. A banner proclaiming this fact once hung in every church.

The major theme of the United House of Prayer is *joy in the House of the Lord.* Members come to services to dance for God and for Grace, to sing the jazz spirituals that are the root of black music, and to shout during sermons. Visitors are always greeted after services with "Did you enjoy?" The emotions of the faithful, restricted by poverty and sect regulations, are poured out to the tunes of good bands and tambourines. The words of the Bible come to life when the congregation does indeed make a joyful noise unto the Lord, and for a time hell's fires are dampened by the stream of "God's Truth." At the front of the church stands the "Holy Mountain", a raised platform occupied by an overstuffed easy chair. This chair is reserved for the Bishop during his visits. On either side of the Bishop are seated teenage "mountain girls," who fan him during the service. The theatrical aspect of the service is increased many fold by the presence of the leader. The church is always filled to overflowing. Visitors come from neighboring branches and each congregation attempts to outdo the other with the pageantry of welcome and the elaborateness of its program. Trance periods are longer and more people "get the Holy Ghost." Daddy Grace's gift of language is reflected in his followers who speak in tongues, uttering incantations to God in "all the languages of the world." Visiting preachers vie for the spotlight with fluid extemporaneous sermons, which are greeted with shouts of approval and encouragement to continue. The subject of the sermon is less important than the preacher's ability to ad-lib, and the sense of his words is often lost in a flood of shouting. Content gives way to emotion as the congregation "goes higher." The cathartic, or "cleansing," effect of these services is infectious and spectators often join in the fun. Even skeptics are caught up in the rhythm as they sit or stand in the pews and rock to the beat of the band.

Members of the Church differ little from one another in background and income. Within the church they share membership in an institution that many outsiders consider strange. Thus, they are drawn together by internal and external factors. As an institution the United House of Prayer also provides the membership with a number of social and political positions that are denied them in the society at large. Almost everyone in the church can become either an officer or a member of a special subgroup. Officers are tied tightly into a chain of command, while members of special groups add to the pageantry of church events. The latter positions are powerless but highly visible, since special uniforms mark every one of them.

The various church positions and their accompanying uniforms provide members with a chance to stand out proudly within the church. Participation at church pageants is a happy affair, and much energy and time go into their preparation. In addition to the usual Christian holidays, which are all celebrated in the church, there are many special events that keep the membership busy throughout the year. The most important of these is the annual convocation. June 26th is Grace's Day, celebrated as a grand birthday.

Members of the United House of Prayer are almost exclusively poor urban blacks. Many of them are recent immigrants from the South and few have an education beyond elementary school. Many are on welfare. The members' energy is literally poured into church activities. Outside activity is restricted by the rules against drinking and dancing, while the church itself is seen as a place for both sacred activity and pleasure. The biblical dictum "Make a joyful noise unto the Lord" is taken seriously and nightly services are punctuated by shouting and the popular music of black culture. If members "live clean," that is, follow church rules, they have few, if any, social contacts beyond the Church. This isolation is increased by their low status within the local community. Their church is considered an oddity.

Although poor, members of the United House of Prayer manage to donate a good deal of money to the church. The overt equation of money with power was used by Daddy Grace to show the faithful, as well as outsiders, that the United House of Prayer was no ordinary sect. Grace himself lived in great luxury. Wherever there was a church there was also a "castle," ready to be used exclusively by Grace and his retinue. In most cases these were large Victorian mansions in the fashion of European castles.

During the Depression the United House of Prayer provided one effective way of keeping money within a segment of the black community. That is, many members lived in Grace apartments, ate in Grace cafeterias, and bought Grace products. That faith can have such an economic side effect has been demonstrated more recently with the success of the Black Muslims.

The Grace Church was very much a Depression phenomenon. It, and churches like it, had a great attraction for the less-educated, poor, recent immigrants to the North. Brought up in the tradition of fundamentalism, they were ready in the urban environment to find spiritual, social, and even economic comfort in the bosom of the church. Father Divine and Prophet Jones, other famous sect leaders in the thirties and forties, followed a pattern similar to that of Grace. As the black community became more militant and as blacks became more aware of their potential role in the community, power at large, in both religious and secular forms, began to replace the more passive message preached in the United House of Prayer. Pentecostalism has not died out—far from it—but many sect members have changed their view of society to demand more than salvation in the next life. In addition, there has been a tendency among socially mobile blacks to join more established churches that display patterns close to those of churches frequented by the white middle class. Those sects that were successful have tended to become closer to the mainstream of American religious life. Even the Black Muslims, who began as a movement quite distinct from Islam as practiced in Arab and other Moslem countries, have recently moved toward orthodox Islamic belief and practice.

An examination of the development, growth, and relative decline of the United House of Prayer shows us one way that the poor organize themselves within their own communities and also in the face of the wider society. The United House of Prayer provided satisfaction to its members, not only because it promised them salvation (other churches made the same promises), but because it objectively improved their economic status within the community. Members' lives were enriched by the alternate social structure provided by the Church, as well as by the material benefits that accrued to them. The decline in social pathology (alcoholism, drug addiction, and crime) among the faithful was a further benefit that resulted from the solidarity provided by the formation of a real community of the faithful.

The analysis shows that the poor—and probably any subculture embedded in a larger cultural system—can only be fully understood in the context of wider social relationships. It also shows that although material forces played a major role in the development and orientation of the Church, the evolving system was shaped not only by its social environment, but also by its own cultural elements. The United House of Prayer was not just an adaptation of the poor to American society in some abstract sense. Instead the Church developed out of historical and cultural roots that existed as part of rural black subculture. The United House of Prayer was more successful than other Pentecostal churches because it responded adaptively to objective conditions, but it could not have been invented out of nothing, even by one so clever as Daddy Grace.

This study demonstrates that the anthropology of complex societies must maintain a continuity with anthropological theory in general. The culture concept placed in a proper context has not lost its usefulness for an understanding of the modern world.

The real lesson of the culture-of-poverty studies is that anthropologists are not uncontaminated by the orientation of their own culture. Middle-class anthropologists fell readily into the trap of accepting a narrow view of middle-class American culture as some sort of standard for the whole of American society. Working from this viewpoint, it was not difficult to label *economically* deprived poor children as *culturally* deprived or to label what culture they had as somehow pathological. With this preconception, they then began to search for the roots of social disorganization.

The theory behind the culture-of-poverty concept is that poverty itself can be explained, at least partially, by the culture of its bearers, which is self-perpetuating and self-defeating. The poor, particularly the ethnic poor, as well as other subgroups in American society *do* have their own cultures, which are a blend of American culture at large and specific differences (like the one's seen among the members of the House of Prayer). These real cultural differences, however, cannot be used to explain poverty. Poverty can only be understood in terms of economic relationships among groups within a society.

The Moynihan Report

In the 1960s Daniel Patrick Moynihan, a sociologist, advisor to President Nixon, and subsequently senator from the state of New York, issued a report on the black family in America. Moynihan thought he had found the reason for social problems in the black community and, in a fashion similar to Lewis, located it in black culture. Borrowing a page from a famous black sociologist and historian, Franklin Frazer, who wrote in the early part of the twentieth century, Moynihan reasoned that the shattering effects of slavery, particularly its destruction of family units among blacks, provided the root cause of maladaptive family structure in the modern black community. According to this theory, the corrosive effects of brutal slavery had so weakened black social structure and African culture that it had never recovered. Blacks in America passed into freedom permanently handicapped by the effects of the slave system. One of the major outcomes of slave trading was the destruction of the nuclear family. Wives and husbands were separated by traders and as a result a new family form, the *matrifocal family*, emerged. This is an incomplete economic unit composed of a mother and her offspring. Because no permanent unions could develop under this system, women had a series of consorts who fathered their children. This structure led to the development of strong women but weak men who participated little in family life and who contributed little or nothing to the economic well-being of women and children.

Recently a few historians have attempted to show that slavery was not as brutal an experience for blacks as was once thought. They argue that most plantations were run as efficient business organizations and, as such, were not likely to mistreat slaves. Thus, most slaveholders, acting out of their own self-interest rather than a high moral sense, were not overly cruel, and, in many cases, provided adequate living conditions. In addition, it is claimed that they did not interfere with many aspects of the slaves' social organization. This theory suggests that a relatively happy slave was a better worker than a mistreated slave.

Massive new evidence and a series of systematic critiques, however, have reaffirmed the notion that slavery was indeed a harsh and degrading experience that imposed great suffering on black Africans brought unwillingly to the New World. But these new analyses have also brought to light evidence that blacks never submitted to the system. Once freed, blacks all over the South were able to organize rapidly for self-help and education. In spite of severe privation, black culture and social organization did survive the slave experience, although they were changed by it. One of the best documented and most interesting accounts of this survival is a book by the historian Herbert Gutman. Disturbed by Moynihan's explanation of the matrifocal family, Gutman dove into historical records running from the slave period all the way to modern times. He examined data from both slave and free communities of blacks in the North and South. He found that in spite of consistent destructive attempts (intentional and unintentional), nuclear family units among American blacks persisted. The breakdown found in some urban black communities comes very late in history. Gutman sees it as the outcome of the most severe depression in American history, that of the 1930s, and the effect of particular welfare laws. These make a father's absencc more valuable for a poor family than his presence. According to this view, the matrifocal family, which is the late result of specific economic and legal conditions imposed from the outside, is an economic adaptation rather than a sign of social pathology in black culture.

Events in the city of New York in the 1970s have shown that the fate of even so great an urban center is determined both within and beyond its borders. The city, composed of several subcultures and classes, is itself only part of a larger national system. The high cost of social services in New York can be attributed to the heavy migrations to the city from poor rural areas, particularly from the South and from the island of Puerto Rico. A city that, to an unusual extent, cared about its poor and had a long tradition of mobility from the poverty of the slums into the middle class was forced to its knees financially by the lack of equal treatment provided to citizens in other states and the refusal of the national government to take responsibility for them.

POVERTY ON A WORLD SCALE: IS LESS MORE?

Among the major world problems that anthropologists may be called on to deal with are two issues that obviously go hand in hand, conservation and population. The ecology movement, which began as a social protest primarily from a marginal group on the political left, has grown into a national concern with pollution and the conservation of resources. On one side, the President of the United States has called for a vast program of energy conservation in the context of continued economic growth. On the other side, many have called for a decrease in production and a rethinking of national and international goals in order to reduce consumption, recycle materials, and control population. A famous report published by the Club of Rome, *Limits to Growth,* suggested that the world is in for serious problems in the near future if industrial production is not slowed and population growth stopped. Since then, the notion that "less is more" has been widely disseminated, particularly in middle-class white America. The reaction of the Third World and other poor countries has been mixed. The Club of Rome report, in particular, has been criticized in this country by many authorities on ecology. They point out that the affluent nations continue (in spite of minor conservation practices) to consume well over their proportion of resources and energy in the world population at large. At the same time, there are still a vast number of underprivileged people in the world who suffer from a lack of basic life-sustaining materials. Substandard housing, clothing, and nutrition are more the rule than the exception in the world. A sudden reduction in productivity, on a world scale, would condemn the Third World to perpetual poverty.

Some reply to this argument that poverty is not the fault of the rich and that rich nations should not be pulled down to the level of the poor. To do so would not, they say, appreciably affect the world standard of living. This reasoning is often bolstered by the claim that poverty is the result of poor planning, poor management, and rapidly increasing population. The latter is taken to be the result of benefits derived from Western science that lowered the death rate, combined with an unwillingness to curtail births. This aspect of the problem can be summed up by the proverb, "the rich get richer and the poor get children."

As I pointed out earlier, the poor may *need* children. Where capital investment is lacking, labor intensification (working harder) is the only way to increase production. Under colonial domination, when the "mother" country drained its colonies of natural resources and taxed its subjects, the only way for the latter to meet increasing demands was to intensify labor. There are limits to how hard a single individual can work. Yet there are tasks that must be done at certain peak periods of the agricultural cycle by a large number of hands. The solution is to increase the number of laborers by having many children. In cases of this sort, it is likely that it was Western greed rather than Western science that contributed to rising populations in the Third World. It is a well-known fact of demography that urbanization and industrialization lead to a decrease in birth rates. The same people who in the country produced large families begin to produce small numbers of children under these economic conditions. As I have noted above, a partial explanation of this phenomenon comes from a cost-benefit analysis of having children. Where labor is in great demand and children can perform economically useful tasks, the benefit of having children is high; if the local system is stressed by economic demands from some outside center, then population tends to rise. Conversely, where capital investment is high and the demand for labor lower, and where children are relatively expensive to have and maintain, population tends to stabilize or drop. Labor-intensive Java, with its rapidly rising population, can be compared with capital-intensive Japan, with its stable population.

These facts suggest that population is the cart put before the horse of social and economic conditions. If so, the growing conviction in rich nations that *less is more* makes no sense in the poor nations. For the poor, *less is simply less.*

The United States with only 200 million people, consumes more resources than India with 800 million. If consumption is put on a per capita basis, each American uses far more of the world's resources than each Indian. The cold statistics are that, with six percent of the world's population, the United States consumes 40 percent of the world's resources. Conservation, fairer distribution, and slower growth in the richer nations would appear to be at least one partial solution to the problems of the Third World. But rich countries also have their poor. Any decrease in production at the present state of development and income distribution would lead to an immediate negative effect on the poorest sectors of our own socio-economic system. From the point of view of a world economic system, many scholars feel that planned growth must continue, but with redirected goals and more equitable distribution. This is precisely what the various organizations of poor nations are calling for in their demands that a greater percentage of the world's wealth be shared with them.

Whatever the cause of population growth and increasing consumption, it is clear that a contradiction exists between growth and environmental health. It is ecologically impossible to continue for very long along the path of environmental destruction that we have been following. Sooner or later the world community, an interdependent human population that shares a global ecosystem, is going to have to decide on a set of priorities that will meet these complex problems. There are no easy solutions. There is a web of cause and effect in any one nation and among nations that makes the notion of isolated cultures totally obsolete. Pollu-

Margaret Mead, who died in 1978, was an advocate for many causes, among them anti-hunger campaigns and the Equal Rights Amendment. She combined an academic with an activist approach to anthropology.

tion, overpopulation, the distribution and use of natural resources, and the relation between rich and poor constitute *a* global problem.

Anthropologists can make a contribution to the future health of the world system by continuing to study local cultural variation because real adaptation can only occur when local conditions are considered thoroughly. On the other hand, anthropologists must study their populations, whether they be urban cultures, rural peasants, or the remaining preliterate cultures in relation to the world economy of which they are only a part. The future of each culture depends on how it fits into the total system and what share it gets of world resources. In the best of all possible worlds local cultures will continue to exist and thrive under a situation in which people have a free and informed choice over which changes to adopt and which to reject. Under these conditions cultural diversity will, no doubt, persist as one feature of the human condition.

Summary

The majority of people living in the world today are either small-scale agriculturalists or urban dwellers. While the traditional societies studied by anthropologists in the past are disappearing, the new nations in which they live are becoming more and more vocal on the international scene. Major world problems today revolve around development and underdevelopment, the dislocations caused by rapid change, an unequal distribution of the world's resources. Modern anthropology must take these problems into account as it attempts to remain relevant in the face of modern human history.

This chapter has dealt with peasants, rural poor, and urban populations. It has examined them in relation to social and economic inequality and the continuing problem of racism. It has raised problems of major concern for anthropology and has attempted to show how anthropology can meet the challenge of the modern world.

Peasants are rural cultivators whose surpluses are transferred to a dominant group that uses the surpluses both to underwrite its own standard of living and to distribute to groups in society that do not farm. Peasants have often been described as backward and conservative, yet the major revolutions of the twentieth century with the exception of the Russian Revolution have been successfully carried out by peasant populations. When examined in historical perspective, as well as by contemporary anthropological field work, peasants turn out to be conservative, when they are, because of the social situation in which they find themselves. Peasant economy in general is labor-intensive. Landlords and other possible investors in the agricultural sector of societies with peasants as the major producers of surplus hesitate to make capital investments or lend money. The peasants' conservatism is due to a need to stick to well-tried methods in the face of possible disaster as the result of failed experimentation. When given the opportunity, they respond well to land reform, as has been demonstrated in Tepoztlan, a Mexican peasant village studied by Robert Redfield in 1940 and again by Oscar Lewis in 1947. Nonetheless, landownership is not enough to free peasants from economic dependence. Even when they own land, they are generally unable to control or influence such crucial economic factors as supply and demand. In many cases they live in the most backward parts of their countries and have little access to modern conveniences ranging from uncontaminated water and basic medical services to consumer products that reduce individual drudgery.

Although much of the poverty in the ex-colonies has been attributed to excess population, it is probable that population increase in these countries is the result and not the cause of such poverty. The only way the rural poor can keep their families alive is to increase the labor force. In such areas the cost of having and keeping children is low compared to the value of their labor.

Programs designed to aid the world's poor have often failed. In many cases the aid destined for the poor never reaches them. Corruption is a direct cause of the maintenance of the *status quo,* but there are other reasons as well. In many cases the local situation is poorly understood by government agencies and even planners. Change is often imposed on people from the outside without their consent and without adequate explanation. Anthropologists have documented many cases of this type and have aided in designing projects that avoid these pitfalls.

Economic exploitation is often justified on the basis of race or sex. Yet racism and sexism are often analyzed apart from the economic system of which they are a part. The anthropologist Marvin Harris has explained different attitudes toward race in North and South America on the basis of different labor needs in the two regions. A rigid, caste-like system based on color developed in North America, according to Harris, because slaves came in great numbers rather late and could be controlled and used by a rather large and established white population. In Latin America, particularly Brazil, there was a severe labor shortage and few white colonists. A class of mixed race was needed to control the large slave-labor force. The free "half-castes" occupied necessary roles that placed them between the slaves and the white masters.

It cannot be denied that cultural factors also play a role in defining and reinforcing racist attitudes. In Japan long-held notions about the colors white and black and the belief on the part of the Japanese themselves that they were white led to the development of self-hatred among many Japanese when they saw themselves in comparison to lighter Europeans.

A major trend in the modern world is the movement of rural populations into urban centers. Recently some anthropologists have turned their attention to these movements and to the urban populations themselves. In general their focus has been on the urban poor. In the 1950s the concept of the culture of poverty was developed by Oscar Lewis based on his work with urban Mexicans and, later, Puerto Ricans. Lewis suggested that poverty tends to create a self-perpetuating and maladaptive system of values. Critics of the culture-of-poverty concept claim that many of the characteristics attributed to the poor by Lewis either do not exist among them or are common to them and the middle class as well. In addition, while few anthropologists would deny that both ethnic and class subgroups in society have their own subcultures, this fact does not mean that these subcultures are responsible for their poverty or its perpetuation. An examination of the members of the United House of Prayer shows that, although they do share many ideas and behaviors that mark them off as a subculture, they do not display many of the characteristics described by Lewis. In addition, an analysis of the dynamics of the church shows that it is an adaptation to poverty rather than a sustainer of it.

Sooner or later the world community is going to have to decide on a set of priorities that will meet the complex problems caused by overuse of resources by the rich nations, overpopulation, global pollution, and the relations between rich and poor nations. Anthropologists can make a contribution to the future health of the world system by continuing to study local cultural variation, because problems will have to be solved in relation to local conditions. On the other hand, these populations must be studied in relation to the world economy and ecology as well, since each population is only a small part of a global system. The future of each culture depends on how it fits into the total system and what share it will get of world resources.

Bibliography

Frank, A. G. 1969 — *Capitalism and Underdevelopment in Latin America: Historical Studies of Chile and Brazil.* New York: Modern Reader Paperbacks. The historical development of underdevelopment analyzed by a radical economist.

Friedl, J. and N. J. Chrisman, editors 1975 — *City Ways: A Selective Reader in Urban Anthropology.* New York: Crowell. Urban anthropology from various perspectives.

Gutman, H. 1976 — *The Black Family in Slavery and Freedom, 1750–1925.* New York: Pantheon. Masterful documentation of the strength of the black family up to the Great Depression. Refutation of the Moynihan report.

Harris, M. 1964 — *Patterns of Race in the Americas.* New York: Walker. Social, historical, and ecological analysis of different racial relations in North and South America.

Leacock, E. B., editor 1971 — *The Culture of Poverty: A Critique.* New York: Simon and Schuster. Critical articles on the culture-of-poverty concept.

Lewis, O. 1960 — *Tepoztlan: Village in Mexico.* New York: Holt, Rinehart, and Winston. Excellent small study extracted from a larger work on culture and history of a Mexican peasant village.

Lewis, O. 1959 — *Five Families.* New York: Basic Books. Study of five Mexican families based on taped interviews. Beginning of the culture-of-poverty concept.

Piven, F. F. and R. A. Cloward 1971 — *Regulating the Poor: The Functions of Public Welfare.* New York: Random House. The effect of the economic forces in society at large as they touch upon the poor.

Moynihan, D. P. 1965 — *The Negro Family: The Case for National Action.* Washington, D.C.: United States Government Printing Office. The matrifocal family explained as part of black culture of poverty.

Valentine, C. 1968 — *Culture and Poverty.* Chicago: University of Chicago Press. Critique of the culture-of-poverty concept.

Wagatsuma, H. 1967 — The Social Perception of Skin Color in Japan. *Daedalus* 96:407–43. Discussion of race and color, particularly Japanese attitudes toward black and white.

Wolf, E. R. 1966 — *Peasants.* Englewood Cliffs, New Jersey: Prentice-Hall. Short introduction to peasant societies and culture.

Wolf, E. R. 1969 — *Peasant Wars of the 20th Century.* New York: Harper & Row. Twentieth-century revolutions in agrarian societies analyzed by an anthropologist of complex and peasant societies.

CHAPTER 27
THE NATURE OF HUMAN NATURE

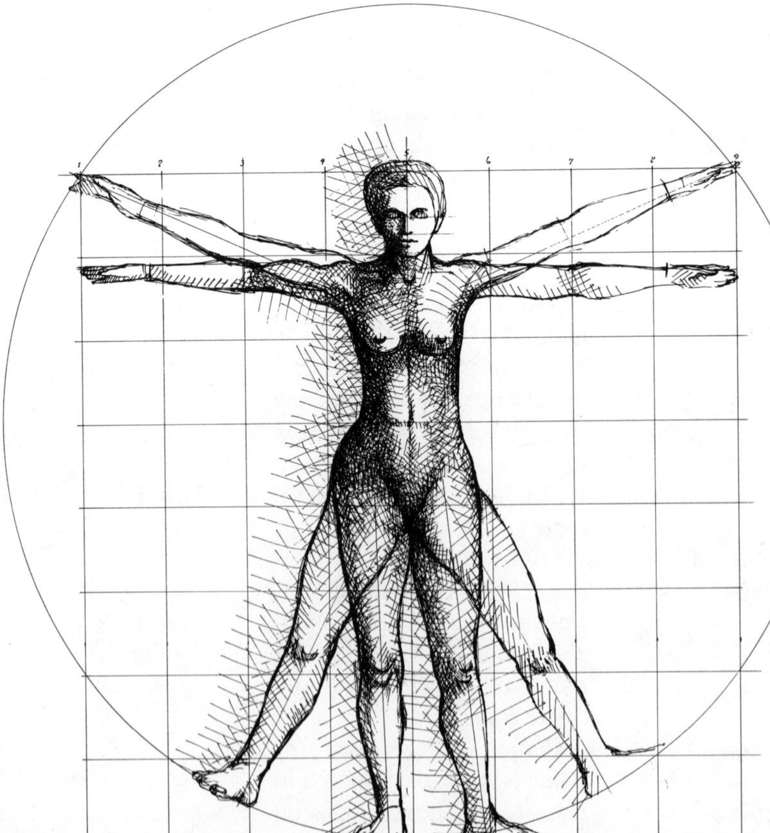

The Ik
The Death Camps
What Is Human Nature?

All organisms are the product of their genes and their environment. Human beings are no exception. The difference between ourselves and other animals is our species-specific adaptation, *culture.* As we have seen, culture is rooted in our biological past. All humans share a basic physical structure and all have highly developed brains that allow us to learn and store a tremendous amount of information. The human brain is the tool with which we are able to learn and use language and culture. If there is such a thing as "basic human nature" it lies in this capacity for culture. Anthropologists and biologists argue over how specific this capacity is. Some believe that, now evolved, culture and language are completely open systems and vary at random. Others believe that patterns of thought are severely restricted by the brain so that all languages and all cultures develop from a common base located in the central nervous system. It is probable that the most interesting theoretical and empirical work in anthropology, linguistics, and human biology in the next decade will touch on this problem.

Current discussions about human nature also often address the question of whether humans are innately "good" or innately "bad." This is really not a biological question. It has its roots in literature and speculative philosophy. During the eighteenth-century Enlightenment philosophers argued about "original" human nature. Some assumed that humans are innately bad, but that the restraints of culture permitted social life. If humans were taken out of society and freed of rules, they would immediately revert to savagery. Other philosophers saw the true human in the image of the "noble savage." War, greed, and other types of behavioral "illness" were seen as the result of the social process. Society and culture were responsible for all that was evil in human behavior.

This argument has not ended. Many ethologists, particularly those who write popular books (among them Desmond Morris and Konrad Lorenz), believe that aggressive and territorial tendencies rooted in biology are responsible for major social problems. For them humans are basically dangerous animals. According to these authors, if we are to survive we must find ways of taming our innate biological tendencies.

On the other side of the issue are many cultural anthropologists and physical anthropologists who believe that culture is the great liberator, that with the emergence of culture, humans have been freed from the bondage of basic instincts. Culture alone, they hold, is responsible for both the good *and* the bad in human social life. Some push the argument one step further by arguing that human beings are basically moral and that morality itself has its roots in the cultural process. For them, human nature *is* cultural nature. Therefore, it makes no sense to speak of biologically determined human nature, since stripped of society and culture the human is stripped of humanity as well.

Finally, there are those in both camps who believe that humans are neither good *nor* bad. The human response to environmental and social problems depends on specific conditions. Culture plays a major role in these adaptations, but the full role of biology in behavior remains to be discovered. We can study the biological aspect of human behavior without assuming that values themselves are derived from human biology. We might very well discover that, in certain circumstances, humans behave in ways that are abhorrent to our own particular value system. To call this behavior a return to "basic human nature," however, is to put the question aside. An examination of the circumstances may well show us why a certain kind of behavior occurs. In order to do this, wc must be sure not to operate with prior assumptions about the species as a whole. As we shall see in this chapter, the lumping of different historical and cultural events only leads to misunderstanding.

In this chapter I have chosen to examine a study of survival in the Nazi concentration camps and an ethnography by Colin Turnbull of the Ik, a mountain group of hunters and gatherers who live in Uganda. In the specific cases to be dealt with here, I shall look at the human response to extreme deprivation and immediate threats to survival. I have picked these examples because biological determinists are fond of telling us that such conditions lead to the expression of the basic and unchangeable side of human nature. The authors of the two studies both argue that the will to survive (which is, I agree, strong in humans) is sufficient to explain the events and outcomes described. Yet, as we shall see, the end results in each group were in fact quite different. In both instances, also, counterarguments to the authors' conclusions can be found in their own material. A comparison of the two will show how different cultural circumstances led to different results in the struggle for self-preservation.

THE IK

We have met the author of the Ik study before. He is Colin Turnbull, who wrote so sensitively about the Mbuti. While in the Ituri Forest, Turnbull developed a strong identification with the Mbuti and their society. His field work in Uganda, with a far more aggressive and difficult people, left him disturbed and shattered by the cruelty he observed. The Mbuti live in relative abundance and in a relatively undisturbed environment. The Ik live under constant deprivation and the erosion of their native culture. Turnbull came to the conclusion that the Ik, in their present circumstances, represent true human nature—humans stripped of culture. Thus, in *The Mountain People* he writes:

The Ik appear to have disposed of virtually all the qualities that we normally consider are just those qualities that differentiate us from other primates; and yet they survive without seeming, if we are honest, to be greatly different from ourselves in terms of behavior.

The much-vaunted gap between man and the so-called "lesser" animals suddenly shrinks to nothingness, except in this case most "lesser" animals come off rather well by comparison, displaying many more of those "human" qualities than the Ik did.

What are the Ik like? Ik culture was originally based on nomadic hunting and gathering. Before they were settled in the mountains by the Ugandan government they lived much the same way as the Mbuti. Cooperation and sharing were necessary for survival. Social harmony was a major feature of standard behavior. Living in small mobile bands the Ik had no real chiefs and no rigid political hierarchy.

With the establishment of a game park in their territory, the Ik were forced into permanent agricultural settlements. The Ik's way of life was suddenly destroyed. Their new economic situation was aggravated by poor climatic and soil conditions. Although they were apparently willing to try agriculture, frequent droughts brought crop failure and severe famines. The Ik, even in rare times when food was plentiful, lived in the constant shadow of hunger. In order to survive, they were forced to turn to illegal means. Agricultural production was soon supplemented by poaching and by exploiting the hostile competition between two nomadic cattle peoples. The Ik supplied both groups with arms, spied for each, and, whenever possible, set one group against the other.

The bulk of Turnbull's work was carried out during a major drought. He found the Ik to be sneaky, uncaring, and devious in their relations with others, including members of their own families. Turnbull was particularly struck by the callous manner in which children and old people were treated. At the age of three, children were literally thrown out on their own. Ik parents were delighted when their children hurt themselves. When a young child plunged its hand into a fire, a group of adult men found this highly amusing. According to Turnbull, the mother in this instance was pleased that her child could bring such pleasure to adults. Children themselves were fond of teasing the sick or mentally retarded (one can find instances of this in any schoolyard in our own culture), whether these were young or old. The aged were not frequently left to die but were pushed toward death by cruelty, neglect, and malicious treatment. The death of an individual was often hidden from Turnbull so that relatives could benefit from food given by him for a sick or starving member of the family. What little cooperation Turnbull saw among the Ik occurred among young adults in the prime of life and health. Even then little love was lost between individuals. Although he notes a few exceptions, his account of Ik cruelty is illustrated by a long series of anecdotes, all of which contribute to a picture of what, in our culture, would have to be referred to as "inhumanity."

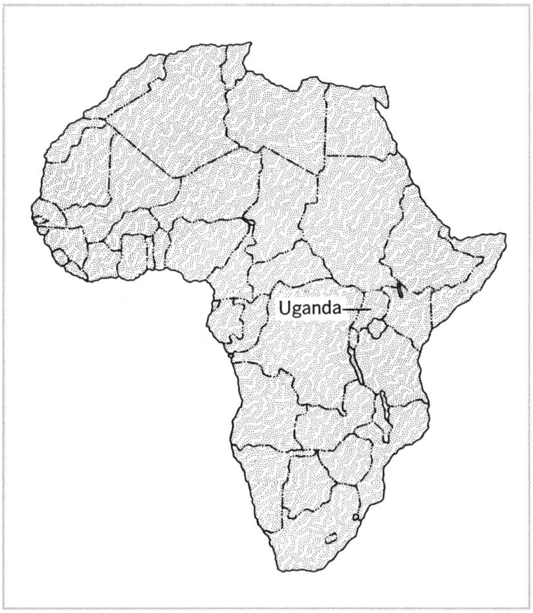

Figure 27.1
Location of the Ik.

Living along the migratory routes of two cattle peoples—the Turkana and the Dodo—the Ik consistently encouraged raiding between these groups. This conflict provided a fertile ground for arms running, an Ik specialty. Ik women sold themselves as prostitutes to both Turkana and Dodo men and were encouraged to do so by their fathers and husbands. Ik men spied on both the Turkana and Dodo, relaying information to rivals. In short, they took what they could from each other and from outsiders, including local police, other ethnic groups, and the anthropologist who lived in their midst.

THE DEATH CAMPS

Terrence Des Pres, the author of *The Survivors,* paints quite a different picture of survival strategies under conditions at least as debilitating as those facing the Ik. Concentration camp victims were systematically deprived of every sort of human dignity. They were fed a minimum of food, lacking in necessary nutrients ranging from vitamins and minerals to simple calories, so hunger was a constant feature of camp life. Cleanliness was impossible to achieve. The lack of hygienic facilities, coupled with poor diets and heavy work loads, led to many epidemics in the camps. Even privacy was systematically denied camp inmates. Those who did not die from frontal attacks on their health and personalities were in constant danger of being chosen, often at random, to be gassed. Yet, although death rates were high, certain individuals survived. In Des Pres's book it becomes clear that it was the maintenance of human feelings and a strong sense of cultural identity that allowed people to survive under hellish conditions. Why were they so different from the Ik?

The will to survive the camps was described by many victims as a will to bear witness. They lived in order to tell their story to others so that the holocaust could never recur. Des Pres quotes many survivors who eloquently described this need to tell their story.

In setting down this personal record, I have tried to carry out the mandate given to me by the many fellow internees at Auschwitz who perished so horribly. This is my memorial to them. (Olga Lengyel in Five Chimneys)

There were things I had to do, words I had to speak, moments which I had to dissect in order to show the world what I had seen and lived through, on behalf of the millions who had seen it also—but could no longer speak. Of the dead, burnt bodies, I would be the voice. (Eugene Heimler in Night of the Mist)

Des Pres points out that statements like these not only show the need to speak out but also the compassion and loyalty of victims to their fellow victims. Many of these people had a strong sense of identity with the group.

Survivors, faced with the constant threat of disease, were forced to live in their own and others' filth. This was not the result of accidental neglect on the part of camp directors but rather part of an overall plan to humiliate prisoners.

At the outset the living places, the ditches, the mud, the piles of excrement behind the blocks, had appalled me with their horrible filth. . . . And then I saw the light! I saw that it was not a question of disorder or lack of organization but that, on the contrary, a very thoroughly considered conscious idea was in the back of the camp's existence. They had condemned us to die in our own filth, to drown in mud, in our own excrement. They wished to debase us, to destroy our human dignity, to efface every vestige of humanity, to return us to the level of wild animals, to fill us with horror and contempt toward ourselves and our fellows.

With this insight either came an abandonment of hope or a renewed will to survive:

But from the instant when I grasped the motivating principle . . . it was as if I had been awakened from a dream . . . I felt under orders to live . . . and if I did die in Auschwitz, it would be as a human being, I would hold on to my dignity. I was not going to become the contemptible, disgusting brute my enemy wished me to be. . . . And a terrible struggle began which went on day and night. (Pelagia Lewinska, Twenty Months in Auschwitz)

Although conditions in the camps can be partially ascribed to hatred and contempt toward the prisoners, there was also a functional psychological reason for them. The debasement of concentration camp prisoners allowed those who ran the camps to think of their victims as subhuman. Once this psychological distance was achieved, it was easier to participate in extermination programs.

Prisoners were able to predict with a high degree of accuracy who would survive and who would not. Of course, survival depended partially on the age and physical state of the individual prisoner, but there were other factors as well. Those who lost the will to survive died. Those who abandoned social ties were seen as living dead by their fellow prisoners. Although there were instances of cruelty among prisoners and survival sometimes came at the expense of others, for many the maintenance of social bonds was crucial. Rather than abandoning everyone for the sake of one's own life, prisoners organized camp undergrounds that saved lives.

Ghetto and camp regulations were designed to make life impossible. Survival, therefore, depended on an "underworld" of activities, all of them illegal, all of them risky, but all essential to life.
In the language of a political prisoner, the word "organize" means to acquire a thing you need without wronging another prisoner. For instance: to take a shirt from a warehouse full of underwear left to rot and be gnawed by rats because a German Kapo would rather see it destroyed than give it to prisoners, is to organize. But to take someone else's shirt, which she washed and put on the grass to dry, is not to organize—that is stealing. When a prisoner gives other prisoners a few loaves of bread, filched from the supply room—this is organization. But when the block supervisor takes loaves from the rations of other prisoners and hands them out to privileged prisoners, for some underhanded additional services—this is theft. (Seweryna Szmaglewska, Smoke Over Berkenau)

Survivors, particularly those who had had political experience before they were sent to the camps, realized that the key to life was organization.

Unlimited egoism and a consuming desire to save their own lives, at the expense of their fellows, were common phenomena among prisoners who were politically backward, for such people were quite incapable of realizing that in this way they merely strengthened the hand of the SS against the prisoners. . . . Our experience of other concentration camps (prior to Auschwitz) had taught us the vital need to live collectively. Political consciousness and contact with others in the struggle against Nazism were necessary conditions of success; it was this that gave people a sense of purpose in life behind barbed wire and enabled them to hold out. (Ota Kraus and Erich Kulka, The Death Factory: Document on Auschwitz)

Des Pres sums up this aspect of camp survival by criticizing the claim that there was no moral or social order in the camps. He goes so far as to note that the "state of nature" did not exist. The maintenance of culture was more than a mere set of cooperative networks in which individuals worked together for individual survival. A vivid demonstration was the rich cultural life maintained in the camps until the very end of the war. Musical and theatrical performances continued in secret in the camps under the noses of the guards. These performances required organization and involved both professional and amateur actors and musicians. Plays ranged from serious drama to comedies, from music hall to Shakespeare. In many cases features of concentration camp life were parodied and anti-Nazi themes were common. These plays provided occasions for both self-expression and group activity. They were treasured by inmates as a vital aspect of their survival.

Although he makes an excellent case for the role of culture in survivorship, at the end of his book, Des Pres takes a surprising biological tack.

Behavior which proves successful, for any particular species over the long run, *enters its genotype and becomes "innate." To be sure, this happens by chance, with many failures, and through unimaginably long ages of time. From phylum to phylum, furthermore, the elements of such patterns differ greatly, but each will possess some fixed response to danger, some settled way of meeting major needs, including those of defense and repair. Survival in this case depends on a basic fund of "biological wisdom," to use C. H. Waddington's phrase, with which all living creatures are endowed. Stripped of everything but life, what can the survivor fall back upon except some biologically determined "talent" long suppressed by cultural deformation, a bit of knowledge embedded in the body's cells. The key to survival behavior may thus lie in the priority of biological being—which is to say that the properties of life itself may best account for the rather surprising fact that under dehumanizing pressure, men and women tend to preserve themselves in ways recognizably human.*

WHAT IS HUMAN NATURE?

How ironic that both Turnbull and Des Pres end their works on a biological note, as if they have explained survival on the basis of some simple genetic mechanisms. Turnbull sees a return to "basic animal nature" while Des Pres suggests that humaneness is in some biological way a characteristic of our species. Survival demands an awakening of humaneness and allows individuals and groups, under stress, to react in adaptive ways.

Certainly the will to survive has its roots in biology. Suicides are rare, even in those cultures where it is an acceptable form of behavior, yet even this "biological" will can be overcome. This is amply demonstrated by cases of mass suicides under very special historical conditions. When they realized that they could not fend off the Roman armies, the Jews of Masada apparently killed themselves. When it became apparent to Balinese princes that they would be defeated by the militarily superior Dutch armies, they marched directly into the Dutch guns. Hundreds of Japanese soldiers in Saipan at the end of World War Two killed themselves by jumping off a cliff rather than surrender. The Jonestown massacre in which over 800 followers of the cult leader Jim Jones killed themselves is a particularly poignant example of mass suicide from the recent past. Evidently the people of the Jonestown commune were convinced by their leader that their community was about to be destroyed by outside forces. In what sense were all these individuals acting out their wills to survive?

But even if we were to accept the will-to-survive notion at face value, what could it tell us about human nature? How can it help us understand different human responses to extreme privation? Why did the Ik turn *against* one another? Why did a large number of concentration camp victims turn *toward* one another in the struggle for survival? Were the Ik less human than the Nazi victims? Turnbull notes carefully that in former times the Ik shared the same human traits we find in other cultures.

The explanation for these differences can only be found in particular cultural and historical circumstances. The Ik could only survive by turning outward and exploiting a situation existing beyond the boundaries of their own group. Stealing from one another and individual acts of cruelty were actually minor factors in Ik survival. The major strategy involved playing the Turkana and the Dodo against each other. When they could, the Ik exploited any outsiders for their food resources. Concentration camp survivors could not turn outward to any great degree. When they could, they tricked and exploited their captors, but they could only do so successfully with a carefully organized internal effort. The Turkana and Dodo were not intent on exterminating the Ik. The Nazis *were* intent on exterminating their prisoners.

It is always easier to exploit and cheat outsiders than members of one's own group. Identification with the group (which no doubt has roots in biology—we are a social species) inhibits in-group cruelty. When the out-group can be defined as somehow not human, it becomes easier to treat them with a totally different set of standards. This is precisely why the Nazis dehumanized their victims. It allowed them to exterminate without guilt. The Ik not only exploited outsiders, but they also made themselves essential for the survival of both Turkana and Dodo. They cheated and were nasty but they were necessary. Exploitation of the Turkana and Dodo was primarily an individual effort. Since they were able to use an external situation, primarily as individuals, the social glue that bound Ik to Ik disintegrated. Nastiness to one another became a way of life for many but not all Ik. Reading *The Mountain People* one does find instances of both compassion and cooperation.

Inside versus outside social relations are not the only difference between these two cases, however. Although in its original state Ik culture no doubt contained an oral tradition and philosophy, they had no traditions stressing that suffering was a part of life. The daily existence of hunters and gatherers, under normal environmental and social conditions, is relatively easy. Famine is rare and cooperation among individuals the mode. Thus, there was probably nothing in the past experiences and traditions of the Ik that prepared them for suffering and deprivation. Under normal conditions the Ik lived out their lives in harmony with nature and with infrequent contact with other ethnic groups.

Most of the concentration camp victims were Jews, who had a folklore of suffering. Strong internal community feelings were always part of their traditional resistance to deprivation and discrimination. Happiness was seen as tentative and a brief aspect of life. Harmonious social existence depended on community awareness of the potential dangers from outsiders. Jewish political and social history was formed in the experiences with alien and frequently hostile groups, among whom Jews have lived for centuries.

These two cases have one thing in common. They demonstrate that under stress humans will attempt to survive. How they will survive, however, depends on conditions, including traditions and past experiences. What results can only be explained as a cultural response. Culture as a human trait (as the human adaptation) is rooted in biology, but it is not based on a set of automatic genetic responses. The genius of culture is its openness. Genes that affect behavior more or less directly tend to produce stereotypic automatic responses. The situations in which humans find themselves are highly variable. Under these conditions automatic mechanisms (excepting perhaps the will to survive, which is too general to explain actual process) would be maladaptive so often that they would be selected against. The human condition has led to an open adaptive system based on culture. Culture may have its own set of biological restraints. Mental patterns may be partially shaped by genes, but these can only set the outer limit on the range of possible human behavior. Actual behavior, in specific conditions, can never be understood without an understanding of the cultural and historical process that shapes it. The nature of human nature is essentially cultural.

Bibliography

Des Pres, T. 1976 — *The Survivors: An Anatomy of Life in the Death Camps.* New York: Oxford University Press. The culture of the death camps explained with a sociobiological tack.

Turnbull, C. 1974 — *The Mountain People.* New York: Touchstone. The Ik of Uganda viewed as a case of culture in conditions of extreme deprivation.

GLOSSARY

absolute dating those archeological dating techniques which can assign a specific age in years to an **artifact.** See **relative dating.**

acculturation process whereby the people of one culture take on the characteristics of another culture. This occurs most often in situations of contact between two cultures of very different levels of technological achievement.

acephalous societies "headless" societies; those without centralized political authority, governed instead by consensus.

adaptation process of modification whereby organisms come to fit environmental conditions.

adaptive polymorphism phenomenon in which two **alleles** of a gene both appear with relatively high frequency in a population. This may occur as in the case of **sickle cell anemia** in West Africa, when the **heterozygote** has some advantage over both **homozygote** types.

adenine one of the four bases of the **DNA** molecule.

afferent neural responses which travel from sense organs toward the central nervous system; sensory inputs.

affine relative by marriage; an in-law.

age grade one of a number of sequentially arranged social categories, all of which the members of each **age set** will eventually occupy. Each age grade has different rights and duties.

age set group of individuals, usually males, born within a specified period. An age set will, through time, occupy a number of sequentially organized **age grades.**

aggression unprovoked attack of an organism on another organism of the same species.

agnatic pertaining to kinship traced through male links.

agriculture plant cultivation using plows.

allele alternative form of a **gene.**

all-purpose money type of **money** that can be exchanged for any economic good or service.

allomorphs **phonetically** different versions of the same **morpheme.**

allophones sounds which are pronounced somewhat differently but do not change word meanings because they never occur in the same sound context. Such sounds are considered to be mere variants of a single **phoneme.**

alphabet set of written symbols which stand for the sounds of a language.

altruistic behavior sacrifice on the part of one organism for the good of others.

alveolars linguistic sounds whose production involves touching the bony ridge just behind the upper teeth with the tip of the tongue.

ambilineal descent group see **cognatic descent group.**

ambilocal residence post-marital residence pattern in which the couple may live with either the bride's or the groom's family.

amino acids organic molecules which combine to form proteins.

animatism belief in the existence of impersonal spiritual forces.

animism belief that everything in nature contains conscious spirits.

Anthropoidea **primate** sub-order that includes monkeys, apes and humans.

anthropomorphism attribution of human qualities to non-human entities.

applied anthropology application of anthropological theory, data, and method to the planning and implementation of programs designed to help native populations adapt to a changing world.

arbitrary symbol a sign which bears no inherent similarity to the thing it stands for.

arboreal tree-dwelling.

arboriculture cultivation of tree crops.

archeology the subfield of anthropology concerned with the reconstruction and analysis of past cultures.

archeomagnetism technique for dating **artifacts** that were exposed to fire in their making or use, such as pottery, bricks, or hearths, on the basis of shifts in the earth's magnetic poles. When such objects are heated, the iron particles in them align with the prevailing magnetic field, and a knowledge of the temporal sequence of shifts in this field can allow the dating of these objects.

archeopallium in evolutionary terms, the relatively ancient areas of the cerebral cortex of the brain, including the limbic system, rhinencephalon, etc. In developmental terms, these are the early-maturing areas of the cortex. Distinguished from **neopallium.**

art play with form, the purpose of which is to produce an aesthetically successful object or performance.

artifact entity created or altered by humans.

assemblage the totality of **artifacts** and other remains of an archeological **site.**

association cortex that part of the outer layer of the brain (cerebral cortex) which functions to connect areas of the cerebral cortex specialized to process information from single sensory modes or information about motor (muscular) activity.

Aurignacian Upper **Paleolithic** stone- and bone-tool industry from southwestern France. May be a refinement of **Mausterian.**

Australopithecine member of the genus ***Australopithecus.***

Australopithecus genus of **fossil hominids** of wide African distribution, dating between one and six million years ago. Dentition and posture were humanlike, but cranial features were apelike and brain was quite small.

Australopithecus afarensis small-brained but erect-walking species of *Australopithecus* whose date of over three million years BP and **morphology** suggest it is ancestral to both *A. africanus* and *A. robustus.*

Australopithecus africanus relatively small (possibly 60 lbs.) ***australopithecine*** **species** living in South Africa at least three million years ago until perhaps one million years ago. Characterized by cranial, facial, and dental **morphology** suggesting the possibility of a vegetable diet supplemented by meat. Bipedal.

Australopithecus robustus relatively large (possibly 100 lbs.) **australopithecine species** living in South Africa and possibly East Africa between three and three-quarter million years ago. Characterized by massive cranial and facial features and believed to have been largely or exclusively vegetarian on the basis of dental evidence. **Bipedal.**

avunculocal residence post-marital residence of the couple with or near the groom's mother's brother.

Aztec last native **civilization** of Mesoamerica. It was centered in Tenochtitlan, a massive urban center which is now the site of Mexico City, flourishing from around 1300 AD until contact with Europeans in 1521. The Aztecs are noted for a religious complex based upon large-scale warfare and human sacrifice.

balanced reciprocity type of **reciprocity** in which the exchange is balanced and direct; that is, reciprocity is essentially immediate.

base one of four chemicals—adenine, guanine, cytosine and thymine—found in **DNA** molecules, the sequential arrangement of which provides the basis for **heredity.** (In the **RNA** molecule, thymine is replaced by uracil.)

bifurcate merging system see **Iroquois terminology.**

big man individual in societies of Oceania who acquires prestige and non-coercive authority through elaborate display of generosity made possible by entrepreneurial manipulation of wealth derived from kin.

bilabials linguistic sounds whose production involves the bringing together of both lips.

bilateral in kinship, pertaining to both the maternal and paternal sides of a family.

bilateral symmetry characterized by the same **morphological** features on each of two opposite sides of the body.

biological anthropology see **physical anthropology.**

bipedalism **locomotion** using only the two hindlimbs.

blade tools flake stone tools, bifaced and at least twice as long as they are wide, appearing during the Upper **Paleolithic.**

boreal pertaining to the north.

bottleneck effect chance alterations in a **population's gene** frequencies, resulting from a relatively sudden decrease in population size.

bound morpheme **morpheme** which only occurs attached to other morphemes, such as the plural morpheme or past-tense morpheme in English.

brachiation specialized form of arm-swinging **locomotion** in which the arms are fully extended and the organism describes wide arcs in its motion; characteristic of gibbons.

bride price payment in **money** or goods from the husband and his kin group to the bride's group in exchange for rights over her and/or her offspring.

bride service work required of a groom on behalf of his wife's family before, during, or after the marriage ceremony.

burin chisel-like stone tool appearing during Upper **Paleolithic.** Used for working bone and antler.

C_{14} dating Archeological dating on the basis of the half-life of Carbon 14. This isotope decays into Carbon 12 at a known rate. When an organism dies it ceases to take in "new" C_{14}. Thus the ratio of C_{14} to C_{12} in an organic specimen should be an indication of how long ago the organism died.

calendrical rite type of ritual that occurs in a cyclical pattern, the length of the cycle being anywhere from one day to many years.

Callithricidae more primitive of the two families of New World monkeys.

canines teeth used for grasping and tearing. In humans, they are usually more pointed than **incisors.**

cargo cult native political-religious movement found in colonial contexts in which members advocate the destruction of native goods in the expectation that this will induce **supernatural** powers to overturn colonial authority and provide the native population with the products of Western consumer society.

carrying capacity regarding humans, the maximum number of people a given area could support without undergoing resource diminution.

caste **endogamous,** occupationally-specialized group, membership in which is inherited from one's parents. Such a group is one of many in a hierarchically structured caste system.

catarrhines the Old World monkeys.

Cebidae one of two families of New World monkeys, similar in form to Old World monkeys.

celibacy willful abstinence from sexual intercourse and/or marriage.

channel perceptual mode, such as a visual or auditory, used to receive **messages.**

Chellean-Acheulian late-lower **Paleolithic** toolmaking industry characterized by finely chipped, bifaced **hand axes.**

chiefdom society in which territory and kinship function together as major forms of integration and having a centralized political authority wielding some degree of coercive power.

chimpanzee one of four living genera of apes, they are found in and around the rain forests of central Africa. Chimpanzees are **knuckle-walking** fruit-eaters who live in troops of 40-50 members. These troops are highly variable in terms of sex and age composition as well as day-to-day membership.

Chimu Peruvian **civilization** that dominated the coastal valleys of Peru during the fourteenth and fifteenth centuries.

chinampas artificial islands constructed in Lake Texcoco by Aztec farmers. These consisted of fertilizing plant materials, human wastes, and lake bottom ooze and were utilized in an intensive form of **agriculture.**

chordate possessing a dorsal nerve chord.

chromosome structure in the cell nucleus which contains **DNA** molecules.

circulating connubium form of marital alliance that results from the practice of **generalized exchange.**

circumlocution substitute term used in place of a term the mention of which would be undesirable.

civilization a **state** society characterized by **urbanism** (usually), a complex division of labor, social **stratification,** full-time government officials, extensive trade, a full-time army, a national religion, and a high development of the arts and science.

clan **unilineal descent group** whose members claim to be related to one another by descent from a common ancestor but cannot demonstrate the genealogical links involved. A clan may be subdivided into **lineages.**

class a form of **stratification** in which one group owns the means of production and controls access to it.

climax forest forest community which appears as the final stage of ecological **succession.** Theoretically, the composition of a climax community will remain stable barring human intervention or extraordinary natural events.

cline gradient in the distribution of a **gene** or trait through space among populations of a single species.

Clovis North American Indian culture identified by an arrow type and associated with the hunting of species of horse and mammoth. Dates between 11,000 and 9500 years ago.

coding systematic way in which **information** is translated into ***signals*** for communication.

codominant if, in a **heterozygote,** both of the **alleles** present manifest themselves to some extent, these alleles are said to be codominant to each other. See **dominant.**

cognatic descent group type of descent group in which membership is acquired by descent from the founding ancestor through male and/or female links.

collateral relative relative who is not in ego's direct line of descent; that is, is neither a descendant nor an ancestor of ego.

complex marriage structure marriage system in which one is constrained in choosing a spouse only by *negative* rules; that is, rules specifying the types of kin one cannot marry.

conical clan form of political **ranking** in which relative age combines with descent to determine one's rank. For example, first-born sons of first-born sons are of higher rank than second-born sons of first-born sons since the formere are genealogically closer to the founding ancestor of the clan.

connotation associations that a word or phrase elicits that are not part of its strict, "dictionary" definition. See **denotation.**

consanguineal relative by "blood"; a genetic relative.

consonants linguistic sounds produced in part by obstructing the flow of air either completely or partially.

consumption aspect of **economics** concerning those activities and social relations involved in the utilization of goods and services.

crime wrong that, regardless of the identity of the immediate victim, is taken to be an **offense** against the **state** itself. Distinguished from **tort.**

Cro-Magnon Fossil form of *Homo sapiens.* They are associated with the cave-painting cultures of Spain and France, and lived at the very end of the **Paleolithic.**

cross cousin offspring of ego's mother's brother or of father's sister. Thus, cross-cousins are offspring of siblings of opposite sex. See **parallel cousin.**

crossing over form of **mutation** in which portions of **homologous chromosomes** are exchanged for each other.

crow terminology system of kin-type categories, associated almost exclusively with matrilineal societies, in which members of ego's father's **matrilineage** are distinguished only by sex.

cultigen cultivated plant.

cultural anthropology subfield of anthropology concerned with the traditional behavior of humans in a social context.

cultural ecology school of anthropology, founded by Julian Steward, that is concerned with the effect of different **environments** on the organization of work and of this organization's effect on other aspects of culture.

cultural materialists those anthropologists who consider material variables as opposed to ideological ones to be the real determinants of cultural differences and similarities.

cultural relativism doctrine advocating that the elements of a culture should be judged or analyzed only in terms of *that culture's* values and internal structure rather than in terms of the values of one's own culture or some universal system of values or analysis.

culture the totality of a human society's tradition of thought and its expression in behavior.

cytoplasm area of a cell outside of the cell nucleus.

cytosine one of the four **bases** of the **DNA** molecule.

deep structures innate mental principles, shared by all humans, for organizing sense data and knowledge.

deletion form of **mutation** resulting from the breaking of a **chromosome** and the loss of genetic material.

demography study of the characteristics of populations.

dendrochronology technique for dating certain **artifacts** made from temperate-zone wood or artifacts of other material in the same site. It involves matching the annual growth rings in the wooden artifact with a master sequence which reaches the present and counting back from the present to the outer ring of the specimen, which yields the year at which the tree was cut.

denotation the strict, "dictionary" definition of a word or phrase. See **connotation.**

dental formula description of the kinds and numbers of teeth of an organism. Calculated from the midline toward the back of the jaw, it is written as a ratio of the upper quadrant over the lower.

dependent variables factors which, within a specific **hypothesis,** are viewed as being caused by other factors.

derivational morpheme bound morpheme which changes the part of speech of the word to which it is attached.

diachronic a study which focuses on the changes through time of the object of study is a **diachronic** study. See **synchronic.**

dialect variation of a language spoken by a subgroup of the population sharing the language. Speakers of different dialects of a language understand one another without great difficulty.

diffusion the spread of an idea, style, or practice from one culture to others.

distribution aspect of **economics** concerning those activities and social relations involved in the process of getting goods and services from the source of **production** to the point of **consumption.**

DNA (deoxyribonucleic acid) chemical basis of **heredity.** DNA is a double-stranded molecule composed of chains of sugar-phosphate molecules chains attached to one of four chemicals called **bases.** The two strands of the molecule are wrapped about each other in a corkscrew or helical fashion. It is the sequence of bases in these chains which conveys genetic messages.

dominance formation of precedence hierarchies for feeding, sexual access, etc., among members of a group of social animals.

dominant if, in a **heterozygous genotype,** one **allele** manifests itself in the **phenotype** and the other doesn't, the former allele is said to be dominant to the latter, which is **recessive** to the former. See **codominant.**

double descent system of descent in which every individual is a member of both a patri-group and a matri-group; patri-group membership is inherited from the father and matri-group membership from the mother.

double helix corkscrew arrangement of the two strands of a **DNA** molecule.

dowry goods, or **money** that a wife gives to her husband or his family upon marriage.

drift see **genetic drift.**

Dryopithecus genus of **fossil** apes appearing during the **Miocene.** This group of species includes the ancestors of living apes and probably of *Homo sapiens* also.

duplication form of **mutation** in which a portion of a broken **chromosome** is joined to its **homologue.**

ecological evolutionists anthropologists who view cultures as **populations** and study the intricacies of population-**environment** interactions from a short-term and micro-level perspective or in terms of the long-term evolution of major cultural traditions.

ecology study of the relationships among groups of organisms and their environment. Also, these relationships themselves.

economics aspect of society concerning activities and social relations that involve the **production, distribution,** and **consumption** of goods and services.

efferent neural impulses which travel from the central nervous system toward locomotive or other organs. Behavioral outputs.

ego that component of Freud's model of the personality which mediates between the demands of the **id** and the realities of the social and physical environment.

elementary marriage structure marriage system in which rules specify the precise category of kin from which a spouse must be chosen.

emic aspect of a culture consisting of natives' perceptions, thoughts, and values.

endemic disease disease present, at least at a low level, in a population most or all of the time. See **epidemic disease.**

endocannibalism consumption, usually in a **ritual** context, of the remains of members of one's own social group.

endocast mold taken from the inner surface of a skull.

endogamy rule-governed practice of acquiring a spouse from inside one's defined social group. See **exogamy.**

endoskeleton internal body support system.

energy the capacity to perform work.

environment usually taken to mean the complex of material elements and physical phenomena within which a **population** exists. However, from another perspective, other populations as well as members of one's own population may be considered as part of one's environment.

Eocene geological epoch extending from approximately 58 million to 44 million years ago. During this period there is **fossil** evidence of the radiation (rapid increase in number and type) of **primate** species.

epidemic disease rapidly spreading and disappearing disease which attacks periodically in the same geographic zone. See **endemic disease.**

Eskimo terminology system of kin-type categories in which no **lineal** and **collateral** relatives are referred to by the same term.

ethnocentrism judging another culture by the standards of one's own culture.

ethnographic present common anthropological practice of describing traditional cultures with the present tense as they were before contact.

ethnography description and analysis of particular cultures.

ethnology the derivation of generalizations about human culture on the basis of **ethnography.**

ethnosemanticists who focus on the way different groups perceive and classify their natural **environments.**

ethnosemantics study of the way native **informants** order and categorize various aspects of their universe.

ethology study of the behavior of organisms, especially in terms of ecology and evolution.

etic aspect of a culture consisting of natives' actual, objectively verifiable, behavior.

eugenics measures to "improve" the human **gene pool** by preventing the breeding of bearers of "undesirable" **genes** and/or promoting that of those bearing "desirable" ones.

evolution, theory of includes three principles: 1) there is a natural source of variation among members of a **population,** 2) the **environment** "selects," i.e. favors, some variant forms over others, and 3) successful variants transmit the source of their success to offspring.

exogamy rule-governed practice of acquiring a spouse from outside of one's own defined social group. See **endogamy.**

exoskeleton external body-support system, such as the chitin of insects and crustaceans.

extensive agriculture agriculture characterized by low inputs of labor and materials and relatively large quantities of land, resulting in fairly low yields per unit of land. See **intensive agriculture.**

external adaptation process that occurs as a result of **natural selection.**

F_1 generation in genetics experiments or abstract models of the hereditary process, the first filial generation; that is, the offspring of the **parental generation.**

fallow period in which soil is allowed to replenish itself following the harvesting of a crop.

falsification disproving a **theory** through experiment or observation.

familism primary loyalty of an individual to the nuclear family.

family of orientation family into which one is born (parents, self, and siblings). See **family of procreation.**

family of procreation family that results when an individual marries and has children. See **family of orientation.**

features major characteristics of an archeological **site,** such as houses, graves, and other large structures.

field any setting in which anthropological research is conducted is referred to as **the field.**

fitness measure of **adaptation** in terms of **selective fertility.** It is an intra-specific measure. One form within a species may be said to be more fit than another, if, within a given environment, it typically produces more offspring.

Folsom North American Indian culture identified by fluted arrowheads and associated with bison-hunting, appearing around 10,000 years ago.

foramen magnum opening at the base of the skull where the spinal cord enters the brain.

fossil remains of a plant or animal that have petrified or have left impressions in mineral formations.

founder effect chance **gene** frequency differences between a derivative and original **population** when the former is founded by a small number of individuals.

free morpheme morpheme that can occur by itself, that is, as a whole word.

fricatives linguistic sounds whose production involves a narrowing of the air passage and resulting friction.

functionalism several theoretical approaches to culture which have in common an emphasis on the function that cultural institutions serve either in meeting biopsychological needs of individuals (Malinowski's version) or in insuring the integration and perpetuation of cultures themselves (Radcliffe-Brown's approach).

gamete sperm or egg cell.

gametogenesis formation of **gametes** through **meiosis.**

gene fundamental unit of **heredity.** Genes are segments of **DNA** molecules which carry instructions for the production of single proteins.

gene flow contribution of an organism's **genes** (by way of offspring) to the **gene pool** of a different **population** from the one into which it was born.

gene mutation see **mutation.**

gene pool totality of **genes** of a breeding population.

genealogy set of marriage and "blood" relationships of an individual within a group.

generalized adapted to a variable ecological **niche** or to several niches.

generalized ecological zone ecological zone characterized by a large number of **species,** each of which is relatively low in population.

generalized exchange marital alliance among three or more kin groups in which each group obtains its wives from a certain group and gives its own women to another. Also known as indirect exchange.

generalized reciprocity type of **reciprocity** in which the parties involved give goods and services without concern for balance or promptness of reciprocity.

generate in linguistics, to produce or make possible the production of utterances.

genetic drift chance variation in **gene** frequencies between generations in a **population.**

genotype genetic make-up of an organism, either at a single **locus** or considered in its entirety.

geronticide cultural practice of directly or indirectly killing old people.

ghost supernatural being which is a dead human

"misplaced" in some sense.

gibbon smallest of the four living genera of apes, they are found only in the rain forest of Southeast Asia. They are fruit-eaters who move through their habitual **arboreal** habitat by **brachiating.** Gibbons form solitary life-long pair bonds.

Gigantopithecus very large **fossil** ape dated to the **Miocene** in India and the **Pleistocene** in China.

glottochronology method of estimating the time of historical divergence of related languages based on the assumption that basic vocabulary changes at a regular and measurable rate.

gorilla one of four living genera of apes, the largest **primate.** Found in the rain forests of central Africa, they are ground-dwelling, **knuckle-walking** herbivores who live in nomadic troops of around 15 members.

grammar system of rules for combining the sounds of a language into meaningful utterances.

Gravettian late Upper **Paleolithic** stone-tool industry based in eastern Europe and associated with mammoth-hunting.

Green Revolution widespread attempt to introduce high-yield varieties of rice and wheat into agricultural systems of underdeveloped countries. The effort failed because the new varieties required techniques and materials beyond the means of most **peasants.**

Grimm's law model of certain regular sound correspondences among **Indo-European** languages.

guanine one of the four **bases** of the **DNA** molecule.

hand ax tear-shaped, fist-sized, stone tool with a point and sharp edges.

Hardy-Weinberg law mathematical equation describing the relationship between a population's **genotype** frequencies and its **gene** frequencies. It also demonstrates that, in the absence of conditions promoting evolutionary change, these frequencies will not change from one generation to the next.

Hawaiian terminology system of kin-type categories in which relatives are distinguished only by sex and generation.

hemizygous having only one **gene** at a **locus,** with no **homologous** locus. This is a condition of **sex linkage,** where human males are hemizygous for genes on the X **chromosome** because they have no homologous loci (plural of locus) on the Y chromosome.

heredity component of an organism's structure and function obtained through the process of transmitting genetic information across generations. Also, this process itself.

heritability measure of the genetic component in a variable trait. It tells what percentage of the variation in that trait *within* a population is due to **heredity.**

heterozygous regarding a particular **locus,** having a different **allele** on each of the **homologous chromosomes.**

homeothermy ability to maintain constant body temperature by internal mechanisms, characteristic of birds and mammals. Warm-bloodedness.

hominid of the family Hominidae, including ancient and modern human **species.**

Hominidae family of **primates** consisting of extinct and living **species** of humans.

hominization evolutionary development of humans.

hominoid of the superfamily Hominoidea, including ancient and modern apes and humans.

Hominoidea superfamily of **primates** consisting of extinct and living **species** of apes and humans.

Homo erectus **fossil hominids** of extensive Old World distribution. They were extant between 1.5 and .5 million years ago. Medium brain-sized and with primitive skull features, they stood fully erect and are associated with fire and tool use.

Homo habilis East African **fossil hominid.** A controversial find, it has been classified both as a species of *Australopithecus* and as a species of a competing genus (*Homo*), making it a direct ancestor of modern humans.

Homo sapiens Modern humans and our immediate predecessors from about 300,000 BP to the present, including **Cro-Magnon** and possibly **Neanderthal.**

Homo sapiens sapiens modern human beings; most recent subspecies of *Homo sapiens,* believed to have first appeared sometime between 100,000 and 35,000 years ago.

homologous regarding **genes** or **chromosomes,** matching. Homologous chromosomes, one derived from each parent, carry (homologous) genes controlling the same traits. Homologous chromosomes pair during **meiosis.**

homozygous regarding a particular **locus,** having the same **allele** on both of the **homologous chromosomes.**

horticulture plant cultivation using hoes or digging sticks rather than plows. See **agriculture.**

hydraulic agriculture **intensive agriculture** based

upon construction and maintenance of complex and labor-intensive irrigation systems involving pumping apparatus.

hypergamy marriage to someone of a higher-status social group than one's own.

hypodescent descent rule stating that an offspring of marriage between a member of a socially inferior group and a member of a superior one belongs to the inferior group.

hypothesis a testable conjecture about a class of phenomena designed to support or disprove a **theory,** which is a more general account of the class of phenomena.

iconic symbol a sign which is in some way inherently similar to the thing it stands for.

id that component of Freud's model of the personality which contains instinctual drives. Unlike the other components of the personality, the **ego** and the **superego,** the id is present at birth. It is governed by the **pleasure principle.**

ideographs **pictographs** which represent an idea associated with the object depicted rather than the object itself.

ilium blade of the pelvis.

imprinting combination of innate and learned behavior in certain bird species in which newly hatched birds attach themselves emotionally to the first moving object in their environment.

Inca Peruvian **civilization** of the late fifteenth and early sixteenth centuries. At its apex, the Inca Empire stretched from Ecuador to Chile.

incest taboo cultural prohibition on mating and/or marriage between certain kin.

incisors wedge-shaped front teeth designed in humans for cutting and shearing.

inclusive fitness effect of a **genotype** on the reproductive success (fitness) of its bearer *plus* its indirect effect on the reproductive success of genetic relatives of its bearer.

independent assortment, law of Mendel's observation that some traits appear to be passed on by parents to offspring independently of others. This is now known to occur when these traits are under the control of **genes** on different **chromosomes.**

independent variables factors which, within a specific **hypothesis,** are viewed as causing other factors.

Indo-European major language family including, among others, the Romance, Indo-Iranian, Germanic, and Celtic language groups, and Greek.

inflectional morpheme **bound morpheme** which does not change the part of speech of a word. Examples are the plural morpheme and past tense morpheme in English.

informant in **field** work, an individual who gives the anthropologist information about his or her culture.

information meaning content of a **message.**

innate patterns inborn, automatic behavioral responses that occur under certain environmental conditions.

innate response inborn behavior. Behavior which in the presence of a certain internal state of the organism and the proper **releasing mechanism** appears without modification or variation.

insectivores group of small ground- and tree-dwelling mammals that eat insects.

integration systemic nature of the relationships within and among organisms, **populations,** and communities.

intelligence ability to learn and to understand new or trying situations.

intensive agriculture **agriculture** characterized by high inputs of labor and materials into relatively small quantities of land, resulting in high yields per unit of land. See **extensive agriculture.**

interbreeding see **gene flow.**

internal adaptation maintenance or improvement of a system's integrity.

intonation feature of some languages in which the sequence of **pitches** over whole sentences determines (in part) the meaning of sentences.

inversion form of **mutation** in which the portions of a broken **chromosome** rejoin in an inverted configuration.

Iroquois terminology system of kin-type categories in which parallel relatives are referred to by the same terms as the members of one's immediate family and distinguished from cross relatives.

ischium lower rear area of pelvis.

jargon specialized vocabulary of a professional group.

joint family extended family type consisting of two or more brothers and their families all residing together.

kindred all of the people, on both the maternal and paternal sides, whom an individual regards as relatives.

kinesis elementary behavior in which, in the presence of a noxious stimulus, an organism tends to increase random motion. The farther it happens to remove itself from the stimulus, the more it tends to reduce such motion.

kin selection aiding of genetic kin through **altruistic** acts so that **selection** acts not upon a single organism but upon a group of genetically related organisms.

knuckle-walking form of **quadrupedal locomotion** typical of **gorillas** and **chimpanzees** in which ground contact occurs on the soles of the hindlimbs and the backs of the middle section of the curved fingers.

kula trading network which takes the form of a circle around the participating South Pacific islands, including the Trobriand Islands.

Kuru degenerative brain disease peculiar to highland New Guinea. Because of its unique distribution among only the women and children of a single population—the Fore—it was at first thought to be genetic. Since then it has been discovered to be viral, transmitted through the consumption of incompletely cooked brain material.

labiodentals linguistic sounds whose production involves contact between the upper teeth and lower lip.

labor activity involved in **production.**

laterization transformation of land surface into **laterite,** a hard and infertile crust of iron-bearing soil.

law aspect of **social control** that operates through rules of conduct and their application to behavior.

learning gaining knowledge through experience.

learning theory school of psychology that excludes the importance or existence of innate mental schema and studies the role of stimulus-response dynamics and reinforcement in the acquisition of knowledge.

Levallois Middle **Paleolithic** stone-tool making technique in which a disc-shaped core is first prepared before striking off chips which will be shaped into finished tools.

levirate custom of marriage of a woman to her deceased husband's brother.

lexicostatistics see **glottochronology.**

life-crisis rite type of **ritual** held on the occasion of a major status transition in the life of an individual.

life-history technique research technique in which extensive biographical interviews are conducted with members of the society being studied.

lineage type of **unilineal descent group** whose members consider themselves related to one another because they can all trace descent from a common ancestor through either all-male or all-female links.

lineal relative relative who is a direct descendant or ancestor of ego.

linguistics study of the origin, distribution, and comparative grammar of languages.

locomotion process in which an organism moves itself from place to place.

locus point on a **chromosome** where a single **gene** is located.

Magdalenian Latest **Paleolithic** tool industry. It is associated with stone and bone carvings and the cave murals of southern France and Spain. Dates from around 17,000 to 10,000 years ago.

mana Polynesian concept, a spiritual power residing in certain beings and things.

market exchange in capitalist economies, type of economic exchange in which buyers and sellers try to make a profit from the exchange. Price of goods and services is determined by their supply and the demand for them.

mastoid process projection of the temporal bone, below and behind the ear.

matriarchy political rule by females.

matrifocal family structure in which the permanent residential core consists of a mother and her daughters.

matrilineage corporate kin group whose members are related to one another by descent from a common ancestor through female links.

matrilineality descent through a line of females.

matrilocal residence see **uxorilocal residence.**

Maya civilization of the lowlands of the Yucatan Peninsula that flourished between 200 AD and 900 AD.

meiosis sex-cell division. Pre-gametic cells undergo a first phase comparable to **mitosis,** during which **chromosomes** are duplicated and two daughter cells are produced with normal chromosome number. These cells, however, undergo a second division without chromosome replication and they produce cells with only half of the normal chromosome number—**gametes,** or sperm and egg cells.

menarche occurrence of first menstruation.

meritocracy social structure in which individuals are awarded position in a hierarchy solely on the basis of personal ability.

Mesolithic Middle Stone Age, beginning about 10,000 years ago and ending with the **Neolithic.** It is characterized by the appearance of ground (as opposed to chipped) tools and by **microliths.**

message **information** content of a communication.

messenger RNA chemical that carries a genetic message from the **DNA** to the site of protein synthesis, the **ribosome.**

metabolism process in which an organism converts nutrients into energy used in life-sustaining activities.

metaphor use of an expression for something which it doesn't **denote** in order to suggest a certain similarity between the usual referent and the new one.

microcephalic having an abnormally small skull and brain.

microliths tiny stone chips, used as points, sickle teeth, etc., during the **Mesolithic.**

Miocene geological epoch extending from approximately 25 million to 5 million years ago. During this period, fossils appear which are ancestral to apes and probably to humans as well.

mitosis normal cell division. The essential features of this process are the assortment of **chromosomes** into **homologous** pairs, the replication of these pairs, and the migration of one set of each of the pairs so duplicated to either pole of the cell so that when the cell divides along its equator, each daughter cell contains the species' normal number of chromosomes.

mode of production totality of a society's system of **production** and **distribution** of goods and services, including technology, the organization of work, and the **social relations of production.**

moiety organization division of a society into two social groups, frequently exogamous, membership in which is inherited unilineally.

molars broad-surfaced, 4- or 5-cusp teeth (in humans) used for crushing and grinding.

money any general-purpose medium of exchange.

monocropping cultivation of a single plant species.

monogamy marriage consisting of one husband and one wife.

monotheism belief in a single god.

morpheme smallest unit of language which has meaning. Can be a whole word or part of a word.

morphology study of the physical form of an organism. Also, this form itself.

Mousterian complex technological and artistic culture of the Middle **Paleolithic,** associated with **Neanderthal** fossils.

multilinear evolutionists those anthropologists, especially followers of Julian Steward, who allow for a number of recurrent cultural-evolutionary pathways, each one occurring in one of several major types of **environment.**

mutation change in genetic structure. Mutations may occur at a single point on a **chromosome** or may involve relatively large areas of whole chromosomes.

mutation rate frequency of **mutation** of one form **(allele)** of a **gene** into another. These rates are usually stable for any given gene.

myth religious account of the origins of humans and the **supernatural.**

nasal sound when the production of a linguistic sound involves the expulsion of air out the nose as well as the mouth, it is a nasal sound.

nativism doctrine advocating that a people unite themselves in the face of political and religious domination by colonizers.

natural selection effect of **environment** in favoring one form of a **gene** over another. It may be measured in terms of its effect on the **fitness** or relative reproductive success of different varieties of an organism.

Neanderthal subspecies of *Homo sapiens* inhabiting Europe, Asia, and Africa between about 150,000 and 35,000 years ago.

negative reciprocity type of **reciprocity** in which the parties involved try to come away from an exchange with more than they gave.

neocortex most recently evolved portion of the mammalian brain and the site of information processing and storage.

neofunctionalists group of **human ecologists** who develop explicit models of the way in which cultural institutions function to maintain certain vital relationships between environmental and cultural variables, especially **demographic** ones.

Neolithic New Stone Age. Period beginning 10,000 to 2,000 years ago in various parts of the Old World and noted for the widespread adoption of **agriculture** and the advent of large sedentary populations. Tools were ground and polished as well as chipped.

neolocal residence post-marital residence pattern in which the couple sets up a household removed to some degree from the relatives of both.

neologism newly developed term.

neopallium in evolutionary terms, the relatively modern areas of the cerebral cortex of the brain, including the association areas of the parietal, temporal, and frontal lobes. In developmental terms, these are the late-maturing areas of the cortex. Distinguished from **archeopallium.**

neuroendocrine system the unified behavior-producing and controlling system composed of both the electro-chemical apparatus of the nervous system and the chemical activity of the endocrine (hormonal) system.

niche place occupied by a specific **population** in an ecological system.

nocturnal active at night.

nonrecurrent phenomena phenomena that occur only once.

nuclear family married couple and their children.

null hypothesis in statistical testing of a **hypothesis,** the counter-hypothesis that the relationship among variables argued for in the first hypothesis does not exist.

obsidian hydration dating archeological dating technique for **artifacts** of obsidian based upon the fact that this volcanic material absorbs moisture and lays down a patina at a constant rate. Measuring the patina's thickness will thus yield an indication of when the stone was mined.

Oedipus complex cluster of mainly unconscious ideas and strivings concerning desire for the mother and hostility to the father. According to Freud, normal children of both sexes experience the complex around the age of 4. Its normal resolution involves a renunciation of the mother as an object of sexual desire and identification with the parent of the same sex.

Oldowan East African **pebble-chopper** tradition, dating to around 2.6 million years ago, associated at Olduvai Gorge with *Zinjanthropus* and at East Lake Rudolf and Omo with *Homo habilis.*

Oligocene geological epoch extending from approximately 44 million to 25 million years ago. During this period, **fossils** ancestral to the monkeys appear.

Olmec first Mesoamerican **civilization.** The Olmec inhabited the Gulf Coast of Mexico between 3500 and 2500 BP and are noted for a distinctive style of art.

Omaha terminology system of kin-type categories, associated almost exlusively with patrilineal societies, in which members of ego's mother's **patrilineage** are distinguished only by sex.

omnivorous characterized by a diet consisting of both plant and animal foods.

ontogenetic pertaining to the development of the individual organism as opposed to that of the species.

open-ended interview relatively unstructured and conversational interview.

operationalization in science, the practice of defining a practice, belief, attribute, or material entity in such a way that it can be objectively observed, described, or measured.

opposability ability of many **primates,** especially humans, to rotate the thumb toward the palm of the hand so as to bring the fleshy part of the thumb and fingers into contact. This provides for the ability to precisely manipulate objects.

oral sound when the production of a linguistic sound involves the expulsion of air solely through the mouth rather than mouth *and* nose, it is an oral sound.

orangutan one of four living genera of apes, they are found only in the rain forests of Southeast Asia. Orangutans are tree-dwelling fruit-eaters, and are second in size among the **primates** only to the **gorilla.** They are slow-moving tree climbers, using three or four limbs when moving or stationary. Little is known of their social structure.

oriental despotism notion forwarded by Karl Marx and developed by Karl Wittfogel of the origin and nature of Asian states based on **hydraulic agriculture** with a large bureaucracy and standing army essentially subservient to a monarch.

orthograde posture characterized by a vertically oriented trunk.

ownership social relations concerning rights to use and rights to exchange goods.

Paleocene geological epoch extending from approximately 69 million to 58 million years ago. During this period appear the oldest **fossils** bearing some resemblance to **primates.**

Paleolithic Old Stone Age. Includes period between the first appearance of stone tools **(Oldowan)** up to about 10,000 years ago. It is divided from early to late into Lower, Middle, and Upper stages.

paleontology study of fossils.

palynology technique for determining the climate and floral resources of an archeological **site** on the basis of kinds and frequencies of pollen grains excavated.

parallel cousin offspring of ego's mother's sister or of father's brother. Thus, parallel cousins are offspring of siblings of the same sex. See **cross cousin.**

parental generation in genetics experiments or abstract models of the hereditary process, the first generation of interbreeding organisms.

participant observation method of anthropological research in which the researcher, rather than remaining a detached and isolated observer, integrates himself or herself as a participant into the society being studied in order to better understand it.

patrilineage corporate kin group whose members are related to one another by descent from a common ancestor through male links.

patrilineality descent through a line of males.

patrilocal residence see **virilocal residence.**

peasants rural cultivators whose surpluses are transferred to a dominant group of rulers that uses the surpluses both to underwrite its own standard of living and to distribute the remainder to groups in society that do not farm.

pebble chopper stone tool generally produced from rounded, flat stone, minimally worked at one end. Typical of the **Oldowan** tradition.

pejoration process in which originally positive words or expressions take on a negative or pejorative meaning.

penetrance degree to which a **gene** manifests itself in the **phenotype** as a function of environmental modification of its expression.

percussion flaking technique for stone-tool making involving the striking of a stone with or on another object of stone, bone, or wood. Distinguished from both pressure and grinding techniques.

Perigordian Upper **Paleolithic** stone-tool industry from southwestern France. It may be a refinement of **Mousterian.**

phenotype characteristics of an organism, resulting from the interaction of its genetic make-up **(genotype)** with the **environment** in which it develops.

phone linguistic sound.

phoneme smallest unit of sound which can change the meaning of a word when substituted for another such sound. Phonemes themselves do not have meaning.

phonetics study of speech sounds.

phonology study of the sound system of a language.

phratry loose confederation of clans that recognize kinship ties with one another.

phylogenetic pertaining to the evolutionary history of species of organisms.

physical anthropology the subfield of anthropology concerned with the biological evolution of the human species from its origins to the present our relationship to the other **primate** species, and biological characteristics of present-day human populations. Also known as **biological anthropology.**

pictographs written symbols consisting of drawings of the objects they represent, believed to be the earliest form of writing.

pitch feature of some languages in which vocal chord vibration rate determines (in part) the meaning of a word.

Pithecanthropus erectus Javanese specimen of *Homo erectus.*

platyrrhine the New World monkeys.

pleasure principle behavioral motivation that, according to Freud, governs the **id.** It is the pursuit of pleasure and the avoidance of discomfort.

Pleistocene geological epoch extending from approximately 1.9 million until 10,000 years ago.

polyandry type of **polygamy** (plural marriage) in which a woman has more than one husband.

polygamy marriage in which an individual has two or more spouses of the opposite sex.

polygenetic refers to **phenotypic** traits that are determined by more than one gene acting in concert.

polygyny type of **polygamy** (plural marriage) in which a man has more than one wife.

polyploidy form of **mutation** resulting from a failure of **meiosis.** A **gamete** results with more than the normal complement of **chromosomes.** While polyploidy is typically lethal in animals, it frequently leads to plant forms which, at least from a human point of view, are desirable.

polytheism belief in multiple gods identified with but not identical to natural forms.

population group of organisms of a single **species** occupying a more or less bounded area and interbreeding with one another to the relative exclusion of other groups.

population genetics study of the effect of evolutionary forces on the frequencies of **genes** and **genotypes** in **populations.**

positivism philosophical doctrine contending that experience is the only source of knowledge and that scientists should concern themselves only with empirically testable **hypotheses.**

potassium-argon dating method of archeological dating on the basis of the rate of breakdown of a radioactive isotope of potassium into a stable form of argon. This technique is not applied directly to a **fossil** or **artifact,** but to volcanic rock in which it is embedded.

potlatch redistributive feast sponsored by prestigious individuals among Northwest Coast American Indians, involving distribution and destruction of goods.

preadaptation anatomical, physiological or behavioral **adaptation** to one **niche** which proves to be useful in a niche that is later adopted.

prehensile grasping, as in the flexible **primate** hand.

premolars teeth used for grinding and crushing. In humans, they are intermediate in shape between the **canines** and the **molars,** and have two cusps as compared with the four or five of the molars.

primate mammalian order which includes **prosimians,** monkeys, apes, and humans.

pristine state a **state** which comes into being without the influence of pre-existing state societies. Also referred to as a primary state.

production aspect of **economics** concerning those activities and social relations involved in the creation of goods and services, including work, access to resources, and access to the technological means of performing work.

promiscuous mating mating which is random and lacks permanent pair bonds.

prosimii most primitive **primate** suborder, includes tree shrews, lemurs, lorises, and tarsiers.

psychic unity the modes by which all humans perceive and organize experience.

psychoanalysis school of psychology developed by Sigmund Freud, emphasizing the importance of very early sexual experience and of the **unconscious** in determining thought and behavior.

quadrupedal characterized by **locomotion** on all four limbs.

radial symmetry characterized by **morphological** features radiating from a central point on the body.

ramage type of **cognatic descent group** in which membership is determined by residence as well as descent.

Ramapithecus earliest putative **fossil hominid.** Dating from the middle **Miocene,** it has been found in Africa, Asia, and Europe.

random sample sample in which every item in the group from which the sample will be drawn has the same probability of being included in the sample.

rank system of differential prestige. In social systems based upon ranking, high prestige does not confer coercive authority over lower ranks.

receiver recipient of a communication.

recessive an **allele** that does not manifest itself in a **phenotype** when it is in a **heterozygous genotype** is said to be recessive.

reciprocal altruism hypothetical mechanism for the **selection** of **altruistic** behavior. An organism genetically inclined to aid other organisms at its own expense might at some future time be itself aided by these organisms if they possessed the same genetically based inclination toward altruism. Thus, the genetic basis for altruism would be perpetuated.

reciprocity "horizontal" mode of exchange in which parties of equal status exchange goods or services of roughly equal value without careful accounting of exchange balance.

redistribution "vertical" mode of exchange in which goods flow upward to a political leader and are then redistributed downward to members of the social group at large.

reification in linguistics, the identification of a term as part of or all of the thing to which it refers.

relative dating those archeological dating techniques which can determine that an **artifact** is older or younger than others in the **site** or a different site, but cannot specify precisely how much older or younger. Obviously, such techniques cannot assign specific ages in years to artifacts, as can **absolute dating.**

releasing mechanism environmental factor which stimulates an **innate response.**

religion set of collective **supernatural** beliefs and practices.

research proposal formal and detailed description of a proposed research project submitted to a granting agency as a request for financial support of the research.

restricted exchange marital alliance between two kin groups who exchange their women with each other; modeled on the exchange of sisters between two groups of brothers. Also known as direct exchange.

revitalization movement political-religious movement in which an attempt is made to recapture old cultural values and/or eliminate foreign political domination.

revivalistic movement see **revitalization movement.**

ribosome structure in the cell body the site of the assembling of **amino acids** into proteins.

ritual invariant behavior that is the acting out of religious belief.

riverine pertaining to rivers.

RNA (ribonucleic acid) single-stranded nucleic acid closely related to **DNA.** In the production of proteins, one form of this chemical, messenger RNA, carries "messages" from DNA in the cell nucleus to **ribosomes** in the cell body. Transfer RNA carries **amino acids** to these same sites where they are assembled into protein chains according to the code carried by the messenger RNA.

Rorschach ink-blot test series of abstract designs which are shown to a subject in order to elicit his or her thought associations provoked by them.

sagittal crest ridge of bone, running from front to back down the middle of the skull, which develops in some **primates** in response to the need for attachment area of growing jaw muscles.

sampling practice of choosing and studying a relatively small proportion of the total number of items in a group rather than studying every one of the items in the group.

scheduled interview interview structured by a set of specific questions.

schema see **deep structures.**

secondary sexual characteristics anatomical features exclusive to males or females which are not part of the genital organs.

sedentarism residence in permanently settled communities.

segregation, law of Mendel's observation that some hereditary traits which appear to be lost in the transmission from parents to offspring may reappear in later generations. This is now known to result from **dominance** or **codominance.** If **recessive** or **codominant** forms of a **gene** happen to reassort in later generations into **homozygote genotypes,** then they will manifest themselves again.

selection see **natural selection.**

selective fertility **natural selection** by way of differential reproductive success among members of a **population.** It is considered to be a more important determinant of evolution than is **selective mortality.**

selective mortality **natural selection** by way of differences in the rates at which different lineages of organisms within a **population** survive to reproduce. It is considered to be a less important determinant of evolution than is **selective fertility.**

self-regulation the maintenance of an organism's stability under varying conditions.

semantics study of the relationship between words and meaning.

sender source of a communication.

seriation technique of **relative dating** based upon the notion that new **artifact** styles become popular gradually, remain so for a certain period, and are then gradually replaced by newer forms. A curve relating the relative popularity of a group of artifact styles to time in a given region can be used to estimate the relative age of the artifact **assemblage** in a new **site.**

settlement patterns distribution of human communities relative to one another and to natural features, as well as the internal geographical layout of individual communities.

sex-linkage refers to **genes** that are located on the sex **chromosomes.**

shaman a person in simple societies who is believed to communicate with **supernatural** beings or forces on behalf of individuals in need of the shaman's help.

sickle-cell anemia blood-destroying disease occurring in **homozygotes** for a **gene** that produces abnormal hemoglobin. This causes the victim's red blood cells to assume a crescent shape, which impedes circulation and the cells' ability to transport oxygen. Among Americans, the disease is most common among those of African descent.

signal physical medium, such as sound or light, which carries **information.**

Sinanthropus pekinensis specimen of *Homo erectus* found in China.

site place where the remains of human activity have been discovered.

slang vocabulary of socially marginal groups which differs from that of the general population.

slash-and-burn cultivation form of gardening in which forest growth in a plot is cut down and burned, after which the plot is planted and harvested, and then left to lie **fallow** until the soil is replenished while other plots are planted. Also known as shifting cultivation and swidden cultivation.

social control regulation of behavior within and between social groups.

social Darwinism spurious use of Darwin's theory of **natural selection** to explain the origin of **class** differences in society.

socialization process in which a child learns the rules, values, and worldview of his or her culture.

social relations of production those social relations concerning access to the material wherewithal of **production** and its products.
sociobiology speculative field of biology, akin to **ethology,** that stresses apparent genetic continuity of social behavior from lower to higher organisms while tending to ignore the role of learning and, in terms of humans, the importance of culture in determining social behavior.
Solutrean Upper **Paleolithic,** European stone-tool industry characterized by laurel-leaf-shaped **blade tools** and by use of pressure (as opposed to **percussion**) flaking.
somatology study of size and shape differences in humans.
sororal polygyny marriage of a man to two or more sisters.
sororate custom of marriage of a man to his deceased wife's sister.
specialized adapted to a relatively limited ecological **niche.**
specialized ecological zone ecological zone characterized by a small number of **species,** each of which is abundant in population.
special-purpose money type of **money** that can only be exchanged for certain goods and services.
speciation process whereby **populations** of a single **species** become separate species through reproductive isolation from one another.
species group of organisms that could potentially breed with one another but not with members of similarly constituted groups. Whereas the **populations** which comprise a species are relatively closed to one another in terms of **interbreeding,** species are absolutely isolated from one another.
state epitome of social **stratification** in which coercive authority is vested in a government with powers to tax, raise an army, and enforce **law.**
stelae tall stone-slab monuments bearing inscriptions or designs.
stem family extended-family type consisting of a married couple and one married son and his family, all residing together.
stimulus diffusion invention stimulated by the knowledge that the desired item exists in another culture.
stimulus generalization principle of **learning theory** stating that entities sharing significant attributes will be mentally grouped under the same category.
stratification process whereby differential status **(rank)** becomes transformed into a structure with real political power and differential access to resources. Also, this structure itself.
stratified sample sample structured to include items drawn from every segment of a group which has distinguishable segments or subgroups.
stratigraphy the study of natural geological deposits. Also, these deposits themselves.
structuralism school of anthropology that views the form of certain cultural domains, especially myth, kinship, and classification systems, as determined by universal mental organizing principles. While the specific contents of these domains will vary from one culture to the next, the way in which these contents are symbolically *structured* will, according to structuralists, conform to these universal principles.
succession in **ecology,** the orderly and predictable replacement of one plant community by another under natural conditions.
Sudanese terminology system of kin-type categories in which each type of relative is referred to by a different term.
superego that component of Freud's model of the personality which contains the capacity for self-criticism. It develops when the child incorporates the parental figures into his or her psyche.
supernatural that domain of phenomena which are empirically unknowable and which are believed to exist outside of the visible universe.
supraorbital torus bony ridge above the eyes.
survival of the fittest notion that the strongest or most efficient members of a species will out-compete all others and thus come to constitute the majority. Originally proposed by Herbert Spencer in sociology, it was later appropriated by Darwin in his **theory of evolution.** In contemporary theory, it is replaced by the notion of **selective fertility.**
swidden cultivation see **slash-and-burn cultivation.**
syllabary set of written symbols representing the syllables of a language.
synchronic a time perspective in which the object of study is viewed as it appears at a single point in time. See **diachronic.**
syncretism a union of beliefs and practices of disparate origins.
syntax rules for forming sentences.

taboo prohibition related to religious belief.
TAT (Thematic Apperception Test) series of drawings of personal and social situations which a subject is asked to respond to by writing a story about them.

taxis elementary form of behavior in which an organism will move directly toward or away from some stimulus, as in the positive photo-taxis of certain moths, or the negative geo-taxis of flies.

Teotihuacan first great urban **civilization** in central Mexico. It flourished from about 2200 BP to around 1300 BP and, at its apex, had a population of between 120,000 and 200,000.

territoriality defense of living and/or breeding space by an organism or group of organisms.

tetrad chromosomal unit produced prior to cell division consisting of a **chromosome** and its replica attached to each other.

theory general principle designed to explain and predict a certain class of phenomena.

thymine one of the four **bases** of the **DNA** molecule.

tone feature of some languages in which **pitch** of individual syllables within words determines (in part) the meaning of words.

tort a wrong conceived of legally as an offense against an individual. Distinguished from a **crime.**

totems natural entities, such as plants, animals, and geographic features, used to symbolize social groups.

transfer RNA chemical that "reads" the genetic message carried by **messenger RNA** and brings appropriate **amino acids** to the **ribosome** for protein synthesis.

transhumance seasonal movement of pastoralists and their herds from one ecological zone to another.

translocation form of **mutation** in which a portion of a broken chromosome is joined to another that is not its homologue.

tundra vegetation zone found above the tree line, consisting of lichens, mosses, and some grasses.

Tupaioidea superfamily of tree shrews, classified by some as primitive **prosimians.**

unconscious that part of Freud's model of the mind which contains thoughts and drives of which the individual is unaware but nonetheless influence conscious thought and behavior.

unilateral in kinship, pertaining to only one side, either maternal or paternal, of the family.

unilineal descent group type of descent group in which membership is acquired by descent from the founding ancestor through exclusively male or female links.

unilinear evolutionists those anthropologists of the nineteenth and early twentieth century who conceived of human cultural development as always following a single course from a stage of simple technology and social organization to a final stage of complex technology and social organization.

universal general grammar basic properties shared by all human languages and believed to derive from universal properties of the human brain.

unvoiced sounds linguistic sounds produced without vibrating the vocal chords.

uracil only **base** that differs between **DNA** and **RNA;** in RNA, it replaces **thymine.**

urban anthropology anthropological study of people in cities.

urbanism complex, permanent settlements with a large resident population of non-agriculturalists specialized into crafts, business, administrative, and religious occupations.

uxorilocal residence post-marital residence of the couple with or near the bride's family. Also known as *matrilocality.*

varve analysis archeological dating technique employing the sedimentary layers that form on a lakeshore as the lake freezes and melts seasonally.

velars linguistic sounds whose production involves touching the soft palate (velum) with the back part of the tongue.

vertebrate possessing a dorsal nerve chord encased in an articulated bony column.

virilocal residence post-marital residence of the couple with or near the groom's family. Also known as *patrilocality.*

viviparous bearing live offspring, as opposed to laying eggs.

voiced linguistic sounds produced with the vocal chords vibrating.

vowels linguistic sounds produced in part by maintaining an unobstructed air flow.

wages money that is exchanged for a person's regular services.

war armed **aggression** by one group against another.

PICTURE CREDITS

Cover Photo: Peter B. Kaplan/Photo Researchers
Chapter Opening Illustrations: Mario Stasolla
Endpaper Maps: John V. Morris
Endpaper Photos: Courtesy of the United Nations; Eastfoto and Sovfoto; The American Museum of Natural History; Marjorie Shostak/Anthro-Photo File; The British Tourist Authority; Japan Trade Center; New Line Cinema; Norwegian National Travel Office.

Chapter 1
Page 10: Megan Bieseli/Anthro-Photo File.
Page 11: A. Ekekyan/Novosti from Sovfoto.
Page 12: Photo by Don Hesse/Wycliffe Bible Translators, Inc., Summer Institute of Linguistics.
Page 13: Peter Menzel.

Chapter 2
Page 21: Rare Book Division, The New York Public Library, Astor, Lenox and Tilden Foundations.
Page 23: Left, Brown Brothers; right, Radio Times Hulton Picture Library.
Page 26: United Press International.
Page 27: Top and bottom, Ira Kirschenbaum/Stock, Boston.
Page 30: Top left, Sdeuard C. Bisserot/Bruce Coleman; top center, top right, bottom center and right, U.S. Fish and Wildlife Service; bottom left, Florida State News Bureau.
Page 33: Left and right, Dr. H. B. D. Kettlewell, University of Oxford.
Page 40: Top, Courtesy of Francois Morel, from Morel, Baker, Wayland, *J. Cell Biol.* 48:91, 1971; bottom, from Marcel Bessis *Corpuscles: Atlas of Red Blood Cell Shapes*, Springer-Verlag.

Chapter 3
Page 59: Ross E. Hutchins.
Page 60: Top, David A. Krathwohl/ Stock, Boston; bottom, Franklin Wing/Stock, Boston.
Page 61: Top, Walter Chandoha; bottom, Nina Lean, Life Magazine © Time, Inc.
Page 63: Bottom left, Ellis Herwig/Stock, Boston; top right, Malcolm/Anthro-Photo File.
Page 64: Top left, The American Museum of Natural History; top right, Eric Hosking/Bruce Coleman; bottom left, Pinney/Monkmeyer; bottom right, Sdeuard C. Bisserot/Bruce Coleman.
Page 65: Courtesy E. P. Reese, Department of Psychology, Mount Holyoke College. Photo by Max Kotfila, from E. P. Reese, "The analysis of human operant behavior," Wm. C. Brown, 1966.
Page 66: Top, Irven DeVore/Anthro-Photo File; bottom, Ray Ellis/Rapho-Photo Researchers.

Chapter 4
Page 86: Top, Ira Kirschenbaum/Stock, Boston; bottom, Jen & Des Bartlett/Photo Researchers.
Page 91: A, Alan Walker/Anthro-Photo File; B, WHO; C, Nicolson/Anthro-Photo File; D, Ira Kirschenbaum/Stock, Boston; E and F, Russell A. Mittermeier/Anthro-Photo File.
Page 93: A, Richard Wrangham/Anthro-Photo File; B, George B. Schaller/Bruce Coleman; C, D. J. Chivers/Anthro-Photo File; D, H. Kanus/Rapho-Photo Researchers.
Page 98: Figure 4.11 bottom, Courtesy Professor J. Buettner-Janusch.

Chapter 5
Page 103: A and D, Russ Kinne/Photo Researchers; B, Hrdy/Anthro-Photo File; C, A. W. Ambler-National Audubon Society Collection/Photo Researchers; E, Ira Kirschenbaum/Stock, Boston.
Page 105: Sarah Bloffer-Hrdy/Anthro-Photo File.
Page 108: Top and bottom, Irven DeVore/Anthro-Photo File.
Page 111: Top and bottom, Joseph L. Popp/Anthro-Photo File.
Page 114: Courtesy Masao Kawai, Primate Research Institute, Kyoto University, Japan.
Page 115: Courtesy of Peter Marler.
Page 117: G. B. Schaller/Bruce Coleman.
Page 119: Richard Wrangham/Anthro-Photo File.

Chapter 6
Page 129: Richard Wrangham/Anthro-Photo File.
Page 131: Paul Hosefros/The New York Times.
Page 136: Whitten/Anthro-Photo File.
Page 137: A, B, and D, Courtesy of The American Museum of Natural History; C, Kathy Bendo; E, Peabody Museum, Harvard Univeristy, photograph by Hillel Burger.
Page 139: A, Courtesy of the Transvaal Museum; B, Courtesy of the National Museums of Kenya; C, Photo Camperapix/Rapho-Photo Researchers; D, Kathy Bendo; E, From the Emergence of Man/The Missing Link, published by Time-Life Books, Inc.
Page 140: Cannon/Anthro-Photo File.

Page 141: United Press International.

Page 142: Left, Courtesy of the National Museums of Kenya; right, Kathy Bendo.

Page 144: Top left, Barney Taxel/The New York Times; bottom left, Kathy Bendo; right, The Cleveland Museum of Natural History.

Page 149: A, Musée de l'Homme; B, Peabody Museum, Harvard University, photo by Hillel Burger; C, Kathy Bendo; D, Courtesy of The American Museum of Natural History.

Page 152: Left, Musée de l'Homme; right, Spanish Information and Tourist Office.

Page 153: Top left, The Stuttgart Museum; top right, Musée de l'Homme; bottom, The Trustees of The British Museum (Natural History).

Chapter 7

Page 162: Left and right, Monkmeyer.

Page 167: Alexander Alland, Sr.

Page 168: Left and right, Smithsonian Institution, National Anthropological Archives.

Page 169: Sylvia Johnson/Woodfin Camp.

Page 170: All, Courtesy of the United Nations.

Page 171: Wide World Photos.

Pages 174 and 175: A, B, D, E and H, Courtesy of the United Nations; C, World Health Organization; F, Tass from Sovfoto; G, Food and Agriculture Organization.

Boxed Chapter

Page 182: Courtesy Professor I. Eibl-Eibesfeldt, from *Ethnology: The Biology of Behavior*, Holt Rinehart & Winston, 1970.

Page 185: Left, Cary Wolinsky/Stock, Boston; right, Marc & Evelyne Bernheim/Woodfin Camp.

Page 188: United Press International.

Pages 190 and 191: A, Photo supplied by the author; B, Albright-Knox Art Gallery, Buffalo, New York. Gift of Seymour H. Knox; C, The Museum of Modern Art, New York. Gift of Mr. & Mrs. David M. Solinger; D, Bruckmann-Art Reference Bureau; E, Kathy Bendo.

Page 192: Left and right, © S.P.A.D.E.M., Paris, 1979.

Chapter 8

Page 199: Laboratory of D. Carleton Gajdusek, M.D.

Page 200: World Health Organization

Page 201: Courtesy of Dr. Paul T. Baker, The Pennsylvania State University.

Chapter 9

Page 208: Top, M. E. Mosely/Anthro-Photo File; bottom, Courtesy of Jacques Barrau.

Page 210: Top left, Musée de l'Homme; bottom right, Irven DeVore/Anthro-Photo File.

Page 211: Peter Menzel.

Page 212: Top, The University Museum, Files of The Tikal Project, The University of Pennsylvania; bottom, Scientific American, February, 1979.

Page 213: Left, M. E. Mosely/Anthro-Photo File; right, from "Early Sedentary Economy in the Basin of Mexico," Niederberger, C. *Science*, Vol. 203, pp. 131-142, Fig. 3, 12 January 1979. Copyright 1979 by the American Association for the Advancement of Science.

Page 215: Photo by James O. Sneddon, Courtesy of the Information Services, University of Washington, Seattle.

Page 217: M. E. Mosley/Anthro-Photo File.

Page 219: Courtesy of The American Museum of Natural History.

Page 220: Left, Cliff Garboden/Stock, Boston; center, Joseph Flack Weiler/Stock, Boston; right, Jeff Albertson/Stock, Boston.

Page 221: Joseph Flack Weiler/Stock, Boston.

Chapter 10

Page 228: Left, From The Emergence of Man/The Missing Link, published by Time-Life Books, Inc.; right, Illustrations from PEOPLE OF THE LAKE, by Richard E. Leakey and Roger Lewin. Copyright © 1978 by Richard E. Leakey and Roger Lewin. Used by permission of Doubleday and Company, Inc.

Page 229: (b) Courtesy of The American Museum of Natural History; (c) Peabody Museum, Harvard University, photo by Hillel Burger.

Page 231: Musée de l'Homme.

Page 232: Courtesy of Professor Ralph S. Solecki, Department of Anthropology, Columbia University.

Page 235: A, Courtesy of The American Museum of Natural History; B, C, and D, Musée de l'Homme.

Page 239: Courtesy of The American Museum of Natural History.

Page 243: K. Cannon/Anthro-Photo File.

Page 246: Lars Smith/Anthro-Photo File.

Page 253: Robert S. Peabody Foundation for Archaeology, Andover, Massachusetts.

Page 255: (a) World Health Organization; (b) Food and Agriculture Organization.

Chapter 11

Page 264: Peter Menzel.

Page 271: NASA.

Page 272: UNESCO, Paris, courtesy of the New York Graphic Society.
Page 274: Top, World Health Organization; bottom, Paolo Koch/Photo Researchers.
Page 277: Georg Gerster/Rapho-Photo Researchers.
Page 278: Robert Feldman/Anthro-Photo File.
Page 279: Left, Dumbarton Oaks, Washington, D.C., right, Peter Menzel.
Page 280: Owen Franken/Stock, Boston.
Page 281: Museum of Anthropology, Mexican National Tourist Council.
Page 283: A, Peter Menzel; B, Kathy Bendo; C and D, M. E. Mosley/Anthro-Photo File.

Chapter 12
Page 292: Kathy Bendo.
Page 293: Pamela R. Schuyler/Stock, Boston.
Page 295: Massachusetts Institute of Technology.
Page 300: Bell Laboratories.
Page 306: United Press International.
Page 307: Courtesy of Dean Naritoku, The Chicago Medical School.
Page 310: Courtesy of Carol Belkin, Vassar College.
Page 311: (b) From E. O. Reischauer & J. K. Fairbank, A History of Eastern Civilization, Vol. I, courtesy of Houghton Mifflin; (c) Department of Antiquities, Ashmolean Museum; (d) The University Museum, The University of Pennsylvania.

Chapter 13
Page 320: La Recherche Magazine, Paris.
Page 326: Left, M. Shostak/Anthro-Photo File; right, Lee/Anthro-Photo File.
Page 327: (a) and (b) Courtesy of the United Nations; (c) World Health Organization.
Page 329: Courtesy of the United Nations.
Page 330: Food and Agriculture Organization.
Page 332: Left and right, Courtesy of R. K. Dentan, Department of Anthropology, SUNY at Buffalo.
Page 333: Smithsonian Institution, National Anthropological Archives.
Page 334: Courtesy of the United Nations.
Page 336: Swiss National Tourist Office.
Page 337: Left, H. W. Silvester/Rapho-Photo Researchers; right, Marc & Evelyne Bernheim/Woodfin Camp.

Chapter 14
Page 344: Kathy Bendo.
Page 346: Left, Marc & Evelyne Bernheim/Woodfin Camp; right, Lee/Anthro-Photo File.
Page 353: Both, Kathy Bendo.
Page 355: Courtesy of Christine Padoch.
Page 358: Courtesy of Eric Ross.
Page 361: Courtesy of Candilario Sarez.

Chapter 15
Page 366: Frank Siteman/Stock, Boston.
Page 367: A and B, David Austin/Stock, Boston; C, Rare Book Division, The New York Public Library, Astor, Lenox and Tilden Foundations; D, Carl Frank/Photo Researchers; E, Thomas Hopker/Woodfin Camp.
Page 374: Abigail Heyman/Magnum.
Page 376: Tony Howarth/Woodfin Camp.
Page 379: Pietro Francesco Mele/Photo Researchers.

Chapter 16
Page 384: David Gillison/Anthro-Photo File.
Page 385: Ellis Herwig/Stock, Boston.
Page 386: Courtesy of Arthur Kurzweil.
Page 391: (a) The British Tourist Authority; (b) National Museums of Canada, Ottawa.

Chapter 17
Page 408: Dr. J. F. E. Bloss, A.R.P.S./Anthro-Photo File.
Page 409: Museum of New Mexico, photo by T. Harmon Parkhurst.
Page 410: Simon Trevor/D.B./Bruce Coleman.
Page 411: Martin Etter/Anthro-Photo File.
Page 412: Courtesy of Warren L. d'Azevedo.

Chapter 18
Page 416: Left, Courtesy of The Stop & Shop Companies; right, courtesy of the United Nations.
Page 419: Top, Food and Agriculture Organization; bottom, U.S.D.A.
Page 420: Louis Renault/Photo Researchers.
Page 421: Left, George Holton/Photo Researchers; right, Bohdan Hrynewych/Stock, Boston.
Page 423: Katrina Thomas/Photo Researchers.
Page 425: Left, Courtesy of Glenn T. Petersen, Baruch College; right, Richard Katz/Anthro-Photo File.
Page 426: Courtesy of The American Museum of Natural History.

Chapter 19
Page 434: Courtesy of R. K. Dentan, Department of Anthropology, SUNY at Buffalo.
Page 435: Napoleon Chagnon/Anthro-Photo File.

Page 437: Top, Marc & Evelyne Bernheim/ Woodfin Camp; bottom, courtesy of the House of Representatives.

Page 439: Left, Richard Katz/ Anthro-Photo File; right, Owen Franken/ Stock, Boston.

Page 443: Copyright 1968 by The Film Study Center, Harvard University.

Page 454: The Metropolitan Museum of Art, Rogers Fund, 1923.

Page 455: A, Picture Files; B, Alinari-Art Reference Bureau; C, Bruce Coleman; D and E, Kathy Bendo.

Page 460: Left, Richard Katz/ Anthro-Photo File; right, Smithsonian Institution, National Anthropological Archives.

Page 462: Georg Gerster/ Rapho-Photo Researchers.

Page 464: Jason Lauré/ Woodfin Camp.

Pages 466 and 467: A, Martin Etter/ Anthro-Photo File; B, Bruce Roberts/ Photo Researchers; C, Library of Congress; D, Richard Katz/ Anthro-Photo File; E, The British Tourist Authority; F, Maybury Lewis/ Anthro-Photo File; G, Marc & Evelyne Bernheim/ Woodfin Camp.

Chapter 21

Page 480: Marbury-Art Reference Bureau.

Page 481: Marc & Evelyne Bernheim/ Woodfin Camp.

Page 485: A, René Burri/ Magnum; B, Ian Berry/ Magnum; C, Photo Researchers; D, United Nations; E, Harvey Stein.

Page 486: A, Richard Lee/ Anthro-Photo File; B, Keith Gunnar-National Audubon Society Collection/ Photo Researchers; C, Desmond Doig/ Magnum; D, Hiroshi Hamaya/ Magnum; E, Owen Franken/ Stock, Boston.

Page 488: A, D, and E, Kathy Bendo; B, The Frick Collection; C, The National Gallery.

Page 489: A and C, United Nations; B, Frédéric Rapho/ Rapho-Photo Researchers; D, Marc & Evelyne Bernheim/ Woodfin Camp; E, Georg Gerster/ Photo Researchers.

Page 491: Norman Myers/ Bruce Coleman.

Page 492: Courtesy of Warren L. d'Azevedo.

Page 493: Courtesy of DeBeers Consolidated Mines, Ltd.

Page 495: Sepp Seitz/ Woodfin Camp.

Page 497: Wide World Photos.

Chapter 22

Page 502: Max Halberstadt, Hamburg.

Page 505: Culver Pictures.

Page 507: Courtesy of The American Museum of Natural History, from the Margaret Mead Collection. Photo by Reo Fortune.

Page 514: Wide World Photos.

Page 517: Wayne Behling, Ypsilanti Press, Michigan.

Chapter 24

Page 542: R. C. Bailey/ Anthro-Photo File.

Page 543: Louis Renault/ Photo Researchers.

Page 545: Christa Armstrong/ Rapho-Photo Researchers.

Pages 557, 562 and 563: Courtesy of The American Museum of Natural History.

Chapter 25

Page 573: James R. Holland/ Stock, Boston.

Page 577: Carl Frank/ Photo Researchers.

Page 579: Smithsonian Institution, National Anthropological Archives. Photo by James Mooney.

Page 580: Novosti from Sovfoto.

Page 581: Cornell University, Department of Anthropology, Vicos Collection.

Chapter 26

Page 588: Left, Franklin Wing/ Stock, Boston; right, United Nations.

Page 589: Cron/ Monkmeyer.

Page 595: The Bettmann Archive.

Page 596: The New York Historical Society.

Page 599: Left, Courtesy of the Smithsonian Institution, Freer Gallery of Art, Washington, D.C.; right, National Portrait Gallery, Smithsonian Institution.

Page 601: Left, Owen Franken/ Stock, Boston; right, George Malave/ Stock, Boston.

Page 603: Brown Brothers.

Page 611: Wide World Photos.

INDEX

ESKIMOS
INGALIK
MONTAGNAIS
TLINGIT
HAIDA
KWAKIUTL
CROW
ALGONGKIANS
IROQUOIS
CHEYENNE
OMAHA
SHOSHONE
HOPI
NAVAJO
PUEBLO
GROUPS
ZUÑI
HAWAIIANS
Teotihuacan
AZTEC
Tepotzlan
MAYA
Ponape
YANOMAMÖ
MUNDURUCU
TROBRIAND
ISLANDERS
SHAVANTE
ACHUARA
Dobu
INCA
Chan Chan
Fiji
SAMOANS
New Hebrides
MAORI